THE ALHAMBRA AT THE CROSSROADS OF HISTORY

THE ALHAMBRA AT THE CROSSROADS OF HISTORY

Eastern and Western Visions in the Long Nineteenth Century

Edhem Eldem

EDINBURGH
University Press

Edinburgh University Press is one of the leading university presses in the UK. We publish academic books and journals in our selected subject areas across the humanities and social sciences, combining cutting-edge scholarship with high editorial and production values to produce academic works of lasting importance. For more information visit our website: edinburghuniversitypress.com

Edinburgh University Press Ltd
13 Infirmary Street
Edinburgh EH1 1LT

First published in hardback by Edinburgh University Press 2024

Typeset in 11/15 EB Garamond by
IDSUK (DataConnection) Ltd

A CIP record for this book is available from the British Library

ISBN 978 1 3995 2487 2 (hardback)
ISBN 978 1 3995 2488 9 (paperback)
ISBN 978 1 3995 2489 6 (webready PDF)
ISBN 978 1 3995 2490 2 (epub)

CONTENTS

List of Figures vi

Introduction: Trailing a Photograph 1

1 North: Western and Spanish Visions of the Alhambra 22

2 South: Visitors from the Maghreb 72

3 East: Ottomans at the Alhambra 144

4 Modernity: Dreams and Ideals 225

Conclusion: Connections, Entanglements and Influences 314

Bibliography 330

Index 370

FIGURES

I.1 Photograph of Khalīl Jawād al-Khālidī, sent to his colleague Hasan Tahsin Bey in 1912 2
I.2 Inscriptions on the back of Khalīl Jawād al-Khālidī's photograph 2
I.3 Osman Hamdi Bey, *Believer Saying His Rosary*, 1905 6
I.4 'Patio del Kadid'. Publicity postcard of Rafael Garzón's photographic studio in Granada 9
I.5 Publicity postcard of Rafael Garzón's studio 9
I.6 A tourist couple posing in 'Moorish' garb in Garzón's *patio* árabe 10
I.7 Albert Frederick Calvert, posing in Garzón's *patio árabe* 10
1.1 'The Alhambra Court, Crystal Palace, Sydenham' 36
1.2 'The Royal Panopticon, Leicester-Square' 39
1.3 The Spanish pavilion at the 1878 Paris Exhibition 40
1.4 Jean-Léon Gérôme, *The Grief of the Pasha*, 1885 53
1.5 Henri Regnault, *Summary Execution under the Moorish Kings of Granada*, 1870 56
1.6 Marià Fortuny, *The Slaying of the Abencerrages*, c. 1870 58
1.7 'Andalusia under the Moors – The Court of the Lions' 61
1.8 Étienne Dinet, *Exhibition of 1900. Andalusia under the Moors* 64
1.9 Title page of *The Tunnels of the Alhambra*, 1862 69
2.1 'The Court of the Lions at the Alhambra', from Laborde's *Voyage pittoresque et historique de l'Espagne* 73

2.2 'A Perspective View of the Court and Fountain of Lions', from Murphy's *Arabian Antiquities of Spain* 74
2.3 Visual account of the Andalusian journey of King Alfonso XII and the Infanta Isabella 81
2.4 Cover of the first register of the Alhambra visitors' book 83
2.5 Inscription left in the visitors' book by Fulgencio Gómez Carrión, 1916 91
2.6 Signatures of members of a Moroccan embassy in the visitors' book, 1885 101
2.7 Photograph of the members of the Moroccan embassy, 1885 103
2.8 Inscriptions left in the visitors' book by the scholars Shinqīṭī and Wardānī, 1887 118
2.9 'Sid Abdesslam Esuisi during his visit to the palace of the Alhambra', 1877 122
2.10 Inscription left in the visitors' book by the 'poet from Tétouan', Malek Salem, 1876 134
3.1 'Fuad Pasha, Kâtib Efendi of the Ministry of Foreign Affairs at the Ottoman Porte', 1858 146
3.2 Inscriptions left in the visitors' book by ambassador Fuad Efendi, his secretary Mehmed Kâmil Bey, and his servant, Mikhail Dimitriadis, 1844 147
3.3 Fuad Pasha's mausoleum, c. 1870 166
3.4 Inscription left in the visitors' book by Midhat Pasha, 1877 177
3.5 Title page of the second edition of Ziya Pasha's *History of al-Andalus*, 1889–90 182
3.6 Title page of *The Story of the Conquest of al-Andalus*, by Abdülhak Hâmid 1905 190
3.7 Obverse and reverse of the third-class badge of the *Osmani* order 201
3.8 The Ottoman Exhibition building in Istanbul, 1863 205
3.9 The *Seraskerat* Gate, 1867 208
3.10 The imperial tribune erected for Empress Eugénie's visit, 1869 210
3.11 Empress Eugénie visiting the baths of the palace of Çırağan, 1869 211
3.12 Triumphal arch erected for Empress Eugénie at Pera, 1869 212
3.13 Empress Eugénie at the palace of Gezira, Cairo, 1869 218

4.1 Inscription left in the visitors' book by the Ottoman minister Turhan Bey, 1889 227
4.2 Inscription left in the visitors' book by Mehmed Kâmil Bey, 1892 234
4.3 Inscription left in the visitors' book by Aḥmad Zakī Bey, 1893 238
4.4 Title page of Aḥmad Zakī's *Journey to the Congress*, 1894 240
4.5 Inscription left in the visitors' book by Khalīl Jawād al-Khālidī, 1904 257
4.6 Portrait of Shakīb Arslan taken in Rafael Garzón Herranz's studio in Cordoba, 1930 265
4.7 Portrait of Khalīl Jawād Khālidī in the Court of the Maidens, the Alcázar, Seville, 1932 267
4.8 Sheikh Muḥammad 'Abduh with Princess Nazli and Ali Kemal Bey, Paris c. 1900 277
4.9 Inscription left in the visitors' book by Tunalı Hilmi Efendi, 1900 280
4.10 Postcard of the Alhambra sent by Tunalı Hilmi to his brother, 1902 282
4.11 Postcard of the mosque of Cordoba sent by TunalHilmi to his brother, 1901 283
4.12 Portrait of Tunalı Hilmi Efendi as a globetrotter in Garzón's *patio* árabe, 1900 292
4.13 Portrait of Tunalı Hilmi Efendi in Roma costume in Garzón's *patio* árabe, 1900 294
4.14 Portrait of Chorrojumo, 'Prince of the Gypsies' in Garzón's *patio* árabe, c. 1900 295
4.15 The Ottoman minister Samipaşazade Sezai Bey in the Court of the Lions,1914 301
C.1 Contemporary photograph of a tourist posing in a studio bearing traces of Garzón's *patio* árabe 326

INTRODUCTION
TRAILING A PHOTOGRAPH

This project started with the purely fortuitous discovery I made of a photograph dated 1912, representing an Arab man in his traditional costume, posing in the corner of a Moresque-style room or courtyard. I owe this discovery to a friend and colleague, Esra Gençtürk, who had shown me this image, handed down by her family, hoping that I might be able to tell her something about it. Thanks to the inscription on the back, I had no difficulty identifying the subject and recipient of the photograph. The man was Khalīl Djawād al-Khālidī (1864–1941), a member of the famous Jerusalemite Palestinian Khālidī family, posing, as noted in his handwritten inscription, 'in an apartment of the palace of the Alhambra, located in the city of Granada, in al-Andalus'.[1] The photograph was addressed to one Hasan Tahsin Bey, 'prosecutor at the Beirut court of appeal', my friend's great-grandfather. Khālidī identified himself as 'former judge of Diyarbekir' (Figures I.1 and I.2).[2]

[1] As Khālidī's case will be taken up further in this work, his biography will be treated in due course. For the moment, suffice it to say that he was an *'ālim* (scholar) trained in the Islamic tradition, who served in several posts of the Ottoman judiciary and that he travelled twice to the Maghreb and to southern Spain (see below, n. 85, p. 256).

[2] We have practically no information on Hasan Tahsin Bey, except for his great-granddaughter's stating that he served for about twenty years in the Arab provinces of the empire as an official in the judiciary.

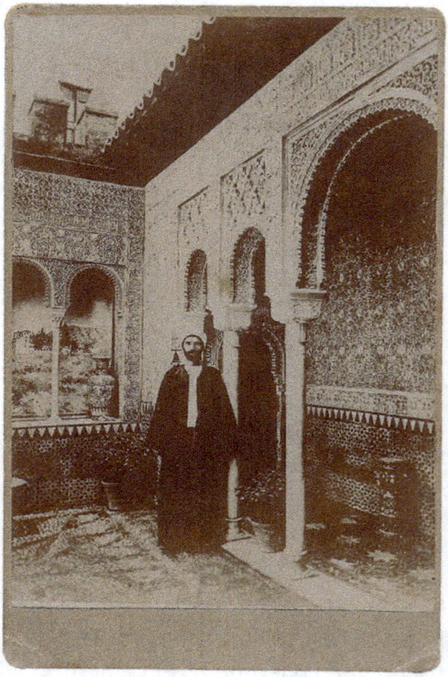

Figure I.1 Photograph of Khalīl Jawād al-Khālidī, sent to his colleague Hasan Tahsin Bey in 1912. Esra Gençtürk collection, Istanbul. The photograph was taken in Rafael Garzón's *patio árabe* in Granada, probably on 26 June 1904.

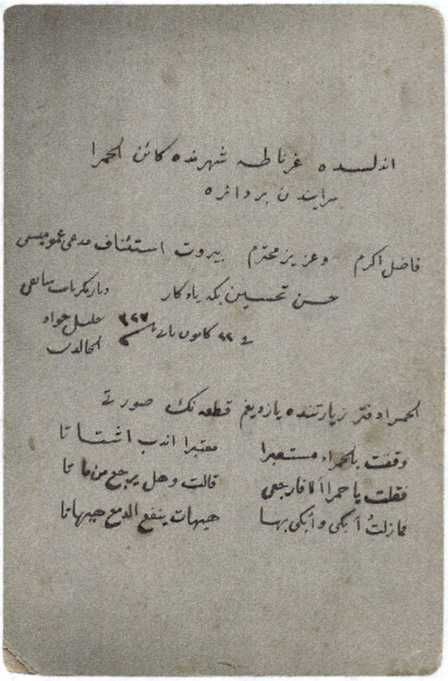

Figure I.2 Inscriptions on the back of Khalīl Jawād al-Khālidī's photograph, 1912. Esra Gençtürk collection, Istanbul. The upper half of the inscription is a dedication to Hasan Tahsin Bey, while the lower part contains a poem Khālidī claimed he had inscribed in the visitors' book of the Alhambra.

There was nothing exceptional to such an exchange between two colleagues, who were probably also friends. In the last decades of the nineteenth century, photography had made remarkable progress in the Ottoman Empire and had spread considerably throughout society.[3] Signed portraits had thus become a popular and efficient tool of sociability among the middle class and elite.[4] However, Khālidī's memento was not as common as the photographs his contemporaries frequently exchanged. First, this was a full-length and 'contextualised' portrait, much rarer than the conventional studio headshots or bust-size portraits produced by most professional photographers.

Moreover, the image was taken away from home, which is all the more surprising when one considers that Ottoman subjects – particularly Muslims – hardly had a reputation as globetrotters. In fact, when they did happen to travel outside the empire, or even in the provinces, postcards turned out to be a much more accessible and affordable way of sending greetings to parents and friends while at the same time offering them a peek of the place(s) they were visiting. Finally, and perhaps most importantly, the setting Khālidī had chosen for his portrait was certainly not ordinary. The sight of a Muslim Arab posing in front – or rather, in – one of the most celebrated monuments of Arab and Islamic culture was quite meaningful, as suggested by the inscription on the back, which included a short poem, which Khālidī claimed to have also inscribed in the 'visitors' book of the Alhambra'.

[3] There is a rich literature on the history of photography in the Ottoman Empire, but of varying merit. For an excellent synthesis, see B. Öztuncay, *The Photographers of Constantinople: Pioneers, Studios and Artists from Nineteenth-Century Istanbul*. Unfortunately, most works on the topic tend to concentrate more on the production – photographers, studios, techniques, etc. – rather than on the diffusion and consumption of images; moreover, they also display a bias towards 'high-end' photography, represented by the major studios, famous sitters, Orientalism, sites and monuments – at the cost of more common and demotic practices. I have addressed this issue in E. Eldem, 'Powerful Images: The Dissemination and Impact of Photography in the Ottoman Empire, 1870–1914', and E. Eldem, 'The Search for an Ottoman Vernacular Photography'.

[4] See, in particular, B. Öztuncay, *Hâtıra-i Uhuvvet: Portre Fotoğraflarının Cazibesi, 1846–1950*. Öztuncay's book, whose title reclaims a formula frequently used when signing a portrait to a friend (*hâtıra-i uhuvvet*, meaning 'brotherly memento'), is entirely devoted to signed photographs. Although most of the cases recorded in the volume belong to the upper crust of Ottoman society, the phenomenon was growingly common among the middling classes.

Although this image and its context immediately triggered my interest and curiosity, it was apparently not enough to incite me to carry out the kind of systematic research that might have enabled me to delve further into the matter. The language barrier was partly the reason, given that the inscription on the back was bilingual, Turkish and Arabic. As Khālidī's poem was in the latter language, it remained largely incomprehensible to me. Most of all, to a historian whose work had almost always focused on the empire's capital city, the thought of engaging in a quest concerning the life and career of an Arab and Arab-speaking provincial scholar seemed to exceed by far my competence.

Years later, a combination of factors made me reconsider the document with renewed curiosity. The main reason was a growing interest in Orientalism, particularly in its Ottoman version, mostly a consequence of my research and work on the famous Ottoman intellectual, painter and museologist Osman Hamdi Bey (1842–1910). Generally speaking, I had always wondered at the ease with which some art historians credited this artist with ideas and intentions on the mere basis of a 'critical reading' of his paintings. To them, despite the Orientalist style and outlook of his works, Hamdi Bey was using his brush to 'speak back' to Orientalism,[5] or even to 'subvert' this ideology by appropriating its style only to throw it back in the face of its representatives.[6]

This vision of a 'proto-Saidian' consciousness seemed highly unconvincing, all the more so because my own work on Hamdi Bey, grounded in textual evidence, especially his own correspondence, proved – to me, at least – that, far from rebelling against Orientalism, he actually had the mind and soul of an Orientalist, both in terms of his artistic production and of his overall perception of his country's engagement with the West and with modernity. True, there was much ambiguity in his stance, but it remained quite comprehensible given the intellectual, ideological and political context of the time. As an intellectual formed in Paris in the 1860s and convinced of Western superiority, particularly of the necessity for the empire to Westernise itself for its own survival, he had understandably internalised the major tenets of the ideology that ruled over the relations between Europe and the Ottoman Empire. Ottoman

[5] See, for example, Z. Çelik, 'Speaking Back to Orientalist Discourse'.

[6] See, particularly, W. K. Shaw, 'The Paintings of Osman Hamdi and the Subversion of Orientalist Vision'.

Orientalism was an integral part of imperial modernity, to the point of influencing many statesmen and administrators, who had no qualms about – in fact, often revelled in – appropriating and projecting the major Orientalist stereotypes of the West on several sections of the population, from the 'savage' Bedouin to the 'fanatic' Muslim.[7]

Osman Hamdi was no exception, except perhaps with regard to the excess of his own Orientalism, a direct consequence of a 'super-Westernised' identity, in Şerif Mardin's terms,[8] which made him particularly vulnerable to such ideological contamination. It seems to me, then, that the efforts of 'over-reading' and 'over-interpretation' deployed to prove Hamdi Bey's imperviousness, or, even better, resistance, to Orientalism, far from corresponding to any form of reality, betray wishful thinking. This approach is heavily tainted with anti-Orientalism and crypto-nationalism, together with an inability – or unwillingness – to accept that, in the context of the period, Orientalism had come to dominate the minds of all linked, in one way or another, to the notion of Westernisation, including the populations targeted by this ideology, as long as they were committed to the path of modernity.

This digression allows me to recontextualise the way in which Khālidī's photograph made its way back to the centre of my preoccupations. The impact of my growing familiarity with Osman Hamdi Bey and his oeuvre on my renewed perception of Khālidī was double. The first shock was purely visual, a sort of dejà vu, as it were, triggered by a striking resemblance to one of the artist's canvases. His *Believer Saying His Rosary* (1905), a self-portrait in 'Oriental' garb in front of the entrance to Rüstem Pasha Mosque, displayed an astonishing parallel with the setting of the Palestinian scholar's photographic portrait (Figure I.3). Of course, this was pure coincidence – if not obsessive delusion on my part – but a coincidence that warranted some reflection on the strange convergence between an almost 'Gerôme-ian' scene imagined by an Ottoman Orientalist and the pose of a 'genuine' Arab in a courtyard of the Alhambra.

Beyond this fortuitous resemblance, the true question inevitably has to do with the conformity or not of Khālidī's portrait with the ideological norms and bearings of the time. By dint of being exposed to an Orientalist

[7] See, for example, S. Deringil, '"They Live in a State of Nomadism and Savagery"'.

[8] Ş. Mardin, 'Super Westernization in Urban Life in the Ottoman Empire'.

Figure I.3 Osman Hamdi Bey, *Believer Saying His Rosary*, 1905. Oil on canvas, 210 × 120 cm. Istanbul Museum of Painting and Sculpture, Mimar Sinan University of Fine Arts. A typical example of Hamdi Bey's later works, which represented a character in Oriental garb in a partial setting clearly identifiable as Islamic. In this particular case, the setting is the entrance of Rüstem Pasha Mosque, in Istanbul, and the model for the character is the artist himself.

iconography caricaturing the Orient and its peoples, we are disconcerted at the sight of an Arab willingly posing in his own costume in one of the most iconic sites of Western Orientalist fantasy. Where, then, should we situate this image? Had Khālidī slipped through the net of Orientalism to acquire a space of freedom, where he could flaunt his allegiance to his own past, or even claim back a heritage from which he felt he had been estranged and deprived?

Fortunately, contrary to Hamdi Bey's paintings, Khālidī's photograph comes with a text. The inscription on the back provides numerous, concrete clues likely to reveal the details of the story. This was the main incentive behind my decision to pursue in a rigorous and systematic manner a quest of Khalīl Djawād al-Khālidī's Andalusian adventures. I soon had two epiphanies that decisively changed the course of my research. I owe the first to a friend and colleague, the art historian Avinoam Shalem, who saved me from a dead-end in which I had found myself regarding the visual setting of the document. As a historian with an almost obsessive proclivity for hard documentary and textual evidence, I had taken Khālidī's inscription quite literally and had started looking, by all possible means, for the precise spot in the Alhambra where the photograph had been taken. It took Avinoam Shalem just a look at the photograph to put an end to this frustrating and utterly sterile quest: this was not a corner of the Alhambra but the set of a photographer's studio, as revealed by the chimneys visible above the awning and by the fake view – apparently a photographic print – framed by the window to the scholar's right.

I will not dwell upon the lesson in humility I drew from the discovery of the power of insight and analysis unleashed by a method I had so often criticised. Obviously, the text was lying, but the image spoke the truth, at least for those who knew how to 'read' it properly. Once past this hurdle and with the help of the web, it did not take much time to identify the setting. This was the studio of the Granada photographer Rafael Garzón Rodríguez (1863–1923),[9] located close to the Alhambra, whose principal attraction was the '*patio árabe*',

[9] Rafael Garzón Rodríguez started working as an apprentice with the French photographer Charles Mauzaisse (1823–1885), who settled and married in Granada, and whose daughter Louise/Luisa married Rafael's elder brother, Nicolás. He took over Mauzaisse's studio in 1883; this is probably when he started proposing 'Moorish' portraits to visiting tourists, whom he would photograph in the courtyards and halls of the Alhambra, wearing costumes he provided. From 1898 to 1904, he worked in partnership with another col-

or Arab courtyard, which the photographer had set up to offer visitors the chance to take home 'the loveliest and most surprising keepsake . . . from the Alhambra of Granada'(Figures I.4 and I.5).[10] A pure example of 'consumer Orientalism',[11] as witnessed on scores of images of tourists, Spanish and foreign, men and women, posing at the exact same location as Khālidī, dressed in 'Moorish' costume and surrounded by a paraphernalia of vases, tables, hookahs and rifles provided by the resourceful Garzón (Figures I.6 and I.7).[12]

What a revelation! The dignified *'ālim* from Jerusalem had found nothing better than to emulate vulgar tourists to send a memento of this momentous episode in his peregrinations through the Maghreb and Andalusia. Obviously, there were some extenuating circumstances, starting with the difficulty of

---

league, Rafael Señán González (1864–1911). Garzón expanded his business to Cordoba and Seville, where he used similar Moorish sets. He had also specialised in photographs of Andalusian views and monuments, especially the Alhambra, in all shapes and formats – watercolours, photographs, albums, postcards and publications. The catalogue of a recent exhibition recounts Garzón's career and works, but with a stress on his Cordoba studio: A. J. González (ed.), *Los Garzón: Kalifas de la fotografía cordobesa*, pp. 28–54. I am particularly grateful to Pascual Sellés Cantos, from the Department of Architectural Projects at the Polytechnical University of Valencia (Universitat Politècnica de València) for his help and advice on Garzón.

10 'Patio árabe de Garzón', *La Mañana*, 3,610 (15 November 1919), p. 13. Garzón's *patio árabe* was inaugurated in 1900, probably towards the end of the summer. The setting was inspired by the Court of the Harem (*patio de Harem*) at the Alhambra and from the gallery at the end of the Court of the Myrtles, in front of the entrance to the Hall of the Ambassadors. The model for the columned double window (*ajimez*) seems to have been quite freely borrowed from that of the Tower of the Captive (*torre de la Cautiva*).

11 E. Eldem, *Consuming the Orient*.

12 'Its owner, Mr. Garzon, has had the rich idea to establish a photographic workshop in that courtyard, provided with a wardrobe room, well supplied with Arab costumes, and where many tourists visiting Granada have their photographs taken: some peeking out of a window, admiring the splendid landscape; others reclining on a soft cushion, smoking; yet another with his beautiful sultana; and in thousands of other such picturesque poses' ('Patio árabe de Garzón', *La Mañana*, 3,610 (15 November 1919), p. 13). An advertisement from 1892 reveals that Garzón had by then already started proposing 'Moorish portraits', although he did not yet have an appropriate studio. He would offer to take 'group [photographs] in the Arab palace with stylish costumes provided by the house to those who wish ('*Gran centro de fotografías*').

Figure I.4 'Patio del Kadid'. Publicity postcard of Rafael Garzón's photographic studio in Granada, n.d. Author's collection. The two men wearing 'Moorish' costumes, evidently provided by the photographer, are standing in the corner where most of Garzón's clients posed, including Khālidī.

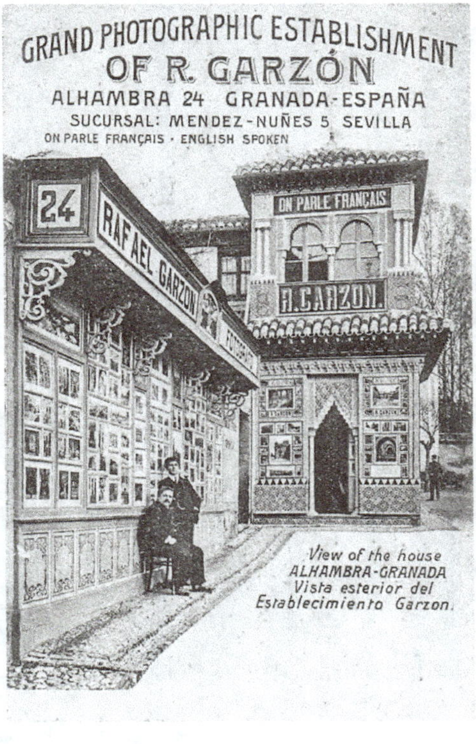

Figure I.5 Publicity postcard of Rafael Garzón's studio showing him and (probably) his son posing in front of his shop next to the Alhambra. The walls are covered with examples of his merchandise; the Moresque door most likely leads to the 'Arab patio', where tourists would be photographed.

Figure I.6 A tourist couple posing in 'Moorish' garb in front of the fake window of Garzón's *patio árabe*, n.d. Author's collection. The photograph is mounted on cardboard boasting the studio's address on the back. It should be noted that the photographic view placed in the window is not the same as on Khālidī's portrait. The view represented here is that of the 'Court of the Water Canal' (*patio de la Acequía*) at the Generalife.

THE AUTHOR IN THE ALHAMBRA

Figure I.7 Albert Frederick Calvert (1872–1946), posing in Garzón's patio, c. 1906. A. F. Calvert, *Granada and the Alhambra*, pl. 309. Calvert is standing at the exact same spot as Khālidī and the fake view from the window is the same on both images. It is rather amusing to note that Calvert had captioned this image as 'The Author in the Alhambra', thus creating the same fiction as Khālidī. Nevertheless, he did acknowledge in his book that Garzón had provided him with photographs of the Alhambra (ibid., p. x).

having one's portrait taken at the 'real' Alhambra.[13] Moreover, his pose and general attitude clearly set Khālidī apart from Garzón's typical clients. His sober costume, evidently authentic, his convincing beard, his upright – even a bit stiff – and somewhat frozen pose bore no similarity with 'white' tourists in their farcical clothes, sprawling over cushions or casually leaning against a Moresque window or a stucco column. Nevertheless, there was still a highly unexpected intersection, an astonishing overlap between mass Orientalism and an Arabo-Islamic identity of the most serious and committed sort.[14]

My second discovery, which had an even greater impact on the turn that my project would take, was essentially textual, and therefore perfectly compatible with my documentary penchant. As Khālidī had clearly indicated that he had written his poem in the 'visitors' book of the Alhambra', I set out to find this document, and was ready to go all the way to Granada if its existence and preservation were confirmed. To my utter surprise, I discovered – on the web, of course – that not only had this book been kept and preserved since 1829, but that it was integrally accessible online.[15] Thanks to this extraordinary resource,

[13] A 1913 guidebook mentions that 1½ peseta was asked of tourists who wanted to take photographs inside the monument (R. K. Wood, *The Tourist's Spain and Portugal*, p. 230). The cost was not forbidding, providing the visitor had a camera, which seems unlikely in Khālidī's case.

[14] This 'discovery' reminds me of Christina Civantos' experience, as described in the following short passage from the preface of her study *The Afterlife of al-Andalus*: 'The earliest beginnings of this book can be traced far back. I grew up seeing a framed photograph of my parents decked out in faux Oriental garb in a real-life "Oriental" palace. The photo was taken in 1976 during one of my father's first trips back to Spain since leaving with his family during the civil war, he was accompanied by my Cuban mother, who was visiting for the first time the Andalusia from which some of her grandparents hailed. A stop in the portrait studio set up inside Granada's Alhambra palace was de rigueur. Seeing that photograph every day and the many questions that it raised in my mind certainly contributed to my pursuit of this project' (C. Civantos, *The Afterlife of Al-Andalus*, p. vii). It is amusing to note that despite being conscious of the device of costumes, Civantos seems to have been tricked by the set, which she thought was authentic. The tradition of the 'Arab' portrait in the studios surrounding the Alhambra continues today, as suggested, among others, by the following website and its fascinating gallery of such images: 'Alhambra Foto, Galería fotográfica Ruiz Linares, desde 1886', see at: https://alhambrafoto.com/en/home.

[15] Patronato de la Alhambra y el Generalife, Archivo de la Alhambra (AA), *libros de firmas*, 42 to 51 (1829–1955). See at: https://www.alhambra-patronato.es/ria/handle/10514/813; https://www.alhambra-patronato.es/ria/handle/10514/822.

I started looking for Khālidī's poem in register 49, covering the period from 8 February 1911 to 2 July 1916. Nothing. Had Khālidī lied about this, too? Yes and no. Browsing through the other registers, I finally came across a tiny inscription in his hand dated 12 *Rabiulakhir* 1322 (26 June 1904).[16] I had made the mistake of treating this photograph like a postcard bearing the date of a visit. In fact, the date on the back was only that of the signing, when Khālidī, wishing to honour a colleague or to express him his friendship, had apparently picked a copy from a pile of identical photographs he had purchased from Garzón in 1904, at the time of his visit to the Alhambra. The existence of a second copy, dated 1905 and signed to a close parent, al-Ḥājj Rāgheb Khālidī,[17] confirms that this must indeed have been the case.[18]

Therefore, it was not a lie to have post-dated his portrait; however, what was more difficult to understand was that Khālidī's poem changed each time, with additions, omissions or variations on the two signed copies and on the original version inscribed in the Alhambra visitors' book. This situation, which could be accounted for by a memory lapse or by a certain licence, had no direct incidence on my research, and we will have the occasion to return to this poem and its context later. For the time being, I will be content with noting the crucial realisation that came out of this exposure to the registers: Khālidī was not alone. Throughout the pages I discovered one individual after another whose use of a very particular script set apart from the mass of signatures and comments.

[16] AA, *libros de firmas*, 47, fol. 13 v.

[17] Al- Ḥājj Rāgheb bin Na'mān bin al-Shaikh Rāgheb bin Muḥammad 'Alī bin al-Sayyid 'Alī bin Muḥammad bin al-Shaikh Khalīl bin al-Shaikh Muḥammad Ṣan'allah al-Khālidī (?–1966), was educated in Jerusalem and in 1899 established the famous Khālidiyya Library, inaugurated the following year in the mausoleum of Barakat Khan (http://khalidi.org/23.htm, last accessed in 2016, but unavailable today).

[18] This document was accessible on the Khālidī family website (http://khalidi.org/17.htm, last accessed in 2016, but unavailable today). Interestingly, although the document was not identified as the inscription on the back of a photograph – also absent from the site – its nature would be clear to anyone aware of the example I had published. Indeed, the text was formatted in almost identical fashion, but was entirely written in Arabic: a description of the setting ('a section of the Alhambra'), an address to the recipient, and a poem claimed to have been inscribed in the 'visitors' book of the Alhambra'.

That is how I came to realise that contrary to my initial belief that this must have been a rather unique case, tens of other individuals of a similar profile had visited the Alhambra, each time leaving a trace of their passage in the famous registers invented and inaugurated by Prince Dolgorukov and his travel companions, one of whom was the famous Washington Irving.[19] Of course, my use of the notion of a 'similar profile' begs for an explanation. Given that my curiosity had been triggered by Khālidī, it was clear that I would focus on those visitors whose identity was likely to present the same kind of 'tension' with the Alhambra and with the notions linked to that monument in the nineteenth century: a 'Moorish' past, Islamic civilisation, Muslim identity, Moresque architecture, and, of course, Orientalism under all its guises. The goal was therefore to sift through the registers to collect those names that bore religious, ethnic, cultural or linguistic features that would allow me to lump them in a vague category covering the Orient, Islam and Arab culture.

This selection process involved a self-imposed practical dimension. Signatures and comments in the Arabic script were easy to spot, enabling me to pick them across the pages with a bit of patience and not too much effort, despite the extraordinary volume of the documentation. This was a considerable advantage, especially compared with, say, a colleague wishing to work on Belgian tourists at the Alhambra. On the other hand, this advantage also came with shortcomings, however small, such as the difficulty in spotting Arabs, or other Orientals, using the Latin script, especially in French or English. Eventually, however, this risk was largely offset by the unexpected discovery of numerous 'fake Arabs', Westerners dabbling in a script they generally had not mastered to impersonate Arabs.

Ironically, this procedure had much in common with the odious practice of profiling, morally criticised and condemned by all, but still so often used by Western and 'white' authorities to screen individuals belonging to 'high-risk' countries and communities. Indeed, looking for 'Arab' or 'Oriental' signatures in a series of registers, the pages of which are covered with signatures of British, American, French, German and, of course, Spanish tourists amounted to hunting down 'alien' elements. Embarrassing as this

[19] See below, pp. 82–4.

may seem, this is, after all, the main objective of the project: to find fault lines in a system known to be predominantly Western, to flush out 'misfits', who, like Khālidī, looked out of place in a documentary and iconographic mass homogenised by nineteenth-century Western culture. Indeed, we should not forget that the 'long' nineteenth century is to a large extent a period during which a common culture rapidly took over Europe, only to spread out to the rest of the world through modernity and its armed wings, colonialism and imperialism. Most of the notions, trends and ideologies that exerted a strong influence on the perception and reception of the Alhambra during this period were born or reached their peak during this century. This is true of Orientalism, of course, but also of romanticism and medievalism, two currents of thought inseparable from the image of the monument that formed during the century, and of which the visitors' book constitutes tangible proof.

Faced with the scope of the task, I decided to limit myself to a context with which I was more familiar and focused on Ottoman subjects. I also used this angle to study the perception and impact – if any – of the Alhambra in Ottoman culture during the long nineteenth century, including the oft-observed phenomenon of the Moresque style adopted in the design and construction of many buildings built in Istanbul in the 1860s. The result was a series of articles, which, each through a slightly different angle, addressed the issue within a predominantly Ottoman framework.[20]

I owe the opportunity and the courage to carry this project further, beyond its initial Ottoman limits, to the invitation that was extended to me in 2018 by the Academy of the Kingdom of Morocco. I was invited to present the work I had done until then on the Ottoman dimension of the question, but I took this occasion to mention the very considerable presence of visitors from the Maghreb, most particularly from Morocco, a phenomenon I had barely touched upon in my articles. The very fact of speaking on this matter in a Sharifian institution, in front of a predominantly Moroccan audience, and under a magnificent dome in Andalusian style convinced me that I could no longer avoid the option of widening my quest to make it as inclusive and exhaustive

[20] E. Eldem, 'Ottomans at the Alhambra'; E. Eldem, 'The Ottomans and the Alhambra'; E. Eldem, 'Turcos y árabes en la Alhambra'.

as possible. In fact, such a perspective had already been in the making: as some of my Ottomans, such as Khālidī himself, were of Arab language and culture, I had to venture outside my scholarly comfort zone into a linguistic and cultural context with which I was not familiar. Thanks to the guidance and support of colleagues and friends who had previously lent me a helping hand in the initial phase of my project, I decided to launch a 'total' project on the discovery of the Alhambra by those whose history and heritage it was supposed to represent. The Academy of the Kingdom of Morocco, who had only requested the text of my conference, was kind enough to sponsor a new version, enlarged to the dimensions of the present work.

The goal was therefore to widen my approach to the subject, together with the database I had established from the visitors' book, in such a way as to include all possible variations of the 'Oriental' profile as I had defined it: North Africans, of course, but also Arabs from the Mashreq, both Muslim and Christian Ottoman subjects, whose different perception of the Alhambra I had already sensed. Compared with their fellow countrymen of Turkish language and culture, they seemed to possess and express more conscious, more learned, more intense feelings towards the celebrated monument.

For the study to be exhaustive and consistent, I needed to add a third dimension, that of Westerners, covering a wide spectrum of nationalities extending from the United States to the major nations of Europe, and generally restricted to the most affluent strata of society. Indeed, travelling to Spain was not affordable to everyone, and it is only at the turn of the twentieth century that one can start to speak of a relative democratisation of what had remained a rather posh and exclusive activity for decades.

Obviously, there was no way I could apply to Western visitors the method I had devised for Orientals, as it would have meant combing through thousands of pages filled with names and inscriptions in the same script. This would have been impossible and rather useless, given that, after all, the discovery of the Alhambra by the West in the nineteenth century is a well-known subject. All I had to do, then, was to cherry-pick some of the most significant inscriptions, the context of which was likely to bring some novelty to the main narrative. To be honest, the mere recourse to the visitors' book was a novelty in itself, considering that it had not been done before, with the exception of a few compilations of 'celebrity' signatures towards the end of the nineteenth century.[21] Moreover, even though the Western narrative was well-known, I believed it would be useful to re-trace its outline, if only to bring together elements and perspectives that were often handled separately. To be sure, works devoted to the Alhambra's architectural aspects and their (re)production by artists such as Owen Jones or Ludwig von Zanth have not necessarily featured the perceptions of the same monument in literature by authors like François-René de Chateaubriand or Washington Irving.

Even greater omissions can be observed in the treatment that Spain and the Spaniards receive in most of the studies devoted to the discovery of the Alhambra in the nineteenth century. In many cases, Spain and its population are perceived as forming part of a South, or an Orient, directly integrated into the image of the Alhambra, almost as a complement to the exoticism and romanticism that dominates the visions and perceptions of Western authors and observers. This was an additional reason to widen my perspective on the 'Orientals' in this study, given that the Spaniards formed an integral part of the Alhambresque scene and setting in Europe's imagination. And yet, in reality, the Spaniards had themselves already trodden this path, sometimes much earlier, by creating a popular literature on the Arab past of their country, by documenting the Alhambra and its heritage, and by progressively constructing their own Orientalism and their own Andalusian myths.

The ultimate goal, then, will be to build a general overview to analyse these different perspectives converging on the Alhambra. That is how this work will

[21] L. Seco de Lucena, *Poesías y pensamientos del álbum de la Alhambra*, 1878, 1883, 1889; C. del Castillo Tejada, *Poesías, pensamientos y firmas que se encuentran en los cuatro albums de la Alhambra*; R. Sánchez Valdivia, *Brevísimo guía del palacio árabe*. Of course, the sheer volume of the information contained in the registers perfectly justifies the absence of any research based on their systematic exploitation. Indeed, the number of inscriptions rises geometrically in time: the first register covered no less than forty-three years (1829–1872); the second, eleven years (1872–1883), the following three, seven years each (1883–1890, 1890–1896, 1896–1903), and the following four, approximately four years each (1904–1907, 1907–1911, 1911–1916, 1916–1920). The size of each register shows slight variations in time, from 700 pages (1829–1883) to 600 (1883–1896), and finally to 500 (1896–1920). Finally, one should not forget that the nature of the inscriptions varies greatly from one register to the other. The most concise, consisting of a signature and a date, constitute the overwhelming majority, which only causes an increase in the number of people to be inventoried.

try to distinguish itself from numerous predecessors, generally characterised by a narrower focus on a certain aspect or a particular dimension of this vast topic. Without claiming to have written a 'total' history of the Alhambra in the nineteenth century, nevertheless I may propose a new reading of a phenomenon of a complex and fascinating nature. By bringing up differing but also interconnected visions of the same monument, I hope to be able to give an impression of the intertwining and entanglement of images, ideas, references, clichés and fantasies characterising the cultural history of the interaction between centre and periphery, North and South, East and West, throughout the almost never-ending century of modernity.

* * *

I believe that the number of acknowledgements an author feels necessary to list is inversely proportional to their skills and competence. At least, this is how I intend to justify the length of the following list of individuals and institutions I need to thank for their precious support, without which this work would have been impossible. Understandably, I shall start with the person who provided me with Khalīl Djawād al-Khālidī's photograph, my friend and colleague Esra Gençtürk, presently president of Özyeğin University, Istanbul. None of this would have been possible without that first and crucial stimulus.

I owe to the precious help of very many people the ability to have used the documentary evidence that was available to me, but often required linguistic skills that I did not possess. With regard to sources in Arabic from the Mashreq, I would like to express my gratitude to Esra Karabacak, formerly at Boğaziçi University, and presently at the Near East University of Cyprus; to Karam Nachar, then a doctoral candidate at Princeton University, and now teaching at Işık University, in Istanbul; to Paule Fahmé-Thiéry, the École pratique des hautes études, Paris; to Walter Scott Sasson Chahanovich, doctoral candidate at Harvard University; to my friends Zainab Bahrani, Columbia University, Akram Zaatari, Beirut, and Nasser Rabbat, the Massachusetts Institute of Technology. Regarding North African inscriptions in the visitors' book, I have greatly benefited from the help and guidance of Loubna Lamrhari and Romana Khalef, the University of Montpellier III and of Driss

Mekouar, the Collège de France, who, additionally, was kind enough to verify and correct Malek Salem's inscription from 1876. I have also received much guidance regarding this latter inscription from Mehdi Ghouirgate,the University of Bordeaux-Montaigne, and from Mohamed B. Bouabdelli. Joshua Picard, Princeton University, was kind enough to decipher a Judeo-Spanish inscription. As to Persian texts, I have received the help of Mohammad Ali Amir-Moezzi, the École pratique des hautes études, and of Fatemeh Faridi Majid, the Iranology Foundation, Tehran. Greek inscriptions were kindly read and translated for me by Katerina Stathi, the Laskaridou Foundation, Elektra Kostopoulou, Rutgers University, Antonis Anastasopoulos, the University of Crete, and Christine Angelidi, the Institute of Historical Research at the National Hellenic Research Foundation. My former student, Aylin Koçunyan, Notre-Dame de Sion, Istanbul, provided me with similar support regarding Armenian inscriptions.

As my shortcomings were not limited to languages, I am indebted to an impressive number of friends and colleagues who have helped me better understand and contextualise many of the sources I needed to use, and who, very often, have helped me avoid errors and mistakes I would have most probably made. Avinoam Shalem, Columbia University, rescued me from an embarrassing position by revealing the true nature of Khālidī's photograph, with which it all started. My timid incursions into Arab history and culture would have been impossible had it not been for the insight and advice of Salim Tamari, the Institute for Palestine Studies, Beirut, and the Institute of Jerusalem Studies, Jerusalem; of Khader Salameh, director of the Islamic Museum, at al-Aqsa, Jerusalem; and of Orit Bashkin, University of Chicago. I am particularly grateful to my colleague and friend Dana Sajdi, Boston College, who guided me through the maze of literary references relevant to the Arab poems with which I was faced; to Anne-Laure Dupont, the University of Paris-Sorbonne, whose careful review of a previous version of this work was of invaluable help; and to Renaud Soler, the Centre for the History of the Nineteenth Century at the Sorbonne, who patiently answered my incessant queries on some of the texts. My friends and colleagues Adam Mestyan, Duke University, and Seif el-Rashidi, the Institute for Historical Research at London University, have enlightened me on many issues concerning some Egyptian authors and intellectuals. Malika Slaoui, with whom, years ago, I had the honour to work on the project 'Consuming the Orient', was kind enough to provide me with the image of a magnificent poster by Étienne Dinet.

Regarding the Spanish dimension of the project, I have greatly relied on the support and advice of José Antonio González Alcantud, the University of Granada, whose work undoubtedly embodies the most critical and sophisticated discourse on the topic. My thanks also go to Nieves Paradela Alonso, the Universidad Autónoma de Madrid, for sharing her own work on Arab visitors to Spain. I have greatly benefited from the experience of David Sánchez Cano, a historian specialising in Andalusian and Moroccan photography, and of Pascual Sellés Cantos, the Department of Architectural Projects at the Polytechnical University of Valencia, passionate *aficionado* of the Granada photographer Rafael Garzón Rodríguez. I owe the use of a particularly interesting photograph of Chorrojumo, *príncipe de los Gitanos*, to Carlos Sánchez and to Javier Piñar Samos, one of the most eminent specialists of Andalusian photography.

Although it lies within my specialty, the Ottoman and Turkish part of the project would have remained incomplete without the help of numerous scholars. My friend and colleague, Sinan Kuneralp, owner of the Isis publishing house, in Istanbul, has always provided me with documents and information regarding the Ottoman elite of the nineteenth century; this project was no exception, and I am in his debt for many clarifications on some of the major figures in this narrative and for original documents concerning them. İnsan Tunalı, Koç University, as the grandson of Tunalı Hilmi Bey, who plays a central role in this work, has given me access to the fascinating photographs and postcards dating back to his grandfather's visit to the Alhambra. Alyson Wharton, a specialist of the Balian family, Lincoln University, has provided me with several documents on the role of these architects in the development of a Moresque style in the 1860s. I must also thank my former student Murat Şiviloğlu, now teaching at Trinity College, Dublin, for sharing some of his observations on Ottoman perceptions of al-Andalus. My friend Bahattin Öztuncay, director of the Meşher art gallery, in Istanbul, and one of the greatest specialists of photography in the Ottoman Empire, has given me access to a photograph from the 1860s, preserved in the extraordinary collection of Ömer M. Koç, to whom I also wish to express my most heartfelt gratitude. I cannot thank enough Ahmed Salcan, from the İş Bankası publishing house, for having allowed me to reproduce an image taken from his magnificent collection of the *Illustrated London News*. Finally, my thanks go to Kasım Hızlı, from the Turkish State Archives, who kindly drew my attention to Khalīl Djawād al-Khālidī's personnel record at the Sheikhulislamate archives.

Several institutions have helped and supported me in various ways throughout the realisation of this project. I would like to thank the Institute for Palestine Studies, Beirut, particularly Mona Nsouli; the library of the Diputación de León, particularly Alberto González Fierro; the Istanbul Metropolitan Municipality Atatürk Library, particularly Metin Tekden; the National Library of Turkey, Ankara; the Mohammed Daoud Foundation for History and Culture, Tétouan; the Istanbul Museum of Painting and Sculpture, at the Fine Arts University of Mimar Sinan; the French National Library, Paris; the Joslyn Art Museum, Omaha, Nebraska; the Getty Research Institute, Los Angeles; the Victoria and Albert Museum, London; the British Library, London; the National Library of Spain, Madrid; the State Archives of the Republic of Turkey, section of Ottoman State Archives, Istanbul; finally, of course, the Archives of the Directorate of the Alhambra and Generalife whose fabulous collections stand at the very heart of this work.

I should also express all my gratitude to those who have made the realisation and publication of this work possible. By inviting me to present my ongoing research on the Alhambra 'seen from the Orient', the Academy of the Kingdom of Morocco was the origin of my decision to widen my perspective to the scope of this book; moreover, by accepting to sponsor the first version of this book in French with the Belles Lettres publishing house, this institution has extended its support to include the logistics of the project's realisation. I would like to express my deepest gratitude to the Academy in the person of its Perpetual Secretary, Abdeljalil Lahjomri, and his collaborator, Bachir Tamer, who also contributed to my quest for documents concerning the Moroccan dimension of the question. My thanks also go to the publishing house of Les Belles Lettres, Paris, for their immediate interest and support of my project. More particularly, I would like to thank Nicolas Filicic, who, with patience and enthusiasm, accompanied me throughout the very demanding process of preparation leading to the publication of the original French version. Ever since its publication in May 2021, my mind had been set on working towards the publication of an English version of the book. For the realisation of this dream, I have Edinburgh University Press to thank, and more particularly, Rachel

Bridgewater, senior commissioning editor for Islamic and Middle Eastern History, Isobel Birks, assistant editor, Eddie Clark, managing desk editor, and Lyn Flight, their freelance copy-editor.

Finally, last but certainly not least, and in a much more intimate context, I must express all my gratitude to Simin and Mia for their unwavering support and patience, which I have been able to put to the test by asking them to edit the first draft of my translation. As to Sedef, all I have done to this day has been with her and thanks to her; this book is no exception to this rule.

1

NORTH: WESTERN AND SPANISH VISIONS OF THE ALHAMBRA

A Western Passion

The Alhambra, the celebrated palatial structure of the Nasrid dynasty located in the last Arab capital of the Iberian Peninsula, Granada, was (re)discovered during the first half of the nineteenth century. Let us immediately note that this discovery was essentially Western: French, British and, later, German. Its genealogy is complex and convoluted, but it is marked by milestones consisting of texts and images produced by authors who have greatly contributed to the construction of one of the major myths of romanticism. Already in the last decade of the eighteenth century, Jean-Pierre Claris de Florian (1755–1794) introduced his *Gonzalve de Cordoue ou Grenade reconquise* (*Gonzalo of Cordoba, or Granada Reconquered*) with a 'historical summary on the Moors of Spain', a section of which was devoted to a 'description of the Alhambra'. In it, the author described the contrast between the palace's chaotic exterior and its lavish apartments, dwelling at length on the Court of the Lions – the famous *patio de los Leones* – and its alabaster fountain.[1] In a guidebook for travellers dated 1805, more than half of the description of Granada was devoted to the Alhambra, 'one of the most complete and most

[1] J.-P. Claris de Florian, 'Description de l'Alhambra', *Gonzalve de Cordoue ou Grenade reconquise*, pp. 110–19.

magnificent edifices built by the Moors in Spain'.[2] Between 1807 and 1818, Count Alexandre de Laborde (1773–1842) published his monumental *Voyage pittoresque et historique de l'Espagne* (*Picturesque and Historical Travels to Spain*). True to the passion for the 'picturesque' that had invaded travel literature during the past few decades, Laborde's work included lavish plates of the palace, its main halls and courts, inscriptions and other decorative elements, and a section on the Court of the Lions.[3]

And yet, although it is true that the French and the British figured prominently in this discovery in the first decades of the nineteenth century, one needs to do justice to the role the Spaniards played in this process, most notably through the realisation of a major project involving the drawing and documentation of the monument as early as the mid-eighteenth century. This undertaking was partly sponsored by King Carlos III (r. 1759–88) and especially by the Royal Academy of Fine Arts of San Fernando, established in Madrid in 1752. Ignacio de Hermosilla (1718–94) had started the project in 1756, when, as secretary of the academy, he commissioned the artist Manuel Sánchez Ximénez to copy the frescoes of the Alhambra. By 1761–2, Diego Sánchez Sarabia (1704–79) had taken over the mission, drawing a great number of decorative elements, particularly tiles, frescoes and inscriptions, as well as plans and elevations of the monument. Following doubts expressed as to the accuracy of these documents, a third mission was organised in 1766–7 with the objective of correcting Sarabia's drawings. Two young architects, Juan de Villanueva (1739–1811) and Juan Pedro Arnal (1735–1805) were recruited for the occasion and placed under the supervision of the military architect and engineer José de Hermosilla Sandoval (1715–76), Ignacio's brother. Rather than correct their predecessor's errors, the team started the whole project from scratch, with the addition of plans of the famous mosque of Cordoba. The result was the *Antigüedades árabes de España* (*Arab Antiquities of Spain*), a work containing twenty-nine plates, the first twenty-one of which were devoted to the Alhambra, the following three to the cathedral of Granada and the remaining five to the mosque of Cordoba.[4] The work's publication

[2] H. A. O. Reichard, *Guide des voyageurs en Europe*, vol. I, pp. 97–9.

[3] A. de Laborde, *Voyage pittoresque et historique de l'Espagne*, vol. II, Part I.

[4] Hermosilla (ed.), *Antigüedades árabes de España*.

was delayed by the authors' wish to add the drawings and translations of the Arab inscriptions of the monument. The task had been entrusted to Miguel Casiri de Gartia (1710–91), a Maronite priest, born Mikhail al-Ghazīrī (مخايل الغزيري), who completed his translation work in 1775. It was only in 1787, twenty years after the last mission and thanks to the support and encouragement of Count Floridablanca (1728–1808), then secretary of state, that a first volume of plates was finally published, without waiting for the epigraphical section, so still deemed incomplete. The publication, in 1779, of Henry Swinburne's (1743–1803) travelogue, a section of which, containing six plates, was devoted to the Alhambra, seems to have played a role in this decision.[5] The second volume, consisting of the epigraphical drawings and their translation by Casiri, revised and corrected by the king's librarian Pablo Loranzo (1749–1822), came out only in 1804.[6]

About a decade later, the Irishman James Cavanah Murphy (1760–1814), putting to good use the seven years he had spent in Andalusia, from 1802 to 1809, published a truly remarkable work on the *Arabian Antiquities of Spain*, illustrated with nearly a hundred plates.[7] About ten of these had to do with Cordoba; the rest was entirely devoted to the Alhambra: general views, plans, interior views, façades, sections, architectural details, tiles, frescoes, inscriptions etc. In his single-page introduction, Murphy mentioned his Spanish precursors' publications – which probably explains why he used their title, translated word for word – and saluted the way in which these authors had 'contributed to remove, or at least to mitigate, this prejudice' that encouraged the Spaniards to 'demolish the works of infidels, whom it was accounted both pious and popular to deride'. He concluded these considerations by evoking the extraordinary beauty of the monument, stressing 'the very high state of

[5] Swinburne, *Travels through Spain*. Letter XXIII is entirely dedicated to the Alhambra (pp. 171–88). Swinburne's plates could hardly compete with the quality of the plates in *Antigüedades árabes de España*, but his travelogue had the advantage of an earlier publication date, of a reprint in 1787 in quarto format, and, the same year, of a translation in French by Jean-Benjamin – not Alexandre – de Laborde.

[6] A beautiful work published on the occasion of an exhibition on this topic staged at the Royal Academy of Fine Arts of San Fernando in 2015 recounts this adventure in great detail: A. Almagro Gorbea (ed.), *El legado de al-Ándalus*.

[7] J. C. Murphy, *The Arabian Antiquities of Spain*.

excellence, to which the Spanish Arabs [*sic*] attained in the Fine Arts, while the rest of Europe was overwhelmed with ignorance and barbarism'.[8]

Evidently, the Alhambra had started to trigger dreams and fantasies. Nothing illustrates the situation better than the frequency with which the monument appeared on canvases exhibited at the yearly exhibition of living artists, known as the Paris Salon. The kick-off was given in 1802 by Citizen (*citoyen*) Dutaillis, whose *Danse du boléro* (*Bolero Dance*) took place in 'the gallery of the Generalife, from where one can see part of the Alhambra and the city of Granada'. In fact, this was a scene that would grace one of the plates of Laborde's *Travels*.[9] In 1808, Jean Lubin Vauzelle (1776–1839) exhibited no less than five 'Moorish' works, two of which – the 'Court of the Lions' and the 'Queen's Robing Room' (*tocador* or *peinador de la Reina*) – took their inspiration from the Alhambra.[10] Vauzelle turned this into a trademark, as he exhibited three views of the Alhambra in 1812, two in 1814, one in 1817 and two in 1819.[11] Victor Texier (1777–1864) exhibited two engravings in 1812 and 1814, both part of his work for Laborde's publication.[12] If anything, this

[8] Murphy, *The Arabian Antiquities of Spain*, 'Introduction', n.p.

[9] *Explication des ouvrages*, an X (1802), p. 18. The commentary triggered by this engraving some ten years later in the press constitutes an exceptional collage of clichés worth citing in extenso: 'The engraving representing the *Bolero* dance is no less remarkable: it gives a perfect idea of this national dance that charms all Spaniards; they are even so passionate by this exercise that if one were to suddenly enter a court of law playing the *Bolero* tune, the judges, the lawyers, the people, would all start dancing. One can find in this dance all the passions that stir the soul: fear, desire, delight spring forth one after the other and form a rapid sequence' ('Voyage pittoresque en Espagne', *Le Miroir des spectacles, des lettres, des mœurs et des arts*, 855, 30 May 1823).

[10] *Explication des ouvrages*, 1808, p. 91.

[11] 1812: 'View of the Entrance to the Court of the Lions at the Palace of the Alhambra, in Granada', 'View of One of the Galleries of the Palace of the Alhambra' and 'View of the Portico and Small Garden of the Generalife in Granada' (*Explication des ouvrages*, 1812, p. 101); 1814: 'View of the Entrance of the Court of the Lions at the Palace of the Alhambra, in Granada' and 'View of the Galleries of the Palace of the Alhambra' (*Explication des ouvrages*, 1814, p. 95); 1817: 'The Massacre of the Abencerrages' (*Explication des ouvrages*, 1817, p. 89); 1819: 'View of the Court of the Alhambra in Granada' and 'View of the Resting Room, After the Bath, in the Palace of the Alhambra, in Granada' (*Explication des ouvrages*, 1819, p. 125).

[12] 'View of the Hall of Justice, at the Palace of the Alhambra, in Granada' (*Explication des ouvrages*, 1812, p. 133) and 'Interior of the Alhambra, in Granada' (*Explication des ouvrages*, 1814, p. 129).

proves the central role that Laborde and his *Voyage pittoresque* played in the emergence and circulation in France of an increasingly rich iconography of the celebrated palace of Granada.

If Laborde was responsible for the dissemination in France of images of the splendid ruins of the Alhambra, François-René de Chateaubriand (1768–1848) is probably the author who has most contributed to the birth of a romanticised myth of the monument and its history. His travels to the Levant had ended in Spain: he left La Goulette on 9 March 1807, landed at Algeciras and reached Cadiz on 6 April. He discovered Cordoba, then Granada: 'The Alhambra seemed to me worthy of being viewed, even after the temples of Greece.'[13] Among the mementos he brought back from his travels was a 'moulded plaster of the Alhambra'.[14] All of this is quite dry and laconic, even though one can imagine that the monument and his history may have impacted him retrospectively, as he was writing down his impressions of the Levant. Indeed, that is when he compared the Omayyad monuments of Jerusalem to the Alhambra, which he called a masterpiece of Arab architecture, 'much like the Parthenon is the miraculous genius of Greece'.[15] Likewise, when speaking of the Maghreb district of Jerusalem, he lamented that the 'proud heirs of the Abencerrages, those elegant architects of the Alhambra' should have been reduced to earning their livelihood as gatekeepers and messengers.[16]

Was this commentary a premonitory sign of his celebrated novella, the *Adventures of the Last Abencerrage*?[17] Certainly, but under conditions that were quite different to the author's claim. As Louis Stinglhamber very wittily demonstrated, it appears that Chateaubriand spent only a short day at the Alhambra and that he drew his inspiration for the location of the short story from the work by Laborde, his friend, whose plates on Granada he had viewed as early as 1807, well before the publication of the volume that contained them. Ironically, it appears that the source of inspiration for the novella, apart from a few earlier publications, was Nathalie, Countess of Noailles (1774–1835), Count de Laborde's sister, who happened to be in Granada at

[13] F-R. de Chateaubriand, *Itinéraire de Paris à Jérusalem*, vol. III, pp. 211–12.

[14] Chateaubriand, *Itinéraire de Paris à Jérusalem*, vol. I, p. 209.

[15] Chateaubriand, *Itinéraire de Paris à Jérusalem*, vol. II, p. 364.

[16] Chateaubriand, *Itinéraire de Paris à Jérusalem*, vol. II, p. 334.

[17] Chateaubriand, *Aventures du dernier Abencerage*.

the time, helping her brother in his undertaking. Thus, towards 1807, after a hurried discovery of the Alhambra shortened by an amorous encounter with her, Chateaubriand developed a passion for a story he built up from the documentation provided by his lover's brother and which he wrote during the following two years, only to publish it in 1826.[18] As Scipion Marin noted in 1832, written in 1810 but published more than fifteen years later, this work had largely missed its intended audience.[19]

To be sure, Chateaubriand had not invented anything, given that the myth of the Abencerrages was already in circulation, carried by many publications, especially the *History of the Factions of the Zegri and the Abencerrages* by Ginés Pérez de Hita (1544–1619), who, at the turn of the seventeenth century, invented the story of the quarrel between the Zegris and the Abencerrages.[20] Plate XXXVI of Laborde's book described the 'Hall of the Abencerrages', where, 'according to tradition . . . the fierce Boabdil, king of Granada, had the valiant tribe of the Abencerrages massacred'.[21] This event was mentioned in a review of the book in 1823 in terms that proved to what extent architecture and tragedy could mix: 'One view represents the Court of the Lions in the Alhambra; this is where the Abencerrages were massacred. This monument is the most perfect type of Moresque architecture.'[22] The plate was by Vauzelle, who, in 1817, exhibited a painting titled the *Massacre of the Abencerrages*, the description of which was taken from Pérez de Hita's *Histoire chevaleresque*.[23]

It should be noted that the stress on the 'discovery' of the Alhambra by Europe should not make us forget that Spanish literature, especially from

[18] L. Stinglhamber, 'Chateaubriand à Grenade?'

[19] S. Marin, *Histoire de la vie et des ouvrages de M. Chateaubriand*, vol. II, pp. 293–309.

[20] G. Pérez de Hita, *Historia de los bandos de Zegríes y Abencerrajes*. A French translation was available to Chateaubriand: G. Pérez de Hita, *Histoire chevaleresque des Maures d'Espagne*. See also, B. Matulka, 'On the European Diffusion of the "Last of the Abencerrajes" Story in the Sixteenth Century'.

[21] Laborde, *Voyage pittoresque et historique de l'Espagne*, vol. II, Part I, p. 19 and pl. XXXVI. Boabdil is the name given in Spain to Abū ʿAbdallah Muḥammad bin ʿAlī (1459–1533), also known by the dynastic name of Muhammad XII, the last ruler of Granada, from 1486 to 1492. In Arab sources, he is often nicknamed '*al-Zughbī*' ('the Unfortunate') and in Spanish '*el Chico*' ('the Young'), to distinguish him from a homonymous predecessor.

[22] 'Voyage pittoresque en Espagne'.

[23] *Explication des ouvrages*, 1817, p. 89.

Granada, was already rich with texts that glorified Andalusian heritage through monuments, inscriptions, and regional custom and traditions. Juan Velázquez de Echeverría's (1729–1804) *Strolls in Granada and its Surroundings* (*Paseos por Granada y sus contornos*), the first edition of which dates to the mid-eighteenth century, constitutes a fascinating example of this phenomenon. Designed as a dialogue between a citizen of Granada (*Granadino*) and a stranger (*forastero*) roaming the city and its environs along about sixty itineraries, this book demonstrates to what extent the Islamic heritage was still present in local memory. One finds in it a detailed description of the Alhambra, a fascinating mix of history and legends as well as an impressive number of translations of the main Arabic inscriptions.[24] Echeverría had at least one follower, Simón de Argote, whose *New Strolls* (*Nuevos Paseos*) were presented as a work bringing those qualities that were allegedly lacking in his predecessor's, particularly order, clarity, accuracy and a true history of the Moorish kings.[25]

Although it is certain that this local knowledge must have influenced, often in convoluted ways, the discovery of the monument by European authors and artists, one can only lament that this rich and original documentation has been generally ignored by the Western sources that would come to dominate the main narrative of the Alhambra in the nineteenth century.[26]

[24] J. de Echeverría, *Paseos por Granada, y sus contornos, que en forma de diálogo traslada al papel Don Joseph Romero Yranzo*, 1st edn, 1764; J. de Echeverría, *Paseos por Granada y sus contornos, o descripción de sus antigüedades y monumentos dados a luz por el célebre Padre Juan de Echeverría*, 2nd edn, 1814.

[25] S. de Argote, *Nuevos paseos históricos, artísticos, económico-políticos por Granada y sus contornos*. On this subject, see J. Calatrava Escobar, 'Un retrato de Granada a principios del siglo XIX'; Calatrava Escobar, 'La Alhambra, entre las luces y el romantismo'; J. M. Barrios Rozúa, 'El Generalife y las ruinas árabes'. Argote acquired a terrible reputation: *afrancesado*, or collaborator with the French invaders, he had corresponded with Laborde (Barrios Rozúa, 'El Generalife y las ruinas árabes', p. 33). He is also held responsible for the plundering of works of art by General Sébastiani during the French occupation (Ford, *A Hand-Book for Travellers in Spain*, vol. I, p. 383).

[26] Another publication in this local genre, which deserves better visibility, is the 'Traveller's Guidebook' published by M. Lafuente Alcántara, *El libro del viajero en Granada*. This historian was also the author of history of Granada and its region in four volumes: *Historia de Granada*.

From Romanticism to Exoticism

From the 1820s on, the two basic elements of the 'reinvention' of the Alhambra were solidly in place: on the one hand, a romanticised legend consisting of mystery and bloody episodes and, on the other, a growing fascination with Moresque architecture and motifs. With his novella on the last of the Abencerrages, Chateaubriand had in effect placed the Alhambra at the centre of a medievalist and exotic version of romanticism.[27] Behind the monument, one could sense the vague image of the fall of Granada, that last episode of the *Reconquista*, bringing together an Arabo-Muslim tragedy and a Hispano-Christian triumph.[28] Florian had already celebrated Gonzalo of Cordoba – Gonzalo Fernández de Córdoba y Aguilar (1453–1515) – who had negotiated the surrender of Granada in 1492. In 1816, the French dancer and choreographer Armand Vestris (1786?–1825) staged a 'heroic ballet' at London's King Theatre, which used the name of this hero of the *Reconquista*, with sets that represented the 'interior of the palace of the Alhambra'.[29] A few years later, Count Auguste de Forbin (1777–1841) exhibited a painting immortalising that very moment: *Gonzalo of Cordoba seizes in 1492, under the reign of Ferdinand and Isabella, the Alhambra of Granada, palace of the Moorish kings* (*Gonzalve de Cordoue s'empare, en 1492, sous le règne de Ferdinand et Isabelle, de l'Alhambra de Grenade, palais des rois maures*).[30] Immediately after, Victor Hugo

[27] For a British counterpart, see D. Saglia, 'The Exotic Politics of the Domestic'.

[28] The preference of many contemporary authors for a glorification of the *Reconquista* is perfectly illustrated by Count Alexis de Saint-Priest's travelogue: 'But how small, how shrunken, how petty is the whole of it. How devoid of grandeur! How typical a residence for a sensual despot! There were probably sofas surrounding these frail galleries. There, the last Moorish kings nonchalantly smoked their pipes amidst women, eunuchs, and pages. Only one single sublime idea can arise in one's soul at the sight of this edifice: the memory of the conquest of Granada. Ferdinand and Isabella, with their court in armour, kneel before a hastily improvised altar. The *Te Deum* resonates in this infidel cloister. Such a scene elevates the Alhambra: from elegant it becomes sublime' (A. de Saint-Priest, *Monumens, souvenirs, mœurs de l'Espagne*, pp. 22–3; A. de Saint-Priest, *L'Espagne. Fragment d'un voyage*, p. 32).

[29] 'Théâtres de Londres'.

[30] *Explication des ouvrages*, 1822, pp. 58–9. The painting was described in great detail: 'The city of Granada is burning as the result of a long siege and a deadly assault. In the middle of the

(1802–85) would incorporate the image of the Alhambra into his visions of the Orient,[31] devoting an entire ode of his *Orientales* to Granada, which he described as unique among all the cities of Spain because 'it has the Alhambra'.[32]

There was some irony in Hugo's passion for Granada, if one considers that his father, Joseph Sigisbert Léopold Hugo (1773–1828), was a general in Napoleon's army, who took an active part in the French occupation of Spain, which nearly caused the destruction of the Alhambra. Indeed, his companion in arms, Horace Sébastiani (1772–1851), had made the monument his headquarters, with ambiguous consequences, to say the least, for its state of preservation. On the one hand, he had the roofs and many sections repaired in order to make them liveable, but on the other hand, he had also caused considerable damage while at the same time engaging in a systematic plunder of the monument.[33] Sébastiani himself, evidently still under the influence of his residency in Constantinople as ambassador (1806–8), revelled in a setting he had entirely Orientalised, where he acted like a nabob.[34] A tragedy unfolded in 1812, when he had to evacuate Granada and decided to blow up the entire

---

night, Gonzalo has forced open the gates of the palace of the Alhambra. He compels the old Boabdil, last king of Granada, to incline before the cross borne by the grand master of the Order of Calatrava, followed by his religious knights. One of Gonzalo's young squires places at the foot of the Crucifix the insignia taken from the Moors. Boabdil's first eunuch has not abandoned his master. One of Gonzalo's pages carries his lance, his shield, and walks at the head of the men-at-arms. In the foreground of the painting, Moraïm dispenses care to the young Almanzor, who expires after having fought with intrepidity. Fragments of armour and Saracen costumes prove that the victory was disputed for a long time, even inside the palace. At middle ground, one can see the Fountain of the Lions, famous in the history of Granada, and a section of the waterspouts that used to cool the delicious garden of the Generalife. The sea closes the horizon.' A painting by Forbin bearing this name and corresponding in every detail to this description, but dated 1831, can be seen at the Granet Museum, Aix-en-Provence. Could it be a later copy by the painter of the canvas he exhibited in 1822? I shall leave this mystery pending.

31 V. Hugo, 'Les deux îles', ode VI (July 1825), *Odes et ballades*, vol. I, pp. 267–80; Hugo, 'La fée et la péri', ode XV (July 1824), *Odes et ballades*, vol. II, pp. 447–61.

32 V. Hugo, 'Grenade', ode XXXI (April 1828), *Les Orientales*, vol. III, pp. 291–2.

33 On the occupation of Granada by Napoleon's troops, see J. M. Barrios Rozúa, *Granada napoleónica*.

34 'His headquarters were then located in Granada, where he lived like a true satrap. The *corregidores* [provincial officials] had been forced, under his orders, to furnish in Oriental style and cover with sofas the Alhambra, that ancient residence of the Moorish kings. General

citadel after him. According to some sources, it was one José García, brigadier in the veterans' unit (*cuerpo de inválidos*), who, at the risk of his life, averted the catastrophe by defusing the explosives that were meant to trigger a chain reaction. The Alhambra nevertheless lost eight of its towers in the event.[35]

An Architectural Wonder

If, on the one hand, the Alhambra kindled fantasies and flights of lyricism, on the other, its architecture contributed to its growing visibility and popularity beyond Spain. Initially, well before the publication of the famous architectural studies of the decades to come, it seems that this role fell almost exclusively on the Fountain of the Lions, by means of a growing number of copies. The fountain of the water tower on Bondi Boulevard in Paris, designed by the engineer Pierre-Simon Girard (1765–1836) and inaugurated in 1811, constitutes a particularly interesting case, due to the ambiguity with which it was received. Indeed, while several comments mentioned the fact that it was inspired by the Fountain of the Lions at the Alhambra, it seems that it drew mostly on an Egyptian model, which makes sense if one considers that Girard was a veteran of Bonaparte's Egyptian expedition of 1798–1801. If the overall look of the fountain confirms that it had very little in common with the Fountain of the Lions, the fact that several authors should have perceived it as such suggests that the monument in the Alhambra was well-known enough to be mentioned, but perhaps not sufficiently to be properly visualised.[36] At any rate, it

---

Sébastiani, perfumed, embroidered and gilt, would hold court in the hall known as the ambassadors', cross-legged like a pasha on red satin cushions. All the officers of the Fourth Corps will remember having witnessed this strange sight. Over four thousand piastres of the city's budget were spent to drive out the old palace's ancient spiders and straighten it up with some splendour' ('Lettres sur les hommes d'État de la France', p. 705). See also, Barrios Rozúa, 'El Generalife y las ruinas árabes', p. 32.

[35] Ford, *A Hand-Book for Travellers in Spain*, vol. I, p. 365.

[36] The booklet published on the occasion of the fountain's opening ceremony mentions 'ancient lions' (Aubry, *Description du château d'eau situé sur l'esplanade du boulevard de Bondi*, p. 7). In his service record, Girard calls it simply 'monumental' (P-S. Girard, *État des services de M. P.-S. Girard*, p. 10). A publication of 1817 speaks of 'eight Egyptian lions with water spouting from their mouths' ('Fontaine ou château d'eau sur le boulevart de Bondi, à Paris', *Nouveau voyage pittoresque de la France*, n.p.). According to Jean-Baptiste de Saint-Victor, the

is clear that the fountain project designed a few years later by a certain Herbert for the Place des Vosges in Paris, although never carried out, was directly modelled on the Alhambra's monument.[37] By the 1830s, reconstitutions of the Alhambra of more or less good taste had become rather common in very diverse contexts, from ephemeral constructions to actual buildings. Prince Stanisław Poniatowski (1754–1833), who lived in exile in Italy, had a *casino* built in the environs of Rome, 'of Moresque architectural style, [representing] a miniature copy of the Alhambra'.[38] At around the same time, during the visit of the King of Naples, the Spanish ambassador in Paris had a copy of the Court of the Lions built, thus giving the press an opportunity to report on the beauty of the site and, at the same time, its bloody past.[39]

These numerous, but after all rather modest, references to the Nasrid palace were followed by a true surge of works, which, this time, were entirely devoted to the monument. Baron Taylor's *Picturesque Travels in Spain* (*Voyage pittoresque en Espagne*), published in 1832, formed a sort of link between the two genres, since it took over the style and contents of Count de Laborde's work, but with even more romantic illustrations.[40] Of course, the true pioneer of this new passion was Washington Irving (1783–1859), who, after a *Chronicle of the Conquest of Granada* (1829),[41] in 1832 published his famous *Tales of the Alhambra*. This collection of short stories drew its evocative power from the combination of a traveller's observations with the

monument 'seems copied from the famous Fountain of the Lions of the Alhambra, but is far from producing as beautiful an impression' (J-B. de Saint-Victor, *Tableau historique et pittoresque de Paris*, vol. II, p. 791). In 1835, Abel Hugo ascribed its project to the 'famous Arab Fountain of the Lions at the Alhambra' (A. Hugo, *France pittoresque*, vol. III, p. 109).

[37] Laborde, *Projets d'embellissement de Paris*. See also, J. M. Barrios Rozúa, 'La recreación orientalista del Patio de los Leones', pp. 230, 240.

[38] 'Souvenirs de l'Italie', p. 318.

[39] 'M. d'Ofalia had the excellent idea of reproducing for the eyes of the King of Naples, who possesses in his kingdom the most beautiful and elegant *casini* in the world, that most remarkable spot of the palace of the Alhambra, called the Court of the Lions, famous for the Koranic inscriptions that grace its walls. These revered inscriptions, however, failed to save the Abencerrages from a treacherous death that was plotted, sworn and executed under these celebrated vaults' ('Bal de M. d'Ofalia').

[40] Baron Taylor, *Voyage pittoresque en Espagne*.

[41] W. Irving, *Chronicle of the Conquest of Granada*.

narrative of a storyteller. In it, the reader found a most lively description of the charms of a rundown palace, inhabited by the spectres and memories of Boabdil or the Abencerrages, but also by Andalusian characters that lent the book a strong local colour.[42] Irving had evidently read Chateaubriand,[43] but he also claimed to have been influenced by the stories he had heard on site from local storytellers.[44] It is probably no coincidence that only a few years after Irving's discovery of the Alhambra as a 'real tourist',[45] several artists also made extended stays in Granada, often at the Alhambra itself. David Roberts (1796–1834), better known for the numerous lavish illustrations of his travels in Egypt and Palestine, had visited Spain a few years earlier, in 1832. The artist and future pioneer of photography, Joseph-Philibert Girault de Prangey (1804–92) resided there in 1832–3; the Orientalist painter John Frederick Lewis (1804–76) did so in 1833–4; the architect Jules Goury (1803–34) died of cholera while he was drawing plans of the palace, and his colleague Owen Jones (1809–74), who had accompanied him then, returned to the site in 1837. In less than five years, the Alhambra had become the target of an interest that clearly exceeded simple curiosity; from collecting picturesque views of the site, the objective had started moving towards a desire to document the monument's every detail.

Among the many works that resulted from these sojourns, those by David Roberts and Frederick Lewis were most clearly connected to the lineage of the picturesque travels of the previous decades, but with the addition of a very strong touch of romanticism. In both these volumes, the main views of the Alhambra, both exterior and interior, were drawn with great precision, but with a particular stress on the dilapidated state of the monument and on the

42 Irving's *Tales of the Alhambra* were published under several names, all in 1832: W. Irving, *The Alhambra: A Series of Sketches and Tales of the Moors and Spaniards*; G. Crayon [alias W. Irving], *The Alhambra*; W. Irving, *The Alhambra; or the New Sketch Book*. For a detailed analysis of Irving's relation to the site of the Alhambra, see J. Rubin-Dorsky, '*The Alhambra*: Washington Irving's House of Fiction'.

43 R. L. Kagan, *The Spanish Craze*, p. 138.

44 G. Crayon [alias Irving], 'Recollections of the Alhambra'.

45 I have taken the liberty of borrowing this expression from the French version of the book, used to translate 'rambling expedition' in the English original (Irving, *L'Alhambra. Chroniques du pays de Grenade*, p. 1).

local colour provided by numerous 'typical' characters such as muleteers, peasants, Romani, women in mantillas and guitar players.[46] The point was not just to document an architectural wonder, but to convey the atmosphere of an edifice in ruins and of the colourful figures who still haunted it. Roberts and Lewis' plates would have perfectly illustrated Irving's tales.[47]

Only with Girault de Prangey did romanticism gradually start to give way to an increasingly exclusive attention given to architecture and decoration. Interestingly, his stay at the Alhambra resulted in two publications. The first, published in 1837, was more conventional in the way it used a great number of plates reminiscent of those of his precursors: the accuracy of the exteriors and interiors was mixed with the romanticism and exoticism of local scenes. And yet this work already included several plates of a much more sober character, devoted to architectural details and decorative motifs, as well as two double plates dedicated to a plan of the site and to 'sections, elevations and details of the palace'.[48] As suggested by its title, *Essay on the Architecture of the Arabs and Moors* (*Essai sur l'architecture des Arabes et des Mores*), Girault de Prangey's second publication, which came out four years later, focused unequivocally on Moresque architecture in general, and that of the Alhambra in particular. Its plates, entirely devoid of any form of local fantasy, focused exclusively on the reproduction of architectural details, decorative motifs and inscriptions, to which an entire section was devoted.[49]

However, it was with Jules Goury and Owen Jones that this trend reached its peak. The publication, in 1842 and 1845, of the two volumes of their joint venture – posthumously in Goury's case – marked the consecration of the Alhambra as the unique embodiment of Moresque architecture and decoration. Rather significantly, these volumes reflected this somewhat binary vision of the monument. The first volume contained fifty-one plates, the

[46] D. Roberts, *Picturesque Views of Spain and Morocco*; J. F. Lewis, *Lewis's Sketches and Drawings of the Alhambra*. See also, A. Gámiz Gordo, 'Los dibujos originales de los palacios de la Alhambra de J. F. Lewis'.

[47] In fact, Roberts and Lewis' engravings were used to illustrate some of the later editions of Irving's *Tales*. See, for example, Irving, *Tales of the Alhambra*.

[48] J-Ph. Girault de Prangey, *Monuments arabes et moresques de Cordoue, Séville et Grenade*.

[49] J-Ph. Girault de Prangey, *Essai sur l'architecture des Arabes et des Mores, en Espagne, en Sicile, et en Barbarie*.

overwhelming majority of which consisted of architectural plans and details; the last plates of this volume, as well as all those of the second volume, reproduced in rather systematic fashion the principal decorative motifs of the palace: frescoes, stuccos, mosaics and every other form of ornamentation.[50]

In more than one way, Owen Jones' work constitutes a decisive turn in the history of the Alhambra, which saw the monument's popularity spread across the world in the following decades. As the last link in a long chain of narratives, images and plans of the Nasrid palace, this work gave it a final consecration as an artistic monument and a masterpiece of Moresque art. This style would thus take its place in Jones' *Grammar of Ornament*, which he published in 1856 in an attempt to list the basic principles regulating the interaction between forms and colours in the formation of architectural and decorative styles.[51] A theoretician of decorative arts, a committed champion of polychromy and an impresario of historicist architecture, Owen Jones contributed to the dissemination of the image of the Alhambra well beyond the publication of his *Grammar*. He fed it indirectly into the Crystal Palace exhibition at Hyde Park in 1851 through the use of a tricolour decoration of blue, red and yellow, but even more when he was entrusted, together with Matthew Digby Wyatt (1820–77), with the addition to the building, transferred to Sydenham in 1854, of a series of 'historical courts' meant to give a concise vision of the history of civilisation. Next to those of Egypt, Nineveh, Greece and Rome, the 'Alhambra Court' was formed of the interconnected copies of the Hall of the Abencerrages, the Hall of Justice and, finally, the Court of the Lions with its famous central fountain (Figure 1.1).[52]

Jones was the first to explicitly and quite literally use the reference to the Alhambra by making a near-identical copy of architectural elements taken from the Nasrid palace. Nevertheless, he had some more 'flexible' precursors. When the Colosseum at Regent's Park in London, which was built in 1827

[50] J. Goury and O. Jones, *Plans, Elevations, Sections, and Details of the Alhambra*.

[51] O. Jones, *The Grammar of Ornament*. Chapter Ten, devoted to Moresque ornamentation, contained nine pages of text and eight plates, all of which were taken from his *Plans, Elevations, Sections, and Details of the Alhambra*.

[52] O. Jones, 'The Alhambra Court in the Crystal Palace'; *Views of the Crystal Palace and Park*, pp. 28–9, pl. XI; K. Ferry, 'Owen Jones and the Alhambra Court at the Crystal Palace'.

Figure 1.1 'The Alhambra Court, Crystal Palace, Sydenham'. Detail of a photograph by Philip Henry Delamotte, c. 1855. Prints, drawings and paintings collection, Victoria and Albert Museum, London, available at: https://collections.vam.ac.uk/item/O155277/the-alhambra-court---photograph-delamotte-philip-henry. A view of Owen Jones' partial reconstitution of the Court of the Lions at Crystal Palace as part of his series of historical courtyards.

by the architect Decimus Burton (1800–81) on the model of the Pantheon of Rome to house Thomas Hornor's (1785–1844) panorama of London changed hands in 1843, many novelties were introduced, each more eclectic than the next. Among these, the two winter gardens or conservatories flanking a Gothic aviary were remodelled in the Moresque style, while an external pathway wound through fake classical ruins. The illustrated press of the time praised this 'tasteful combination of the Moorish and the Gothic':

> In the centre is a Gothic Aviary, superbly fitted up with gilt carvings, and looking-glass, and 'such as Isabella of Castile might have been supposed to have commanded to be erected amidst the relics of a Moorish Palace: Abd-Abdallah, with true Arabian gallantry, to have conjured up for the solace of some fair Christian captive, within the enchanted walls of his own Alhambra'; and, as Washington Irving observes: 'How many legends and traditions, true and fabulous; how many songs and romances, Spanish and Arabian, of love, and war, and chivalry, are associated with this romantic pile!'[53]

Even before Owen Jones appropriated the Alhambra for good as his trademark, the British market and public had already been strongly impacted by the image of so-called Moresque style and decoration. The very year of the opening of the Crystal Palace Exhibition, a manufacturer of stoves from Sheffield by the name of Stuart & Smith presented a model called 'Alhambra', with an 'arabesque pattern of the richest description', which was purchased by Queen Victoria herself.[54] Two years later, the artist and entrepreneur Robert Burford (1791–1861), who owned an establishment on Leicester Square specialising in the then very popular attraction of panoramas, drew crowds with his 'View of Granada and the Alhambra'.[55] British infatuation with the Alhambra found one of its most imposing expressions in a theatre that bore its name, the Royal Alhambra Theatre of Varieties or Royal Alhambra Palace, which opened in 1856. Ironically, this theatre was located in a building that already presented all the features of an Oriental style carried to its extreme:

[53] 'Re-Opening of the Colosseum, Regent's Park'.

[54] 'Alhambra Stove. By Stuart & Smith, Sheffield'.

[55] R. Burford, *Description of a View of the City of Granada*; 'Panorama of the "Alhambra", Leicester Square'; 'Mr. Burford's Panorama of Granada and the Alhambra'.

a 32 m high façade decorated with doors and windows in Moresque style, topped with an enormous dome in Persian style, flanked by two minarets. This had been Edward Marmaduke Clarke's (1806–59) Royal Panopticon of Science and Art, a sort of spectacle and exhibition hall inaugurated in 1854 and dedicated to arts and sciences, whose architect, Thomas Hayter Lewis (1818–98), explained that he had been inspired by the mosques of Cairo, while at the same time taking into consideration all the 'modifications necessary to the modern customs of Europe'.[56] Most likely, the building's pre-existing eclectic Orientalist style had inspired the name of the theatre that would succeed the Royal Panopticon. After all, when viewed from London, a Cairene mosque and a Moresque palace were not very different. The theatre's publicity booklet thus claimed the building's 'Saracenic architecture', praised its resemblance to 'some of the enchanted palaces described in Oriental fiction', noted that 'the dome, the minarets, the horseshoe arch . . . are strictly in accordance with the Moorish order of architecture', adding that the structure 'constitutes a striking example of the palace and fortress founded by Mohamed I in the 13th century' (Figure 1.2).[57]

The Alhambra's reputation in Britain was solidly established by then, even overrated.[58] In Germany, Ludwig von Zanth (1796–1857) worked from 1842

[56] 'The Royal Panopticon of Science and Art, Leicester-Square'; P. Cunningham, *London in 1853*, p. 302; 'Opening of the Royal Panopticon'; E. Ziter, *The Orient on the Victorian Stage*, p. 119; J. Hamilton, *A Strange Business: Making Art and Money in Nineteenth-Century Britain*, pp. 309–10.

[57] W. White, *The Illustrated Hand Book of the Royal Alhambra Palace, Leicester Square*, pp. 5–6.

[58] The British press of the time perfectly illustrates the Alhambra's success with a wide and diverse public. It is particularly striking to note how the younger generations were targeted. One of the major magazines for children devoted no less than four pages to the monument and advised its young readers to visit the Crystal Palace with that particular issue at hand ('The Moorish Palace of Alhambra'). Women's magazines also contributed to the propagation of this image, even though one could sense some ambiguity due to an underlying Islamophobia. Thus, one article praising the beauty of the monument concluded with these words: 'But Time, the destroyer, is eating it away; and the palace of the Moor must make room for the cottage of the Christian, so surely as Bible truth shall replace the delusive promises of the Koran' ('The Alhambra', *The Ladies' Treasury*). A similar tone dominated another article, published a few years later in the press 'for ladies' and illustrated with the Court of the Lions at Crystal Palace, which presented the Spanish campaign in Africa as a just revenge for the past domination of the Moors over Iberia ('Spain and the Moors').

Figure 1.2 'The Royal Panopticon, Leicester-Square', *The Illustrated London News*, 543 (31 January 1852), p. 96. Ahmet Salcan collection, Istanbul. A detailed depiction of the eclectic building combining a great variety of styles: Persian dome, Cairene minarets, and Moresque, Gothic and Byzantine façade.

to 1847 on the realisation of the palatial complex commissioned by Wilhelm I, King of Wurttemberg, in Bad Canstatt, in the environs of Stuttgart, which included a ballroom (*Festsaal*) and a villa (*Landhaus*) in Moresque style, strongly inspired by the Alhambra.[59]As Zanth had never visited Spain, he had to rely on the authors mentioned above, from Laborde to Jones, and on the help of his master and friend Jacob Ignaz Hittorff (1792–1867), and his student, Christian Friedrich Leins (1814–92).[60] These two major 'schools' of the Alhambresque – the British and the German – ended up conquering the entire world, starting with Spain itself, whose commissioned architects often resorted to this style as an expression of national identity. This is particularly the case for the Spanish pavilions at the world exhibitions, which often mimicked Moresque architecture. Of course, there were always hesitations, since Spain possessed a Catholic national style also, the Plateresque (*plateresco*),

[59] L. von Zanth, *Die Wilhelma*; S. Koppelkamm, *The Imaginary Orient*, pp. 65–75.

[60] F. Giese, 'An Inclination for the Moorish Style'.

which harked back to the splendour of Spain during its 'golden' sixteenth century. Thus, the Spanish pavilion at the 1867 Paris Exhibition took up this style, while the Alhambresque was claimed by a small Prussian pavilion designed by Carl von Diebitsch (1819–1869).[61] Perhaps influenced by comments criticising them for not having used the Moresque style that was so popular at the time, the Spanish government reverted to the Mudejar and Moresque styles in 1873 in Vienna and in 1878 in Paris, respectively (Figure 1.3).[62] The (neo-) Plateresque made a comeback in 1900, in a context that will be analysed later, before a final return to the Alhambresque in 1910 at Brussels.[63]

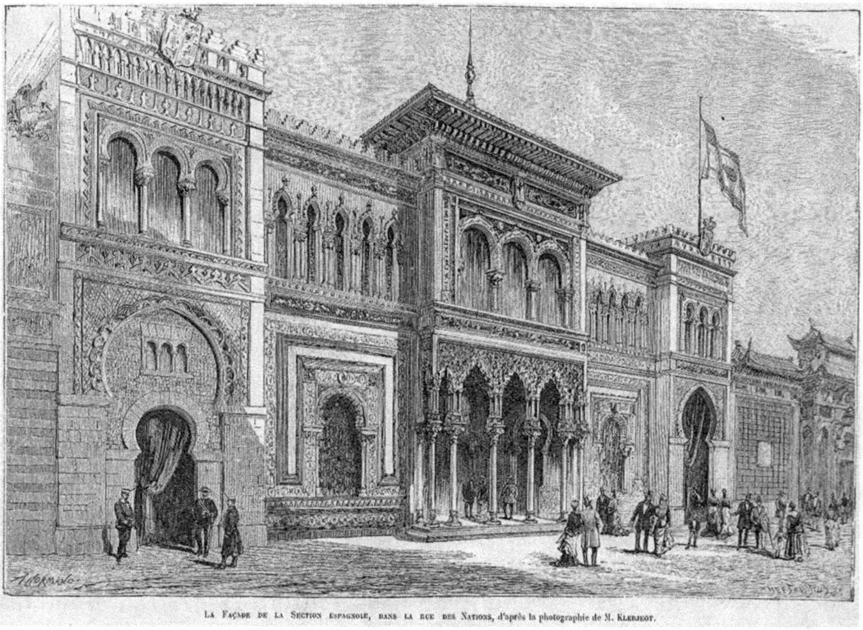

Figure 1.3 'The façade of the Spanish section, on Nations Street', *L'Illustration*, 1, 841 (8 June 1878), p. 365. Author's collection. The architectural and decorative details of this imposing structure designed by Agustín Ortiz de Villajos were picked from a number of Arab and Mudejar structures from Cordoba, Zaragoza, Tarragona and Toledo to produce an overall Moresque style.

[61] A. McSweeney, 'El mudéjar y el alhambresco', pp. 208–10.

[62] McSweeney, 'El mudéjar y el alhambresco', pp. 216–24.

[63] D. Delpechin, 'Orientalism Challenged: The Spanish Pavilion at the 1910 Brussels International Exhibition'.

In Italy, the extraordinary castle of Rocchetta Mattei, built in the 1850s by the famous founder of electrohomeopathy Count Cesare Mattei (1809–96), included a courtyard that imitated – in rather modest fashion – the Court of the Lions. At around the same time, another Italian aristocrat with a huge fortune, Ferdinando Panciatichi Ximenes d'Aragona (1813–97), gradually transformed his Florentine palace of Sammezzano into one of the most outrageous Orientalist fantasies of the century, partly through architectural elements and motifs borrowed from the Alhambra.[64] This fad reached as far as Chile, if one considers the 'Palace of the Alhambra' built in Santiago in the 1860s by the mining magnate Francisco Ossa Mercado.[65] In the United States, already under the charm of Washington Irving's writings, the Moresque style found one of the most fertile grounds in which it could flourish, often combined with the Spanish colonial 'missionary' style, even just in name, if one considers the plethora of theatres and cinemas bearing the suggestive names of Seville, Granada and, of course, Alhambra.[66] Finally, how could one ignore the infatuation of the Jewish communities of Central Europe for this particular architecture and decoration, as witnessed by their use in the construction of so many synagogues?[67] As to the diffusion of the Alhambresque model in the Orient, especially in the Ottoman imperial capital of Istanbul, I shall leave this fascinating but complex issue to another section of this work.

The Black Legend

As mentioned above, Henry Swinburne's travelogue, published in 1779, had made a strong impression on his peers, including the Spanish team in charge of the publication of the *Antigüedades árabes de España* commissioned by the Royal Academy of San Fernando. Swinburne's work combined a lively text, consisting of letters focusing on one topic or site, with plates, which, although

[64] A. Varela Braga, 'Building a Dream: the Alhambra in the Villa of Sammezzano'.

[65] M. A. Emparán Fernández, 'Palacio de la Alhambra: Un orientalismo chileno del siglo xix'. On other examples of Moresque architecture and decoration in Latin America, see R. Gutiérrez Viñuales, 'Alhambras americanas: Memoria de una fascinación'.

[66] See Kagan, *The Spanish Craze*, pp. 305–40.

[67] I. D. Kalmar, 'Moorish Style: Orientalism, the Jews, and Synagogue Architecture'; B. von Orelli-Messerli, 'Gottfried Semper's Dresden Synagogue Revised: An Echo of the Alhambra?'; Hildegard Frübis, 'Die Neue Synagoge in Berlin (1866) und die Alhambra'.

of inferior quality, already prefigured the illustrated works of the decades to come. Three 'letters' were devoted to Granada. Letter XXII praised the wealth and beauty of the city under Moorish rule and lamented the loss caused by the departure of the Muslims, as well as the persecution suffered by the Moriscos only five decades earlier.[68] The second letter described the Alhambra in great detail and insisted heavily on the beauty, perfection, originality and ingenious layout of the site.[69] Finally, a third letter spoke of the contemporary state of the city of Granada, in terms that betrayed Swinburne's lack of admiration or sympathy: 'After the Alhambra, I am afraid the rest of the city will go down but poorly: indeed there is little worth seeing here.' He did recognise its natural charm stemming from the beauty of the site, and its exceptionally pleasant climate, which he believed enhanced its women's beauty and complexion. For the rest, however, he found everything to be ordinary or just ugly. The streets were 'narrow and dirty' and used by the 'common people . . . to perform the filthiest of nature's functions', albeit 'with much decency'. 'Most of the small houses are Moorish built, or coarse imitations of that manner, the modern masons decorating their walls with uncouth copies of Saracenic mosaics.'[70] Not even the cathedral was immune to Swinburne's disdain; its large chapel had been 'erected by Ferdinand V, at that unfortunate era of the arts, when all the lightness and beautiful caprice of the Saracenic taste was laid aside, to make room for an unwieldy, preposterous mode of building'.[71]

This notion of a striking contrast between the glorious past of al-Andalus and the pitiful state of contemporary Spain, between the beauty and sophistication of the Alhambra and the sight of the miserable towns and edifices of modern Andalusia came up frequently in the publications of the time. To be sure, the message was sometimes more discreet, implicit, as in Murphy's work, quoted earlier, where the author was content with praising the beauty and refinement of the Alhambra against the barbarism of medieval Europe, without implicating contemporary Spain. That was probably why he used that strange expression of 'Spanish Arabs', rather than 'Moors', as most of his peers did.[72] Nevertheless, some have seen in this tendency of non-Spanish

[68] Swinburne, *Travels through Spain*, pp. 162–71.

[69] Swinburne, *Travels through Spain*, pp. 171–88.

[70] Swinburne, *Travels through Spain*, pp. 190–1.

[71] Swinburne, *Travels through Spain*, p. 193.

[72] Murphy, *The Arabian Antiquities of Spain*, 'Introduction', n.p.

authors to stress the contrast between the Andalusian past and present an element of the 'Black Legend', which has targeted Spain ever since the early modern period. Thus, José Francisco Pérez Berenguel does not hesitate to accuse Swinburne not only of having accepted the lies of this legend, but of having contributed to it by adding new ones.[73]

The 'Black Legend' is a delicate issue in Spanish historiography, which I believe deserves our attention in the context of this study. The paternity of this expression can be attributed to the French historian Arthur Lévy (1847–1931), who, probably inspired by Jacobus de Voragine's (*c.* 1230–1298) *Golden Legend* (*Légende dorée*),[74] claimed in his *Intimate Napoleon* (*Napoléon intime*, 1893), that 'by studying the life of the Emperor with honesty, one soon sees the truth emerge from the golden legend, but also from what one is allowed to call the Napoleonian black legend'.[75] According to this earliest usage of the term, a 'black legend' consists of a fundamentally negative perception of a person or event, as opposed to a hagiographic approach – a golden legend – stressing only the positive aspects of the subject. Nevertheless, it was in the context of Spanish historiography that this term acquired a very particular meaning and relevance. With his work bearing the explicit title of *The Black Legend and Historical Truth* (*La leyenda negra y la verdad histórica*, 1914), Julián Juderías (1877–1918) would consecrate the usage of the expression in Spanish and, most importantly, its application to the history of Spain.[76] The following was his definition of the concept:

> By Black Legend, we understand the atmosphere created by the fantastic accounts about our Fatherland that have popped out in almost all countries;

[73] J. F. Pérez Berenguel, 'Las fuentes principales de los *Viajes por España* (1779) de Henry Swinburne', pp. 76–80.

[74] The *Golden Legend* or *Legenda aurea* was a work composed in the 1260s by the Dominican and archbishop of Genoa, Jacopo de Varazze or Jacques de Voragine, on the lives of about 150 Christian saints and martyrs.

[75] A. Lévy, *Napoléon intime*, p. v.

[76] In 1913, Juderías won the prize for historical studies of the illustrated magazine *La Ilustración española y americana* with this text, the conclusion of which was published in the issue of 15 February 1914 (J. Juderías, 'La leyenda negra y la verdad histórica, España ante Europa'). That same year, his essay was published under the title of *La leyenda negra y la verdad histórica: Contribución al estudio del concepto de España en Europa, de las causas de este concepto y de la tolerancia religiosa y política en los países civilizados.*

> the grotesque descriptions that have always been made of the Spaniards as individuals and as a community; the systematic denial, or at least ignorance, of whatever is favourable to, or honours, us with respect to various manifestations of culture and art; the accusations made at all times against Spain on the basis of exaggerated, misinterpreted or entirely false facts and, finally, the claim made in seemingly respectable and truthful books, often reproduced, commented and amplified in the foreign press, that our Fatherland constitutes, from the viewpoint of tolerance, of culture and of progress, a regrettable exception among the community of European nations.[77]

This definition, together with the opposition suggested in the title between the legend and historical truth, prove to what extent Juderías had strayed from Lévy's interrogative stance. Indeed, while he stressed the contrast between the golden and black legends, the French historian did not label one or the other as true or false. To him, the truth would emerge from a scholarly and critical use of both; the danger was to fall for one or the other, forgetting that the truth was necessarily somewhere in between. In his words, 'Napoleon was neither a god, nor a monster, but simply – following the classic formula that one can apply to him – he was human, and nothing human was foreign to him.'[78] To Juderías, on the contrary, there was no hesitation or ambiguity. The Black Legend was the exact opposite of historical truth, a pile of lies, calumny and exaggerations. These claims to a perpetual victimisation of Spain and its history, together with Juderías' repeated references to the 'Fatherland', seriously hampered the historiographical value of the concept he proposed.

Nevertheless, the defensive – not to say paranoid – and clearly nationalist – not to say chauvinistic – character of Juderías' arguments should not make us forget the reality of a perception and representation of Spain by foreign observers, at least since the nineteenth century. Two major events seem to have been at the origin of a negative vision of Spain. On the one hand, the conquest of America and the establishment of a colonial empire had provoked the jealousy and envy of the other European monarchies; on the other, the rise

[77] Juderías, *La leyenda negra*, pp. 14–15.

[78] Lévy, *Napoléon intime*, p. v. Of course, he was borrowing this expression from Terence's famous saying, 'I am human, and I think nothing human is alien to me' ('Homo sum, humani nihil a me alienum puto').

of the Protestant reform had contributed to the stigmatisation of Spain as the bastion of Catholicism.[79] In both cases, its rivals soon developed powerful arguments to demonstrate the barbaric character of Spain.[80] Regarding the conquest of America, the Dominican friar Bartolomé de las Casas' *Brief Account of the Destruction of the Indies* (*Brevísima relación de la destrucción de las Indias*)[81] provided them with the evidence of the inhumane treatment of the indigenous population by the conquistadores. This work was translated into several languages and, more importantly, illustrated and often modified in such a way as to indict the Spaniards with all possible and imaginable cruelties, from torture to cannibalism, including systematic massacre.[82] Not surprisingly, this theme was rehashed in an American pamphlet, published on the occasion of the Hispano-American conflict of 1898.[83]

Rather predictably, the second component of the legend fed on the Spanish Inquisition, perceived not only as a form of violence akin to the treatment of the Amerindian populations, but also as an unmistakable sign of religious – and by extension, political – intolerance, which set Spain apart from the rest of Europe. This explains why many Spanish authors, starting with Juderías, should have chosen to counter this argument by claiming that other European states had always proved to be much more violent and intolerant than Spain.[84] In fact, the country's feeling of having been ostracised by Europe went back to much earlier times. Almost 150 years earlier, in a work published in 1759 and devoted to the 'abuse of royal revenues' ('*Abusos de las*

[79] Kagan, *The Spanish Craze*, pp. 8–9.

[80] For a history of the Black Legend, see, among others, J. P. Sánchez, *The Spanish Black Legend/La Leyenda Negra Española*; J. Pérez, *La Légende noire de l'Espagne*; M. E. Roca Barea, *Imperiofobia y leyenda negra*.

[81] B. de las Casas, *Brevísima relación de la destrucción de las Indias*.

[82] See, for example, *Narratio Regionum Indicarum per Hispanos quosdam Deuastatum Verissima; Le Miroir de la cruelle, & horrible tyrannie espagnole*.

[83] *Horrible Atrocities of Spaniards in Cuba*.

[84] The fourth and last part of Juderías' work was devoted to 'religious and political tolerance in Europe from the sixteenth to the nineteenth century (Juderías, *La leyenda negra*, pp. 127–219). In rather similar fashion, Roca Barea's controversial work includes a section on the 'the Inquisition and *the Inquisition*', where she puts forward an apology of the Spanish Inquisition by stressing the violence and scope of the Protestant inquisition and of witch hunts in Europe (Roca Barea, *Imperiofobia y leyenda negra*, pp. 326–60).

rentas reales'), the *arbitrista* or 'giver of advice' Joaquín de Aguirre had already complained that by means of unfavourable pacts and treaties, other nations were treating Spain 'like the Indies of Europe'.[85]

The matter is too delicate and touchy to allow for a categorical statement on the existence or not of a 'Black Legend', which might have systematically tainted the history of Spain for more than four centuries and continues to haunt Europe's collective memory. Clearly, there is some truth to the legend, but it also serves the purposes of a certain Spanish historiography that instrumentalises these prejudices and clichés to promote an overly positive, and generally apologetic vision of the past. At any rate, in this particular case, it seems clear that the 'Black Legend' is much less relevant to the question of the perception of the Alhambra. I believe that the example of Swinburne's account provides a middle ground between the two extreme positions in the debate. While there is little doubt that he did observe, and attach importance to, the Andalusia of the fourteenth century and that in which he roamed in 1775 and 1776, it would probably be an exaggeration to interpret this as the result of centuries of indoctrination or of a conscious commitment to a cabal directed at Spain's honour and reputation. At a time when romanticism was often coloured with medievalism, it was only natural that the Alhambra, together with other monuments of Arab art and culture in Andalusia, should have triggered feelings of nostalgia for a lavish and exotic past, often at the cost of viewing the present through the filter of these prestigious ruins. In the face of such splendour, even partly imagined, the rest of the landscape could understandably look dull, even at times squalid. Nevertheless, one needs to consider the possibility that if the surroundings of these glorious remains were so often frowned upon, it was not necessarily because they were Spanish, but rather because they were not medieval.

We should not forget that the work that contributed the most, in the short and long run, to the visibility and fame of the site, Washington Irving's *Tales of the Alhambra*, kept a balance between past and present, between the splendour of the Arab palace of yore and the charm of the local population squatting in its ruins. Nothing in his stories denigrated Spain; at most, he may have had a clear tendency to play the card of exoticism by putting forward

[85] J. V. Vives, *An Economic History of Spain*, p. 568.

colourful characters, such as smugglers, bandits, dancers, Romani and story-tellers. As a result, contrary to the opinion of some authors who claim that his work fed into the Black Legend,[86] I would rather agree with Richard Kagan, who sees in Irving's oeuvre a strong dose of Hispanophilia, running counter to the 'then prevalent Anglo-American view of Spain as a dark, sinister, almost gothic country'. According to Kagan, Irving was partly responsible for the emergence of yet another Spanish stereotype, positive this time, that of 'Sunny Spain'.[87] Granada was described as picturesque and beautiful, Spain as a land of adventure and romanticism, and its inhabitants as even more striking than the Italians.[88] Irving himself, now adored by an ever-growing number of American readers, looked back fondly at the striking contrast he had perceived:

> I lived in the midst of an Arabian tale, and shut my eyes, as much as possible, to everything that called me back to every-day life; and if there is any country in Europe where one can do so, it is in poor, wild, legendary, proud-spirited, romantic Spain; where the old magnificent barbaric spirit still contends against the utilitarianism of modern civilization.[89]

Perhaps the best alternative to the somewhat Manichaean interpretation of the Black Legend can be found in Irving's dedication to his friend and travel companion during his trip to Spain in 1828, the Scottish artist David Wilkie (1785–1841):

> You may remember, that in the rambles we once took together about some of the old cities of Spain, particularly Toledo and Seville, we remarked a strong mixture of the Saracenic with the Gothic, remaining from the time of the Moors; and were more than once struck with scenes and incidents in

[86] J. Herlihy-Mera, 'Islamic Spain in American Travel Writing', pp. 129–32. True, the author stresses that under Irving's pen, the Black Legend is much tempered and often reduced to a 'selective exaltation of 'Moorish' symbols in Granada'. Nevertheless, he does note that 'when we scrutinize his interactions with people who are ostensibly Catholic, and his remarks about the cultures of these communities, his perceptions are forcefully negative' (p. 129).

[87] Kagan, *The Spanish Craze*, pp. 8–9.

[88] Kagan, *The Spanish Craze*, p. 140.

[89] Crayon [alias Irving], 'Recollections of the Alhambra', p. 485.

> the streets, which reminded us of passages in the 'Arabian Nights'. You then urged me to write something that should illustrate those peculiarities, 'something in the Haroun Alraschid style', that should have a dash of that Arabian spice which pervades everything in Spain. I call this to your mind to show you that you are, in some degree, responsible for the present work, in which I have given a few 'Arabesque' sketches from the life, and tales founded on popular traditions, which were chiefly struck off during a residence in one of the most Morisco-Spanish places in the Peninsula.[90]

These repetitive references to 'Arab' elements, both in the Moorish past and the Andalusian present, suggest that the leitmotiv of Irving's narrative came very close to contemporary notions of the Orient. Obviously, this was an Orient that was vague enough to suit as much the identity of the former conquerors of the land as its present inhabitants and to allow for daring parallels between Seville and Baghdad and between an Abbasid caliph and the masters of al-Andalus. Given this, in the case of the Alhambra, it seems necessary to break away from the specific context of the Black Legend and to widen our perspective beyond the Iberian Peninsula. Once again, Washington Irving provides us with a clue as to how this could be done in his striking description of the Alhambra:

> Such is the Alhambra. A Moslem pile, in the midst of a Christian land; an Oriental palace amidst the Gothic edifices of the West; an elegant memento of a brave, intelligent, and graceful people, who conquered, ruled, and passed away.[91]

One can immediately discern three levels of discourse. First, the very local and specific level of the history of the Moors, who, after centuries of presence and glory, have finally ceded their place to the Spaniards. Second, emerges the somewhat wider context of two civilisations defined by their religions, Islam and Christianity. Finally, at the third and most general level appears the much vaguer but so powerful dichotomy of East and West, Orient and Occident. A simple pseudo-statistical survey of the frequency of repetition of certain terms

[90] Irving, *The Alhambra*, vol. I, p. iii.

[91] Irving, *The Alhambra*, vol. I, p. 47.

in the book seems to confirm this hierarchy. 'Moor' and its derivatives [Moor*] appear 236 times, undeniably forming the core of the narrative. Arab [Arab*] and Spanish [Spani*, Spain] fall far behind, with 81 and 61 occurrences, respectively. As to the binomial of Islam [Moslem*, Islam*] and Christianity [Christ*, Catho*] this follows closely, at 57 and 59, respectively. Finally, Orient [Orient*] and West [West*, Europe*] are the rarest, but still very present, with 14 and 13 repetitions. Behind Spain, behind Andalusia, behind the Alhambra, one can catch a glimpse of one the most powerful fantasies of the nineteenth century, Orientalism, but packed in Russian-doll fashion. Benjamin Disraeli (1804–81), who visited the Alhambra just a year after Irving, did not hesitate to compare the Alhambra to the Parthenon, the Pantheon, Seville cathedral and the Temple of Dendera.[92] As to the Spaniards, he viewed them as 'kind and faithful, courageous and honest, with a profound mind, that will nevertheless break into rich humour, and a dignity which, like their passion, is perhaps the legacy of their Oriental sires'.[93]

If any doubt subsisted as to the representativeness of Irving's work, one could simply submit to the same test one of the most frequently consulted books of the period, Richard Ford's (1796–1858) *Hand-Book for Travellers in Spain*, first published by John Murray in 1845.[94] The results are striking: the Orient – exclusively under the form of the adjective Oriental – pops up no less than 291 times – against 1,042 for [Moor*] – 103 of which, amounting to more than a third, occur in the 100-page introduction describing the history, culture, customs and traditions of the country. The circumstances under which this term appears leaves no place for ambiguity: every time, it has either to do with a description of some trait or character of the Spaniards, or to a comparison with 'Orientals'. The expression 'like [the] Orientals' is repeated sixteen times, twelve of which are in the introduction. For the rest, the adjective 'Oriental' describes practically every aspect of life in Spain, from resignation to vengeance, from cuisine to dance, from decoration to devotion and from costume to prejudice. One thus discovers that the *toreros* are 'true Orientals'; that 'the airs and tunes, as sung by the

92 B. Disraeli, *Contarini Fleming*, vol. IV, p. 8.

93 Disraeli, *Contarini Fleming*, vol. IV, p. 18.

94 Ford, *A Hand-Book for Travellers in Spain*.

peasants and lower classes, are very Oriental'; that the character of Gipsy dances is 'completely Oriental' and that beating time with the hands is 'a most primitive Oriental custom'; that in medicine, 'dissection is even now most repulsive to their Oriental prejudices'; and that 'the Spaniard is an Oriental of high caste'.[95] An unmistakeable sign of Orientalism, the 'Turk' appears several times as a measure of comparison: 'A Spanish bookseller [is] more indifferent than a Turk'; 'the native, like the Turk, despised [foreigners] and their civilisation alike'; 'The Spaniard, a creature of routine and foe to innovations, is not a locomotive animal; local, and a fixture by nature, he hates moving like a Turk, and has a particular horror of being hurried.'[96] The French *Guides Joanne* had a similar opinion of the local population: 'Generally speaking, and like all the Andalusians, the inhabitants of Granada resemble more the Orientals than their fellow Europeans.'[97]

Orientalisms

Irving and Ford had not invented anything. In 1826, the year Chateaubriand published his *Adventures of the Last Abencerrage*, Alfred de Vigny (1797–1863) had drawn the same parallel between the Spaniard and the Turk in his bestselling novel, *Cinq-Mars*. The long monologue of a Spanish prisoner began by addressing that striking ambiguity:

> The Orient? Exactly, said the prisoner, a Spaniard is a man from the Orient, he is a Catholic Turk; his blood is still or simmers, he is lazy or tireless; indolence enslaves him; ardour turns him cruel; motionless in his ignorance, ingenious in his superstition, he wishes for only one religious book, one tyrannical master; he abides by the law of the scaffold, he rules by that of the knife, he falls asleep at night in his bloody misery, sleeping off fanaticism and dreaming of crime. Who is that, gentlemen? Is it the Spaniard or the Turk? Just guess.[98]

[95] On *toreros*, see, Ford, *A Hand-Book for Travellers in Spain*, vol. I, p. 184; on music and songs, ibid., p. 192; on dances and clapping, ibid., p. 188; on dissection, ibid., p. 175; on Spaniards, ibid., p. 161.

[96] Ford, *A Hand-Book for Travellers in Spain*, vol. I, pp. 138, p. 228; vol. II, p. 799.

[97] A. G. de Lavigne, *Itinéraire descriptif, historique et artistique de l'Espagne et du Portugal*, p. 447.

[98] A. de Vigny, *Cinq-Mars*, vol. II, pp. 368–9.

Théophile Gautier (1811–72), who visited Spain in 1840, had a vision very similar to Irving and Ford's. In his *Travels in Spain* (*Voyage en Espagne*), it was the Orient he saw in the 'perpetual separation of the man from the woman' in Spanish towns;[99] when he discovered the Court of the Myrtles, it seemed that 'an enchanter's wand has carried you to the East of four or five centuries back';[100] and he thought that 'the head of some dark Andalusian servantmaid, looking out of a narrow Moresque casement, now and then produces a very pleasing Oriental effect . . .'[101] To Gautier, however, the determining criterion was not cultural, but geographic. In Spain he saw an extension of Africa, whose traces he could spot in the 'blooming, crimson African mouth' of a waitress in Jaen,[102] and in the 'blooming nature of African mouths' he observed among the Roma.[103] Beyond these strongly racialising considerations, he considered Africa to be a 'natural' model, which suited Andalusia better than any other, with strange political implications:

> What southern Spain requires is African civilization, and not the civilization of Europe, which is not suited to the heat of the climate or to the passions it inspires. Constitutional mechanism can only agree with the temperate zones; above a heat of eighty degrees charters melt or blow up.[104]

The Orient, Africa, Asia, Spain – well before anyone, Victor Hugo recognised to what extent these notions were fluid, interchangeable, like a series of communicating vessels from which romantic authors, starting with himself, could draw inspiration:

> As a result of all this, the Orient, be it as an image or as a thought, has become for both intelligence and imagination a sort of general concern to which the

[99] Th. Gautier, *Voyage en Espagne*, p. 231; Th. Gautier, *Wanderings in Spain*, p. 172.

[100] Gautier, *Voyage en Espagne*, p. 243; Gautier, *Wanderings in Spain*, p. 180.

[101] Gautier, *Voyage en Espagne*, p. 243; Gautier, *Wanderings in Spain*, p. 181.

[102] Gautier, *Voyage en Espagne*, p. 220. Strangely the African reference in this passage disappeared in the English translation but can be found in his quest for the *manola* (young Spanish female beauty) in Madrid, whom he eventually discovers with 'something strangely African in the formation of her face' (Gautier, *Wanderings in Spain*), p. 78.

[103] Gautier, *Voyage en Espagne*, p. 260; Gautier, *Wanderings in Spain*, p. 193.

[104] Gautier, *Voyage en Espagne*, p. 259; Gautier, *Wanderings in Spain*, p. 192.

> author of this book may have unconsciously yielded. Almost of their own will, the colours of the Orient have ended up marking all his thoughts, all his dreams; and his dreams and thoughts, one after the other, almost involuntarily, have become Hebrew, Turkish, Greek, Persian, Arab, and even Spanish, for Spain is still the Orient; Spain is half African, Africa is half Asiatic.[105]

Jean-Léon Gérôme's (1824–1904) painting, *La Douleur du pacha* (*The Grief of the Pasha*, 1885),[106] is a good illustration of this fluidity (Figure 1.4). Inspired by Victor Hugo's poem on the same theme,[107] it represents a cross-legged Oriental 'pasha' grieving over the loss of his tiger, lying on a carpet in the middle of a Moresque hall or court. It functions like a palimpsest of Oriental(ist) clichés of very diverse origins: the setting is borrowed from the Alhambra but paved in Western style; the carpet is Oriental; the candelabras are in Mamluk style; the pasha is in Turkish garb; as to the 'Nubian' tiger, according to Hugo, it is simply impossible, since there are no tigers in Nubia.[108]

One could multiply these examples ad infinitum; they would only confirm my previous observation of an overlap between certain aspects of the Black Legend and Orientalism in its broadest sense. In both cases, there is an obvious connection between centre and periphery, the centre being represented by a vague notion of the West or of Europe, and the periphery, even more elusive and slippery, moving back and forth according to time and perspective. As we have already observed, the distinction between the two is based on values and criteria considered to be fundamental and determining: religion, geography, climate, civilisation, to name the most obvious ones. Everything comes down to an otherness rooted in a form of essentialisation, which, according to Edward Said, is one of the basic characteristics of Orientalism.[109] True, Said never spoke of Spain, since it does not belong in

[105] V. Hugo, *Les Orientales*, vol. III, pp. ix–x.

[106] Jean-Léon Gérôme, *La douleur du pacha*, 1885; Oil on canvas, 91.8 cm × 73.7 cm. Joslyn Art Museum, Omaha, Nebraska.

[107] V. Hugo, 'La douleur du pacha', *Les Orientales*, vol. III, pp. 108–15.

[108] R. Irwin, *The Alhambra*, pp. 173–4.

[109] E. Said, *Orientalism*, p. 97 and *passim*. For an analysis of this Orientalisation and racialisation of Spain in an Anglo-Saxon, particularly American, context, see M. DeGuzmán, *Spain's Long Shadow: The Black Legend, Off-Whiteness, and Anglo-American Empire*.

Figure 1.4 Jean-Léon Gérôme, *La douleur du pacha* (*The Grief of the Pasha*), 1885. Oil on canvas, 91.8 cm × 73.7 cm. Joslyn Art Museum, Omaha, Nebraska. Photograph © Bruce M. White, 2019. A painting describing a pasha grieving over his dead tiger in an Alhambresque setting, inspired by Victor Hugo's poem from 1827.

the Orient on which he focuses; nevertheless, it is striking to observe that all the names mentioned above, with the exception of Irving, are also to be found in his study. To Chateaubriand, Hugo, Vigny, Gautier or Disraeli, the Orient and Spain were quasi-interchangeable notions and, more often than not, common destinations.

These observations easily apply to the very particular, but also meaningful, case of the Alhambra. I have already noted how General Sébastiani, when he set up his quarters in the palace during the French occupation of Spain, transformed its interior by refurbishing it in Oriental style, probably inspired by his two-year stay in Istanbul as ambassador. Evidently, he had no difficulty 'orientalising' the Alhambra, borrowing the expression used by José Antonio González Alcantud and Sandra Rojo Flores to describe the quasi-universal infatuation for the Alhambra from the 1850s, through architecture and world exhibitions.[110] It is no coincidence that, at the same moment, in the 1860s, the monument's caretaker, Rafael Contreras y Muñoz (1824–90), embarked upon a restoration project of one of the two pavilions (*templetes*) of the Court of the Lions by topping it with a small cupola in Persian style, which had nothing to do with the original structure.[111]

Of course, this 'Oriental' character had to be connected to the domination of Spain, and more particularly of Andalusia, by the Moors during the Middle Ages. However, according to some, this character possessed much deeper roots, as suggested by Ford's observation that in the south, in Andalusia, 'the original Oriental tendency was revived by the Arabic influence'.[112] What was at hand, therefore, was a complex interplay between two Oriental civilisations, with different degrees of sophistication, generally to the disadvantage of the Spaniards. The section of Ford's guidebook dedicated to Granada and the Alhambra is a good example,[113] especially when the author attempts a comparison between this city and the wealthy Seville: 'The houses again are smaller, and less Oriental, for Granada was built by impoverished defeated refugees, not, like Seville, by the Moor in all his palmy pride.'[114] He was just short of accusing the inhabitants of Granada of ingratitude: 'The *Granadinos* despise the Alhambra, as a *casa de ratones*, or rat's hole, which indeed they have made it.'[115] Ford was merciless. To him, the citizens of Granada did not understand

[110] J. A. González Alcantud and S. Rojo Flores, 'La Alhambra de Granada: Un fractal orientalista en clave poscolonial', p. 699.

[111] J. A. González Alcantud, 'La reinvención "persa" del Patio de los Leones'.

[112] Ford, *A Hand-Book for Travellers in Spain*, vol. I, p. 81.

[113] Ford, *A Hand-Book for Travellers in Spain*, vol. I, pp. 366–82.

[114] Ford, *A Hand-Book for Travellers in Spain*, vol. I, p. 367.

[115] Ford, *A Hand-Book for Travellers in Spain*, vol. I, p. 367.

the appeal of the Alhambra on foreigners, for '[f]amiliarity has bred in them the contempt with which the Bedouin regards the ruins of Palmyra, insensible to present beauty as to past poetry and romance'.[116]

It is this complexity that encouraged me earlier to resort to the metaphor of Russian dolls to describe this strange blend of myths and stereotypes that click together and interlock, albeit without any precise logic. The Spaniards were at times presented as the deserving heirs of the Moors, and at other times as an uncouth people who had put an end to a superior civilisation. The Moors, too, were tossed around between endless admiration for their artistic achievements and cultural refinement, on the one hand, and the reminder of their violent and bloodthirsty customs, on the other. Interestingly, it seems that these latter traits were given particular prominence towards the end of the nineteenth century, as if Orientalism had suddenly taken a more violent turn, distancing it from the romanticism of the previous decades. How else are we to explain the violence oozing from Henri Regnault's (1843–1871) famous work, *Exécution sans jugement* (*Summary Execution*), a painting of monumental proportions describing the aftermath of a summary execution in a setting borrowed from the Alhambra and inspired by the massacre of the Abencerrages?[117] (Figure 1.5).

True, Robert Irwin, known for his healthy cautioning against a Saidian over-reading of Orientalist works, believes that 'when one considers the abrupt and sanguinary way in which Nasrid sultans and viziers dealt with one another, one cannot claim that Regnault's painting represents a libel on the Alhambra's past'.[118] Nevertheless, leaving aside the problematic nature of the claim that violence might have been intrinsic – not to say essential – to the Nasrid dynasty, I believe that this scene of bloodshed does distinguish itself from former representations of the Alhambra by the fact that the monument is reduced to a simple setting, all the stress being on the executioner, his victim and the blood flowing down the steps of an imaginary space.[119] Moreover,

[116] Ford, *A Hand-Book for Travellers in Spain*, vol. I, p. 363.

[117] Henri Regnault, *Exécution sans jugement sous les rois maures de Grenade*, 1870. Oil on canvas, 301 cm × 143 cm, Musée d'Orsay, Paris.

[118] Irwin, *The Alhambra*, pp. 171–3.

[119] Regnault realised this painting when he was in Tangier. Irwin himself notes that 'the painter has produced a composite version of the Alhambresque, rather than an accurate reproduction of any particular room' (Irwin, *The Alhambra*, p. 172).

Figure 1.5 Henri Regnault, *Exécution sans jugement sous les rois maures de Grenade* (*Summary Execution under the Moorish Kings of Granada*), 1870. Oil on canvas, 301 cm × 143 cm, Musée d'Orsay, Paris. Inspired by the story of the massacre of the Abencerrages, this a gruesome depiction of an executioner standing by the decapitated body of his victim, on a flight of stairs leading to a hall reminiscent of the Alhambra, wiping off the blood from his sword with his cloak.

how can one not note that the Catalan artist Marià Fortuny (1838–74), who was in Granada at the same time as Regnault and his friend Georges Clairin (1843–1919), also painted a scene harking back to the same tragedy, but in a much less gory and violent style than that of the French painter (Figure 1.6).[120] Théophile Gautier – him again – proposes a reading of Regnault's work, which I find open to a much less 'innocent' interpretation than Irwin's. More than thirty years after his own trip to Granada, Gautier had written a detailed account on Regnault on the occasion of a posthumous exhibition dedicated to his oeuvre, organised at the School of Fine Arts of Paris in 1872.[121] In it, he praised several of his canvases, including the *Summary Execution*. Fascinated by its colours, light, costumes and decoration, he saw in the eyes of the 'dispenser of justice' (*justicier*), whom he refused to call an executioner, 'an expression both disdainful and melancholy, of sweet and dreamy cruelty, and imbued with Oriental fatalism'.[122] Africa, Gautier's older reference for Andalusian identity, had completely disappeared, only to be replaced by the Orient lending all its dramatic tension to the painting. Among Regnault's few other paintings, which he studied in detail, Gautier chose two more, whose subjects were closely connected to Spain. One of these represented Salome, waiting to be served John the Baptist's head on a platter she held in her lap.[123] Spain was only implied when he described the innocent, and yet cruel, beauty of the young woman with an expression in Spanish: '*muy gitana*' – 'quite a Gypsy'.[124] The other work was downright Spanish, as it represented General Juan Prim (1814–70), the hero of the 1868 Revolution – *la Gloriosa* – which overthrew Queen Isabella II. The general was represented on horseback with a

[120] Marià Fortuny, *La matança dels Abenserraigs* (*La matanza de los Abencerrajes / The Slaying of the Abencerrages*), *c.* 1870. Oil on canvas, 73.5 cm × 93.5 cm, National Museum of Catalonia, Barcelona. On this, see S. Tabbal, 'Marià Fortunys *Die Ermorderung der Abencerragen*'.

[121] Th. Gautier, 'Henri Regnault', *Œuvres de Henri Regnault exposées à l'École des beaux-arts*, pp. 3–49. We should remember that Regnault, who was in Tangier in 1870, hastily returned to France to join the army during the Franco-Prussian War and that he eventually fell under enemy fire at the battle of Buzenval, on 19 January 1871.

[122] Gautier, 'Henri Regnault', p. 29.

[123] Henri Regnault, *Salomé*, 1870. Oil on canvas, 160 cm × 102.9 cm, Metropolitan Museum of Art, New York.

[124] Gautier, 'Henri Regnault', p. 21.

Figure 1.6 Marià Fortuny, *La matança dels Abenserraigs* (*La matanza de los Abencerrajes / The Slaying of the Abencerrages*), c. 1870. Oil on canvas, 73.5 cm × 93.5 cm, National Museum of Catalonia, Barcelona. A depiction of the famous story, located in the Alhambra's Hall of the Abencerrages, and rendered particularly dramatic by the contrast between architectural detail and the blurred images of the victims and onlookers.

crowd of revolutionaries brandishing arms and flags following him.[125] Free of any Orientalist cliché, this canvas followed the lineage of Velázquez, Goya and Delacroix.[126] At the very end of his commentary on *Salomé*, Gautier drew attention to the contrast between the two paintings in just a few words: 'Prim's portrait is all Spain; *Salomé* is all Orient.'[127] In Gautier's eyes, there was now a new Spain, which the dynamic revolutionary Prim symbolised; the Orient was no longer part of it. Salome may have looked like a Roma; she was essentially, intrinsically, Oriental. The executioner of the Abencerrages, too, belonged to this Orient, whose violence masked its refinement and charms.

[125] H. Regnault, *Juan Prim, 8 octobre 1868*, 1869. Oil on canvas, 315 cm × 258 cm, Musée d'Orsay, Paris.

[126] Gautier, 'Henri Regnault', p. 11.

[127] Gautier, 'Henri Regnault', p. 25.

It was not just violence that was at stake, but rather a wider phenomenon consisting of the dramatisation of scenes which the earlier generation tended to enclose within the domain of architecture and decoration. One needs only to compare the illustrations of the travellers and artists of the 1830s and 1840s to those realised by Gustave Doré (1832–83) for Baron Charles Davillier's (1823–83) *L'Espagne*.[128] Doré had devoted a dozen illustrations of the volume to the Alhambra and the Generalife; they stood out by the force of the local colour he had chosen to bring forth, often to the detriment of the architecture, which, a bit like Regnault, became the backdrop of a 'typical' scene. Thus, a view of the door to the Tower of the Infantas was partly hidden by a couple and their child; a group of Romani and a priest masked most of the famous vase of the Alhambra; the Tower of Comares became the backdrop of women in mantillas and a man in a cape; the gallery of the Court of the Myrtles was besieged by beggars in rags, and the Court of the Lions invaded by peacocks.[129] Preliminary plates of 'native' scenes introduced the reader to the site's atmosphere: ladies from Granada listening to musician dwarves, local beauties at their balcony, rambling musicians, a family of beggars, etc.[130] True, Doré's predecessors had often included more or less colourful characters in their plates, but never to the point of blocking the view and marginalising the central subject of attention, the Alhambra. Fantasy, exoticism and imagination had then been the prerogative of literature, poetry, and of their lyrical and theatrical adaptations. During the last decades of the century, all these genres had begun to converge towards an increasingly exotic image of quasi-colonial character.

This may well be the key to understanding the main causes of this mutation, of the hardening of the Orientalist gaze on Spain and Andalusia. France had already occupied Algeria for over thirty years at this point; Tunisia had emerged as a new target. Queen Victoria was on the verge of being crowned empress of India, and Egypt would soon come under the control of the British Empire. The scramble for Africa and the ensuing international tensions were already in motion. In a colonial context increasingly marked

[128] Ch. Davillier, *L'Espagne*.

[129] Davillier, *L'Espagne*, pp. 155, 159, 165, 175, 178.

[130] Davillier, *L'Espagne*, pp. 139, 143, 145, 147.

by the power and arrogance of the Great Powers, the conflation of Africa, Orient, Islam and Andalusia was becoming more and more perceptible and tangible every day.

The best illustration of this trend can be found in the way Andalusia was handled during the 1900 World Exhibition in Paris. An entire section was reserved to 'Andalusia under the Moors' ('l'Andalousie au temps des Maures'), where visitors were invited to discover the charms and beauties of a quaint and lively world laid out over a surface of 5,000 m^2 with a front of 100 m on the Seine. At first glance, the goal seemed to be the glorification of a time and civilisation recognised as unique, with the additional advantage of a slap in the face to the Germans:

> The domination of the Moors is unquestionably the most brilliant period of the history of Spain. Indeed, together with perfect customs and a highly advanced civilisation, these alleged barbarians brought with them the arts and the sciences, which the Germanic invasions had committed to oblivion.[131]

The major architectural wonders of Andalusia were displayed: once they had passed through the gate of the Alcázar of Seville, the visitors found themselves in the Alhambra's Court of the Lions, over which loomed a 65-m high copy of the Giralda of Seville, accessible thanks to 'little black donkeys wearing Andalusian harnesses' (Figure 1.7). However, this vision of Moorish Andalusia did not end there; it happily spilled over towards the opposite shores of the Mediterranean:

> With . . . the two minarets of the Great Mosque of Tangier, the Aissaoua Mosque of Tétouan, the picturesque Spanish village with its old houses from Toledo and Cordoba, and the Arab huts (*gourbi*), Andalusia under the Moors shows us different aspects of Moresque architecture, of such singular originality, which mixes the Greek, Roman and Byzantine arts brought to Spain by the architects of Constantinople.[132]

[131] J. Dancourt, 'L'Andalousie au temps des Maures', p. 239.

[132] Dancourt, 'L'Andalousie au temps des Maures', pp. 239–40; *Guide Lemercier, publié par les concessionnaires du Catalogue officiel de l'Exposition universelle de 1900*, pp. 184–5.

Figure 1.7 'L'Andalousie au temps des Maures – La cour des lions', *Le Panorama: Exposition universelle* (Paris: Ludovic Baschet, 1900). Bibliothèque nationale de France. One of the main attractions of the Andalusian section of the 1900 Paris Exhibition was, as the caption explains, 'a vast Moresque courtyard, copied from the famous Court of the Lions, the marvel of the Alhambra of Granada'. The people seen posing and strolling, whose images were apparently added afterwards, are the 'native' extras brought from Africa to add a touch of 'authenticity' to the architectural setting.

This confusion reached even more alarming proportions when it came to 'ethnography'. On a terrace, one could admire the dances of 'the chubby Jewish women of Tunis and Tangier'; they would then leave the stage to Kabyle singers and to swordsmen from Lebanon. A bit farther down, some old Romani would tell fortunes, while in the theatre Spanish and Roma women dancers from the troupe of the 'Capitan of Granada' performed.[133] In the middle of the Arab village, labelled a '*gourbi*' – a pejorative term generally used to describe an African village of huts – some craftsmen wove carpets, babouches and jewellery under the astounded gaze of visitors.[134] The principal

[133] Dancourt, 'L'Andalousie au temps des Maures', p. 240.

[134] 'L'Andalousie au temps des Maures', *L'Exposition en famille*, p. 142.

attraction was an arena or track, where a great variety of performances took place: Arab fantasias, tournaments between opposing Moorish and Christian knights, gazelle hunts, caravan attacks, 'and a series of scenes from Moorish and Spanish life'.[135] The albums published for the occasion showed the most striking scenes: Roma women dancing in the street, a crowd admiring a show in the central arena, an Arab *gourbi* with its twenty or so inhabitants wearing tradition garb, actors rehearsing on the theatre stage, Spanish dancers in the midst of a reconstituted village, Africans strolling around the fake Court of the Lions, and the 'Belle Lallah' dancing on a carpet in front of a crowd of Arabs and two camels.[136]

Clearly Andalusia had been drowned in a hodgepodge of shows and settings combining the most common clichés of Orientalism, heavily tainted with colonialism. The performances mixed references to Spain, Romani, the Orient, Morocco, Tunisia and Kabyle culture to create an unending attraction for the visitors:

> To go to the Exhibition at night, the public expects to be somewhat entertained. At the Trocadéro, they have come up with an original idea. Natives have come from all our colonies: Arabs, Moors, Dahomeyans, Hovas, Annamite, Tonkinese, etc. They bring them together every Wednesday evening, give them Venetian lanterns, and exotic music gives the beat. All this crowd starts to move, some happy like the children they are, others solemn in their demeanour, but highly amusing for the public lining the alleys of the Trocadéro, along which they march.[137]

The nature and the framework of this undertaking was revealed in its ultimate goal. 'Andalusia under the Moors' was located at one of end of the Trocadéro gardens, dedicated to the colonial pavilions of the Exhibition. More precisely, it was situated next to the 'French colonies and protectorates'

[135] Dancourt, 'L'Andalousie au temps des Maures', p. 240; 'L'Andalousie au temps des Maures', L'Exposition en famille, p. 143; *Guide Lemercier publié par les concessionnaires du Catalogue officiel de l'Exposition universelle de 1900*, pp. 184–6; 'L'Andalousie au temps des Maures', Guide Chaix.

[136] *Le Panorama: Exposition universelle.*

[137] J. Vermont, 'La Retraite aux flambeaux du mercredi'.

section, which placed it as a continuation of the pavilions of Tunisia, Sudan, Senegal, French Indochina, Guinea, Ivory Coast and Dahomey, not to forget the buildings housing the colonial press and administration.[138] True, Andalusia was neither a French colony nor a protectorate, but each show offered a connection to Algeria, Tunisia and Morocco, whose colonial future was already in the making. The fluidity of Andalusian references is perfectly illustrated by the monumental poster drawn by Étienne Dinet (1861–1929) for the occasion. It featured a 'Moorish' dancer, dancing under a starry sky in front of a group of turbaned men (Figure 1.8). For this work, Dinet had used a model with which he was very familiar, the 'Ouled Naïl' women, the famous 'easy' women of the Algerian desert, whom he knew well from having observed and painted them during his frequent stays in Laghouan, Biskra and, most of all, Bou Saâda.[139] Evidence suggested, to him as well as to the organisers, that it seemed reasonable to assume that in the absence of medieval Moors, Berbers from colonial Algeria would perfectly well do the trick. For that matter, the Ouled Naïl dancers were part of the show, charming the visitors 'with their beauty, their grace and the splendour of their costume'.[140]

One needs only to dig into the origins of the project to understand its true nature. 'Andalusia under the Moors' was a commercial venture, imagined and set up by one Jean-Samuel Roseyro (1867–1926), who had already rented the site by 1897.[141] Apparently, he had come up with the idea after observing the success of the 'Cairo Street' and of the Spanish dancer Soledad[142] at the 1889 World Exhibition, also in Paris, yet another proof, if needed, of the permeability between Spanish, Moorish and Arab themes. Of course,

[138] P. Bineteau, *Exposition universelle de 1900: Plan général*.

[139] L. Thornton, *The Orientalists: Painters-Travellers*, pp. 76–9. On Dinet, see, F. Pouillon, *Les deux vies d'Étienne Dinet, peintre en Islam*. See also, Eldem, *Un Orient de consommation*, pp. 94, 108.

[140] *Guide Lemercier publié par les concessionnaires du Catalogue officiel de l'Exposition universelle de 1900*, p. 185.

[141] *Conseil municipal de Paris. Rapport présenté par M. Thuillier, au nom de la 3e Commission, tendant à donner l'autorisation d'occuper une partie de la rue Le Nôtre et une bande du sol du quai Debilly pour la* 'Reconstitution de l'Andalousie au temps des Maures'.

[142] *Guide Lemercier publié par les concessionnaires du Catalogue officiel de l'Exposition universelle de 1900*, p. 184.

Figure 1.8 Étienne Dinet, *Exposition de 1900. L'Andalousie au temps des Maures*, 1900. Colour lithograph, 252.2 cm × 94.3 cm. Abderrahman Slaoui Foundation, Casablanca. This oversized poster advertising the event was designed by Dinet based on one of his favourite themes, the 'Ouled Naïl' women from the Algerian desert, thus demonstrating the ease with which the Andalusian past could be conflated with the African present.

this rather cheap version of a fantasised Andalusia had nothing to do with Spain, whose national pavilion stood on the 'Street of Nations' built along the Quai d'Orsay, on the left bank of the Seine.[143] And yet all the same the Spanish ambassador in Paris, Fernando León y Castillo, had visited the site and – according to the Parisian press – admired the sculptures in the fake *patio de las Doncellas* (Court of the Maidens) of the Alcázar of Seville as well as the Giralda, and congratulated 'profusely' Roseyro on his success.[144]

Was this simply a visit out courtesy? Perhaps, given that many Spaniards present in Paris during the Exhibition, especially newspaper correspondents, had been shocked by the '*españoladas*' – mock Spanish shows – they had witnessed.[145] The statesman César Silió (1856–1944) was offended to the point of producing a pamphlet he titled *Yet Another Disaster (Spain in Paris)* (*Otro desastre más (España en Paris)*), referring to the Exhibition and to the shows organised at its 'Andalusia under the Moors' attraction:

> Our 'golden legend' was erased two years ago with the *Peace of Paris*.[146] The 'black legend', which depicts us as a people of toreros and braggarts, resistant to modern culture, more African than European, should have also disappeared in Paris, and yet we have failed to kill it. It seems that all our efforts are reduced to letting this legend travel freely and without hindrance throughout the world. *We exhibit singers*, instead of exhibiting machines![147]

143 Bineteau, *Exposition universelle de 1900: Plan général*.

144 'Échos', *Le Rappel*.

145 L. Sazatornil Ruiz and A. B. Lasheras Peña, 'París y la *españolada*'. If one is to believe Benjamin Rogers, Roseyro had obtained the support of the Spanish Minister of Fine Arts, Count de Sequena, whose son was allegedly involved in the preparation of the attraction (B. Rogers, '*Andalusia in the Times of the Moors*', p. 183). This information, which Rogers draws from Roseyros' correspondence, needs to be taken with a pinch of salt, considering that the Spanish Ministry of Fine Arts was not created until 18 April 1900, four days after the opening of the Paris World Exposition (*Guía oficial de España 1901*, p. 613; *Guía oficial de España 1916*, p. 643). Moreover, I have failed to find any reference to a Count de Sequena.

146 The Treaty of Paris of 10 December 1898 put an end to the Hispano-American conflict, as a result of which Spain, defeated by the United States, lost Cuba, the Philippines, Puerto Rico and Guam.

147 César Silió Cortés, *Otro desastre más (España en París)*, p. 52, quoted by Sazatornil Ruiz and Lasheras Peña, 'París y la *españolada*', p. 284.

Silió was rebelling against what he already called – almost fifteen years before Juderías[148] – the black legend of Spain in its folkloric and caricatural version, which turned Spaniards into characters from *Carmen* or from engravings by Gustave Doré. This was precisely the message conveyed by the 'Andalusia under the Moors' attraction, to the great joy of the Parisian crowds, and to the despair of Spanish modernists.[149] The imposing Spanish pavilion had nothing left in common with the Alhambresque antecedents at the previous exhibitions. Designed by José Urioste y Velada (1850–1909) in a historicist neo-Plateresque style, it claimed back the heritage of the 'Golden Century' (*siglo de oro*) of the Spanish monarchy and attempted to restore the tarnished image of a state that had lost its last overseas colonies at the end of a disastrous war against the United States. The pavilion's exhibits focused on the discovery of the new continent as a civilisational project and stressed the technological and industrial progress of the last few years in the hope of erasing the caricatural image of *flamenquismo* – the reduction of Spain to *flamenco* – which had invaded Spain in the past decades.[150]

All these reactions and susceptibilities, such as the doubts shown by Spain throughout the second half of the nineteenth century regarding the image it wanted to convey of itself during the world exhibitions, bring us to the questioning of the most problematic issue of Orientalism in this context, that of its Spanish manifestations. What makes the issue particularly complex is the embedding of Orientalism in a culture that was already its target. This idea may seem surprising, or even contradictory, if we are to stick to an 'orthodox' reading of Orientalism, according to which this vision derives from an unequal balance of power between a centre and a periphery, between a colonising power and a colonised – or perceived as such – territory. And yet Orientalism, in its widest meaning, can reproduce and take root in a peripheral region, especially if the latter has been exposed to Western modernity sufficiently to create an Orient for themselves. As a historian of the Ottoman Empire, I would advance the evidence of Ottoman Orientalism, a concept introduced

[148] Silió seems to have been one of the pioneers of this usage, one year after Cayetano Soler and Emilia Pardo Bazán (R. Barea, *Imperiofobia*, pp. 18–19).

[149] J. A. González Alcantud, 'Andalucía "en el tiempo de los moros": Flamencos en la Exposición Universal de París de 1900'.

[150] Sazatornil Ruiz and Lasheras Peña, 'París y la *españolada*', p. 284.

by Ussama Makdisi,[151] and which generally speaking consists of the appropriation of the main tenets of Orientalism by the Westernised ruling elites, to the point of adopting a self-civilising mission and, more importantly, of projecting this vision onto certain ethnic groups or social classes considered to be – even more – Oriental.[152]

One should not be surprised, then, to see Spain, subjected to the Orientalism of the 'North', following the same path during the nineteenth century. Spanish Orientalism could adopt several forms, the most common being to simply emulate the model provided by British and French authors. Irving's *Tales of the Alhambra* were translated into Spanish as early as 1833, albeit fragmentarily, just a year after their original publication in English, and ten years before they were translated into French.[153] In 1856, Manuel Fernández y González (1821–88), a best-selling author of serialised novels, published an illustrated collection of Arab legends of the Alhambra, much in the style of Irving's tales.[154] This thick volume ended with a chronology of the kings of Granada and, more importantly, a list of all the damage done to the Alhambra since the *Reconquista*, from the destruction of its mosque to the building of Charles V's palace, and from the erection of a Franciscan convent on the remains of the 'wonders of Arab art' to the construction of a garden on top of the abandoned baths.[155] In 1852, the famous poet José Zorrilla (1817–93) composed an 'Oriental poem' in two volumes, bearing the title *Granada*, a brilliant evocation of the city's Muslim past.[156] Many followed suit, such as Rogelia León (1828–70), from Granada, who, in 1857, published a collection of poems inspired by the Alhambra.[157]

I would not be doing justice to the Spaniards by implying that they discovered their Moorish heritage only after others did so, and by following

[151] U. Makdisi, 'Ottoman Orientalism'.

[152] Eldem, 'Les Ottomans, un empire en porte-à-faux'.

[153] Irving, *Cuentos de la Alhambra*. The first integral Spanish translation was published only in 1888 by José Ventura Traveset (A. Gallego Morell, '"The Alhambra" de Washington Irving y sus traducciones españolas').

[154] M. Fernández y González, *Los alcázares de España. La Alhambra, leyendas árabes*.

[155] Fernández y González, *Los alcázares de España. La Alhambra, leyendas árabes*, pp. 540–1.

[156] J. Zorrilla y Moral, *Granada: Poema oriental, precedido de la leyenda de Al-Hamar*.

[157] R. León, *Auras de la Alhambra*.

in their steps. As we have already seen, Spain had been the first to inventory and draw in systematic fashion the architectural and epigraphic remains of Muslim Andalusia, even though the project's diffusion had remained very limited. In fact, this interest in Moorish architecture went further back in time, all the way to the aftermath of the *Reconquista*, albeit in a very different context, often defined by religious concerns and priorities, notwithstanding clear expressions of a genuine admiration.[158] Perhaps even more importantly, Spanish authors had been at the origin of some of the foundational myths of the Alhambresque narrative of the nineteenth century, with Pérez de Hita's *History*, which, among others, inspired Chateaubriand and Irving.[159] Although much more difficult to document, popular literature, often orally transmitted, gave birth to many stories and legends, which must have also greatly contributed to kindling the curiosity of modern travellers and authors. A concrete example of this is the popular chapbook *The Tunnels of the Alhambra*, which revolved around the impossible love between a young Christian maiden, Doña María de Mendoza, and Don Luis de Sotomayor, in reality Aben-Amed, a descendant of the kings of Granada. The lovers, persecuted by María's perfidious cousin, Don Pedro, and threatened by the religious abyss that separates them, still manage to come together and live happily ever after with a child born of their union, thus fulfilling the favourite fantasy of the Moresque novella (*novela morisca*), that of a communion between Christians and Muslims (Figure 1.9).[160] One should add to this list the accumulation, starting already in the sixteenth century, of knowledge in the domain of Arab culture and literature as well as Islam, thanks to numerous scholars and philologists, often Moriscos, who took it upon themselves to study the Muslim heritage of Spain. Even though their efforts were often triggered by a very Catholic zeal or by rather dubious circumstances, such

[158] A. Urquízar-Herrera, *Admiration and Awe: Morisco Buildings and Identity Negotiations in Early Modern Spanish Historiography*.

[159] See, for example, G. Cirot, 'La maurophilie littéraire en Espagne au xvie siècle'; A. Redondo, 'Moros y moriscos en la literatura española de los años 1550–1580'; J. A. González Alcantud, 'The Dream of Washington Irving in the Alhambra or the Endurance of the Myth', p. 32.

[160] *Historia de los subterráneos de la Alhambra, ó los amores de Aben-Amed*. Apart from an undated edition, there are two more editions of this chapbook, dated 1858 and 1894. On the subject of the *novela morisca* focused on Granada, see Luis Morales Oliver, *La novela morisca de tema granadino*.

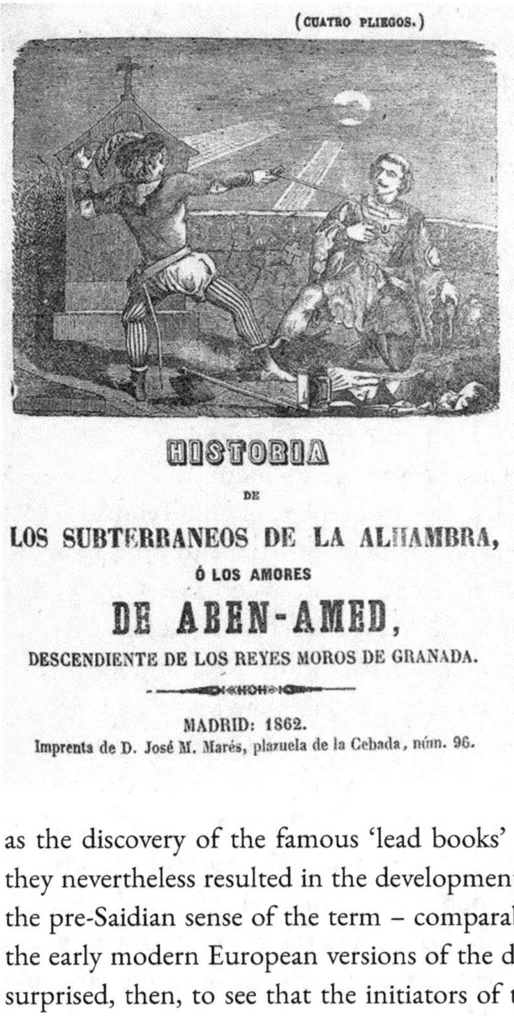
(CUATRO PLIEGOS.)

HISTORIA
DE
LOS SUBTERRANEOS DE LA ALHAMBRA,
Ó LOS AMORES
DE ABEN-AMED,
DESCENDIENTE DE LOS REYES MOROS DE GRANADA.

MADRID: 1862.
Imprenta de D. José M. Marés, plazuela de la Cebada, núm. 96.

Figure 1.9 Title page of *Historia de los subterráneos de la Alhambra, ó los amores de Aben-Amed, descendiente de los reyes moros de Granada* (Madrid: José M. Marés, 1862). British Library, No. T52, Vol. 12330.l.9. *The History of the Tunnels of the Alhambra, or Amorous Adventures of Aben-Amed, Descendant of the Moorish Kings of Granada* is a thirty-one-page chapbook on the popular theme of the impossible love between a descendant of the Moorish kings and a Spanish damsel.

as the discovery of the famous 'lead books' of Sacromonte, in Granada,[161] they nevertheless resulted in the development of a form of Orientalism – in the pre-Saidian sense of the term – comparable, if not superior, to some of the early modern European versions of the discipline.[162] One should not be surprised, then, to see that the initiators of the eighteenth-century Spanish

[161] These documents, 'discovered' in Granada at the turn of the seventeenth century, contained a sort of hagiography of the Virgin Mary in Arabic, strongly marked by Islamo-Christian syncretism. It seems that this was in fact a fraud concocted by the two Moriscos who deciphered and translated these texts, with the objective of creating a favourable environment for the survival of the Arabic language and of Morisco identity, threatened by a hardening of the crown's policy regarding this community and its heritage.

[162] M. García Arenal and F. Rodríguez Mediano (eds), *The Orient in Spain: Converted Muslims, the Forged Lead Books of Granada and the Rise of Orientalism*. While this work addresses primarily the 'lead books', it retraces very convincingly the context of Arab philology and Spanish orientalism in the early modern period.

project of an inventory of Arab monuments were able to complete their architectural survey with a catalogue of Arabic inscriptions, transcribed and translated by two talented philologists, the Maronite Miguel Casiri and Pablo Lozano, royal librarian. It should also be remembered that, albeit in a more common and certainly less erudite genre, Echevarría's *Strolls* (1764) listed not only the main monuments of the city, but also a translation of many Arabic inscriptions, such as the basin of the celebrated Fountain of the Lions.[163]

Spanish Orientalism, which long remained confined to the domains of erudition, on the one hand, and popular culture, on the other, took a decisive turn following the Moroccan War of 1859–60. Pretexting the attacks of tribes from the Rif against the Spanish enclave of Ceuta, the government of Leopoldo O'Donnell (1809–67) had set up a punitive expedition against the Sharifian kingdom. Spain emerged victorious from this four-month conflict, defeating the Moroccan forces and capturing the city of Tétouan on 6 February 1860. The concrete benefits of the campaign were minimal, due to British opposition to the increased Spanish presence in the vicinity of Gibraltar. On the other hand, ideologically speaking, Spain had drawn immense advantages from it, starting with the soaring of patriotism, doubled with a sense of pride derived from having been promoted to the rank of a colonial power.

The result of these developments was a form of Orientalism that bore similarities to the Ottoman Orientalism previously mentioned. On the one hand, the consciousness of an alterity imposed by Western visions would lead to a reshuffling of Spain's Islamic heritage to meet the needs of the image it wanted to convey of it, from Maurophile exoticism to vengeful Catholicism.[164] On the other hand, from then on Spain could claim a colonial policy and vision, directed towards Africa, with the advantage that other powers could not match, of possessing historical links to the continent. In a way, Spain was turning against Europe the argument of its alterity, by using it as the foundation of its African policy.[165] The establishment of the Spanish Royal Society

[163] Echeverría, *Paseos por Granada y sus contornos*, 1st edn, 1764, p. 114.

[164] Martín Corrales, 'Maurophobie/islamophobie et maurophilie/islamophilie dans l'Espagne du xxie siècle', pp. 243–4; J. A. González Alcantud, 'El orientalismo de los viajeros españoles por el Marruecos decimonónico: L'orientalisme des voyageurs espagnols à travers le Maroc du xixe siècle'.

[165] I. Tofiño-Quesada, 'Spanish Orientalism: Uses of the Past in Spain's Colonization in Africa', p. 143.

of Geography (*Real sociedad geográfica española*) in 1876, followed by the Spanish Association for the Exploration of Africa (*Asociación española para la exploración de África*) in 1877 and, finally, by the Spanish Society of Africanists and Colonialists (*Sociedad española de africanistas y colonialistas*) in 1883, one year before the infamous Berlin conference on the Partition of Africa, constituted the milestones of this colonial mission, which remained rather timid until the establishment of the Franco-Spanish protectorate over Morocco in 1912. Nevertheless, this mission gave rise to a very particular ideology, Africanism (*africanismo*), the impact of which would be felt on Spanish politics and culture at the end of the century and, of course, on Spain's relations with the closest and most clearly coveted African power, Morocco.[166] We will now turn in that direction in the hope of understanding whether all this accumulation of knowledge, of images and of legends concerning the Alhambra found any form of echo on the other side of the Straits, in the lands that were supposed to share with Spain the common heritage of this monument and of the Islamic civilisation of al-Andalus.[167]

[166] F. Archilés Cardona, '¿Una cultura imperial? Africanismo e identidad nacional española en el final del siglo xix'. There is a rich literature on Spanish *africanismo*; for some examples, see B. López García, 'Arabismo y orientalismo en España'; C. Viñes Millet, *Granada y Marruecos: Arabismo y africanismo en la cultura granadina*; A. B. Espinosa Ramírez, 'Los judíos marroquíes vistos a través del periódico africanista *La Estrella de Occidente*'.

[167] For an analysis of Spanish colonialist ideological constructs and their link to 'Hispano-Arab' identity under Francoism, see E. Calderwood, *Colonial al-Andalus: Spain and the Making of Moroccan Culture*.

2

SOUTH: VISITORS FROM THE MAGHREB

While the Alhambra was triggering so much interest and so many passions in the West and in Spain, how was it perceived from the Orient, or more particularly from the Islamic world, whose heritage it was allegedly an essential element of? After all, travellers, artists and architects kept reminding their audiences of the place the Alhambra occupied in the evolution of Islamic art and civilisation. Was this discovery being made unbeknown to those who were supposed to be the heirs and worthy descendants of this civilisation? The question is all the more justified if one considers that it was more or less implicitly embedded in some of the works mentioned earlier. Indeed, the illustrated plates depicting the interior of the monument often staged Moors, whose costume and presence contributed to the feelings of exoticism and authenticity sought by these authors. Of course, in most cases, this was a mere artistic fiction, which does not warrant the quest for possible traces in contemporary reality. Nevertheless, some of these images stand out due to the context of a Muslim – or Arab – presence of an unmistakably concrete nature. An excellent example is plate XXXIV in Laborde's work, representing the 'Court of the Lions' (Figure 2.1). There, halfway between the famous fountain and the gallery surrounding the court, a group of three men can be spotted, whose turbans and wide cloaks leave no doubt as to their Muslim, Arab or North African identity. True, Laborde would often spice up his plates with fantasy scenes and figures, such as plate XXXIII, representing the 'Court

Figure 2.1 'The Court of the Lions at the Alhambra', Alexandre de Laborde, *Voyage pittoresque et historique de l'Espagne* (Paris: Pierre Didot l'aîné, 1812), vol. III, pl. XXXIV. The plate is remarkable for its inclusion of contemporary visitors from the Maghreb, namely 'an ambassador of the King of Morocco, who bowed down at the sight of Koranic inscriptions and shed tears upon thinking about his ancestors' history' (ibid., p. 19). Indeed, one can clearly see three turbaned men with a Spaniard wearing a bicorn hat guiding them across the Court of the Lions.

of the Baths', which displayed a naked woman dipping her feet in the pool. However, in the case of the plate mentioned earlier, the fact that the three turbaned men are preceded by a Westerner wearing a bicorn hat and whose gesture suggests that he is guiding them, allows us to assume that this time there was more to it than just a decorative element. The plate's legend lifts any remaining doubt on the issue; after a long description of the court as 'the most perfect type of Moresque architecture', a comment offers context to the scene:

> The view on this plate is taken from one of the sides of the court on the left. It represents the scene that took place in Granada during the passage of an

> ambassador of the King of Morocco, who bowed down at the sight of Koranic inscriptions and shed tears upon thinking about his ancestors' history.[1]

One of the plates in Murphy's work revealed a rather similar setting (Figure 2.2). Once again, the scene was set in the Court of the Lions, viewed from one of the two small pavilions located at its ends. In the foreground, to the right, stand two 'Moors', one of whom seems to be pointing at an architectural detail; on the left side, three others converse in front of the gallery surrounding the court; at the centre, the presence of a couple, the man wearing a bicorn hat, indicates that this is indeed a contemporary scene. Could it be that like Laborde, Murphy represented the visit of a Moroccan delegation, possibly even the same, considering that both authors were

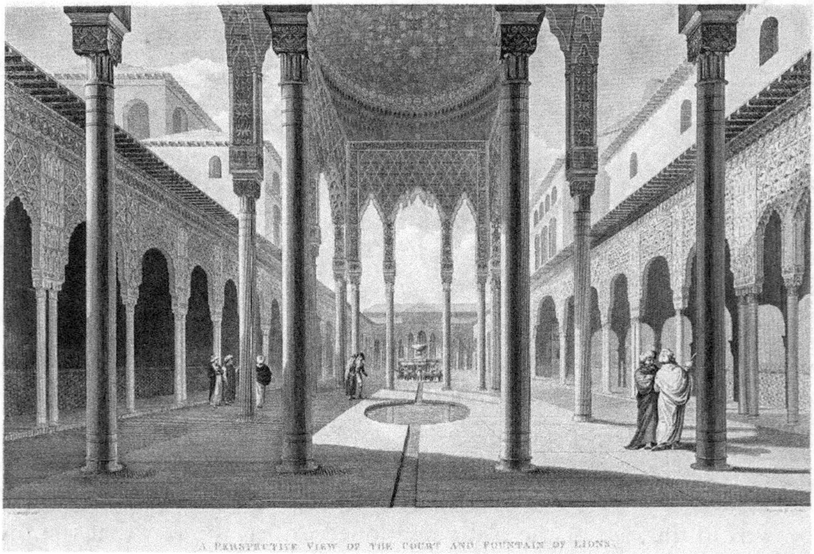

Figure 2.2 'A Perspective View of the Court and Fountain of Lions', James Cavanah Murphy, *The Arabian Antiquities of Spain* (London: Cadell & Davies, 1815), pl. XXXIII. Much like Laborde's, Murphy's plate shows contemporary Muslim visitors in the Court of the Lions, seemingly discussing and admiring the setting. However, unlike Laborde, Murphy does not provide any information as to the identity of these (probably Moroccan) visitors.

[1] Laborde, *Voyage pittoresque et historique de l'Espagne*, vol. III, p. 19, pl. XXXIV.

in Granada at around the same time? It is difficult to tell: Murphy's Arabs were not accompanied; more importantly, the long legend accompanying the image makes no mention of the people represented.[2]

At any rate, the image brought up by Laborde of the Moor shedding tears over the loss of Granada and, more generally, Andalusia, was part and parcel of a rather common stereotype, as suggested by its recurrence in contemporary sources:

> They say that of the many things the Moors have lost in Spain, there is nothing they regret more than Granada, which they mention every Friday during their evening prayer, asking the heavens that it may be returned to them. An ambassador of this nation, who was sent to the court of Spain towards the middle of the past century, having received from the king permission to see Granada, started to weep upon entering the *Alhambra* and could not refrain from crying out: 'How foolishly have my ancestors lost these sweet lands'.[3]

Should one conclude from these scenes that there were indeed Muslim travellers, especially from the Maghreb, who, while visiting the Alhambra, lamented the sad destiny of their forefathers, who had been driven out of Spain? It may be difficult to find a concrete answer to this question. Henri Pérès (1890–1983), who was the first to show an interest in the question of Muslim visitors in Spain, has identified a certain 'Abu'l-'Abbās Aḥmad ibn al-Mahdī al-Fāsī al-Andalusī al-Ḥimyarī al-Ghazzāl (?–1777), who, in 1766, was sent by Sultan Sīdī Muḥammad ibn 'Abdallah (Muḥammad III, r. 1757–90) to negotiate a peace with Carlos III on the occasion of an exchange of prisoners.[4] His mission was primarily diplomatic, but he found the time and opportunity to visit the main Andalusian sites and monuments in Seville, Cordoba and Granada, as witnessed in his travelogue or *riḥla*. With some knowledge about buildings and construction, he gave interesting details concerning the Alhambra and, particularly, the Alcázar of Seville, even though, with respect to the latter monument, he seems to have been unable to recognise the Mudejar additions of

[2] Murphy, *The Arabian Antiquities of Spain*, p. 12, pl. XXXIII.

[3] *Lettres champenoises*, p. 29.

[4] H. Pérès, *L'Espagne vue par les voyageurs musulmans*, pp. 19–40.

Don Pedro's time.[5] Al-Ghazzāl's admirative comments on these monuments did not include any of the lamentations so frequently mentioned by Christian observers, but they do appear in his contemplation of Cordoba, viewed from atop a neighbouring hill:

> When we got close to the city and gazed upon it from a mound, we saw its well-structured buildings, its raised minarets and the distinction of its great mosque towering above the other buildings and encircled by the Islamic wall. Our souls constricted with pity, and how could they not when we remembered the Muslims who used to populate it (may God forgive them). Indeed, the affair is to God before and after! We ask God that he return it to the abode of Islam.[6]

It is quite possible that al-Ghazzāl may have indeed been the ambassador sent 'towards the middle of the past century' mentioned in the *Lettres champenoises*. A Granada chronicle from the eighteenth century, updated at the beginning of the nineteenth, confirms al-Ghazzāl's predilection for the technical and economic aspects of his visit: 'When he passed through this city, after admiring its grandeur and magnificent antiquities, he had several fabrics of raw silk brought to him so he could take them with him to his country as the best products of Spain.'[7]

Al-Ghazzāl was not the first Moroccan ambassador or traveller to narrate his impressions of reconquered Spain. Less than a century before him, in

[5] Pérès, *L'Espagne vue par les voyageurs musulmans*, pp. 33–8.

[6] Pérès, *L'Espagne vue par les voyageurs musulmans*, p. 33. Translation taken from N. F. Hermes, 'Nostalgia for al-Andalus in Early Modern Moroccan *Voyages en Espagne*: Al-Ghassānī's *Riḥlat al-Wazīr fī Iftikāk al-Asīr* (1690–91) as a Case Study', pp. 12–13. See also, A. Ponz, *Viage de España*, vol. IX, p. 161; R. Amador de los Ríos, *Inscripciones árabes de Sevilla*, pp. 45–7, n. 2.

[7] Echeverría, *Paseos por Granada y sus contornos*, 2nd edn, 1814, vol. II, p. 218. As the original version of this text was published in 1764, two years before al-Ghazzāl's visit, it is normal that this ambassador was not mentioned in it. It should also be noted that al-Ghazzāl's travelogue had also drawn the attention of a Spanish author, who reviewed it in the *Estrella de Occidente* (*Western Star*, a journal occasionally published in Arabic under the name of *Najmat al-Maghreb*), whose objective was to promote a rapprochement between Spain and the Maghreb and to inform its readers on Arab culture (F. de Paula Valladar, 'Un embajador de Marruecos en Granada en el año de 1766', 1891).

1690–1, al-Wazīr al-Ghassānī (?–1707) was entrusted with a similar mission by Sultan Ismail (r. 1672–1727) and left a *riḥla* of his travels.[8] However, his itinerary did not include Granada; moreover, if we are to believe Pérès, al-Ghassānī was much less interested in architectural remains than he was in the population and had the soul of an ethnographer rather than a historian.[9] A more recent and closer reading of the same text proposes a somewhat different view of a traveller, who, in fact much more sensitive to history, devoted a major part of his narrative to the conquering Ṭāriq ibn Ziyād and complained about the appalling state of disrepair in which the Spaniards maintained, or rather let crumble into oblivion, the 'remains of an ancient civilisation'.[10] True, his stress is mostly on the descendants of Muslim Spain, be it the Andalusian population, whom he admired for its qualities, obviously inherited from the Arabs, or the Moriscos, whose sad destiny as converts he laments, but the text also leaves a deep feeling of nostalgia for a land lost merely two centuries earlier.[11]

Al-Ghassānī's feelings and observations are meaningful and useful for a better understanding of the mindset of the North African travellers and diplomats who would come after him. Nevertheless, as this study focuses specifically on the Alhambra, it makes sense to avoid the dispersion that would result from addressing the vast topic of Arab nostalgia for al-Andalus. If, therefore, we limit ourselves to the visitors to the Nasrid palace, it seems necessary to take al-Ghazzāl's narrative as our starting point and to seek his successors in this specific context. About a decade later, in 1779–80, another traveller from the Maghreb, Muḥammad ibn 'Uthmān al-Miknāsī (?–1792), sent, like al-Ghazzāl, by Muḥammad III, had the opportunity to visit the Alhambra,

[8] Pérès, *L'Espagne vue par les voyageurs musulmans*, pp. 5–17. For a critical edition of the text, see 'A. Binḥāddah (ed.), *Riḥlat al-Wazīr fī iftikāk al-asīr*. Part of the text has been translated into English in N. Matar, *In the Lands of the Christians: Arabic Travel Writing in the Seventeenth Century*, pp. 118–89. An early French version can be found in H. Sauvaire (ed.), *Voyage en Espagne d'un ambassadeur marocain (1690–1691)*.

[9] Pérès, *L'Espagne vue par les voyageurs musulmans*, pp. 9–10.

[10] Hermes, 'Nostalgia for al-Andalus in Early Modern Moroccan *Voyages en Espagne*', pp. 6–8.

[11] Hermes, 'Nostalgia for al-Andalus in Early Modern Moroccan *Voyages en Espagne*', pp. 9–14.

where he was greeted by Spanish officials.[12] While Pérès did not include him in his study, Nabil Matar studied his travelogue in detail, mentioning his brief visit to the Alhambra. Al-Miknāsī had fallen for the beauty of the site, which he described as 'one of the wonders of the world in the mastery of design and beauty of construction'. He lingered over the inscriptions in Arabic found in the palace, both religious and lay, expressing sadness upon reading some of the poems decorating some of the halls.[13] Rather than laments, al-Miknāsī engaged in curses, reminiscing the calamity that befell Granada when it fell into Christian hands, praying for its return to Islam, and wishing upon Queen Isabella the worst torments in the afterlife and at Judgement Day.[14] One of the officials assigned to his company even showed him the place where the children of al-Sarraj – the Abencerrages – were slaughtered, a reminder that the legend that would mark the nineteenth century was already alive and well in local folklore decades earlier.[15]

Al-Miknāsī was sent to Spain a second time in 1790 by the same ruler, but this time stayed on for two years, seeking asylum due to the change of sovereign that had brought Muḥammad III's son, Yazīd, to the throne. Whatever the circumstances, it seems that this time he did not visit the Alhambra. On the other hand, the archives of the Alhambra preserve the trace of the passage of a Moroccan 'notable' (*magnate*) by the name of 'Abdallah Kitrānī (?), with a retinue of three men, they too, fleeing from the ire of the new sultan. While the documents reveal some practical aspects of their accommodation inside the Alhambra itself, they provide no information as to the circumstances of their stay and, of course, on the way in which the visitors perceived the Nasrid remains that surrounded them.[16]

Pérès' list of travellers, which we left at al-Ghazzāl's embassy, takes a leap of approximately a century to resume with the Moroccan ambassador Abū

[12] Matar, *An Arab Ambassador in the Mediterranean World*. For an Arab edition of the text, see M. al-Miknāsī, *Al-Iksīr fī fikāk al-'asīr*. See also V. Rodríguez Casado, 'La embajada del talbe Sidi Mohamed ben Otman en 1780'.

[13] N. Matar, *An Arab Ambassador in the Mediterranean World*, p. 83.

[14] Matar, *An Arab Ambassador in the Mediterranean World*, p. 85.

[15] Matar, *An Arab Ambassador in the Mediterranean World*, p. 84. We should remember that the legend of the Abencerrage had been in circulation since the publication of de Hita's *Historia de los bandos de Zegríes y Abencerrajes* in 1595.

[16] A. Gámir Sandoval, 'En el siglo xviii, moros en la Alhambra'.

al-ʿAbbās Aḥmad al-Kardūdī (1840–98), who, in 1885, seems to have been much more impressed by the Cordoba mosque than by the Alhambra.[17] He was followed by the Mauritanian Muḥammad Maḥmūd ibn al-Talāmīd al-Turkuzī al-Shinqīṭī and his Tunisian companion, ʿAlī ibn Sālim al-Wardānī al Tūnisī, who visited the palace together in 1887, during a mission ordered by the Ottoman Sultan Abdülhamid II (1840–1918, r. 1876–1909), aimed at establishing an inventory of Islamic manuscripts kept in the libraries of Spain.[18] The other few travellers taken into account by Pérès were all Egyptian: the intellectual and bureaucrat Aḥmad Zakī, in 1893;[19] the lawyer Muḥammad Farīd, in 1901;[20] and, finally, the poet Aḥmad Shawqī, in 1919.[21]

Could the number of Arab and/or Muslim visitors to the Alhambra be limited to this handful of individuals? How are we to explain the long hiatus of over a century between al-Miknāsī and al-Kardūdī? Given the short distance between Spain and the Maghreb – particularly from Morocco – does it really make sense to take at face value this long interruption and accept that there would have been so few visits from just the other side of the Strait of Gibraltar?

The issue is evidently linked to the availability of sources; the few authors who have shown interest in the question have depended on written evidence of a very particular kind, namely *riḥla*s, or travel narratives – sometimes embassy

[17] Pérès, *L'Espagne vue par les voyageurs musulmans*, pp. 42–51. As I will explain later, Pérès is mistaken regarding Kardūdī's duties; he was not the ambassador, but the ambassador's secretary. This information was taken up in P. Wien, *Arab Nationalism*, pp. 57–8, 60, 63. Pérès provides no biographical information on Kardūdī. Thanks to Abdelmajid Kaddouri, we know that Abū al-ʿAbbās bin ʿAbdelqāder al-Kardūdī lived from 1840 to 1898 and that he descended from a Sharifian family of notables from Fez, which had been at the service of the *Makhzen* (government) for a long time. After studying at the University of al-Qarawiyin, he became a notary in his native town, before being appointed secretary at the Ministry of Justice, and, later, secretary to Sultan Ḥasan I for seventeen years (A. Kaddouri, 'Images de l'Europe dans un genre d'écriture marocaine: la *Rihla*', pp. 129–30). It seems that Kardūdī was the son of Abū ʿAbdallah Muḥammad bin ʿAbdelqāder bin Aḥmad al-Gulālī al-Ḥasanī al-Idrisī (1801–49), qadi of Tangier and author of several works on history and jurisprudence (M. Lakhdar, 'al-Kardudi').

[18] Pérès, L'Espagne vue par les voyageurs musulmans, pp. 55–72. Taken up in Wien, *Arab Nationalism*, p. 58.

[19] Pérès, *L'Espagne vue par les voyageurs musulmans*, pp. 72–87.

[20] Pérès, *L'Espagne vue par les voyageurs musulmans*, pp. 88–100.

[21] Pérès, *L'Espagne vue par les voyageurs musulmans*, pp. 100–20.

reports – which cannot be expected from any Arab visitor to Andalusia.[22] Of course, it is quite possible that other *riḥla*s may have survived and are yet to be discovered, but even if that were the case, their number would be highly unlikely to change in any significant way the volume of the corpus available today. The real challenge, then, is to find ways of reaching out to less prestigious, less erudite, more accidental, travellers, or simply to identify such individuals who might not have left a narrative or recollections of their visit to the Alhambra and of the circumstances surrounding it.

To do so, we can count on the unexpected assistance of one of the most extraordinary archival series any historian of culture in general, and of the Alhambra in particular, could ever dream of: a series of registers of visitors to the monument, a visitors' book where they could leave their signature and, often, some personal comments. The advantage of this documentary series is that, contrary to the dominant tradition of guest books at the time, it was not reserved for a careful selection of distinguished guests, but open to all the visitors of the monument (Figure 2.3). Some clues even suggest that the visitors were encouraged and asked to partake in this ritual and that, consequently, the pages of the book come closer to an exhaustive census than to a simple fantasy for a handful of overzealous tourists wanting to immortalise their passage. An American journalist recounts with some humour how exasperated he was by this obligation, expressing his frustration by mentioning three times 'the green book "Presented by Prince --- to the Alhambra" as one reads in gold letters outside'.[23]

[22] Of the seventy-two travelogues inventoried by Daniel Newman, only four concern Spain, far behind those of France (thirty-eight), Great Britain (nine) and Italy (five) (D. Newman, 'Myths and Realities in Muslim Alterist Discourse', p. 27).

[23] 'Our Spanish Correspondence: "H. P. L." in the Alhambra'. This anecdote allows us to 'test' the reliability of the visitors' book. Indeed, as the author of the article hiding behind the initials 'H. P. L.' noted he had signed the book on 30 April 1859, not only have I been able to verify that he was telling the truth and that he had indeed been there on that date at 4:30 pm, but that his full name was Henry P. Leland, and came from Philadelphia (Patronato de la Alhambra y el Generalife, Archivo de la Alhambra (AA), *libros de firmas*, 42, fol. 201 v, 30 April 1859). Leland's exasperation reminds us that many tourists were intimidated or irritated by 'high society' visitors signing the book. An amusing example is that of three travel companions who, on 17 December 1843, described themselves as 'braggarts' (*flambards*), and signed, one after the other, 'Baron Émile, trade ambassador of Lyon', 'Felix Rodrigues, minister plenipotentiary of Parisian industry', and 'A. Ganet, like the above, bankrupted ambassador', thus mocking the often aristocratic character of signatories (AA, *libros de firmas*, 42, fol. 49 v, 17 December 1843).

Figure 2.3 'Granada: 1. General View of the Alhambra (from the Chapiz incline), which His Majesty and Her Highness visited on the 1st of this month; 2. H.M. and H.H. inscribing their names on the visitors' book of the Alhambra; 3. The Watch Tower (*torre de la Vela*), where the royal banner was unfurled on 2 January 1492; 4. The cypress of the sultana, at the Generalife; From Granada to Antequera: 5. Gypsy families admiring the passage of the royal train; Antequera: 6. Types of riders escorting H.M. and H.H. upon their entrance into the town; Cordoba: 7. H.M. and H.H. visiting the *mihrab* of the ancient mosque; 8. H.M. and H.H., followed by a large crowd, heading towards the hermitages on the hills, on the 4th of the month; 9. Types of hermits from the hills of Cordoba' *La Ilustración española y americana*, XXI/XV (22 April 1877), p. 269. Author's collection. This full-page visual account of the Andalusian journey of King Alfonso XII and his sister, the Infanta Isabella, in the most popular Spanish illustrated magazine of the time shows the importance attached to the visit to the Alhambra and, in the upper left corner, the signing of the visitors' book placed just outside of the Court of the Myrtles.

A second advantage, as unexpected and precious to the historian as the former, is that the series starts very early, in 1829, under circumstances that explain to a large extent the nature and goals of this undertaking. The idea of keeping a visitors' book had come to a Russian prince and diplomat, Dimitri Ivanovich Dolgorukov (1797–1867), who was posted to Madrid from 1826 to 1830. It so happens that Dolgorukov was a friend of Washington Irving, whom he accompanied during a journey to Granada in 1829: 'In the Spring of 1829, the Author of this Work, whom curiosity had brought to Spain, made a rambling expedition from Seville to Granada in company with a friend, a member of the Russian Embassy at Madrid.'[24] The cover of the first register of the book bore in engraved golden letters: 'Given to the Alhambra by Prince Dolgourouki', the very inscription that had upset the Philadelphian journalist to the point of refusing to name the generous prince (Figure 2.4). Inside, an inscription in French by the prince explained the reasons behind his decision:

> Several travellers, wishing to perpetuate the memory of their visit to the Alhambra, have disfigured its walls by filling them with their names and thoughts. To ensure a longer existence to the memory of these travellers and at the same time to preserve the building from greater damage, this book has been presented by Prince Dolgourouki.
>
> Alhambra, 9 May 1829[25]

The inscription was followed by the signatures of the individuals who made up the party of visitors on 9 May 1829: Dolgorukov; Washington Irving; Count Alexis de Saint-Priest (1805–51), the French ambassador in Lisbon and his wife Louise;[26] Cavaliere Ermolao Asinari di San Marzano (1800–64), secretary of the Sardinian legation in Madrid; Antoine-Pierre-Charles Favart (1780–1867), painter and author; the painter Pierre-Auguste Biard (1799–1882); Édouard de Lussy, architect in Madrid; M. de Billecocq, secretary of the

[24] Irving, *The Alhambra*, vol. I, p. 3.

[25] AA, *libros de firmas*, 42, fol. 0 r, 9 May 1829.

[26] Author of *L'Espagne. Fragment d'un voyage*, mentioned above in n. 28, p. 29. One needs therefore to remember that this man did not share most of his travel companions' positive feelings about the former rulers of Spain.

Figure 2.4 Cover of the first register of the Alhambra visitors' book, bearing the inscription acknowledging Prince Dolgorouki/Dolgorukov's role in this innovative practice. AA, *libros de firmas*, 42 (1829).

French embassy in Madrid; and one Gustav (?) von Hamelberg.[27] These were the very first of an extraordinary list of names that would resonate with the history of the discovery of the Alhambra. Jules Goury and Owen Jones, 'architects', signed the visitors' book in May 1834, fourteen pages after Dolgorukov and his travel companions.[28] On the same page, at the date of 22 November 1833, a visitor left a short lament in French:

> O silent walls, which I can still see, and
> Who fill my heart with bitter memory,
> Here is my farewell; and as I lament your misfortune
> Far from you, alas! I shall soon die.

This short poem could easily escape the reader's eye; the book is filled with similar moments of lyricism. Nevertheless, it bares a signature that is far from inconspicuous: 'A. Almaric, last French governor of the Alhambra in 1812'.[29] There was more: just beneath Almaric's signature, another visitor, anonymous this time, added a highly sarcastic comment on the poem: 'That was probably what Boabdil must have been thinking while leaving Granada. But he probably wrote better.' A third hand, also anonymous, agreed: 'I have no doubt'.[30]

There could be no better illustration of the amazing potential of this series. These albums (*álbumes*), as they were called before they were renamed *libros de firmas* (signature books), were more than just a list of names awaiting statistical treatment. Comments, poems, drawings, questions, answers, insults accumulate and crisscross over the pages, giving them an extraordinary liveliness that cannot be captured by quantitative analysis. The question, then, is not just to know who visited the Alhambra, but to understand what they may have felt, thought, remembered when in front of the monument, what their references and recollections may have been, how they perceived, and sometimes reacted to, other comments across the pages. Given this wealth of information, one cannot help but wonder why nobody has had the idea of engaging in a

[27] AA, *libros de firmas*, 42, fol. 1 r, 9 May 1829.

[28] AA, *libros de firmas*, 42, fol. 8 v, May 1834.

[29] Adrien-Augustin-Almaric, comte de Mailly, marquis d'Haucourt et de Nesle, prince d'Orange (1792–1878).

[30] AA, *libros de firmas*, 42, fol. 8 v, 22 November 1833.

systematic study of this source, other than in the form of sporadic, and rather old, celebrity hunts.[31]

Clearly, this source is more than just an inventory: thanks to the subjective and personal, and often surprising, comments it contains, it acquires an amazing degree of depth and liveliness. This phenomenon is further intensified by the urge felt by some visitors to comment on, or respond to, previous comments, often in a polemical way. Browsing through the pages, one can find several examples reminiscent of the exchange between Almaric and his detractors, indicating an ongoing tension between French visitors and Spanish readers of their comments. When, in 1879, one Delaunay having cursed 'the day which saw the fall of Granada at the hands of Isabella' and the 'brutality' of Charles V 'who lacerated this page of love, the divine Alhambra', a Spaniard, whose signature remains undecipherable, responded by cursing 'the day the French came to Granada to desecrate the tomb of Gonzalo de Cordoba and to build bridges with the stones of the churches they had demolished'.[32]

Fake Arabs, Maurophiles and Maurophobes

It would serve no useful purpose to expand further this particular aspect of the topic, however amusing; the objective was simply to give a concrete idea of the form that the visitors' inscriptions and comments could sometimes take, and of the advantages that historians could derive from such details. At any rate, such inscriptions constitute a minority, not to say an exception, among an overwhelming number of much more laconic formulas of identification: a date and a signature, generally coupled with a full name and, often, a profession, a nationality, or a city of origin or residence. From the perspective of this study, one has to be content with – even thankful for – the possibility of simply counting Arab or Muslim visitors or, more precisely, visitors using the Arabic script among the thousands of signatures and inscriptions penned in Western languages.[33] This is precisely the advantage that has enabled me to

[31] See n. 21, p. 16.

[32] AA, *libros de firmas*, 43, fol. 194 r, *c.* 25 January 1879.

[33] In 1859, the American journalist Henry P. Leland (see, n. 23, p. 80) had already noted the presence of Arabic signatures in the registers, prompting him to wonder: 'The most striking feature in that register of the Alhambra, "*Presented by Prince ------- to the Alhambra*", as one reads in gold letters outside, was certain names or words written in Arabic. Who knows

undertake an exercise that would have been simply unthinkable for Western visitors, even though skimming through thousands of pages in search for Arabic characters was already a tedious task in itself.

However, before starting this inventory, it should be noted that the Arab, Moorish or Islamic character of the Alhambra was a recurring leitmotiv throughout the comments left in the book, some of which were of a rather polemical nature, by visitors whose identity had no direct connection to the question. In the case of French and Spanish polemists, this was an argument that surfaced sometimes, provoking heated exchanges. Thus, one Albert Duval wrote the following, on 8 November 1878:

> Luckily for the inhabitants and for tourists, the Moors have occupied Spain for a long period of time. It is to these Barbarians that their victors owe the olive trees that feed them and the masterpieces of Arab architecture which attract foreigners. The view of the Alhambra largely compensates for the slowness and the inconveniences of the journey.[34]

Clearly offended by these demeaning remarks, a first commentator, most probably Spanish, responded with a curt 'Written by a beast of burden.' A second one counterattacked by using the same theme: 'It is precisely because the Spaniards were much superior to the Barbarians that they threw them out and have taken advantage of their palace.'[35]

Yet another expressed his disdain for Arab art, which he apparently considered to be less manly than the Gothic style, whose decorative achievements he found much superior to the work of plaster and stucco the tourists admired so much:

> Disillusion of disillusions! All is disillusion! All this would be pretty, not beautiful, if instead of moulding plaster and stucco, the Arabs had carved the marble with a chisel. A work of women! The material on which art is

---

who did it? may be an Englishman; but the characters, at least, suggest that one of the descendants of the former owners came back and wrote therein' ('Our Spanish Correspondence. "H. P. L." in the Alhambra').

[34] AA, *libros de firmas*, 43, fol. 187 v, 8 November 1878.

[35] AA, *libros de firmas*, 43, fol. 187 v, n.d.

executed is half the art; it makes it great if it resists, and small if it yields under its hand.

Of course, the author of these lines, one Auguste Poupart, was soon targeted by others, who, while remaining anonymous, took to the Alhambra's defence by putting Poupart in his place through comments and jibes that made fun of his name and his assumed profession.[36] These references to the Arabs – often called Moors – were part of a wide spectrum of feelings, ranging from hatred to admiration, often tainted with a strange Orientalist condescension. This patronising tone was evident in the comment left by one C. Bonforti, a member of a group that styled itself as 'Frenchmen from Africa', where he expressed regrets at 'not having brought a few Bedouins with him to show them what they had been capable of some centuries ago and to teach them what they should become'.[37] Generally speaking, religious commitment could trigger partisan reactions, sometimes of a rather violent nature. The abbot Georges Frémond, canon of Algiers and Poitiers, provides a blatant example of such bigotry, when, making fun of the famous motto of the Alhambra – 'There is no victor but God' (*lā ghāliba illā Allah*) – prayed for a final victory against the Arabs: 'There is no victor but God! . . . And yet, the Arabs are not vanquished yet; but thanks to Spain, to the noble sons of Ferdinand and Isabella they will soon be.'[38] The same mindset seems to have motivated one Doctor Mérali, of Georgian origin, and physician of the Negus Menelik II (1844–1913, r. 1889–1913), when in 1919, he declared himself to be 'a friend and admirer of Spain, which reconquered its territory from the Moors through a persistent crusade of 500 years (from 711 to 1212).

[36] AA, *libros de firmas*, 42, fol. 34 v, 9 June 1841. 'My dear Poupard, you are but a chubby baby (*poupard* in French). Your style is chubby, and you will always remain a chubby baby'; 'Poupard, grocer in bulk and retail, deals also in cloth! Oh you animal, Poupard, you grocer!' It seems that the said Poupart was Simon Pierre Auguste Poupart de Wilde (1798–1882), author, prefect of Vaucluse (1848), private secretary of Ferdinand Flocon, agriculture minister (1848). He descended from the Poupart de Neuflize family of bankers and clothiers, see at: https://fr.wikipedia.org/wiki/Famille_Poupart_de_Neuflize; https://fr.wikipedia.org/wiki/Liste_des_préfets_de_Vaucluse.

[37] AA, *libros de firmas*, 42, fol. 67 v, 19 June 1847.

[38] AA, *libros de firmas*, 45, fol. 189 v, 24 October 1893.

Long live Georgia and Spain, two soldiers of Christ, one in the Caucasus and the other in the Pyrenees.'[39]

Nevertheless, it would be a mistake to think that this sectarian attitude characterised most comments referring in one way or the other to the Arab past of Andalusia. Quite the contrary, the beauty of the site encouraged many visitors to express out loud their admiration for the civilisation that had built it. In 1846, Charles de Vendegies (1822–97), a French aristocrat and Orientalist dilettante,[40] found no other means to express his amazement than to write down word for word the entire poem describing King Don Juan's love for the city of Granada, dutifully copied from Chateaubriand's *Adventures of the Last Abencerrage*.[41] Seeking to add an exotic and original touch to his long inscription, the young man decided to show off his linguistic skills by appending a distich in Turkish, perhaps of his own composition: 'I have contemplated this rose garden of the world from end to end / I have never seen a rose that did not burn with the fire of torment.'[42]

Under the pen of some Spanish visitors, this mix of exoticism and admiration could sometimes take the shape of a strong nostalgia with surprising undertones: 'Señor ¡Que nos reconquisten los árabes!', 'Lord! May the Arabs

[39] AA, *libros de firmas*, 45, fol. 237 r, 11 June 1919.

[40] Charles-Marie-Vincent Bouchelet de Vendegies's first contact with the Orient dated back to the early 1840s, when he met four Ottoman students during his education in London. He then started to study Turkish, Arabic and Persian in Paris, under the watchful eyes of Orientalists such as Desgranges, Jaubert and Quatremère. Just before obtaining his diploma, in 1846, he undertook a journey to Spain together with his cousin Charles Ewbank, and boasting a recommendation from François Guizot, then Minister of Foreign Affairs. He extended his journey to Tangier, Tétouan and Oran, and retuned to Spain, where he visited the Alhambra. Vendegies finally settled in Cambrai and contributed to the town's cultural development as a local erudite and amateur of art and literature. See A. Berger, 'Notice biographique de M. le comte Charles de Vendegies'.

[41] Chateaubriand, *Aventures du dernier Abencerage*, pp. 152–4.

[42] AA, *libros de firmas*, 42, fol. 64 r, 25 August 1846. The distich reads 'Bu gülistan-ı cihana ser-ta-ser gördüm nazar / Görmedim bir gül ki hâr-ı can-güzarı olmaya'. Having failed to find any Ottoman poem that might have inspired him, I must assume that it was probably of his own composition, as some errors would tend to corroborate. Thus, '*gülistan*' (كلستان rose garden) is misspelled '*gûlistan*' (كولستان) and the expression '*nazar gördüm*' needs to be corrected as '*nazar etdim*'.

reconquer us!' cried out one J. Emilio Ferrero in a rush of Maurophilia, which, if one considers the absence of any reaction or comment, had not offended anyone.[43] Such was not the case, however, when, in September 1889, the realist author and poet Leopoldo Cano y Masas (1844–1934) inscribed a poem, where, faced with 'the sadness of his Granadan Alhambra', he lamented over 'unfortunate Spain' (*pobre España*): 'Due to fanaticism and torpor / the cross always among the ruins / and always in ruin your greatness!'[44] There were no reactions on the pages, but the daily press took it upon itself to publicise Cano's sad reproaches in the weeks that followed his visit. Newspapers became the stage for a political debate over the poet's verses. On 9 October, *El Liberal*, true to its name, gave him its support by publishing the three poems he had composed following this first visit to Granada. The first poem, written before he saw the Alhambra, praised the beauty of the site, but had already set the tone by mentioning 'the palace of a Castilian tyrant' (*palacio de un verdugo de Castilla*), clearly referring to the palace that Charles V had built right next to the Alhambra. The second was the one he had inscribed in the visitors' book. As to the third, even more violent, drove the argument home: 'We have ousted the Moors / who built these palaces / to make more space / to erect our bullrings. / After glorious conquests / envious inquisitors / roasted the peasants / and banished the artists.' What had the *Holy* Inquisition left behind it? he asked: 'A beggar at each street corner, / a cross in every ruin, / many monks . . . and very little faith.'[45] The Carlist and conservative *Siglo futuro*, counterattacked a few days later, devoting more than half a page to the matter, speaking of 'less than mediocre verses circulating in liberal papers', literally building an indictment against the poet and his supporters. Disgusted by the insinuations against Charles V and the Inquisition, the newspaper accused the

[43] AA, *libros de firmas*, 46, fols 237 137, r, November 1899.

[44] '¡Pobre España! ¡Qué tristeza / da tu Alhambra granadina! / Por fanatismo y torpeza / ¡Siempre la cruz en la ruina, / siempre en ruinas tu grandeza!' AA, *libros de firmas*, 44, fol. 271 v, *c.* 27–29 September 1889.

[45] 'Desterramos á los moros / que hacían estos palacios / para aumentar los espacios / donde hacer plazas de toros. / Tras las gloriosas conquistas, / celosos inquisidores / tostaron agricultores / y desterraron artistas.' [ ] 'un mendigo en cada esquina / una cruz en cada ruina / mucho fraile y poca fe' ('Leopoldo Cano en Granada'). See also 'Visitando la Alhambra'; 'Visita a la Alhambra'.

liberals of doing 'Lucifer's work', attributed Spain's ruin to the disaffection suffered by the Church and denounced the utter barbarism of the Arabs: 'They came to Spain as complete Barbarians, and they became Barbarians once again when they left Spain.'[46]

For many Spanish visitors, Maurophile nostalgia could find its expression in a claim to Arab descent. Emboldened by his allegedly Arab-sounding name, Pedro Aliaga Romarosa exclaimed: 'My name is Ali-aga. There is no doubt: I am an Arab. Therefore, I am at home.'[47] Just a line above, one Ramón Friller simply stated: 'I feel like an Arab.'[48] Others, more playfully, wrote down their names in Arabic script, with varying degrees of success: Felipe de Talavera (فليپه ده طلويرا);[49] Francisco Fernández y González, professor of literature in Granada (فَرَنسِيسكو فرنندز و غُنزَلَز پْرُفسُر دا لِترَتُره أن غَرَنَد Fransisqo Fernandez wa Gonzalez profesor da literatura en Gharnad);[50] Rodrigo from Madrid, son of José from Cordoba (روذريق المجريطي ابن يوسف القرطبي Rodhrīq al-Majritī ibn Yūsef al-Qurṭubī);[51] Manuel Pablo Castillanos (مانويل بابلو كسطيانوس).[52] In 1913, one Salvador Ramón Benítez made a point of dating his visit in Arabic: '1913 كنت لهنا اليوم ثمينة يوليو kuntu lehnā al-yawm thamīna yūlyū 1913'.[53] The most striking example is probably that of Fulgencio Gómez Carrión, officer in the Guardia Civil, whose braggartly inscription covered almost all of the page (Figure 2.5):

Fūlkhenzyū Gūmez Karriyūn fāyid al-miyat Guwārdiya
Sībīl khantil ḥūmbrī dhi'l-sulṭān dhi'l-Isbānya

[46] 'La cruz en las ruinas'. Two years later, on the occasion of the festival of the invention – in the sense of discovery – of the Holy Cross, the Catholic daily *El Lábaro* rekindled the debate by accusing the poet of having failed to understand that it was not the cross that had ruined the Arab monuments of the country, but the vandalism of the present century ('La invención de la Santa Cruz').

[47] 'Mi apellido es Ali-aga. No cabe duda: soy árabe. Estoy pues en mi casa' (AA, *libros de firmas*, 45, fol. 185 v, 19 September 1879).

[48] 'Me siento árabe', AA, *libros de firmas*, 45, fol. 185 v, 19 September 1879.

[49] AA, *libros de firmas*, 42, fol. 55 r, 12 April 1849.

[50] AA, *libros de firmas*, 42, fol. 152 v, 29 August 1857.

[51] AA, *libros de firmas*, 43, fol. 101 r, 31 August 1875.

[52] AA, *libros de firmas*, 43, fol. 74 v, 19 June 1876.

[53] AA, *libros de firmas*, 49, fol. 123 r, 8 July 1913.

Mūlāy Alfūnsū al-thuluthāshar itnaʿam Allah wa'l-qārī
āmīn
Gharnāta yawm 30 min shahr Nubānbar sanati 1916
(ʿām 1335 min al-hijra)
wa lā ghāliba illā Allah
Lā ilaha illā Allah wa Muḥammadun rasūl Allah
Salām wa sallam[54]

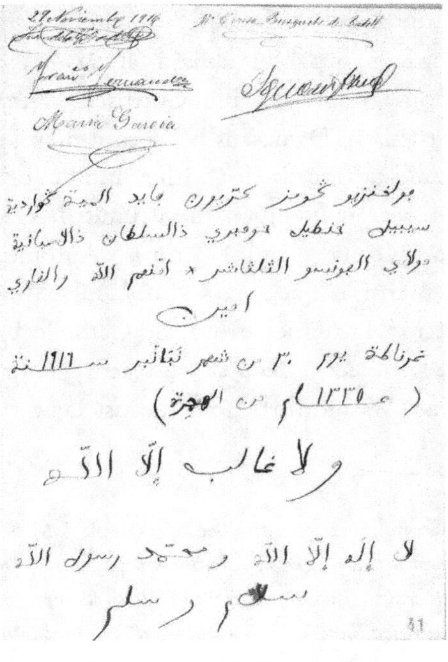

Figure 2.5 Inscription left in the visitors' book by Fulgencio Gómez Carrión, 30 November 1916. AA, *libros de firmas*, 50, fol. 41 r. © Archivo del Patronato de la Alhambra y Generalife. An officer in the Guardia Civil, Gómez Carrión wrote this pompous inscription in rather broken Arabic, filled with neologisms meant to translate Spanish terms, but ended it with the Nasrid motto and the Islamic *shahada*.

[54] AA, *libros de firmas*, 50, fol. 41 r, 30 November 1916:
ڢولخنزيو ݣومز كرّيون ڢايد المية ݣواردية / سيبيل خنطيل حومبري ذالسلطان ذالاصبانية / مولاي الڢونسو الثلثاشر اتنعم الله و القاري / امين / غرناطة يوم 30 من شهر نبّاڢبر سنة ١٩١٦ / (عام ١٣٣٥ من الهجِرة) / و لا غالب إلّا الله / لا إلَه إلّا الله و محمّد رسول الله / سلام و سلم
Fulgencio Gómez Carrión was a career officer who served in the famous Guardia Civil. He participated in the Francoist uprising in Malaga in July 1936, and was consequently executed

Spanish visitors were not the only ones to engage in this exercise; some foreigners, especially Orientalist scholars, who had the required skills did the same, such as Charles William Benton, professor at the University of Minnesota (شارلس ويليم بنتن مدرسة العظيمة من منسوته *Shārls Wilyam Bentun madrasata'l-ażima min Minesūta*),[55] Edward Granville Browne and Edward Denison Ross, both professors of Persian in Great Britain (ادوارد برون الانكليسى معلّم اللسان الفارسى فى دارالفنون كمبريج فى بلاد انكلتره المحروسة و معه ادورد دنيسون روس معلّم اللسان الفارسى فى دارالفنون لندن Edwārd Brūn al-Ingilīsī mu'allim al-lisāni'l-Fārsī fī dāru'l-funūn Kembrīj fī bilādi Ingilteret-i'l-mahrūsa wa ma'ah Edw[ā]rd Denīsūn Rūs mu'allim al-lisān al-Fārsī fī dāru'l-funūn Landan),[56] or the famous Arabist Johann Gottfried Wetzstein (1815–1905), former consul of Prussia in Damascus, who copied and translated a distich in Arabic.[57] One could expand the list with a number of individuals, whose linguistic skills were certainly much more limited: Gustav Antoni from Berlin (جوستاو انطوني برلين Gustāv Anṭūnī Berlīn),[58] Antonio Mifsud, evidently Maltese, and Henry Griffin (انطونيو المفصود - هنرى كريفين Anṭūniyū al-Mifṣūd – Henrī Grīfīn),[59] Henry Heffernet, from the Catholic University of Washington (هنرى هيفرنة معلم في الكلية الكتولكيه في وشينتون Henri Hifirnat mu'allim fī'l-kulliyati'l-Katūlikiya fī Washintūn),[60] to name just a few.

---

the same year by the Republican authorities. See, for example, J. M. Martínez Bande, *Los años críticos: República, conspiración, revolución y alzamiento*, p. 286. Carrión's inscription is rather remarkable for its numerous mistakes and, most of all, for its surprising phonetic renderings and barbarisms: '*Guwārdiya Sībīl*' for '*Guardia Civil*'; '*khantil hūmbrī*' for '*gentilhombre*' (gentleman); '*fāyid al-miyat*', obviously a mistake for '*qā'id al-mia'a*', a neologism for captain, rendered by 'head of a hundred'; '*al-sultān zi'l-Isbānya Mūlāy Alfūnsū al-thuluthashar itna'am Allah wa'l-qārī*', for 'the King of Spain, His Majesty Alfonso XIII, may God and the reader bless him'.

55 AA, *libros de firmas*, 45, fol. 232 r, *c.* 11 August 1894.

56 AA, *libros de firmas*, 46, fol. 148 r, 6 April 1900.

57 AA, *libros de firmas*, 42, fol. 285 r, 10 October 1870: 'هنا نزلنا و من هنا ارتحلنا / كذا الدنيا رحيل و ارتحال' ('We have landed here and we have travelled / Just like this world, which goes and travels').

58 AA, *libros de firmas*, 46, fol. 51 v, May 1897; fol. 116 r, May 1899. The use of the letter *jim* (ج) for the hard 'G' in his name suggests that he was familiar with the Egyptian pronunciation of Arabic.

59 AA, *libros de firmas*, 46, fol, 165 r, 23 July 1900.

60 AA, *libros de firmas*, 46, fol. 201 r, *c.* 16 July 1901.

Visitors from the Maghreb: Moroccan Embassies

Pseudo-Arabs, Spanish and foreign, contributed with a local touch to the diversity of the visitors' book, while many tourists had much to say about the Arabo-Islamic heritage of the monument; but what about real Arabs, especially those from the Maghreb, a few examples of whom we have previously seen? I had expressed doubts as to the long silence of more than a century separating al-Miknāsī (1779–80) from al-Kardūdī (1885); a very substantial number of signatures spotted throughout the pages of the visitors' book confirm this impression. In total, I have counted over fifty visits concerning approximately 150 individuals, whom I have been able to ascertain as originating from the Maghreb.[61] A few general observations may be in order. The chronological distribution of these visits is relatively erratic but increases with time. Unless I am mistaken and have missed an earlier occurrence, the first of these visits seems to date back to 1863,[62] and their frequency starts to increase only after the 1870s, reaching a peak of fifty-six visitors in fifteen visits during the 1900–9 decade. Among those visitors who explicitly state their identity, most originate from Morocco (fifteen visits and thirty-eight individuals), with Algeria (three and twenty-nine) and Tunisia (four and five) lagging far behind. The Algerian numbers are heavily inflated by the visit, on 16 June 1900, of a group consisting of twenty-seven horsemen participating in a fantasia – la *fiesta de la pólvora* or '[gun]powder festival' – held at the hippodrome of los Llanos de Armilla, near Granada. The inscriptions they left in the visitors' book lacked a personal touch. Only two of the inscriptions look like they have been penned by the person concerned. One referred jointly to 'Abdelqāder bin Houari al-Misfīqī and Muḥammad bin Jalūl, while the other was by one Ṭahar ben 'Abdelqāder, from the douar of Suwarkin (?). For the rest, the inscription consisted of two lists containing the names of four and nineteen individuals, respectively, written in the same hand in both French and Arabic, without a single comment.[63] The local press gave a very detailed account of the festival and of the remarkable skills of the Algerian riders during the fantasia. Don

[61] Obviously, this figure is a minimum, considering that I have probably missed some, especially when they signed, as they sometimes did, in French.

[62] One al-Hājj 'Alī bin al-Bashīr al-Sharīf al-Husnī al-Ghrīssī (AA, *libros de firmas*, 42, fol. 244 r, *c.* 8 February 1863).

[63] AA, *libros de firmas*, 46, fol. 162 v, 16 June 1900.

Pascual, writing for the *Defensor de Granada*, noted that the 'Algerian Moors' had outdone the toreros with their presence and agility. To him, 'the Arabs, children of Africa, that continent with a future, displayed a wonderful performance made of intelligent strength, discipline and marksmanship, a brilliant entertainment in time of peace and an admirable preparation for war'.[64] *La Publicidad* also praised the beauty of the show and the agility of the horsemen, whose eyes were brighter than the sun and who claimed to be envious of the light, the heat and the beauty of the women attending. The daily also published a list of the riders and the 'tribes' to which they belonged: Bel-Abbès, Tenera, Mercier-Lacombe (Sfisef), la Mekerra, Amarnas and Assesna. While some of the names did indeed overlap with the list in the visitors' book, most were transcribed with a licence that made them unrecognisable.[65] Clearly obsessed with the beauty and exoticism of the festival, none of the local newspapers touched upon the Algerians' visit to the Alhambra. The palace appeared only as a backdrop in Don Pascual's narrative, where the author made a point of reminding his readers that on that very spot, four centuries earlier, the forefathers of these riders 'were fighting . . . against the best knights of Europe, the invincible warriors of Aragon and Castile'.[66] Spanish Orientalism and Africanism were thus merged into a chauvinistic nostalgia of the glorious days of the *Reconquista*.

A rather similar visit had taken place about thirty years earlier, on 4 December 1871, by the Beni Zoug-Zoug company of acrobats, consisting of thirty individuals. The visitors' book holds only the signatures of five members and their interpreter. The only person whose inscription displayed an origin was al-Ḥājj Aḥmad ben Muḥammad al-Ṭanjawī, from Tangier.[67] The information we already possess on the Beni Zoug-Zoug allows for the identification of al-Ḥajj 'Alī ben Muḥammad, the only one signing in French, albeit in a shaky hand, as the company's impresario and manager, a Moroccan subject naturalised French. With its name borrowed from a famous confederation of Berber tribes, this company had been active since the 1860s and specialised in acrobatic performances, particularly human pyramids. The Beni Zoug-Zoug, introduced as the 'famous company of Algerian Arabs', had performed on

[64] Don Pascual, 'Los moros argelinos', *El Defensor de Granada*, 11, 857 (16 June 1900), p. 1.

[65] 'Granada en fiestas – Correr la pólvora'.

[66] Don Pascual, 'Los moros argelinos'.

[67] AA, *libros de firmas*, 42, fol. 344 r, 4 December 1871.

30 November and 1 December 1871 at Granada's Teatro Principal. The show's programme included performances with evocative names: 'the invocation of Allah', 'the great column of the Nile', 'the magic flask', 'Cheops' pyramid', 'a Moorish pastime'.[68] The reason that only five persons from the company signed the book was probably because most of its members consisted of rather young children, who, as would be later discovered, had been 'purchased' from destitute British families, based on abusive contracts.[69]

If one is to exclude the rather particular cases of Algerian – or allegedly Algerian – horsemen and acrobats, the Moroccan presence in the visitors' book was much more significant and sustained, covering several decades. A striking feature of Moroccan presence at the Alhambra was the frequency and predominance of diplomatic missions. Out of fifteen visits and thirty-eight individuals openly identified as Moroccan, seven visits and twenty-three persons had to do with such a mission. The inscriptions left by these visitors are generally laconic and repetitive. Many were content with writing down their name, followed by a date. Names were often introduced by the expression 'عبد ربه' (*'abdu rabbihi*, servant of God) and followed by a prayer, 'لطف الله به' (*laṭafallah bihi*, may God's grace be upon him). Some also added a surname, their origins or their profession. Diplomats generally enjoyed pompous titles, albeit of a rather repetitive nature. In some exceptional cases, they commented on their visit, occasionally adding expressions of marvel and qualifications underlining the beauty or majesty of the Alhambra. One such exception is that of the first visitor spotted in 1863, al-Hājj 'Alī bin al-Bashīr al-Sharīf al-Ḥusnī

[68] 'Espectáculos', 30 November 1871 and 1 December 1871.

[69] In 1881, during the company's stay in Constantinople, the British consular authorities took action to secure the liberation of these children. Out of a total of seventeen children of British origin, three decided to stay with the company under improved conditions, three joined a company from Marseilles, four were returned to their families and seven were placed in institutions to receive an education ('The "Beni-Zoug-Zoug – Arabs"'). See also, T. J. Barnardo, 'The Beni-zou-zougs!'; L. Simour, *Recollecting History beyond Borders: Captives, Acrobats, Dancers and the Moroccan-American Narrative of Encounters*, pp. 101–5. The company was reformed and renewed after these events. They returned to Granada in 1887, under the name of the 'Imperial Ottoman Company of Baghdad', still under the direction of Sīdī Ḥājj 'Alī ben Muḥammad, 'of the Beni Zoug-Zoug tribe' ('Fiesta de moros'; *La Política*, 172, 25 September 1887, p. 2).

al-Ghrīssī, whose long inscription glorified the Alhambra, while at the same time condemning those who had surrendered it to the enemy:

> Praise be to the One God
> Having arrived at the palace, on this 8th day of Sha'bān of the year 1279, al-Hājj 'Alī bin al-Bashīr al-Sharīf al-Husnī al-Ghrīssī, of noble descent, has been extremely delighted with the fortress. How strange were its inhabitants who abandoned it to have their lives spared and failed to find another of similar beauty. It would have been preferable to see them perish down to the last.[70]

It may well be that this mysterious 'Alī bin al-Bashīr was not the first visitor to the Alhambra from the Maghreb for a century, nor the first to have left such a rich commentary. If we are to believe the Granadan author Francisco de Paula Valladar (1852–1924), in 1846, two 'Moors', accompanying the French consul general in Morocco[71] and his secretary Léon Roches (1809–1900)[72] had asked

[70] AA, *libros de firmas*, 42, fol. 244 r, *c.* 8 February 1863:

الحمد الله و حوا

كان وصولنا هنا الى هذا الفصر العظيم بي اليوم الثامن من شعبان عام 1279 الحاج على بن البشير الشريب الحسنى الغريسى نهيا المشرب اصلا بعجيبنا الفصر غاية العجب بياعجبا لا هسله هربوا منه يطلبون الحيوة و لعلهم مجيدون مثله بى الدنيا بيا حسرتهم لو ماتوا بيه عن اخرهم كان احسن و ابضل

[71] Edme de Chasteau, consul general in Tangier and French chargé d'affaires in Morocco.

[72] Great-nephew of the famous Madame Roland (1754–93), Léon Roches started his career in Algeria, where his father had acquired agricultural lands. Endowed with an excellent knowledge of Arabic, he joined the army as an interpreter. In 1836, he met Emir Abdelkader and became his private secretary. When the emir's relations with France deteriorated, he returned to the army. After a few years, backed and recommended by General Thomas-Robert Bugeaud (1784–1849), he joined the Ministry of Foreign Affairs as an interpreter. In 1846, in the wake of a mission with the Sultan of Morocco, he was appointed secretary at the French legation in Tangier, headed by Edme de Chasteau, his wife Camille's father. In 1841, much like other adventurers such as Richard Francis Burton, he had managed to visit Mecca, wearing local disguise. He was appointed consul in Trieste, Tripoli of Barbary and Tunis, and ambassador to Japan in 1863. He published his – often embellished – memoirs in *Trente-deux ans à travers l'islam (1832–1864)* and *Dix ans à travers l'islam (1834–1844)*. On Roches, see Alpinus, *Quelques pages sur Léon Roches*; 'Léon Roches'; D. Irwin, 'Sheikhs and Samurai: Léon Roches and the French Imperial Project'.

the latter to insert the following inscription in Arabic in the 'album' of the Generalife:

> Praised be the One and Only God
> Only God is permanent
> Peace be upon you, oh Granada! We have watched and admired you and we have said to you: 'Praised be he who has erected you and may [divine] compassion be upon those who built you. Nothing remains, except the Kingdom of the Almighty, the Live One, the Eternal and Immortal.' The author of these lines will always remember you, for in truth he has admired you together with his companions and he has agreed with them that nothing could meet your beauty![73]

Unfortunately, as the album of the Generalife, apparently a later equivalent of the visitors' book of the Alhambra, seems to have been lost, the original inscription is nowhere to be found.[74] We do not know either who the two persons accompanying Chasteau and Roches were, nor why they may have chosen to delegate to the latter the task of writing down their inscription.[75]

As I said earlier, these two examples are exceptional in that their authors expressed strong feelings triggered by the discovery of the Alhambra. The Spanish press took upon itself to fill the documentary void created by the silence of most visitors. Indeed, to the historian's greatest joy, Spanish newspapers and magazines seem to have shown a genuine and sustained interest in these visits, conveying to their readers the comings and goings of these 'Moors'

[73] F. de Paula Valladar, 'El álbum de Generalife' (1902), p. 709.

[74] The only other trace of these registers can be found in Paula Valladar's article mentioned in the preceding note. According to him, this 'album' was inaugurated in 1845 and the first volume ended in August 1865 (Paula Valladar, 'El álbum del Generalife' (1921), p. 329). The administrators of the Alhambra archives have declared that they have no knowledge of the existence of a second series of books devoted to the visitors of the Generalife.

[75] One is tempted to see in these two visitors, members of the Moroccan embassy, which Chasteau and Roches were asked to accompany to Paris in 1845. Unfortunately, however, the dates do not correspond at all, as the embassy left Tétouan on board the *Météore* on 13 December 1845 and returned on 7 March 1846, not to mention that the two journeys were done directly through Marseilles, without any stopover in Spain. On this embassy, see S. G. Miller (ed.), *Disorienting Encounters: Travels of a Moroccan Scholar in France in 1845–1846.*

confronted with the Alhambra and other monuments of Andalusia. While the visit of ʿAbdesselām al-Sūsī, during his embassy in 1877, was hardly mentioned in the daily press – one newspaper just noted that the delegation visited the Alhambra 'with attention' (*con detenimiento*)[76] – the most popular illustrated magazine of the time did bring up the matter in an item describing in some detail the ambassador and his retinue's visit:

> The Moroccans walked slowly through the elegant galleries of the Court of the Lions; they went in a compact group to the beautiful mirador of Lindaraja; they examined meticulously the hall of antiquities; they read the tombstones of the Granadan kings;[77] they visited the other rooms of the palace, the galleries, the turrets, the magnificent gardens and they contemplated the vast plain and the towers of Santa Fe from the windows of the Queen's Robing Room (*peinador de la Reina*).[78]

An engraving complemented the description, showing the delegation on their way to the Hall of the Ambassadors, adjacent to the Court of the Lions.[79] Rather surprisingly, it was only after his departure that some dailies started to circulate information on the 'tears shed by the ambassador and his entourage' upon beholding the Alhambra.[80] This is a theme which we will analyse in greater detail below.

[76] *El Globo*, 6 December 1877.

[77] What is meant here is the museum which was established in 1870. Its major sponsor, Rafael Contreras, the restorer of the Alhambra, wished that this museum be installed inside Charles V's palace (R. Contreras, 'La Alhambra y el museo oriental'). The much more modest final realisation consisted of one hall located on the left of the entrance to the Court of the Lions. Inside had been placed a 'splendid vase . . . enamelled in blue, white and gold, several tombs of Moorish kings, one sarcophagus decorated with reliefs representing lions killing deer, bronze medallions from the palace of Charles V, column capitals, fragments of sculpted and painted beams and other remains of the Moors' (J. and M. Oliver Hurtado, *Granada y sus monumentos árabes*, p. 288; Ford, *A Hand-Book for Travellers in Spain*, 5th edn, p. 376). See also, 'Establecimiento de un museo de antigüedades en la Alhambra'.

[78] 'El embajador marroquí visitando la Alhambra'.

[79] 'Sid Abdesslam Esuisi visitando el palacio de la Alhambra'.

[80] *El Pueblo español*, 10 December 1877; *La Crónica meridional*, 13 December 1877; 'Había motivo', *La Paz de Murcia*, 16 December 1877.

In 1880, it was Sīdī Lʿarbī Brīsha's turn to visit Granada on his way back to Morocco from his mission in Madrid. With a very small group accompanying him, he did not attract much attention. The *Estrella de Occidente* reported briefly on his visit to the Generalife and the Alhambra, insisting on the way the beauty of the site had impacted him and noting that he had signed and dated the visitors' book.[81]

Five years later, in December 1885, another Moroccan embassy would draw much more interest from the Spanish press. The ambassador's audience with the queen, in Madrid, on 13 December, was described and commented on at length.[82] The Spaniards were particularly impressed by one of the members of the delegation, Aḥmad bin Shuqrūn, a colonel in the Sharifian army, who having been taught at the Guadalajara School of Engineers had mastered the Spanish language to the point of being able to give a lecture at the Athenaeum of Madrid. 'It may well be that those whose mosque we have conquered will come and conquer the tribune, that mosque where resonate the prayers of modern nations', commented one of the newspapers, not without condescension.[83] The ambassador and his retinue came to Granada by train on the evening of 23 December and were accommodated at the Siete Suelos (Seven Floors) Hotel, located in the vicinity of the gate by that name.[84] The visit to the Alhambra took place the following day, as testified by an entire page in the visitors' book devoted to it (Figure 2.6).[85] This is how I have been able to correct Pérès' error, who thought that Kardūdī was the ambassador.[86] In fact,

[81] 'Viaje de regreso del embajador marroquí Sidi el Arby Brischa'; AA, *libros de firmas*, 43, fol. 252 v, 22 June 1880.

[82] 'Recepción de la embajada marroquí'.

[83] J. Ortega-Munilla, 'Madrid'.

[84] *La Época*, 24 December 1885.

[85] AA, *libros de firmas*, 44, fol. 107 r, 24 December 1885.

[86] In his defence, Pérès seems to have used only Kardūdī's own account, *At-Tuḥfat as-Saniyyat li'l Ḥaḍrat ash-Sharīfat al Ḥasaniyya bi'l-Mamlakat al-Isbāniyya* (manuscript D 1282, Rabat Library), the title of which says nothing about the ambassador's identity. It is intriguing to see that the ambassador is apparently not even mentioned in this *riḥla* (Pérès, *L'Espagne vue par les voyageurs musulmans*, p. 42 and n. 2). Nieves Paradela, who used the same account, describes the journey without mentioning the Alhambra or Granada (N. Paradela, *El otro laberinto español*, pp. 96–9).

as we learn from the local press, the ambassador was ʿAbdelṣādeq bin Aḥmad al-Rīfī, governor of Tangier, aged about sixty-five, a distinguished old man with a white beard, greatly respected in his hometown for his moral purity and rectitude. Aḥmad bin Muḥammad bin ʿAbdelqāder Kardūdī, approximately fifty years old, was his secretary. He had 'large, expressive and intelligent eyes revealing an aptitude to govern'. Moreover, he was highly educated and had been behind the speeches delivered during the reception at the royal palace. Two other members of the mission were also identified: Aḥmad bin Shuqrūn, already mentioned, who served as interpreter, and ʿAbdelraḥman, Kardūdī's younger brother. The rest of the delegation consisted of seven *qaids* (commanders) in 'Moroccan military uniform', one of whom was 7-ft (2.10 m) tall, 'one good looking black and stocky equerry', Moses Anichar, a Jew, 'wearing his kind's traditional garb and who turned out to be intelligent and shrewd', one Muḥammad el-Tiṭwānī, from the Spanish legation in Tétouan, several Nubian slaves, cooks and other servants.[87] Of all these 'extras' in the delegation, the visitors' book retains only three signatures: that of Moses Anichar, in Judeo-Spanish and in a shaky hand, and those of Lʿarbī bin Ḥussain and Wāṣif Mawlānā, probably two of the *qaids* accompanying the ambassador.[88] The reporter from the *Defensor de Granada* seems to have had an explanation for the small number of signatures: 'Among the other members of the retinue, those who knew how to write signed [the book].'[89]

On the Spanish side, the Moroccan delegation was accompanied by the governor of the province, Alonso Castrillo, the substitute mayor; Joaquín Gavilanes, the governor's secretary; Emilio Vivanco, the head of the development section; José Casado; and lieutenant colonel of the Cuban infantry, Antonio Zendreras. Also present was Mariano Contreras [Granja] (1853–1912), the architect of the province, who signed as 'architect of the Alhambra', and son of the famous Rafael Contreras, in charge of the monument's restoration since 1852. Apart from Juan Vicente Zugasti Dickson (1866–1925),

[87] 'La embajada marroquí', *El Defensor de Granada*, 16 December 1885; 'Desde Granada'.

[88] AA, *libros de firmas*, 44, fol. 107 r, 24 December 1885. Moses Anichar's signature in Judeo-Spanish, ע״ה משה אניג׳אר סירבידור די דיוס reads 'Moshe Anigar serbidor di Dios', as noted also in the *Defensor de Granada*. I owe the transcription of this signature to Joshua Picard, from Princeton University.

[89] 'La embajada marroquí', *El Defensor de Granada*, 26 December 1885.

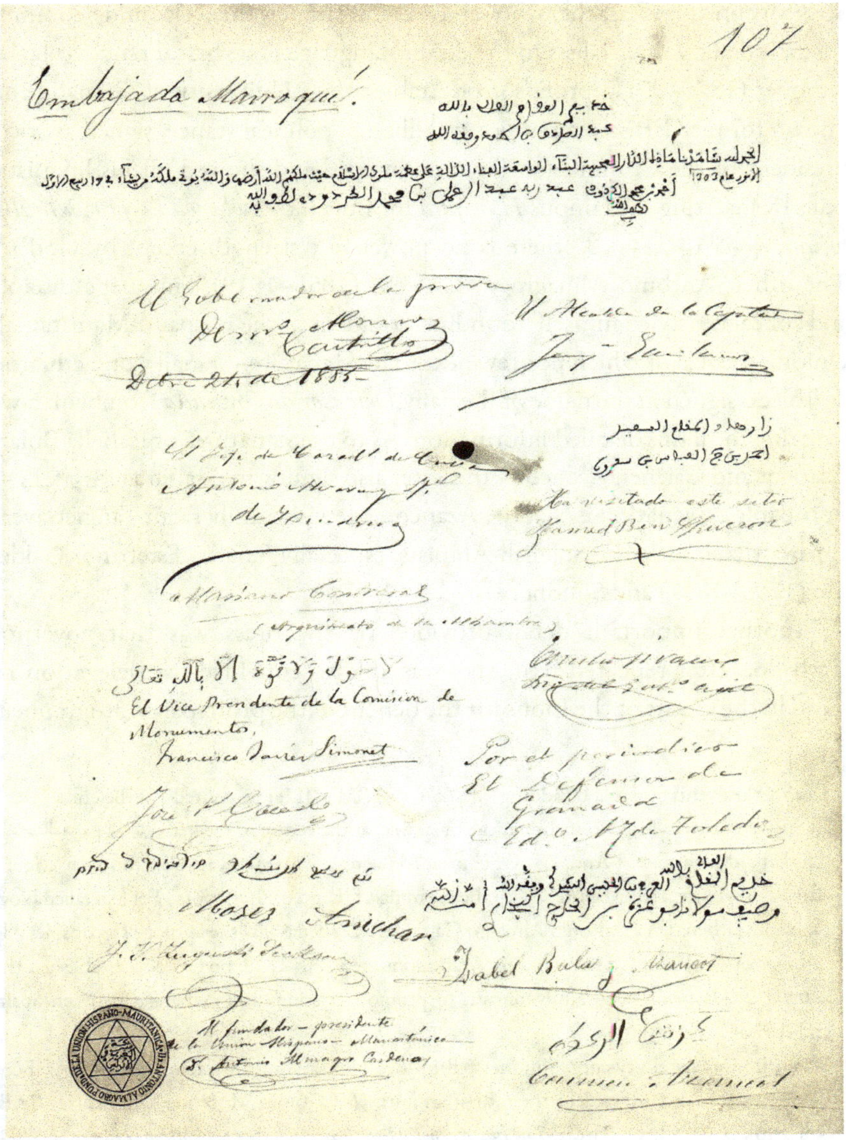

Figure 2.6 Signatures of members of a Moroccan embassy and their hosts in the visitors' book, 24 December 1885. AA, *libros de firmas*, 44, fol. 107 r. © Archivo del Patronato de la Alhambra y Generalife. A whole page of the visitors' book was reserved for this crowded company, which consisted of the Moroccan delegation and local officials and notables, including two Arabist scholars and the caretaker of the Alhambra.

Spanish consul in Larache, who served as interpreter, the welcoming committee included two specialists in the Arabic language. The first, Francisco Javier Simonet (1829–97), a professor of Arabic at the University of Granada and known for his Carlist sympathies and illiberal political stance, signed as 'vice-president of the Commission for monuments' and showed off his linguistic skills by inserting the famous *Ḥawqala* formula (*la ḥawla wa la quwwata illā billah*, لا حول و لا قوة الا بالله, 'there is no power nor strength except by God').[90] The other, Antonio Almagro y Cárdenas (1856–1919), Simonet's disciple and colleague, styled himself 'founding president of the Hispano-Mauritanian Union', the seal of which he drew next to his signature.[91] Finally, one Eduardo de Toledo signed in the name of the daily *Defensor de Granada* from which we have drawn all this detailed information. As to the signatures of Isabella Bula y Azancot and Carmen Azancot – the latter also signing in Arabic as كرمن الزكوط –, a probable explanation is that the Azancot, a Jewish family from Tangier, were apparently close to the Spanish Arabists, especially Serafín Estébanez Calderón (1799–1867) and Simonet.[92]

Another important detail provided by the press was that governor Castrillo, 'after repeated requests', was able to convince the delegation to stand in the Court of the Lions for the benefit of the principal photographers

[90] Simonet uses this formula by adding '*ta'āla*' (تعالى) ('May [He] be exalted') at the end.

[91] In Spanish, 'Unión hispano-mauritánica'; in Arabic, at the centre of the seal, 'شركة المغرب والاندلس / Chirkat al-Maghrib wa'l-Andalus'. Of course, Almagro y Cárdenas was using the term 'Mauritania' as a synonym for Maghreb, with the meaning of 'Land of the Moors'. For a detailed biography of Cárdenas, see 'Antonio Almagro Cárdenas'. Cárdenas was the author of a considerable number of works on Granada and its Arab monuments; in 1879, he had also established the *Estrella de Occidente*, whose mission was to promote relations and exchanges between Spain and Africa.

[92] When he was barely twenty, Simonet fell in love with a young woman from the Azancot family, who had converted to the Christian faith (M. Gómez Moreno, 'Unas cartas de El Solitario', p. 214; J. C. Baroja, *Los Judíos en la España Moderna y Contemporánea*, p. 204; J. A. González Alcantud, *La ciudad vórtice*, p. 90). Moreover, as noted by González Alcantud, Serafín Estébanez Calderón, Simonet's mentor, 'would marry a woman linked to the Azancots, Jews of Tangier' (J. A. González Alcantud, 'La maurophobie dans les cercles intellectuels andalous', pp. 245–6). Knowing that Estébanez had married Matilde Livermore Salas (?–1856), it is not obvious how this woman may have been 'linked' to the Azancots. The Azancot family perhaps descends from Moisés Azancot, who, in 1859, when he was eighteen, was baptised as Leopoldo, Joaquín, Jesús María de los Milagros, Juan José, Ignacio de la Santísima Trinidad

of Granada.[93] The local press was more detailed in its account: the governor having insisted that the ambassador accept being photographed, the latter did so only on condition that the whole group would pose with him.[94] The result was a fascinating image, preserved at the Alhambra archives, signed by [José] Camino, and showing a group of some twenty-six individuals posing in front of one of the two small pavilions (*templetes*) of the Court of the Lions (Figure 2.7). Seated in a row of four chairs were the ambassador and – probably – Kardūdī, flanked, one would imagine, by the governor and

Figure 2.7 Photograph of the members of the Moroccan embassy and their hosts by José Camino, posing in the Court of the Lions, in front of one of the two *templetes* (pavilions), 24 December 1885. AA, *colección fotografía*, F-0013027. © Archivo del Patronato de la Alhambra y Generalife. This fascinating document provides a unique opportunity to put faces on the names that appeared on the corresponding page of the visitors' book.

(*La Correspondencia de España*, 27 November 1859). As to the other woman signing the visitors' book, an item in the press reveals that Isabel Bula y Azancot was the daughter of Captain Melchor Bula y Vázquez, who lost his life during the 'Northern campaign' (*La Correspondencia de España*, 9 June 1878). Given her composite name, she must have been related to the Azancot family through her mother.

[93] 'Desde Granada'.

[94] 'La embajada marroquí', *El Defensor de Granada*, 26 December 1885.

the deputy mayor. In the back, to the left, five top hats and three bowler hats mark the presence of the Spanish members of the welcoming committee. The only Spaniard one can identify with certainty is the officer in uniform, evidently the lieutenant colonel of the Cuban infantry, Zendreras. Among the Moroccans, seven men in white garb stand out behind the ambassador, probably the seven *qaid*s mentioned by the *Defensor de Granada*, one of whom is indeed rather tall, even though he does not seem to measure 7 ft. On their left, to the right of the Spanish officer, stands Aḥmad bin Shuqrūn, the Spanish-speaking officer. The black man to the right is probably the equerry, accompanied by a young groom. Kardūdī's younger brother may well be the man in dark costume at the left of the image, to the extreme right of the *qaid*s. As to Moses Anichar, in all likelihood, he is the man on the right of the image, slightly set back, his back against one of the columns of the *templete*.[95]

The Embassy of 1889

Four years later, another Moroccan embassy triggered much attention in the press, both national and local. This time, the ambassador was Sīdī al-Hājj al-Moʿaṭī bin ʿAbdelkebīr al-Mezāmsī, and he came from Paris, where he had visited the World Exhibition. He had arrived at San Sebastian on 11 October 1889 with over four tons of luggage.[96] From there, the embassy headed towards Madrid, which they reached on 13 October. The ambassador was accompanied by a large entourage, including his first secretary Faqīh Sīdī Aḥmad al-Kardūdī. Was this the same Kardūdī? Yes, as we will see later; at any rate, the *Correo militar* seemed particularly interested in his physiognomy. He was 'tall and portly, with black slanted eyes, a copper complexion, an aquiline nose and a white beard, speaking little, very serious and with gestures that were in perfect harmony with his character of a jurisconsult'. The description followed with the second secretary, El-Amīn Hājj Muḥammad bin Madanī bin Nīs, 'short, very fat, with a fine and trimmed black beard', and the interpreter Hājj Muḥammad, 'also short, with a puffy face and a lighter complexion than the

[95] AA, *colección fotografía*, F-0013027. *El Defensor de Granada* notes that two photographs were taken by José Camino and José García Ayola.

[96] 'La embajada marroquí', *El Correo militar*, 12 October 1889.

former', four attachés, five *qaid*s and twenty-four servants.[97] The ambassador and his retinue arrived at Cordoba on 22 October, where they discovered the famous mosque, which 'provoked the profound admiration of the ambassador and other persons. They read out loud the inscriptions in the 'Arab chapel [*sic*] and remained a long time in meditation, as if they were praying'.[98] On 23 October, they finally reached Granada and were able to visit the Alhambra, leaving – again – a short inscription in the visitors' book, where one can read the ambassador's name, preceded by the title '*al-Bashador*', from the Spanish '*embajador*' (ambassador), as well as those of al-Hājj Muḥammad bin Aḥmad Fāssī and 'Abdesselām Zōzō.[99] Interestingly, these last two names do not appear in the press and, on the contrary, the names listed in the newspapers, especially Kardūdī's, are absent from the visitors' book.[100] Granada's local paper, *El Defensor de Granada*, had some additional details concerning the identity and career of some members of the delegation. We thus learn that the ambassador al-Hājj al-Moʿaṭī was descended from one of the most noble families of Casablanca, that he had held important positions in the administration, that his daughter was one of the sultan's spouses, that he enjoyed the trust of his sovereign and that he was accompanied by his twenty-five-year-old son. As to Aḥmad al-Kardūdī, he was from a noble family from Fez.[101] During the following days, the public was informed of several other details concerning the embassy and its journey. The visit to the Cordoba mosque often came up in

97 'La embajada marroquí', *El Correo militar*, 14 October 1889; 'La embajada marroquí', *La Correspondencia de España*, 14 October 1889.

98 *La Unión católica*, 22 October 1889.

99 AA, *libros de firmas*, 44, fol. 276 r, 23 October 1889.

100 The two signatures that follow the ambassador's were identified in the press as 'El siervo de su Señor, Ahmed-ben-Mohamed-ben-Abd el-Kader-el-Kardudi, protéjalo Dios' and 'Ab-Abselem Mezeuzeu' ('La embajada marroquí', *La Iberia*, 26 October 1889). While the second signature is clearly a deformation of Abdesselām Zōzō's name, it seems difficult to connect this version of Kardūdī's signature with the one seen in the visitors' book. This is all the more surprising given that the expressions that precede and follow his name are accurate translations of the formulae so often found in Moroccan inscriptions (*'abdu rabbihi* and *laṭafallah bihi*), but not in this case. For an explanation of this inconsistency, see pp. 111–12 below.

101 'La embajada marroquí', *El Defensor de Granada*, 23 October 1889; 'La embajada marroquí en Granada', *El Popular*, 23 October 1889.

the reports, with particular emphasis on the fact that they had spent over half an hour contemplating and examining the *mihrab* down to its minutest detail, reading verses from the Koran and jotting down some of the inscriptions. When asked about it, the interpreter declared that there existed two similar *mihrabs* in Morocco, but that he had never seen any as magnificent as that of Cordoba.[102] Regarding Granada and the Alhambra, the newspapers were surprised to see that the Moroccans had remained emotionless in the presence of Boabdil's sword, and that most of them did not even know who that was.[103] Nevertheless, they translated some of the palace's inscriptions, copying also the verses carved on the Fountain of the Lions.[104] When asked about progress and modernity in Europe, they answered that they had no wish for railways, roads or the telegraph, claiming that they were much better off without these innovations.[105]

Nevertheless, it seems that this visit was much more serious and thorough than the newspapers suggested. The *Defensor de Granada* provides us with an extremely lively and detailed description, which deserves special attention. The delegation was ready by 6 am; they left the hotel at 10 am, in company of local notables and, once again, the Arabists Simonet and Almagro y Cárdenas. The visit started at the Gate of Justice (*puerta de la Justicia*), whose inscriptions they examined in great detail. They were particularly interested in an inscription in 'monastic' (Gothic) script located close to the altar.[106] The ambassador stood 'sadly contemplative' before this plaque and conversed for a few minutes with his secretary, Kardūdī, and one of the imams who accompanied him. Interestingly, the imam held in his hands 'a manuscript guide of Granada in Arabic'. After that, they headed towards the Place of the Cisterns

[102] 'La embajada marroquí', *La Iberia*, 25 October 1889; 'Los marroquíes'.

[103] Boabdil's (Abū 'Abdallah Muḥammad bin 'Alī, or Muḥammad XI) sword fell into Castilian hands in 1483, at the battle of Lucena.

[104] 'Los turbantes'; 'Los marroquíes'.

[105] 'Los turbantes'; 'La embajada marroquí', *La Monarquía*, 25 October 1889.

[106] Evidently, this was the commemorative plaque of the cistern (*aljibe*) built by Iñigo López de Mendoza, Count of Tendilla, who took possession of the Alhambra after the conquest of 2 January 1492. This plaque is located inside the Gate of Justice, next to an altar/chapel containing an altarpiece. On this matter, see Lafuente Alcántara, *El libro del viajero en Granada*, pp. 88–9; Ford, *A Hand-Book for Travellers in Spain*, p. 370.

(*plaza de los Aljibes*) and, once they had reached the Gate of Wine (*Puerta del Vino*), they asked for detailed information about its history.[107] They then proceeded to the ramparts, where they remained for some time, 'absorbed in the contemplation of Granada'. The ambassador chose that moment to ask the authorities about the Albaicín, the ancient Arab district of Granada, expressing regret that he did not have the time to visit its numerous remains of the Muslim presence.

At that point a man known as Chorrojumo, who styled himself as the 'prince of the Gypsies' (*príncipe de los gitanos*) and made a living by selling his portrait in a colourful costume to visitors and tourists came to them. He bowed several times to the ambassador, who, unaware of the man's identity, responded in courteous fashion. When Chorrojumo tried to sell him his photographs, his Spanish hosts talked him out of doing so, explaining what it was all about; all the same, one of his secretaries gave him a coin.[108]

They then proceeded towards the Garden of the Adarves, where they spent some time before heading to the Tower of the Candle or Watch Tower (*torre de la Vela*). This gave them the opportunity to stop and examine the

[107] According to tradition, the name of this gate goes back to the sixteenth century, when the wine destined for consumption by the inhabitants of the Alhambra was stocked before retail (Lafuente Alcántara, *El libro del viajero en Granada*, p. 90). It has also been proposed that this name might derive from its original name, Bib el-Hamra, or the 'Red Gate', with a semantic shift from *ḥamra* (red) to *khamr* (wine).

[108] Mariano Fernández Santiago (1824–1906), known by the nickname of Chorrojumo (a contraction of *chorro de humo*, 'smoke stream'), sometimes called 'Chorro é jumo', was a Roma who built his career by posing in traditional grab and selling his photographs to tourists and visitors in Granada and at the Alhambra. He came up with this vocation after the famous artist Mariano Fortuny painted him in as a Goyesque *gitano* character around 1868 (see, in Spanish at: https://es.wikipedia.org/wiki/Chorrojumo). He had turned this into a sales pitch, repeated on a sticker placed on the back of the photographs he sold to tourists: 'príncipe gitano, modelo de Fortuny'. An anecdote concerning Chorrojumo's encounter with the heir to the Prussian throne, Friedrich Wilhelm (1831–88) – the future Friedrich III – is a perfect illustration of this colourful character. During his visit to Granada in 1883, struck by the Roma's extravagant costume, Friedrich Wilhelm had asked him who he was. Chorrojumo had replied he was the 'King of the Gypsies', to which the Prussian prince snapped back 'Very well, then! We are colleagues' ('De potencia a potencia'). A whole page of the visitors' book is dedicated to Friedrich Wilhelm's visit (AA, *libros de firmas*, 44, fol. 35 r, 11 December 1883).

tunnel at the entrance of the tower. Seeing that the visitors were particularly interested, the photographer Rafael Garzón[109] gave some explanations in French to one of the members of the mission who spoke the language. This, he explained, was an underground passage that connected the Alhambra with the Albaicín from beneath the Darro and where, according to local tradition, the Arabs had left buried treasures.[110] In 1879, an Englishman, enticed by this legend, rushed into the tunnel without telling anyone, and, due to a fall, remained there for three days before they could rescue him with great difficulty. 'The Moors laughed a lot upon hearing this story, whispering about the tradition of treasures', and started climbing the stairs leading to the top of the tower. Once there, the ambassador and Kardūdī asked to be shown the Sierra Nevada and requested explanations as to the use of the famous bell atop the tower.[111]

Only then did they begin their visit of the palace proper, with 'great emotion', starting with the Court of the Myrtles (*patio de los Arrayanes*). Charmed by what they saw, they spent much time reading the inscriptions. Kardūdī himself read the inscription decorating the 'babouche holder' (*babuchero*) of the Hall of the Boat (*sala de la Barca*),[112] as well as the *qaṣīda* (ode) running along the mosaics of the Hall of the Two Sisters. He was the

[109] On Garzón and his studio, see pp. 7–11.

[110] This is an occasion to remember the chapbook mentioned earlier, *Historia de los subterráneos de la Alhambra*.

[111] According to the Baedeker guidebook, this bell, known as the *campana de la Vela* (watch or candle bell) and weighing over 12 tons, was used to regulate the opening and shutting of irrigation channels in the Vega – the plain surrounding Granada – by ringing it at night every five minutes. The same source notes that on the afternoon of every second day of January, the anniversary of the conquest of Granada by the Catholic monarchs, the young women from Granada and from throughout the Vega climbed to the top of the tower between 3 pm and 4 pm to ring the bell, which, according to popular beliefs, would guarantee them a fiancé (K. Baedeker, *Espagne et Portugal*, pp. 332–3, 354–5). While the historian Lafuente Alcántara corroborates the tradition of 2 January, it seems that the nocturnal use of the bell was somewhat more complicated: two rings at a short interval from vespers to ten, four at ten, then two until eleven, thirty-three at eleven, etc. until dawn (Lafuente Alcántara, *El libro del viajero en Granada*, p. 175).

[112] This is a niche, called *babuchero*, because it was then thought that visitors placed their babouches there before entering the throne room.

one who took it upon himself to write down the inscription on the basin of the Fountain of the Lions.[113]

When passing through a spot from where one could see Charles V's palace, the ambassador asked about this 'magnificent building'. When he was told that it had been erected on the ruins of the winter palace of the Alhambra, he could not hide his disappointment and lamented that this 'artistic marvel' should have been lost.[114] In the Hall of the Ambassadors, the visitors could examine the tiles and inscriptions; they took their time admiring the scenery through the mullioned windows embedded in the thick walls (*ajimeces*). In another interesting episode, the photographer approached the group and showed them a photograph taken during the embassy of 1885. Of course, this must have been the image discussed earlier, even though it seems surprising that Garzón should have advertised his trade with a photograph taken by his competitors, José Camino and José García Ayola. The newspaper noted that some members of the present embassy could be seen on this earlier pose, 'including the first secretary', which proves that it was indeed the same Kardūdī in 1885 and 1889. The visitors were very pleased and pointed musingly at the men they knew and recognised. Kardūdī then asked the ambassador whether he wanted to do the same, but the latter 'made a gesture expressing his displeasure and, as it were, turned his back on him'. One member from his entourage explained that this should not come as a surprise, since their religion forbade them from having their photograph taken.

The visit continued through Charles V's dining room, the *mirador* of Lindaraja, the Hall of Justice, and that of the Two Sisters. In the latter two

[113] The *qaṣīda* in the Hall of the Two Sisters, as well as the poem of the fountain, are by Ibn Zamrak (1333–93).

[114] What would he have said if he had known that the construction of this palace had started in 1526 thanks to 10,000 ducats out of the 80,000 that were paid to Charles V by the Morisco community of Granada in order to be spared the confiscation of their assets and other harassments wished for by the Christian population of the city? Tempted by this offer, the sovereign had cancelled the confiscation decree and authorised the converts to continue wearing their Moorish costume. Thus, noted Lafuente Alcántara, evidently siding with the Catholics who had been frustrated in their thirst for vengeance, 'the foundations of this edifice were laid with the tears of many families and, consequently, with a destiny of gloom', referring to the fact that the palace was never completed, nor inhabited (Lafuente Alcántara, *El libro del viajero en Granada*, p. 95).

halls, the visitors were so impressed by the beauty of the ceramic tiles that they could not help but complain that those produced in Morocco were not only of much lower quality, but also much more expensive. Struck by the quality of the stucco imitations of tiles, they inquired about the possibility of bringing workers and artisans specialised in this trade to Morocco. The restorer of the Alhambra, Rafael Contreras, explained that these imitations were manufactured at the palace itself, but he did not know whether this request could be met.

From there, they went to see the museum, where they read 'with some ease' the funerary inscriptions and admired the great porcelain vase, asking about its purpose.[115] Almagro y Cárdenas explained that it was used to hold flowers to decorate the rooms. They then visited the *Rauda* (*rawḍa*, garden), as the location of the graves of Arab rulers was known, before proceeding to the baths, the restoration of which they highly praised, albeit expressing some disappointment that there should not have been running water to take a bath and do their ablutions.

Once the visitors' book had been signed, the visitors returned to town, leaving the visit to the Generalife for the afternoon. The *Defensor* went as far as to provide its readers with a detailed commentary on the lunch served to the guests: roast chicken seasoned with garlic and onion, in a marinade of oregano,

[115] Two large vases or jars of the Alhambra, which can be seen in many illustrated works, have been the object of several articles in the press. One of these was decorated with gazelles and the other with crests, hence their respective names of 'vase of the gazelles' (*jarrón de las gacelas*) and 'vase of the crests' (*jarrón de los escudos*). Both were drawn by Sarabia (Almagro Gorbea, *El legado de al-Ándalus*, pp. 202–5) and are represented in Hermosilla, *Antigüedades árabes de España*, pls XVIII and XIX, and in Laborde, *Voyage pittoresque et historique de l'Espagne*, vol. IV, pls XLV and XLVI. That of the crests can be seen in Murphy, *Arabian Antiquities of Spain*, pl. XLVII; that of the gazelles in Goury and Jones, *Plans, Elevations, Sections, and Details of the Alhambra*, pl. XLV. Jones notes that the vase 'is at present to be seen in a small chamber of the Court of the Fishpond, in which are deposited the archives of the palace', adding that another vase – that of the crests – 'was broken a few years ago, and the pieces sold to a passing traveller', as confirmed in Ford's *Hand-Book for Travellers in Spain*, vol. I, p. 375. There are presently some twenty vases of this type, most of which were discovered after those of the gazelles and of the crests, dispersed throughout the world in collections from Paris to Stockholm and from St Petersburg to New York.

ground chili, vinegar, salt and parsley; ram's liver cooked in the same sauce; biscuits from the convent of the Comendadoras de Santiago (in Granada); watermelon, grapes, peaches, apples and figs. 'They did not take wine or coffee' added the daily. After lunch, the ambassador received the local authorities, 'without ever ceasing to pray while telling the beads on his ivory rosary'.[116]

At around three in the afternoon, the embassy started again, this time to visit the Generalife. They first made a stop at the *casa de los Tiros* (the House of Shots) to see Boabdil's sword.[117] The description of this visit helps us to recontextualise the comments in the national press on the alleged ignorance of the Moroccans about their own history:

> They held in their hands the sword of the unfortunate Boabdil; the first secretary examined it carefully and it seems that he was the only one who knew something about this Boabdil and what he represented in the history of the Arab Kingdom of Granada.[118]

Once at the Generalife, the visitors were invited to sign the visitors' book. Had they not signed it already? Once again, we are confronted to the existence of a second series of registers, that of the Generalife, which has apparently not survived to this day.[119] This is probably the reason behind the differences noted between the inscriptions observed in the visitors' book and those reported in the press, which were apparently taken from the Generalife album, where the

[116] 'La embajada marroquí en Granada', *El Defensor de Granada*, 24 October 1889, p. 3.

[117] The *casa de los Tiros*, a fortress-like structure, was built in the sixteenth century. Its first owner, Sidi Yahya el-Nayyar (al-Najjār), converted in 1489 and took the name of Pedro de Granada, thus founding the house of Granada-Venegas, which, in 1643, acquired the title of marquis of Campotéjar. This family kept this building until 1921, when it passed to the state and became a museum (see, in Spanish, at: https://es.wikipedia.org/wiki/Casa_de_los_Tiros and https://es.wikipedia.org/wiki/Cid_Hiaya). The information in the *Defensor* goes against the general wisdom that this sword, exhibited today in the Military Museum of Toledo, was initially kept by the descendants of Fernández de Córdoba at the Palace of Viana in Cordoba, before it was bequeathed by the first Marchioness of Viana at the turn of the twentieth century (see, in Spanish, at: https://es.wikipedia.org/wiki/Espada_de_Boabdil).

[118] 'La embajada marroquí en Granada', *El Defensor de Granada*, 24 October 1889, p. 3.

[119] See p. 97.

signatures were more substantial and included that of Kardūdī.[120] Finally, the *Defensor*'s detailed account of the visit to the Generalife also brings a useful precision on the visitors' alleged lack of interest for the benefits of progress and modernity. During the visit, the conversation between the delegation members and their hosts had come to the point of their Parisian stay. When asked about it, the Moroccans had declared that 'they had much enjoyed Paris and that the [1889] Exhibition was marvellous, especially the Eiffel Tower, which they had found impressive'. At that point, the Arabist Almagro y Cárdenas had asked one of the them, a *qaid* from Fez, why they did not set up such novelties in Morocco by building railways and roads. The *qaid*'s answer was brief: 'We are better off without all that.'[121]

Towards a Trivialisation?

The visit of the 1889 embassy covered more than three columns, the equivalent of almost a full page, of the Granada daily *El Defensor*. This was a clear indication of the degree of interest it had sparked among the local public, not to mention the numerous repercussions of the event in the national press.[122] What was particularly striking was the level of detail and precision in this account, which – I hope – justifies the space I have dedicated to it in this work. Compared with the embassies of 1877 and 1880, this Moroccan mission constituted a form of peak in the public interest triggered by the presence of visitors, whose identity was intimately linked to that of the Alhambra itself. The years and decades that followed would be characterised by a marked drop in the visibility of such missions in the press. In March 1895, the *Defensor* noted that the embassy of Sīdī 'Abdelkerīm Brīsha, had drawn only a very

[120] Here is the text of the inscription, as it appeared in translation in the *Defensor*: 'Praises be to the One God. We have visited this abode and have seen the splendid remains that testify to the greatness of the Only One and Almighty. On this 27th of *Safar al-khair* of the year 1307. El Hajj el-Moati ben Abdelkebir el-Mazamisi, may God protect him. The servant of his lord Ahmed ben Mohammed ben Abdelkader el-Kerdudi, may God protect him. Abdesselam Siusu' ('La embajada marroquí en Granada', *El Defensor de Granada*, 24 October 1889, p. 3).

[121] 'La embajada marroquí en Granada', *El Defensor de Granada*, 24 October 1889, p. 3.

[122] It is striking to see that, for example, the account of the 1889 embassy was taken up even in the local press of the Canary Islands ('Los marroquíes en Granada').

small number of curious onlookers to the railroad station and along the mission's route to the Washington Irving Hotel. The visitors seem to have followed more or less the same itinerary as their predecessors, but its description in the Granada newspapers was much more succinct.[123] The visitors' book holds only three signatures, those of the ambassador, his secretary, 'Abdelkerīm bin Slīmān, and one Sīdī Muḥammad Tamṭamun, whose duties were not noted.[124] Nevertheless, some details made it into the newspapers, such as the gallantry of the visitors towards 'various ladies and damsels' with whom they conversed in good Spanish, as well as the manner in which a curious crowd formed to admire the Moroccans, who, from the summit of the Watch Tower, admired the landscape of the Vega, the plain surrounding Granada. In town, the visit to the cathedral had to be cancelled due to the intransigeance of the priests, who insisted that the visitors take their headgear off before entering. Despite this disappointment, the day ended in a good mood with a ball improvised at the hotel and in which several notable families of the city participated.[125] An amusing detail of the journey was that well before the visit to Granada, the moment he had set foot in the city of Cadiz, the ambassador had been confronted by one of the many imitations of the Alhambra: 'After dinner, the Moors visited the aristocratic casino of Gadino, which contains a superb Arab patio, imitated from the Alhambra. They admired it greatly and deciphered its inscriptions.'[126]

The following embassy, in May 1902, was even less visible. One barely learns from the press that the mission had arrived by train from Madrid, that the visitors were lodged at the Washington Irving Hotel, that they visited the municipality, that they would perhaps attend a bullfight and that they were looking forward to moving on to Malaga to see the Feast of Corpus Christi, to be held on 29 May that year. Despite the presence in the visitors' book of the

123 According to the *Defensor*, the ambassador was 'an elderly man of pleasant looks, short, with a thick white beard, rather fat' and originating from Tétouan ('La embajada', *El Defensor de Granada*, 5 March 1895, pp. 2–3).

124 AA, *libros de firmas*, 45, fol. 252 r, 5 March 1895.

125 'La embajada'. The national press provided even less detail, limited to a few items fed by the local press: *El Correo militar*, 5 March 1895; 'El viaje de los moros'; 'La embajada marroquí', *La Unión católica*, 6 March 1895. See also, *El Popular* and *La Publicidad* of 5 and 6 March 1895.

126 'La embajada marroquí', *Las Baleares*, 1 February 1895, p. 2.

signatures of the ambassador and two of the members of his retinue,[127] the visit to the Alhambra was not mentioned, let alone described in the local press.[128] Four years later, in 1906, the embassy of Qaddūr el-Ghāzī was treated in the same casual fashion by the local press, which was content with noting that contrary to their custom, which forbade them from expressing the least admiration in presence of strangers, the Moroccans could not refrain from crying out 'God is Great!' in the face of the monument's beauty.[129]

The following embassies clearly confirm this trend. Although L'arbī bin Aḥmad el-Ḥarīshī and his secretary, 'Abdelkerīm, did sign the visitors' book on 12 September 1908,[130] this mission does not seem to have left any trace in the local press. Aḥmad bin el-Mowāz's embassy in 1910 also went unnoticed, despite the presence of a familiar name, Muḥammad bin Aḥmad al-Kardūdī, most probably a relative of the 'great' Kardūdī of the 1885 and 1889 embassies, perhaps even his son.[131] Even worse, the visit of the famous Grand Vizier Muḥammad El-Mokrī (1852?–1955) on 4 October 1916, although perfectly recorded in the visitors' book,[132] was not even mentioned in the local or national press. Was it because this was a private journey, as he was on his way back from Paris, where his son was studying?[133] Perhaps so, but it nevertheless is surprising that the presence of a Moroccan statesman of such stature should have gone completely unnoticed.

[127] AA, *libros de firmas*, 46, fol. 234 v, 28 May 1902. The book was signed by the ambassador, Aḥmad bin Mohammed al-Torris, Larbi bin Dahman and Mohammed Ragón.

[128] 'La embajada marroquí', *El Defensor de Granada*, 28 and 29 May 1902; 'La embajada marroquí', *El Triunfo*, 28 May 1902; 'La embajada marroquí', *La Publicidad*, 28 May 1902.

[129] 'La embajada marroquí', *El Defensor de Granada*, 13 June1906; 'La embajada marroquí', *El Noticiero granadino*, 13 June 1906.

[130] AA, *libros de firmas*, 48, fol. 92 v, 12 September 1908.

[131] AA, *libros de firmas*, 48, fol. 228 v, 16 October 1910. Abu al-'Abbās Aḥmad Kardūdī having died in 1898, it cannot be him. Given this Kardūdī's patronym is 'bin Aḥmad' it may well have been his son.

[132] AA, *libros de firmas*, 50, fol. 24 v, 4 October 1916.

[133] El-Mokrī had made a stop in Cordoba and visited its monuments in mid-August, coming from Morocco via Algeciras and on his way to Madrid and Paris, where his son was studying ('Viaje del Mokri'). On his way back, he stopped in Madrid on 2 October before heading for Andalusia ('El Mokri, en Madrid'; 'El Mokri').

Should we conclude from this information that there was a form of disenchantment, at least on the Spanish side, concerning the rediscovery of the Andalusian past by its alleged heirs, or perhaps a form of saturation of the public of Granada with the historicist exoticism provided by the rather steady spectacle of 'Moors' wandering around the courts, halls and gardens of the Alhambra? Possibly, even probably; after all, the frequency and emphasis with which these visits were recorded in the press must have been related to the degree of interest and attention they sparked within the local population, represented by the newspapers' readership. Although I cannot possibly ascribe any serious form of statistical value to a total of nine embassies over a period of about three decades, I believe that the elusive nature of the comments in 1877 and 1880, followed by the excitement of 1885 and 1889, the drop witnessed in 1895, 1902 and 1906, and finally the absence of any proper mention in 1908 and 1910 do follow a bell-shaped curb that describes a rising infatuation followed by what seems to have been a growing indifference to the matter. Should one link this to a form of banalisation or trivialisation that ended up prevailing over curiosity and exoticism? Could the political developments of the time have been partly responsible, especially with respect to Morocco's gradual loss of prestige and autonomy, ending with the joint protectorate of Spain and France after 1912?

Giving a precise answer to these questions is beyond my competence. Moreover, I must stress that the main objective of this study, rather than measuring the reactions of the Spanish public, is to understand under what circumstances and in which state of mind these visitors from the Maghreb discovered the Alhambra. Therefore, if I have paid so much attention to the accounts of these visits in the Spanish and Granadan press of the time, the main reason is that I wanted to compensate for the extreme dryness of most of the inscriptions in the visitors' book by attempting to fill in the blanks left behind to try and reconstitute the context in which these visits were taking place. I believe that I have been able to do so only within the limits of a few embassies, to the detriment of a considerable number of more modest travellers, who inevitably fell through the cracks. I can therefore only claim half-success, but I believe that will have to do until new sources, especially from Morocco, might enrich and complement this information. Yet one particular dimension of the matter remains to a large extent unexplored, namely, that of the 'subjective' aspects of these visits, in the sense of the way the visitors mentioned earlier lived, perceived and experienced this heritage- and possibly emotion-laden site. Indeed, to this point, I have mostly tried to analyse and elucidate the material, factual and practical aspects of these visits; and yet many of these accounts included comments that claimed to describe and interpret the visitors' feelings, sometimes going as far as putting words in their mouths or exclamations of admiration, joy or sadness at the sight of the monument. This qualitative dimension of visits from the Maghreb is evidently essential to a proper understanding of the emotional and cultural context in which these moments of discovery took place.

Feelings by Proxy?

Kardūdī's visit may be a reasonable starting point for this investigation, if only because this is the only journey from the Maghreb that has been studied in sufficient detail to allow for such an exercise. Pérès, who pioneered works on this question, noted that Kardūdī's real interest lay with purely technical matters relating to fortifications and armament; as such he ascribed very little cultural or historical sensitivity to this traveller. In Madrid, he 'examined some twenty Arab manuscripts' at the National Library;[134] in Granada, he did not seem to be interested in the Generalife; in Cordoba, only the mosque seems to have drawn his attention; in Seville, although he did visit the Alcázar, his focus was almost exclusively on a review of artillery batteries and the manufacture of cannon, cartridges and shells at the arsenal.[135] Nevertheless, this general lack of curiosity for things cultural did not exclude some strong reactions in the face of a lost heritage. In Cordoba, the sight of the treasures contained in the mosque triggered rather violent thoughts against Christians, as he wished that 'God may turn all this into booty for the Muslims.' As he exited the monument, he was overcome by a feeling of anguish at the idea that destiny 'had caused this mosque of great importance to pass from Muslim hands to those of the infidels'. As he returned to his hotel, he felt that 'the fire of sorrow (*asaf*) was burning inside [his] heart!' Granada seems to have

[134] Pérès, *L'Espagne vue par les voyageurs musulmans*, p. 45.

[135] Pérès, *L'Espagne vue par les voyageurs musulmans*, pp. 45–6. Taken up by Wien, *Arab Nationalism*, p. 57.

caused much less exaltation, as he was content with noting that he came back from the Alhambra 'torn between joy and sorrow'.[136]

Much later, Abdelmajid Kaddouri corroborated Pérès' verdict by stressing the practical and technical nature of his journey: 'The author came back bearing the image of a technical Europe.'[137] According to Daniel Newman, Kardūdī's journey was 'tantamount to an intelligence gathering mission'.[138] More recently, Peter Wien has taken up these observations, but with a clear effort towards fleshing out the diplomat's character and feelings. According to him, Kardūdī

> did not consider his journey a visit to a realm of lost glory, but rather as a mission to alien territory. He considered the de-Islamization of Muslim monuments an outrage, but, different from many other travellers who came after him, he did not historicize this loss as part of a narrative of a competition between Christian and Muslim civilizations, in which the latter had lost ground since the period of the Reconquista. For him, the current margin between Islam and Christendom was rather a technical matter.[139]

When it comes to Kardūdī's contemporaries, the Mauritanian Muḥammad Maḥmūd ibn al-Talāmīd al-Turkuzī al-Shinqīṭī and his Tunisian travel companion, 'Alī ibn Sālim al-Wardānī al Tūnisī, who visited the palace in 1887, one could understandably expect a clearer and stronger awareness of the historical and memorial context of Andalusia. After all, these were two scholars who had been commissioned by Sultan Abdülhamid II to discover and catalogue Islamic manuscripts kept in Spanish libraries. Yet their inscription in the visitors' book betrays no such attitude: Shinqīṭī's major concern was apparently to list his numerous titles and merits; as to Wardānī, he seems to have felt a need to boast his cosmopolitan knowledge by signing exclusively in French (Figure 2.8).[140] The two men have left very different traces of their journey to Spain. Shinqīṭī's interest was limited to composing archaic-sounding poems

[136] Pérès, *L'Espagne vue par les voyageurs musulmans*, p. 48.

[137] Kaddouri, 'Images de l'Europe dans un genre d'écriture marocaine: la *Rihla*', p. 133.

[138] Newman, 'Myths and Realities in Muslim Alterist Discourse', p. 32.

[139] Wien, *Arab Nationalism*, p. 57.

[140] AA, *libros de firmas*, 44, fol. 185 r, 28 October 1887.

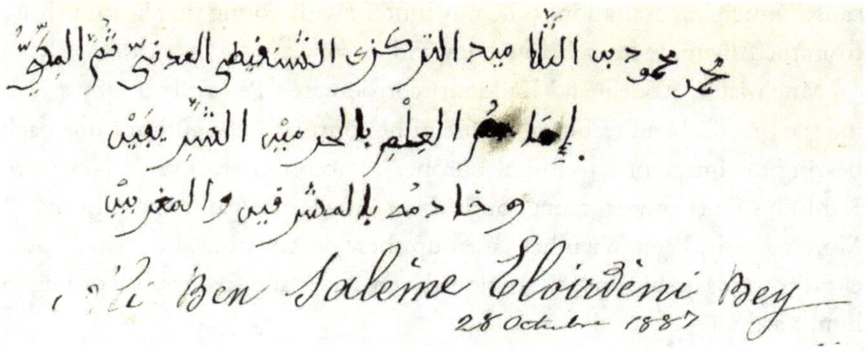

Figure 2.8 Inscriptions in the visitors' book by the Mauritanian Muḥammad Maḥmūd ibn al-Talāmīd al-Turkuzī al-Shinqīṭī and the Tunisian 'Alī ibn Sālim al-Wardānī al Tūnisī, 28 October 1887. AA, *libros de firmas*, 44, fol. 185 r. © Archivo del Patronato de la Alhambra y Generalife. The two scholars had been entrusted by the Ottoman Sultan Abdülhamid II with a scientific mission consisting of identifying Islamic manuscripts kept in Spanish libraries. Shinqīṭī's inscription consisted of a long list of his titles and qualifications, while Wardānī seems to have made a point of signing in French.

on 'reactionary' themes comparing the beauty and purity of his own civilisation to the barbaric modernity of the West. Regarding the monuments of al-Andalus, only the mosque of Cordoba triggered his interest, or rather his ire, as he witnessed its profanation by the Christian religion; the Alhambra is nowhere to be seen in his angry poems.[141]

His secretary, interpreter and travel companion, 'Alī Wardānī (1861–1905), a protégé of the famous 'Tunisian' Hayreddin Pasha (*c.* 1822–90),[142] was younger than him and certainly less bitter and more curious. In his travelogue, which was published shortly after his return in the Tunisian journal

[141] Pérès, *L'Espagne vue par les voyageurs musulmans*, pp. 55–61. Nieves Paradela mentions only Wardānī, the only one of the two who left an account of his travels (Paradela, *El otro laberinto español*, pp. 100–4).

[142] Born into an Abkhaz family and brought up as a slave in a major household of Istanbul, Hayreddin was sold to the palace of Aḥmad Bey of Tunisia (r. 1837–55), where he received further education and training, thus becoming one of the leading reformist political figures of the time. Minister of the Navy in 1857–62 and Chief Minister in 1873–7, he served for less than a year as Grand Vizier of the Ottoman Empire in 1878–9.

al-Ḥāḍira in 1888–90,[143] he stood out due to the genuine interest he showed for the Islamic monuments of Spain, in Toledo, Cordoba, Seville and, of course, Granada. The Alhambra received all his attention, and he did not try to mask his emotion at the sight of the palace, admitting he lacked the courage to even try to describe it properly; in his words, 'it would require a whole volume'. Particularly striking to him was the interest the monument triggered among Western audiences, especially tourists: 'More than a hundred tourists come and visit it every day, most of them British . . . Their eagerness to visit the Alhambra with such enthusiasm informs the observer of its importance throughout the civilised world (*al-ʿālam al-madanī*)[144] and demonstrates its value to the industrial society of the West.'[145] He was evidently conscious of the role played by the numerous illustrated publications on the history of the Arabs in Spain and on the exceptional beauty of this architectural wonder. He visited it in the company of a very learned and competent guide, most probably the same Javier Simonet who had accompanied several Moroccan embassies, and engaged in a conversation with him on the Arab past of Andalusia.[146] This apparently included a short argument about the number of Spaniards who died during the efforts to dislodge the Arabs from Spain. Millions, insisted his guide, upon which Wardānī took some pleasure in remarking that Tarik – Ṭāriq ibn Ziyād – had conquered the peninsula with merely 21,000 men.[147] Nevertheless, apart from monuments and history, Wardānī was also interested in Spanish society

[143] There are two recent editions of this travelogue, one by ʿAbd al-Jabbār al-Sharīf (1984) and the other by al-Ḥabīb al-ʿAwwādī (2008). See, Paradela, *El otro laberinto español*, p. 100, n. 30; J. L. Roldán Romero, '*Al-Riḥla al-Andalusiyya* de ʿAlī Sālim al-Wardānī al-Tūnisī (1861–1905): Estudio preliminar', p. 299.

[144] This fashion of qualifying the Western world as 'civilised', not unlike an admission of barbarism, may come as a surprise to the reader. In fact, this was a rather common occurrence, at least among the Ottoman bureaucratic elite since the 1840s, especially when it came to justifying an innovation borrowed from the West, by explaining its merits among 'civilised nations' (*milel-i mütemeddine*). While this expression clearly reflected the 'self-civilising mission' on which the Ottoman state had embarked following the *Tanzimat* decree of 1839, it is probable that those who used it were not entirely conscious of the perception of the empire it implied.

[145] Paradela, *El otro laberinto español*, p. 143.

[146] This point is corroborated by Paradela, *El otro laberinto español*, p. 89, see also, p. 105, n. 34.

[147] Paradela, *El otro laberinto español*, p. 89.

and culture, from bullfighting to politics and from traditions to linguistic borrowings from the Arabic language.[148] The sultan's Tunisian envoy was a man of diverse interests, who knew how to observe and appreciate Andalusia's Arab heritage. One could at most reproach him for not allowing himself to develop his emotions and personal opinions beyond simple expressions of admiration and wonder.[149]

By the way, was that not one common denominator of all the visitors from the Maghreb? As I have already noted, the inscriptions left by these travellers showed the same extreme concision and the general lack of personalised comments. The rare exceptions to this rule seem to confirm Wardānī's attitude. At most, they expressed an admiration for the monument, without ever ceding to the emphasis so typical of European or Spanish comments. In 1863, the earliest visitor recorded, al-Hājj 'Alī bin al-Bashīr, spoke of a 'magnificent palace' (*qaṣr al-'aẓīm*);[150] in 1880, the ambassador Brīsha mentioned a 'sacred abode' (*dār al-mubāraka*);[151] in 1885, Kardūdī described 'these wonderful buildings, proof of the greatness of the sovereigns of Islam';[152] in 1895, the embassy's secretary 'Abdelkerīm bin Slīmān transcribed a few ancient verses on the glory of past rulers and of their architectural remains;[153] in 1910, the young Kardūdī spoke of 'great feats';[154] finally, in 1919, one Aḥmad bin Aṣaf 'Abdallah declared, in three languages, how 'enthralled and charmed' he had been by his visit.[155]

There was much admiration, to be sure, but few, if any, feelings or strong emotions. Did this really stem from indifference, or should we interpret it as a kind of restraint, a desire not to indulge in lamentations or in any

148 Pérès, *L'Espagne vue par les voyageurs musulmans*, pp. 62–72. See also, Wien, *Arab Nationalism*, pp. 58–9.

149 We will have the opportunity to revisit Wardānī's journey and his comments on the mosque of Cordoba (see pp. 231–2).

150 AA, *libros de firmas*, 42, fol. 244 r, *c.* 7 February 1863.

151 AA, *libros de firmas*, 43, fol. 252 v, 22 June 1880.

152 AA, *libros de firmas*, 44, fol. 107 r, 24 December 1885.

153 AA, *libros de firmas*, 45, fol. 252 r, 5 March 1895. We will take up these verses again later, see pp. 130–2.

154 AA, *libros de firmas*, 48, fol. 228 v, 16 October 1910.

155 AA, *libros de firmas*, 50, fol. 248 r, 25 July 1919.

attitude that might be incompatible with the generally official nature of these visits? If we are to believe the contemporary Spanish press, there was much more to say about the feelings of visitors from the Maghreb. The way in which ambassador 'Abdesselām al-Sūsī's mission in 1877 was covered and illustrated in the *Ilustración española y americana* is a perfect example, which demonstrates to what extent the magazine gave importance to the visitor's emotions:

> A trustworthy correspondent tells us that the elderly Sīdī Abdesselam al-Soussi, deeply moved at the sight of the Court of the Lions, covered his swarthy face with his hands, shed some tears and cried out in despair:
>
> 'It seems impossible that those who possessed all of this should not have had themselves killed rather than abandon it!'[156]
>
> Then, suddenly pulling himself together and bowing his head in humility, as if the weight of fatality had burdened it, he added with resignation:
>
> 'God is great! May we respect His will, which gives and takes power from men and peoples.'[157]

An image reproduced a few pages later drove the message home. One could see the ambassador 'and the Africans of his retinue mournfully roaming the galleries adjacent to the sumptuous Hall of the Ambassadors'.[158] The artist had made a special effort to capture that dramatic moment when the ambassador, followed by half a dozen other men wearing a white burnous like him, overwhelmed by emotion, hid his face behind his hands (Figure 2.9).[159]

[156] Obviously, a reference to the fact that the last ruler of Granada capitulated and surrendered the keys of the Alhambra to the Spanish invaders. Interestingly, this remark echoes very closely the inscription left by al-Ghrīssī in 1863: 'How strange were its inhabitants who abandoned it to have their lives spared and failed to find another of similar beauty. It would have been preferable to see them perish down to the last' (see, p. 96).

[157] 'El embajador marroquí visitando la Alhambra'. This last quote seems to echo partly verse 3:26 of the Koran: 'Say, "Lord, sovereign of all sovereignty. You bestow sovereignty on whom you will and take it away from whom You please; You exalt whoever You will and abase whoever You will. All that is good lies in Your hands. You have the power to will anything".' See n. 24, p. 234.

[158] 'El embajador marroquí visitando la Alhambra'.

[159] 'Sid Abdesslam Esuisi visitando el palacio de la Alhambra'.

Figure 2.9 'Sid Abdesslam Esuisi during his visit of the palace of the Alhambra, on the 4th of this month', *La Ilustración española y americana*, XXI/XLVIII (30 December 1877), p. 413. Author's collection. The image from the popular illustrated magazine shows the ambassador and his retinue in the gallery between the Court of the Myrtles and the Hall of the Ambassadors. More importantly, it recreates the scene of 'Sid Abdesslam Esuisi and the Africans in his company walking sadly along the galleries next to the magnificent Hall of the Ambassadors' (ibid., p. 403) and depicts the ambassador expressing his grief by covering his face with his hands.

The words ascribed to the ambassador, the emotion he allegedly felt at the sight of the palace's wonders, the way he covered his face with his hands in a gesture of despair as depicted in the engraving, everything was meant to convey to the readers the sense of an overwhelming feeling of distress triggered by the beauty of a site that was supposed to remind the travellers of their forefathers' past glory. Was this true, or were the reporters and artists just assuming that the visitors were bound to experience such feelings and emotions? Was this attitude caused by sentiments of empathy, or was it rather a form of condescension mixed with a strange feeling of pride at the thought of having dispossessed the Moors of the most magnificent gems of their civilisation?

One can hardly answer these questions with categorical certainty; it is likely that the truth was somewhere in the middle. The visitors most probably expressed some interest in the site they were discovering, after which it was left to the Spaniards to interpret – or overinterpret – this admiration through the array of emotions they believed made sense, It is rather meaningful that although it was barely covered by the press, the embassy of 1877 triggered in half a dozen newspapers a chain reaction of references to a letter allegedly received from Granada, which linked the ambassador and his entourage's presumed tears to those shed by Boabdil, the last king of Granada, exactly 385 years earlier.[160]

This typically Spanish vision of events would generally start by loading meaning onto the journey itself, stressing the historical motivation that lay behind the desire of these 'Moorish' travellers or emissaries to undertake this visit, almost like a pilgrimage. This was the explanation brought in 1880 to the ambassador Sīdī L'arbī Brīsha's wish to visit his ancestral lands:

> Sidi Larbi . . . did not wish to return to his homeland without visiting the Arab monuments of Andalusia and without reminding himself, under the glorious sky of this privileged region, of the glorious memories of his forefathers.[161]

[160] *El Pueblo español*, 10 December 1877; 'Los moritos'; 'Había motivo'; *La Paz de Murcia*, 16 December 1877.

[161] 'Viaje de regreso del embajador marroquí Sidi el Arby Brischa'.

Once his dream had come true, this noble descendant of the Andalusians of yore fell under the spell of the extraordinary beauty of the site and its monuments, among which the Alhambra stood out:

> The city of Granada and, most of all, its unique Arab alcázar produced on Brisha's soul an effect that one would have expected . . . Sidi Larbi is a child of Tétouan, of this beautiful odalisque, which the Moors so rightly name the Granada of Africa, for it was founded by Granadans . . . Gazing from the field of the Martyrs,[162] the child of Tétouan let out a mysterious sigh . . . When he set foot on the white ground of the Arab alcázar, the ambassador let out another sigh, even deeper. As we heard him say, the palace shone in his eyes with a beauty as lively as the sunlight . . . Understandably so, for the genius of the Orient was able to create in Spain works of such splendour thanks to the civilising influence of Christianism.[163]

The setup was just perfect. Parallels were drawn with Morocco, especially with the city of Tétouan, while many innuendos were meant to capture the sensitivities and meet the expectations of the Spanish public. This was particularly the case with the final reference to the 'fertilisation' of Oriental genius with Christian civilisation, a convoluted but very efficient means of praising the enemy of the past without questioning the merits of Spanish identity, as defined in its commitment to the Catholic faith. One may remember the quarrel, which, in 1889, had followed Leopoldo Cano's outburst of Maurophilia. The conservative press had blamed him for suggesting that the Catholic conquest had brought misery and oppression upon a once fertile and blissful land. In the eyes of conservatives and nationalists, Andalusian civilisation constituted merely a parenthesis in the overall barbary of Muslims, between the Moors arrival in, and departure from, Spain. It was therefore obvious that if this civilisation had shone during this period, it was not due to the invaders, but rather to the civilising effect of Spain itself.[164]

[162] Campo de los Mártires, or rather Carmen de los Mártires, was the name of a seven-acre garden located a short distance south of the Alhambra. It owes its name to the Christian captives who were martyred in Arab dungeons (see, in Spanish, at: https://es.wikipedia.org/wiki/Carmen_de_los_Mártires).

[163] 'Viaje de regreso del embajador marroquí Sidi el Arby Brischa'.

[164] 'They came to Spain as complete Barbarians, and they became Barbarians once again when they left Spain' ('La cruz en las ruinas'), see, p. 90.

The other striking element in this description was the series of sighs ascribed to Brīsha. He let out a first and 'mysterious' one from atop the Carmen de los Mártires, apparently while contemplating the Alhambra. It was followed by a second, 'even deeper' one, upon his entrance into the Alhambra. Were these sighs triggered by the vision of these splendid ruins? Certainly, but any Spaniard reading those lines would have recognised an unequivocal reference to the dramatic end of Granada in 1492. Indeed, the expression '*suspiro del moro*' or 'the Moor's sigh' corresponded to that tragic moment when Boabdil, after his capitulation and the surrender of the keys of Granada to the Catholic monarchs, on his way to his small fief of exile in the Alpujarras, had paused to look back one last time upon the city and the palace he had just lost. He had then let out a deep sigh and burst into tears, only to be severely scolded by his mother who blamed him for 'weeping like a woman over that which he had not been able to defend like a man'. The name had been given to a pass in the Sierra Nevada, some 12 km south of Granada, where this scene was supposed to have unfolded.[165] It was thus a much more subtle rehash of the reminder from 1877 concerning the continuity in tears shed by the 'Moors' despite the passage of almost four centuries. In a way, Moroccan visitors were suspended, frozen in time, as if they had been cursed to shed over and over again the tears of their ancestors ousted from Granada in 1492. Thirty years later, during the last embassy covered in some detail in the press, a very similar feeling was once again ascribed to the ambassador, before he even beheld the site: 'As they were heading towards the Alhambra, when the governor's carriage passed beneath the Arch of Grenades (*arco de las Granadas*),[166] the ambassador entered a dark mood.[167]

[165] According to the historian Leonardo Villena, the myth of Boabdil's 'sigh' was invented about 1526 by Bishop Antonio Guevara to impress Charles V (see at: https://www.ideal.es/granada/prensa/20070302/provincia/bulo-para-poder-lucirse_20070302.html). We should also remember that this is also the title Salman Rushdie chose for his fifth novel, *The Moor's Last Sigh*. On this, see P. A. Cantor, 'Tales of the Alhambra: Rushdie's Use of Spanish History in *The Moor's Last Sigh*'.

[166] The Arch or Gate of the Grenades is a monumental gate in the form of a Roman triumphal arch erected in 1526 on the occasion of Charles V's marriage, which gave access to the Gomérez slope, leading to the Alhambra.

[167] 'La embajada marroquí', *El Noticiero granadino*, 12 June 1906.

The embassy of 1885, the one most followed together with that of 1889, provides us with ample material to study the modus operandi of the Spanish press, especially the local press. Reporters followed closely the meanderings of the mission, which included Kardūdī. The visitors were awed by the sheer beauty of the *mihrab* of the mosque of Cordoba: 'The Moors, clearly moved, did not realise the magnificence of the basilica. They moved on to the chapel of the cardinal, where the treasures are kept, which they examined attentively, before walking down the various naves.'[168] In all evidence, Kardūdī must have kept his comments for later. During their visit to the Alhambra, 'upon arriving at the mosque, today standing as an abandoned chapel, most probably overwhelmed by so many emotions hidden behind his solemn and respectable attitude, [the ambassador] must have felt somewhat affected'.[169] The assumptions interspersed in this sentence – and recognised as such – betray the Spanish reporter's 'method': to interpret the feelings of a visitor whose culture does not allow for emotional outpourings. According to the *Defensor de Granada*'s correspondent, the wonderful panorama from the top of the Watch Tower

> impacted the southern imagination of Abdelsadeq and his companions, who contemplated with melancholy the snowy mountains, which, like a Moorish cape, hide the Moroccan land of this nation, who shares with the people of Granada half its history and has given us half of the blood that flows in our veins and half of the sparkle that shines in the wonderful eyes of our so beautiful women.
>
> From the Watch Tower, the group headed towards the Palace of the Alhamares,[170] which they visited carefully, recalling the glorious memory of their ancestors. When he entered the mihrab, Abdelsadeq could not hold back the strong emotions that raged through his mind and was forced to pause.[171]

[168] *La Unión*, 26 December 1885.

[169] 'Desde Granada'.

[170] Another name for the Alhambra, from Alhamar, a Spanish deformation of 'al-Aḥmar', one of the nicknames of Muḥammad ibn Yūsuf ibn Naṣr (Muḥammad I, *c.* 1195–1273), better known as 'al-Ghālib bi'llah' (Victor by the grace of God) and 'ibn al-Aḥmar' ('the Red'), founder of the Nasrid dynasty and first ruler of the Emirate of Granada (*c.* 1238–1273).

[171] 'La embajada marroquí', *El Defensor de Granada*, 16 December 1885.

The journalist was evidently having a field day, putting his own Maurophile Andalusianism to the service of a fertile and romantic imagination, thus ascribing dramatic emotions and a historical consciousness to the visitors. In contrast, the comments left in the visitors' book were much shorter and cooler, with the relative exception of the elder Kardūdī, who did express his admiration for 'these wonderful buildings, proof of the greatness of the sovereigns of Islam',[172] an inscription that was immediately taken up by all the newspapers reporting on the visit.

It is rather difficult to find the right balance between the interest the visitors must have certainly shown in the remains of 'their' culture and Spanish wishful thinking concerning their expectations of strong and dramatic emotions. We should not forget that by then the Alhambra had become, in Spain as well as in the rest of Europe, a kind of historic symbol laden with romantic references further reinforced in arts and literature. There is little doubt that the visitors from the Maghreb were conscious of the Andalusian past and of its connection both to Islam and to their own history. Yet had they developed a rhetoric that could be compared with Western romanticism? Should we, on the contrary, imagine that even though their perception of Muslim and Arab remains in Andalusia triggered strong feelings and deep emotions, they did not possess the appropriate forms and means of making the same use of these sentiments as Europeans, and that consequently it fell upon the Spanish press and observers to self-appoint themselves as their interpreters and spokespersons?

Obviously, by leaving the ground to the local press, the Moroccan ambassadors' silence does not make it any easier for the historian to counter these arguments. However, it is also true that Spanish commentators displayed so much bias, so many exaggerations and inconsistencies, that one is bound to consider them only with the greatest suspicion. One of the major contradictions had to do with the clear tendency of these observers to ascribe to these men deep emotions and a strong historical consciousness, while at the same time stressing their profound ignorance, which could often turn into a general indifference to the sites they visited. Thus, during the 1889 embassy, the

[172] AA, *libros de firmas*, 44, fol. 107 r, 24 December 1885.

Moroccan delegation was blamed for not having shown sufficient interest or emotion for the remains of their own civilisation:

> The stay of the Moroccans in Granada has not produced the poetic impact some expected. The Moors strolled around the place more or less as they would have elsewhere, without shedding tears upon the memory of lost grandeur.[173]

With its references to poetic expectations and to disappointment due to the absence of tears and sighs, this passage reveals to what extent the Spanish discourse was full of preconceived ideas and stereotypes that determined the turn the account of the visit would eventually take. We should remember that it was precisely during this embassy that the local press had expressed surprise at the realisation that the visitors did not know of Boabdil, whose sword they had been shown, and noted that they were opposed to any form of material and technological progress. And yet, it was also during this embassy that the newspapers had noted the interest shown by the ambassador for the old Arab district of the Albaicín, his lamentations upon seeing Charles V's palace erected on the former location of the winter palace and the fact that he and his retinue spent time reading the inscriptions in the palace and the epitaphs of the tombstones kept in the museum. Clearly, the journalists were pulling out all the stops, pushing in one direction or another as they saw fit. At any rate, they had one more cliché at their disposal to explain the visitors' silence and, consequently, to justify why they should step in and speak on their behalf: the reserved and taciturn character of the 'Moors' and their reluctance to publicly express admiration for things they did not own. That is why the embassy of 1906 seems to have left a memorable impression for the simple reason that the visitors' wonder was such that they could not hide it and that they could not help but let out emotional outpourings allegedly so contrary to their nature:

> Although the Moors always try to feign indifference before anything that is not from their land, awe-inspiring as they may be, the magnificent alcázar broke the spell and exclamations of 'Wonderful!', 'God is great!' were constantly springing from the lips of the Moroccans in the mission at the sight of the beauty of

[173] 'Los marroquíes'.

the Vega and of the gates and walls of the palace, whose inscriptions they read with true delight.[174]

Apparently, their surprise was such that one of the Spanish hosts wrote down in the visitors' book, just below the signatures, a comment that went in exactly the same direction and may well have been the source of inspiration for the account published in the *Defensor*.[175] What should one think in the face of such insistence? Should one espouse the famous saying that there is no smoke without fire and conclude that despite a clear predilection for Orientalist clichés and wishful thinking, the Spanish witnesses to the scene could simply not have made up the whole set of reactions they ascribed to the Moroccan visitors?

As I suggested in an earlier instance, I believe the truth stands somewhat midway between the two extreme positions. There is little doubt that the Spaniards, perhaps sometimes unconsciously, detected in their guests' attitude the signs of emotions that they had no difficulty in overinterpreting in a way that flattered their own self-esteem or met their expectations of exoticism and Orientalism. On the other hand, there is no reason to reject the possibility that Moroccan reactions could vary greatly, from indifference – feigned or genuine – to powerful feelings, such as amazement or deep sorrow. The problem evidently stems from the fact that we have much more information on Spanish perceptions and stereotypes than on the way the visitors from the Maghreb actually behaved before the monument. After all, the Spaniards had at their disposal a rather limited set of references, which made their reactions all the more predictable: Boabdil and his sword, the 'Moor's sigh', Arab inscriptions, Isabella and Ferdinand, the *Reconquista* . . . depending on the choice or dosage of these elements, the Spanish discourse could become more

[174] 'La embajada marroquí', *El Defensor de Granada*, 13 June 1906.

[175] AA, *libros de firmas*, 47, fol. 156 r, 12 June 1906. The three individuals signing the book were the ambassador, Qaddūr el-Ghāzī; Ṣādeq Akhardhān, his councillor; and Muḥammad al-Misfīqī, his secretary. The comment said: 'Los moros guardan siempre su admiración ante los extraños, pero hoy ante la Alhambra Kaddur-El-Gasi exclamó ¡Dios es grande! Y Mohamed el Misfiqui ¡Mejor que Tetuán!' ('The Moors always keep their admiration to themselves in the presence of strangers, but today, before the Alhambra, Kaddur al-Gazi cried out God is great! And Mohammed el-Misfiqui, Better than Tétouan!').

or less nostalgic, more or less jingoist, more or less Orientalist. With regard to the North Africans, on the contrary, the absence or scarcity of sources obscures the scene; to make matters worse, we have very little information as to what cultural and intellectual material and references were at their disposal. While it appears that one of them did take advantage of a manuscript guidebook in Arabic, it seems difficult to assume that they were all likewise equipped. At any rate, the gravest error would be to think of them as a monolithic group. The difference between one ambassador, in 1885, accepting a group photograph being taken, and his successor, four years later, who refused to even hear about it is telling enough of the variety that must have characterised the cultural and intellectual profile of these visitors.

Voices from the Maghreb?

A concrete example of the way some visitors stood out from their travel companions by a more 'emotional' attitude is that of 'Abdelkerīm bin Slīmān, secretary to the ambassador 'Abdelkerīm bin Muḥammad Brīsha in 1895, whose solitary and meditative character was duly noted by the *Defensor*:

> It was the secretary-poet Soliman who showed the greatest admiration, when, once the visit had ended, did not follow his companions but stayed in the alcázar until two o'clock in the afternoon, after which he returned to the hotel.
>
> He asked for a chair and, during all that time, remained absorbed in the contemplation of the wonderful scene of the Court of the Lions, thinking out loud every so often. He expressed to some persons who accompanied him a deep regret that he could not stay longer to contemplate and study the palace as he wished.[176]

Of course, the point is to again avoid falling into the trap set by Spanish witnesses by taking too literally remarks that may well be little more than a reflection of their own fantasies. Yet it also seems difficult, not to say impossible, to discard altogether this mention of a member of the delegation separating from the rest and voluntarily seeking isolation to better enjoy this moment of contemplation of the monument. One may always approach with caution the attribution of some feelings to a visitor, but details concerning his

[176] 'La embajada', *El Defensor de Granada*, 6 March 1895.

whereabouts or his isolation constitute the kind of information that one can hardly assume to have been completely made up.

However, there is one very important clue that encourages me to think that the said 'Abdelkerīm bin Slīmān did indeed stray from the herd, or at least stood out from the rest of his companions in a very particular way. The *Defensor* noted that he was a 'secretary-poet', and this hybrid qualification is indeed reflected in the rather uncommon inscription he left in the visitors' book, consisting of a quatrain:

If kings want their zeal to gain in glory
As you can see, it is by the language of edifices.
For if a building rises, full of majesty,
It will continue to remind us of the glorious.[177]

The verses were not his; he had borrowed them from a prestigious author, 'Abdelraḥman III al-Nāṣir li-Dīn Allah (891–961), Omayyad emir and caliph of Cordoba from 912 to 961, who, according to al-Ṣafadī (1296–1363)[178] and al-Maqqarī (1578–1632),[179] composed this poem in praise of the palatial city

[177] AA, *libros de firmas*, 45, fol. 252 r, 5 March 1895. Strangely, the author of this inscription had two goes at it, crossing out a first version to replace it with a second and definitive one:

هِمَمُ الْمُلُوك إِذَا تَعَاظَم شَأَنُه   إِو مَا تَرَى فَبِأَلْسُنِ الْبُنْيَانِ
إِنَ الْبِنَاءَ اذا تَعَاظِم شأَنهْ   أضحْى يَدلُّ عَلى عَظِيمِ الشانِ

[178] S. Al-Ṣafadī, *Kitāb al-Wāfā*, vol. XVIII, p. 137:

و مدَحَه الشعراء، و كَثُر العلماءُ في أيامه. و من شعر الناصر عبدالرحمن [الكامل]:
هِمَمُ الملوك إذا أرادوا ذكرَها * من بعدهم فبأَلسُنِ البنيانِ
إن البناء إذا تَعاظَمَ شأنُه * أضحى يدلُّ على عظيم الشانِ

[179] A. Al-Maqqarī, *Kitāb Nafḥ al-Ṭīb*, vol. I, p. 243:

رجع الى أخبار البنيان ولا خفاءَ أنه يدلّ على عظيم قدر بانيه و لذلك قال امير االمومنين الناصر المروانى بانى الزهراء رحه حسبما نسبهما له بعض العلماء و بعض ينسبهما لغيره و سياتيان فى ترجمة نورالدين بن على منسوبين
هِمَمُ الملوك اذا ارادوا ذِكْرَها * من بعدهم فبأَلْسُن البنيانِ
ان البناءَ اذا تعاظم قدرُه * اضحى يدلّ على عظيم الشانِ

p. 269:

فى اخبار المغرب فانه اتمُّ فائدةً اذقال رحمه الله دخل منذر ابن سعيد يوما على الناصر بانى الزهراء و هو مُكِبّ على الاشتغال بالبنيان فوعظه فانشده عبدالرحمن الناصر
هِمَمُ الملوك اذا ارادوا ذكرَها * من بعدهم فبالسُن البنيانِ
أَوَ ما ترى الهرمَيْن قد بقيا وكم * ملك مَّحاه حوادثُ الازمانِ
ان البناءَ اذا تعاظم قدرُه * اضحى يدلّ على عظيم الشانِ

of Madīnat al-Zahrā (Medina Azahara), which he had founded in 936. The caliph's verses were remarkablely successful, if one considers the number of times they were taken up by later authors. In the fifteenth century, al-Maqrīzī (1364–1442) took up verses 1, 2, 5 and 6 in his *Topographical Description of Egypt*, when speaking of the 'commentaries on Cairo and its entertainments'.[180] The three first verses also appear in the story of Caliph al-Ma'mūn (786–833) and the destruction of the pyramids, corresponding to the 398th night of the Calcutta edition in Arabic of the *Thousand and One Nights*, where they are used as part of a poem describing the pyramids, with the addition of a last verse stressing the unchanged nature of these monuments.[181] Finally – and this is certainly not the last example to be found – Rifā'a Ṭahṭāwī (1801–73) went as far as to use these verses in his famous travelogue to praise the beauty and majesty of the edifices of Paris.[182]

What should one make of this quote? Should we conclude that 'Abdelkerīm bin Slīmān knew his 'classics' well and that he had seen a perfect opportunity to revive the small poem a great Andalusian had composed to exalt the beauty of a site lost by then? Was he conscious that he was quoting from a caliph of the tenth century, that the reference was to Madīnat al-Zahrā, and not the Alhambra? Had he on the contrary found inspiration in a more demotic oral tradition, made up of anonymised poems and quotes, sometimes distorted or truncated with the passage of time?

I am in no position to answer these questions, as I do not know if there exist works on the cultural and literary repertoire available to Moroccan elites at the turn of the twentieth century that might shed some light on the question. In the particular context of this study, this quote, as incidental as it may seem, allows for a questioning of the apathy and indifference that Spanish observers so often ascribed to visitors from the Maghreb. It does seem that 'Abdelkerīm bin Slīmān can be credited for writing out loud what others said or recited in a

---

As appears from the second quote by Maqqarī, the caliph's poem consisted of six verses; in his version, 'Abdelkerim Slīmān omitted the second and fourth verses. Moreover, his first verse was wrong, given that it ends with the second half of the penultimate one. These errors and omissions were most probably due to an approximative memorisation, thus suggesting an oral, rather than written, transmission.

[180] N. A. Al-Maqrīzī, *Kitāb al-Mawā'iẓ wa al-I'tibār bi-Dhikr al-Khiṭaṭ wa al-Āthār*, p. 187.

[181] W. H. Macnaghten (ed.), *The Alif Laila or Book of the Thousand Nights and One Night*, p. 414.

[182] R. Ṭahṭāwī, *Takhlīṣ al-Ibrīz ilā Talkhīṣ Bārīz*, p. 52.

whisper, thus leaving a precious clue as to the existence of feelings and cultural references triggered by their visit of the monument.

Interestingly, there is another written testimony confirming a similar attitude, which, moreover, is of a much earlier date than the verses scribbled by the ambassy secretary in 1895. In 1876, almost twenty years earlier, the visitors' book had received a long and dense inscription by one Malek Salem (Figure 2.10):

> Thus spoke Malek Salem before the Alhambra: Oh, palace of the Alhambra! I have come from distant lands to admire you, thinking that you were as a garden in the spring, yet I saw you as a tree in the autumn. I thought that my heart would fill with joy upon seeing you, but on the contrary, tears sprang from my eyes. Lucky he who could see you in those happy days, when Granada had thousands of palaces, hundreds of thousands of inhabitants, and the splendour of a crown. You would then rise like a beautiful sultana, crowned with battlements of gold and covered in forests of pearls. Then, the hues of your chambers surpassed in beauty the flowers that perfume the banks of the Darro and the sky reflecting in the mirror of its waters. During the day, you are but a slave; and that is why your garments are torn and colourless, and in your misfortune, you have only one consolation: when the birds that come from Africa start to flutter over your battlements, you seem to be happier. It is because you hear them repeat endlessly, 'blessed be the Alhambra'. They learnt this phrase in the African desert. When the *shūb*[183] whips the forehead of the unfortunate who has no place to take shelter, he remembers the welcome shade of your forests, which his parents praised to him, and he exclaims with sorrow: 'Blessed be the Alhambra'. If one day, the enmity disappeared between Christians and Muslims, and between Spaniards and the inhabitants of Africa, and if, all of them being like brethren, those whose forefathers had lived under the rule of the Nasrid came to Granada without fear, you would once again wear your mantle of a lady. Yet do not lose hope: such a day may come. A Christian king built a palace next to you, which, like you, now lies deserted. Perhaps you are both awaiting to be inhabited by a monarch under whose sceptre Christians and Muslims shall live like brethren.[184]

[183] An erroneous transcription of *shawb* (شوب), meaning 'intense heat', probably used to describe a hot wind blowing from the desert. For a discussion of this word and the implications of its use, see below, n. 201.

[184] AA, *libros de firmas*, 43, fol. 86 r, 2 or 3 December 1876. The text is undated, but it is preceded by an inscription dated 2 December and followed by another of 3 December. The text below is a corrected version of the original inscription, which contains several errors, which

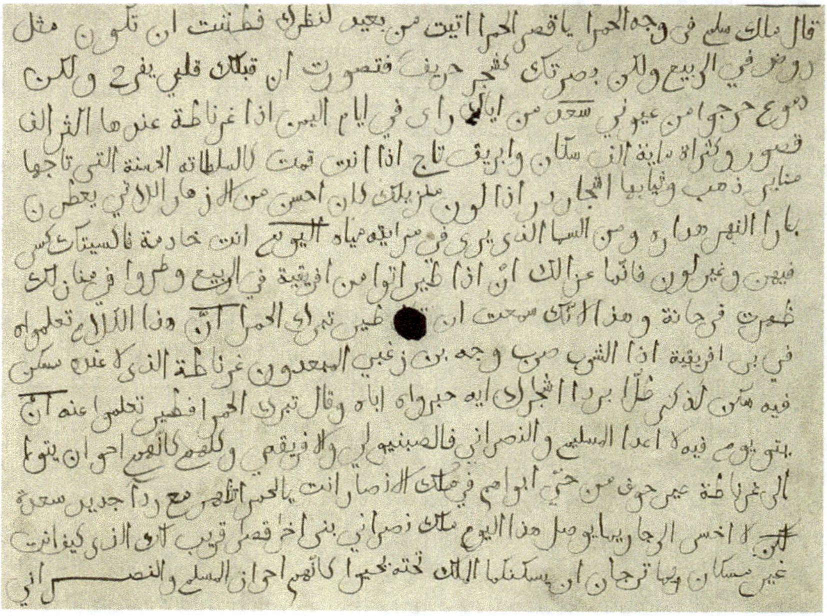

Figure 2.10 Inscription left in the visitors' book by the 'poet from Tétouan', Malek Salem, 2 or 3 December 1876. AA, *libros de firmas*, 43, fol. 86 r. © Archivo del Patronato de la Alhambra y Generalife. The nostalgic tone of this long inscription and its surprising wish for the unification of Christians and Arabs under a single sovereign cast serious doubts as to the identity of its author, possibly a 'soft' promoter of Spanish colonialism.

---

the reader may identify on its photographic reproduction. The translation above is based on the Spanish translation by Antonio Almagro y Cárdenas, published in *El Globo* on 2 September 1877, amended thanks to a careful re-reading of the original Arabic text by Driss Mekouar, from the Ottoman library at the Collège de France:

قال ملك سلم فى وجه الحمرا يا قصر الحمرا اتيت من بعيد لنظرك فظننت ان تكون مثل روض في الربيع و لكن بصرتك كشجر خريف فتصورت ان قبلك قلبي يفرح و لكن دموع خرجوا من عيوني / سعد من اياك راى في ايام اليمن اذا غرناطة عندها اكثر الف قصور و كثراة مائة الف سكان و ابريق تاج اذا انت قمت كالسلطانة الحسنة التي تاجها منابر ذهب و ثيابها اشجار در اذا لون منزلك كان احسن من الأزهار اللاتي يعطرن بارا النهر هداره و من السماء الذي يري في سرايته مياه / اليوم انت خادمة فاكسيتك كسر فيهن و غير لون فإنما عزالك انّ اذا طيراتوا من افريقية في الربيع و طاروا في منازلك ظهرت فرحانة و هذا الانّك سمعت ان [. . .] طير تبارك الحمرا / انّ هذا الكلام تعلموا في بر افريقية اذا الشوب ضرب وجه بن زغبي المبعدون غرناطة الذي لا عنده سكن فيه سكن لذكر ظلّ بردا اشجارك ايه خبروه آباءه و قال تبارك الحمرا فطير تعلموا عنه / انّ يتو يوم فيه لا اعدا المسلم و النصراني فالصبنيولي و الافريقي و كلهم كانّهم اخوان يتوا الى غرناطة غير خوف من حيّ ابواهم في ملك النصارى انت يالحمرا تظهر مع رداء جديد سعدة / لكن لا اخسر الرجا ربما يوصل هذا اليوم ملك نصراني بني اخر قصر قريب لك الذي كيف انت غير مسكون ربما ترجوان ان يسكنكما الملك تحته يحيوا كانّهم اخوان المسلم والنصراني

Compared with the usual silence and laconic inscriptions of visitors and diplomats from the Maghreb, Malek Salem's looks simply extraordinary. So much so, that the Spanish press took hold of it less than a year later, when the daily *El Globo* republished a translation into Spanish of the inscription, by the philologist, linguist and future 'Africanist' Antonio Almagro Cárdenas, who, as we have seen earlier, accompanied the Moroccan embassies of 1885 and 1889.[185] 'We are copying here the words penned in the album of the Alhambra of Granada by the Arab Meleksalom on the occasion of his recent visit, for we believe it deserves to be reproduced', noted the Madrid newspaper in its preliminary remarks on the translation.[186] In the following days, *La Época* and *El Pabellón nacional* reprinted it in full.[187] The following year, the same translation, preceded by an introduction celebrating the feelings of 'fraternity between all the nations and races' expressed in it, was published in the *Revista de Andalucía*. According to the author, Aureliano Ruiz, the poet was a 'wealthy trader from the interior of the neighbouring Kingdom of Morocco'.[188]

One can understand why the Spanish press and public loved Malek Salem's declamation. It embodied many of the elements of 'Andalusist' exoticism and nostalgia we have seen earlier. Filled with a form of irenicism that must have charmed many readers, the words of this mysterious 'Moor' kept being repeated for decades in the Spanish press and other publications. In1878, an in-depth article published in *El Globo* on the preservation of Andalusian heritage felt the urge to ask: 'Who should be held responsible for the sorrow felt by the Moor Melek-Salom at the sight of the mistreated *slave*?'[189] In 1881, on the occasion of a detailed article on Cárdenas's career, *El Defensor de Granada* reminded his readers of how he had been the first to publish a translation of

[185] The first translation was published in the Granadan daily *La Lealtad* ('Antonio Almagro Cárdenas'). Given that *El Globo* did not quote this article and that the surviving collections of *La Lealtad* are incomplete – the years 1876 and 1877 are missing altogether – it seems impossible to guess at what exact date Cárdenas published this first version of it.

[186] 'Variedades', *El Globo*, 2 September 1877, p. 3.

[187] *La Época*, 5 September 1877, p. 3; *El Pabellón nacional*, 7 September 1877, p. 2.

[188] A. Ruiz, 'Un poema árabe'.

[189] 'Dos joyas'.

this text in the local press.[190] In 1882, during the visit of the infantas Paz (1862–1946) and Isabella (1851–1931) of Bourbon, when the princesses were invited to sign the visitors' book,[191] Almagro Cárdenas was there to offer a reading of his translation of Malek Salem's poem, which gave the press yet another occasion to publish the text. According to the *Defensor*, 'the infantas could only admire this composition, which is without any doubt, the most beautiful in the book'.[192]

In 1883, Malek Salem and his text resurfaced, this time on the occasion of the debates concerning a project for the 'coronation' of the poet José Zorrilla, already mentioned as the author of an 'Oriental' poem in two volumes by the name of *Granada*.[193] The city of Granada wished to celebrate its 'national poet' by organising a festival at the Alhambra, in Charles V's palace. The plan was to invite poets from each province of Spain; but it was also 'possible that Moroccan poets attend the event, among whom Melch Sulem [*sic*] of Tétouan, author of a brilliant poem, inscribed in 1876 in the album of the Alhambra'.[194] This was the first time that a precise information was given on the origins of the mysterious poet: he was from Tétouan.

Where did this information come from, knowing that it had been absent from all the initial translations? There is no indication whatsoever as to its source; at any rate, Malek Salem would be nowhere to be seen during the event itself, held in June 1889.[195] Nevertheless, his name and his poem would remain on the agenda and would be brought back to the attention of the public at regular intervals, often with a full quotation of his text, in numerous publications, such as *La Alhambra*, a local journal,[196] or in many of the guidebooks on Granada and the Alhambra, including compilations of signatures and comments taken from the visitors' book, which never failed to

190 'Antonio Almagro Cárdenas'.

191 A whole page of the visitors' book is dedicated to the princesses (AA, *libros de firmas*, 43, fol. 299 v, 1 April 1882).

192 *El Defensor de Granada*, 554, 2 April 1882, p. 3.

193 Zorrilla y Moral, *Granada: Poema oriental, precedido de la leyenda de Al-Hamar*.

194 *Diario oficial de avisos de Madrid*, 2 May 1883, p. 3; 'Coronación de Zorrilla'.

195 M. Sancho y Rodríguez, *Crónica de la coronación de Zorrilla*.

196 '"La Alhambra" en el Mogreb'; R. Gago y Palomo, 'El tiempo de los moros'.

cite the Moroccan poet's inscription.[197] In 1886, an extraordinary embassy from Morocco – which, by the way, does not seem to have left a trace in the visitors' book – was allegedly 'pleasantly surprised, while leafing through the album, to find a tender poem penned in Arabic by the African poet so full of inspiration, the Moroccan Meleksalón [*sic*]'; this remark was followed by yet another rehash of Cárdenas' translation.[198] In reality, the fact was rather improbable, considering that no less than ten registers had been filled since the one containing Malek Salem's inscription. Clearly, this was again a sort of wishful thinking, unless the officials in charge of the monument had the idea to bring the register concerned from the archives, just to proudly show it to the visitors.

Fraud or Ideological Pamphlet?

All these inconsistencies cast a shadow of doubt over the identity of this author, and even on the authenticity of the inscription. In many ways, the text was 'too good to be true' and stood in astonishing contrast to the extremely laconic style witnessed in the inscriptions left by the other visitors from the Maghreb. The absence of any serious follow-up on Malek Salem's identity and the way this text was overexploited to the point of becoming a romantic cliché linked to the Alhambra have only increased my scepticism on the matter.

Much more concretely, the possibility of fraud was suggested by several colleagues, whose competences allowed them to go much further than my initial reaction, intuitive at best.[199] It was thus pointed out to me that both its style and script suggested that the text might have been rather of Oriental

[197] This is particularly the case with several publications by Luis Seco de Lucena: *Poesías y pensamientos del álbum de la Alhambra*, pp. 25–6; *Practical and Art Guide of Granada*, pp. 304–6; *Idearium de la Alhambra*, p. 190. For other examples, see Castillo Tejada, *Poesías, pensamientos y firmas que se encuentran en los cuatro albums de la Alhambra*, pp. 7–8; Sánchez Valdivia, *Brevísimo guía del palacio árabe*, pp. 133–4; Wood, *The Tourist's Spain and Portugal*, pp. 228–9.

[198] *La Correspondencia de España*, 13 August 1886, p. 1; *La Época*, 16 August 1886, p. 4.

[199] I am very grateful to Anne-Laure Dupont, Paris-Sorbonne University, to Mehdi Ghouirgate, Bordeaux-Montaigne University, and to Mohamed B. Bouabdelli, whose comments have allowed me to verify these doubts by providing concrete arguments, which I would have been incapable of bringing up myself.

origin.[200] A closer look at the text reveals spelling and vocabulary details that seem to also betray its non-Maghrebi origin.[201] To make matters worse, a few awkward turns of language – Western, mostly French – could even indicate that, beyond differences between Maghreb and Mashreq, the text may have even been written by a non-Arab, perhaps a Westerner having a go at a language they had not mastered to perfection.[202]

Of course, one is immediately tempted to assume that the translator himself, Almagro y Cárdenas, might have been involved in the operation. For a young man of twenty, with a remarkably early graduation at sixteen, who was trying to build a career on the Arab remains of the Alhambra and by making use of his linguistic and philological knowledge of the Arabic language, this would have been a rather clever publicity stunt. While some clues tend to exonerate him from such fraudulent behaviour,[203] it remains that this mysterious text, whoever may have penned it, overlapped perfectly with some of the Spanish political trends of the time.

Indeed, below a strong varnish of nostalgia and irenicism, this text was much less innocent that it seems at first glance. When the poet expressed his wishes for the reunification of Spaniards and Moroccans, Christians and

[200] Mehdi Ghouirgate is categorical on this point, noting that it is only after the 1920s that Oriental graphic forms started to be used in the Maghreb and adding that this inconsistency can be traced also in the syntax and style of Malek Salem's text.

[201] The letter 'fa' should have had a dot beneath (ب), but has it above (ف), as done in the Mashreq and the 'qaf' has two dots (ق) instead of one (ف), betraying a similar practice. Similarly, the word *shawb* (شوب) used in the sense of 'intense heat' belongs to the Syro-Lebanese dialect and does not exist in the Maghreb, where the equivalent would be *ṣahd* (صهد). On this topic, see the discussion on the WordReference forum at: https://forum.wordreference.com/threads/all-dialects-the-weather-is-hot.3573430.

[202] For example, Mohamed Bouabdelli notes the expressions 'في وجه' ('in the face of') used in the sense of 'before' and 'قبلك' ('before you') used for 'in front of you', as well as the fact that the Alhambra is addressed in masculine form, while any proper speaker of the Arabic language would know that this name is feminine. My friend and colleague Nasser Rabbat, from the Massachusetts Institute of Technology (MIT), also confirmed that the text did not seem to have been penned by a true Arabic speaker, if only due to numerous grammatical errors. To him, the author might have been European.

[203] Mohamed Bouabdelli notes that he transcribes *shawb* (شوب) as *schub*, suggesting that he did not know the word and that, therefore, it seems absurd that he should have written a text including a word unknown to him.

Muslims, under the rule of a single sovereign who would then reside at the palace of the Alhambra, there is little chance that he had in mind the sultan of Morocco. Quite the contrary, one gets a strong feeling that this mission of peace and unity would have to be entrusted to the king of Spain, at the time Alfonso XIII, who, at the young age of nineteen had been on the throne for merely two years.

Such a vision was perfectly in line with the evolution of Spain's African – or rather, Moroccan – policy. We should not forget that the country had embarked upon a first colonial adventure in 1859–60, when the Spanish army, led by General Leopoldo O'Donnell, using the pretext of Berber attacks against the Spanish towns of the North African coast, had attacked and defeated the troops of Sultan Muḥammad IV (1810–73). This victory had given Spain the opportunity to enlarge and establish in perpetuity its territories of Ceuta and Melilla and to occupy the city of Tétouan, pending the payment of the heavy indemnity imposed on the kingdom of Morocco. One of the consequences of this success was a growing enthusiasm for an expansionist policy emulating the colonial achievements of France and Great Britain. Although it is true that it was only after the famous conference for the partition of Africa held in Berlin in 1884–5 that a true colonial ambition developed in Spain, this first experience nevertheless triggered a wave of interest for Arab culture, language and history.[204]

It should therefore not come as a surprise that the expedition of 1860 was marked by another 'poetic' episode, which had striking similarities to that of Malek Salem in 1876. Then, too, the story revolved around a poet from Tétouan, who had greeted the Spaniards with open arms, by putting his mansion at the disposal of a group of officers from the occupying army. Shorby, as he was called, thus struck up a friendship with the Spanish author Pedro Antonio de Alarcón (1833–91), who served in the army as an officer, and wrote an account of this communion between a Spanish conqueror and a conquered Moroccan in his *Diary of a Witness of the African War*.[205] Almost ten years later, the same Shorby went to Madrid to visit his former guests,

[204] González Alcantud, 'La maurophobie dans les cercles intellectuels andalous', p. 253.

[205] P. A. de Alarcón, *Diario de un testigo de la Guerra de África*, pp. 265–77. On this topic, see G. R. Nunley, *Scripted Geographies: Travel Writings by Nineteenth-Century Spanish Authors*, pp. 123–68; J. A. González Alcantud, *Qué es el orientalismo*, pp. 168–80.

among whom Alarcón, who had brought him fame. The news of this reunion appeared in the Spanish press, which noted that the real objective of Shorby's journey was 'an artistic expedition throughout the towns of Spain boasting monuments of Arab architecture'.[206]

Unfortunately, the poet vanishes from the press after that, and I have not been able to find any trace of his possible visit to the Alhambra. At any rate, without really suggesting that he way have inspired Malek Salem, fictional or not, it seems clear that Shorby's case was feeding into a new ideological and intellectual current, that of Spanish *africanismo*, a combination of Orientalism and colonialism, which was born out of the African campaign and would rapidly develop in the 1880s.[207] Antonio Almagro y Cárdenas was fully engaged in the most conservative wing of this movement, much like his mentor, Francisco Javier Simonet. These two men's undeniable competences regarding the Arab language, philology and history did not temper in the least their colonialist – sometimes even racist – stance, all the more amplified by their political conservatism and Catholic fundamentalism.[208]

Once again, my point is not to suggest, let alone prove, that Malek Salem's text was actually penned by Cárdenas or by his mentor, Simonet. If indeed Malek Salem never existed, we will probably never know with certainty who was hiding behind this pseudonym. Nevertheless, it seems obvious that this text needs to be taken into consideration within the framework of the Africanist context prevailing at the time, and that consequently it was most probably deliberately inserted in the visitors' book by a partisan or at least a loyal supporter of the cause. Under these circumstances, the pseudonym itself

[206] *La Correspondencia de España*, 6 October 1869, p. 2; *La Época*, 7 October 1869, p. 4; *La Esperanza*, 10 October 1869, p. 4; *La Iberia*, 10 October 1869, p. 4.

[207] See above, p. 71.

[208] See, for example, Simonet's biography by his disciple: A. Almagro Cárdenas, *Biografía del doctor D. Francisco Javier Simonet*. For an excellent analysis of Maurophobia among Spanish Arabists, particularly Simonet, see J. A. González Alcantud, 'Pasión fría y objeto fóbico: El círculo orientalista Estebánez, Cánovas, Simonet'; González Alcantud, 'La maurophobie dans les cercles intellectuels andalous', pp. 253–9; J. A. González Alcantud, 'El mito fallido sacromontano y su perdurabilidad local a la luz del mozarabismo de F. J. Simonet'; M. Guerrero Moreno, 'Entre maurofobia y maurofilia: formación e impacto del pensamiento historiográfico de Francisco Javier Simonet'.

may even acquire a hidden and highly symbolic meaning: Malek Salem, the 'King of Peace',[209] or, in other words, the – obviously Spanish – king, whose reign would bring about the realisation of the still timid dreams of Spanish colonialists. Let us not forget that in 1885, Cárdenas signed the visitors' book in the capacity of the founding president of the Hispano-Mauritanian Union. The avowed goal of this association, established in 1883, immediately in the wake of the Spanish Society of Africanists and Colonialists (Sociedad española de africanistas y colonialistas), was to tighten the links and friendship between Spaniards and Africans and to promote trade between the two areas.[210] Nevertheless, ideologically speaking, the project was much more ambitious, as revealed in the twice monthly and (partly) bilingual – Spanish and Arabic – journal managed by Cárdenas, the *Estrella de Occidente* (1879–93). The inauguration of this publication was preceded by an article by Cárdenas with the highly symbolic title of '2 January 1879: Memories and projects' – 2 January was the anniversary of the conquest of Granada by the Catholic monarchs in 1492 – in which the author put forward the idea that 'the work of the *Reconquista* did not end with the fall of Granada' and that 'it invited the Spanish nation to fulfil the mission that Providence had assigned it in the Empire of Morocco'.[211] In 1892, Cárdenas organised a congress of Africanists in Granada, to which he ascribed a central role in the spreading of the influence of Spain in Morocco.[212]

It is therefore not just coincidence that Malek Salem's text resurfaced many years later and in a context that lent itself to a much more aggressive interpretation of his message of peace and communion between the two nations. In 1906, the text was brought up again in a newspaper of Melilla, *El Telegrama del Rif*, at the precise moment when the famous Conference of Algeciras was

[209] My thanks go to Mohamed Bouabdelli for this suggestion.

[210] See, in Spanish, at: https://es.wikipedia.org/wiki/La_Estrella_de_Occidente; Viñes Millet, *Granada y Marruecos: Arabismo y africanismo en la cultura granadina*, p. 104.

[211] Almagro y Cárdenas, 'El 2 de enero de 1879: recuerdos y proyectos'. I have not been able to find a copy of this article, even though Cárdenas himself claims in the magazine's third issue to have published exactly a year earlier (Almagro y Cárdenas, 'El 2 de enero de 1880'). Nevertheless, the main idea behind the article is summarised in his biography published later in the *Defensor de Granada* ('Antonio Almagro Cárdenas').

[212] J. A. González Alcantud, 'Reflejos de la Conferencia de Algeciras', p. 254.

being held, whose outcome would eventually lead to Spain being granted the right to a protectorate in Morocco.[213] A very similar conjunction of circumstances led to the publication in 1911 – by the same author – of an article citing the inscription in extenso, at a moment when Morocco was in the midst of a domestic crisis that would result, the following year, in the definitive establishment of the Franco-Spanish protectorate over the country. Apart from arguments calling for the development of a commercial and cultural influence over Morocco, the article added an intriguing point of detail to the mystery that surrounded Malek Salem, by claiming that he was not a poet, but a very wealthy and respected merchant of a town in Northern Morocco.[214] Malek Salem would make one more appearance as late as 1931, this time under the pen of the poet and historian from Tétouan, Mohammed Daoud (1901–84), who, rejoicing at the news of the proclamation of the Spanish Republic, addressed a letter of 'greetings and deep gratitude' to Granada through the mediation of the *Defensor*: 'A I remember the words of Saled Melan [*sic*] inscribed in the album of the Alhambra, I hope that, based on the past and thanks to the rapprochement between Moors and Andalusians, you, oh Granada, will place again on your forehead the crown of greatness and splendour our forebears had placed on it'.[215] Malek Salem managed even to

213 G. de Azcárate, 'Pensamiento de un Muslim'. This short articles quoted the last sentences of Malek Salem's text and ended with a wish: 'May God make that many of Meleksalom's compatriots share these feelings!' On the Conference of Algeciras and the role played by Granada and its Africanists, see González Alcantud, 'Reflejos de la Conferencia de Algeciras'.

214 G. de Azcárate, 'Intereses político-económicos de España en Marruecos'. This claim is all the more unlikely considering that it is based on the testimony of the Ottoman Grand Vizier Midhat Pasha, who had allegedly provided this information after seeing the inscription during his visit of the Alhambra. Although it is true – as we will see later – that Midhat Pasha did visit the Alhambra on 26 April 1877 and that his own inscription appears in the same volume as Malek Salem's, there is simply no reason or possibility that he should have known him. As to his qualification as a 'wealthy merchant', it is probable that the author had fished this information from Aureliano Ruiz's article published in the *Revista de Andalucía* in 1878 (see p. 135).

215 M. A. Daoud, 'Acercamiento andaluz: Cordial saludo de un moro de paz'. The text of this letter was republished two years later by one 'Doctor Pschrr' ('Acercamiento hispano-musulman: Granada y el mundo islámico'). We will come across Mohammed Daoud again later in a different context, as the recipient of a very interesting photograph of Shakīb Arslān taken

make inroads into Francoism: in 1951, when calling for the 'civilising mission' of France in Morocco, the Phalangist magazine *Nueva Alcarria* recalled once more the memory of 'Meleksalom', who 'begged for a common nationality between Christians and Muslims, between the descendants of the victors of the *Reconquista* and the sons of those fathers who fertilised our fields under the rule of the Nasrid dynasty'.[216]

---

in Cordoba (see, pp. 263–6). I find it interesting that a historian from Tétouan should have quoted from Malek Salem's text, despite its rather dubious character. Should we deduce from this that Mohammed Daoud considered him as likely to have existed and trustworthy, or did he simply find the text useful in message of communion addressed to the Granadan public? I cannot really say, but the documentation preserved at the Mohammed Daoud Foundation for the History and Culture of Tétouan may well offer some clues.

[216] E. Romero, 'Desde los Pirineos hasta el Atlas: nuestros apellidos'.

3

EAST: OTTOMANS AT THE ALHAMBRA

An Ottoman Ambassador in Granada

Although the connections between the Alhambra and the Maghreb and, more particularly, Morocco, were heavily marked by historical intimacy, the monument's cultural impact on the Arab and Islamic world throughout the nineteenth century extended all the way to the Orient – the Mashreq – and even beyond. Once again, the visitors' book reveals the existence of many travellers from these faraway lands, whose inscriptions form expressions of a – sometimes silent – homage paid to this monument of Arabo-Islamic civilisation.

Rather surprisingly, the first Muslim visitors to appear on the pages of the visitors' book of the Alhambra were not the Moroccans and other North Africans we have discovered in the preceding chapter, but Ottoman subjects coming from much more distant regions, both geographically and culturally. Of course, this statement is valid only as long as we exclude the Moroccan embassies from the seventeenth and eighteenth centuries mentioned earlier. Nevertheless, if we limit ourselves to the romantic vision of the Alhambra created by French and British authors in the early decades of the nineteenth century, and which came to dominate the mindset of travellers signing the visitors' book, one cannot help but observe that visitors from the Maghreb had disappeared from the scene, only to resurface – if my information is correct – in 1863. Yet it was twenty years earlier, on 19 July 1844, that the first Ottoman subject signed the visitors' book. This visitor was Keçecizade

Mehmed Fuad Efendi (1815–69), the ambassador sent on an extraordinary mission to Madrid to convey Sultan Abdülmecid's congratulations to Queen Isabella II (1830–1904, r. 1833–68) on the occasion of her coming of age, on 8 November of the preceding year (Figure 3.1).

Fuad Efendi had in common with the eighteenth-century Moroccan travellers and most of their successors of the second half of the nineteenth century the official nature of his mission, which set him apart from most of the Western visitors. From the Ottomans' point of view, this was a first, given that his closest predecessor, Ahmed Vasıf Efendi (?–1806), sent to Spain in 1787, had not been to Granada. Despite a residency of almost a year, his contact with Islamic remains had been limited to a visit to the library of the Escorial, where the sight of 'some ten Korans in ancient calligraphy and of countless works of jurisprudence, theology and prophetic tradition' had caused him 'nostalgia and sorrow'.[1] The inscription left by Fuad Efendi in the book matched the nature of his mission; he just listed his titles and qualifications, in Turkish and French: 'Fuad, envoy extraordinary of H. M. the Emperor of the Ottomans at the court of H. M. the Queen of Spain' (Figure 3.2).[2]

The ambassador was not the only one to sign the register. His secretary and brother-in-law, Mehmed Kâmil Bey (?–1879), known by the nickname the 'Pony of the Apocalypse',[3] introduced himself as 'secretary of the Imperial embassy' and signed in French, 'Kiamil'.[4] The third member of the delegation was Greek, most certainly an Ottoman subject, one Mikhail Dimitriadis, who styled himself, in his native language, as a 'guest of His Excellency the

[1] E. I. Menchinger, 'The Sefaretname of Ahmed Vasıf Efendi to Spain', p. 357. See also, *Relación Nueva en la que se describe el arribo y desembarco, que ha hecho en la ciudad de Barcelona el día 28. de julio de este año de 1787. el exc.mo señor enviado de la Sublime Puerta Otomana cerca de S. M. Católica*.

[2] AA, *libros de firmas*, 42, f° 52 v°, 19 July 1844. In Turkish: 'Taraf-ı Devlet-i Aliyye'den İspanya Devlet-i fahimesi nezdinde sefaretle memur Mehmed Fuad Efendi'. In French: 'Fuad, envoyé extraordinaire de S. M. l'Empereur des Ottomans près la cour de S. M. la Reine d'Espagne'.

[3] A popular nickname describing either a person of small height, or a schemer. Interestingly, Fuad Pasha's obituary in *The Times* humorously refers to him: '[Fuad] had with him at the time a secretary, of very small stature, whom he used to introduce as his miniature' (*The Times*, 26,362, 16 February 1869, p. 5).

[4] 'Mehmed Kâmil Bey kâtib-i sefaret-i seniyye'.

Figure 3.1 'Fuad Pasha, Kâtib Efendi (Secretary) of the Ministry of Foreign Affairs at the Ottoman Porte and Minister Plenipotentiary at the Paris Conferences, from a photograph by [Gustave] Legray', *L'Illustration*, 802 (10 July 1858), p. 17. Author's collection. A portrait of Fuad Efendi, now Fuad Pasha, some fifteen years after his mission to Spain, when he had risen to a prominent position in the Ottoman bureaucracy. With Mustafa Reşid Pasha's death in 1858, he would become one of the top two statesmen of the empire, together with Âli Pasha.

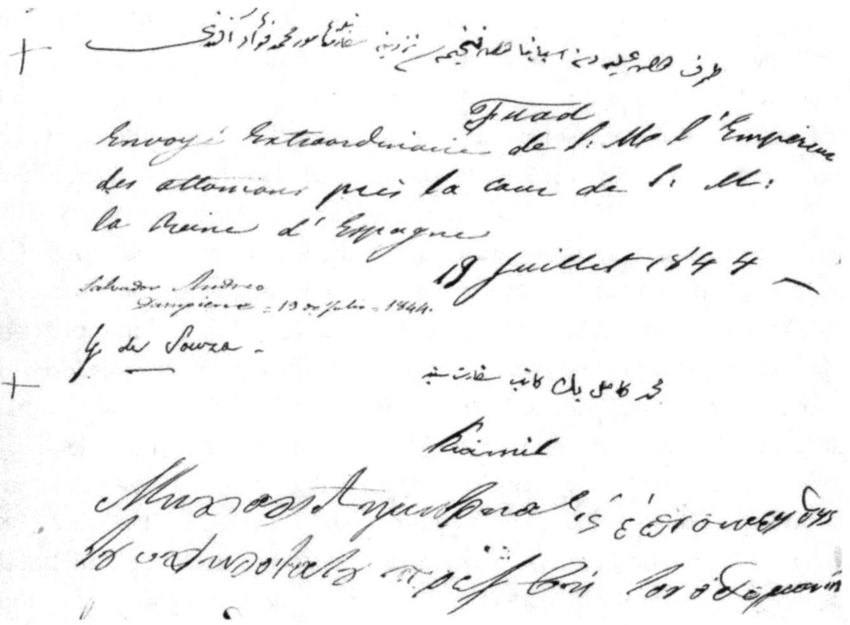

Figure 3.2 Inscriptions in the visitors' book by the ambassador Fuad Efendi, his secretary Mehmed Kâmil Bey, and his servant, Mikhail Dimitriadis, 19 July 1844. AA, *libros de firmas*, 42, fol. 52 v. © Archivo del Patronato de la Alhambra y Generalife. Fuad Efendi wrote down his titles and attributions in Turkish and in French; Kâmil Bey in Turkish and signed in French; Dimitriadis chose his native language to describe himself as the ambassador's 'guest'.

ambassador of the Ottomans',[5] although a report in the Granadan press seems to suggest that he was in fact Fuad Efendi's servant, which would probably explain the iffy spelling in his inscription.[6] Two Spanish signatures completed the party, corresponding to the two hosts accompanying the Ottoman mission. The first was Gerardo de Souza (?–1871), an official from the Ministry of Foreign Affairs, who, well acquainted with all things Ottoman thanks to several postings there, had been in charge of Fuad Efendi ever since his arrival

5 'Μιχαήλ Δημητριαδης επισκεπθης του υψηλοταατου πρεζβή τον cθομανόν' (*sic*, for Μιχαήλ Δημητριάδης επισκέπτης του υψηλοτάτου πρέσβη των Οθωμανών).

6 It was noted that Fuad Efendi was accompanied by his brother-in-law, M. Souza and a servant (*criado*) ('Llegada del embajador estraordinario de la Sublime Porta').

at Barcelona.[7] The second was Salvador Andreo Dampierre (1812–79), from Granada, representing the local government.[8]

Fuad Efendi's inscription was dry and lacked any trace of feelings or admiration. Yet he was not just anybody. As the son of the famous judge and poet Keçecizade İzzet Molla (1786–1829), he had started studying medicine before shifting to the Translation Bureau at the Sublime Porte, the hothouse of bureaucratic and diplomatic careers during the *Tanzimat* period of reforms. Following a posting as secretary at the Ottoman embassy in London during the Egyptian crisis of 1839–40, he had been appointed second interpreter of the Porte in 1843. That was when he was selected for a diplomatic mission with queens Isabella II of Spain and Maria II of Portugal. Promoted to the rank of pasha in 1855, several times minister of Foreign Affairs and Grand Vizier, Fuad Pasha became one of the major statesmen of the period, alongside Mustafa Reşid Pasha (1800–58) and Mehmed Emin Âli Pasha (1815–71). Apart from this brilliant political career, Fuad Efendi/Pasha was a man of culture, both Eastern and Western, who perfectly embodied the ideals and goals of the modernisation and Westernisation movement that started with the promulgation of the *Tanzimat* (reorganisation) edict of 1839. Given this profile, it seems impossible to imagine that he should have visited the Alhambra without a substantial intellectual and cultural background. Unfortunately, the few words he had scribbled on the page of the visitors' book make it impossible to guess his thoughts and emotions; once again, we will have to resort to other sources to try to give some meaning to this visit.

Luckily, as in the case of the Moroccan embassies, the Spanish press, both national and local, comes to our rescue by providing precious details on this

[7] The Spanish diplomat Gerardo de Souza y Castro had started his career in Constantinople as a '*jeune de langue*' or apprentice dragoman, studying Turkish and other Oriental languages. He was legation secretary from 1831 to 1841 and twice minister plenipotentiary in Constantinople, in 1847–52 and 1854–61. He was appointed minister at the Holy See in 1861–4 and retired in 1864, after which he passed away in January 1871.

[8] Following a degree in law, Dampierre became solicitor in 1834. As a prosecutor (*fiscal*) and military judge (*auditor de guerra*), he participated in the defence of the government of Granada against the Carlist movement in the 1830s. He played a significant role in the establishment of a high school and an academy in his town, as well as in the campaign for the restoration of the Alhambra in 1851.

mission. The reason for this was simple: this was the first time, in almost sixty years, that a 'Turk' had come this way, which was bound to titillate the curiosity of Spanish public opinion. Of course, this curiosity was heavily loaded with many clichés and stereotypes inherited from a common past that was, to say the least, rather ambiguous. It was also embedded in a more recently formed perception of the Orient as essentially different and particularly marked by exoticism. And yet, to the astonishment of the public, the man who landed in Barcelona on 23 May 1844 turned out to be rather disappointing in many ways:

> [Fuad Efendi] seems to be thirty to thirty-five years old; he is of ordinary height, with a dark complexion, expressive black eyes, black hair and an interesting, but hardly beautiful, physiognomy. He wears a European suit, speaks better French than Turkish and understands Italian and Spanish. He has a secretary, who is his wife's brother. His demeanour is very distinguished, and he seems to have frequented the salons of our society all his life. He has four servants, two French and two Turkish.[9]

During his stay in Barcelona, Fuad visited the archives of the Crown of Aragon, leaving a dedication in Turkish to the curator general, the historian Próspero de Bofarull y Mascaró (1777–1859).[10] On 11 June, he was received by the queen, to whom he presented his letter of credence with a short speech in French to which the sovereign replied in the same language.[11] On 8 July,

[9] *El Clamor público*, 36, 11 June 1844, p. 4. An almost identical portrait of Fuad Efendi was published in 'Fuad-Efendi, enviado estraordinario de la Sublime Puerta'. See also, *Oesterreichischer Beobachter*, 187, 5 July 1844, pp. 733–4. His obituary in *The Times* also bore witness to this, with a considerable dose of 'reverse' racism: 'His agreeable manners made him universally popular. In society he was the gayest of the gay, and he spoke French so fluently that but for his fez he might have passed for a Frenchman . . . Indeed, people could hardly believe that the elegant and cultivated person who spoke so well, who told such good stories and uttered witticisms that Talleyrand would not have disowned, and whose manners were so polished, could be a Turk' (*The Times*, 26,362, 16 February 1869, p. 5).

[10] M. Milá y Fontanals, *Noticia de la vida y escritos de Don Próspero de Bofarull y Mascaró*, p. 49, n. 1.

[11] *El Católico*, 1 547, 15 June 1844, p. 571; *El Clamor público*, 41, 16 June 1844, p. 1. For the text of Fuad Efendi's speech, see *Journal de Constantinople* II(108) (6 July 1844): 1.

he boarded the *Villa de Madrid*, with the intention of visiting the main towns of Andalusia before heading for Madrid.[12] He landed at Valencia on 9 July, where he was greeted by the mayor, José Campo Pérez (1817–89) and hosted by the Marquess of Serdañola. The press once again took note of his surprisingly European attire, 'with the exception of the bright red Greek cap from which hung a thick silk tassel'. His general outlook and his attitude 'revealed a cultivated man and a diplomat, very different from the idea that has formed in the past of the nation he belongs to'. During his short stay, Fuad Efendi found the time to visit the hospital, the prison, the cathedral and its relics, and to enjoy the panorama of the city from atop the medieval Tower of Miguelete.[13] The following day, 10 July, he reached Alicante, where he stayed for only a few hours, enough to visit his host, the Marquess of Algorfa's collection of paintings.[14] Two days later, he landed at Almeria and headed the same day for Malaga.[15]

In Granada, the municipality had previously prepared to host him at the archbishop's palace. However, fearing that the sight of a Muslim staying at such a holy abode might trigger some reactions, it was decided that he would be accommodated at the *fonda* de Minerva, an inn on the Plazuela de los Lobos.[16] The local press was looking forward to his arrival and had already expressed its expectations of a communion between this Muslim envoy and the very particular past of the city: 'The Turkish ambassador will find much to admire in this Oriental paradise, and it is to be hoped that he will remain some days more in this city.'[17] Fuad Efendi reached Granada by stagecoach on the evening of 17 July and was greeted by a crowd, 'who expected to find a prince wearing a great turban and a gorgeous Oriental costume, but whose illusions vanished at the sight of a young man in European garb, with no other distinguishing feature from an ordinary suit than a Greek cap with a thick silk tassel'.[18] Once he reached Granada, the local daily, *La Campana de la vela*,

[12] *El Católico*, 1 571, 11 July 1844, p. 91.

[13] *El Católico*, 1 573, 13 July 1844, p. 108.

[14] *El Clamor público*, 70, 20 July 1844, p. 3.

[15] *El Católico*, 1 580, 20 July 1844, p. 164.

[16] *Eco del comercio*, 575, 18 July 1844, p. 2. 'Among the best [hotels] are the new *Fonda de las Diligencias, La Minerva . . .*' (Ford, *A Hand-Book for Travellers in Spain*, vol. I, p. 359).

[17] *La Campana de la vela*, 40, 28 June 1844, p. 2.

[18] *El Espectador*, 952, 24 July 1844, pp. 3–4.

took over from the national press the duty of narrating in great detail the ambassador's sojourn. One thus learns that the local authorities had reconsidered their decision regarding his accommodation and had secured the archiepiscopal palace for him.[19] There, Fuad Efendi received the city's notables 'with much kindness and courtesy and conversed with them at length in very proper French'. A dinner was organised in his honour, and he drank to the health of all present. The announcement that was made to him of the decision to lodge him in the archbishop's palace offered him yet another opportunity to flaunt his excellent manners. After expressing all his gratitude and admiration for the hospitality with which he had been greeted everywhere in Spain, he added that his only regret was 'that the archbishop was not alive to grant him his blessing, as he had received that of the archbishop of Barcelona'.[20]

Clearly, Fuad Efendi was demolishing every cliché and stereotype associated with his identity one after the other. The following day, 18 July, was also filled with surprises that unfolded as the Ottoman envoy visited the city, guided by the Granadan authorities. At noon, he was taken to the cathedral and to the monastery of San Jéronimo, both located in the heart of the city, amidst a curious crowd, especially women. According to the *Campana de la vela*, he was highly impressed by the architecture of the monastery, the work of Diego de Siloé (1495–1563), and even more by the main chapel of the cathedral, as well as by the 'robust and harmonious music of the great organ':

> He examined with interest the paintings and sculptures by Cano, pausing with obvious attention before his beautiful Conception.[21] The same occurred in the

[19] The archbishop's palace was located between the squares of Bib-Rambla and Alonso Cano, just across from the cathedral and the Sagrario church, Ford, whose rather poor opinion of Granada I have already mentioned, calls this palace a '*casa de ratones*', a mousehole, taking up the expression, which, he claimed, the Granadans used for the Alhambra (Ford, *A Hand-Book for Travellers in Spain*, vol. I, p. 385).

[20] 'Llegada del embajador estraordinario de la Sublime Porta'. The Archbishop of Granada, Blas Joaquín Álvarez de Palma had died in 1837 and was replaced only in 1848, by Luis Antonio Folgueras y Sión (see, in Spanish, at: https://es.wikipedia.org/wiki/Anexo:Obispos_y_arzobispos_de_Granada).

[21] Ford gives a detailed description of this section of the cathedral: 'The dome is painted in white and gold. The effigies of Ferd. and Isab. kneel at the sides of the high altar: above and let into circular recesses are the colossal heads of Adam and Eve, carved and painted by Alonzo Cano;

> royal chapel, before the tombs of the great conqueror Ferdinand V and Isabella the Catholic. At the sight of the standards used during the triumphal entrance to Granada, he asked about the Arab banners, and then seized with veneration the sword, sceptre and crown of the Catholic king.[22]

The ambassador's day ended on a high note: 'At night, he went to the theatre, where he fulfilled one of his greatest wishes, that of watching a dance with castanets, and the municipality made sure that they performed five national *jaleos*.[23] There remained only one visit to be carried out, the most important one according to the local press. Indeed, given the interest Fuad Efendi had shown in the splendours of Catholic Granada, how could one not imagine that he must have been dying to contemplate the pearl of Muslim architecture that dominated the city?

> No sooner had he caught sight of Granada than he asked about the Alhambra, which he wished to admire. He also wanted to be given all the information available about his ancestors, and to do so, the political chief [of the province] proposed to introduce him to the young and distinguished Miguel Lafuente

---

by him also are the seven grand pictures relating to the Virgin, whose temple this is. They are her "Annunciation", "Conception", "Nativity", "Presentation", "Visitation", "Purification", and "Ascension". They can be closely examined from an upper gallery, and are coarsely painted, because destined to be seen from below, and at a distance' (Ford, *A Hand-Book for Travellers in Spain*, vol. I, p. 386). See also, Lafuente Alcántara, *El libro del viajero en Granada*, pp. 233–4. On the organ, the French *Guides Joanne* had this to say: 'The organ, of bad taste, has a very powerful sound and varied manuals' (Lavigne, *Itinéraire descriptif, historique et artistique de l'Espagne et du Portugal*, pp. 452–3).

22 'Llegada del embajador estraordinario de la Sublime Porta'. In his long description of the royal chapel, Ford does not mention standards or banners, but only 'the shields and badges of the Catholic sovereigns'. He does mention, without locating them, the royal attributes bequeathed to the chapel by the monarchs: 'the royal sword, with a singular semi-circular guard, a plain gold crown, a Gothic cross, two pixes . . . and the queen's own "missal"' (Ford, *A Hand-Book for Travellers in Spain*, vol. I, pp. 388–9). Lafuente Alcántara's guidebook is more accurate: 'Venerable antiquities are preserved in the sacristy: the very missal used by the Catholic queen for her prayers . . .; the sceptre, crown and sword of the Catholic king; the banners that the Christians flew from the crenels of the Alhambra . . .' (Lafuente Alcántara, *El libro del viajero en Granada*, p. 242).

23 'Llegada del embajador estraordinario de la Sublime Porta'.

> Alcántara, chronicler of the Kingdom of Granada and one of the persons most capable of providing him with an account of all the monuments.[24]

The choice of Miguel Lafuente Alcántara (1817–50) as cicerone was a wise one. This young solicitor and historian from Malaga was a great specialist of the region and the city; he had published a very detailed guidebook of the city for travellers, soon to be followed by a history of Granada and the neighbouring provinces in four volumes.[25] We have already seen, in the case of Moroccan ambassadors, to what extent the Spanish press was inclined to ascribe to these Muslim visitors intentions and feelings, which actually corresponded to their own expectations. In Fuad Efendi's case, while it is possible, even probable, that he did not qualify the Moors of Granada as his ancestors, it is almost certain that he did express as strong desire to visit the Alhambra. The following issue of the *Campana de la vela* gave an account of this visit, which seems to corroborate this interest:

> The ambassador Fuad-Effendi has visited the Alhambra with enthusiasm and has enjoyed in an extraordinary way these ruins. He read with extreme ease and translated into French the inscriptions on the walls, thus demonstrating his archaeological knowledge, for we know well that most of the inscriptions of the Alhambra are in the Kufic script. He also went to the Cartuja and at the sight of the ravages of the revolution, he exclaimed with indignation: 'The hordes of Africa would not have done this much'.[26]

Compared with the treatment Fuad Efendi's arrival received in the press, this short paragraph is somewhat disappointing. One would have wanted to learn more. Luckily, we have two additional witnesses, who allow for a slightly better understanding of the conditions under which this visit unfolded. The first is the German botanist Heinrich Moritz Wilkomm (1821–95), who, during his botanical explorations in Spain, happened to be at the Alhambra on the day of the Ottoman envoy's visit. He left a very lively testimony of this moment,

[24] 'Llegada del embajador estraordinario de la Sublime Porta'.

[25] Lafuente Alcántara, *El libro del viajero en Granada*; Lafuente Alcántara, *Historia de Granada* (see n. 26, p. 28).

[26] *La Campana de la vela*, 47, 23 July 1844, p. 4.

which once again takes up the theme of the public disappointment caused by Fuad Efendi's 'civilised' outlook:

> I would have missed this pleasure if the Turkish ambassador Fuad Efendi had not come to Granada on 19 July. A remarkable spectacle was organised in his honour, and I was thus given to see the Alhambra in all its splendour from the times of Boabdil and Mulay-Hassan.[27] There was a huge crowd at the palace that day, for everyone in Granada was impatient to see a Turk, be it only once. But all these good people were quite disappointed, since the Muslim did not appear as they had imagined him, like a true Moor wearing a turban and a caftan, with a sabre to his waist, but dressed in a French-style modern tailcoat and no other clue than his fez to reveal that he was a faithful Muslim and a subject of the Porte. Fuad-Effendi, of ordinary presence, stayed several days at the Alhambra to study the Arab inscriptions of the palace.[28]

The second witness to the scene was none other than Miguel Lafuente Alcántara, the young historian who had been assigned to accompany Fuad Efendi at the Alhambra and to inform him on the monument's history. When he published his history of Granada, one year after Fuad Efendi's passage, he included two anecdotes concerning his encounter with the Ottoman envoy. The first had to do with a square-shaped Almohad coin, discovered in Almeria, which he presented to Fuad Efendi, who 'was kind enough to accept it'.[29] The second was related to the famous representation of ten Moorish kings painted on the ceiling of the Hall of Kings, which Lafuente Alcántara believed dated from the Nasrid period, contrary to those who thought it was of a later – therefore Spanish – time, due to the Koranic prohibition against human and animal figures. The historian based his argument on other examples of such representations, starting with the lions of the fountain, and ended up referring to the authority of the Ottoman ambassador on this matter: 'Fuad Efendi, the

[27] Abū al-Ḥasan ʿAlī (?–1485), or Muley Hacén in Spanish, was the penultimate Nasrid ruler of Granada (1464–82 and 1483–5) and the father of the last sultan, Muḥammad XII, better known as Boabdil. He is one of the rulers accused of having perpetrated the massacre of the Abencerrages.

[28] M. Willkomm, *Zwei Jahre in Spanien und Portugal*, vol. II, p. 142.

[29] Lafuente Alcántara, *Historia de Granada*, vol. III, p. 123, n. 1.

ambassador extraordinary of the Sublime Porte, who visited Granada last year, in 1843 [*sic*], admitted that there existed many monuments of this kind, albeit imperfect, throughout Muslim states'.[30]

All this information suggests that Fuad Efendi's visit had indeed been very active and that he had personally engaged in conversations with the people around him, most notably his guide. He had left a very good impression, proving that he had sufficient knowledge to decipher some of the inscriptions and to come up with general remarks on Islamic art and civilisation. Should one take literally the mention of his 'archaeological knowledge' and deduce that he had really attempted an epigraphic survey of the monument? Probably not, considering the limited mastery of Arabic by most Ottomans, even educated, especially when it came to deciphering the truly challenging Kufic script. Most likely, perhaps incited by some of those present, he just read some of the most obvious ones, such as the ubiquitous Nasrid motto of 'There is no victor but God' (*la ghāliba illā Allah* لا غالب الا الله), or any other inscription, made legible by its Koranic origin. That would most certainly have been enough to convince and impress the onlookers, even though for the more erudite, such as Lafuente Alcántara, reading the inscriptions would have proved to be absolutely useless, as all the texts had been well known for quite some time.

Fuad Efendi: Mind and Soul

What overall assessment can we derive from this relatively well-documented visit, considering both the observations and expectations of the Spaniards, on the one hand, and the actions and probable intentions of Fuad Efendi, on the other? Once again, the laconic character of his inscription in the visitors' book does not allow for speculation on the nature of his feelings; yet it seems possible to draw some conclusions from the bits and pieces of information we have gathered on his comings and goings. First, we should note a rather remarkable balance between the Catholic and Islamic remains of the city he visited. Fuad Efendi spent one day visiting the cathedral and monastery and devoted the other to the discovery of the Alhambra. In both cases, they seem to have been 'studious' visits, engaging the diplomat's curiosity, be it in the case of the Arab inscriptions or of Cano's *Immaculate Conception*. Unlike the Moroccan

[30] Lafuente Alcántara, *Historia de Granada*, vol. III, p. 152, n. 1.

visitors we have already seen, Fuad Efendi is presented as being erudite, showing a greater penchant for history than for emotions. While the Granadan press did ascribe him a wish to learn about the fate of his 'ancestors', it never suggested that the visit to the Alhambra triggered the tears and lamentations so often expected from Moroccan visitors.

It seems likely that this balance corresponded rather accurately to the Ottoman ambassador's cultural stance. A cultivated polyglot familiarised with Western ways and customs, it seems plausible that Fuad Efendi was aiming at learning about both sides of a history he probably knew about through Western sources. The scene where he is depicted as holding Ferdinand's sceptre, crown and sword – all three at a time? – is simply fascinating to anyone familiar with the way in which Western travellers visited the museum that would be opened in Constantinople only two years later. Indeed, when the Ottomans, in their desire to imitate the West, turned the Hagia Eirene Church, neighbouring the Hagia Sophia and the imperial palace, into the semblance of a museum,[31] European visitors discovered in its nave a collection of arms, armour, standards and other martial objects going back to the conquest of Constantinople and even to the Crusades. In 1850, Gustave Flaubert described his visit in the following terms:

> A nice gun room with vaults and a dome, its naves filled with rifles in poor condition; at the back, on the upper floor, invaluable ancient weapons, Persian helmets inlaid in Damascene style, coats of mail, most of them ordinary, great Normand swords to be held in two hands. Mohammed's sabre, straight, wide and flexible, like a whalebone, its hilt covered in a green skin; everybody took it and brandished it, except me.[32]

Frenchmen brandishing Mehmed the Conqueror's sabre in Istanbul and an Ottoman seizing Ferdinand's in Granada – pure coincidence, of course, but one that shows to what extent Fuad Efendi had internalised this historicist modernity, which viewed with curiosity the relics of bygone civilisations now relegated to the romantic imagination of the West. If one needed yet another

[31] On the extremely superficial and ephemeral nature of this first version of the Imperial Museum, see Eldem, 'The (Still)Birth of the Ottoman "Museum": A Critical Reassessment'.

[32] G. Flaubert, *Voyage en Orient (1849–1851)*, p. 248.

proof of his deep acculturation, it would suffice to recall his alleged words during the visit of the Cartuja (Charterhouse) of Granada: 'The hordes of Africa would not have done this much.' The context had to do with the Carlist War of the 1830s, which led in 1836 to the *desamortización*, that is the confiscation of Church properties under the Mendizábal government, including this particular Carthusian monastery, already plundered by Sébastiani during the French occupation, which was eventually sold to a Sevillian speculator. The new owner had demolished its beautiful cloister, most of the monks' cells, as well as the abbot's residence, while part of the decorative elements, including splendid tiles, were sold by auction.[33] Why had they brought Fuad Efendi to view the ruins of this monastery, located at the other end of the city? We will probably never know; at most can we surmise that his hosts had Carlist sympathies and wanted to share with him the memory of their suffering.[34] Whatever the context may have been, the striking point from the perspective of this study is to note the clearly Europocentric, not to say colonialist, undertones of the expression 'African hordes' he had used to express his indignation at the mention of such spoliation. Without going as far as to interpret it as an insult to the Andalusian heritage he had come to admire – there is little doubt that the Africa he had in mind was much more southern – this remark showed to what extent Fuad Efendi could appropriate a Western discourse, in what sounds like a prophetic sign of the Orientalist attitude that would eventually characterise a sizeable portion of the Ottoman political and cultural elite in the following decades.

The Ottoman ambassador stayed in Granada for a few days longer. Did he really spend them at the Alhambra, studying the inscriptions of the palace as Moritz Wilkomm claimed? At any rate, the press does not say anything about it but records only one last activity in which Fuad Efendi participated while still in Granada, namely, attending a reception given by the captain general of the garrison of Granada, José Laureano Sanz (1793–1868) on the

[33] Lafuente Alcántara, *El libro del viajero en Granada*, pp. 257–9; Ford, *Hand-Book for Travellers in Spain*, vol. I, p. 391; J. M. Barrios Rozúa, *Reforma urbana y destrucción del patrimonio histórico en Granada*, pp. 142–78, 520–9.

[34] Interestingly, Fuad Efendi's remark was recalled almost fifty years later in *El Liberal* when referring to the plunder of convents and monasteries in the 1840s (*El Liberal*, 51, 18 March 1890, p. 3).

occasion of Saint Christine's day, whose name the queen mother bore. Toasts were made to the health of the sovereigns, of the ministers and administrators of the realm, of the pope and even of the Ottoman sultan; Fuad Efendi himself raised his glass to the queen's health and to Granadan hospitality.[35] The *Campana de la vela* gave no details on this, but if we are to believe the *Heraldo*, the Ottoman envoy 'toasted only with pure water'; however, his secretary and brother-in-law Kâmil Bey 'had no qualms about honouring the excellent wines he was served'.[36]

Fuad Efendi left Granada on the evening of 26 July, after spending over a week in the city. However, his departure was much less glorious than his arrival. Once again, his Westernised demeanour was cause for disappointment, but this time with no extenuating circumstances:

> On the night of Friday 26, Fuad-Effendi and his secretary Kiamil left our city in order to roam the other provinces of Andalusia. Upon his departure, all those who had served him expected a gesture of Oriental generosity from him, but he acted like a Jew taking French leave. He was educated in Paris and was still following these customs: very sweet words, the most cordial propositions and very few good deeds. Had he grown up in these lands, he would have been very different with regard to generosity.[37]

On this wrong note, which the national press seems to have dutifully ignored, the Ottoman envoy headed for Malaga, where he boarded a ship to Cadiz, after a short stop at Algeciras.[38] On 1 August, he reached Cadiz, where he was hosted by Don Sebastián Martínez Pinillo's widow.[39] From there, he proceeded to Seville, where he arrived on 5 August and was accommodated in a mansion known as 'Andueza', property of one Miguel María Domínguez.[40] On 8 August, he was still in Seville, whose major monuments he visited,[41] before

[35] *La Campana de la vela*, 48, 26 July 1844, p. 4.

[36] *El Heraldo*, 660, 31 July 1844, p. 3.

[37] *La Campana de la vela*, 30, 2 August 1844, p. 3.

[38] *El Castellano*, 2 492, 6 August 1844, p. 2.

[39] *El Clamor público*, 86, 8 August 1844, p. 4; *Eco del comercio*, 593, 8 August 1844, p. 4.

[40] *El Clamor público*, 88, 10 August 1844, p. 3; *El Heraldo*, 669, 10 August 1844, p. 4; *El Clamor público*, 89, 11 August 1844, p. 3.

[41] *El Clamor público*, 90, 13 August 1844, p. 4.

embarking on the last leg of his Spanish journey, Madrid, where he arrived on 15 August and was lodged at the Palace of Buena Vista.[42]

Fuad Efendi's tour of Spain had lasted over a month, during which time he had been completely diverted from his diplomatic mission, which proved, if need be, the importance he attached to this expedition. His own silence was compensated by the wealth of information published in the Spanish press, especially local, which has enabled us to reach some conclusions on the meaning and circumstances of his journey. Fuad Efendi was undoubtedly conscious of the historic and artistic significance of the monuments he visited, both Arab and Spanish, and much more so than his Moroccan colleagues of the years to come. On the other hand, he seemed to lack the emotional engagement the Spanish press ascribed to the visitors from the Maghreb. Was it because he was not an Arab and, consequently, incapable of connecting with the cultural roots and references that would have enriched his curiosity with an emotional dimension available only to the descendants of al-Andalus? Or else, was he too 'white', too Westernised, to allow for such outpourings? If that was the case, should we see in the 'medievalist' scene that unfolded in the royal chapel an expression of a form of romanticism he might have espoused in emulation of the West?

It is greatly frustrating not to be able to answer these questions due to the lack of any documentation on the Ottoman side, both in terms of Fuad Efendi/Pasha's personal life and of possible traces of his career in the Porte's diplomatic and administrative archives. Indeed, despite the importance of the question of whether his Andalusian journey was from the start planned as part of the mission to which Fuad Efendi had been assigned, or whether, on the contrary, it was the result of his personal initiative, the Ottoman documentation does not provide any form of information on this matter. True, the first items in the Spanish press, even before he landed at Barcelona, already claimed that 'Fuad-Effendi considers visiting our beautiful southern provinces',[43] which would imply that this trip had already been planned well before. Towards the end of June, dispatches from Barcelona announced that 'it seems that Fuad-Effendi will leave soon for Andalusia, in order to visit, upon express orders

[42] *El Católico*, 1 605, 16 August 1844, p. 362.

[43] *El Clamor público*, 14, 20 May 1844, p. 4.

of His Majesty the Sultan, the Arab monuments located in these provinces'.[44] Was that really part of his mission, or was the daily just pre-empting what it thought was evidently the case?

On the contrary, a Spanish document found in the Ottoman archives seems to suggest that the decision was taken on Fuad Efendi's own initiative, and not commanded by his sovereign. Indeed, in a letter addressed to him on 8 July, Queen Isabella assured the sultan that 'Your envoy wishing to travel through some provinces of our Realm', everything would be done to ensure that his journey should be as comfortable as it would be enjoyable, and that he would be greeted with all the honours worthy of his rank in every land he visited. Interestingly, in the Turkish version of the letter, the verb 'travelling' (*recorrer*) in the original had been translated as '*seyr ü temaşa etmek*' (viewing and admiring), which corresponded word for word to the most common formula used by the Ottoman bureaucracy to describe (and authorise) the activity of Western diplomats and travellers wishing to visit ancient sites and curiosities, especially the mosques and palaces of the capital.[45] Alas, there is nothing in the Ottoman documentation as to the reasons that might have incited Fuad Efendi to undertake a journey to Andalusia. A draft of an answer to one of his letters simply notes that he would have to spend about three months in Spain.[46] As to his own reports, they consisted only of a list of the presents, decorations and dispatches he had received in his name and in that of his master. Unfortunately, he seems to have felt no need to write an account of his embassy (*sefaretname*) or a travelogue (*seyahatname*) that might have enlightened us on this matter.

And yet, despite the absence of any concrete information on the reasons behind his Andalusian tour, his death, twenty-five years later, triggered a flood of explicit references to his personal commitment to the heritage of

[44] *El Clamor público*, 33, 3 July 1844, p. 4. Without referring to his official mission, the *Diario constitucional de Palma* came to the same conclusion: 'We know that [Fuad Efendi] will go directly to Malaga, from where he will head to Granada, Cordoba, Seville and other towns of southern Spain, which have preserved so many memories of the past rule of the Arabs in this land' (*Diario constitucional de Palma*, 18, 18 July 1844, p. 4).

[45] 'Deseoso Vuestro Enviado de recorrer algunas provincias de nuestro Reino, procuarémos que para él sea este viage cómodo y agradable, y no dudéis que en todas partes será recibido con afecto, tratado con agasajo y aprecio' (Turkish State Archives, Ottoman Archives (BOA), İ HR 27/1254, Barcelona, 8 July 1844).

[46] BOA, A DVN 9/49, n.d., c. July 1844.

al-Andalus. Fuad, now a pasha, had attained the highest positions in government, coupled with an international reputation that mirrored the role he had played at the very top of the Ottoman administration. His demise in Nice thus gave the international press an opportunity to celebrate the memory of this great man and to remind the public of his brilliant career. Only a few days after his death, a two-column obituary in the French daily *La Presse* noted that he had returned from his mission in Spain 'covered in decorations and bringing with him, on the one hand, a charming poem on the Alhambra and, on the other, a report to the sultan, which spoke of the width and perspicacity of his political mind'.[47] The same information was taken up by other newspapers, such as the *Morning Post*,[48] the *New York Tribune* and the *Chicago Tribune*,[49] *The Times*,[50] *Freeman's Journal and Daily Commercial Advertiser*,[51] the *Manchester Courier and Lancashire General Advertiser* and the *Nottinghamshire Guardian*,[52] *The Sunday Times*,[53] *La Época*,[54] and the *Illustrated London News*,[55] among many others.

[47] 'Fuad-Pacha', *La Presse*, 15 February 1869, p. 1.

[48] *Morning Post*, 29,699, 15 February 1869, p. 4: 'Also, what may not be so generally remembered, he was the author of a poem entitled "The Alhambra" . . .'.

[49] 'Obituary. Fuad Pasha', *New York Tribune*: 'He was possessed of superior literary attainments, proof of which he has left behind in an Ottoman grammar, and a poem entitled "The Alhambra", outbodying his recollections of Spain during his mission to that country'; 'Obituary. Mehmed Fuad Pasha', *Chicago Tribune*: '. . . on his return from Spain, he embodied his recollections of that country in a very popular poem, "The Alhambra"'.

[50] *The Times*, 26,362, 16 February 1869, p. 5: 'He visited Granada and composed a poem, which was said to have considerable merit, on the Alhambra '.

[51] 'Death of Fuad Pasha': 'About this time, Fuad published his poem, "The Alhambra", which embodies his recollections of Spain, and gained for him great popularity with his countrymen.'

[52] 'The Late Fuad Pasha', *Manchester Courier and Lancashire General Advertiser* (text identical to that of *The Times*); 'The Death of Fuad Pasha', *Nottinghamshire Guardian* (text identical to that of *Freeman's Journal*).

[53] 'Obituary', *The Sunday Times*, 2,393, 21 February 1869, p. 8: 'At 30 years of age he published a poem, entitled "The Alhambra," which was very popular.'

[54] *La Época*, 22 February 1869, p. 2: 'The son of the famous Turkish poet, Izzed Mollah, he was known for light poems; he did not forget this youthful passion when he went to Spain in 1846 [*sic*] as ambassador extraordinary, as he brought back from this journey a poem on the Alhambra.'

[55] 'Fuad Pasha', *Illustrated London News*, 1,527, 27 February 1869, p. 219: 'He was the author of a poem entitled "The Alhambra" . . .'

Where did this information come from? It seems that it originated from Gustave Vapereau's (1819–1906) famous biographical dictionary, whose first edition (1858) included a detailed record on Fuad Pasha, describing his numerous merits and achievements. A passage from this text emphasised his talents as a diplomat and the success of his mission to Isabella II:

> Soon enough he was assigned to the mission of complimenting the Queen of Spain on the occasion of her accession and he obtained the greatest success at the court of Madrid. Nothing in him betrayed the old Turk. He spoke French to perfection, was as witty as M. de Talleyrand and displayed the gallantry of an Abencerrage. He fulfilled a similar mission with Queen Dona Maria [of Portugal] and was bestowed the grand collar of the Tower and Sword, after having received that of Isabella the Catholic. He brought back to Constantinople, after an absence of seven to eight months, a poem on the Alhambra, much acclaimed by the literati, and a report to the Sultan, whose novel and interesting views have been praised by statesmen.[56]

In all evidence, it was in this biographical note, immediately accessible upon the pasha's death, that the press and contemporary authors found all the relevant information on his career, including his Spanish adventure.[57] The vision of an Oriental 'redeemed' by his knowledge of French was a compliment which the French paid only with parsimony; on the other hand, thanks to Chateaubriand and his followers, the reference to the 'gallantry of an Abencerrage' was a rather common Orientalist cliché that seemed particularly appropriate in this context. This leaves us with two concrete elements that cannot be reduced to simple rhetoric: the poem on the Alhambra and the report submitted to the sultan. The latter is obviously of no great significance

[56] 'Fuad-Mehmed-Pacha', G. Vapereau, *Dictionnaire universel des contemporains*, p. 708.

[57] See, for example, in chronological order, 'Fuad Pasha', *The Spectator*, 17 August 1861, p. 15; B. Poujoulat, *La Vérité sur la Syrie et l'expédition française*, p. 327; 'Fuad, Mehmed Pasha', *Men of the Time*, pp. 334–5; *Diario de Pernambuco*, 6 September 1867, p. 2; 'Fuad-Méhémet-Pacha', *Annuaire encyclopédique*, cols 697–9; 'Fuad, Mehmed', *The American Annual Cyclopædia*, vol. IX, pp. 285–6; 'Fuad, Mehmed Pasha', *Beeton's Modern European Celebrities*, p. 95; F. I. Scudamore, *France in the East*, p. 215; 'Fuad Pasha, Mahmud [*sic*]', L. C. Sanders, *Celebrities of the Century*, p. 457; 'Fuad Pasha, Mehmed', *The Encyclopædia Britannica*, vol. IX, p. 707.

for this study; moreover, it seems likely that it might have derived from a confusion with the pamphlet the pasha published anonymously in 1853 on the 'Holy Places' of Jerusalem to counter Russian claims and which received much attention on the eve of the Crimean War.[58] From our perspective, then, it would be quite sufficient to focus on the poem he allegedly composed to prove that his visit to the Alhambra had indeed left an emotional, intellectual and literary mark on the young Fuad Efendi. However, the said poem is nowhere to be found. Worse, I have not been able to find the slightest mention of it in contemporary Ottoman or later Turkish sources. This is all the more surprising if one considers the extensive coverage that Fuad Pasha's death received in the local press – in Turkish, French or English – especially during the days following his funeral in Istanbul. All these newspapers listed the details of the statesman's life and career, including his short mission to Spain, but without any reference to his mysterious poem on the Alhambra.[59]A single exception seems to confirm the rule: on 15 February 1869, a few days after his demise in Nice and two weeks before his funeral, the daily *La Turquie* devoted a paragraph of its obituary to the missing ode:

> After having fulfilled a similar mission with Queen Dona Maria of Portugal, he returned to Constantinople, bringing with him a poem on the Alhambra, much acclaimed by the literati and the only copies of which, we have been told, were lost in the fire that consumed his *konak* (mansion) in 1864, and a report to the Sultan on the men and manners of Europe.[60]

The explanation provided by *La Turquie* is tempting, but the description of the poem is too close to Vapereau's wording not to seem suspicious. One can

[58] *La Vérité sur la question des lieux-saints par quelqu'un qui la sait.*

[59] See, for example, *Ruzname-i Ceride-i Havadis*, 1,093, 3 Zilkade 1285/17 February 1869, p. 4,369; 1,101, 17 Zilkade 1285/1 March 1869, pp. 4,401–2; 1,103, 19 Zilkade 1285/3 March 1869, pp. 4,409–11; 1,104, 20 Zilkade 1285/4 March 1869, p. 4,413; 1,107, 25 Zilkade 1285/9 March 1869, pp. 4,425; 1,112, 2 Zilhicce 1285/16 March 1869, p. 4,445; 1,115, 6 Zilhicce 1285/20 March 1869, pp. 4,457–78; 'The Burial of Fuad Pasha'; 'Funérailles de Fuad Pacha' *The Levant Herald*, 1 March 1869, p. 3; 'Les funérailles de Fuad Pacha', *La Turquie*, 1 March 1869, p. 2; 'Fuad Pasha', *The Levant Herald*, 2 March 1869, p. 2; 'Funérailles de Fuad Pacha', *La Turquie*, 5 March 1869, p. 2; 'Réminiscences de Fuad Pacha'.

[60] *La Turquie*, 15 February 1869, p. 2.

imagine that the anonymous author of the item, having read the pasha's biography in Vapereau's dictionary, copied it as did everybody else, but also tried to investigate locally what the fate of the poem might have been. It seems, however, that they came up with little more than hearsay ('we have been told'), which sounded more like an educated guess than a proven fact. Indeed, if the poem had been known for some twenty years before its only copy was lost in a fire, would there not have been a trace of it, as for the pasha's other works? Moreover, if the information in *La Turquie* was accurate, would it not have been taken up by numerous other publications published in the following days, months or years? And yet, all the works of some significance which one would have rightly expected to reflect any additional information on the subject remain absolutely silent on the matter. Ahmed Lutfi Efendi's chronicle,[61] Şemseddin Sami's encyclopaedia[62] or the biographies of the last grand viziers by İbnülemin Mahmud Kemal İnal[63] mention at most some of his works of poetry without ever referring to an ode to the Alhambra. Like all published sources, a manuscript anonymous biography preserved in the Ottoman state archives is also content with noting the success of his mission to Spain and the wonder caused by his Western appearance.[64] Strangely, the only 'Oriental' source that does mention this poem seems to have been a compilation of biographies published in 1899 in New York, in Arabic, by one Yūsuf Naʿmān Maʿlūf, where the pasha is said to have returned from Spain with a *divan* (a collection of poetry) bearing the title of the Alhambra. This inflated version of the story is hardly credible, as Maʿlūf's misspelling of Alhambra in Arabic

[61] Ahmed Lutfi, *Vak'anüvîs Ahmed Lûtfî Efendi Tarihi*, vols VI–VIII, p. 1153. Lutfi says practically nothing on Fuad's mission to Spain.

[62] 'Fuad Paşa', in Şemseddin Sami, *Kamusü'l-A'lâm*, vol. V, pp. 3,440–1. Şemseddin Sami Bey praises his knowledge of Arabic and Oriental literature, his poetic skills in Turkish, his wit, his command of French and the excellent grammar he published with Cevdet Pasha, but says absolutely nothing of a poem on the Alhambra.

[63] 'Mehmed Füad Paşa', in İ. M. K. İnal, *Osmanlı Devrinde Son Sadrâzamlar*, vol. I, pp. 149–95. İnal, whose almost obsessive passion for systematically collecting anecdotes about the individuals whose biographies he wrote is well-known, speaks of Fuad Pasha's poetic merit and even lists some of his poems, but does not say a word on the Alhambra, or even on Andalusia or Spain.

[64] BOA, Y EE 31/31, 'Biographie de Son Altesse Fuad Pacha', n.d.

as الهمبره (Al-Hambra) instead of الحمراء (Al-Ḥamra') is an unforgivable barbarism that betrays his use of Western sources.[65]

The discrepancy between Western sources claiming that Fuad Pasha had composed an ode to the Alhambra and the silence of Ottoman and Turkish sources on this matter is not a minor one. This dilemma could be solved by speculating in either direction. On the one hand, one could easily claim that there cannot be smoke without fire and that Western authors, starting with Vapereau, had no reason to come up with this anecdote had there not been some truth to it. This is all the more plausible if one considers that the biographical dictionaries of the time generally collected their information from the individuals themselves and, in any case, gave them the possibility of going over the record before publication.[66] Given this, it seems unlikely that wrong or fictive information could have appeared in Vapereau's who's who without the consent of the individual concerned, unless they were complicit. On the other hand, one would be justified in claiming that if such a poem did really exist, a trace of it would necessarily have remained in Ottoman sources. I must admit that I feel torn between these two extremes. While my strong propensity for scepticism incites me to doubt the very existence of the poem, I cannot either discard the possibility that I may simply have failed to find the clues that would have led me to it, while earlier researchers have simply never looked for it. After all, is there any stronger argument in favour of Western documentation than the simple fact that, without the information provided by the European – and more particularly Spanish – sources I have used, the Ottoman and Turkish documentation alone would never have allowed me to discover that Fuad Pasha had visited the Alhambra?[67] To make matters worse, or

[65] Y. N. Ma'lūf, *Khizānat al-Ayyām fī Tarājim al-'Iẓām*, p. 211.

[66] 'Finally, before addressing the question of publicity, we have no fear to contact all the persons interested in our work, and request the most recent information from those whose life or achievements draw the attention of the public and make them worthy of the honour of a biography' (Vapereau, *Dictionnaire universel des contemporains*, p. iii).

[67] The only trace I have been able to find in the Ottoman press of Fuad Efendi's visit to the Alhambra is a short item published in the French-language press of the imperial capital on 26 August 1844, no less than a month and a half after the event: 'Fuad Efendi has visited the Alhambra with enthusiasm; he has translated with great ease into French the inscriptions carved on the walls' (*Journal de Constantinople*, II (118), 26 August 1844, p. 2). There is little

rather more complicated, I should bring up one last convergence that seems to have connected Fuad Pasha to the Alhambra at the very end of his life. Indeed, the mausoleum, which was erected on the site of his grave was in the purest Moresque style, like many other public and religious edifices built in the 1860s (Figure 3.3).[68] Many art historians have noted this peculiarity, which they have interpreted as yet another reflection of an imperial policy aimed at using this

Figure 3.3 Fuad Pasha's mausoleum. Photograph by Félix Bonfils, undated, after 1870. Getty Research Institute, Los Angeles (96.R.14 (C14.3)). The mausoleum was built in 1869–70, following the pasha's demise in Nice on 12 February 1869, in the purest Moresque style. Was this choice linked to his Andalusian journey some twenty-five years earlier, or just the result of the popularity of this style in Istanbul during the 1860s?

---

doubt that the newspaper got this information from the French press, which in turn borrowed it from the Spanish newspapers: 'The Ottoman ambassador, Fuad-Effendi, is presently visiting the main monuments of Spain. At the Alhambra, he has demonstrated his familiarity with archaeology; he has fluently translated into French the inscriptions covering the walls, despite their being written in the Kufic script. From there he went to the Charterhouse; while contemplating the ruins of this edifice, which suffered so much at the hands of the revolutionaries, *El Castellano* claims that he exclaimed: "The hordes of Africa would not have done this much"' (*La Presse*, 2 August 1844, p. 3). Interestingly, of all the information provided by *La Presse*, the *Journal de Constantinople* kept only the epigraphic anecdote.

[68] H. Eraktan, 'Fuad Paşa Camii ve Türbesi'; T. Saner, 'Fuad Paşa Türbesi'.

style in order to give a historical character to the architectural realisations of Sultan Abdülaziz's reign (1861–76). This, however, is a complex issue to which I will return further in the study.

Ottoman Diversity

In many ways, Fuad Efendi played a pioneering role. He was at the same time the first Muslim and the first Ottoman subject to sign the visitors' book of the Alhambra. Moreover, his visit was a momentous one, both for him, if we are to believe the Granadan press and the literary merit that was ascribed to him later, and for the witnesses and observers of this first highly publicised confrontation of an 'Oriental' with the remains of his presumed forebears. That said, one should not overestimate the significance of a contact between the Ottoman Empire and the Andalusian heritage, which would remain for long a rare, if not unique occurrence. After all, if almost sixty years earlier, despite a stay of over a year in Spain, the Ottoman ambassador Vasıf Efendi did not visit Andalusia and the Alhambra, it may well have been because he lacked the cultural references that would have made this journey meaningful and worthwhile. Fuad Efendi, on the contrary, belonged to a new elite, whose intellectual profile and horizon had been widened by the empire's opening towards the West. In all likelihood, if he had managed to grasp the importance of the Alhambra and of the Islamic heritage in Spain, it was through the mediation of Western works, all the more so since it would take another fifteen years before the publication of the first book in Turkish on the topic, Ziya Pasha's (1829–80) *History of al-Andalus*, which we will take up later. In a sense, Fuad Efendi was the exception confirming the rule of a general lack of interest and knowledge on part of the 'Turks'.

The use I have just made of 'Turk' to qualify the identity of some Ottoman subjects is evidently problematic. Normally, I make it a point to refrain from this laxism in terminology, whose main danger is to reproduce ahistorical categories so typical of both Western Orientalism and Turkish nationalism. Clearly, at least until the rise of Arab and Turkish nationalism at the turn of the twentieth century, the main criterion of differentiation among Ottoman citizens was still religious, despite some timid efforts at the establishment of a notion of equality borrowed from the West. However, I believe that the use of the ethnonyms 'Turk' and 'Arab' is justifiable in the context of this study for the simple reason that its focus is on a monument considered to represent the heritage of a civilisation defined not only in religious, but also in cultural and linguistic terms. Consequently, as long as they are cautiously framed by quotation marks, following the now well-established tradition of the social sciences and humanities, these terms come in handy to qualify and distinguish groups and identities also defined through cultural and linguistic criteria. Indeed, one cannot help but observe that, when confronted with the Alhambra and other remains of Islamic presence in Andalusia, Ottoman 'Turks' of some standing and education were likely to have fewer cultural references and linguistic skills at their disposal than 'Arabs' of similar profile. As I have already suggested in Fuad Efendi's case, a learned 'Turk' would have mastered enough 'dog-Arab' to identify the most basic and common inscriptions of the Nasrid palace, but he would have certainly floundered when faced with a complex and original text, such as the verses of the Fountain of the Lions, or with an overly archaic or complex script, as was often the case with Kufic calligraphy.

Fuad Efendi may have preceded his North African counterparts in the modern 'discovery' of the Alhambra, but his way of appreciating the monument probably lacked a similar degree of intimacy and familiarity. If the Moroccan ambassadors and their retinue remained silent to the point of inciting the Spanish press to guess their thoughts and feelings and express them in their stead, this did not necessarily mean that they did not have any, but rather that they did not share the same cultural and linguistic registers with their hosts. Fuad Efendi, on the contrary, knew exactly what his interlocutors meant; even worse, his own perception of the site and the set of references he used to express his opinion were derived from a knowledge and a discourse he had acquired, not from his own culture, but from that of an increasingly powerful and hegemonic Europe.

It should not come as a surprise that Fuad Efendi's Ottoman successors were few and, for quite some time, of very different cultural roots. The next visitor that one can surmise to have been an Ottoman subject was in all evidence an Arab, what is more a Christian: 'Abdallah Khalīl Dāvud signed the visitors' book in 1849 with his name (عبدالله خليل داود) in a rather coarse, not to say hesitant, hand, with the addition of the date 'كانون اول ١٣', or 13 December.[69] Nothing in the inscription allows for the identification of

[69] AA, *libros de firmas*, 42, fol. 75 v, 13 or 25 December 1849.

this person, other than his patronym and the use of the Christian calendar, which show that he was a Christian Arab, probably from the Levant, and with a rather average education, if one is to judge from the quality of his handwriting.

Should we link this early presence of a Christian Arab in Spain to a web of older connections between the two ends of the Mediterranean? We may recall the case of Miguel Casiri, a Maronite from Tripoli of Syria, who had migrated to Spain and became a prominent Arabist in the eighteenth century; was there a form of continuity in these relations, revealing a religious network, especially in the case of Maronites, the Catholics of the Levant? While it is impossible to verify this point beyond simple speculation, one cannot help but notice that Christian Arabs did appear rather frequently among the signatories of the visitors' book of the Alhambra, in fact well before their Muslim compatriots, who would not do so before the last decade of the century. Moreover, it is striking to see to what extent these visits were concentrated in time: between 1879 and 1884, no less than ten Christians from Syria or Lebanon signed the book. In 1879, Ibrāhīm Sāleḥ 'Abīd and Ibrāhīm Na'īm, travelling together, both identified as Lebanese Maronites, the former from Daraya and the latter from Raskifa.[70] Less than a year later it was the turn of two other Maronite travelling companions, al-Khūrī Jebrā'il and Ilyās al-Lubnānī,[71] followed by one Yūhanā Mīkhā'il, a 'Maronite from Lebanon', who declared he had seen 'this ancient palace' during his journey, on 16 May 1881, the very same day as Pablo de Sarasate (1844–1908).[72] The following year, Panayot and Nicolas al-Khūrī Ilyās, two Greek Orthodox brothers from Bethlehem signed the book together.[73] In September 1883, Ibrāhīm Na'īm, a Maronite from Raskifa, whose first passage in 1879 we have already noted, was back, this time in the company of a certain Ḍoumit Mema'a, from Daraya.[74] The series ends with Benjamin Trad, priest of the Church of Beirut, who visited the site on 7 May 1884.[75]

[70] AA, *libros de firmas*, 43, fol. 215 v, 8 July 1879.

[71] AA, *libros de firmas*, 43, fol. 234 v, c. 1 March 1880. The two signatures in Arabic script are followed by 'E. Maronita' in Latin characters, probably for Elias.

[72] AA, *libros de firmas*, 43, fol. 276 v, 16 May 1881.

[73] AA, *libros de firmas*, 43, fol. 311 r, c. 20 June 1882.

[74] AA, *libros de firmas*, 44, fol. 24 r, 1 September 1883.

[75] AA, *libros de firmas*, 44, fol. 58 v, 7 May 1884.

How are we to explain such a high concentration of Christian Arabs, almost all Maronites, over such a short period of time? Should the repeated visit of Ibrāhīm Naʿīm in 1879 and 1883 be taken as an indicator of the existence of religious, or perhaps even commercial, networks between Lebanon and Spain, particularly Andalusia, as I have suggested earlier? Bits and pieces of information found in local publications and newspapers seem to suggest that there may indeed have existed such a connection. A late edition of Echeverría's *Paseos* included a conversation between a Granadan host and his visitor, concerning the 'lead books' of Sacromonte and their 'Solomonic' calligraphy, where the guide mentioned the expertise of a Maronite priest by the name of Abu Yuhanna bin Suf (?), who 'passed through here during his journey, without begging for alms as many others like him', thus implying that there were quite a number of Maronite clerics, who, without going as far as Casiri, ended up settling and were roaming Spain in their quest for support and solidarity.[76] One should therefore not be surprised to see the Maronites getting much coverage in the Andalusian and Granadan press. In 1858, the daily *La Alhambra* published across three issues and on its first page a 'historical study' on the Christians of Lebanon and the Maronites, which ended with a call to Spanish Catholics for fraternity and generosity on behalf these martyrs of the Orient.[77]

A more detailed study of the press reveals interesting overlaps between the visitors' book of the Alhambra and Maronite missions to Spain. For example, a short item in Almagro Cárdenas' *Estrella de Occidente* mentions the visit to Granada of two Maronites from Aramoun, a Maronite village of Mount Lebanon, some 30 km to the north of Beirut. One of them was Gabriel Spahat [*sic*], presented as the founder of the School of Fraternal Charity in Aramoun; the other, Elias Monasa, was a language teacher at the same institution. Both were in Spain in the hope of collecting funds to meet the expenses of their

[76] Echeverría, *Paseos por Granada y sus contornos*, 2nd edn, 1814, vol. I, p. 301.

[77] J. García, 'Estudios históricos: Los cristianos del Líbano. Los maronitas'. Much later and in a much more political context, in 1890–1, the Arabist Simonet published a long series of articles on Lebanon, in which he compared the role played by France in this region with the one he believed Spain should play in Morocco, particularly in Tangier (F. J. Simonet, 'Francia en Siria y España en Marruecos').

establishment.[78] A closer look at the documentation reveals that one Father Gabriel Spath (Shbat in Arabic) had indeed established a college by this name in Aramoun in 1860 and that he had frequently travelled to Europe to collect money for his undertaking.[79] One needs only to translate Gabriel into Arabic to realise that the two Maronite visitors to the Alhambra in March 1880, al-Khūrī Jebrā'il and Ilyās al-Lubnānī, were no other than Father Spath and his companion Elias Monasa, and that in the case of the former the term 'al-Khouri' that preceded his name needs to be taken literally as 'priest' and not as a surname. Moreover, it should be noted that the peregrinations of Maronites in Spain were not all about faith. Another visitor that I have been able to trace in the press seems to have been in Andalusia for much more mundane reasons. Benjamin Trad, who signed the visitors' book on 7 May 1884 as priest of the Church of Beirut, had posted an advertisement in Jerez's daily *El Guadalete*, informing the public of a bargain he proposed 'only for a few days': 'Coming from Beirut, capital of Syria [*sic*], a trader from this land, of the Christian faith, has just arrived in our city, bringing a rich and diverse choice of Oriental goods'. A long list of objects followed: Turkish and Persian carpets, shawls, belts, slippers, bracelets, rose essence, kohl from Mecca, etc.[80]

Given the absence of the slightest remark to that effect in their inscriptions, it seems highly unlikely that these Levantine visitors should have felt any form of intellectual or sentimental commitment to the monument. Rather, it is plausible to imagine that these visits were the result of a desire to do as the others and to admire a site, whose reputation had by then reached far beyond the borders of Western Europe. One cannot exclude either a phenomenon of contamination, easily justifiable amidst a rather small community sharing a restricted network of contacts in Spain. At any rate, how can one not note that these visitors almost systematically put forward their Maronite identity, so

[78] *La Estrella de Occidente*, II(8), 15 March 1880, p. 4. These two Maronite travellers are mentioned in Simonet's biography by Cárdenas, as having provided the Arabist with precious remarks on his Arabo-Spanish chrestomathy (Almagro Cárdenas, *Biografía del doctor D. Francisco Javier Simonet*, p. 58).

[79] 'Nouvelles d'Orient. Mont Liban. Une courageuse entreprise'.

[80] 'Sólo pocos días', *El Guadalete*, XXX(8), 573, 29 February 1884, p. 3 and XXX(8), 578, 6 March 1884, p. 3.

much so that one wonders if the visit to the Alhambra was not for them a symbolic re-enactment of a Christian – and what is more, Catholic – victory over Islam, well before it could acquire a historic and cultural meaning connected to their Arab identity. As we will see, it would take some time for the first signs of a political and ideological reclaiming of the Alhambra by Arab nationalists, including Christians.

While the Maronites and other Christian Arabs formed a rather homogeneous group of Ottoman subjects of Arab culture and language visiting the Alhambra almost accidentally, the other Ottomans – or associated with – spotted among the pages of the visitors' book in the decades following Fuad Efendi's passage constitute a very diverse set, to whom it seems difficult to ascribe clear intentions and a concrete vision. This is the case, for example, with the few Armenians I have managed to identify and whose presence can hardly be explained otherwise than by a 'Western' curiosity concerning a physician[81] and two brothers sharing a business,[82] all of them from Constantinople. One could probably qualify in the same way a few Greek visitors, be it Themistocles Cartali from Volos, claiming that 'whoever has the opportunity to visit the Alhambra and does not, does not deserve to have been brought to the world',[83] or an individual with an undecipherable signature who saw nothing else in the monument than 'the victory of the cross of Jesus Christ and the glory of God'.[84]

Other than the fact that, for practical reasons, Ottoman non-Muslims, except for those writing in Arabic, are difficult to spot among the mass of signatures and inscriptions in the book,[85] it is also true that they belonged to a cultural tradition and environment less likely to find a form of historical

[81] 'Dr Mihran Boyadjian (بوياجيان Պոյաճեան) Constantinople' (AA, *libros de firmas*, 44, fol. 296 v, *c.* 11 April 1890).

[82] Agop and Miguirditch Indjoudjian (AA, *libros de firmas*, 47, fol. 92 v, 24 October 1905).

[83] 'Ὁ δυνάμενος νὰ ἐπισκεφθῇ τὴν Ἀλάμπραν καὶ δὲν τὴν ἐπισκέπτεται εἶναι εἰ νὰ μὴν ἔλθῃ εἰς τὸν μάταιον τοῦτον κόσμον' (AA, *libros de firmas*, 46, fol. 158 v, 24 May 1900). Themistocles Cartali was one of the sons of Hajiantonis Cartali from Volos, a city in Thessaly that was ceded to Greece by the Ottomans in 1881. My gratitude goes to Christine Angelidi for her transcription and translation of this text, as well as for the identification of Cartali.

[84] 'Κοινις ουδεν Ενικησεν ο σταυρος Ιεσου Χριστου – Θεῳ δοξα' (AA, *libros de firmas*, 43, fol. 164 v, *c.* 4 May 1879). The transcription and translation are by Christine Angelidi.

[85] The script is the main reason for this. Although Greeks and Armenians used particular scripts, they do not stand out as clearly from the Latin script as the Arab script, which makes them

inspiration or 'ancestral' familiarity. For that reason, I believe it may be more useful and reasonable to focus on those Ottomans whose identity was more compatible with an 'Oriental' vision of the monument, be it through language or religion, or, at least by a mission and duties that linked them to an imperial administration that could be expected to be receptive to a form of recognition or even of claim of a common heritage.

Fuad Efendi's immediate successors fall precisely into this last category; yet even for diplomats serving the Ottoman Empire, such duties and qualifications did not necessarily come with a sense of cultural affinity, however vague, with al-Andalus and its heritage, if only because of their very identities. Thus, the second Ottoman diplomat who visited the monument, fifteen years after Fuad Efendi, was not even an Ottoman subject, but Belgian. Eugène de Kerckhove (1817–89), just jotted down the date and time of his passage – five o'clock in the afternoon, on 7 April 1859 – and signed with a Hispanised form of his name, 'Eugenio'.[86] To those who may wonder at this Belgo-Ottoman hybridity, suffice it to say that Kerckhove, who had been secretary at the Belgian legation in Constantinople, had entered Ottoman diplomatic service in 1849. He was appointed minister in Brussels in 1855 and Madrid in 1858, where he would remain in position until 1860. It was as an Ottoman minister that he went to Granada; it remains to be seen whether this was a mission associated with his official duties as representative of the Ottoman Empire, or simply the result of a personal initiative, whence he was emulating tens of Belgian tourists at the time.[87] The visit, in 1882, of Stephanos/Étienne Karatheodori

much more difficult to spot when browsing hundreds of pages of the visitors' book. Moreover, Greeks and Armenians had a higher propensity to use the Latin script, which makes them simply invisible at first glance. It is probably not a coincidence that both the Armenian inscriptions I have noted were written at least partially in Turkish, which made them much more 'visible'.

[86] AA, *libros de firmas*, 42, fol. 199 v, 7 April 1859. On Kerckhove, see, S. Kuneralp, 'El primer representante permanente otomano en Madrid'.

[87] The fact that Kerckhove wrote only 'M^{tro} Plenipot^{o}' (*ministro plenipotenciario*) under the column reserved to the visitor's profession (*calidad de persona*) without mentioning the state he was representing speaks against the probability of an official mission. Likewise, the presence of the signature of one 'J. Mommaerts' – most likely also Belgian – just after Kerckhove's suggests the possibility that this was a compatriot who accompanied him, thus strengthening the hypothesis of a private journey.

(1836–1907), was very similar to Kerckhove's. Not that Karatheodori was a foreign national, he was as Ottoman as an Orthodox Greek could get at the time; but the reasons that brought him to Granada had an even less official character. Karatheodori was also an Ottoman diplomat, but in post at Brussels since 1875, which shows that his journey had nothing official to it and that he was probably travelling for pleasure. In his comment, although he signed with his name and duties in Turkish, Karatheodori seems to have made a point of putting forward his cultural – and religious – identity by using Greek:

> Stephanos Karatheodori of Byzantium, Ottoman ambassador in Brussels, has admired this masterpiece of Arab art, perhaps for the first time in Greek in this book.[88]

Given all this cultural diversity and mixed identities, one should probably not be surprised to find that the first Ottoman to have *really* followed in Fuad Efendi's steps had a very similar profile. Midhat Pasha (1822–84) was an Ottoman bureaucrat and statesman, a Muslim of Turkish culture, who had recently acquired international celebrity as the hero of Ottoman reformism. He was the instigator of the coup that had brought Sultan Abdülaziz's reign to an end (1876), the architect of the first Ottoman constitution promulgated on 23 December 1876, and the first grand vizier during this new phase in the destiny of an empire heading towards a constitutional monarchy inspired by European examples.[89]

[88] AA, *libros de firmas*, 43, fol. 278 r, 8 October 1882. In Greek: 'Στέφανος Καραθεοδωρή Βυζάντιος, του των Οθωμανών Αυτοκράτορος εν Βρυξέλλαις πρεσβευτής πρώτος ίσως εν ταύτη τη Βίβλω Ελληνικοίς γραμμάσι, το μοναδικόν εν τω κόσμω αριστούργημα Αραβικής τέχνης εθαύμασε. Εν Αλχάμπρα τη 8 Οκτωβρίου αωπβ'. It was followed by a signature in Turkish: '*Kara-Todori, Devlet-i Aliyye-i Osmani'nin sefir-i Brüksel*'. The Greek includes a few mistakes; the Turkish inscription has syntactical errors.

[89] Ahmed Midhat Şefik Pasha was one of the leading Ottoman reformers associated with the opposition movement that developed in the 1860s. He acquired this reputation during his governorship of Niš (1861–4), of the Danubian provinces (1864–8) and of Baghdad (1869–71). Following a short term as grand vizier in 1872, he took the lead in the coup he organised with Hüseyin Avni and Süleyman pashas in May 1876 against Abdülaziz, after which he was appointed president of the Council of State before becoming grand vizier on 19 December 1876, four days before the promulgation of the constitution.

Despite the very similar profile of the two men as Ottoman bureaucrats and statesmen, the context and circumstances of their journeys to Spain were very different. Contrary to Fuad Efendi, Midhat Pasha did not visit Spain on an official mission, but as a fallen grand vizier and political exile, both of which had contributed even more to his fame throughout Europe. On 5 February 1877, less than two months after his appointment as grand vizier, Midhat Pasha had been dismissed and banished overnight by Sultan Abdülhamid II, who had turned against this ambitious statesman Article 113 of the constitution, which granted the sovereign the 'exclusive power to expel from the territories of the Empire those who, following trustworthy information collected by the police administration, have been known to endanger the security of the state'.[90] A state ship had taken him to Brindisi, whence he had reached France. Once in Nice, rumours started to circulate that the former grand vizier intended to visit Spain. As with Fuad Efendi, the Spanish press immediately got hold of this information and set out to follow Midhat Pasha's every move. From the very start, the idea of a journey to Andalusia was present in many of the dispatches.[91] Just like Fuad Efendi, Midhat Pasha surprised the public with his 'civilised' outlook, all the more so considering that upon his arrival at Barcelona, on 16 April, he took off his fez to don a top hat.[92] As to the objective of his mission, it was even clearer in the mind of the Spanish press than it had been for Fuad Efendi:

> There is no doubt that [Midhat Pasha] has come to this land, so rich in glorious historical recollections of such melancholy interest to Muslims, to admire the greatness still visible in the remains of the powerful empire of the caliphs of

[90] *La Constitution ottomane du 7 Zilhidjé 1293 (23 décembre 1876)*, p. 49. After long travels through Europe, Midhat Pasha was pardoned in 1878 and returned to the empire to serve as governor of Syria (1878–81) and of Aydın (1881). In May 1881, he was arrested and charged with the assassination of Sultan Abdülaziz. Following a mock political trial engineered by Abdülhamid, he was sentenced to death. Although his sentence was commuted to life imprisonment in the fortress of Taif, in the Hejaz, he was eventually strangled in 1884 on the orders of the sultan.

[91] See, for example, *La Correspondencia de España*, 7,057, 29 March 1877; *La Iberia*, 6,258, 3 April 1877, p. 3.

[92] *La Época*, 8,924, 19 April 1877, p. 3.

> Cordoba and of the opulent and magnificent Islamic civilisation, not with feelings of vexed and bitter fanaticism, but in a spirit of reflection and erudition. Granada, Cordoba, Malaga and Toledo, as well as a hundred other towns, will reveal to Midhat's artistic genius a rich and variegated treasure of memories, emotions and lessons.[93]

The same item also mentioned the possibility that, on the contrary, Midhat might prefer to devote his attention to observing the progress and variety of Spain. In any case, it is striking to note that the Spanish press had a clear idea of what Andalusia was supposed to mean to a Muslim statesman: admiration mixed with melancholy and political lessons to be drawn from these ruins. This was more than what had been expected of Fuad Efendi some thirty years earlier; in all evidence, the Spanish perception of the confrontation of 'Moors' with their past was becoming clearer every day, based on two fundamental notions: memory and regret. These feelings combined made it possible to view them as the heirs to a glorious past, but also as the losers of a conflict from which Catholic Spain had come out victorious. The tears and sighs ascribed to Muslim visitors thus became the attributes of a pathetic connection with the Andalusian past. We should remember that it was in precisely that year, in 1877, that 'Abdesselām al-Sūsī's embassy had given the Spanish press the opportunity to promote a theme that would become a sort of leitmotiv for the Moroccan visits of the following decades. It seems that Midhat Pasha, much like Fuad Efendi before him, was not a perfect fit for this cliché. He was a Muslim, but not Moroccan; he came from the Orient, but looked modern. Consequently, even if one could still assume that his profile would make him sensitive to the appeal of the remains of the Andalusian past, the discourse used to suggest this was much less emotional and stood halfway between erudition and melancholy.

The former grand vizier left Barcelona on 19 April and arrived at Malaga on 26 April, using more or less the same itinerary as Fuad Efendi through Valencia, Alicante and Murcia.[94] He visited the Alhambra the same day, as appears from the comment in Turkish he left in the visitors' book. Should one

[93] *La Época*, 8,914, 9 April 1877, p. 2.

[94] *El Imparcial*, 3,559, 22 April 1877, p. 2; and 3,560, 23 April 1877, p. 2; *La Época*, 8,929, 24 April 1877, p. 3; *El Siglo futuro*, 383, 3 May 1877, p. 2.

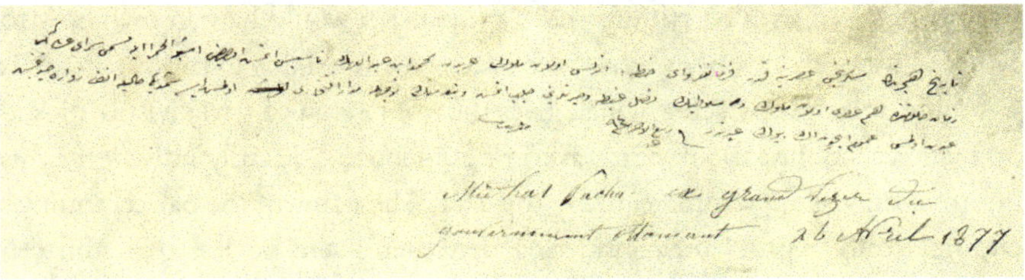

Figure 3.4 Inscription in the visitors' book by Midhat Pasha, 26 April 1877. AA, *libros de firmas*, 43, fol. 102 r. © Archivo del Patronato de la Alhambra y Generalife. The famous Ottoman statesman and leader of the coup carried out against Sultan Abdülaziz the preceding year had been dismissed from the grand vizierate and banished by Sultan Abdülhamid II. Three months into his exile, Midhat Pasha decided to embark on a tour of Spain and made a stop in Granada, where he visited the Alhambra.

conclude that he was more eager to do so than Fuad Efendi, who had spent a whole day visiting the city before he climbed the famous hill? Not necessarily, nevertheless, his inscription suggests that he had much more to say than his predecessor (Figure 3.4):

> What a great example it is for all to see to what extent this sublime palace by the name of Alhambra, established by Muḥammad son of 'Abdallah, one of the Arab kings who ruled over the lands of al-Andalus until the eighth century of the Hijra and who caused the envy and wonder of contemporary kings and sultans as well as the pride of his subjects, constitutes, in its present state, an example before the astonished eyes of visitors.

The inscription was followed by his name in Turkish, 'Midhat', and his name and titles in French: 'Midhat Pasha former grand vizier of the Ottoman government'.[95]

The inscription was quite disappointing. Not to mention the inexplicable misspelling of '*ottoman*' as '*ottomant*' in French,[96] the Turkish text was awkward,

[95] AA, *libros de firmas*, 43, fol. 102 r, 26 April 1877.

[96] I am truly at a loss to propose an explanation for this error. The rest of the sentence proves that Midhat Pasha had a decent command of French, and even if that were not the case 'Ottoman' is certainly the last word an Ottoman pasha would have misspelt. I have no other argument than to suggest a moment of inattention.

wordy and filled with repetitions that a proper pen would have known how to avoid.[97] However, beyond its very poor style, what is striking in this paragraph is its highly didactic character, which gives the impression of trivia hastily picked up from a school textbook or a traveller's guidebook.[98] Hastily indeed, for this information was approximate, to say the least. The name of the palace's builder was not really a problem, considering that there were no less than thirteen Muḥammads among the Nasrid; however, none of these had a father named ʿAbdallah. The confusion probably stemmed from the fact that the ruler who completed the construction of the Alhambra was *Abū ʿAbdallah* Muḥammad V Ghanī Billah (r. 1353–91), whose father was named Yūsuf. At any rate, the chronology proposed was not any better: the eighth century of the Hijra corresponds to the fourteenth century of the Common Era. Depending on the inclusive or exclusive meaning one might give to the expression 'until the eighth century', Midhat was depriving the Nasrid of one or two centuries of rule.

Clearly, the pasha's historical knowledge had its limits. He was far from enjoying the same degree of erudition as Fuad Efendi, both East and West. Midhat Pasha, an ambitious and pragmatic man, had clearly understood that a journey to Andalusia and a visit to the Alhambra would be laden with political meaning. He was perhaps already thinking of the immediate risk – of which he was greatly responsible – of a Russo-Ottoman conflict in the wake of the Balkan crisis. Whatever his actual intentions may have been and although he lacked Fuad Efendi's erudition and refinement, it was clear that Midhat Pasha was much more conscious of the meaning and impact the Alhambra could acquire in the political symbolism of modernity. Fuad was curious; Midhat was committed.

A Growing Awareness

Had the circumstances changed so radically in thirty years as to make Midhat Pasha a less cultivated but more 'modern' visitor to the Alhambra?

[97] The words 'example' (*ibret*) and 'wonder/astonishment' (*hayret*) are both twice repeated in this short text. By Ottoman standards, this denotes, to say the least, a lack of elegance.

[98] Given the importance that Baedeker's guidebook will acquire in the last part of this study, I would have loved to prove that this was Midhat's source of inspiration, but I have to admit it is simply impossible, considering that the first edition of this work was published in 1897. At any rate, Midhat Pasha's inscription is too short to be subjected to a textual analysis in contemporary guidebooks or history books.

Some intellectual and cultural developments in the Ottoman world seem to suggest so. At the top of the list was the publication, already mentioned in passing, of Ziya Pasha's *History of al-Andalus* (*Tarih-i Endülüs*), the two volumes of which came out in 1860 and 1863.[99] This was a translation, or rather an adaptation, of Louis Viardot's (1800–83) *Histoire des Arabes et des Mores d'Espagne*, published in 1833 and again in 1851.[100] The circumstances in which Ziya Pasha undertook this work are not well known. Some claim that this was initially an exercise in translation that was suggested by Edhem Pasha (1818?–1893), a former student of the École des Mines in France and a perfect speaker of French; others, that it was a rewriting by Ziya Pasha of a translation by the same Edhem Pasha. Given the absence of any concrete information, it seems impossible to find an answer to this – after all rather futile – question. It is much more important to note that this was the first work in Turkish on the history of Andalusia under Muslim rule and that it consequently triggered a new consciousness on a subject that had until then remained totally unknown to the vast majority of the Turkish-speaking public.

The work's quality was far from remarkable, if only because Viardot's original was already outdated in the 1860s. Moreover, it relied on a very 'free' translation, closer to an adaptation, with many additions, as well as omissions.[101] To

[99] Ziya Pasha, *Endülüs Tarihi*, vol. I, 1276/1860; vol. II, 1280/1863.

[100] L. Viardot, *Essai sur l'histoire des Arabes et des Mores d'Espagne*; L. Viardot, *Histoire des Arabes et des Mores d'Espagne*.

[101] There is no systematic study of Ziya Pasha's text. A Masters thesis has the merit of analysing, however succinctly, some of the peculiarities of the work, particularly its eclectic usage of numerous sources, both European and Islamic, as well as the author's frequent commentaries and digressions (Z. Gözütok, 'Ziya Paşa'nın Endülüs Tarihi'). More recently, Ahmet Ersoy has also stressed this aspect, noting that it 'was not a direct translation but a hybrid text based upon and improvised from Viardot's original', and suggesting that it should be seen 'more [as] an Ottoman critical edition of Viardot's work than a translation' (A. Ersoy, *Architecture and the Late Ottoman Historical Imaginary*, pp. 98, 270, nn. 21–2). This may be an overestimation of Ziya Pasha's literary and intellectual merit, unless we lend a political meaning to the term 'critical', as reflected in the author's frequent remarks, where he counters or corrects passages from Viardot, which he considers unfair towards Islamic society and civilisation.

give an idea of this rather particular method, it would suffice to quote a short passage on the construction and merits of the Alhambra:

> King Bani Aḥmar had a magnificent palace built for himself in Granada, which was very vast, beautiful, solid and charming, by the name of the fortress of al-Ḥamra'; its wonderful location caused the admiration of the mind and fantasy of engineers and its pleasant style triggered the wonder of artists throughout the world; its decoration, inside and out, had nothing to envy to the fortress of Khawarnaq[102] and each one of its apartments reminded one of the following verses:
>
> Like the dome of Khosrow, it is adorned with images
> Like the Book of Mani, it is covered with drawings
> It shines like the sun and rivals in beauty the paradise
> It is blessed like the Kaaba and pleasant like the garden of Eden.[103]
>
> Faithful to the meaning of these verses, this was truly a marvel among the marvels of this world and worthy of paradise. Subsequently, as the Christians who conquered Granada have apparently not destroyed this unrivalled edifice, it remains whole today and causes the admiration of travellers who journey through Spain.[104]

Needless to say, the Persian quatrain Ziya Pasha used to praise the beauty of the Alhambra was nowhere to be found in Viardot's work; the 'translator' had inserted it to comply with the traditional Ottoman style, which interspersed flowery verses throughout a text in prose. However, Ziya Pasha's meddling with the original text did not stop at that. In his work, Viardot hardly ever mentioned the Alhambra, except in passing, and for good reason: he referred

[102] A palace built by the Lakhmids at a close distance from Najaf, which pre-Islamic poetic tradition included among the thirty marvels of the world.

[103] چون قبهٔ کسری بتصاویر مزین / چون نامهٔ مانی بتماثیل منقش / چون چشم فلك روشن و چون خلد برین خوب / چون بیت حرم فرخ و چون باغ ارم خوش I owe the translation of these verses, together with the correction of a few errors by Ziya Pasha, to Mohammad Ali Amir-Moezzi, from the École pratique des hautes études in Paris. It appears that these verses were not authored by a known poet but rather were part of a popular repertoire.

[104] Ziya Pasha, *Endülüs Tarihi*, vol. II, p. 253.

the reader to his own description of the site in an earlier publication,[105] where some forty pages had been devoted to the monument, with no possible comparison to Ziya Pasha's paragraph and a half.[106] At any rate, this short commentary provided no useful information about the palace; there were no dates, but only the name of a sovereign that was vague enough to fit almost any Nasrid ruler and stereotypical superlatives and comparisons to praise its beauty. Other than that, the only somewhat concrete information had to do with the infatuation of tourists with the Alhambra.

Bits and pieces of information gleaned from the Ottoman archives tell us that the first edition – for there was a second one in 1888–9 (Figure 3.5) – faced some minor difficulties, which may explain the delay in the publication of the second volume. Indeed, an inspection of the first volume had come up with a few 'unacceptable expressions', which required that unsold copies be seized in July 1860, only months after publication.[107] Did Ziya Pasha spend the following three years cleansing the second volume of 'unacceptable' expressions? Whatever the circumstances may have been, it was only in January 1863 that the second volume was approved by the Council for Public

[105] The section devoted to architecture, while noting the perfection of the Alhambra, deals only with the mosque of Cordoba and the palatial city of Madīnat al-Zahrā (Viardot, *Histoire des Arabes et des Mores d'Espagne*, vol. II, pp. 71–81).

[106] Viardot, *Les Musées d'Espagne, d'Angleterre et de Belgique*, pp. 174–210. The introductory statement of this description titled 'The Alhambra' perfectly illustrates to what extent the monument had already become popular by the early 1840s: 'I am afraid that upon seeing this title, many readers will exclaim with exasperation: "The Alhambra again! Granada again! Oh! My God, there is not a single tourist riding across Spain who has not fleetingly visited the Moorish kings' old castle and has not, upon their return, considered it their duty to give us their impression of this eighth marvel of the world. We know it by heart"' (p. 174).

[107] Permission for publication was granted in February 1860 (BOA, İ DH 451/29844, 14–15 Receb 1276/6–7 February 1860). However, in May, based on the opinion of 'some persons who have examined it', it was decided that the work contained 'some expressions incompatible with the language of the time', that 'such remarks are harmful and unacceptable at this juncture' and, therefore, that unsold copies should be withdrawn from sale (BOA, HR MKT 333/3, 10 Şevval 1276, 1 May 1860). In July, realising that this decision had been made after the publication had been authorised, the government recognised the validity of a complaint [by Ziya Pasha?] concerning losses incurred (BOA, HR MKT 340/53, 18 Zilhicce 1276/7 July 1860). Unfortunately, all this administrative documentation omits any information as to what the unacceptable terms and expressions may have been.

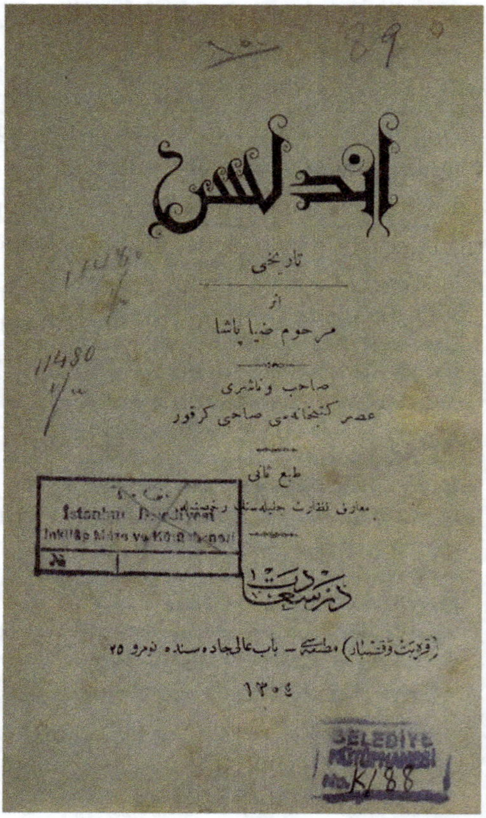

Figure 3.5 Title page of the second edition of Ziya Pasha's *Endülüs Tarihi* (Istanbul: Karabet ve Kasbar Matbaası, 1304/1888–9). Istanbul Metropolitan Municipality Atatürk Library. Ziya Pasha had first published his *History of al-Andalus* in 1860/63. A striking detail of the title page in this second and posthumous edition is the use made of ornate Kufic characters for *Endülüs*, reflecting the contemporary infatuation for this script in historicist contexts, not unlike the use of the Gothic script in Europe during the same period.

Education, which decreed that this was 'a useful work'.[108] Consequently, the following month, the Supreme Council remarked that contrary to the first volume, which had received 'some criticism', this one was 'free of any objection' and that there should be no obstacle to its publication, thus leading to the government's final imprimatur.[109] The publication, some twenty-five years later, of a second edition should probably be read as the sign of a relative success.[110] As to the prohibition that struck the new edition ten years later, it seems that it had nothing to do with its contents, but only with its author,

[108] BOA, İ MVL 482/21842, 29 Receb 1279/20 January 1863.

[109] BOA, İ MVL, 482/21842; 24 Şaban 1279/14 February 1863; 26–7 Şaban 1279/16–17 February 1863.

[110] Ziya Pasha, *Endülüs Tarihi*, vols I–III, 1304/1888; vol. IV, 1305/1889.

whom Abdülhamid could still not forgive for his political allegiances, despite his death almost twenty years earlier.[111]

Leaving aside the rather uneven quality of Ziya Pasha's work, it is clear that it had a considerable impact on the learned Ottoman public. True, it is rather difficult to measure this impact with any precision, considering that we do not even know its print run. According to some, such as Bernard Lewis (1916–2018) or Ahmet Hamdi Tanpınar (1901–62), the book had a large readership and, despite its mediocre quality, played an important role in the creation of many works covering the same theme in years and decades to come.[112] It should also be noted that when Ziya Pasha published his famous anthology of poets in 1874, he devoted a significant space to about ten Andalusian authors.[113]

In February–March 1860, at the very moment when Ziya Pasha's history was published, an article published in the first issue of a periodical by the name of *Mir'at* (*Mirror*) addressed the question of the 'sources of wealth' (*esbab-ı servet*) – the Ottomans had not yet come up with a definitive neologism for 'economy' – in the form of an imaginary dialogue between an elderly wise man (Kâmil) and a brilliant youth (Âkil) on the conditions leading to economic success.[114] As Kâmil presented Spain as an example of economic failure due to the absence of productive activity despite the wealth brought from America, young Âkil asked whether there was also a connection with the wars the Spaniards waged against Muslims. Finding this digression useful, Kâmil embarked upon a long description of the Arabs' achievements in Spain, their conquests, their love and support of arts and sciences, but concluded by observing that the period of the *taifa*s, by bringing disorder and by creating dissension among Muslim principalities, was the cause for the defeat that eventually led to the destruction of Islamic presence in Spain. Âkil was impressed by this tirade:

[111] BOA, MF MKT 394/8, 14 Zilkade 1315/5 April 1898; 4 Zilhicce 1315/26 April 1898; A. Birinci, 'Osmanlı Devletinde Matbuat ve Neşriyat Yasakları Tarihine Medhal', p. 345.

[112] 'Very widely circulated at the time, it inspired a series of Turkish poems, of plays and of tales, which familiarised a new generation of Turkish readers with the glories of al-Andalus' (B. Lewis, 'Quelques thèmes andalous de la littérature turque au xixe siècle', p. 188; A. H. Tanpınar, *19uncu Asır Türk Edebiyatı Tarihi*, p. 328. See also, A. Yalçınkaya, *Learned Patriots*, p. 111.

[113] Ziya Pasha, *Harabat*, pp. 258–71.

[114] 'Esbab-ı Servet'.

'God knows to what extent your remarks have moved your servant'; to which the elderly Kâmil responded: 'It is indeed the case, but what use is it to be moved and to lament the events of the past? We should rather draw a lesson from the fate of the Andalusians.'[115]

It seems difficult, if not impossible, to connect this article to Ziya Pasha's work. Nevertheless, the coincidence of these two publications in time is an indication that the history of Muslim Andalusia had made an inroad, however modest, into the repertoire of historical references for a somewhat wider section of the Ottoman public than the tiny minority, which, until then, had depended on Western sources. Moreover, it should be noted that Ziya Pasha was also the author of another contemporary translation, which, much more modestly, contributed to the central theme of Spanish history. This was a *History of the Inquisition* (*Enkizisyon Tarihi*), which he wrote in 1860–1 (1277 AH), but was published only in 1882 (1299 AH), two years after his death, by Ebüzziya Tevfik Bey (1849–1913), who had found and acquired this manuscript from the pasha's dispersed estate.[116] This work, too, consisted of a translation, but only of a chapter from a popular history of Spain, published in Firmin Didot's famous 'l'Univers' series.[117] Finally, is it simply a coincidence that the following year, an article in *The Times* reported that when the Dominican priests of the Church of Saint Peter and Paul in Galata had requested that their church, which had been confiscated in the fifteenth century, be returned, they had been answered that 'the Sultan is prepared to restore this church of the Spaniards, so soon as the Spaniards shall restore all the mosques which they seized from the Sultan's co-religionists in Spain'.[118]

115 'Esbab-ı Servet', pp. 6–7.

116 Ziya Pasha, *Enkizisyon Tarihi*. A second edition was published in 1888 (1305 AH).

117 J. Lavallée and A. Guéroult, *Espagne*, pp. 453–70. It is very disappointing to see that most authors – particularly Turkish – believe that the work translated by Ziya Pasha was by Théophile Lavallée and Adolphe Chéruel, or by Joseph Lavallée (1747–1809), the author of the *Histoire des inquisitions religieuses d'Italie, d'Espagne et de Portugal*. The only exception is Johann Strauss: J. Strauss, 'What was (Really) Translated in the Ottoman Empire? Sleuthing Nineteenth-century Ottoman Translated Literature', pp. 64–5.

118 'Archaeology in Turkey'. The Church of Saint Peter and Paul, then served by the Dominicans, was established in 1475, after that of Saint Paul was seized. Saint Paul's was later turned into a mosque and granted to the Morisco refugees from Andalusia, hence the name it was given of Arap Camii (mosque of the Arabs).

Although all these texts form a highly heterogeneous, even erratic, array, they do seem to converge around a vague notion of accounts to be settled with Spain. They had in common a glorification and victimisation of Muslims, together with an effort to put before their readers the barbaric behaviour of the Catholic conquerors, even though in the case of the Inquisition, the Jews had been their main target. To an Ottoman and Muslim audience, this amounted to a most welcome inversion of the stereotypes to which they were themselves subjected. At a time when Europe was rapidly increasing its domination over the Muslim world and when this power was coupled with a cultural arrogance that reduced Islam to an image of violence and barbarism, the notion of an Islamic civilisation that Westerners themselves praised for its perfection and sophistication, combined with that of a primitive and uncouth Christianity, formed a contrast that could only reassure Ottoman Muslims in their belief that they had been wronged by the West. After all, did this vision not encompass the two fundamental elements of any form of proto-nationalism, pride and victimisation? In 1867, an article devoted to libraries in the Islamic world, published in *Mecmua-i Fünun* (*Journal of Sciences*), proposed a rehash of this theme by reminding its readers of the diffusion of Islamic sciences all the way to the Holy See:

> At a time when Europe was still drowning in the darkness of ignorance, the cities of Baghdad, Cairo, Fez and Cordoba had become beacons of science. Even the famous Pope Sylvester II had gone to Andalusia at the beginning of his education to learn geometry; upon his return he was accused of sorcery because he drew circles and angles.[119]

True, one swallow does not a summer make, and it would take more examples to solidly prove that Ziya Pasha's work had really made an impact. Nevertheless, a few other concrete examples, albeit of later date, do confirm such a trend. Thus, the inauguration of the Imperial University, on 20 February 1870, became the occasion for the listing of references to the role played by the Arabs, particularly in al-Andalus, in the scientific revival of the Middle Ages and the diffusion of knowledge. In his speech delivered

[119] A. ibn Embasevi, 'İslam Kütüphaneleri', p. 28.

in French, Jean Aristoclès, member of the Higher Council for Public Education, had insisted on this Islamic heritage, with a particular stress on Andalusia and Cordoba:

> The University of Cordoba, established by Al-Hakem, gained great reputation; in the said city, there was a library allegedly containing over 500,000 volumes. While Europe was plunged in barbarism and weak glimmers of light had barely started to show, a shining light of science, literature, art and philosophy flooded Baghdad, Cordoba, Basra, Samarkand and all the other capitals of Islam.[120]

The Minister of Public Education, Safvet Pasha (1814–83), echoed the same thoughts in his own speech, praising the achievements of Arab civilisation in Spain.[121] A closer look at his words, however, revealed striking resemblances with Ziya Pasha's work. Indeed, according to the minister, the 'Arabs of Spain' (*İspanya Arabları*) had revived those sciences that had remained 'hidden for several centuries in the clouds of ignorance that had followed the dismemberment and devastation of the Roman Empire under the influence of the Barbarian nations'. The list he gave of these sciences followed, with minimal changes, the order in which Ziya Pasha himself, copying Viardot, had enumerated the Arabs' scientific and technological innovations: medicine, surgery, pharmacy, chemistry, mathematics, algebra, astronomy, zoology, botany, geology, music, paper, gunpowder, compass, etc.[122] There is no doubt that Safvet Pasha had leafed through Ziya Pasha's *History of al-Andalus*, among other sources, when preparing his speech.

Much later, the famous author and intellectual Namık Kemal (1840–88) provides us with yet another concrete example of Ziya Pasha's influence. As several researchers have already noted,[123] this patriotic poet's

[120] 'Discours prononcé par Jean Aristoclès'.

[121] Yalçınkaya, *Learned Patriots*, p. 143.

[122] 'Maarif-i Umumiye Nazırı devletlü paşa hazretleri tarafından irad buyurulan nutuk'. Ziya Pasha lists, in that order, medicine, surgery, natural history, mathematics and geometry, astronomy . . . paper and gunpowder (Ziya Pasha, *Endülüs Tarihi*, vol. II, pp. 512–22, 532–7). Needless to say, Ziya Pasha's observations are a very abbreviated version of Viardot's in his *Histoire des Arabes et des Mores d'Espagne*, vol. II, pp. 93–102, 142–66.

[123] Gözütok, 'Ziya Paşa'nın Endülüs Tarihi', p. 25.

correspondence reveals that in 1883, during his exile on the island of Mytilene (Lesbos), he had asked Menemenli Rifat Bey to send him, among other books, Ziya Pasha's work.[124] The use he intended to make of it is meaningful. On 29 March 1883, Ernest Renan (1823–92) had given his famous lecture on 'Islam and science', where he defended his thesis that Islam had always fought against science and curbed its development.[125] Like many other intellectuals throughout the Islamic world, Namık Kemal felt the urge to counter this argument and had immediately started working on a rebuttal. Although he wrote it in just a few months, he eventually changed his mind and decided not to publish a text he was not satisfied with.[126] It was only in 1910, well after his death, that this refutation was published among his collected works.[127] His arguments were not very convincing,[128] and they bore no trace of Ziya Pasha's work. Nevertheless, what really counts is that the author should have expected to find some material there to strengthen his arguments against Renan, most probably by stressing the flourishing of arts and sciences in medieval Andalusia.

However, apart from a sort of revanchism directed at Europe through the proxy of Andalusia, the history of Muslim Spain gave the Ottomans occasion to ponder about their own destiny. After all, how could one ignore the feelings barely hidden behind the two first verses of a poem (*ghazal*) composed by Ziya Pasha in November 1870 during a stay in Genoa?

> I have visited the lands of the infidels, filled with cities and mansions
> I have roamed the lands of Islam, where I saw nothing but ruins[129]

Let us not hastily jump to the wrong conclusion. Ziya Pasha was not of those who saw unconditional Westernisation as the only path to salvation. Quite the contrary, he believed that imitating Europe was corrupting the nature

[124] F. Abdullah, 'Namık Kemal'in Midilli'de Yazdığı Manzum ve Mensur Eserler', pp. 88–9.
[125] E. Renan, *L'islamisme et la science: Conférence faite à la Sorbonne le 29 mars 1883.*
[126] Abdullah, 'Namık Kemal'in Midilli'de Yazdığı Manzum ve Mensur Eserler', pp. 89–90.
[127] Namık Kemal, *Rönan Müdafaanamesi.*
[128] See, Ş. Mardin, *The Genesis of Young Ottoman Thought*, pp. 324–6.
[129] Ziya Pasha, *Külliyat-ı Ziya Paşa*, p. 203.

of Islamic society and making it forget the very roots in which it should seek its revival:

> They say that it is Islam that impedes the state from progressing
> This rumour did not exist in the past; that is a novelty.
> By forgetting our identity in everything we do
> We submit to the ideas of Europe; that is a novelty.[130]

This fear of failure was part and parcel of the mindset of many members of the empire's political and intellectual elite. However, all were not as idealistic – and old-fashioned – as Ziya Pasha. What could be more natural, after all, if one considers that committing to the path of modernity through Westernisation amounted to a certain extent to admitting failure and recognising the superiority of the West as a civilisational model. The reason why Renan's accusations were so hurtful and difficult to digest was that, deep down, many Ottomans thought he was right. Obviously, the vision of a past Islamic civilisation taunting a barbaric Europe could provide some solace, but it was not sufficient to conjure the feeling of defeat at the sight of a weakened and crumbling empire confronting the growing power of contemporary Europe. However glorious it may have been, the history of al-Andalus inevitably ended up acquiring a much darker and ominous aspect in the eyes of the Ottoman Muslims who had just discovered it. Some could not help but see it as a premonitory sign of their own destiny, or at least as a warning against the dangers resulting from the precarious situation in the empire's Balkan provinces. After all, it was clear that the Ottomans were losing their hold in Europe; would they, too, end up being expelled, like the Arabs four centuries earlier?

This may be one way to understand Kâmil's answer to Âkil, where he advised him to cease lamenting the fate of the Andalusians and think instead of drawing a lesson from it. Yet it seems also rather difficult to ascribe an Ottoman author such a defeatist attitude at such an early date. The circumstances of the empire and the vision of its near future may have already looked grim in the 1860s, but they had not yet reached the degree of desperation that would characterise the following decade. It was really with the *annus horribilis* of 1876 and its immediate aftermath that a true wind of panic swept across

[130] Ziya Pasha, *Terci'-i Bend: Terkib-i Bend*, p. 10.

the government and elites, as the notion of the empire's collapse reached an unprecedented level of probability. The bankruptcy of October 1875; the coup against Abdülaziz in May 1876; the failure of the international conference in January 1877; the dismissal and exile of Midhat Pasha in February; Russia's declaration of war in April; the crushing defeat that followed within less than a year; followed by the closing down of parliament and the suspension of the constitution – it would have taken much less to drive to despair the rulers and intellectuals of an empire, who felt more and more cornered by Europe, by Russia and by the rise of nationalism in the Balkans. In a diatribe against the Turks, William Gladstone (1809–98) famously claimed that they should be banished from Europe: 'Their Zaptiehs and their Mudirs, their Bimbashis and their Yuzbachis, their Kaimakams and their Pashas, one and all, bag and baggage, shall, I hope, clear out from the province they have desolated and profaned.'[131] Was this not the signal of a new Crusade, a *Reconquista* aiming to purge Christianity of its invaders? Russia would eventually be the one to realise Gladstone's dream: following the Russo-Ottoman conflict of 1877–8, hundreds of thousands of Muslims had to leave the Balkans to take refuge in Anatolia.

Not surprisingly, this disaster triggered a second and much more powerful wave of Andalusian references throughout Ottoman letters. At the very beginning of the crisis, two tragedies were published with the fall of Granada as its backdrop. The first, *Seydi Yahya* by Şemseddin Sami [Frashëri] (1850–1904), published towards the end of 1875, told, in an excessively convoluted and heavy style, the drama of some of the survivors of the defeat, particularly the valiant warrior Seydi Yahya and his daughter Halime.[132] The following year, Abdülhak Hâmid [Tarhan] (1852–1937) published *Nazife*, a very short play named after a young and beautiful Muslim woman of Granada, who, rather than submit to the advances of King Ferdinand, chose to kill herself in front of him, shouting 'my corpse will be your only booty!'[133] Abdülhak Hâmid continued this streak with two more plays on the same theme. In 1879, in *Ṭāriq, or the Conquest of al-Andalus*, which he had already completed in 1875, he recounted the glorious times of the Arab conquest of Spain, under the

[131] W. E. Gladstone, *Bulgarian Horrors and the Question of the East*, pp. 61–2.

[132] Ş. Sami, *Seydi Yahya. Beş Fasıldan İbaret Facia*.

[133] Abdülhak Hamid, *Nazife*. The plot unfolds in the Alhambra.

leadership of Ṭāriq ibn Ziyād (?–*c.* 720) and Mūsà ibn Nuṣayr (640–716).[134] The following year, he published *Tezer*, the story of a thwarted love between a young Spanish woman and the caliph of Cordoba, ʿAbdelraḥman III (891–961).[135] The series ended with a last play, written in 1881 (1297 AH) but published in 1917, *İbni Musa yahud Zatü'l-Cemal*, a tragedy in prose forming a sequel to *Tarık*.[136] It should also be noted that his *Conquest of al-Andalus* was translated into Arabic in 1905 (Figure 3.6).[137]

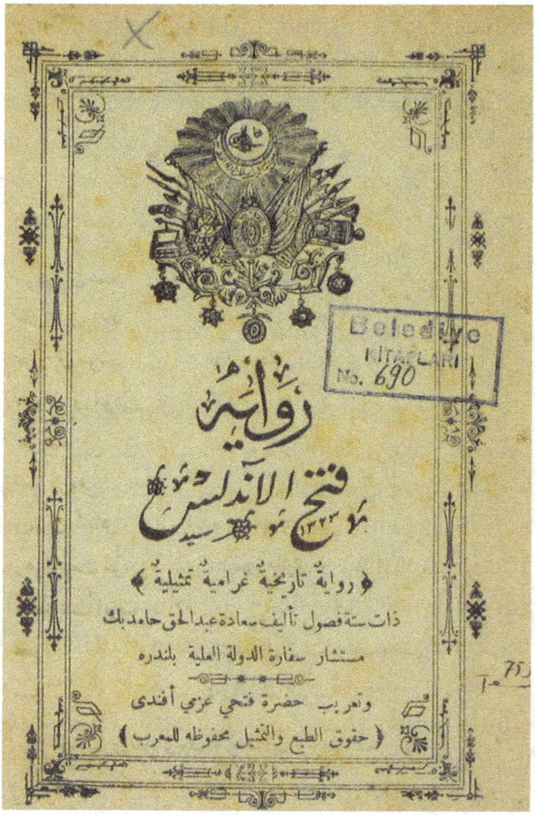

Figure 3.6 Title page of *Riwāyat Fatḥ al-Andalus* (*The Story of the Conquest of al-Andalus*) (Istanbul(?): n.p., 1323/1905), a translation into Arabic by Fethi Azmi Efendi of Abdülhak Hamid's *Tarık yahud Endülüs Fethi* (*Ṭāriq, or the Conquest of al-Andalus*), published in 1879. Istanbul Metropolitan Municipality Atatürk Library. Although the place of publication is not specified, the very prominent presence of the Ottoman coat of arms suggests that it was published in Istanbul.

134 Abdülhak Hamid, *Tarık yahud Endülüs Fethi*.

135 Abdülhak Hamid, *Tezer yahud Melik Abdurrahman el-Salis. Manzum ve Kavafi-i Mukayyedeyi Havi bir Facia-i Tarihiyedir*.

136 Abdülhak Hamid, *İbni Musa yahud Zatü'l-Cemal*.

137 The translation is by one Fethi Azmi Efendi (Abdülhak Hamid, *Riwāya Fatḥ al-Andalus*). According to Lewis, there were also Persian, Serbian and Bosnian translations of the play (Lewis, 'Quelques thèmes andalous de la littérature turque au xixe siècle', p. 189).

Evidently, Abdülhak Hamid had capitalised on a popular theme and one can rightly wonder whether his real objective might not have been to become an Ottoman Corneille or Racine.[138] Nevertheless, it seems unrealistic to assume that such a concentration of works on the same subject during such a short period of time should have been merely the result of a literary fad. In 1882, two other publications were added to the repertoire. First, a Turkish translation by one A. [Abdullah?] Tahir of Chateaubriand's *Adventures of the Last Abencerrage*. It seems meaningful that the title was doubled with an explanatory subtitle – 'about al-Andalus' (*Endülüs'e Dairdir*) – from which we can deduce that a reference to al-Andalus had become useful to draw the readers' attention and to give meaning to a title that was far from suggestive. We should also note that in his short preface, the translator stressed the fact that the decline and fall of al-Andalus had been the result of immorality (*su-i ahlak*) and dissension (*nifak*).[139]

This was precisely one of the central themes of a second work published that same year, Muallim Naci's (1849–93) *Musa bin Eba'l-Gazan*. Contrary to most other works, this was not a play, but a sort of gest in verses celebrating the feats of the eponymous hero, a valiant warrior of Islam, who, rebelling against his lord's decision to surrender and after having tried in vain to rally his companions to his cause, had ended up launching an attack on the enemy alone, thus finding in death an alternative to captivity.[140] This short epic summarised most of the clichés that had taken root in Ottoman culture by then. It recalled the superiority of Arab civilisation over medieval Europe, while at the same time bringing up with much bitterness the reversal of which the Ottoman Empire had become a victim:

> Europe is now selling us back
> The knowledge it acquired from them.[141]

[138] Lewis, 'Quelques thèmes andalous de la littérature turque au xixe siècle', p. 189.

[139] Chateaubriand, *İbni Serrac Âhir: Endülüs'e Dairdir*.

[140] Muallim Naci, *Musa bin Eba'l-Gazan*. The Alhambra appears as the meeting place of the Arab warriors whom Musa tried to convince of the need to resist: 'All the commanders came together / Inside the palace of the Alhambra' (*İctima eyledi bütün ümera / Oldu mücemma' saray-ı [Elhamra]*) (p. 13).

[141] 'Avrupa ondan aldı irfanı / Bize satmaktadır henüz onu' (Muallim Naci, Musa bin Eba'l-Gazan, p. 8).

The main message in the work was strongly linked to the work's alternative title, *Hamiyyet*, or 'devotion', soon to become the Turkish translation of 'patriotism'. It was the moral of the story: Musa had sacrificed his life for his nation, preferring a tragic death to the disgrace of surrender. From the very start, Muallim Naci addressed his readers by reminding them of the lesson to be drawn from the decline of Arab civilisation in Spain: the fragmentation of power witnessed during the rule of the *taifa*s had ended up undermining the foundations of the former conquerors' political and military might:

> If union had been in the nature of the nation
> Would the state ever come to perish?
> The calamity for the state is dissension amidst the nation
> And its soul resides in the union of the nation.[142]

In about twenty years, the history of Andalusia and of the Arabs in Spain had moved from anonymity to a central position in the historical imagination of the Ottoman elite, gradually acquiring an ideological meaning intricately emmeshed in the almost existential crisis faced by the empire. A handful of influential authors had discovered in this previously ignored episode in the history of Islam an inspiration allowing them to reclaim the glory of a civilisation that had surpassed that of the West, at a moment in time when Europe turned to be more invasive, arrogant and menacing than ever in its relations with the Orient and with Islam. Apart from offering an antidote to an increasingly dominant inferiority complex, Andalusia provided the first timid ideologues of Ottoman patriotism, heavily tainted with Islamism, a collective identity that enabled them to hark back to an idealised past. If this wave started to recede in the 1890s before fading away,[143] it was probably due

[142] 'İttihad olsa tab'-ı milletde / Hiç olur mu zeval devletde / Mülke âfet şikak-ı milletdir / Ruh-ı mülk ittifak-ı milletdir (Muallim Naci, Musa bin Eba'l-Gazan, p. 5).

[143] Works of comparable scope with the epics and tragedies of the 1870s and 1880s disappear altogether, with the exception of two plays by Abdülhak Hamid, *Abdullah e's-Sagir* (Boabdil), completed in 1915 and published in 1917, together with a re-edition of *Nazife* (Abdülhak Hamid, *Abdullah e's-Sagir – Nazife*) and *İbni Musa yahud Zatül-Cemal*, completed in 1881 but published in 1917. For the rest, most of the production consists of short articles in the – sometimes illustrated – press.

to the refocusing of Turkish proto-nationalism on Anatolia, the Middle East and a historical narrative more directly linked to the Ottoman and Turkish past.[144] It seems particularly meaningful that the Arabs – both Ottoman and post-Ottoman – who took over this trend and appropriated Andalusia as the catalyst of their own nascent nationalism.

Architectural Inspirations?

A particularly striking parallelism can be witnessed between the Ottoman discovery of the history of Andalusia and the adoption of a Moresque style in a growing number of public edifices built in the Ottoman capital during the 1860s. The observation of such an infatuation with an architectural style so intimately linked to the image of Arab civilisation in Spain immediately brings to mind the probability of a connection between the two, which would enable us to link the rise of the Moresque to the impact among intellectual circles of Ziya Pasha's work and of other publications that followed. I must say right away that I believe it is extremely difficult, not to say impossible, to establish a convincing link between the two phenomena. Nevertheless, many researchers, especially art and architectural historians, have been tempted into seeing in the Ottoman Moresque much more than a simple imitation of a style, which European architectural realisations – many examples of which I have already mentioned – had rendered popular.

> To a certain extent, the alhambresque in the Ottoman context can be interpreted as a local domestication of this Western Orientalism.
>
> But, as I have indicated, the different interpretations of the alhambresque in non-Western contexts are evidence that there the alhambresque was not an unthinking adoption from the West but a knowing and deliberate use of

[144] The idea of finding inspiration in the history of the early Ottoman conquerors had already emerged under Sultan Abdülaziz, whose efforts to promote a dynastic cult and foundational discourse are well-known (E. Eldem, *Pride and Privilege*, pp. 216–22). However, it was during the reign of his nephew and successor, Abdülhamid II, that this phenomenon reached unprecedented proportions and that systematic attempts were carried out to feed the Ottoman and Islamic past into the state's ideology (S. Deringil, *The Well-Protected Domains*, pp. 31–7; Ersoy, 'The Sultan and his Tribe: Documenting Ottoman Roots in the Abdülhamid II Photographic Albums'.

> the style for a variety of complex reasons. Outside Europe the alhambresque represented an absorption of European practices, true, but it also represented a self-conscious manipulation of a historic style associated with an idealized Islamic past in an attempt to create a visual sense of continuity with the contemporary.[145]

Such a vision is obviously interesting and appealing. First, it ascribes meaning to architecture, which, in art and architectural history, is understandably a useful way of avoiding the stigma of too formal and descriptive an approach. Moreover, in the context of a phenomenon observed in a non-Western context, ascribing conscious choices and agency to the major actors is a useful way of restoring the kind of dignity and autonomy that Orientalist scholarship tends to deny them. The notion that the adoption of a Moresque style, copied from European Orientalist realisations, cannot be reduced to a simple imitation and needs to be viewed as the reflection of a conscious and deliberate desire to make use of this style for ideological purposes, constitutes a counter to the conventional argument of the slavish and thoughtless emulation of the West by Ottoman elites.

The problem, however, is to work out if, their evident appeal aside, these claims can really be supported by solid and reliable evidence, beyond assumptions and wishful thinking. True, there is no dearth of studies on the topic, especially since the 1990s; many researchers have examined, on the one hand, the important role played by architecture in Ottoman modernisation and Westernisation and, on the other, the very particular way in which 'Oriental' forms and styles were appropriated in the second half of the nineteenth century.[146] Many of the cases discussed in these studies belong to the general category of 'Moresque', renamed 'Alhambresque' by some to give a

[145] A. McSweeney, 'Versions and Visions of the Alhambra', p. 64.

[146] See, in particular, Z. Çelik, *Displaying the Orient: Architecture of Islam at Nineteenth Century World's Fairs*, pp. 157–8; T. Saner, '19. Yüzyıl Osmanlı Eklektisizminde "Elhamra'nın Payı"'; F. Yenişehirlioğlu, 'Continuity and Change in Nineteenth Century Istanbul: Sultan Abdülaziz and the Beylerbeyi Palace'; T. Saner, 'Orientalism in Architecture'; Ersoy, 'Ottoman Gothic: Evocations of the Medieval Past in Late Ottoman Architecture', pp. 218–25; Ersoy, *Architecture and the Late Ottoman Historical Imaginary*, pp. 195, 214–23.

more precise idea of the principal source of inspiration for decorative forms and motifs. What we do know with certainty is that the Moresque style did invade the architectural scene in the Ottoman capital in the 1860s; we are also able to identify, both in their overall aspect and in details, the linkages between these edifices and their source of inspiration, very often the Alhambra itself. The real challenge, however, remains that of documenting the way in which architects or their patrons came to choose these specific examples and, most of all, of revealing the objectives behind these choices. Finally, if we do indeed manage to grasp the intentions behind the artists' and their sponsors' decisions, we will still have to measure the impact of this architectural programme by trying to evaluate its perception and reception with as much precision as possible, through a contemporary documentation that might confirm – or contradict – the assumptions brought up to this day by these scholars.

The greatest obstacle in our way, as is so often the case in Ottoman history, especially in its cultural dimension, is the dearth of available documentation and sources. Anyone who has had to deal with questions relating to cultural or artistic realisations in the Ottoman Empire will have certainly faced at one point or another the archival silence concerning the 'immaterial' dimension of these phenomena. While the documentation concerning the financing or construction of a public or imperial edifice – mosques or palaces, to name only the most visible – is generally abundant, the archives will very often remain silent with respect to the less concrete and more qualitative issues concerning the choices made, the reasons behind them and the perception and reception of these undertakings by the greater public. These limitations tend to force art and architectural historians to jump through hoops and to use the tiniest bit of information in the hope of making up for these gaps in the documentation.[147] They may also incite them to take shortcuts and to overcome the absence of evidence by deductions and reasoning based on the observation of common points that are likely to indicate some form of causality. Thus, conscious

[147] See, for example, the work by Ünver Rüstem on the Ottoman Baroque of the eighteenth century, where the author tries to force architectural realisation to 'speak up' in order to defend the use of this term despite the absence of concrete evidence to this effect in contemporary Ottoman sources (Ü. Rüstem, *Ottoman Baroque: The Architectural Refashioning of Eighteenth-Century Istanbul*).

of the problem and wishing to liberate himself from the documentary void mentioned earlier, Ahmet Ersoy proposes to avoid the 'burden' of 'historicist causality' by resorting to 'the very contingencies of a world of intense global interconnectedness and reciprocity'.[148]

While it is certainly sometimes useful – even necessary – to free oneself from an overly rigorist approach and methodology, and from an overzealous commitment to documentation, I still believe that one does not exclude the other and, most of all, that speculations and interpretations of a somewhat more daring nature should be resorted to only once the available documentation has been truly exhausted. At any rate, it should be noted that despite their rather clear propensity to favour interpretive reasoning, art historians have always tried to present concrete clues suggesting the existence of concrete links between the Ottoman Moresque style and the intellectual or political trends observed amidst the Ottoman elite of the time.

Some have thus stressed the synchronicity, mentioned earlier, between the publication of many popular works on the history of Andalusia, starting with Ziya Pasha's history, and the construction of edifices in Moresque style in Istanbul.[149] While it is true that there is a certain degree of overlap between the two phenomena, one must also admit that this overlap remains very limited, considering that most of these texts were published after 1875, at a point in time when the Moresque style had already been supplanted for some years by the neo-Gothic. More importantly, it should be noted that none of these works contained the least evocation of the architecture of the period described. We have already seen that the only paragraph that Ziya Pasha devoted to the Alhambra did not include a single concrete detail that would have enabled a visualisation of the edifice. The plays published during the two following decades were as oblivious to architecture, with one or two references at most to the Alhambra, without any form of physical description of the palace. The claim that Edhem Pasha, as both the translator of Viardot and the mind behind the publication of the monumental compilation on Ottoman architecture prepared for the 1873 Vienna Exhibition,[150] might have provided a link between

[148] Ersoy, 'Ottoman Gothic', p. 217.

[149] Ersoy, *Architecture and the Late Ottoman Historical Imaginary*, pp. 208–9; McSweeney, 'Versions and Visions of the Alhambra', p. 63.

[150] Edhem Pasha (ed.), *Usul-ı Mimari-i Osmani – L'Architecture ottomane.*

literature and architecture is hardly convincing, considering that there are serious doubts as to his involvement in the translation work and that his role in the publication of the *L'Architecture ottomane* was limited to his patronage of the project as Minister of Public Works.

Some efforts have also been made to explain the phenomenon through the knowledge, preferences and taste of the major actors of this architectural endeavour, especially members of the Balian family of architects and, of course, the main sponsor of these projects, Sultan Abdülaziz himself. The suggestion that the sultan had 'probably' met Owen Jones during his visit to London in 1867 is irrelevant,[151] first, because there is no confirmation of such an encounter in the British press of the time and, more importantly, because most of the Moresque edifices of Istanbul had already been built or designed well before that date.

As to Abdülaziz's role in the development of this style, we do have Sarkis Balian's (1835–99) testimony, whereby he declared that 'every time I have worked for His Majesty, He was the one who made the drawings, chose the marbles, stones and ironworks, as well as decorative elements'.[152] Of course, such humility and admiration on behalf of the sultan's chief architect is likely to have more to do with sycophancy than reality.[153] Nevertheless, it is also true that Abdülaziz did have true artistic skills,[154] and it is perfectly plausible to imagine that he should have had something to say about the style of the numerous buildings he commissioned throughout the decade. The testimony of Sopon Bezirdjian (1839–1915), in charge of the decoration of the edifices built by Sarkis Balian, is probably more reliable, if only because it was published in 1889, more than ten years after the sultan's deposition and death. According to him, Abdülaziz had eventually become 'exceptionally fond of

151 McSweeney, 'Versions and Visions of the Alhambra', p. 56.

152 A. de Caston, 'Le grand mouvement architectural dans l'Empire ottoman', p. 418.

153 With less severity, Ersoy speaks of 'a highly qualified witness . . . displaying the extreme loyalty and humility of an ideal bureaucrat' (Ersoy, *Architecture and the Late Ottoman Historical Imaginary*, p. 235).

154 Abdülaziz's artistic merit has always been recognised by historians. See, on this issue, E. Z. Karal, *Osmanlı Tarihi*, vol. VII, pp. 113–14; Yenişehirlioğlu, 'Continuity and Change in Nineteenth Century Istanbul', p. 66; Ersoy, *Architecture and the Late Ottoman Historical Imaginary*, pp. 234–5; McSweeney, 'Versions and Visions of the Alhambra', p. 56; M. Roberts, *Istanbul Exchanges: Ottomans, Orientalists, and Nineteenth-Century Visual Culture*, pp. 37–74.

purely decorative arts'. He had commissioned 'vast and gorgeous palaces . . . in the true Oriental style'. Still according to Bezirdjian, he was 'passionately fond of Turkish, Arabian, and Persian styles of art'.[155]

One may deduce from these observations that Abdülaziz was aware of the existence of these styles and that his role in the realisation of these projects certainly exceeded the limits of simple and passive patronage. Nevertheless, are they really sufficient to back the hypothesis of the sultan's conscious and truly historicist intentions regarding the choice of a Moresque style? Quite the contrary, I believe that his awareness of the existence of three 'Oriental' styles suggests that he would have been capable of distinguishing Moresque motifs from those attributed to a 'Turkish' heritage. After all, even Owen Jones' famous *Grammar of Ornament* included a short section devoted to 'Turkish ornament'. Its weakness, however, is that it was both very short and not very flattering.[156] In fact, this may well have been the crux of the problem: convinced that the 'Turkish' style was not developed and sophisticated enough to support an ambitious architectural programme, the architects and their imperial patron may have fallen for the appeal of a universal Oriental(ist) style, already recognised and approved by Europe.

Finally, we need to address the claim made by Pars Tuğlacı that artists were sent to Spain and the Maghreb by the architect Agop Balian (1838–75) on a quest for sources of inspiration for the imperial projects in Istanbul.[157] Unfortunately, as Tuğlacı does not provide any form of documentation to back this

[155] S. Bezirdjian, *Albert. Fine Art Album – L'Albert: Album des Beaux-Arts*, p. 4. I am grateful to Alyson Wharton, who has kindly provided me with a copy of this very rare booklet.

[156] The section of Jones' work dedicated to Turkish decorative arts consisted of three pages and three plates, against ten and five, respectively, for the Moresque style. More importantly, Jones considered Turkish art to be deficient, base and inferior, noting that 'the Turks have rarely themselves practised the arts; but that they have rather commanded the execution than been themselves executants'. The reason for this, according to him, was that they 'have been the first of the Mohammadan races to abandon the traditional style of building of their forefathers, and to adopt the prevailing fashions of the day in their architecture; the modern buildings and palaces being not only the work of European artists, but designed in the most approved European style' (Jones, *The Grammar of Ornament*, pp. 61–3, pls XXXVI–XXXVIII and pp. 65–74, pls XXXIX–XLIII).

[157] P. Tuğlacı, *The Role of the Balian Family in Ottoman Architecture*, p. 318; taken up in McSweeney, 'Versions and Visions of the Alhambra', p. 61.

assertion, and as I have combed the visitors' book for the period without finding a single Armenian signature, the question remains unresolved, with the only possible clue being a few sketches by Sopon Bezirdjian that may indeed stem from an otherwise undocumented journey to Spain and/or Morocco.[158]

Of course, I should add to the list my own contribution to the question, namely, the possibility of a connection between Fuad Pasha's Moresque mausoleum and his Andalusian past, unknown to all to this day. I am well aware of the irony of the situation, considering that my discovery of this connection does look like a 'smoking gun' confirming the arguments of the partisans of a 'voluntarist' vision of the Ottoman fad for the Moresque in the 1860s. However, as I intend to demonstrate below, this would have merely added yet more purely circumstantial evidence feeding the frequent error in history of mistaking correlation for causality.

I believe the problem has to do with some scholars' irrepressible wish to see in the architectural realisations of the 1860s a historicist project and not just an Oriental(ist) one. This would imply that the Ottoman elite at the time would have already acquired a clear enough notion of a correspondence between medieval Islamic architecture and their own past. While it is certainly possible that the architects themselves should have entertained such a fantasy under the influence of Owen Jones' perception of Andalusian art as superior to its Anatolian counterpart, we lack any concrete indication suggesting that Abdülaziz and his entourage also shared such a vision. Moreover, one should not forget that the very notion of the Middle Ages was a very recent and extremely marginal addition to Ottoman historiography, which would not gain any substance before the end of the century.[159] The mistake, I believe, consists simply in interpreting as historicism what really amounts to little more than Abdülaziz's desire to produce an Oriental effect.

Indeed, we should remember that this architectural fashion constituted only one of the many facets of a much wider phenomenon observed during Abdülaziz's reign. Ever since his accession in 1861, the new sultan had tried to set himself apart from his older brother and predecessor, Abdülmecid, by

[158] A. Wharton, 'The Unknown Craftsman Made Real: Sopon Bezirdjian, Armenian-ness and Crafting of the Late Ottoman Palaces', pp. 86–8.

[159] Strauss, '*Kurûn-ı Vustâ*: la découverte du Moyen-Âge par les Ottomans'.

fashioning a more traditional identity for himself, in the hope of meeting the expectations of a conservative Muslim public, frustrated and antagonised by the excessive Westernisation of the previous reign. This involved as much his physical appearance – he was nicknamed *Pehlivan*, 'wrestler' – as his religiosity; however, it was principally with respect to iconography and symbolism that he subjected his empire to a campaign of de-Westernisation based on two major themes: Islam and the Ottoman dynasty. His creation of the *Osmani* order in 1861 was one of the most blatant examples of this effort. Compared with Abdülmecid's *Mecidi*, whose outlook imitated some of the major European orders of the time, the *Osmani* made conscious use of forms and motifs echoing the new leitmotivs of the empire: 'Turkish' red, combined with the green of Islam, reinforced by an Arabic motto inscribed around the name and titles of the sultan; an 'Oriental' look provided by a seven-pointed star with a crescent in the middle; and on the back, the martial motif of two janissary drums and two crossed banners, topped with the date of 699 of the Hijra (1299 CE), that of the alleged foundation of Osman's state (Figure 3.7). To drive the message home, Abdülaziz had made a pilgrimage to Osman Gazi's mausoleum in Bursa, where he had pinned the diamond-set insignia of the new order on his ancestor's cenotaph.[160]

The parallelism with architecture is striking: in both cases, the goal was to use forms and motifs that could suggest an image of Ottoman identity through easily recognisable visual references, doubled with likewise evocative or explicit text and symbols. Just like the palace of Dolmabahçe, built in an eclectic style mixing neoclassicism with rococo, or the *Mecidi* order and its European outlook spoke of Abdülmecid's commitment to the West, the Moresque style of the palace of Çırağan and the Orientalising insignia of the *Osmani* reflected Abdülaziz's allegiance to Islam and tradition. The new reign was undeniably engaging with history, through religion and the cult of the forefathers; but this implication remained at a discursive level and did not attempt to – in fact, could not – create a historicist and revivalist repertoire of references. That is why the Moresque style developed in Europe came in handy, given that it was already universally recognised as Oriental and/or

[160] Eldem, *Pride and Privilege*, pp. 216–21, 230–4; E. Eldem, 'The Changing Design and Rhetoric of Ottoman Decorations', pp. 36–8.

Figure 3.7 Obverse and reverse of the third-class badge of the *Osmani* order. Author's collection. On the obverse, the Arabic inscription on the red enamelled central piece reads 'Abdülaziz Khan, sovereign of the Ottoman State, who relies on Divine guidance' (*'Abd al-'Azīz Khān Malik al-Dawlat al-'Othmāniya al-Mustanid bitawfiqāt al-Rabbāniyat*). On the reverse, on top of two crossed banners and kettledrums symbolising the janissaries. a cartouche bears the alleged date of the foundation of the Ottoman Empire, 699 AH (1299 CE).

Islamic, not unlike the crescent or the colour green. Some twenty years later, the same logic incited the empire, after decades of hesitation, to finally adopt an official coat of arms, inspired by Western practice and examples adapted to an Ottoman context. The goal behind this undertaking was not to come up with a medievalist design, but simply to acquire an official emblem that could compare with those of the principal monarchies of Europe.[161]

Through the mediation of architects such as the Balian brothers, the inventors of the Moresque style, principally Owen Jones and Ludwig von Zanth, provided Abdülaziz with the perfect formula to attain his goal. Showy, majestic and universally recognised as an evocation of Islamic civilisation, Moresque architecture offered a foolproof combination of Oriental symbolism

[161] Eldem, *Pride and Privilege*, pp. 281–6.

and Western modernity. It should therefore not come as a surprise that it was transferred as is, in copy–paste fashion, without any real thought being given to its cultural and historical meaning. In the same way as the Baroque had been adopted about a century earlier with a vague sense of novelty but without any notion of its origins, the Moresque style, reduced to its simplest expression, invaded the Ottoman capital under the incentive of a ruler intent on marking his reign with the double imprint of the Orient and of modernity. As a result, it is likely that only very few members of the Ottoman elite, including the sultan himself, would have possessed the knowledge required to identify the original inspiration behind this fad, namely, the Alhambra.

Of course, nothing is more arduous than proving the absence of an intent or of an impression. All a researcher can do at best is to sift through the entire documentation available on the phenomenon and to make sure that there is indeed no reference whatsoever in support of the existence of such intent or impression. The case of Fuad Pasha's mausoleum may well provide us with a testing ground for the existence of a particular intent, beyond a simple fad, justifying the adoption of the Moresque style in the construction of the monument. The question is simple: does what we now know of Fuad Pasha's career allow us to assume that the style of his mausoleum reflects a deliberate choice that can be linked to his Andalusian journey twenty-five years earlier? Given the number of edifices built in this particular style throughout the 1860s, would the connection of a mausoleum constructed in 1869 to the deceased's nostalgia for al-Andalus really provide a key to the mystery behind the infatuation for this style during the first decade of Abdülaziz's reign?

Contingencies and interconnectedness may well be an antidote to a naive and obsessive submission to documented causality; yet can one really discard altogether the common sense in the suggestion that 'if we are to unearth the intentions of the architects and their clients, then we must base ourselves on contemporary textual and architectural evidence', to take up the formula used in the context of a study on the adoption of this particular style in the construction of Ashkenaz synagogues in Western Europe and the United States in the nineteenth and early twentieth centuries?[162] True, the Ottoman documentation available is much poorer than what can be found on the

[162] Kalmar, 'Moorish Style: Orientalism, the Jews, and Synagogue Architecture', p. 70.

fashion for 'Oriental' synagogues, but it seems that the actual problem has to do with the fact that the existing documentation, however meagre, has not been exploited systematically enough to allow for a proper treatment of the comments and information it contains or, on the contrary, of its absence.

The contemporary press is probably what comes closest to a systematic survey of public opinion and of a general awareness of the architectural and decorative changes taking place in the city. Comments on, and appraisals of, the outlook of new edifices might thus allow us to grasp the way in which they were perceived – or on the contrary, ignored – by the local public, thus filling in one of the major voids in Ottoman art and architectural history. Fuad Pasha's mausoleum could thus become a testing ground for this hypothesis by trying to ascertain if its design and construction might correspond in one way or another to the assumptions made on its style.

In fact, the press seems to have shown interest not only in the mausoleum, but also in the neighbouring mosque, which the pasha had vowed to have restored. On 3 March 1869, in a long description of the funeral, following a biography of the deceased, the *Ruzname-i Ceride-i Havadis* noted that he was buried next to the mosque he wished to have repaired according to the stipulations of his testament.[163] The following week, the same daily revealed that a document found among his belongings mentioned his intention to have the mosque and his own mausoleum built and included two chronograms intended for each of these edifices.[164] This information eliminates any form of doubt concerning the construction of the mosque and mausoleum, proving that they were erected after his death. The French- and English-language press of the city confirms that the work on the mausoleum began immediately[165] and that its estimated cost of 5,000 liras would be covered by the sultan himself.[166] The bulk of the work having to do with excavation and foundations, it was not before July that the first stone was laid during a ceremony attended by the entire cabinet.[167] By the end of November, the work

[163] *Ruznâme-i Cerîde-i Havâdis*, 1,103, 19 Zilkade 1285/3 March 1869, p. 4,410.

[164] *Ruznâme-i Cerîde-i Havâdis*, 1,107, 25 Zilkade 1285/9 March 1869, p. 4,425.

[165] *The Levant Herald*, 15 March 1869, p. 3.

[166] *The Levant Herald*, 27 March 1869, p. 3. This information was taken up by the French daily *La Presse*, 31 March 1869, p. 2.

[167] *The Levant Herald*, 8 July 1869, p. 2.

on the mausoleum and mosque was progressing well and it was hoped that the construction would be completed by spring.[168] In April, 'the construction work of the magnificent *djami* (mosque) and *turbe* (mausoleum) dedicated to the memory of Fuad Pasha [were] about to be completed'.[169] And then, nothing – not a word. Was it because this was only a secondary project, which had been completely occulted by the terrible event of the huge fire of 5 June 1870 that destroyed half of the 'European' district of Pera? A month later, the Franco-Prussian War would monopolise the public's attention. Fuad Pasha's mausoleum seems to have simply fallen through the cracks of a particularly dense and sensational agenda.

That being said, if a final report in the press had announced the completion of the work, what would it have said? That it had espoused the forms of the deceased's nostalgia for the Alhambra? That it was a monument erected to honour the past glory of al-Andalus? Certainly not, if one considers that during approximately a year of press coverage – however patchy – not a word had been written on its style, its inspiration, or even on the architect's name. In all likelihood, a last item would have mentioned the cost incurred and stressed the magnanimity of the sultan, while praising the beauty of the edifice, probably using the buzz word of 'Moresque' to describe its style in the middle of a stereotypical sentence. After all, that was the most frequent way in which the press described, without ever explaining it, the infatuation of the imperial capital with this novel style.

Leafing through the press reveals how superficially and repetitively the architectural novelties of the city were described. One of the first examples is undeniably the famous building that was erected in the middle of the Hippodrome (At Meydanı) to house the first – and last – Ottoman Exhibition in 1863. This temporary structure, which emulated, at a much more modest scale, the palaces and halls built in Europe for the great universal exhibitions, had been realised in two months by the French architect Marie Auguste Antoine Bourgeois (1821–84) (Figure 3.8).[170] The building was of a rather eclectic style, as noted by

[168] *The Levant Herald*, 29 November 1869, p. 2.

[169] *La Turquie*, 1 April 1870, p. 2.

[170] Marie Auguste Antoine Bourgeois was a student of Auguste Caristie. He had worked as inspector at the Tuileries Palace from 1848 to 1852 and had restored the castle of Anet between 1860 and 1866 (P-A. Planat, *Encyclopédie de l'architecture et de la construction*, vol. I, p. 159; J-C. Daufresne, *Louvre & Tuileries. Architectures de Papier*, pp. 247–8).

Figure 3.8 'View of the main façade of the exhibition palace at Constantinople', *L'Univers illustré*, 257 (16 April 1863), p. 153. Author's collection. The image depicts the structure built by the architect Bourgeois on the Hippodrome to house the Ottoman exhibition. The building's Moresque style is particularly visible in the arches of the gallery.

the *Illustrated London News*: 'With regard to the architecture of the building, no one style has been adhered to; but as in the columns and the arches of the interior, a kind of Composite Mauresque predominates'.[171] *L'Illustration*, on the other hand, noted that it was a 'beautiful edifice, in the style of the period of Mahomet II'.[172] As to the *Univers illustré*, it thought that 'the architect ha[d] managed to pleasantly mix to the style generally used for such constructions the Moresque architectonic style'.[173] Pierre Baragnon's publication devoted to the exhibition read like a eulogy of the edifice's beauty:

> This palace of solid, elegant and light construction is reminiscent of the style introduced in Europe and generally adopted under the rule of the first Ottoman emperors. Its decoration, in a style echoing that of the building,

[171] 'The Ottoman Exhibition, Constantinople'.

[172] 'Exposition à Constantinople'.

[173] *L'Univers illustré*, 257, 16 April 1863, p. 155.

> the models for which have been selected with perfect taste among the most charming realisations of Asiatic decorative art, was entrusted to a skilled artist, M. Léon Parvillée, who was also in charge of the overall control of the construction and of the design of its details. These various works have been achieved with a zeal and intelligence deserving the greatest praise.[174]

One may wonder what the author understood by a 'style introduced in Europe and generally adopted under the rule of the first Ottoman emperors', but it is clear that opinions went back and forth between the generic term of Moresque and vague references to the early examples of Ottoman architecture in the city. A short item in *La Turquie*, where the famous fifteenth-century building known as the 'Tiled Pavilion' (*Çinili Köşk*) located inside the imperial palace gardens was qualified as a 'Moresque edifice' proves that some viewed this construction as a local version of the Moresque style.[175] This confusion can be justified by the similarities researchers have recently established between this kiosk and the exhibition hall of 1863.[176] In all probability, Bourgeois must have used the former as an inspiration for the latter; on the other hand, it seems that contemporary observers had simply sensed this resemblance by associating the term Moresque with a vague notion of 'Turkish' architecture in the fifteenth century.

The most surprising – and frustrating – aspect of this architectural episode is the deep silence observed in the Turkish-language press regarding the description of this new building erected right in the middle of the capital city. True, there were numerous comments, but they were all exclusively devoted to the exhibition itself, that is, to the contents of the building and not to its overall aspect and even less to its style.[177] The first issue of *Mir'at* (*Mirror*) included the entire regulation of the exhibition, together with two plans and

[174] P. Baragnon, *Coup d'œil général sur l'Exposition nationale à Constantinople*, p. 13.

[175] *La Turquie*, 2 February 1866, p. 2.

[176] Ersoy, *Architecture and the Late Ottoman Historical Imaginary*, pp. 228–9.

[177] See, for example, *Cerîde-i Havâdis*, 1,119 (1 Cemaziyülahir 1279/24 November 1862), p. 1; 1,120 (8 Cemaziyülahir 1279/1 December 1862), p. 1; 1,123 (29 Cemaziyülahir 1279/22 December 1862), p. 1; 1,126 (21 Receb 1279/12 January 1863), p. 1; 1,127 (28 Receb 1279/19 January 1863), p. 1; 1,128 (5 Şaban 1279/26 January 1863), p. 1; 1,130 (20 Şaban 1279/10 February 1863), p. 1; 1,131 (27 Şaban 1279/17 February 1863), p. 1; 1,132 (4 Ramazan 1279/23 February 1863), p. 1.

two views of the building, including its 'Moresque' façade. And yet not a word was said about the building's general outlook or style. Ironically, this was precisely the issue of the periodical in which the dialogue between Kâmil and Âkil on Spain and the fate of the Arabs of Andalusia had been published.[178]

The difference between the local press in Turkish and in foreign languages is of crucial importance. Apparently, references to the style of the new buildings belonged to a lexical and cultural repertoire, which had no equivalent in the Turkish vocabulary. As a result, it was only in the French- or English-language press that the term 'Moresque' continued to be used with the same insistence, but also with the same vagueness. By 1866, the monumental gate of the War Ministry, also built by Bourgeois, became the new focus of attention of the press of Constantinople. The German historian Philipp Anton Dethier, director of the Austrian high school, saw in the style of this new edifice the 'ennobled style of Oriental architecture'.[179] A few years later, the same Dethier, now director of the Imperial Museum, had apparently decided to bring more precision to this vague notion by proposing to qualify it as 'of a distinguished taste of a revival of the Ottoman style',[180] thus echoing the trend observed among architects in the 1870s of celebrating the birth of an Ottoman style, but this time openly claiming historic roots.[181] The *Seraskerat* (Office of the Commander-in-Chief) gate, as it was called in Turkish, constitutes, I believe, the only example of a building on whose style the Turkish-language press did comment:

> We do not need to remind [our readers] that the War Ministry was previously a wooden building about to collapse; it was demolished a year or two ago and rebuilt in stone. We are publishing in our humble pages the image of the two kiosks and of the majestic gate, which have been completed by now. According to architectural practice, the said kiosks belong to the category of known as that of Arab edifices.[182]

[178] *Mir'at*, I/1, pp. 14–16 and 4 pl. n.p.

[179] Ph. A. Dethier, 'Le Monument de Théodose II'.

[180] Ph. A. Dethier, *Le Bosphore et Constantinople: Description topographique et historique*, p. 26.

[181] On this topic, see the many articles by Pietro Montani published in the press from 1870 on, as well as the previously mentioned volume on the *Architecture ottomane* prepared on the occasion of the Vienna Exhibition of 1873. For more details, see Ersoy, 'Ottoman Gothic'.

[182] 'Daire-i Umur-ı Askeriye'.

This short description was coupled with a centrefold image representing the famous gate, flanked by the two kiosks, evidently drawn by a local artist of rather modest skills (Figure 3.9).[183] There is no doubt that the qualification of 'Arab' betrayed an effort at translating 'Moresque' into Turkish. One can derive from this the conclusion that despite the recent publication of Ziya Pasha's work, the term '*Endülüs*' had not come to the mind of the magazine's editors. Rather ironically, by qualifying the style of these buildings as Arab or Moresque, the commentators were oblivious to the fact that this time, Bourgeois had drawn his inspiration from the rear façade of the Tiled Pavilion.[184]

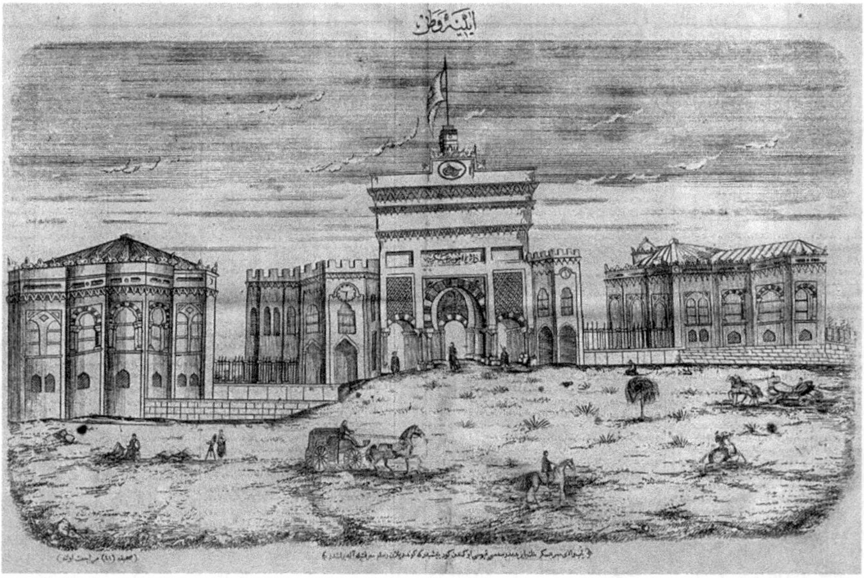

Figure 3.9 'View from the entrance of the madrasa of Bayezid of the Seraskerat Gate, drawn by an artist sent to the location'. *Âyine-i Vatan*, I/2 (24 January 1867), pp. 7–8. National Library of Turkey, Ankara. A rather rough rendition by a local artist of the monumental gate flanked by two pavilions designed by the architect Bourgeois for the War Ministry (*Seraskerat*). The horseshoe arches of the main entrance and pavilion windows give the building a clearly Moresque touch.

[183] *Âyine-i Vatan*, I/2, 24 January 1867, pp. 7–8.

[184] Ersoy, *Architecture and the Late Ottoman Historical Imaginary*, pp. 228–9.

The list of the other Moresque buildings of Istanbul is long. Two imperial palaces were among the most prestigious examples of this fad: Beylerbeyi (1861–5) and Çırağan (1861–72), located on both sides of the Bosphorus. The *Seraskerat* gate, described earlier, gave access to the building bearing the same name, which would later be known as the War Ministry (1864–6). The Admiralty also gained its own Moresque palace on the Golden Horn, close by the Arsenal of Kasımpaşa (1865–9). The end of the decade seems to have been particularly fruitful in this respect. In March 1869, as the restoration of the main gate to the old imperial palace (*Bab-ı Hümayun*), which had been destroyed by a fire, was about to be completed, the *Levant Herald* noted that it had been 'rebuilt in the Moresque style'.[185] About two months later, it was announced that M. Karakiahia had sponsored the reconstruction 'in the Moresque style' of a small mosque located next to his property at Büyükdere, on the Bosphorus.[186] In October of the same year, during the visit of the French Empress Eugénie, the sultan and his guest had attended a military parade at Hünkâr İskelesi, on the Asian side of the Bosphorus, from a 'Moresque kiosk' designed by Agop Balian, admired by all for its 'delicious style and taste' (Figure 3.10). Moreover, 'charmed by the new bath of Tcheragan Palace', the empress 'had asked Agop Bey to make and send her its plan to France, where Her Majesty wished to have a reproduction of this masterpiece of Oriental ornament and architecture' (Figure 3.11).[187] Likewise, Eugénie was greeted in the 'European' district of Pera with the erection of a triumphal arch in the purest Moresque style (Figure 3.12).[188] In December, the mosque of Âli Pasha, inaugurated in the district of Bayezid, was celebrated as 'a wonderful example of Moresque architecture'.[189] At the end of the month,

[185] *The Levant Herald*, 29 March 1869, p. 4.

[186] *The Levant Herald*, 31 May 1869, p. 3.

[187] *The Levant Herald*, 25 October 1869, p. 3.

[188] *Le Monde illustré*, 656, 6 November 1869, p. 293.

[189] *The Levant Herald*, 3 December 1869, p. 3. This mosque was commissioned by Âli Pasha from the Italian architect Bariori to replace that of Yakub Agha, lost in a fire. Although its style is generally qualified as eclectic, it is also true that its octagonal plan and some of the decorative elements give it an Arabesque look (H. Arlı, 'Âli Paşa Camii ve Sebili'). At any rate, the extremely vague manner in which this terminology was used by contemporary observers speaks for itself of the power wielded by the 'Moresque' throughout the period.

when a modest monument was designed to replace a sheikh's mausoleum, which had been demolished to allow for the widening of the main street at Salıpazarı, it was noted that the new edifice would be erected in white marble and 'surrounded with Moresque arches'.[190] The following year, when Midhat Pasha, then governor of Baghdad, made preparations for the visit of the Shah of Iran, thousands of kilometres away from the capital city, he chose to erect

Figure 3.10 'Kiosk at Beycos'. Photograph by Basile (Vasilaki) Kargopoulo, 1869. Ömer M. Koç collection. Previously published by Bahattin Öztuncay, *Vasilaki Kargopulo: Hazret-i Pâdişâhî'nin Serfotoğrafı* (Istanbul: BOS, 2000), pp. 236–7. This temporary structure, designed by the architect Agop Balian, was erected as a platform from which Sultan Abdülaziz and his guest, the French Empress Eugénie, could attend a military parade organised in her honour at Hünkâr İskelesi, in the vicinity of Beykoz, on the Asian side of the Bosphorus. A copy of this construction would be built in Iraq the following year by the governor Midhat Pasha on the occasion of the shah's visit to this province. This architectural fantasy is probably one of the most fanciful examples of the Moresque craze of the 1860s.

[190] *The Levant Herald*, 30 December 1869, p. 3.

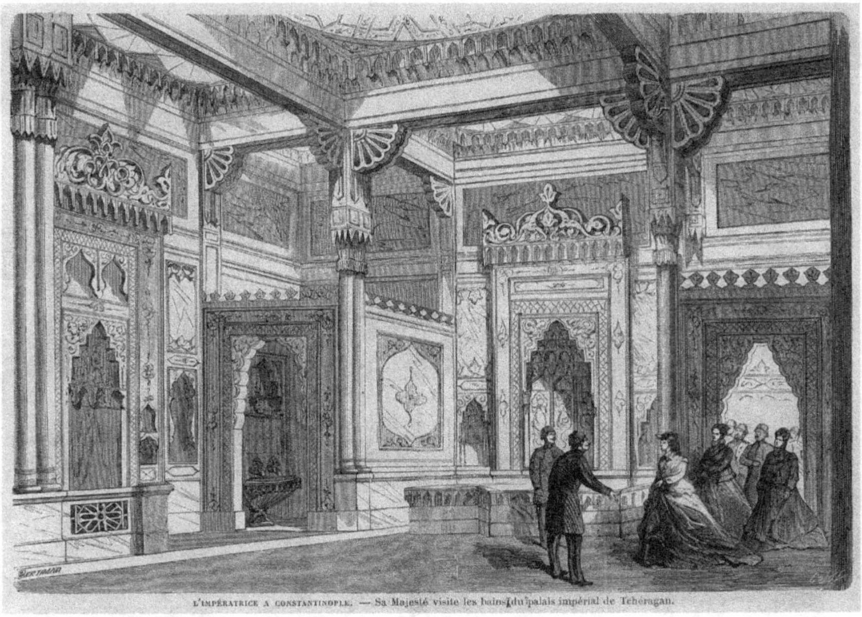

Figure 3.11 'The Empress in Constantinople: Her Majesty visiting the baths of the Imperial Palace of Tcheragan', *Le Monde illustré*, 660 (4 December 1869), p. 356. Author's collection. Designed by the Balians, the palace of Çırağan was the epitome of the application of Moresque architecture in Istanbul. During her stay in Istanbul on her way to Egypt, Eugénie visited the palace and, according to the local press, was 'charmed by the new bath of Tcheragan, and asked Agop Bey [Balian] to have its plan made and sent to her in France, where Her Majesty intended to have a copy made of this masterpiece of Oriental ornament and architecture' (*The Levant Herald*, 25 October 1869, p. 3).

a copy of the kiosk the sultan had commissioned for the empress' visit a few months earlier; rather predictably, the press praised the beauty of 'this elegant example of Moresque architecture'.[191]

All this information suggests a rather consistent pattern: an almost instinctive and catch-all use of 'Oriental' and 'Moresque' by the European and foreign-language local press; their absence from the Turkish-language press; the predominant role played in this by the palace and, most of all, by a handful of

[191] *The Levant Herald*, 25 August 1870, p. 3.

Le corps municipal de Constantinople présente une adresse à l'Impératrice, à l'entrée du faubourg de Péra.

Figure 3.12 'The municipal corps of Constantinople submits an address to the Empress, at the entrance of the suburb of Pera', *Le Monde illustré*, 656 (6 November 1869), p. 293. Author's collection. As the empress was expected to visit the 'European' district of Pera to attend mass at the Armenian Catholic church on 17 October 1869, a triumphal arch in typical Moresque style was erected, at the foot of which she received the homage of the municipal officers.

Western or Westernised architects; and a general indifference, not to say ignorance, of the greater public. The Ottoman Moresque style was embedded in an architectural and ornamental programme closely linked to the Alhambra and its derivative products, but managed by local actors who drew their inspiration directly from the West. All this amounted to a recycling and mixing of Moresque elements created and transferred through different means: Owen Jones' designs and models, their reinterpretation by the Beaux-Arts tradition,[192] or concrete realisations such as the Wilhelma Palace in Stuttgart.[193] The front line of the movement was formed by a small group of architecture and decoration professionals revolving around the palace and ruling elite: Léon Parvillée (1830–85),[194] Pietro Montani (1828–87),[195] and, of course, the elusive Bourgeois. At the top of the pyramid were the Balian brothers, who knew exactly how to manage the delicate balance between the architectural and decorative milieu and imperial whims. What could be more meaningful than the extraordinary versatility that allowed this family to maintain itself in place for three consecutive reigns, redesigning the 'official' style each time according to the circumstances of the day and their master's preferences?[196]

It is much more difficult to grasp the motivations and intentions behind the patrons, starting with the sultan himself. Generally speaking, their mastery of historical and cultural references seems to have been much patchier and more superficial than that of the architects. While there is no doubt that Abdülaziz was intent on distinguishing himself from his brother by espousing a profile and a register of a more local nature and much more rooted in history, I believe that the Balians' and other artists' genius resided in their ability to exploit this penchant by offering him the most efficient means of attaining this goal through the Moresque repertoire created and developed in Europe. This enabled the creation of a 'national' image that satisfied both the expectations

192 A. Wharton, 'The Balyan Family and the Linguistic Culture of a Parisian Education'.

193 Saner, '19. Yüzyıl Osmanlı Eklektisizminde "Elhamra'nın Payı"', pp. 136–8, 144; Koppelkamm, *The Imaginary Orient*, pp. 65–75.

194 M. Aoki Girardelli, 'Léon Parvillée and the Discourse on "Turkish" Architecture'.

195 On Montani's career and personality, see Ersoy, *Architecture and the Late Ottoman Historical Imaginary*, pp. 118–24.

196 A. Wharton, *The Architects of Ottoman Constantinople: The Balyan Family and the History of Ottoman Architecture*.

of a Western audience already marked by Orientalist stereotypes and shortcuts, and the ambitions of a sovereign who wished to catch up with the West while at the same time paying lip service to the traditions and history of his domains.

However, one needs to distinguish two very different registers. On the one hand, architecture and decoration and, on the other, history and literature. The first, of a formal nature, was content with using a pre-set 'kit', ready to use,[197] which needed only to be transferred and applied according to predefined modalities, without any need for contextualisation. The second, on the contrary, although borrowed from the same sources, had to be submitted to a textual and discursive treatment to be inserted into a cultural context, by means of history and ideology. The difference between the two is significant enough to forbid comparisons and connections bearing the risk of being random or, at best, circumstantial. The reason the Turkish-language press did not mention any of the cultural and historical references linked to the buildings and did not bring up any connection to the few 'Andalusian' publications of the time, was precisely because the two phenomena were completely disconnected. On the other hand, the fact that the French- and English-speaking press used the term 'Moresque' almost automatically stemmed from the absence of any other reference among its readers apart from this cultural shortcut.

In the face of such linguistic compartmentalisation, one cannot ignore that a real and deep disconnection existed between the architectural realisations of the 1860s, the historical context from which they drew their inspiration through the mediation of European architects and models, and the way they were perceived by the general public in Istanbul. Under such circumstances it seems simply impossible to accept the idea of a historicist attitude on behalf of the sultan and the elite; at best, one could imagine their satisfaction at the sight of projects, which combined a feeling of novelty with an Oriental look easily identifiable by anyone who had some familiarity with the architectural fantasies of the world exhibitions and of some of the European capitals. This explains that despite its being the original source of inspiration for all these derivatives of a European fad, the Alhambra was never explicitly referred to in the foreign-language press of the city. It may not come as a surprise, then,

[197] Saner, 'Orientalism in Architecture', p. 61.

that a Spanish daily was the first – and only? – publication to establish such a connection, albeit years later.[198] As to the reception of the Moresque style by the population, I believe that the absolute silence of the Turkish-language press in this respect suffices to show that the claims put forward by some historians as to the dissemination of a message intended for the greater public amounted to wishful thinking.[199]

Of course, there were some very rare exceptions that only confirmed this rule. In a letter to the British archaeologist and future diplomat Sir Austen Henry Layard (1817–94) on 18 August 1856, the diplomat and future pasha, Ahmed Vefik Efendi (1823–91), mentioned his project of 'building a true small Alhambra, which will measure 35 feet of length by 29 of width, with a cut-stone exterior' at a cost of 700 Turkish liras (approximately £630).[200] Alas, as no physical or documentary trace of Vefik Pasha's building has survived, it is impossible to imagine exactly what he had in mind, or even to ascertain whether the project was eventually realised. Given its rather modest dimensions (11 m × 9 m) it was probably meant as a small kiosk – perhaps even his famous library – somewhat like contemporary architectural fantasies in Europe. Nevertheless, it seems certain that Ahmed Vefik Efendi knew exactly what he was talking about, if one is to judge from the inventory of his library, as published for the auction organised a few years after his death. Indeed, the catalogue included three editions of *Don Quixote*, several novels by Cervantes, four histories of Spain (Hereford, 1808; Paquis and Dochez, 1838; Lavallée and Guéroult, 1844–7; Romey, 1839–50), four histories of the Arabs in Spain (Cardonne, 1765; de Circourt, 1846; Dozy, 1861; Ziya Pasha,

[198] 'There is nothing more marvellous and beautiful than this palace [of Beylerbeyi] located on the Bosphorus, next to the ruins of the bridge used by Darius's armies and, centuries later, by the Ottoman army conquering Constantinople. Everything is made of marble; in it, the Oriental architecture with its baths and fountains in the rooms and the mementos of the Alhambra come together with European comfort' (*La Época*, 12,978, 24 September 1888, p. 2).

[199] This is particularly the case with McSweeney's 'assessment' that 'the Ottoman world was displaying itself to Europe and all the Muslim world in an architectural language that its own people and foreigners alike would not fail to understand' (McSweeney, 'Versions and Visions of the Alhambra', p. 62).

[200] S. Kuneralp (ed.), *From an Ottoman Gentleman to his English Friend*.

1860–3) and, of course, Owen Jones' famous plans and elevations of the Alhambra (1845).[201]

Ahmed Vefik Efendi was about a decade ahead of Abdülaziz regarding the adoption of a Moresque style in architecture, which allows us to imagine that he might even have made fun of the sultan's infatuation with a style he knew was tainted with fantasy, not to say cheap. After all, it is striking to see to what extent the Ottomans made a different use of it when compared with European practice. While the West considered this style as an exotic fantasy generally used in fairgrounds and theatres, in Istanbul, it was suddenly promoted to a status worthy of the sultan's palaces and some of the most prominent governmental and public buildings.[202] While the imperial architecture of the previous decades was already characterised by bad taste verging on kitsch, as with the Palace of Dolmabahçe, the 1860s slathered on top of it a layer of Orientalism with a strong colonial undertone.[203]

What other proof of the superficial and thoughtless nature of the Ottoman Moresque does one need than the sad realisation that it was never subjected to a comparable depth and wealth of scholarly analysis as the Moresque style used in Ashkenaz synagogues, thanks to a coherent and continuous documentation?[204] Indeed, how can one not admit the fact that once these edifices are described and parallels are made and illustrated with the examples – real or imaginary – of Moresque architecture that have inspired them, the silence and

[201] *Catalogue de la bibliothèque de feu Ahmed Véfyk Pacha*, pp. 85, 189–90, 206, 230–1, 233–4, 237, 253.

[202] M-L. Crosnier Leconte, 'Oriental ou colonial? Questions de styles dans le concours de l'École des beaux-arts au xixe siècle'.

[203] Once again, I can only qualify as wishful thinking McSweeney's efforts to see in this difference of uses a 'subversion of Orientalism': 'By adopting a style that both Ottomans and Europeans clearly understood as Islamic in origin, they were subverting the Orientalist fantasies of their European counterparts by situating the alhambresque not in bathhouses or smoking rooms but in monumental facades and palace structures' (McSweeney, 'Versions and Visions of the Alhambra', p. 62).

[204] The use of the Moresque style in the architecture of – especially Ashkenaz – synagogues is a phenomenon, which, contrary to Ottoman practice, is based on decades of efforts devoted to imagine, justify and apply an Oriental style to find a way of expressing Jewish identity in Western Europe and the United States (Kalmar, 'Moorish Style: Orientalism, the Jews, and Synagogue Architecture').

apathy of the documentation only confirms the intensity of the intellectual void that accompanied this abundance of forms? Finally, how can one not note the ephemeral nature of this fad, which can be explained only by its lack of any form of connection to Ottoman society, other than the sultan's infatuation and the enterprising spirit of a handful of architects?

A comparison may come in handy with an extremely similar phenomenon observed in Egypt during the exact same decade. Immediately after his accession to power in 1863, Ismail Pasha (1830–95), governor and then Khedive of Egypt from 1867 to 1879, had embarked upon a vast programme of urban construction and refurbishment in Cairo. Many among these works were designed in Moresque style; however, contrary to Istanbul, most of these Cairene projects were signed by some of the greatest names in the profession, leaving little doubt as to the ruler's intentions and his knowledge in the field. Owen Jones himself had been commissioned in 1863 to decorate from afar the Gezirah Palace in the style of the 'tombs of the caliphs in Old Cairo', not surprisingly, with a strong Andalusian touch. Carl von Diebitsch, well-known for his Alhambresque architectural fantasies, brought another layer of fantasy to the same palace by adding a 'neo-Moresque portico in moulded cast iron', followed by a monumental kiosk in the same material to welcome Empress Eugénie, whose visit was expected in November 1869 for the inauguration of the Suez Canal (Figure 3.13). The similarities with Istanbul are striking, even though the Cairene examples seem to have displayed more fantasy and more eclecticism, bringing together Alhambresque motifs and elements directly borrowed from the Egyptian capital's medieval architecture.[205] Here lies, it seems to me, a fundamental difference when comparing the two cases. The Ottomans did not yet have a medieval model from which to draw inspiration; Istanbul's medieval architecture was Byzantine, and it would take several decades before they could appropriate Anatolian architecture to create a 'national' style. In the meantime, they would have to make do with whatever Europe had to offer: a Moresque Orient in the 1860s and a revisited Gothic style in the 1870s. In Cairo, on the contrary, the idea of finding an inspiration

[205] M. Volait, 'Appropriating Orientalism?'; M. Volait, 'Dans l'intimité des objets et des monuments: l'orientalisme architectural vu d'Égypte', pp. 234–5; McSweeney, 'Versions and Visions of the Alhambra', pp. 50–6.

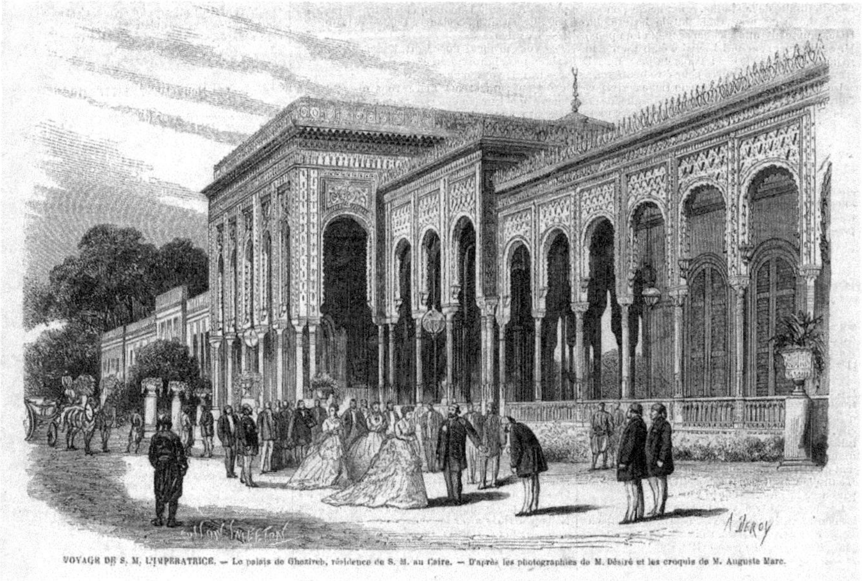

Figure 3.13 'H.M. the Empress' journey to Egypt. The Palace of Gezirah, H.M.'s residence at Cairo', *L'Illustration*, 1, 394 (13 November 1869), p. 312. Author's collection. Although the Palace of Gezirah was built in neoclassical style, the addition of a portico designed by Carl von Diebitsch gave it a resolutely Moresque look.

in the city's vernacular medieval architecture had not taken long to mature, albeit predominantly in the minds of European artists and architects, such as Richard Phené Spiers (1838–1916), Achille Joyau (1831–73), Ambroise Baudry (1838–1906), Henri Saladin (1851–1923), followed by at least two Egyptians, Husayn Fahmi Pasha *'al-mi'mār'* (1827–91) and Saber Sabri (1855–1915).[206]

Contrary to Abdülaziz, whose personal choices and preferences cannot be documented, probably because he was guided and led by the Balians and a few other architects, Khedive Ismail Pasha seems to have had a much greater knowledge and awareness of the architectural and decorative trends of the time. His repeated – and documented – contacts with Owen Jones and Carl von Diebitsch prove that he was indeed personally involved in this programme

[206] Volait, 'Dans l'intimité des objets et des monuments', pp. 234–5.

and that he knew how to directly draw on an architectural practice that suited the modern and cosmopolitan identity he wished to fashion for himself.[207] All this renders a comparison with Abdülaziz even more complicated: on the one hand, a sultan seeking European recognition as an autonomous Oriental power, on the other, his vassal who saw no other viable future than a form of quasi colonial submission to the Great Powers.[208] This may well be the explanation behind the somewhat paradoxical situation of a provincial governor more aware of the ways of Europe than his suzerain, and a province more advanced than the capital city with respect to modernity and to a historical awareness regarding local architectural and monumental heritage. After all, how can we ignore that in the 1870s, while Cairo, after a brief flirtation with the Moresque, developed a locally inspired neo-Mamluk style,[209] Istanbul was still obstinately seeking to transplant Western styles adapted to the needs of a very dubious argumentation.

Indeed, by 1870, the Moresque style was already out of fashion in Istanbul. Ironically, when the government-sponsored daily *La Turquie* published, on 30 July 1870, a letter by a 'Muslim subscriber', accusing of frivolity 'any architect who would fail to admire the Alhambra of Granada and the Giralda and Alcázar of Seville',[210] this was the first time a direct reference had been made to the monument in the press – by the way, without any connection to a recent edifice – but the Moresque had already begun to be supplanted by a new imperial whim, that of the Ottoman neo-Gothic. The difference, however, was that this time, the new stylistic adventure would be accompanied by

[207] McSweeney, 'Versions and Visions of the Alhambra', pp. 50–6.

[208] We should remember this remarkable quote attributed to the Khedive in 1878: 'My country is no longer in Africa, we now are part of Europe' (G. Charmes, 'Un essai de gouvernement européen en Égypte', p. 776; McSweeney, 'Versions and Visions of the Alhambra', p. 55). According to some, the Khedive had already made this statement during the inauguration of the Suez Canal, in 1869 (E. Mercinier, 'L'Égypte actuelle: aperçus de géographie sociale et économique, nationalisme et internationalisme', p. 3).

[209] Without providing any reference, Ersoy notes that 'Forms evoking the Mamluk past, for instance, were studiously avoided in the Ottoman center for obvious political reasons, although these were among the most popular elements of the European Orientalist repertoire' (Ersoy, *Architecture and the Late Ottoman Historical Imaginary*, p. 220).

[210] 'L'islam devant le siècle', p. 2.

a conscious effort to provide it with a context embedded in an ideological and historical argumentation. Ahmet Ersoy has rightly underlined the power of this new wave and its – this time, documented – connection to the monumental volume of *L'Architecture ottomane* published on the occasion of the Vienna Exhibition of 1873.[211] In fact, one could even pull back for a few years this new architectural turn by taking into account the first articles published in the press in 1870 and penned by Pietro Montani, recently appointed 'director of decoration at the imperial palaces'.[212] It was this self-proclaimed ideologue of a 'national' architectural style who took upon himself the duty and honour of celebrating the birth of an Ottoman architecture worthy of this mission:

> For an art to become the pride of a nation, it needs to be measured against the means at this nation's disposal; to build beautiful edifices with means borrowed from abroad merely amounts to producing an ephemeral sparkle, which, far from shining on the nation, will barely present it under the dullest of lights . . . These conditions have been perfectly understood by those who have aspired to save Ottoman art from oblivion . . . Only those who have had the opportunity to see the baths of Tcheragan Palace can get an exact sense of the splendour that has suddenly been reached by Ottoman art. Their admiration will only increase when they realise that all of it has been achieved with the means available in our city. To be sure, this is national art in all its force.
>
> The imperial platform at Beicos[213] also constituted a shining sample of modern Ottoman art, but it has vanished today, and only its memory and photographic image remain; yet, if this work has been lost, others of a more durable character will be offered to the admiring gaze of the public. One of these is the mosque of the Sultana Valide.[214]

Apparently, Montani's goal was to provide an *a posteriori* justification for the Moresque undertakings of the 1860s and to establish a link with the new architectural campaign that had begun with the construction of the mosque

211 Ersoy, 'Ottoman Gothic'; Ersoy, *Architecture and the Late Ottoman Historical Imaginary*, pp. 91–240.

212 *La Turquie*, 10 January 1870, pp. 1–2.

213 The Moresque structure built at Hünkâr İskelesi for Empress Eugénie's visit, located near the village of Beykoz.

214 P. Montani, 'La nouvelle mosquée de la Sultane Validé'.

of Abdülaziz's mother Pertevniyal Valide Sultan (*c.* 1810–84), built between 1869 and 1871 in neo-Gothic style.[215] Although he stressed continuity by qualifying recent and future projects as national, in truth the construction of this mosque constituted a stylistic turning point. It was probably Montani again, who, on 30 September 1872, published a long review of *L'Architecture ottomane*, which was being prepared under the auspices of the Minister of Public Works, Edhem Pasha, for the world exhibition that would be held the following year in Vienna. The first paragraphs deserve to be quoted *in extenso* to give an idea of the arguments put forward to defend the idea of the existence of a 'Turkish' style:

> Western artists are generally unaware of the existence of an Ottoman art. Most of them confuse its production with those of the Persians and Arabs, either under the highly inappropriate name of Moresque style or under the much too vague one of Oriental style.
>
> With particular respect to architecture and the arts linked to it, such as sculpture and decorative painting, some of the most learned among them will admit to the existence of three sections in Oriental art: the Persian style; the Arab style, admirably defined by the marvellous edifices of Granada, Cordoba, Seville, the Alhambra, the Generalife, etc.; and finally, the *Saracen* style, which has given birth, at the time of the Crusades, to the style erroneously named Gothic.
>
> The Saracen style, introduced in Anatolia by the Turkish sultans of the Seljuk dynasty, has brilliantly shone under the reign of Alaeddin. After having inspired, in conjunction with the Arab monuments of Sicily, Norman, Flemish and German artists, who have covered the lands of France, England, Germany and Belgium with so many unique masterpieces: Notre Dame in Paris, the Holy Chapel, the cathedrals of Cologne, Bruges, Antwerp, Rouen, and whose first endeavour, the cathedral of Santa Rosalia in Palermo is already in itself a masterful work, the Saracen style gave birth in the Orient to another offspring no less worthy of it than the first: Ottoman art.[216]

215 Ersoy, 'Ottoman Gothic'; Ersoy, *Architecture and the Late Ottoman Historical Imaginary*, pp. 223–34.

216 'Variétés. Bibliographie. L'Architecture ottomane'.

This denial of the Moresque and Oriental styles to promote the idea of a common 'Saracen' ancestry with the European Gothic confirmed the intention to turn the page on the neo-Moresque, and to supplant it with the neo-Gothic style of which the Pertevniyal Mosque constituted the first concrete example. However, given that the construction of the last of the Moresque craze of the 1860s, Çırağan Palace, had just been completed, an urgent need was felt to include it in the positive assessment Montani was trying to give of the architectural 'revolution' in the making. Thus, using a very Christian metaphor, he turned these two edifices into the living proof of the miracle performed by Abdülaziz by bringing back to life the Ottoman art, which had been condemned to the sepulchre by the decadence and depravations of a Western-inspired architecture in effect since the eighteenth century:

> Like Lazarus, Ottoman art, sealed in the sepulchre, awaited its saviour ... Like Lazarus, it was merely asleep, and now, upon the sovereign call of Abd-ul-Aziz Khan, he breaks through the stone of his grave to reappear before our eyes fully alive, albeit still slightly held up by the wrapping of his funerary bandages.
>
> Nevertheless, it does not stagger. On the contrary, its strides are firm and confident. The Tcheragan Palace, the Mosque of Ak-Serai,[217] are its victorious stages.[218]

I shall not dwell any further on the irony behind this bold comparison between Jesus and a sultan intent on revamping his empire with an Islamic makeover; in the context that concerns us here, what counts is to understand that Montani was trying to bury as discreetly as possible the Alhambresque style that had dominated for a decade and to make as smooth a transition as possible to a new style of which he had become the self-proclaimed advocate and promoter.

From then on, the Alhambra and its architectural and decorative derivatives were reduced to the level of occasional reminders and architectural nods, such as the motto '*lā ghāliba illā Allah*' used in the decoration of Khedive Ismail's mansion on the heights of Altunizade, on the Asian side of

[217] Another name for the mosque of Pertevniyal Valide Sultan, derived from its location in the district of Aksaray.

[218] 'Variétés. Bibliographie. L'Architecture ottomane'.

the Bosphorus.[219] This ephemeral infatuation faded away as an increasingly eclectic Oriental(ist) style developed, which would ultimately dominate the Ottoman architectural scene, especially in Istanbul, until the beginning of the twentieth century. Another unmistakable sign was that from the 1870s on, the Alhambra, much like the Alcázar, would turn into a stereotypical reference in the world of entertainment in the empire's major cities. This was one of the settings the famous novelist Ahmed Midhat Efendi (1844–1912) chose for his character the singer Finette in his novella *Happiness*, published in 1885 but set in the cosmopolitan Pera of the 1870s:

> If, for example, one was to mention to the regulars of that world the name 'Finette', they would immediately recognise it and say: 'She was a singer who drew the crowds to the Alhambra.' They are mistaken. It is at the Flamme [theatre] that Finette had gained fame and when the audiences began to tire of her and her glory tarnished, she had taken refuge at the Alhambra to shine once again under [that theatre's] thousands of gaslights.[220]

The Alhambra was a theatre – actually, a singing café – located on the Avenue of Pera, the main artery of the city's 'European' district.[221] Each of the cities with some connection to Europe had its own Alhambra, which could take the shape of a café, a brasserie, a concert house or even a hotel, before cinemas took over the name from the 1910s on.[222] Fallen from the heights of the imperial palaces along the Bosphorus, reduced to an exotic cliché completely uprooted from its origins, the image of the Alhambra was diluted within an *alla franca* modernity, which, with some delay, led to the fate that it had met with in the main capitals and cities of the West.

[219] T. Toros, 'Yapı Kredi Bankası'nın Bağlarbaşı'ndaki Mecid Efendi Köşkü'; A. Batur, 'Abdülmecid Efendi Köşkü'.

[220] Ahmed Midhat, *Bahtiyarlık*, p. 25.

[221] E. de Amicis, *Constantinopoli*, vol. I, p. 193.

[222] The 'Petit Alhambra', operated by Antoine Zott, was on the same Avenue of Pera (*L'Indicateur ottoman*, 1881, p. 283). In the provinces, 'Alhambra' was the name of a cabaret operated by one Calerghis, on the quays of Izmir (*L'Indicateur ottoman*, 1881, p. 504), of a summer theatre in the same city (*Annuaire oriental*, 1891, p. 824), of a café with a garden and restaurant on the quays of Salonica (*Annuaire oriental*, 1891, p. 779) and of a hotel in Mytilene, owned by Malacou Brothers (*Annuaire oriental*, 1891, p. 836).

Paradoxically, the same modernity that had contributed to the banalisation of the Alhambra to the point of pulling it down to the level of a decontextualised cliché had also contributed to increasing the heightened sensitivity and awareness of Ottoman subjects who found themselves in the position of visiting the actual monuments after the end of the 1880s. The impact of architecture had evidently been ephemeral and, most of all, too muddled to allow for the growth of a true awareness with respect to Andalusian heritage. This was not the case with literary and historical sources, which left a far deeper imprint on their readers. True, not everyone had read Ziya Pasha, Abdülhak Hamid or Şemseddin Sami, but the most basic work of universal history published from the end of the 1870s onwards would have included at least a section dedicated to the history of Muslim presence in Spain.[223] While the mention of the Alhambra brought to the mind of an average Ottoman, at best, little more than a place of entertainment, those who had received a proper education and, *a fortiori*, those who had had a chance to visit the monument, now possessed the necessary intellectual tools and references to replace it in a historical and cultural context of some depth. Under the influence of a growingly invasive modernity, the Ottoman visitors of the turn of the century would be able to unleash a much more powerful and much denser vision of these iconic remains of Islamic civilisation. However, this heightened awareness was far from being uniform; it was characterised by an increasingly widening gap between Turks and Arabs, most notably due to the linguistic and cultural familiarity, which would provide the latter with the means of a much more meaningful engagement with the heritage and patrimony of al-Andalus.

[223] Ahmed Midhat, *Tarih-i Umumi*, vol. II, pp. 225–9, 254–5, 273–9, 342–50, 419–42; Mehmed Murad [Mizancı], *Muhtasar Tarih-i Umumi*, pp. 185–6; A. Tevfik, *Fezleke-i Tarih-i Umumi*, vol. II, pp. 63–6; Strauss, '*Kurun-ı Vusta*: la découverte du Moyen-Âge par les Ottomans', pp. 238–9.

4

MODERNITY: DREAMS AND IDEALS

The Beginnings of an 'Enlightened' Diplomacy

Ottoman diplomatic missions to the Spanish court started anew after the legation was re-established, following an interruption of over twenty years. Hüseyin Sermed Efendi (1832–86), a career diplomat, took over the mission in 1881 and died in Madrid in 1886, while still in post. On 25 February 1883, he visited the Alhambra and left a short inscription in the visitors' book: 'Here is the palace of the exemplary kings and sultans of Islam'.[1] Such concision does not allow for much interpretation; nevertheless, it is worth noting that he was the only one on the page to have felt the need to leave more than just a signature behind. The Granadan press, once so excited at the sight of a 'Turk' seemed indifferent: 'After spending a few days at the Alhambra in the magnificent hotel of Siete Suelos, the Turkish ambassador in Madrid has left [Granada] to pursue his journey through Andalusia.'[2] If we assume that he visited the Alhambra and signed the book immediately upon arrival, on 25 February, it seems that Sermed Efendi spent about a week in Granada, lodged right next to the monument. Should we take this as an indication of a curiosity that the press simply did not see worthy of comment?

[1] AA, *libros de firmas*, 43, fol. 290 v, 25 February 1883.

[2] 'Embajador'.

Not necessarily;[3] nevertheless, it should be noted that visiting Granada and touring Andalusia had become one of the conventional duties of Ottoman ministers in Madrid.[4]

Sermed Efendi's successor, Turhan Hüsnü Bey (1846–1927),[5] who filled this post from 1886 to 1894, visited the Alhambra on 1 May 1889. The inscription he left in the visitors' book suggests that a new stage had finally been reached concerning Ottoman awareness. The text was so rich that a note in Spanish called it 'a poem written by the ambassador of Turkey'. Actually, it was only prose, but Turhan Bey had undeniably embarked upon a lyricist streak (Figure 4.1):

> There is no victor but God. Oh, Alhambra, pride of Islamic civilisation and source of bewilderment in the minds of countless visitors. How could the believers prostrated before you in astonishment not cry? You were once the magnificent palace of kings who applied the precepts of the Koran in this land of al-Andalus for eight centuries. You were the gate of justice of a nation of warriors, who, like the radiant sun, came from the lands of the Orient and

[3] One could uselessly speculate on the fact that Sermed Efendi's personnel file mentions that he had taken lessons in Arabic, Persian and jurisprudence from private tutors. In all likelihood, this would have been a very elementary form of education if one considers that the linguistic skills mentioned in the same files consist only of Turkish and French, together with a basic understanding of German and English (BOA, DH SAİDd 2/996, p. 996).

[4] In a letter to the Minister of Foreign Affairs, Ârifi Pasha, Sermed Efendi expanded on the diplomatic significance and success of the journey to Spain of the German crown prince, Friedrich Wilhelm, adding that he had 'left Madrid yesterday for a short excursion to Andalusia', mentioned earlier in a very different context (see n. 108, p. 107). However, this remark shows no sensitivity to the historic dimension of this region, which suggests that contrary to his successor Turhan Bey (see, pp. 228–30), Sermed Efendi did not consider it worth an Ottoman diplomatic engagement (BOA, HR SYS 15/52, 8 December 1883).

[5] Turhan Hüsnü Bey [Përmeti] (1846–1927), later pasha, was ambassador to Rome (1877–80) before he was appointed in 1886 to Madrid, where he remained until 1894. He was then appointed governor of Crete (1894–5), Minister of Foreign Affairs (1895), again governor of Crete (1896), Minister of Pious Foundations (*Evkaf*) (1904–8) and ambassador to St Petersburg (1908–14). In 1914, he returned to his – now independent – native Albania, where he was twice prime minister (1914 and 1918–20). He then left Albania and settled in Rome, and eventually died in Neuilly in 1927 (S. Kuneralp, *Son Dönem Osmanlı Erkân ve Ricali*, p. 124; see at: https://sq.wikipedia.org/wiki/Turhan_pashë_Përmeti).

spread the true faith. Despite your pitiful state today, you deserve every word one could write about you, for you are a place that resembles paradise. I consider myself happy to have had the opportunity of visiting you and I leave you in tears, while addressing to the Lord my endless prayers for the protection of the lands of Islam from all calamities as long as the earth keeps turning.[6]

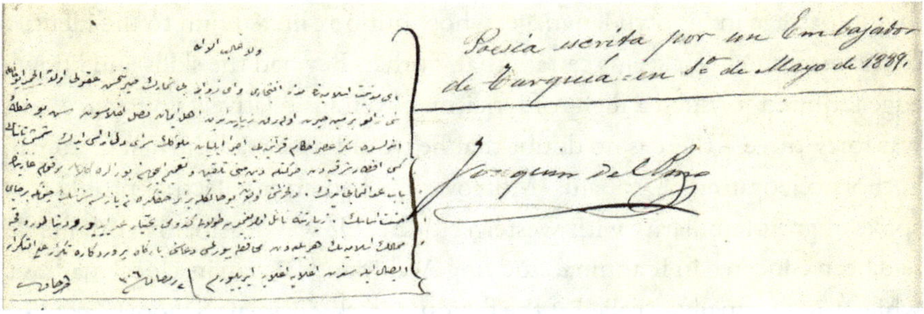

Figure 4.1 Inscription left in the visitors' book by the Ottoman minister in Madrid Turhan Bey, 1 May 1889. AA, *libros de firmas*, 44, fol. 251 v. © Archivo del Patronato de la Alhambra y Generalife. The length of the inscription must have convinced the Spaniard who left a note on the margin that this was a poem.

Leaving aside Malek Salem's more than suspect inscription of 1876, the Ottoman minister's comment was of unprecedented force. Much more than Midhat Pasha, whose text left the impression of a half-digested lesson learnt for the occasion, Turhan Bey managed to exploit the main feelings the Alhambra was expected to trigger in a Muslim visitor. The idea of harking back to the motto that covered the walls of the Nasrid palace was excellent; for the rest, a clever balance between the glorification of Islam and the deep sorrow caused by the expulsion of the Arabs from Spain perfectly suited the notion of a 'lesson' (*ibret*) for the visitors. The lesson was a double one: on the one hand, it was about learning of and appreciating the greatness of Islamic civilisation and, on the other, it involved the recognition of the misfortunes that befell it while at the same time being prepared for the dangers that lurked in the present. Repeated references to the tears shed over this sad fate gave the text a dramatic dimension the Spaniards were so fond of, as we have already observed.

[6] AA, *libros de firmas*, 44, fol. 251 v, 1 May 1889.

Turhan Bey had gone much further than his predecessors, be they diplomats or simple visitors.

The inscription was sophisticated, both in form and in content, which suggests that he had prepared it beforehand. True, its impact was seriously reduced due to the language barrier, but it seems clear that the ambassador, although perfectly capable of writing the same text in French, had made a point of marking his passage in his own language, whose outlook linked him to the identity of the monument. It seems certain that Turhan Bey had the skills and knowledge required for such a flight of lyricism. Given his relatively young age – he was forty-three – there is no doubt that he would have read the first Ottoman authors celebrating al-Andalus. Moreover, he had an intellectual profile that spoke of great familiarity with Western culture. He was of Albanian origin and had been educated in Ioannina, studying Arabic and Persian in a local madrasa, while being formally enrolled at the famous Greek Zosimaia School (Ζωσιμαία Σχολή), from which he graduated. He had then gone on to study at the Athens Law School, while taking private classes in Roman and international law, as well as economics. He read and wrote in Turkish and French, and knew Albanian, Greek, Italian and even some Spanish.[7] Without going as far as calling him a universal mind, it seems obvious that he was part of a new generation of Ottoman bureaucrats and statesmen, who could boast a staunchly modern education and culture.

Turhan Bey had more to offer than pathos and feelings. As a proper diplomat, he had noted as early as 1888 that the Granadan heritage constituted a good opportunity to promote the image and fame of his sovereign as sultan and caliph:

> The historic city of Granada, the cradle of Islamic civilisation in Andalusia, is visited every year by a great number of African Arabs. In my humble opinion, this situation makes it necessary to establish an honorary consulate.[8]

The minister's observation is extremely interesting from our perspective. Indeed, it comes as a confirmation of one of the major arguments I have put

[7] BOA, DH SAİDd 47/84, pp. 165–6.

[8] BOA, HR MTV 36/54.

forward in the first part of this work, that is, the noteworthy presence of visitors from the Maghreb in Andalusia and more particularly in Granada. The problem, however, is that my own records are far from documenting such a crowded presence at the time when Turhan Bey sent this note to the ministry of Foreign Affairs. There are several ways one can account for this discrepancy. It is quite possible, if not probable, that some of the visitors were content with visiting the city and skipped a visit to the Alhambra. Those who did climb up the hill, may have refused or forgotten to sign the visitors' book. Moreover, we can easily assume that the minister's remark was not based on concrete and recent data, but rather on a general impression he may have formed from information gathered through multiple contacts. After all, just three years earlier, ambassador Rīfī's visit had been widely reported on and had probably left a lively memory of Moroccan presence in Granada.

Whatever the circumstances, it is worth noting that Istanbul reacted promptly and very positively to this suggestion. By January 1889, the state apparatus had been set in motion for the establishment of a consulate as suggested by Turhan Bey:

> Considering the historic and present significance of this city where Islamic civilisation once shone, as well as the large number of its African Muslim and foreign visitors, it is highly important and essential that the Sublime Sultanate, as protector of the true faith of Islam, should hold a consulate there.[9]

There was only one glitch: the financial situation did not allow for the mobilisation of the funds required for a proper consulate. The administration thus reverted to the minister's initial suggestion and one Francisco Morales Fernández was appointed honorary consul, with Andrés Arenas Pérez as his second.[10] That being said, even though the initiative of opening a consulate in Granada was based on arguments directly linked to a novel vision of the 'Moorish' potential of the city, the importance of this decision needs to be relativised by noting that by the preceding year the Ottoman Empire already

[9] BOA, İ HR 314/20061, 10 Şaban 1306/11 April 1889.

[10] BOA, İ HR 316/20304, 25 Rebiyülahir 1307/18 December 1889; *Guía oficial de España 1890*, p. 146.

had consular representation in no less than twenty Spanish cities, including seven in Andalusia: Almeria, Cadiz, Cartagena, Cordoba, Jerez, Malaga and Seville.[11] We should also remember that it was in 1887 that the two scholars Shinqīṭī and Wardānī, as mentioned earlier, were sent by the imperial government to draw up a list of Islamic manuscripts preserved in Spanish libraries.[12] It was Turhan Bey, appointed to Madrid only a few months earlier, who had to deal with the details and logistics of Shinqīṭī and Wardānī's journey to Spain. The detailed report he sent to the palace on 26 October 1887, just after the two men had arrived, allows for a better understanding of how their mission had been imagined and realised. From the very start, the focus had been set on both the 'antiquities' and the 'very rare Islamic works' to be found in Spain.[13] However, a memorandum by the minister revealed that, much more than science, the sultan was interested in the publicity that could be derived from the mission:

> Upon the arrival of Sheikh Muḥammad Shinkitī's (*sic*) and his interpreter Ali Efendi's scientific commission, the *Época*, the best known daily in Spain, has published an article on the true superiority of His August Imperial Majesty over his glorious predecessors regarding his noble personal efforts, acknowledged by all, concerning the highly significant question of the preservation and publication of Islamic antiquities.[14]

That was not all. The minister also explained that he accompanied the two men to Toledo and that a local daily had 'brought up with great respect His Majesty's constant efforts for the happiness of the loyal subjects of God's shadow on earth'. The report ended by noting that the two scholars 'had left for al-Andalus in view of examining the Islamic monuments located in Southern Spain and [that] the said mission had made an excellent impression here'.[15] Turhan Bey's memorandum said a lot about the institutionalisation of

[11] *Guía oficial de España 1889*, pp. 141–2.

[12] See pp. 117–18.

[13] BOA, Y PRK EŞA 7/13, 14 Teşrin-i evvel 1303/26 October 1887.

[14] Turhan Bey misspelled the Mauritanian scholar's name by replacing the original 'qaf' (ق) and 'ṭa' (ط) by a 'kef' (ک) and 'te' (ت) and my omitting the long 'ī' (ي).

[15] BOA, Y PRK EŞA 7/13, 14 Teşrin-i evvel 1303/26 October 1887.

sycophancy under Abdülhamid's autocratic regime. Although it was true that the press had commented on the arrival and presence of the two men, these reports never exceeded the size of small items mentioning their mission, without ever praising the sultan as suggested by his envoy.[16]

Nevertheless, even if we discard these exaggerations, the diplomat's memorandum proved that the Ottoman government was trying to build up a cultural and diplomatic policy aimed at promoting an Ottoman presence in a region of Europe, which was connected to Islam and the Maghreb through history and geography.[17] One particularly interesting account reveals how some Ottoman representatives engaged with this newly discovered Islamic heritage. The Tunisian historian Ḥasan Ḥusnī Abd al-Wahhāb, who knew Wardānī and recorded his words, recounted the way he told him about his recollections of a memorable visit to the mosque of Cordoba:

> When we entered the mosque and examined its columns, I was overwhelmed by a feeling of sorrow, to the point that I took refuge in a distant corner to hide my eyes filled with tears, which betrayed my emotion. As I surrendered to sorrow and emotion, I felt a hand on my shoulder. It was the Turkish consul, who said to me, smiling: 'It looks like the sight of a mosque converted into a church has upset you. You should know that this has happened in every country whose conquests have extended East and West. Do not forget that if we have lost a mosque, where today Christian rites are celebrated, we still hold what has greatest value in the eyes of these vandals: the Holy Sepulchre. Remember this and you will feel comfort.' I thanked him for having pulled me away from my distraction and joined my companions, delighted by what I had just heard.[18]

[16] *Correspondencia de España*, 18 and 23 September 1887; *Diario de Córdoba*, 25 September 1887; *Revista de geografía comercial*, II(46), p. 24, 30 September 1887; *El Liberal*, 22 October 1887; *La Época*, 22 October 1887; *El Día*, 23 October 1887; *El País*, 24 October 1887; *La Unión católica*, 25 October 1887.

[17] After their journey to Andalusia, the sultan's two envoys were sent to Morocco to present their master's compliments to Sultan Ḥasan bin Muḥammad, also known as Ḥasan I (*La Paz*, 29 November 1887).

[18] Ḥ. Ḥ. 'Abd al-Wahhāb, *Waraqāt 'an al-Ḥaḍārat al-'Arabiyya bi-Ifrīqiyat al-Tūnisiyya*, pp. 464–5, trans. and quoted Roldán Romero, '*Al-Riḥla al-Andalusiyya* de 'Alī Sālim al-Wardānī al-Tūnisī (1861–1905): Estudio preliminar', p. 293.

A wonderful story, but one complicated by the fact that, like in all cities of Spain, the Ottoman consul in Cordoba was Spanish. In 1887, this was José Escalambre, honorary vice-consul, whom one can hardly imagine gloating at the idea of the Holy Sepulchre being in Ottoman hands.[19] It could not have been the ambassador either, considering that he had stayed in Madrid, from where he had reported on the two men's departure for Andalusia. One possible explanation is that this 'consul' was in fact the embassy's secretary, Şekib Efendi, or the military attaché, Turgudzade Şekib Bey, whom Turhan Bey might have instructed to accompany the two scholars in their journey.[20]

The conjunction of all these elements shows to what extent the government and its officials had gained awareness of the symbolic potential borne by the Muslim heritage of Andalusia.[21] True, this was still far from a proper policy, but the Ottoman state archives preserve traces of a few cases that may well have indirectly contributed to make the issue more visible and more sensitive. A case in point may be the letter received in 1884 from a Moroccan visitor, who, struck by Sultan Abdülhamid's munificence he had been able to observe during his pilgrimage to Mecca, had decided to spend some time in Istanbul before returning home, where he intended to sing the praises of the Caliph to a Moroccan audience.[22] Likewise, a notable of the island of Chios by the name of Nafiz Bey had sent a Koran written in the Kufic script on parchment, dating from 538 AH (1143–4) and originating from Cordoba, to the Imperial Treasury. The generous donor

[19] *Guía oficial de España 1888*, p. 143.

[20] *Guía oficial de España 1888*, p. 96.

[21] It is worth noting that among the arguments put forward in favour of the establishment of a consulate in Granada, apart from the city's historic significance and the number of visitors it attracted, the ministry mentioned that 'the Imperial Government occasionally sent officials entrusted with duties of inspection and other matters', probably a reference to Shinqīṭī and Wardānī's mission (BOA, İ HR 314/20061, 3 Cemaziyülevvel 1306/5 January 1889).

[22] BOA, Y PRK TKM 7/84, 1301/1884. The letter, written in the Arabic of the Maghreb, is accompanied by an abstract in Turkish. The author claimed to be a descendant of the Prophet and from a Yemenite family that had migrated to Andalusia and then taken refuge in Fez after the fall of Granada.

was rewarded with the fourth-class insignia of the *Osmani* order and a gold watch worth 30–40 liras.[23]

The Muslim Mashreq Steps In

With Turhan Bey, the very superficial connection of Ottoman visitors to the Alhambra seems to have taken a sharp turn. For the first time, history and feelings were skilfully brought together to form a strong image that could finally claim to compete with the one the West had been producing for decades. While the honour of having triggered this awareness falls upon a 'Turk' of Albanian origins, the pages of the visitors' book reveal that from the 1890s on, the torch was taken up by Muslim Arab subjects of the empire, who developed a very particular style, made up of modernity and nostalgia, to celebrate the memory of the Alhambra and of the past glory of al-Andalus.

This situation was all the more surprising because it was rather unpredictable. Until then, apart from visitors from the Maghreb, the only Arabs signing the visitors' book, who had come from the Mashreq had been Christians, more particularly Maronites, which reduced considerably the evocative powers of the Alhambra, especially if one considers that these visits to the monument seem to have consisted of an interlude of curiosity amidst activities linked to a network of religious solidarity uniting the two ends of the Mediterranean. As a result, it was after a silence of some fifty years that the first Muslims from the Mashreq reappeared in the visitors' book of the Alhambra.

The first of them was one Mehmed Kâmil Bey (1853–4–c. 1901), fifth secretary at the Imperial Palace, as he proudly noted in three languages – Arabic, Turkish and French – at the bottom of the long inscription he left in the register (Figure 4.2). He was an Arab, more precisely Syrian, a native of Homs, a detail that varied according to language: in Arabic, he was 'Muḥammad Kāmel, son of Naʿmān Duwwāmī from Homs in the province of Syria'; in Turkish, 'Mehmed Kâmil, son of Numan Efendi from Homs'; in

[23] BOA, İ DH 1046/82198, 11 Teşrin-i Sani 1302/23 November 1886 and 2 Eylül 1303/15 September 1887; Y MTV 38/50, 26 Mart 1305/7 April 1889; Y PRK BŞK 15/60, 3 Nisan 1305/15 April 1889 and 17 Şaban 1306/18 April 1889. In a telegram addressed to the palace, Nafiz Bey explains that this Koran was 'a legacy of his ancestors', without any additional detail about his family's possible ties to Cordoba or Andalusia.

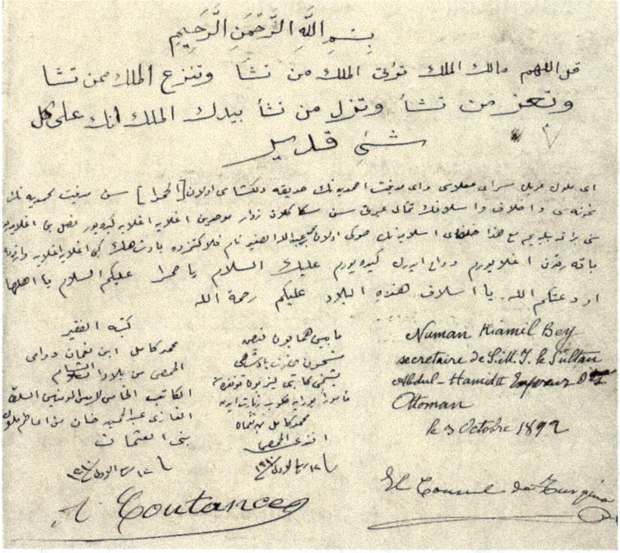

Figure 4.2 Inscription in the visitors' book by Mehmed Kâmil Bey, fifth secretary at the Imperial Palace, 3 October 1892. AA, *libros de firmas*, 45, fol. 126. © Archivo del Patronato de la Alhambra y Generalife. The lengthy inscription consists of the *basmala*, followed by a verse from the Koran, a long comment in Turkish and a prayer in Arabic. Kâmil Bey signed this hybrid text in three languages: Arabic, Turkish and French.

French, all ethnic and geographic references were left out. At any rate, it is clear that what he valued most was the fact that he served Sultan Abdülhamid II, whose pompous titles he made a point of enumerating in all three languages. Mehmed Kâmil Bey represented the kind of hybridity Abdülhamid particularly liked: an Arab – preferably Muslim, but not necessarily – at the service of the Ottoman sultanate and caliphate.

This hybridity had spilled over into the inscription itself. It started with the *basmala*, followed by a citation from the Koran, in a large and vocalised script: 'Say: "O Allah, Lord of all dominion! You give dominion to whom You will, and take away dominion from whom You will, and You exalt whom You will, and abase whom You will. In Your hand is all good. Surely You are all-powerful".'[24] It was followed by a comment in Turkish, with some blunders

24 قُلِ اللَّهُمَّ مَالِكَ الْمُلْكِ تُؤْتِي الْمُلْكَ مَنْ تَشَاءُ وَتَنْزِعُ الْمُلْكَ مِمَّنْ تَشَاءُ وَتُعِزُّ مَنْ تَشَاءُ وَتُذِلُّ مَنْ تَشَاءُ بِيَدِكَ الْخَيْرُ إِنَّكَ عَلَى كُلِّ شَيْءٍ قَدِيرٌ (*Koran*, 3:26).

that clashed with the rather advanced education he had received.[25] The text itself was much more interesting, both in content and in style:

> O Alhambra, exalted palace of the Arab kings and pleasant garden of Islamic civilisation, you are the model of Mohammedan civilisation and the image of the example of ancestors and descendants alike. The Muslim visitors who come to you depart in tears. How can I leave you without shedding tears? Just like your unfortunate sovereign Mohammad bin Abdallah the Young, the last of the caliphs of Islam, I look behind my shoulder and cry, I leave and bid you farewell.
>
> [In Arabic] Peace be upon you, o Alhambra; peace be upon its people. Farewell, o ancestors of this land, may the mercy of God be upon you.[26]

Mehmed Kâmil Bey's text was less sophisticated than Turhan Bey's, but it still had a lot in common: it addressed the Alhambra directly and in the first person; it repeatedly used the leitmotiv of estrangement and tears; it glorified Islam and lamented the fate of the monument and of the Arabs of Spain. What it lost in elegance it compensated for with a verse from the Koran and a litany in Arabic about farewell and benediction at the end of the tirade. He also managed to include the folkloric reference of the anecdote of Boabdil – 'Abdallah al-Ṣaghīr – shedding tears at the sight of the Alhambra as, on his way to exile, he turned back one last time to gaze from afar at his lost citadel. True, calling

[25] According to his personnel record, Mehmed Kâmil Bey graduated from the Imperial Lycée [of Galatasaray], where he studied Turkish literature, world history and geography, philosophy, cosmography, natural sciences, chemistry, natural history, accounting, algebra and Latin literature. He then studied international law, commercial law, economics, international order, finance and administration at the School of Administration (*Mekteb-i Mülkiye*). He also gave private lessons in French and taught geography and history at the Imperial Lycée. He was the author of a geography of the Ottoman Empire and Egypt, which he published at the age of twenty under the title *Arusetü'd-Dünya*, literally 'the World's Bride', a term he used to qualify the Ottoman Empire for its beauty and natural wealth (BOA, DH SAİDd, 1/133, p. 262; Mehmed Kâmil, *Arusetü'd-Dünya: Coğrafya-yı Umumi-i Devlet-i Aliyye ma Hıdiviyet-i Celile-i Mısriyye*). Two years later, Mehmed Kâmil Bey attended the Tenth Congress of Orientalists held in Geneva, where he gave a speech on 'the truth about Islamism and the Ottoman Empire', which was translated and published in Turkish the following year (N. Kâmil, *İslamiyet ve Devlet-i Aliyye-i Osmaniye Hakkında Doğru Bir Söz.*

[26] AA, *libros de firmas*, 45, fol. 126, 3 October 1892.

this unfortunate ruler 'the last of the caliphs of Islam' was a serious faux pas that Abdülhamid would have never forgiven, but the Spaniards, if they still had some interest in exotic visitors to the site, would have been delighted to see that they had finally started to react 'properly' by reminiscing the past glory of their civilisation, lamenting their forebearers' sad fate, and sighing and whining as they were expected to.[27]

One detail made Mehmed Kâmil Bey's visit even more exceptional. He had been sent on a mission by his government as a delegate to the Tenth Congress of Orientalists to be held in Lisbon from 23 September to 1 October 1892.[28] However, due to disagreements among the Orientalist community, the Portuguese government ended up using the pretext of a cholera epidemic to cancel the event about ten days before the planned date.[29] Some delegates had already arrived, as seems to have been the case with Mehmed Kâmil Bey, who had to return empty-handed, but apparently chose to make a detour through Granada on his way back.[30] All these elements point at a rather interesting profile for our visitor: an Arab from Homs, in Syria; a pen-pusher at the Imperial Palace of Yıldız; the author of a textbook on the geography of the empire; and an official delegate at the international congress of Orientalists.

[27] With respect to Mehmed Kâmil Bey, the *Defensor de Granada* just mentioned under 'Travellers' in its 'Miscellaneous news' section, that 'Sunday night His Excellency M. Kiarnich Bey [*sic*], secretary of the Sultan of Turkey and Ottoman delegate at the Congress of Orientalists at Lisbon has arrived in Granada Sunday evening and is lodged at the Washington [Irving] Hotel . . . A man of great knowledge, H. E. Kiarnich was met by M. Francisco Morales, Turkish consul in Granada' (*El Defensor de Granada*, 5,069, 4 October 1892, p. 2).

[28] His signature in Turkish is the only one that includes this detail: '. . . arrived here as delegate to the Lisbon congress' (AA, *libros de firmas*, 45, fol. 126, 3 October 1892).

[29] See, in particular, G. W. Leitner, *Xe Congrès international des orientalistes*, invitation published March 1892; *Congrès internacional* [*sic*] *des orientalistes: 10e session*, circular of 28 April 1892; 'Congresso orientalista'; 'Congresso dos orientalistas'; 'Sanskritica'; 'Congresso em Lisboa'; 'Malogrado congresso orientalista em Lisboa'; 'Xe congrès international des orientalistes'; A. Nepomuceno, 'Les brumes de l'orientalisme: brève histoire d'une rencontre fantomatique'; TECOP, Textos e contextos do orientalismo português, X Congresso de Lisboa, see at: http://tecop.letras.ulisboa.pt/np4/congLisboa.html.

[30] The invitation of March 1892 mentioned that 'excursions are planned to Cintra, Batalha and Evora in Portugal and to Seville, Cordoba and Granada in Spain' (Leitner, *Xe Congrès international des orientalistes*).

By a rather striking coincidence, just a few months later a man with a very similar profile visited the Alhambra and left a long comment in the visitors' book. This time, however, the visitor was a man of somewhat greater fame, an Egyptian bureaucrat and intellectual by the name of Aḥmad Zakī (1867–1934) – Ahmed Zeki in Ottoman sources. Zakī was not Syrian, but Egyptian, albeit born to a Moroccan father and a Kurdish mother. Most of all, he was highly educated and cultivated, to the point of being nicknamed the 'dean of Arabism' (*shaikh al-'Urūbah*) due to his knowledge of the Arabic language, and Arab literature and philology. The combination of these skills with a perfect mastery of French had opened a path for a brilliant administrative career. As he noted at the end of his inscription, he had become 'chief clerk at the Council of Ministers of His Highness the Khedive's government', a position he kept until 1921.[31] Evidently, Mehmed Kâmil Bey was only a pale copy of Zakī, but both men had an interesting point in common. Zakī, too, had visited the Alhambra on his way back from a congress of Orientalists, the ninth, which had been held in London in September 1892. This he noted at the bottom of his inscription, which he signed, a bit like Mehmed Kâmil, both in Arabic and in French. Contrary to Mehmed Kâmil Bey's aborted programme in Lisbon, the congress in London had taken place and Zakī, the delegate for the Egyptian

[31] Aḥmad Zakī went to the Qurabiyya and Tajhiziyya preparatory schools in Cairo before enrolling in the Scool of Administration. By 1888, he had been recruited at the press office of the Interior Ministry and, as translator and editor, at the official gazette, *al-Waqāyi' al-Miṣriyya*, while at the same time working as a translator at the Khedivial School and as professor of Arabic at the French Archaeological Institute of Cairo. The following year, he was appointed as translator at the Cabinet of Ministers and rapidly climbed the administrative echelons within this body. His intellectual merit being recognised both in Egypt and abroad, he joined the Institut d'Égypte, the Royal Society of Geography and the Royal Asiatic Society. He was elected to the executive board of al-Azhar University and of the Egyptian University, where he held the chair of Islamic civilisation. As a philologist and lexicographer of great erudition and a prolific writer, he very soon joined the nationalist cause and became the first secretary general of the Oriental League (*al-Rābiṭa al-Sharqiyya*) ('Zakī, Aḥmad', *Biographical Dictionary of Modern Egypt*, A. Goldschmidt Jr (ed.), pp. 236–7). According to Umar Ryad, his mother was Egyptian (U. Ryad, '"An Oriental Orientalist": Aḥmad Zakī Pasha (1868–1934), Egyptian Statesman and Philologist in the Colonial Age', p. 133).

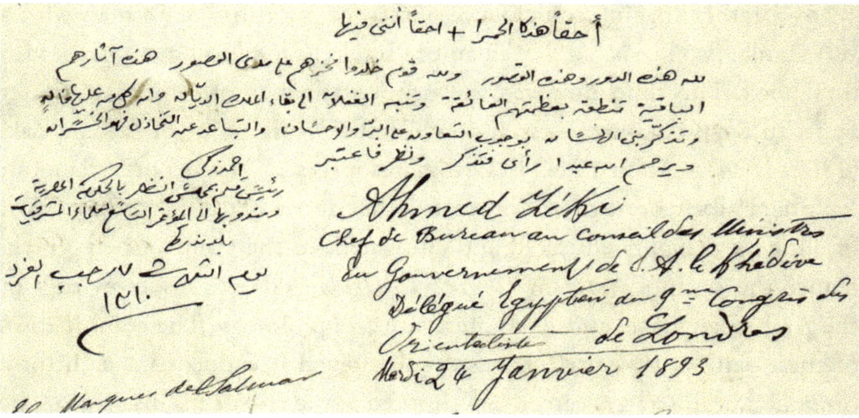

Figure 4.3 Inscription in the visitors' book by Aḥmad Zakī Bey, 24 January 1893. AA, *libros de firmas*, 44, fol. 147 v. © Archivo del Patronato de la Alhambra y Generalife. The Egyptian scholar and bureaucrat's inscription was entirely in Arabic and combined pride in the past with a strong touch of piety.

government, had made quite an impression.[32] His inscription in the visitors' book, dated 24 January 1893, was remarkable for its synthesis of historical pride and pious morality (Figure 4.3):

> Is this really you, al-Ḥamra'? Am I really in it?
> God's are these palaces and these mansions! God's are these people who immortalized their glory and merits. These are their remaining traces, which

[32] Zakī, who had the duty to 'represent modern education', presented a number of works he had transcribed or written himself, after which Sheikh Muḥammad Rāshid, representing al-Azhar University, had spoken, in Arabic, on the history and characteristics of the Cairene dialect, before presenting his new commentary on the poet al-Ḥarīrī (1054–1122). During the closing session, Muḥammad Rāshid recited a poem he had composed for the occasion, which Zakī had then translated into French. 'Mr Ahmed Effendi Zéki (translator at the Council of Ministers) has brought to the attention of the Arabists several ancient manuscripts belonging in part to the Khedivial Library and in part to H. E. Suleiman Pasha Abaza's magnificent collection. There is no doubt that this young and tireless worker will fulfil the promises he has made to the Congress regarding these manuscripts, which are certainly of great value' (E. D. Morgan (ed.), *Transactions of the Ninth International Congress of Orientalists*, vol. I, pp. xii, xiv, xxxviii, liii; K. Vollers (ed.), *Le neuvième congrès international des orientalistes*, pp. 9, 14; Ryad, '"An Oriental Orientalist"', pp. 139–40).

> proclaim their utmost greatness, and alert those unaware of the Omnipresent Lord and Judge. All that is on this earth will perish, and it reminds humanity of the necessity of cooperating in piety and benevolence, and of staying away from disunion, which is the greatest loss. God bless this slave who has seen and recorded, who has looked and reflected.[33]

Alas, there is no trace of Zakī's passage in the Granadan press. As we have noted earlier, 'exotic' visitors drew less and less attention from the public. However, in Zakī's case, it seems that he had the additional misfortune of visiting the Alhambra at the very moment when the death of the 'national poet' Zorrilla, which had happened the day before, monopolised the press for several days.[34]

Zakī is often considered to be the pioneer of a nostalgic vision of al-Andalus as a lost paradise of Arab civilisation.[35] That is not entirely accurate; dubious as his identity might have been, the poet from Tétouan, Malek Salem, had preceded him by almost twenty years. More concretely and reliably, the comments we have just seen signed by the Ottoman minister Turhan Bey and the (fifth) imperial secretary Mehmed Kâmil Bey prove that feelings and expressions of nostalgia had been there for quite some years already. Nevertheless, what sets Zakī apart is that he was the first to disseminate these impressions in a travelogue he published the same year as his journey to Spain. This is the main reason behind the importance that has been attached to him in all works concerning Muslim visitors to Spain, given that from Pérès to Paradela, the common denominator behind all these researchers is that they depend exclusively on written sources – generally *riḥla*s or travelogues – to document this presence. What made Zakī special in this respect is that he was the author of the first Arab travelogue with a section devoted to Spain and

33 AA, *libros de firmas*, 44, fol. 147 v, 24 January 1893.

34 'La muerte del poeta nacional', *El Defensor de Granada*, 5,953, 24 January 1893, p. 1.

35 On Zakī's journey to Spain, see, among others, Pérès, *L'Espagne vue par les voyageurs musulmans*, pp. 72–87; P. Martínez Montávez, *Al-Andalus, España, en la literatura árabe contemporánea*, pp. 26–31; Paradela, *El otro laberinto español*, pp. 112–25; M. Cortés García, 'Andalucía: realidad y mito en la perspectiva intelectual árabe', pp. 272–3; J. Stearns, 'Representing and Remembering Al-Andalus: Some Historical Considerations Regarding the End of Time and the Making of Nostalgia', pp. 369–70; González Alcantud and Rojo Flores, 'La Alhambra de Granada: Un fractal orientalista en clave poscolonial', p. 707.

Andalusia that was published *alla franca*, in Western style, following a style that was inaugurated by the famous Rifāʿa Ṭahṭāwī (1801–73) sixty years earlier, when he published his *Takhlīṣ al-Ibrīz fī Talkhīṣ Bārīz* (*The Extraction of Pure Gold in the Abstract of Paris*).[36] This time gap is probably responsible for the much more mundane – modern – title Zakī gave to his account: *Journey to the Congress* (*Al-Safar ilà al-Muʾtamar*), whose two consecutive editions prove its success (Figure 4.4).[37]

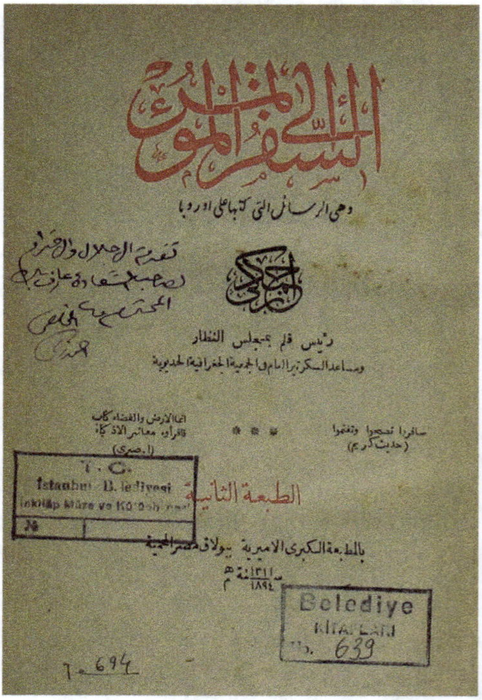

Figure 4.4 Title page of Aḥmad Zakī, *Journey to the Congress* (*Al-Safar ilà al-Muʾtamar*), 2nd edn (Cairo: Bulaq, 1311/1894). Istanbul Metropolitan Municipality Atatürk Library. This copy of the book is signed by the author to one Ârif Bey.

[36] Ṭahṭāwī, whose duty it was to accompany a group of Egyptian students, stayed in France from 1826 to 1831. From this stay he derived a travelogue, the first edition of which dates from 1834: R. Ṭahṭāwī, *Takhlīṣ al-ibrīz fī talkhīṣ Bārīz*. While this title literally means 'The extraction of pure gold in the abstract of Paris', it is known in French as *L'or de Paris* ('the gold of Paris'). This work was translated into Turkish by Besim Rüstem as early as 1839: [Ṭahṭāwī], *Tahlisü'l-ibriz ila telhis-i Paris*. For commented and annotated translations in English and French, see Ṭahṭāwī, *An Imam in Paris* and *L'or de Paris*.

[37] A. Zakī, *Al-Safar ilà al-Muʾtamar*, 1st edn, 1311/1893, 2nd edn, 1311/1894. The first edition had 400 pages; the second, of better quality, had 520 and included, among other additions, a number of reviews praising the work, published in the Egyptian press.

There are more differences between the two travelogues than this time gap. The most striking is probably that while Ṭahṭāwī discovered France together with Western modernity, Zakī, already transformed by modernity, was rediscovering the Islamic past in a remote region of Europe.[38] What makes Zakī's account particularly significant from our perspective is its overlap with the inscription in the visitors' book. Indeed, he had made a point of recording a very accurate version of his comment in his travelogue, preceded by an account of the circumstances that had led to it: 'At the gate, they held out the book of visitors, where I wrote down the following words from memory, my hand shaking, with a lump in my throat and my eyes filled with tears.'[39]

Memory, Culture and Literature

What did Zakī mean when he noted that he had written his comment 'from memory'? One imagines that, like Turhan Bey a few years earlier, Zakī had prepared his text in advance, which allowed him to reproduce it without the slightest error or omission in his travelogue. This shows how much importance he gave to the event and that he wanted to record it forever with the solemnity and emotion it deserved. In fact, his travelogue mentioned another moment of comparable intensity, immediately after the visit, just before signing the book. 'I exited [the Alhambra] and I addressed her in the words of the poet.' There followed the eight verses he claimed to have recited then:

> I stood in tears in the Alhambra; at her sight,
> I lamented her broken fragments
> And I said: 'O Alhambra, no, come back'
> And she answered: 'Can one return from the dead?'
> I kept crying, and I cried there,
> But, alas, tears are of no use whatsoever.
> The remains of those who have left resemble
> The wailers who mourn the dead.[40]

[38] This observation does not exclude the fact that Zakī, too, devoted much of his work to a very detailed and admiring description of Britain and France. See, for example, Ryad, '"An Oriental Orientalist"', pp. 139–43.

[39] Zakī, *Al-Safar ilà al-Mu'tamar*, 1st edn, p. 365, 2nd edn, p. 406.

[40] Zakī, *Al-Safar ilà al-Mu'tamar*, 1st edn, pp. 364–5. 2nd edn, p. 406.

Zakī did not reveal the name of the poet he was quoting. In fact, it turns out that it was none other than Abū al-Qāsim Khalaf bin Faraj al-Ilbīrī, a poet of the second half of the eleventh century from Granada, more commonly known as al-Sumaysir ('the little broker').[41] It was his elegy, except that Zakī had tweaked it to suit his purpose. The original poem did not mention the Alhambra, which did not exist at the time, but the sumptuous palatial city of Madīnat al-Zahrā (Medina Azahara), which was built in the mid-tenth century and plundered less than a century later. It was this destruction that Sumaysir lamented in his poem, but Zakī just replaced 'Zahrā' with 'Ḥamra'' in the first and third verses to adapt this elegy to the disappearance, or rather the loss, of the Alhambra.

This was not the first time that Zakī quoted a poem in his travelogue. On the train that was taking him from France to Spain, just before reaching Irun, he had silently reminisced the verses of the Andalusian poet al-Rundī (1204–85) on the fall of Seville in 1267.[42] Of course, he was well versed in the classics of Arab literature; Maqqarī's famous *Whiff of Perfume of the Flowery Branch of al-Andalus* (*Kitāb Nafḥ al-Ṭīb min Ghuṣn al-Andalus al-Raṭīb*), which recounted the history of Muslim Spain through the major Andalusian authors, had just been republished in Cairo in 1885.[43] There is little doubt, therefore, that Zakī was familiar enough with this compilation, which included an impressive number of poems, including Sumaysir's, to be able to pull out a quote whenever he felt it was appropriate. Did he really recite this poem by heart then and there? Maybe not, for if he did, how would he have resisted the urge to write it down in the visitors' book? Nevertheless, it is very likely that he remembered it and made a note to include it in his travelogue. At any rate Zakī's comments and references prove to what extent notions of splendour, of beauty, but also of loss and nostalgia were firmly anchored in the Arab imagination of the Andalusian past. Tears shed at the sight of ruins and a dialogue between the author and the remains of past splendour were recurrent tropes

[41] P. Lirola Delgado, 'Al-Sumaysir, poeta satírico testigo de las taifas', p. 204; A. E. Elinson, *Looking Back at Al-Andalus*, pp. 6–7, 155; Maqqarī, *Kitāb Nafḥ al-Ṭīb min Ghuṣn al-Andalus al-Raṭīb*, vol. I, p. 247.

[42] Zakī, *Al-Safar ilà al-Mu'tamar*, 1st edn, pp. 338–40, 2nd edn, pp. 376–80; Ryad, '"An Oriental Orientalist"', p. 143.

[43] Maqqarī, *Kitāb Nafḥ al-Ṭīb min Ghuṣn al-Andalus al-Raṭīb*.

of Arab literature, especially in the realm of poetry.[44] This was also true of the image of a golden age, which, whenever brought up, took the form of a lost paradise in the eyes of these nostalgic authors.[45] Under these circumstances, it should not come as a surprise that two ruins of a same past should have been interchangeable. Madīnat al-Zahrā and the Alhambra could thus trigger the same kind of sorrow in a poet who would see both as the embodiment of past splendour and decline. What we do not know for sure is whether this substitution – which the very similar prosody of Zahrā and Ḥamra' made particularly easy – was Zakī's own initiative, or if it belonged to a sort of poetic licence used by others before him. I leave this question to the specialists of Arab poetry.

Zakī's visit marks a new peak in the phenomenon we have observed since the end of the 1880s. Muslim visitors from the Orient were increasingly engaged and their voices were getting stronger at the sight of a heritage that they now knew better how to appreciate and claim. Arabs from the Mashreq clearly stood out compared with other Muslims, be they from the Maghreb or from the Turkish-speaking core of the Ottoman Empire. They enjoyed the advantages of language and culture, which allowed them to perceive and experience the monument with much greater intensity than the others. True, the case of individuals from the Maghreb still needs to be studied in greater detail and from local sources, but it seems that a lower degree of awareness and, probably, lesser knowledge, accounts for the relative silence of Moroccan travellers in the visitors' book. Yet it was between 'Turks' and Arabs that the greatest contrast could be observed, not just because of linguistic and cultural differences, but also because of a growing political and ideological divergence. The Arab 'awakening' or 'Renaissance' of the time, known as the *Nahḍa*, was probably one of the major factors behind this drift.

This should not be taken as a divorce, pure and simple. On the contrary, we should remember that when Abdülhamid sent out Shinqīṭī and Wardānī on a mission to Spain in 1887, he was acting in accordance with his 'pan-Islamist' claims by promoting his own image and role as caliph and protector of the Arabo-Islamic world. We should not forget either that in Istanbul, the sultan

[44] Elinson, *Looking Back at Al-Andalus*, pp. 71–5.

[45] A. Shalem, 'The "Golden Age" in Al-Andalus as Remembered, or How Nostalgia Forged History'.

made sure to surround himself with Arab bureaucrats and scholars, some of whom acquired great power under his arbitrary and autocratic rule. Mehmed Kâmil Bey, although just an underling at the palace, when signing the visitors' book in Arabic made a point of informing potential readers that he was 'fifth secretary of the Commander of the Faithful (*Amīr al-Mu'minīn*), Sulṭān el-Ghāzī 'Abd al-Ḥamīd Khān, from among the greatest sovereigns of the house of 'Othmān'.[46] He was certainly motivated by a combination of pompousness and sycophancy, but he was also recognising and promoting Abdülhamid's claim to an aura among the empire's Arab population. Although much less self-serving than Mehmed Kâmil Bey, Arab notables and intellectuals across the imperial domains were not systematically anti-Ottoman, to the point that many of them remained loyal to the empire as the last independent Islamic state until its collapse after 1918. Nevertheless, it needs to be said that the *Nahḍa*, especially during its second phase at the turn of the twentieth century, was predominantly focused on a form of Arabism, combined with modernity, heavily influenced by Western sources and ideas. It should not come as a surprise, then, that most of this intellectual and political activity could be found in Egypt, and more particularly Cairo, a fertile ground where it could compete against the imperial capital, Istanbul.

As a meaningful actor of this movement, Aḥmad Zakī gave an excellent illustration of this growing rift between Istanbul and Cairo. In a conference in which he took part in 1913 on 'the past and future of Muslim art', he had qualified the Ottoman conquest of 1517 as a 'blow to Muslim art', comparable to the invasion by the Crusaders. While he mentioned his 'feelings of sincere sympathy . . . for the noble race of the Ottomans', he nevertheless ended up speaking of the 'Turkish hordes' responsible for the cultural and artistic impoverishment of Egypt, which had thus been reduced to the status of a province depending on a warrior empire.[47] Of course, this was said some twenty years after his visit to the Alhambra, but it seems plausible to imagine that he was already then committed to the notion of an Arab revival to which Abdülhamid II's crumbling empire might have posed a much greater threat than the colonial ambitions of an enlightened Europe. It is probably

[46] AA, *libros de firmas*, 45, fol. 126, 3 October 1892.

[47] M. Volait, 'L'ingénieur, le réformateur et le collectionneur', pp. 285–6.

not a coincidence that in 1895, Turhan Bey, now Minister of Foreign Affairs, felt the urge to reassure his sovereign with respect to Aḥmad Zakī's loyalty, by referring to an interview he had with him during his trip to Spain:[48]

> When I had a meeting with Ahmed Zeki Bey, chief of the secretariat of the Egyptian Cabinet of Ministers, upon his return from London, where he had been sent to the Congress of Orientalists by His Excellency the Khedive, I entrusted to a special envoy his publications, both original and translated, which he had given to Your humble servant in order to be submitted at the feet of His Majesty the Caliph's celestial throne and I have been able to ascertain during this conversation that he was among the most loyal and devoted subjects of our Master, the most holy and most powerful Caliph and most sublime Emperor.[49]

There is little doubt that Aḥmad Zakī was trying to keep both parties sweet, not out of cynicism, but rather because he knew how to separate politics from culture, or even from ideology. Egypt, even under British control and a strong French influence, remained nominally Ottoman; there was no reason to question this de jure suzerainty, which, after all, had no real impact on Khedivial policy, the main tenets of which were being decided in Europe. Culturally and ideologically speaking, however, it was a wholly different matter. As a convinced partisan of the need for an Arab revival by the Arabs, led by the Egyptian intelligentsia, it was this mission and the identity that came with it that motivated him when signing the visitors' book of the Alhambra and, even more, when writing the section of his travelogue devoted to his Andalusian journey.[50]

48 Zakī also mentions this meeting, but only to praise this talented and cultured diplomat, whose linguistic skills seem to have impressed him (Zakī, *Al-Safar ilà al-Mu'tamar*, 1st edn, p. 349, 2nd edn, p. 390).

49 BOA, Y PRK HR 20/71, 26 Haziran 1311/8 July 1895.

50 'The accounts, full of emotion, concerning the greatness of London, the magnificence of Paris, the artistic and archaeological curiosities of Portugal and especially of Spain, where one finds so many remains of Arab civilisation, everything is thought and said with infinite charm . . . In his work, M. Zéki is particularly addressing Egyptians, his compatriots and, based on this, the author's achievement is not just a beautiful work, but also a good deed' ('Bibliographie' published in the *Phare d'Alexandrie* of 15 November 1893 and reproduced in the annex to Zakī, *Al-Safar ilà al-Mu'tamar*, 2nd edn, pp. 495–6).

Politics and Ideology

Mehmed Kâmil Bey and Aḥmad Zakī had kicked off a series of Arab and Muslim visits, most of them by Egyptians. Two Christians came in between shortly after, but with not much to say. On 22 September 1895, one Edward Elias Bey, from Cairo, just signed the book in French and in Arabic.[51] On 20 April 1897, a young Dimitri Nicolas Tadros (1873–1937), from Jerusalem, left a similarly fugacious and laconic trace, probably linked to tourism, on which he would soon build his own career in his native land.[52] One has therefore to wait for the visit of the next Muslim from the Mashreq to be able to follow up on the strong feelings described earlier. This visitor arrived on 3 August 1897 and left a rather striking comment:

> O Granada, your name spreads over all countries and [the story of] your power fills most of the history of al-Andalus. You were the arrow stuck in the heart of the Franks. I have come to pay you a visit as a passionate believer, whose fervour you have doubled. I was astonished by the light of your beauty after all the vicissitudes fate has imposed on you. I came out of the Alhambra with thousands of burning embers in my heart and thousands of regrets that it should have fallen under Christian rule, its mosques turned into churches, its most beautiful parts destroyed to make place for Charles V's palace. I have devoted all my efforts to draw it from every angle to enjoy the pleasure of contemplating it when I will be far away. I implore God's satisfaction on its builders and on the Muslims who inhabited it. I leave it with passion, hoping

[51] AA, *libros de firmas*, 45, fol. 283 r. The name is too common to warrant an identification based on so little information. At best, one can assume that the English nature of his first name may indicate a Protestant identity, in contrast to the French text of the inscription.

[52] AA, *libros de firmas*, 46, fol. 45 r. Given his name, Tadros was Orthodox, but the mention in English 'of Jerusalem' suggests that he may have been Anglicised through education, like many of his Palestinian and Syro-Lebanese contemporaries. From the 1910s on, he worked in Jaffa as a travel agent, representing the Cruising Co. & Continental Travel Ltd (S. Gibson, Y. Shapira and R. L. Chapman, *Tourists, Travellers and Hotels in Nineteenth-Century Jerusalem*, p. 25, n. 33). It is probably him who was appointed Norwegian honorary consul in Jaffa in 1928 (*Official Gazette of the Government of Palestine*, 222, 1 November 1928, p. 680). Moreover, he seems to have been married to Fanny Emma Tadros, buried at the Zion cemetery in Jerusalem (see at: https://commons.wikimedia.org/wiki/File:Tadros,_Fanny_Emma_Zionsfriedhof_Jerusalem.jpg).

> for God's mercy upon all of us. His omnipotence is great. Muḥammad Tawḥīd al-Silaḥdār, grandson of Muḥammad Salīm Pasha al-Silaḥdār – may God grant him His mercy.[53]

Its vindictive tone makes this text rather unique. While earlier visitors had excelled in expressing laments and mourning, deploring the loss of the Alhambra and its abandonment, Muḥammad Tawḥīd al-Silaḥdār went much further, pointing at those who were responsible for this tragedy, the Christians. Much more than a lament, his was an act of accusation against those who had destroyed, disfigured and despoiled the Islamic heritage in Spain. Rather than sorrow, anger dominated the tone of his comment, prefiguring a form of vengeful challenge that would gain force in the years to come.

Yet who was this angry man? His signature suggests an Ottoman descent, rather easy to identify. Indeed, he seems to have been the grandson of Mehmed Selim Sırrı Pasha (1771–1831), known as 'Benderli', because he was born in the Moldavian town of Bender (Tighina), who had a brilliant career in the Ottoman administration, most notably as grand vizier from 1824 to 1828, at a very critical moment of Mahmud II's reign (1808–39). Indeed, he had been partly in charge of the formation of the new army that would eventually replace the janissaries, and he was at the helm of the government when the janissaries' revolt was crushed in a bloodbath in June 1826. Nevertheless, he was dismissed and exiled two years later, as he was held responsible for setbacks during the Russo-Ottoman War. He was pardoned in 1830 and appointed governor of Aleppo and then of Damascus, where he was confronted by a rebellion of the local inhabitants, stirred up by Muhammad Ali of Egypt, who was preparing an invasion of Syria. He held the citadel against the assailants for forty days before surrendering, after which, despite a promise of safe passage, he was burnt alive by the rebels.[54]

How was Muḥammad Tawḥīd al-Silaḥdār descended from this pasha and, more importantly, why did he live in the capital of the province whose former governor caused his grandfather's death, albeit indirectly? All that we know is that Benderli Selim Sırrı Pasha had two sons, Mehmed Nazif Bey and Aziz

[53] AA, *libros de firmas*, 46, fol. 62 v. All my thanks for the translation go to Renaud Soler, from the Centre d'histoire du XIXe siècle at the Sorbonne.

[54] H. Selçuk, 'Benderli Mehmed Selim (Sırrı) Paşa', pp. 150–64.

Mahmud Bey. The former apparently lived a life of destitution; in 1895–6, he was still receiving a monthly pension of 750 piastres. Mahmud Bey fared better and climbed the echelons of the Ottoman religious hierarchy to become a mullah before he died in 1895, at the age of ninety-two.[55] Was Muḥammad Tawḥīd al-Silaḥdār the son of one of these two siblings? I have been unable to verify this; at any rate, it seems clear that he was of 'Turkish' origin, that he was well established in Egypt and perfectly acculturated into the intellectual environment at the turn of the twentieth century. For the rest, the little information we have on his life and career is limited to bits and pieces gathered from the web.[56] We know that in 1901 he married Munīra Ḥamdī (1884–1944), of the Khedivial family;[57] that he managed the periodical *al-Miṣr al-Fatāt*;[58] that he was secretary at the Egyptian legation in Ankara during the 'tarboosh incident' of 29 October 1932;[59] and, finally, that he was one of the collaborators of

[55] Selçuk, 'Benderli Mehmed Selim (Sırrı) Paşa', pp. 171–2.

[56] I am most grateful to Renaud Soler, Walter Scott Sasson Chahanovich, doctoral candidate at Harvard University, Adam Mestyan, from Duke University, Seif el-Rashidi, from the Institute for Historical Research at London University, and Yasmine Dorghamy, from Cairo for their help in trying to identify this individual. I owe to Adam Mestyan the following information, taken from a work by Yaḥyà Ḥaqqī (1905–92), *Nās fī al-Zill wa-Shakhsiyyāt Ukhrā, 3: al-Maqālāt al-Adabiyya*. According to this source, Muḥammad Tawḥīd al-Silaḥdār started working as a young journalist in the 1890s, publishing in *al-Liwa'* and *Miṣr al-Fatāt*. He was very close to Muṣṭafà Kāmil and as a committed member of the latter's National Party, he is said to have greatly contributed to its finances through his personal fortune. He then went on to live a modest life, occupying several minor bureaucratic positions and taking up his activities as a journalist and literary critic in the 1930s. He is said to have died in 1963. Ḥaqqī also notes that his spoken Arabic was much better than his written Arabic, due to the fact that he was among the *awlād al-dhawāt* (children of nobility), describing the descendants of the Turkish-speaking elite of Ottoman origin.

[57] Munīra was the daughter of Maḥmūd Ḥamdī Pasha (1863–1921), son of Khedive Ismail Pasha and of Princess Zeyneb/Zainab (1860–1918), herself the daughter of Ibrahim Ilhami Pasha (1836–60), the son of Khedive Abbas Hilmi I (1813–54, r. 1848–54).

[58] Rif'at al-Sa'īd, فرح أنطون يعلمنا كيف يكون الثوري رومانسيًا, see at: https://www.albawabhnews.com/2232430.

[59] On 29 October 1932, the president of the Turkish Republic, Mustafa Kemal Pasha, the future Atatürk, arrived visibly tipsy at a reception at the Ankara Palace Hotel and lashed out at the Egyptian representative, 'Abd al-Malik Ḥamza, who was wearing a tarboosh, and ordered him to remove the headgear that he had outlawed in his own country. To avoid any diplomatic

Aḥmad Ḥasan al-Zayyāt's (1885–1968) magazine, *a'r-Risāla*, published from 1933 to 1953.[60] In other words, we have very little to munch on, but perhaps enough to sketch a rough portrait of a young man – he was probably in his twenties at the time of his visit – whose enthusiasm, not to say fervour, at the sight of the Alhambra heralded a political and ideological commitment to the path of Arabism and Egyptian nationalism.

This was precisely the profile of one of the next visitors from the Mashreq, Muḥammad Farīd (1868–1919), who signed the book on 24 July 1901. True, Farīd was much less talkative than Muḥammad Tawḥīd, perhaps due to his somewhat more mature age and to his status as 'solicitor in Cairo', as he indicated when signing his comment. Nevertheless, the line and a half of text he inscribed possessed a depth that betrayed the existentialist emotion he seems to have felt at the sight of the monument: 'Eternity is God and existence is God; God was when nothing existed and will continue to be when nothing more exists.'[61] Of course, we cannot dissociate this interpretation from what we do know about this famous Egyptian intellectual and political activist. Indeed, after a long career in the administration (1887–96), he established a legal office in Cairo (1896–1904). That was when he became acquainted with the nationalist leader Muṣṭafā Kāmil (1874–1908)[62] and became the vice-president of the National Party (*al-Ḥizb al-Waṭanī*), which the latter founded in 1907, and took over the leadership after his death the following year. A nationalist and an Arabist, and a Freemason since 1892, he nevertheless remained loyal to the Ottoman Empire, especially after the Young Turk Revolution of 1908, although he later opposed the Turanian and Turkist policies put forward by

---

incident, the Egyptian diplomat gave in and handed it over to a waiter, who took it away on a silver tray. Al-Silaḥdār, who was then legation secretary, was a witness to this incident, which was closed after formal apologies from the Turkish Ministry of Foreign Affairs (Nagdat Fatḥī Ṣafwat, حكايات دبلوماسيّة, accessed through Google Books).

[60] On *Arrissalah*, see at: https://en.wikipedia.org/wiki/Arrissalah and, in Arabic, https://ar.wikipedia.org/wiki/ الرسالة (مجلة).

[61] AA, *libros de firmas*, 46, fol. 201 v, 24 July 1901. In Arabic, 'الدوام الله و البقاء الله كان الله و لا شيء و يبقى الله و لا شيء'. Muḥammad Farīd signed as 'solicitor in Cairo' (*al-muḥāmī bi-Miṣr al-Qāhira*).

[62] 'Kamil, Mustafa', *Biographical Dictionary of Modern Egypt*, A. Goldschmidt Jr (ed.), pp. 101–3.

the Committee of Union and Progress.[63] True, when he visited the Alhambra in 1901, he was not yet formally active in politics, but he had already established a periodical, *al-Mawsūʿāt*, where he expressed his nationalist and anti-British ideas.[64]

His visit to the Alhambra was part of a long journey through Spain, Morocco and Algeria, an account of which he published under a resolutely modern title: *From Egypt to Egypt, a Journey in 1901* (*Min Miṣr ilà Miṣr: Riḥla sanat 1901*).[65] However, much like his stay in Spain of approximately two weeks, his description of Andalusia was filled with some leitmotivs that had by then become commonplace: the backwardness, even barbarism, of medieval Europe compared with Arab culture and science, the impregnation of the landscapes of Spain with Islamic remains and traditions, the unfair treatment of the Moriscos and the tragedy surrounding the loss of Granada. The Alhambra was barely mentioned, for it was once again on the mosque of Cordoba that the author insisted most, lamenting its conversion into a cathedral, the absence of Muslims and even bringing up the similar fate that had befallen many other lands recently lost and surrendered to Christianity.[66]

The overlap between the Egyptian nationalist and Arabist movement and the rediscovery of al-Andalus was striking. In 1893, the year of the publication of Zakī's travels to Europe and Spain, Muṣṭafā Kāmil, Muḥammad Farīd's mentor, had written a play in five acts titled *The Conquest of al-Andalus* (*al-Fatḥ al-Andalus*). Kāmil was only nineteen at the time; he had apparently found inspiration in Sédillot's (1808–75) *Histoire des Arabes*, published in 1854 and 1877 and translated into Arabic by ʿAlī Mubārak in 1892.[67] One cannot ignore the possibility that he may also have been influenced by Abdülhak Hâmid's play celebrating the same event, published in Turkish in 1879, even

[63] 'Farid, Muhammad', *Biographical Dictionary of Modern Egypt*, A. Goldschmidt Jr (ed.), pp. 53–4; Paradela, *El otro laberinto español*, pp. 153–5.

[64] Paradela, *El otro laberinto español*, p. 154.

[65] M. Farīd, *Min Miṣr ilà Miṣr: Riḥla sanat 1901*; Paradela, *El otro laberinto español*, p. 155.

[66] Paradela, *El otro laberinto español*, pp. 155–9.

[67] D. Walker, 'Egypt's Arabism: Mustafa Kamil's 1893 Play', p. 51; A. Mestyan, *Arab Patriotism*, pp. 298–301; L. A. Sédillot, *Histoire des Arabes*; trans.: *Khulāṣat Tārīkh al-ʿArab*. Mestyan interprets it as a sort of allegory of Khedive Abbas Hilmi II's struggle with Great Britain (pp. 298–9).

though it was not translated into Arabic before 1905.[68] It should also be noted that one of the arguments of the play was to show that the Arab conquest had been made possible by the dissent that reigned among Christians, while the warriors of Islam had all closed ranks around a common goal.[69] It should be remembered that this was a theme that Ottoman authors of the previous decade were particularly fond of, as with Muallim Naci, who insisted on the role played by disagreement and internal struggles in the final defeat of the Muslims of Spain.[70] Obviously, while the Ottomans were worried about losing their territories in the Balkans, for Egyptian nationalists, the true challenge was to liberate themselves from the yoke of colonialism and imperialism. Reminiscing the conquest of Spain was a way of convincing themselves that the domination to which they were subjected presently was not irreversible and that if the Muslims – or Arabs – had once conquered parts of Europe, nothing could stop them from freeing themselves from colonial rule.[71]

Ten years later, Jurji Zaydān (1861–1914) published his famous historical novel bearing the exact same title, *The Conquest of al-Andalus*.[72] Zaydān was born in Beirut to a Christian Orthodox family; he was educated at the Protestant College of Beirut – today's American University of Beirut (AUB) – and had rapidly espoused modernity through individualism, social Darwinism and Freemasonry. He left in exile to Cairo in 1882 and thus joined the heart of the *Nahḍa*, where he chose to live off his pen, but also to embark upon a civilising mission guided by his own writings. He started a periodical titled *al-Hilāl* in 1892 and, a few years later, started a series of publications that would eventually form a corpus of novels and history books aimed at educating the greater public by initiating it to the principles of Arab identity.[73] Popular historical novels were a powerful tool of vulgarisation, much more than the accounts and commentaries published until then. The success of Zaydān's novels,

[68] See p. 130.

[69] Walker, 'Egypt's Arabism: Mustafa Kamil's 1893 Play', p. 50.

[70] See pp. 191–2.

[71] Walker, 'Egypt's Arabism: Mustafa Kamil's 1893 Play', pp. 52–3.

[72] J. Zaydān, *Fatḥ al-Andalus*; J. Zaydān, *The Conquest of Andalusia*.

[73] On Zaydān, see, in particular, A-L. Dupont, *Ǧurǧī Zaydān (1861–1914), écrivain réformiste et témoin de la Renaissance arabe*; Th. Philipp, *Jurji Zaidan and the Foundations of Arab Nationalism*.

starting with *The Conquest of al-Andalus*, opened the path to many disciples who continued to exploit this combination of nostalgia, nationalism and the continuously renewed image of Andalusia under Muslim rule.[74]

The growing instrumentalisation of Andalusian heritage by Arabist ideologues had not escaped the attention of Western observers. Louis Bertrand (1866–1941), who published his impressions during a journey to Turkey and Egypt around 1906, very cynically claimed that the past had become the main instrument of defence – even of attack – of such thinkers and activists in their struggle against Western domination:

> Journalists and speakers are no longer content with complaining, they sometimes blow the trumpets of war. They recall the ancient victories of Islam; they reminisce the long gone centuries when all of Christianity was on the verge of collapsing before the attacks of the Crescent. It is undoubtedly the Arabs' as well as the Turks' right to commemorate their old triumphs and to boast about them. Yet why is it that all this national crowing should barely mask ulterior motives of revenge and retaliation? When these patriots' conquering imagination is unleashed, it embraces and mobilises the entire ancient Empire of the Caliphs and in its flight towards the West it barely stops at the battlefield of Poitiers.[75]

Bertrand was not fundamentally opposed to the nationalism and to the hopes of autonomy he observed among Arab intellectuals; in fact, he was even supportive of them, if one is to judge from the entire chapter he devoted to a very sympathetic portrait of Muṣṭafā Kāmil, whom he met in Cairo.[76] He was rather exasperated with the overly easy way in which the argument of past glory was over-exploited to restore the image of the Arab nation. For example, he resented one speaker, who he heard declare that France owed to Islam 'its civilisation and its sciences', 'half its vocabulary' and 'the best in the character and mentalities of its population'.[77] Given his ambiguous, to the say the least, political leanings – he sympathised with Egyptian nationalism, but defended

[74] W. Granara, 'Nostalgia, Arab Nationalism, and the Andalusian Chronotope in the Evolution of the Modern Arabic Novel', pp. 61–3.

[75] L. Bertrand, *Le Mirage oriental*, p. 209.

[76] Bertrand, *Le Mirage oriental*, pp. 188–99.

[77] Bertrand, *Le Mirage oriental*, p. 209.

French colonialism – and his rather dark ideological career,[78] Bertrand should definitely not be taken too seriously. It is clear that he was seduced by the anti-British dimension of Arab nationalism, but that there were limits to how much criticism and Oriental arrogance he was ready to accept regarding France. Nevertheless, from the viewpoint of this study, one of his remarks concerning the Arab nationalists' sources of pride was particularly interesting:

> In the meantime, Egypt responds to our past military invasions by invasions of tourists, in growing numbers every year. The Egyptians visit much more France than we visit their land. Nay, it is now a fad among fervent nationalists to go as far as Spain and to go and meditate on the bygone splendours of Western Islam while strolling in the gardens of the Alcázar of Seville or in the courtyards of the Alhambra of Granada.[79]

Of course, as usual, he was exaggerating; yet there was some truth to what he said mockingly about Egyptian 'nationalist tourists' swooning at the sight of the Alhambra, even though his estimates were inflated beyond credibility. The Alhambra, as source of pride and proof of civilisation can be spotted in the writings of yet another Egyptian intellectual of the second wave of the *Nahḍa*, Dusé Mohamed (Dūsī Muḥammad, 1866–1945), whose Nubian maternal descent later pushed towards pan-Africanism.[80] In the introduction to his work on the recent history of Egypt, published in 1911, he objected to the arrogance with which Westerners – especially the British – viewed and treated Orientals – especially Egyptians – and countered this form of racism with proofs of the architectural achievements of these nations, deemed inferior. He mentioned the magnificent edifices of India, but also Andalusian architecture, whose splendour he linked directly to the genius of the Arab people:

> Those who have visited Spain, gazing admiringly on the Alhambra and other remnants of Moorish architecture, wrought by the forebears of that very Arab

[78] A committed Dreyfusard in his youth, Bertrand became Catholic and nationalist, and in 1936 published a flattering portrait of Hitler, after having attended the Nuremberg rally of 1935. However, after the French debacle of 1940, he retired from public life and died the following year, see at: https://en.wikipedia.org/wiki/Louis_Bertrand_(novelist).

[79] Bertrand, *Le Mirage oriental*, p. 210.

[80] On Dusé Mohamed [Ali], see I. Duffield, 'Duse Mohamed Ali and the Development of pan-Africanism, 1866–1945'.

> stock who at present inhabit the Delta, must perforce admit that these edifices were the results of Oriental intellect unaided by the 'veneer of European culture and civilisation'.[81]

Clearly, by the beginning of the twentieth century, Arab Andalusia and, at its centre, the Alhambra, had become one of the main symbols of Arabism. On the one hand, they both stood at the heart of an increasingly focused effort by *Nahḍa* intellectuals to convey to the people an awareness of past glory and to mobilise a feeling of pride and confidence that would feed into the nationalist movements of the period; on the other hand, they were instrumentalised to serve the purposes of a struggle against the West, which oscillated between the two extremes of a sometimes simplistic revanchism and an anti-colonial challenge advocating the emancipation of the Arab population living under the domination of the French and, especially, the British, empires. It was striking to what extent this discourse was centred on Egypt, almost to the exclusion of the rest of the Arab world, which normally should have had a say on the issue of Andalusian heritage. Dusé Mohamed's shortcut between the Alhambra and the Nile Delta literally bypassed the entire Maghreb, despite its direct connection to both the conquest and the loss of Spain. These silences and absences echo the rather insidious way in which most historical and fictionalised works of the *Nahḍa* excluded Berber – today Amazigh – identity from the grand narrative of conquest, which these intellectuals were trying to disseminate among the greater public. Thus, Jurji Zaydān went as far as to demonise the Berbers, almost to the level of Christians, in a story whose major hero, Ṭāriq ibn Ziyād, was actually of Amazigh origin.[82] This helps us to understand the very recent trend among some writers from the Maghreb, such as Driss Chraïbi (1926–2007), to try to set the record straight by restoring the dignity and visibility of Amazigh heroes and characters – starting with Ṭāriq – they had been refused by pan-Arabist narratives.[83]

It seems that this discrepancy also had to do with the time gap in historical awareness between the Mashreq and the Maghreb. At a moment when

[81] M. Dusé, *In the Land of the Pharaohs*, p. 5.

[82] Granara, 'Nostalgia, Arab Nationalism, and the Andalusian Chronotope in the Evolution of the Modern Arabic Novel', pp. 64–5.

[83] Civantos, *The Afterlife of Al-Andalus*, pp. 130–7; D. Chraïbi, *Naissance à l'aube*.

the *Nahḍa* was spreading from Cairo and creating a de facto monopoly over the historical and civilisational discourse about Arab identity and Islam, the Maghreb remained silent, apparently unwilling, or perhaps not able, to produce an alternative or complementary narrative to the one that Cairene intellectuals were rapidly developing and bringing to perfection. We have already seen to what extent visitors from Algeria and Morocco remained silent – textually speaking – compared with Egyptians, despite the fact that they had preceded them by almost two centuries, when considering the *riḥla*s studied by Pérès and Matar. The question was not that they lacked curiosity or feelings. Even though their comments were much less developed, and it often fell upon the Spanish press to ascribe them emotions, we have seen that Moroccans did know how to admire the edifice and lament its loss. What they seem to have lacked, rather, were the means to channel these feelings into a historical framework that might establish links to the Andalusian heritage and lead to the construction of a political discourse capable of, or likely to, respond to the rising pressure of French colonialism and of Spanish colonial hopes. Of course, there is always a chance that I might myself be subject to a 'Levantine' bias and therefore missing all sorts of contemporary sources from the Maghreb that would invalidate part, or all, of my present claims. Nevertheless, I am convinced that if most of the literature focusing on the nostalgia and instrumentalisation of Andalusia throughout the Arab world until the 1930s still remains exclusively linked to 'Oriental' authors and intellectual trends, this situation needs to be interpreted as the result of a real imbalance, both qualitative and quantitative, in the manner in which these two major areas of the Arab world have perceived the heritage of al-Andalus in a context of confrontation with diverse forms of modernity.

Emulation and Diffusion

Three years after Muḥammad Farīd, it was yet another Arab, a Palestinian this time, who signed the visitors' book on 13 Rabiulakhir 1322 or 26 June 1904 (Figure 4.5).[84] Khalīl Jawād al-Khālidī – that was his name – had a much more

[84] The exact date is probably 27 June, given that the inscription is placed just below the signature of 'Mrs. J. McMillan Ayer', dated 27 June, and above that of Arthur and Ethel Melville, dated 30 June. This point of detail has incited me – as the result of a historian's obsessive-compulsive

modest profile compared with the diplomats and intellectuals mentioned up to this point, but he remains of crucial importance in the context of this study.[85] The first reason for this is purely personal, given that – as I explained at length in the Preface – it was the discovery of his photograph that triggered my

behaviour – to find out to what extent new research technologies – particularly the web – allowed for in-depth, detailed and, most probably, futile investigations. I tried therefore to see whether the visitors whose signatures framed that of my subject could be identified, knowing that their only distinctive feature was that they had signed the book before and after him. I very rapidly discovered that 'Mrs. J. McMillan Ayer' was born Annie Dana in Fryeburg (Maine) in 1842, that she was the widow of James McMillan Ayer (1839–92), that she had lived in Buenos Aires until her husband's demise and that she had then settled in Pasadena, where she died on 14 December 1921. As to the Melville, Arthur was a Scottish impressionist painter of some renown, who had married Ethel Croall in 1899 and died on 29 August 1904 in Surrey from a typhoid fever he had contracted during his journey in Spain. In 1914, his widow married the French-born painter Théodore Casimir Roussel (1847–1926), widowed in 1909. I think this digression may have proven the power of this new technology, but also its inherent risk of becoming an end in itself and, consequently, of generating information, which, if not entirely useless, is likely to be only marginally relevant. In all honesty, I do not think that I have been completely immune to this danger and temptation throughout this work.

[85] Since the publication of the original version of this book in 2021, I have been able to access, thanks to the guidance of Kasım Hızlı, researcher at the Ottoman section of the Turkish State Archives, Khalīl Jawād al-Khālidī's personnel file among the Sheikhulislamate Personnel Records (MŞH, SAİD, 30/11/198, 20 May 1330/1 June 1914). This has allowed me to revise and refine the biographical information on this individual. Born in Jerusalem in 1281/1864–5, Khalīl Jawād Badr Muṣṭafà Khalīl Muḥammad Ṣan'allah al-Khālidī received his primary education in his native city. He was then taught by the Shafii mufti Muḥammad As'ad Efendi, from whom he received his diploma (*icazet*). In 1896, he went to Cairo, where he received instruction from Sheikh 'Abdelraḥman al-Sharbīnī, from al-Azhar. He then went to Istanbul, received complementary instruction from Âsım Efendi and enrolled in the 'School of Naibs' (*Mektebü'l-Nüvvab*), from which he graduated on 1 Muharrem 1313/24 June 1895. He went to Tunis to study at the Zeytuna Mosque, after which he moved on to Fez, where he studied at the Qarawiyin Madrasa, under the supervision of Ja'far ibn Idrīs al-Kattānī (1830–1905) and Aḥmad bin Muḥammad al-Khayyāṭ, from whom he received his diploma on 14 Muharrem 1322/31 March 1904. He mastered both Arabic and Turkish and had notions of French. He was the author of a book called *Ümmehat-ı Kütüb-i İslamiye* (*The Sources of Islamic Books*) and claimed to have summarised Maqqarī's, *Kitāb Nafḥ al-Ṭīb*, to have written a *Travelogue of the West and Andalus* (*Garb ve Endülüs Seyahatnamesi*), a book titled *İhtiyarat* (*Choices/Selections*) on literature and a detailed memorandum on the science of meaning in language (*ilm-i vaz'*). His administrative career started with his appointment as *naib* (judge)

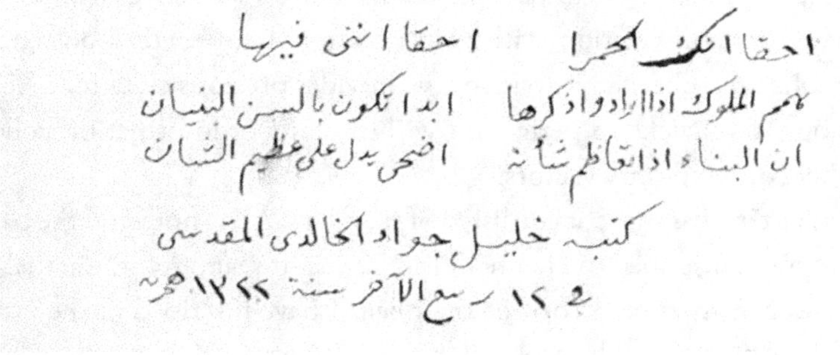

احقا انك الحمرا　　احقا انني فيها
همم الملوك اذا ارادوا ذكرها　　ابدا تكون بالسن البنيان
ان البناء اذا تعاظم شأنه　　اضحى يدل على عظيم الشان
كتبه خليل جواد الخالدي المقدسي
في ١٢ ربيع الآخر سنة ١٣٢٢ هجـ

Figure 4.5 Inscription in the visitors' book by Khalīl Jawād al-Khālidī, 26 June 1904. AA, *libros de firmas*, 47, fol. 13 v. © Archivo del Patronato de la Alhambra y Generalife. The Palestinian scholar's inscription consists of an address taken from Aḥmad Zakī's travelogue and four verses borrowed from a poem by ʿAbdelraḥman III al-Nāṣir li-Dīn Allah, emir and caliph of Cordoba, praising the beauties of his palatial city of Madīnat al-Zahrā.

curiosity and was eventually responsible for this book. The second reason has to do with the photograph itself, because my realisation – with some help – that it had been taken in the fake Alhambra of Rafael Garzón's studio opened up the 'Russian doll' of an Arab appropriating an Orientalist setting to create a memento of his presence in Andalusia that he would send out to his friends

to the district of Jabal Samʿān (Mount Simeon), in the province of Aleppo (1901–3). Followed by the same position in Kalkandelen (Tetovo) in Kosovo (1906) and Metroviçe (Mitrovicë), in the same province (1907–8). In 1909, he was sent to Hungary with a delegation of scholars and at the end of the year, he was appointed judge in Diyarbekir, where he stayed for about two years. In April 1914, he was appointed to the Sheikulislamate's Council for Shar'i Examination (*Meclis-i Tedkikat-ı Şeriye*), a post he held until he left Istanbul for Jerusalem in early 1920. There, he was appointed vice-president of the Shar'i court of appeal. When the mufti of Jerusalem, Kāmil al-Ḥusaynī, died in May 1921, Khālidī was one of the candidates to the succession, but the British High Commissioner, Sir Herbert Samuel, gave his preference to al-Ḥājj Muḥammad Amīn al-Ḥusaynī. Disappointed by this turn of events, Khālidī devoted himself to scholarship and travel. In 1932, he went again on a tour of Andalusia. He officially retired in 1934 and died in Cairo on 10 Ramadan 1360/4 October 1941. See MŞH, SAİD, 30/11/198, 20 May 1330/1 June 1914; 'Al-Khālidī (al-Shaikh Khalīl)', Y. al-ʿAwdāt (ed.), *Min Aʿlām al-Fikr*, pp. 153–5; 'Khalīl Jawād al-Khālidī', Kh. Ziriklī (ed.), *Al-Aʿlām*, 1969, vol. II, p. 366, 2002, vol. II, pp. 316–17; Kh. Salameh, 'Al-Shaykh Khalīl al-Khālidī'; http://khalidi.org/17.htm, accessed in 2016 but no longer available.

and colleagues. Finally, the importance of Khālidī's visit derives from the fact that the text of his inscription, with all its variations between the book and two photographs I have been able to identify, provides precious clues for a 'textual archaeology' that clicks to perfection with the bits of information collected from other contemporary visitors.

Khālidī's text was short; it consisted of six verses. As he noted on the back of the photograph inscribed to Hasan Tahsin Bey eight years after the actual visit, these verses consisted of 'a copy of the poem I have inscribed in the visitors' book of the Alhambra'. The problem, however, was that the verses in the book had nothing to do with those on the back of the photograph. The poem in the visitors' book was as follows:

> Is this really al-Ḥamra'?
> Am I really in it?
> If kings want their zeal to gain in glory
> As you can see, it is by the language of edifices.
> For if a building rises, full of majesty,
> It will continue to remind us of the glorious.[86]

No tears, no laments; just an expression of surprise, even disbelief, at the idea of being inside an edifice so often dreamed, followed by a short praise of the edifices representing the glory of their builders. There could be nothing more logical in the context of a visit to the Alhambra. However, there are two striking peculiarities about this poem. First, the first two verses, which have nothing to do with the following four, are almost identical to the exclamation at the very beginning of the inscription left by Aḥmad Zakī eleven years earlier.[87] As to the quatrain that followed, it was practically the same as the one left in March 1895 by 'Abdelkerīm bin Slīmān, the Moroccan delegation's secretary, whom the *Defensor* reporter claimed to have seen meditate in the Court of the Lions. I should add that I have previously identified these verses as having been copied – with a few minor mistakes – from 'Abdelraḥman III al-Nāṣir li-Dīn Allah, emir and caliph of Cordoba, to celebrate his city and palace of Madīnat al-Zahrā.[88]

[86] AA, *libros de firmas*, 47, fol. 13 v, 26 June 1904.

[87] See p. 238.

[88] See pp. 131–2.

The first overlap is easy to explain. Given that Zakī had signed the visitors' book eleven years and three registers before him, we can dismiss the possibility that Khālidī could have spotted his predecessor's inscription while browsing the book that was handed to him. In all likelihood, Khālidī had read Zakī's travelogue; he may even have carried it with him during his journey through Andalusia. At any rate, this constitutes a concrete example of the manner in which texts circulated at the time, inspiring not only those, who, like Khālidī, possessed the means to travel, but also numerous readers, who, in Cairo, Beirut, Damascus or Istanbul, could visualise the beauty and majesty of these historic sites built by their forebears.

In fact, we have yet another clue proving that Khālidī was inspired by Zakī's work. As I noted in the Preface, this Arab scholar had purchased several copies of his Andalusian portrait in order to present them to several of his acquaintances well after he had returned to Jerusalem. As a result, every time he prepared a new portrait, he would modify the dedication on the back of the photograph, probably due to an imperfect or patchy recollection of what he had actually written in the visitors' book in 1904. These verses were completely different from those he had inscribed on the back of the photograph presented to Hasan Tahsin Bey in 1912. The copy he gave his cousin, al-Ḥājj Rāgheb Khālidī, in 1905, only a year after his journey, was much closer to the original, albeit with some striking differences. Indeed, the quatrain from the visitors' book was there, but this time it was preceded by six other unrelated verses. And yet these additional verses were none other than the three first distiches of the lament that Aḥmad Zakī claimed he had recited upon exiting the Alhambra, before signing the visitors' book.[89] Once again, Khālidī, who had probably omitted to make a note of the inscription he had left, had resorted to Zakī's account, from which he borrowed six verses to complement the basic quatrain. Ironically, when he sent the same photograph to his colleague Hasan Tahsin Bey in 1912, the original quatrain had simply disappeared, with only the six verses taken from Zakī left.

If we set aside Khālidī's probable memory lapses, these variations come to show that he used a 'cut-and-paste' method to create a rather fanciful collage of verses borrowed from two different poems to which he had added Zakī's exclamation, reformatted as a distich for the occasion. I believe this should give

[89] See pp. 241–2.

us a sense of the flexibility and fluidity with which such cultural references and cultural borrowings were handled by individuals possessing a certain level of culture, without necessarily having remarkable erudition. While it seems plausible to imagine that Zakī, a bona fide expert of Arab literature and language, had a sufficient familiarity with tenth- and eleventh-century Andalusian poetry to allow for some licence, and that he had all the necessary publications, including Maqqarī's compilation, within reach, it is more than probable that Khālidī had a more limited choice of mostly secondary sources at his disposal, including Zakī's travelogue. Under these circumstances, it should not come as a surprise to see that he juggled with verses, which he rather freely rearranged to constitute the semblance of a poem.

On the other hand, the question of the source for the quatrain he inscribed in the visitors' book of the Alhambra remains open. As these verses do not appear anywhere in Zakī's travelogue, he must have taken them from elsewhere. Given that the lineage linking these verses to the original poem by Caliph 'Abdelraḥman III is not particularly easy to track down, one can legitimately doubt that Khālidī himself was aware of the connection. I also believe that a form of 'contamination' from the earlier inscription by the Moroccan embassy secretary is highly unlikely. He had been there in 1895 and his verses were in register 45 of the series, while Khālidī wrote his in number 47. I believe the answer is closer to the explanation I suggested while discussing 'Abdelkerīm bin Slīmān's comment, namely, that these verses circulated quite freely in the oral tradition, to the point that they could be 'recycled' by various authors in very diverse contexts and at different points in time. Maqrīzī made use of them in the context of Cairo; the author of the *Thousand and One Nights* adapted them to the pyramids; and Ṭahṭāwī drew on them in his description of Paris.[90] The errors in bin Slīmān's transcription, the adaptation of these verses to different contexts, the use made of four- or six-verse versions are all indicative of the malleability that characterised the diffusion and circulation of extracts and borrowings from 'classical' works. We shall probably never know who or what inspired Khālidī, but after all it does not really matter. What does count is to understand that, by the turn of the twentieth century, the Alhambra could become the inspiration for a Palestinian judge or for a Moroccan official of

[90] See pp. 131–2.

the same verses that sang the praise of historic edifices and their builders, even though the said verses had been – once again – composed in honour of the magnificent palatial city of Madīnat al-Zahrā.[91]

One would probably be able to say more on this if the *riḥla* that Khālidī is supposed to have written was to be found.[92] To complicate matters even more, let us note that another family member, Rūḥī Khālidī (1868–1913), Ottoman consul in Bordeaux,[93] also visited the monument, merely three years after his cousin. In much more laconic fashion, Rūḥī had chosen to inscribe a short

[91] Interestingly, in his personnel record kept at the Sheikhulislamate, Khālidī claimed to have written an abridged version of Maqqarī's, *Kitāb Nafḥ al-Ṭīb* (see n. 85, p. 256). Unfortunately, he provides no date for this undertaking, which does not seem to have been published. One would like to think that this was a result of the curiosity provoked by his Andalusian journey. At any rate, the fact that he should have abridged Maqqarī's does not necessarily imply that he had memorised all the poems in the compilation. The fact that both the poems he chose presented differences with their versions in Maqqarī, and that, like Zakī before him, he chose to transpose Zahrā into Ḥamra', seems to indicate that it was not the original text but rather its later – and looser – versions that he used.

[92] Although several biographies mention the existence of a 'travelogue to the Maghreb and Andalusia' (رحلة إلى بلاد المغرب و الأندلس), I have been unable to locate or access this text. See, 'Al-Khālidī (al-Shaikh Khalīl)', Y. al-'Awdāt (ed.), *Min A'lām al-Fikr*, pp. 153–5; 'Khalīl Jawād al-Khālidī', Kh. Ziriklī (ed.), *Al-A'lām*, 1969, vol. II, p. 366, 2002, vol. II, p. 317; Salameh, 'Al-Shaykh Khalīl al-Khālidī', pp. 52–3. It does not appear in the catalogue of manuscripts kept at the Khalidiyya Library (N. al-Ju'beh et al (eds), *Fihris makhṭūṭāt al-Maktabah al-Khālidīyah*). Any doubts as to the existence of this travelogue or as to the possibility that it may have concerned his 1932 journey can be eliminated by the discovery of his personal record kept at the Sheikhulislamate (see n. 85, p. 256), where he declares himself as having written a 'Travelogue of the West and Andalus' (*Garb ve Endülüs Seyahatnamesi*). Although one can clearly read 'West' (*Garb*), it seems likely that he actually meant to write 'Maghreb' (*Mağrib*).

[93] Rūḥī Yāsīn Muḥammad 'Alī al-Sayyid 'Alī Muḥammad Khalīl Ṣan'allah al-Khālidī was the son of Yāsīn al-Khālidī, first secretary at the Shar'ia court of Jerusalem and the nephew of Yūsuf al-Khālidī, mayor of the city from 1899 to 1907. In 1880, he left for Istanbul together with his uncle, 'Abdelraḥman Nāfiẓ Efendi. Upon his return to Jerusalem, he studied at al-Aqṣā, learnt French at the Alliance israélite universelle school and with the 'White Fathers' (*Pères blancs*), after which he was schooled at the Beirut Imperial Lycée. He left Palestine in 1887 for Istanbul, where he enrolled in the School of Civil Administration (*Mekteb-i Mülkiye*) and met the famous journalist and novelist Ahmed Midhat Efendi, who then owned the daily *Tercüman-ı Hakikat*. He graduated in 1893, spent some time in Jerusalem, but eventually

inscription referring to his Jerusalemite origins and to his passion for literature, with a touch of piety: 'The servant of science, Rūḥī al-Khālidī al-Maqdisī, may God forgive him.'[94] During the following years, other Arabs from the Levant and from Egypt followed in the footsteps of their prestigious predecessors. One Jean-Antoine Melhamé – was he related to the Melhamé '*malfamés*'?[95] – signed the visitors' book with a lyricism that suggested he had not been indifferent to the image of al-Andalus created by the authors and thinkers of the *Nahḍa*: 'My beloved friends, if something else than death had affected you, I would have blamed death, but death does not let itself be swayed.'[96] A month earlier, another 'Levantine', this time a Druze, marvelled at the splendour of

---

returned to Istanbul, where he frequented Jamāl al-Dīn al-Afghānī. Continuously tailed by Abdülhamid's spies and secret police, he fled to Paris to study Islamic sciences and philosophy at the Sorbonne. He published with some success several articles on Islam and Arab culture, while at the same time joining Freemasonry. He was appointed Ottoman consul in Bordeaux in 1898 and stayed in that post until 1908. He married a Frenchwoman, with whom he had a son. After the Young Turk Revolution of July 1908, he was elected deputy of Jerusalem and re-elected in 1912. He died of typhoid fever in 1913. Although he was strongly opposed to Zionism and to Jewish immigration into Palestine, he did not join the Arab nationalist movement and remained loyal to the Ottoman Empire (R. Khalidi, *Palestinian Identity*, pp. 76–84; http://khalidi.org/18.htm, accessed in 2016, but no longer available). For a genealogy of the Khālidī family, see al-Juʻbeh et al. (eds), *Fihris makhṭūṭāt al-Maktabah al-Khālidīyah*, pp. 45–9. Several authors claim that Rūḥī al-Khālidī had written an account of his Andalusian journey; I believe this is due to a confusion between the two Khālidī cousins (A. G. Chejne, 'Travel Books in Modern Arabic Literature', pp. 212–13; Newman, 'Myths and Realities in Muslim Alterist Discourse', p. 65; Paradela, *El otro laberinto español*, p. 91).

94 AA, *libros de firmas*, 47, fol. 224 v, 23 or 24 April 1907. خادم العلم روحى الخالدى المقدسى غفراه له

95 The Maronite family from Beirut of the Melhamé became famous for the close association of six brothers – Salīm, Najīb, Habīb, Philippe, Alexandre and Shukrī – with Abdülhamid's autocratic and corrupt regime. They all had to flee the country after the Young Turk Revolution of 1908 (J. Hanssen, '"Malhamé–Malfamé": Levantine Elites and Transimperial Networks on the Eve of the Young Turk Revolution'). The only concrete information I have been able to access on Jean-Antoine is a contract, dated from 1925, where he appears as a solicitor (at: http://earsiv.sehir.edu.tr:8080/xmlui/bitstream/handle/11498/16293/001635770019.pdf?sequence=1&isAllowed=y, accessed in 2018, but today displaced due to the shutting down of Şehir University by presidential decree on 30 June 2020).

96 AA, *libros de firmas*, 48, fol. 232 v, 2 November 1910. The verse is attributed to ʻAlī ibn Abī Ṭālib (601–61), son-in-law of the Prophet and fourth caliph of Islam. My thanks go to Renaud Soler for the identification and translation of this verse.

the monument: 'Behold the most beautiful edifice of humankind, the pride of all hearts.'[97] This was none other than Amīn Arslān (1868–1943), a member of the great Druze family of the Arslān. Although a Young Turk and Freemason, he had been coaxed by Abdülhamid into accepting a consular post in Bordeaux. After the Young Turk Revolution of 1908, he had refused a position of consul in Paris and asked to be appointed to Buenos Aires, where he eventually settled, once he had been dismissed and sentenced to death in absentia by the new regime. He had travelled through Spain on his way to Argentina, and he had made a stop in Granada to visit the Alhambra on 5 October 1910.[98]

Of course, Amīn Arslān's name immediately brings to mind that of his cousin, Shakīb Arslān (1869–1946), whose much greater fame is built on his written contributions to the Arab nationalist and Islamist cause. True, it was only much later, in 1930, that he visited the Alhambra; nevertheless, his interest in al-Andalus can be dated to much earlier times, more precisely to the moment when his enthusiastic discovery of Chateaubriand's *Adventures of the Last Abencerrage* incited him to translate this work into Arabic. It was published in 1897, with the addition of a short history of al-Andalus.[99] With this undertaking Arslān came close to the main protagonists of the *Nahḍa*; however, he stood apart from most of his contemporaries with his predominantly Islamist, rather than Arabist, stand, which found its expression in his unwavering loyalty to the Ottoman Empire, which he perceived as the last stronghold of pan-Islamist resistance against Western colonialist and imperialist encroachment. It was only around 1925 that his commitment to this cause started to fade and that, seeing that the empire had indeed died for good, he shifted toward Arabism. That was also when he undertook a journey to Spain, from which he drew the inspiration for a history of al-Andalus, titled *The Brocade Robes about Andalusian Messages and Relics*.[100]

While Arslān's Andalusian journey happened after the limits imposed on this study, one detail nevertheless deserves all our attention, namely, the photograph he inscribed and sent to Mohammed Daoud, the historian from

[97] AA, *libros de firmas*, 48, fol. 228 v, 5 October 1910. هذه اجمل ما بناه البشر و بقى فخر في القلوب

[98] S. Kuneralp, 'L'émigration syro-libanaise'; P. Tornielli, 'Hombre de tres mundos'.

[99] Sh. Arslān, *Riwāyat Ākhir Benī Sarrāj*.

[100] Sh. Arslān, *Al-Hulal al-Sundusiyya fī al-Akhbār wa-l-Āthār al-Andalusiyya*; see also, Paradela, *El otro laberinto español*, pp. 201–12.

Tétouan, whose letter of friendship addressed to the *Defensor de Granada* on the occasion of the establishment of the Spanish Republic I have previously mentioned.[101] The photograph shows him in front of the forest of columns, so characteristic of the mosque of Cordoba. An inscription in his own hand, signed and dated, confirmed the location: 'Our image in the Mosque of Cordoba, taken in 1930. Shakīb Arslān' (Figure 4.6).[102] Of course, to the eyes of the – now aware – specialist, it was clear that this was not actually the mosque itself, but a typical backdrop of those photographic studios that offered a 'Moorish' setting to visiting tourists. In this particular case, it was once again Garzón's workshop, more particularly its Cordoba branch, run by Rafael Garzón Herranz (1889–1966), the son of Rafael Garzón Rodríguez, who had died in 1923.[103] Arslān, wearing a loose burnous and a turban, is sitting up straight on a sofa covered in an Oriental rug, flanked by a small hexagonal table in 'Arab' style, on which a tray with a teapot and three cups had been placed.[104]

What is even more intriguing, is that it was precisely this photograph that Arslān chose to illustrate his work published in 1936. Peter Wien has already noted the artificial character of this setting, as well as the costume Arslān was wearing, and the 'undefined Oriental-ness' that stemmed from so much Oriental eclecticism. Wien correctly deduced from all this that it was a studio photograph, displaying a 'make-believe' Orient, which contradicted

[101] See p. 142.

[102] Photograph inscribed to Mohammed Daoud, dated 11 Shawwāl 1350/18 February 1932, Fondation Mohammed Daoud pour l'histoire et la culture, Tétouan. Shakīb Arslān seems to have been strongly attached to Mohammed Daoud, whom he called 'our son' – Arslān was thirty-two years older – on at least two other photographs he sent him, also kept at the Fondation Mohammed Daoud. The first, dated 8 Sha'bān 1350/18 December 1931, shows Arslān at age sixteen; the second, dated 5 Ramaḍān 1350/14 January 1932, is a portrait taken when he was twenty-one. U. Ryad, S. Spaan, A. Tirtan and M. Sajid, 'Muslims in Interwar Europe', see at: https://muslims-in-interwar-europe.com/Gallery3.html. The original photograph is preserved at the Mohammed Daoud Foundation for History and Culture, in Tétouan.

[103] González, *Los Garzón: Kalifas de la fotografía cordobesa*, pp. 54–7. See, in the same work, a photograph of father and son Garzón posing in front of the same backdrop (p. 55), as well as images of individuals and groups wearing Moorish costumes in the same setting (pp. 65, 69, 72).

[104] Of course, the sofa, table, tray and tea set can be seen on many photographs taken in the Garzón studio (González, *Los Garzón: Kalifas de la fotografía cordobesa*, pp. 65–7, 69, 72–3).

Figure 4.6 Portrait of Shakīb Arslan taken in Rafael Garzón Herranz's studio in Cordoba, 1930. Mohammed Daoud Foundation for History and Culture, Tétouan. Arslan sent this photograph to his friend Mohammed Daoud from Tétouan with the following comment: 'Our image in the Mosque of Cordoba, taken in 1930.' Interestingly, Arslan had chosen to pose in a costume borrowed from the photographer in front of a backdrop representing the 'forest of columns' of the famous mosque.

the manner in which Arslān tried to fashion himself 'in suit and tie as a respectable spokesperson of Arab modernity'.[105] He also noted that the published image bore a caption that read 'image of the author in front of the Mosque of Cordoba', by which he seemed to have tried to avoid the deception that the preposition 'in' would have caused.[106] According to Wien, what was at hand was a desire to 'create his own Orientalist Arab–Andalusian imaginary', thus revealing 'the entanglement between the authenticity of

105 Wien, *Arab Nationalism*, pp. 53–6.

106 Wien, *Arab Nationalism*, p. 55. It should be noted, however, that this was indeed the expression he used on the photograph sent to Daoud.

the place (Mezquita–Cordoba), its position in a historical narrative, and its central position in an identity-shaping imaginary'.[107]

While I do not subscribe entirely to this overly 'conscious' interpretation, there is no doubt that there was a radical difference between Arslān's portrait and that of Khalīl Jawād al-Khālidī, taken twenty-five years earlier. The latter, too, probably for lack of any other means, had submitted to an Orientalist exercise; however, he had carefully avoided the costumes and numerous props that the photographer proposed to his ordinary clients. He had chosen to stand upright in a corner of the 'patio' in his own sober garb, thus drawing a striking contrast to Garzón's habitual customers in their Orientalist costumes and poses. Arslān, on the contrary, seems to have played along, shedding his Western suit to don a farcical costume and, although he did not go as far as to sprawl over the sofa, he apparently saw no harm in surrounding himself with the studio's Oriental paraphernalia. The difference in the attitude of the two men becomes all the more striking if we consider that when Khālidī revisited Andalusia in 1932, practically at the same time as Arslān, and that he again had his portrait taken, the venerable Palestinian scholar – almost seventy by then – stood in exactly the same pose as in 1904, not to mention that one of his portraits had been taken inside an actual monument, namely the Alcázar of Seville (Figure 4.7).[108]

Somewhat younger than Arslān, and of a very different profile, considering he was a Maronite who had left Lebanon at the age of twelve to settle in the United States, Amīn Rīḥānī (1876–1940) owed to the Alhambra the (re)discovery of his native culture and identity. As he himself put it, this epiphany had been triggered by Washington Irving's famous *Tales of the Alhambra*, still a bestseller in the American environment in which he had grown:

> After I read the book on the Alhambra, something of an oriental phantasm became blended into my English–French–American mentality. I began to have dreams about the glorious past as if I were living in it, or as it were alive before me. I returned to my homeland sad carrying a book but wishing that there were one hundred and one books instead. I knew then very little about my language and its literature, and proceeded to plunge into its vault without lamenting my conditions.[109]

[107] Wien, *Arab Nationalism*, pp. 54–5.

[108] Eldem, 'Ottomans at the Alhambra', p. 252, ill. 9; p. 254, ill. 13; p. 254, ill. 13.

[109] Rīḥānī, *Mulūk al-'Arab* (1924), quoted in Chejne, 'Amīn al-Rīḥānī and al-Andalus: A Journey into History', pp. 11–12; N. Hajjar, *The Politics and Poetics of Ameen Rihani*, p. 36.

Figure 4.7 Photograph of Khalīl Jawād Khālidī in the Court of the Maidens (*patio de las Doncellas*) of the Alcázar of Seville, by the photographer Abelardo Linares of Seville, 1932. The caption reads 'Khalīl Khālidī in the palace of the Banī 'Abbād in Ishbīliya (Seville), among the cities of al-Andalus, in 1351'. Jawhariyyeh Collection, Athens, album 3, ref. J-3/28-88. Courtesy of the Institute for Palestine Studies. Some thirty years after his first visit to Andalusia, Khālidī had finally managed to have his photograph taken in a real setting.

Rīḥānī's immersion into his native land and culture happened at the turn of the century. A long stay in Lebanon transformed him into a prolific writer and an intellectual increasingly committed to the struggle for the independence of Arab peoples. It was in 1917, twenty years after having read Irving and at a moment when he had started fighting for the recognition and support of the Arab revolt against the Ottomans, that he was finally able to behold the object of his dreams:

> I was able in those days (1917) to visit al-Andalus. I stood in the hall where Washington Irving wrote his precious book. As I stood there, I heard voices calling me in the name of nationalism and patriotism inviting me to the birthplace of Revelation and Prophecy.[110]

[110] Chejne, 'Amīn al-Rīḥānī and al-Andalus: A Journey into History', p. 12; Hajjar, *The Politics and Poetics of Ameen Rihani*, p. 36.

This visit took place at a crucial point in his adoptive country's destiny. The United States had just declared war on Germany in April 1917, while Rīḥānī was in Spain. He described the way he felt torn between his two allegiances in a 'Letter to Uncle Sam', whose 'bread and salt' he had eaten for twenty years, while enjoying 'the freedom of his commons':

> But now that your Uncle is at war, Rihani, what are you going to do about it? Will you continue to dawdle and dilly-dally among monuments of your brave ancestors, deciphering couplets on the walls of the Alhambra and lamenting the vanished glory of Beni Omayia and Beni Ahmar, while the country in which you were reared and schooled and entertained, is now preparing for battle? Will you for all the beauty and loveliness of Andalusia forego your right to join in the combat?[111]

Rīḥānī was saved from this dilemma by his poor health exempting him from active duty. From then on, he devoted himself to the Arab cause by his writings, by his Arabist and anti-Zionist activism and, taking advantage of his dual culture, by diplomatic action with leading Western figures and institutions, as well as with the new local political actors who had emerged during the restructuring of the Middle East in the wake of the First World War and the collapse of the Ottoman Empire, starting with Ibn Saoud (1875–1953, r. 1932–53).

While I have not been able to find the least trace of Rīḥānī's passage in the pages of the visitors' book of the Alhambra, I have found consolation in the discovery I made of the signature of yet another celebrity of the Arabist movement of the time, namely, the Egyptian nationalist poet Aḥmad Shawqī (1868–1932). As in the case of many others, Shawqī's first contacts with Andalusia had been of an abstract and literary nature, but they already fell in line with the political discourse of the time. Indeed, his ode (*qaṣīda*) bearing the title *Al-Andalus al-Jadīda* ('the New Andalus'), dated 1912, was directly linked to the political agenda of the day. In it, the poet drew a parallel between the fall of Granada and that of Edirne (Adrianople), which he described as the 'sister of al-Andalus', following the Ottoman defeat at the end of the Balkan

[111] Rīḥānī, 'Letters to Uncle Sam', 2001, pp. 11–12, quoted in Hajjar, *The Politics and Poetics of Ameen Rihani*, p. 16.

War.[112] Shawqī was one of those Arab intellectuals who remained loyal to the empire, which made perfectly sense if one considers his commitment to Khedive Abbas Hilmi II (1874–1944, r. 1892–1914), whose anti-British feelings encouraged him to cautiously support nationalist intellectuals and politicians, who were often targeted by the colonial authorities. Shawqī was one of them and, in 1914, the year that Abbas Hilmi was deposed by the British, he was 'invited' to exile himself due to his poems that criticised the British administration and supported the Ottoman Empire.[113] He thus chose to go to Spain, more precisely to Barcelona, a choice motivated by practical considerations rather than any form of nostalgia for al-Andalus.[114] This explains why his visit to the Alhambra, marked by a short mention of 'a visitor of these noble monuments', took place only in 1919, more than four years after he had settled in Spain.[115] Interestingly, Aḥmad Zakī seems to have played an important role in this decision, considering that he sent Shawqī several books, among which were his own travelogue and Maqqarī's work on the history of Muslim Spain.[116]

His exile in Barcelona had already begun to transform Shawqī by instilling in him a powerful feeling of longing for Egypt. His journey to Andalusia brought this experience to a climax by offering him a magical vision of past splendour, which inspired his famous *sīniyya* – a poem rhyming in *sīn* (s) – that emulated the one that al-Buḥturī (821–97) had composed to celebrate the beauty of the remains of the arch and palace of Chosroes (Khosrow) in Ctesiphon. By adopting the double role of a visitor admiring monument after monument and of a scholar feeding on the works of poets and authors of

[112] Pérès, *L'Espagne vue par les voyageurs musulmans*, pp. 102–3; C. C. Arslan, 'Translating Ottoman into Classical Arabic: *Nahḍa* and the Balkan Wars in Aḥmad Shawqī's "The New al-Andalus"', pp. 279–86; İ. Doğru, 'Elegy to the Balkans in the Arab Poetry: Fall of Edirne, Sister of Andalucia'.

[113] He most notably published in 1907, 'A Farewell to Lord Cromer', where he strongly criticised this former consul general – in fact, governor general – of Egypt (1883–1907), and 'The Anniversary of Dinshaway' to commemorate the bloody reprisal by British troops in 1906 against the inhabitants of the village bearing this name (N. Kadhim, *The Poetics of Anti-colonialism in the Arabic Qaṣīdah*, pp. 2–34; T. Abdel Nasser, 'Shawqi, Ahmed', p. 360.

[114] Wien, *Arab Nationalism*, p. 61.

[115] AA, *libros de firmas*, 50, fol. 237 v, 12 June 1919. زائر هذه الرسوم الكريمة

[116] Wien, *Arab Nationalism*, p. 61.

those bygone times, he turned his long poem, titled 'Journey to al-Andalus' (*al-Riḥla ilà'l-Andalus*), into the expression of a new national subjectivity built upon a common heritage.[117] From an initial vision of Andalusia tainted with the disaster of the Balkan Wars but also carrying hope for an Ottoman revival, Shawqī eventually chose to retreat into a historical vision of the Arab past, deeply rooted in his Egyptian identity.[118]

A Turkish Twist

From Aḥmad Zakī to Aḥmad Shawqī, in less than thirty years a powerful image of Andalusia had formed around the history, literature and remains of the Arabo-Islamic presence in Spain. This image could greatly vary in intensity and in terms of focus. For some, it took the form of a nostalgia for past greatness; for others, it constituted a lesson from which wisdom should be drawn for the present. Some versions of this image were openly political and aimed either at recreating a past utopia, made of communion and revival, or at mobilising a determination to resist and shake off the yoke of colonialism and imperialism. While the Islamic nature of this heritage and of the dreams and projects that derived from it was often stressed, the common denominator remained a feeling of Arab-ness shared by authors and intellectuals of rather diverse origins. That is why the Alhambra, even more than the mosque of Cordoba, offered its Syrian, Lebanese, Egyptian, Druze, Christian and Muslim visitors a reference and a symbol that fed into a vision of a common identity, a common past and, often, a common future. This feeling of a shared Arab identity was strongly concentrated in the Mashreq, and more precisely in Egypt, whose predominant role in the development of the *Nahḍa* had turned it into the cultural and intellectual capital of the Arab world.

Despite a promising start, the 'Turks' – I am using this term once again only for the purpose of distinguishing them linguistically and culturally

[117] Pérès, *L'Espagne vue par les voyageurs musulmans*, pp. 108–15; Martínez Montávez, *Al-Andalus, España, en la literatura árabe contemporánea*, pp. 45–7; Y. Noorani, 'The Lost Garden of Al-Andalus', pp. 237–41; Wien, *Arab Nationalism*, pp. 61–2.

[118] Pérès, *L'Espagne vue par les voyageurs musulmans*, pp. 118–20; Arslan, 'Translating Ottoman into Classical Arabic: *Naḥda* and the Balkan Wars in Aḥmad Shawqī's "The New al-Andalus"', pp. 291–93.

from the Arabs mentioned earlier in this chapter – seem to have a followed a significantly different trajectory, almost opposite in many regards. We have already seen that despite a marked cultural distance, it was in Istanbul that the first modern works on the history of Muslim Spain had been published. History books, novels, plays, translations followed one after the other for over two decades, triggering an interest, which, albeit limited, ended up influencing many of the intellectuals of the *Nahḍa*, who were apparently more receptive to this message than Turkish-speaking Ottoman subjects. We should also remember that by the end of the 1880s, the Ottoman government seem to have committed to a policy targeting Andalusia and the Maghreb as part of the broader framework of Abdülhamid II's attempts at pan-Islamism. Shinqīṭī and Wardānī's mission and the efforts of the Ottoman minister in Madrid, Turhan Bey, constituted a concrete illustration of this process, even though the results obtained remained very modest, not to say non-existent. The inscription left by Mehmed Kâmil Bey in 1892 stands like a turning point leading to a gradual predominance of Arabs.

Compared with this rapid rise of an Arab presence and discourse in the pages of the visitors' book of the Alhambra, Turkish visibility seems to have been waning steadily. This does not mean that the number of individuals was dropping significantly, but rather that they were becoming silent, especially when compared with the increasingly strong and committed statements of the Egyptians and other Arabs from the Levant visiting the Alhambra. When the new Ottoman minister in Madrid, who had occupied this post since Turhan Bey's departure in 1894, visited the monument a year and a half later, he just signed his name in the book, with no comment whatsoever.[119] This is all the more surprising if one considers that the new minister, Mehmed Feridun Bey (1847–1903), was the son of Mehmed Kâmil Bey, the 'Pony of the Apocalypse', who, exactly fifty years earlier, had visited the same monument as secretary to the ambassador Fuad Efendi. The following minister, Necib Pasha (?–1899) did not even visit Granada and the Alhambra, which may be due to a series of calamities that befell him during his mission. He lost his daughter in July 1898 and by September, his own health had deteriorated so much that he had to ask to be recalled, he spent several

[119] AA, *libros de firmas*, 45, fol. 288 v, 7 February 1896.

months trying to recover in Barcelona and eventually died, still in his post, in November 1899.[120]

His successor, İzzet Fuad Pasha (1852–1925), was minister from 1900 to 1908, and he did visit the Alhambra on 31 January 1903. Much like Feridun Bey, the last Ottoman diplomat to sign the visitors' book before him, İzzet Fuad Pasha had been content with inscribing his name and titles, in Turkish and in French. This very short inscription gave the impression that his identity and his mission were of much greater importance to him than the historical context of the monument he was visiting: 'General Izzet Fuad Pasha, minister and envoy of the Sultan of Turkey.'[121] This slightly pompous concision seems to echo the inscription left in 1844 by Fuad Efendi, the Ottoman envoy, who happened to be his grandfather. We have the advantage of additional clues that may contribute to a better understanding of the pasha's character and of the possible reasons behind his apparent indifference to Andalusian heritage. Indeed, this was not his first visit to Granada. The previous year, at around the same time of year, he had been invited by the extremely wealthy Julio Quesada-Cañaveral, Count of Benalúa, Duke of San Pedro de Galatino (1857–1936) to participate in a hunting party in his domain of Láchar, some 20 km west of Granada. İzzet Fuad Pasha shot seventy-three animals, posting the second best score among a party of sixteen.[122] The following year, his visit to the Alhambra once again followed a partridge hunt organised by the same Count of Benalúa in Láchar, to which many aristocrats and celebrities were also invited, including Prince Anatole Demidoff (1874–1943).[123] A socialite and a snob, a womaniser and a braggart, İzzet Fuad Pasha had very little in common with the passion for, and commitment to, culture and history that characterised his Arab contemporaries. To him, in all evidence, the Alhambra was a touristic detour amid exclusive social events in the environs of Granada.

Apart from a clear penchant for such festive and select occasions, İzzet Fuad Pasha seems to have deeply internalised Orientalist feelings of an *alla turca* nature. Tunalı Hilmi Efendi (1871–1928), who was then secretary at the

[120] BOA, HR UHM 320/46, 10 July 1898; Y PRK EŞA 31/62, 20 September 1898; Y A HUS 393/73, 22 January 1899; HR MTV 678/1, 11 November 1899.

[121] AA, *libros de firmas*, 46, fol. 237 v, 31 January 1903.

[122] 'Cacería en Láchar', 26 January 1902.

[123] 'Partida de caza'; 'Cacería en Láchar', 1 February 1903.

Ottoman legation in Madrid, provides us with a lively and very entertaining description of İzzet Pasha's attitude and comments when faced with the state of disrepair and abandonment in which he found the premises of the Ottoman delegation upon his arrival in Madrid. This passage, which would deserve a choice place in an anthology of Ottoman Orientalism, reveals another trait of the pasha's character, which perfectly fits the tentative portrait I tried to draw previously:

> What on earth is all this? It looks like vestiges from Sermed Efendi's time . . . Oh my God! What to say of all this *Oryan* ['Orient', phonetically borrowed from the French]? One feels like in the home of a religious judge (*kazasker*).[124] With all this old janissary stuff, all we are missing is a yataghan! Look at these armchairs, this sofa: some are missing a leg, the other an arm. It looks like they were loaded on a market boat in Beykoz at the end of the summer and then dumped here.[125] As if they had piled up in a corner of the home.
>
> (In another room) My dear Sir, these were objects of value, but they were left in complete disrepair to rot in a corner! That is so typical of us! Just open a dictionary and look for the equivalent of *antrötyen* [phoneticised form of the French '*entretien*' (upkeep)]. I swear to you that you will not find it. At any rate an *espiri dantrötyen* [again phoneticised from the French '*esprit d'entretien*' (sense of upkeep)] does not exist among this nation.[126]

In October 1899, the visit of a rather exceptional Turco-Egyptian group seems to have been dominated by a very similar context of Westernisation combined with high social status. The group included women, which in itself was truly

[124] In the 'classical' Ottoman system, there were two high-ranking judges known as *kazasker*, one for Rumelia, and the other for Anatolia. Of course, the pasha uses this expression with much Orientalist sarcasm, to mock the traditional, religious and outdated character of an environment that had failed to catch up with modernity.

[125] This colourful metaphor is understandably opaque to anybody unfamiliar with everyday life in the Istanbul of the time. Well-off families would leave the city at the end of spring to settle on the shores of the Bosphorus, only to return at the end of the summer. This would involve a lot of moving of people and furniture by boat. In this particular case, however, the reference to Beykoz, a distant and much more modest village on the Bosphorus, and to a 'market boat' (*pazar kayığı*), a sturdy type of boat used for the transport of common goods and people, indicates a combination of snobbishness and Orientalism aimed at his predecessor.

[126] A. Hilmi [Tunalı], *Rezalet: Yine İspanya'da*, pp. 55–6.

exceptional, if one considers to what extent women have been absent from the sample under study.[127] What made this even more extraordinary was that the group consisted of a majority of women, three, against just one man. Two of the women were celebrities in their own right. The first was none other than the Egyptian princess Zainab Nazli, in Turkish Zeyneb Nazlı (1853–1913), the daughter of Mustafa Fazıl Pasha, one of Muhammad Ali's grandsons, who had settled in Istanbul after having been removed from the Egyptian line of succession, and who eventually moved to Paris in the late 1860s due to his support for the Young Ottoman opposition. Nazlı was famous for her excellent education, her linguistic skills, her independent character and for the literary salon she held in Cairo, which was attended by the intellectual elite of Egypt. The second woman, Leyla Şerife Hanım (*c.* 1868–1945), was the daughter of Halil Şerif Pasha (1831–79), an Ottoman bureaucrat and statesman, best known for his incredible collection of paintings, including Courbet's *L'Origine du monde*, which he sold in Paris in 1868. Her mother was his mistress, Marie-Anne Detourbay (1837–1908), who rose to fame as the *demi-mondaine* Jeanne de Tourbey before she finally settled by marrying the Count of Loynes. To make matters more complicated, we should note that Princess Nazlı had married Halil Şerif Pasha in 1872, but had soon divorced; nevertheless, that made her the ex-stepmother of her travel companion. As to the third woman in the group, she was of a much more modest background: '*Çerkes Sazkâr*' or 'Sazkâr the Circassian' was evidently the slave of one or the other of the two ladies, but 'modern' enough to be able to sign also in French as 'Sazikar' and to date the group's visit. In other words, she was an enslaved person, whom modernity and Westernisation had turned into a *dame de compagnie*. Finally, the man who accompanied the three women was Ali Kemal Bey (1869–1922), a young journalist and intellectual, who, following a flirtation with the Young Turks during his years in Paris and Geneva (1886–8) had grown

[127] The only other 'Oriental' woman I have been able to spot in the visitors' book is one Cemile Hanım, who noted on 20 September 1907 in Turkish that 'Cemile Hanım came to visit [this place]' (AA, *libros de firmas*, 48, fol. 9 v, 20 September 1907). Therefore, there is no doubt that she was a Turkish speaker, although it seems surprising that she should have chosen to date her inscription in the Gregorian calendar, but in Arabic characters, a rarity among 'Turks'.

closer to Abdülhamid's regime, to the point of betraying some of his former comrades during his studies in Paris (1894–9). In 1897, he was appointed secretary at the Ottoman embassy in Brussels and, in 1899, graduated from the School of Political Sciences in Paris. He eventually settled in Egypt, where he was employed as the administrator of a farm belonging to Princess Nimetullah (1875–1945), daughter of Khedive Ismail, and to Mahmud Muhtar Pasha (1867–1935). He returned to Istanbul only after the Young Turk Revolution of 1908.[128] It was therefore at the beginning of his career in Egypt, perhaps during a journey from Paris to Cairo, that Ali Kemal, together with two Egyptian ladies and their slave/companion, visited the Alhambra. We also know that the young man was very close to Princess Nazlı, whom he served like a modern-day knight. The comments left by these visitors were extremely succinct, but sophisticated.[129] Princess Nazlı just signed on top; Leyla Şerife let out two small 'Alas!'; Ali Kemal wrote down the words full of mystical wisdom attributed to Sultan Ahmed II, 'God suffices, the rest is fancy' (*Allah bes, baki heves*); as to Sazkâr the 'Circassian', not only did she sign her name in both Turkish and French, but she also seems to have taken up a secretarial role by dating the inscription for all – again both in Turkish and in French – and by adding one line beneath each of the women's signatures, spelling out their noble lineages, albeit only in Turkish. It is striking to note that all four of them, the princess,

[128] Ali Kemal met with a tragic end. As an opponent of the Unionist government, he was twice exiled after his return to Istanbul. He kept a low profile during the First World War and took up his journalistic career only after the defeat of 1918 and the flight of the Unionist leaders. As Minister of the Interior for a few months in 1919 and as an editorialist, he strongly opposed the nationalist movement in Ankara, which he considered to be a successor to the Unionists. He paid a high price for this stand, which was aggravated in the eyes of the nationalist public by his support of the Armenian survivors of the genocide. Following the decisive victories won by the Kemalist forces, in November 1922, he was arrested under the pretence of being taken to Ankara for a trial, but instead was handed to the military commander in Izmit, 'Bearded' Nureddin Pasha, who turned him over to a mob he had provoked and who lynched him. On a side note, Ali Kemal had married in 1903 one Winifred Emma Marie Brun, with whom he had a son and a daughter. His son, Osman, who was later renamed Wilfred Johnson, was former British Prime Minister Boris Johnson's grandfather.

[129] AA, *libros de firmas*, 46, fol. 135 v, 20 October 1899.

the lady, the journalist, and the 'modern' slave, were perfectly fluent in their use of French.[130]

The difference with Arab visitors is striking. True, Princess Nazlı was Egyptian, and she stood as a protector of the Egyptian intellectuals and artists she often received and entertained at home, but she was of Turkish culture and descent and, more importantly, a highly Westernized aristocrat to whom the emancipation of women and charity towards the most destitute ranked higher than the nationalist and Arabist feelings that inflamed most partisans of the *Nahḍa*. The same was true of Leyla Şerife Hanım: with her 'Turkish' origins and her proximity to the Khedivial family, she came very close to the princess's profile. As to Ali Kemal, he, too, was very much 'Turkish' and much too Westernised – and politically conservative – to adopt the discourse of his Egyptian or Syro-Lebanese contemporaries. I believe a photograph of Princess Nazlı and Ali Kemal taken in Paris together with the modernist and reformist Sheikh Muḥammad 'Abduh (1849–1905) illustrates perfectly the profile of the group of visitors who signed the book of the Alhambra: aristocrats and upper-class bourgeois, who, while rubbing shoulders with people of very diverse backgrounds to support 'enlightened' causes, remained essentially anchored in the comfort of a highly cosmopolitan dilettantism (Figure 4.8). One can easily picture these Egyptian women wearing Parisian dresses and holding umbrellas, accompanied by a young Ottoman dandy in a hat and suit, strolling through the courtyards and galleries of the Alhambra, chattering in French, undistinguishable from the other tourists.

Ottoman diplomats, Turco-Egyptian aristocrats and 'Turkish' intellectuals stood clearly apart from their *Nahḍist* contemporaries by their lack of emotion and of political or ideological commitment. Cultural differences were certainly responsible for much of this discrepancy. They lacked a proper mastery of the

[130] One could speculate almost endlessly on some of the details of this collective inscription. First, it clearly follows a social hierarchy: the princess signed first, followed by her noble companion, her 'knight' and, lastly, the slave/companion. Without claiming graphological skills, I believe both the princess' signatures look self-confident, almost arrogant. Leyla Şerife's seems more understated, and she may have played the role of a private secretary, considering that her two 'Alas!' are not aligned, as if she had written one for the princess and the other in her own name. Interestingly, she has feminised her name in French by adding a silent 'e' at the end, spelling it 'Chérifée' instead of the more conventional 'Chérifé'.

Figure 4.8 'A historic image of the Master, Imam and Sheikh Muḥammad 'Abduh when he lived in Paris. To his right is Princess Nazlı and sitting before her the Turkish journalist Ali Bey Kemal, who was hanged by the Kemalists', 'Ṭarā'if nādirat 'an: al-Sheikh Muḥammad 'Abduh', *Al-Athnayn wa'l-Dunya*, June 1945, p. 7. The three other women are not identified and the photograph is not dated. It is quite possible that one of them may have been Leyla Şerife Hanım; as to the date, it may well have been close to that of the ladies' visit to the Alhambra.

language, they had very few literary references at hand and the historical context was not that familiar to them. Incapable of quoting Maqqarī or even of reading Zakī, they had to resort to sources in Turkish, which were rather rare, and, most of all, to Western authors who were probably more familiar and, in the case of the Baedeker and other similar guidebooks, more accessible.

It seems clear, however, that apart from these cultural limitations, the relative indifference of non-Arab Ottomans had to do with very different political and ideological priorities. The *Nahḍa* movement fed on the sense of urgency triggered by a growingly powerful desire for political and ideological emancipation in the hope of laying the foundations of a new Arab – and partly Islamic – identity and unity. While European colonialism stood as the major obstacle to the realisation of this project and the West appeared as the principal target of the movement, the notion of 'Turkish' domination was not entirely irrelevant to some of its actors' feelings of frustration and animosity. After all, we should not forget that, well before the oppression attributed to Cemal Pasha at the start of the First World War, Abdülhamid and the Young Turks had already put into action a policy of assimilation and Turkification of the Arab populations of the empire, especially through language and education.[131] We should add to this the phenomenon of Ottoman Orientalism already mentioned, which, very often, targeted the same populations by claiming that they 'lived in a state of nomadism and savagery'.[132]

It should therefore not come as a surprise that while the infatuation of intellectuals with Arabism did not systematically lead to anti-Ottoman feelings, it did not find any substantial echo in the culturally and linguistically Turkish circles of the empire, especially in its capital. The 'Turkish' agenda was quite different. If there were indeed deep concerns regarding the capacity of the empire to survive so much adversity, it was not in the Arab past that Turkish intellectuals chose to find some solace and hopes for a better future. As noted earlier, a brief period of curiosity had brought to the fore the image of an Andalusian golden age; however, this distant vision had soon been replaced by a much more local one, based on the early stage of the Turkish presence in Anatolia and on the glorious achievements of the first sultans of the house of Osman. While Abdülhamid was still intent on taking advantage of pan-Islamism and of the caliphate, this was a policy that was essentially geared towards the international scene and the context of potential confrontations with the British and French empires, which by then controlled the majority of the global Muslim population.[133] Within the empire, his discourse was acquiring an increasingly Turkish overtone, and while it is true that the sultan did his best to warrant the loyalty of his Arab and Muslim subjects, he tried to do so by promoting the present state of his empire and caliphate, rather than by espousing a nostalgia for a glorious Arab past that could always turn against him.

131 Deringil, *The Well-Protected Domains*, pp. 99–104; H. Kayalı, *Arabs and Young Turks*, pp. 82–98.

132 Deringil, '"They Live in a State of Nomadism and Savagery"'.

133 For a critical study of Abdülhamid's image as a caliph and his pan-Islamist policies, see, C. Aydın, *The Idea of the Muslim World*, pp. 65–98.

Perhaps the most blatant proof of the deepening rift between Turkish and Arab perceptions of Andalusia can be found in the inscription in the Alhambra visitors' book left on 7 September 1900 by Tunalı Ahmed Hilmi Efendi, whose description of İzzet Fuad Pasha's Orientalist antics was mentioned earlier. Hilmi Efendi was not just anyone, or rather he would not remain anonymous for long. He had joined the Young Turk movement at the Imperial School of Medicine and had fled Istanbul in 1895 to settle in Geneva, one of the main places of refuge for political dissidents of the Hamidian regime. After resisting Abdülhamid's threats and blackmail for several years, young Hilmi finally yielded and accepted a post of secretary for correspondence in Turkish at the Ottoman legation in Madrid, with the intention of making some money to sustain his subversive action.[134] This was a short respite; after barely a year, he was dismissed for seditious activity and fell back on his former Young Turk networks. He returned to Istanbul only after Abdülhamid's fall and started an administrative and political career that was crowned by two terms at the Grand National Assembly in Ankara, where he stood out as one of the most progressive deputies, with workers and women as his major causes.[135]

The inscription he left in the visitors' book was – to say the least – rather extraordinary, both in style and in content (Figure 4.9):

> The sun rises in the East, and sets in the West; this is natural and in reality it does not set, neither does it rise. This is a manner of speech, one can engage in philosophy and find consolation, but generally, every sunrise provides a joyful pleasure, while every sunset causes melancholy; and these feelings are natural. Especially as every sunset is as sad as it is bright, dark, red.
>
> Behold the Alhambra! . . .
>
> O visitor . . . O Oriental! When defeated by melancholy – in the face of black and red clouds – the feelings of those who are of strong essence need to be charged with thunderbolts; rather than shedding tears, their eyes should project rays of light, shining thoughts, as if they were lightning striking through the obscurity, as if to destroy the conquering darkness! Remember that there

[134] BOA, HR SYS 1790/8, 14 Şubat 1315/26 February 1900; A. Hilmi [Tunalı], *On Birinci Hutbe*, pp. 10–11.

[135] For a biography, see, S. Ateş, *Tunalı Hilmi Bey*.

is only one sun in the world that unites it all. Otherwise, harmony and order would fail. Weak and strong, everything would vanish.

Behold the fate of two rivals: Look at Iraq and Syria . . . Look at Al-Andalus! . . .

O visitor! If your quest is for truth, look at this landscape with impartiality, as a 'human', and as a Muslim with the Koran in his hand and on his lips! . . .

O residents of Yıldız, o you who live in the inauspicious shadow of 'Yıldız'! Answer me: Here are the Spaniards, here is their king . . . Where are the Andalusians of yore, where their king?

Today the 'Alhambra' is not even a painting of the setting sun anymore . . . It barely amounts to the traces of that painting, as they remain in memories, as far as one can remember!'[136]

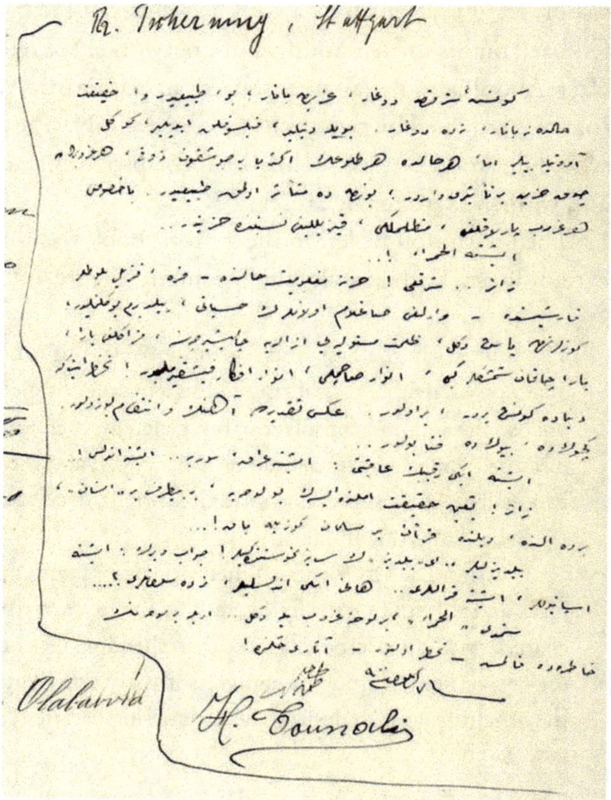

Figure 4.9 Inscription in the visitors' book by Tunalı Hilmi Efendi, 9 September 1900. AA, *libros de firmas*, 46, fol. 166 v. © Archivo del Patronato de la Alhambra y Generalife. Tunalı Hilmi's revolutionary 'stream of consciousness' uses the image of the Alhambra as a pretext to attack another fortress on a hill, Abdülhamid's Palace of Yıldız.

[136] AA, *libros de firmas*, 46, fol. 166 v, 7 September 1900.

Like his compatriots for some time already, Tunalı Hilmi clearly stood out from the monument's Arab visitors with the tone and content of his commentary. If anything, however, he could not be accused of being laconic. As in a fit of logorrhoea, he had poured onto the page a flow of remarks, which, despite several references to the monument, had practically nothing to do with the Alhambra. Two-thirds of the text consisted of a stream of consciousness around the theme of light and darkness, with flights of lyricism on atmospheric phenomena. This decidedly modern and modernist style, feeding on a direct and plain language, will sound familiar to anyone who has been confronted with the 'New Literature' (*Edebiyat-ı Cedide*) current in the last decade of the nineteenth century. The goal was to burn bridges with traditional forms of literature by emulating the Parnassian and Symbolist movements of Europe.

In Hilmi Efendi's case, much more than a literary exercise, the point was to use his words to serve the political cause of the Young Turks and of the struggle they were leading against Abdülhamid's autocracy. This kind of literary symbolism perfectly suited the purpose. Words derived from the Arabic root *ż-l-m* (ظلم) offered the possibility of playing on the ambiguity between darkness (*zulmet*) and tyranny (*zulüm*). All it took was to add a metaphor of light to obtain a vision of the opposition between good and evil, freedom and oppression. Losing its own identity, the Alhambra thus became the backdrop of an apocalyptic landscape where Hamidian obscurity and Young Turk brightness were pitched against each other.

The end of the text dropped all this symbolism and reverted to a more concrete evocation of the Alhambra and of its history, yet the focus remained exclusively political. A vague reference to the rivalry – quite an understatement – between the Umayyads and the Abbasids gave Hilmi an opportunity to draw a lesson for the present. While Syria and Iraq were still under the rule of Islam, Andalusia had fallen into Christian and Spanish hands. The lesson was intended for the 'residents of Yıldız', in other words the microcosm of Hamidian autocracy, whose headquarters were located at the palace of Yıldız, in Istanbul. Like Andalusia, whose rulers had disappeared and been replaced by the Spanish Crown, 'Hamidia' was also bound to disappear. This was a radical inversion of the vision that was so often repeated by most Oriental visitors, especially Arabs from the Mashreq: the Alhambra was no longer perceived as the consecration of past glory, but as the embodiment of decline and doom.

A postcard he sent to his brother Fehmi two years later shows to what extent Hilmi still clung to the comparison between the Alhambra's destiny and the fate he wished upon Abdülhamid, by drawing a rather facile parallel between the location of the two palaces at the top of a hill. In the middle of a very dense text, only a short passage referred to the Alhambra, a view of which graced the front of the postcard (Figure 4.10):

> This card is a souvenir of Al-Andalus: in the past, this hill, too, was a sort of 'Yıldız'. And today, nothing! Not really nothing, but rather a place that teaches a lesson . . . This Palace of the Alhambra has fallen into the hands of the Spaniards. Let us work so that our 'Yıldız' does not fall into other hands, but into the depths of the earth.[137]

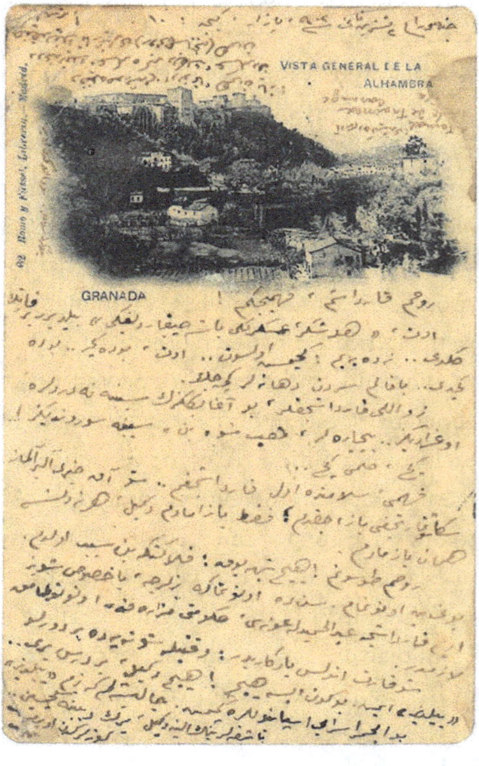

Figure 4.10 'General View of the Alhambra, Granada', Romo y Füssel, Madrid. Postcard sent by Tunalı Hilmi to his brother Fehmi, in Geneva, 2 November 1902. İnsan Tunalı collection, Istanbul. Once again, the Alhambra gives Tunalı Hilmi an opportunity to rant about Abdülhamid and his Palace of Yıldız.

[137] Postcard from Tunalı Hilmi to his brother Fehmi, Geneva, 2 November 1902. Courtesy of İnsan Tunalı.

What better proof could there be of how much, in the young man's mind, the political agenda of Istanbul prevailed over any form of nostalgia of a golden age. Moreover, it should also be noted that apart from this obsession, Tunalı Hilmi's attitude towards Arab heritage and history in Spain, when he did mention it, differed radically from that of his Arab contemporaries by the casualness and frivolity with which he referred to it. Proof of this indifference can be found in yet another postcard to his brother, which represented the interior of the mosque of Cordoba (Figure 4.11). As he had apparently been unable to find a connection between the building and Abdülhamid, he had resorted to describing its beauty and majesty, but in terms that would have offended most Muslim visitors of the time:

> Cordoba: This was the capital of al-Andalus. I have seen this place, too. This picture shows part of the famous great mosque, unrivalled in the world. They still call it 'La Meskita' [*la mezquita*], which must mean mosque. Today it is

Figure 4.11 'Cordoba: The Mosque', Hauber y Menet, Madrid. Postcard sent by Tunalı Hilmi to his brother Fehmi, in Geneva, 14 January 1901. İnsan Tunalı collection, Istanbul. The text on the postcard reveals to what extent Tunalı Hilmi was influenced by his travel companion, Baedeker's *Spain and Portugal*.

> a church! In order to convert it into a church, they asked *Şarlken* ['Charles Quint', Charles V in French], who was then king, for permission and he gave it. However, when he saw that they were demolishing the central part of the mosque to build a place devoted to the priests' prayers, he said: 'Had I known that you would commit such an absurdity, I would never have granted you permission. Know that what you have built can be found anywhere; what you have destroyed was unique and matchless in the world.[138]

Compared with the admiration of visitors from the Maghreb or to the tears shed by Wardānī during his visit to the mosque, Tunalı Hilmi's detached tone and especially his apology of Charles V is truly surprising. And yet, as I will try to show, this was part and parcel of his intellectual and ideological profile, which represented – perhaps in an extreme way – the very different nature of the 'Turkish' approach to Andalusian heritage.

The reason why Tunalı Hilmi is particularly suited to this kind of exercise is not just the 'sharpness' of his comments and political stand; it is also that he has left a considerable number of texts, which allow for a more in-depth analysis of the question without having to depend on a small number of documents, whose representativeness can always be questioned. The two postcards mentioned earlier are a useful complement to the inscription he left in the visitors' book, but it is really in his travelogues that one finds sufficient original material to be able to contextualise the sporadic reactions noted up to here. At any rate, one cannot insist enough that the simple fact that he published a travelogue – in fact, two, one for Spain and the other for Portugal – is in itself exceptional. If we set aside Vasıf Efendi's embassy report, dated 1787,[139] this is the only account of a journey to Spain written and published by a non-Arab Ottoman subject.

Quite surprisingly, Tunalı Hilmi's travelogues have not been studied, at least not as such. The reason for this neglect is rather obvious and understandable. Both works have suffered greatly from the highly political character of their author, which overshadowed them to the point of occulting their basic character as travelogues. It is understandable if one considers that they both bare the same general title of *Rezalet* – 'Shame' or 'Scandal' – which was followed by a more discrete geographical reference, *Portekiz* (Portugal) and *Yine İspanya'da*

[138] Postcard from Tunalı Hilmi to his brother Fehmi, Geneva, 14 January 1901. Courtesy of İnsan Tunalı.

[139] Menchinger, 'The Sefaretname of Ahmed Vasıf Efendi to Spain'.

(Again in Spain).[140] If one considers that the idea of 'shame' in the title referred – of course – to the Hamidian regime, but also to Hilmi's own admission of having sold out by signing a pact with the sultan, that more than half the volume on Spain consisted of copies of documents and telegrams exchanged with the palace of Yıldız, that both texts were replete with anti-Hamidian comments[141] and that they were both published secretly in Switzerland,[142] it becomes easier to understand how they were almost exclusively – but still too infrequently – studied as the political tracts they were meant to be.

And yet, despite all their political baggage, Tunalı Hilmi's travel accounts are a fascinating read, both in terms of their lively, and often funny, style and of the information they provide on the way in which this young Ottoman activist roamed and perceived Spain and Portugal during his short tenure in Madrid. Understandably, it is very tempting to compare this text with Aḥmad Zakī's, published eight years earlier. The differences are striking and reveal an almost diametrically opposite attitude on all the points of interest in this study. One disappointment awaits us, however: despite the fact that we know that he toured Andalusia, Tunalı Hilmi did not include this region in his travelogue, for reasons he explains right at the start in his preface:

> One generally comes to Spain for the 'Alhambra' of 'Granada'.[143] One just sees that and then leaves. Strangely, although it contains scenes and passages describing

[140] [Tunalı] A. Hilmi, *Rezalet. Portekiz and Rezalet: Yine İspanya'da*.

[141] I would give as an example a fantasy that came to his mind while he was about to go to a bullfight in Lisbon: 'Oh, if [Abdülhamid] could only come this way, if I could only take him to a bullfight and throw him amidst the bulls. I would place myself right across from him and watch the show. Oh, what a delicious bullfight that would be. His innards to one side, his guts to the other!' ([Tunalı] Hilmi, *Rezalet: Portekiz*, p. 12).

[142] For a file on the investigation led by the palace on Tunalı Hilmi's subversive activities, especially his pamphlets published in Switzerland, see BOA, HR SYS 1795/8, 10 October 1900–22 March 1901. The most entertaining piece in the file is a telegram from İzzet Fuad Pasha to the Ministry of Foreign Affairs, where he reacted to the order he had received to submit Hilmi Efendi to questioning: 'Hilmy Effendi is back and he answers evasively the questions he is asked; given that it is not in my taste to deal with such matters, I have suggested that he should write directly to whomever was in charge' (18 December 1900).

[143] The frequency with which Tunalı Hilmi uses quotation marks in his texts should not come as a surprise. He belonged to a generation that discovered the joys of Western punctuation adapted to a language that did not have any. This infatuation sometimes resulted in

> places that no one has seen yet and which – due to our unfortunate lack of interest for travel and trade – no one will see any time soon, '*Shame*' is missing the two most celebrated locations of al-Andalus – Granada and Cordoba – as if this work had been born from the idea that 'given that all everyone wants is to see this place, they end up seeing it, we can therefore skip it'; we can only hope that this gap will be filled. As we have already said, '*Shame*' goes on; if it were to be interrupted just now, it would be completed upon the first opportunity.[144]

Hilmi did not keep his promise; there would be no sequel to his travel account, evidently because he had other priorities. Nevertheless, his comment above about the over-rated nature of Andalusia was valid; most of all, his description of other places in Spain and Portugal – Toledo, Zaragoza, Barcelona, Lisbon – were truly interesting. In fact, he was perfectly aware of this:

> If one counted, say, a hundred Muslims or Ottomans who had set foot in Spain, not one of them would have made as many journeys and observations as there are in '*Shame*'. It should be remembered that we are the guardians of the mausoleum of al-Andalus! And yet, we do not possess the least booklet on this topic. That is also what '*Shame*' is about![145]

Once again, it made sense, although it is not entirely clear whether by 'guardians of the mausoleum of al-Andalus' he meant that some sort of responsibility befell the Ottomans with regard to the preservation of Andalusian heritage. At any rate, given the way he perceived this heritage, it is likely that this remark was mostly rhetorical. Nevertheless, even without any description of Andalusia, his account provided a wealth of details with a more or less direct connection to the remains of Muslim and Arab presence in Spain.

Immediately upon his arrival at Toledo, after having rapidly roamed the city and reminded the reader that it was called Tuleytula 'in Andalusian' [*sic*],[146] he sat at the Café Imperial, the decoration of which immediately drew his attention: 'It is built entirely in Arab style. The walls are decorated with Oriental

---

an excessive and often abusive use of certain punctuation signs, especially parentheses and quotation marks, which were often used to emphasise a word or an expression.

144 [Tunalı] A. Hilmi, *Rezalet: Yine İspanya'da*, pp. ix–x.

145 [Tunalı] Hilmi, *Rezalet: Yine İspanya'da*, pp. viii–ix.

146 [Tunalı] Hilmi, *Rezalet: Yine İspanya'da*, p. 5.

mouldings and motifs.'[147] He then discovered the cathedral, noting that it dated back to the Visigoths, that it was converted into a mosque by the Arabs in 712 and that, finally, it was converted back into a church when Alfonso VI took the city in 1185 [*sic*, for 1085], which he contextualised with an interesting remark: 'Could this be a case of *men daqqa duqqa* (one reaps what one sows)?'[148] He came across a few other mosques converted into churches, but refused to visit them, not out of resentment, but simply because there was an entrance fee. Regarding one of them, he expressed regrets, for he had been told it was a splendid example of Arab architecture and noted that 'it is today the chapel of Santo Dolaloz, where Alfonso VI attended the first mass after he had conquered the city in 1085'.[149]

Such a degree of precision comes as a surprise, but Hilmi soon reveals how he accessed it: 'Toledo – according to Baedeker – is one big museum.'[150] We thus understand that he had been visiting the city with the 1900 edition of the Baedeker guidebook on Spain and Portugal, evidently in its French version. Indeed, the guidebook contains all the details of his narrative, from the museum-city[151] to the cathedral[152] and, of course, to the mysterious chapel of 'Santo Dolaloz', which turns out to be the chapel of Santo Cristo de la Luz.[153] This also explains the text of the postcard of the mosque of Cordoba he sent to his brother: the regrets he attributes to Charles V at the sight of the choir built in the middle of the mosque was taken almost word for word from the same guidebook.[154]

147 [Tunalı] Hilmi, *Rezalet: Yine İspanya'da*, p. 6.

148 [Tunalı] Hilmi, *Rezalet: Yine İspanya'da*, p. 7.

149 [Tunalı] Hilmi, *Rezalet: Yine İspanya'da*, pp. 7–8.

150 [Tunalı] Hilmi, *Rezalet: Yine İspanya'da*, p. 8.

151 '[Toledo] has been well described by Wörmann as "a gigantic open-air museum of the architectural history of Early Spain, arranged upon a lofty and conspicuous table of rock"' (Baedeker, *Spain and Portugal*, p. 129). I have taken this and the following quotes and references from the 1898 English version of this guidebook. As noted above, Hilmi would have used the French version, which was to a large extent identical.

152 Baedeker, *Spain and Portugal*, p. 130.

153 Baedeker, *Spain and Portugal*, pp. 143–4.

154 'Charles V himself expressed this feeling in the words he addressed to the cathedral chapter on visiting Cordova in 1526: "You have built what you or others might have built anywhere, but you have destroyed something that was unique in the world"' (Baedeker, *Spain and Portugal*, p. 316).

We have no reason to blame Hilmi Efendi for having followed his Baedeker so closely. As a conscientious tourist, he intended to get the best information possible. What could be more normal than that? However, this also meant that he would have to be exposed to a viewpoint that was essentially different from that of his Muslim contemporaries. There were no laments about the fate of mosques or the loss of cities in the Baedeker guide, but only mentions of Christian conversions and conquests, with no qualms whatsoever, to the point of ascribing to Charles V the selfless and noble role of a protector of Islamic heritage. Nevertheless, a closer reading of Hilmi's travelogues and other texts suggests that this did not really feel like a sacrifice or a frustration to him, and that he sometimes went even further than the Baedeker. The idea that the conversion of a mosque in Toledo into a church could have been a case of 'reaping what one had sown' does not appear anywhere in the guidebook; it was clearly Hilmi's own comment. Moreover, if he chose to present this piece of wisdom by using a proverb in Arabic – '*men daqqa duqqa*' – could it be that he was adding an additional layer of irony to it, almost as if he was thumbing his nose at the Arabs?[155] It is quite possible, especially if one considers that he tended to use Arab sayings in a somewhat comical way, as in '*fülus mafiş*' ('not a penny').[156]

However, I believe that one of his comments concerning Lisbon is of crucial significance to understand Tunalı Hilmi's stand on religious matters.

155 The original expression is '*man daqq bāb ghayruhu daqqu bābihi*', which can be translated as 'whoever knocks on one door will see someone knocking on their door'. Obviously, only the shorter version seems to have been in Ottoman Turkish culture, with the additional advantage of a strong alliteration. After consulting with Seif el-Rashidi, it seems that that this expression has to a large extent vanished from Arab popular culture and that the main reason it has survived in Turkish is probably that it 'sounds' like Arabic, and that it is easy and funny to repeat. Tayyip Erdoğan seems to be an adept of this expression, which he uses repeatedly as a form of warning against political adversaries: Bachar al-Assad in 2012, the European Union in 2017, the United States in 2018 and, in 2019, all who would offer support or protection to Fethullah Gülen. That year, he was himself targeted by a '*men daqqa duqqa*' by Temel Karamollaoğlu, leader of the Felicity Party (*Saadet Partisi*), of Islamist tendency, which would suggest that the expression is particularly popular among right-wing Islamists, perhaps because it is of Arab origin.

156 [Tunalı] Hilmi, *Rezalet: Yine İspanya'da*, p. xii.

After having noted, again thanks to Baedeker,[157] that the city's cathedral was a mosque that had been converted into a church in 1150, inspired by the resemblance between Lisbon and Istanbul, he started to think aloud:

> Lisbon at this end, Istanbul at the other. Over there, a church – the Hagia Sophia – became a mosque . . . Here, a mosque has become a church. Let us be impartial: both are the result of the same baseness, the same immorality, or else, it may well be a fruit picked by the same leonine character, by the same required morality. Yes, but this one causes sorrow, while the other provokes pride . . . I wonder why? . . . Come on, come on . . . Stop babbling like a fool, you 'sick man', look at yourself, rather!'[158]

So much relativism and impartiality seems strange, especially when compared with the attitude adopted in most of the narratives and comments we have observed this far. Yet one should not underestimate to what extent modernisation and political liberalism in the Ottoman Empire at the time were often coupled with a nascent secularisation that challenged the very essence of the identity that Abdülhamid's regime was trying to impose on his empire and on the majority of his subjects. True, Tunalı Hilmi stood at the other extreme, enjoying the freedom of exile and the comfort of provocation that he derived from his status as a dissident and opponent of the Hamidian regime. Nevertheless, I believe that he was saying out loud what others thought very quietly. With such a mindset, far from being a source of nostalgic dreams, Spain became an occasion to question his own identity and, at the same time, that of his country, to which he seemed to be alluding when he called himself a 'sick man'. His visit to Zaragoza, again under Baedeker's guidance, thus became an opportunity to reflect on his own identity, on the past and the present, on heritage and modernity, on Spain and the Ottoman Empire:

> Abstract: The effect of Zaragoza on me has been to make me feel European. Then I remembered where I was from, from which country I came, the state of each of our cities and towns, their ruins. I said to myself: 'Baedeker insists that one should absolutely visit this place; I wonder what he would have said had he

[157] Baedeker, *Spain and Portugal*, pp. 527–8.

[158] [Tunalı] Hilmi, *Rezalet: Portekiz*, p. 11.

> seen our ruins of the early Middle Ages'. That being said, Zaragoza is not just a town inhabited by a people who has managed to establish a constitutional regime, it also possesses a new university and a school of medicine, whose style, like that of all the churches, is fundamentally different.[159]

That was what distinguished his narrative from those of his contemporaries, who were less radically committed to the path of modernity. To Hilmi, the Arab past of the Iberian Peninsula was only a parenthesis in time, a bygone era. What he was more interested in was contemporary Spain, whose contrasts and contradictions between tradition and modernity he observed with a curiosity sharpened by his conviction that there was much food for thought there for an Ottoman who fought for change and modernity in his own country. That is probably why his historical comments are relatively limited and mostly picked from the tourist bible of the time, which apparently never left him. For the rest, however, he never ceased observing the immediate reality that surrounded him, many aspects of which he found fascinating, either because he interpreted them as the embodiment of dogmatism, tradition and religion,[160] or, on the contrary, because they revealed a form of freedom and modernity he craved for.[161] His visit to Barcelona was particularly meaningful. He was conquered by the beauty and wealth of the 'Paris of Spain'. He watched *La Sirène* at the Teatro Catalá, known for staging only plays in Catalan, which gave him

[159] [Tunalı] Hilmi, *Rezalet: Yine İspanya'da*, p. 91.

[160] Immediately upon his arrival in Spain, he was struck by the importance attached to the last rites, and explained that any priest charged with this ritual had the right to stop any carriage for this purpose and that everyone would take their hats off on its passage ([Tunalı] Hilmi, *Rezalet: Yine İspanya'da*, pp. 5–6). During his visit to Zaragoza, inside a church, he was shocked to see a woman, who, while contemplating an image of the Virgin, hawked and spat right in front of it. At the same moment, a 'properly dressed *mademoiselle*' entered the church, kneeled before another image and started kissing 'the floor that had been trampled by everybody's shoes' (pp. 86–7).

[161] As there are numerous examples, I will pick only a few. He is impressed to see the queen and her daughter pass by in an ordinary carriage, without any escort. 'How unpretentious ... How courageous! And back home? What a shame ...' ([Tunalı] Hilmi, *Rezalet: Yine İspanya'da*, p. 47). In the train on his way to Barcelona, he finds himself in a compartment with three women. Two of them were praying. 'The other took out a novel and started reading. This is the first time I see this during travel. Until then, in all of Spain, I have not seen a single man busy reading during travel' (p. 92).

the opportunity to speak of Catalan independentists.[162] He also described the city's nightlife, the destitution of prostitutes, the poverty of young people living on the streets, the misery of a man making a living from collecting cigarette butts . . .[163] He noted, not without a tinge of envy: 'Barcelona is the meeting place of anarchists in Spain, nay, in the whole world![164]

Tunalı Hilmi and his Spanish adventure's exceptional character did not end at that. To my greatest satisfaction, the young revolutionary had left one more trace of his visit to the Alhambra: two photographs. What made this all the more striking is that both were taken in precisely the same studio where Khālidī would pose four years later, namely, Rafael Garzón's famous *patio árabe*. In fact, it seems that Tunalı Hilmi may have been among Garzón's first customers to have enjoyed his brand-new set.[165] However, what really makes these two photographs extraordinary, is that Hilmi chose a different costume and pose for each, a fact that once again set him completely apart from his contemporaries. In the first, he was leaning against one of the stucco columns of the portico forming one side of the make-believe courtyard, posing as a globetrotter. Wearing a light suit and walking shoes, he has a relaxed attitude, further enhanced by a left hand negligently clinging to his belt. A suitcase in his right hand puts a finishing touch to the portrait of the perfect tourist. The quality of the photograph reveals an amusing, and somewhat touching, detail: one of the two books he holds in the same hand as the suitcase is his trusted Baedeker. The only detail that distinguishes him from the average European tourist is his fez and, of course, the fact that he had chosen not to wear one of Garzón's 'Moorish' costumes (Figure 4.12).[166]

And yet Tunalı Hilmi was not one to shy away from disguises. The second photograph shows him in the same studio, but this time in exactly the same corner as Khālidī. His costume looks Spanish: he is wearing a kerchief on his head, a tight waistcoat, a thick fabric wrapped around his waist, tight trousers

162 [Tunalı] Hilmi, *Rezalet: Yine İspanya'da*, pp. 96–7; Baedeker, *Espagne et Portugal*, p. 228. This theatre is not mentioned in the 1898 English edition of the guidebook.

163 [Tunalı] Hilmi, *Rezalet: Yine İspanya'da*, pp. 98–100.

164 [Tunalı] Hilmi, *Rezalet: Yine İspanya'da*, pp. 99–100.

165 Construction of the *patio árabe* had started in April 1900 and the first news items appeared in the press by mid-October. Given that Tunalı Hilmi's photographs were dated 8 September, it is highly probable that he was among the first clients to have enjoyed this setting (see n. 10, p. 8).

166 Portrait of Tunalı Hilmi Efendi as a traveller in Rafael Garzón's *patio árabe*, Granada, 8 September 1900. Courtesy of İnsan Tunalı.

Figure 4.12 Photograph of Tunalı Hilmi Efendi posing as a globetrotter in Rafael Garzón's *patio árabe*, Granada, 8 September 1900. İnsan Tunalı collection, Istanbul. At the antipodes of Khalīl Jawād Khālidī, who would pose in the exact same setting four years later, Tunalı Hilmi adopted a resolutely modern attitude to fashion himself for this memento of his visit to the Alhambra.

and leather spats. He holds a long stick in his left hand as the other rests on the ledge of the fake Moorish window, next to a pointed hat with pompoms (Figure 4.13).[167] A quick search among contemporary photographs reveals that this was precisely the costume worn by the famous Chorrojumo, 'Prince of the Gypsies', as can be seen in a photograph taken in the exact same corner of Garzón's patio (Figure 4.14).[168] After the tourist, the Roma . . . Hilmi had left the Alhambra with an exotic memento, without falling into the trap of Orientalism. While he distinguished himself from his fellow Muslims – assuming he considered himself to be one – by posing as the tourist he actually was, he also stood out by his choice of local exoticism for a fantasy portrait.[169]

That was not all. Tunalı Hilmi also inscribed the back of the two photographs in a style and context we are now rather familiar with. On the back of the 'globetrotter' portrait, he composed a decidedly modern poem, which, despite some efforts at rhyming, ignored all traditional poetic conventions:

> A memento of apostasy[170]
> Behold the 'Alhambra' today, this faint shadow of a glorious past,
> Losing my humanity, I have turned into a tombstone!
> The greatest condition is to turn into stone. Come and look at this world in ruins,
> Watch, reflect, gain awareness and never shed a tear!
> My silence echoes in the calm full of meanings
> Do not keep quiet! Shut up, and stop! Move, get out and turn into an idol, o living creature![171]

[167] Portrait of Tunalı Hilmi Efendi as a Roma in Rafael Garzón's *patio árabe*, Granada, 8 September 1900. Courtesy of İnsan Tunalı.

[168] Mariano Fernández Santiago, AKA Chorrojumo, 'Prince of the Gypsies', in Rafael Garzón's *patio árabe*, *c*. 1900. Private collection, Granada.

[169] Although the unavailability of Garzón's archives or of an exhaustive collection of his studio photographs does not allow for any generalisation, based on the information and images gathered on the web, I believe it may be safe to say that compared with 'Moorish' portraits and scenes, the 'Gypsy' portrait, especially for men, was more of a rarity.

[170] 'Apostasy' (*irtidad*) is a term that Hilmi often uses to describe his pact, albeit temporary, with Abdülhamid.

[171] The inscription is addressed to 'my Ziya'; a later note, from 1948, explains that this was Ali Ziya Zalamanoğlu, who served the Young Turks as a courier.

Figure 4.13 Photograph of Tunalı Hilmi Efendi in a borrowed Roma costume in Rafael Garzón's *patio árabe*, Granada, 8 September 1900. İnsan Tunalı collection, Istanbul. Tunalı Hilmi's quest for exoticism made him choose a 'typically Spanish' costume, which turns out to be that of the eccentric 'Prince of the Gypsies', Mariano Fernández Santiago, better known as Chorrojumo.

Figure 4.14 Photograph of Mariano Fernández Santiago, AKA Chorrojumo, 'Prince of the Gypsies', posing in his traditional costume in Rafael Garzón's *patio árabe*, *c.* 1900. Private collection, Granada. Chorrojumo, a colourful character haunting the Alhambra, made a living of selling his portrait to tourists and, possibly, of providing photographers with a model that would inspire their clients, as in the case of Tunalı Hilmi.

Another poem, in very similar style, graced the back of the 'Gypsy' portrait:

> Even for an impartial philosopher, the scene is tragic
> Everywhere ruins of the 'crescent'. . . Everywhere a sun occasionally darkened
> Even the paradise of the Generalife[172] is a burning hell
> Even if you were Spanish, the heavens would not cease to cry!
> My eyes mirror the terror of the present and of the past
> The stars (*yıldız*)[173] shine in the East, and departures are always inverted![174]

[172] He uses the original Arab expression of '*Cennetü'l-arif*' or 'paradise of the architect', which gave its name to the Generalife. Of course, he has this information from his Baedeker guidebook (*Spain and Portugal*, p. 367), which explains that he should have misspelt it as '*'ārif*' (عارف) instead of '*'arīf*' (عريف), the latter being very rarely used in Ottoman Turkish.

[173] Evidently, yet another allusion to Abdülhamid's Palace of Yıldız ('Star').

[174] Addressed to the same person as the previous photograph.

Rather than engage in an unlikely explanation of a text of dubious clarity and logic, I will just emphasise some of its aspects, which I believe are particularly interesting from the perspective of this study. First, one notices an obsession with ruins, a recurrent motif and metaphor in descriptions of the fate of the Alhambra and of Islamic civilisation in Spain. This theme was embodied in the expression 'everywhere ruins of the crescent', which in a weird way seems to echo Cano's verses: 'Due to fanaticism and torpor / the cross always among the ruins / and always in ruin your greatness!'[175] There was no connection, of course, given that Hilmi's crescent was itself in ruins, whereas Cano's cross was the cause of his 'poor' Spain's ruin. Nevertheless, if Tunalı Hilmi chose to imitate Volney before the Alhambra, it was not because he had a vision of past glory and splendour or because he lamented the crescent's defeat, but rather because the monument inspired in him a feeling of decline and degradation, encouraging him to embrace the present and a future he hoped would be better.

Tunalı Hilmi was not the last 'Turk' to visit the Alhambra before the First World War. I have already mentioned the visit of one Cemile Hanım in 1907,[176] about whom we unfortunately know nothing, despite the fact that it would have been quite unusual, in fact unthinkable, to see a Muslim woman travel alone abroad. She may have been accompanied by a 'Captain L. Trapani', whose signature, bearing the same date, can be seen next right to hers. Yet would that not have made her journey even more inappropriate? At any rate, given that her inscription simply stated her presence, there is little more we can do than just record her passage. A year later, on 16 August 1908, one Ali Kemal Sırrı expressed his admiration for the monument: 'I swear to God that this day of my visit to the Palace of the Alhambra is the happiest day of my life. What a magnificent edifice, my God. And there is no victor but God and Muhammad is His prophet'.[177] Clearly, this visitor did not share Tunalı Hilmi's secularising cynicism. However, once again, as it seems impossible to identify him,[178] we

[175] See p. 89.

[176] See n. 127, p. 274.

[177] AA, *libros de firmas*, 48, fol. 87 v.

[178] The absence of a surname or family name for the overwhelming majority of 'Turkish' Muslims makes it extremely difficult to identify an individual based only on their given names. The only Ali Kemal Sırrı who surfaces more or less clearly in the documentation of

must leave it at the simple observation that his was a statement of endless admiration, probably somewhat exaggerated, mixed with a strong sense of piety, but without any reference to Arab heritage.

Between Tunalı Hilmi and Cemile Hanım, I cannot ignore Münir Süreyya Bey (1871–1932), a career diplomat,[179] who took advantage of his posting as consul general in Barcelona to visit Andalusia in 1902 and subsequently published – eight years later, in 1910 – a short account of this experience in a periodical known for its Islamist allegiances, but close to the Committee of Union and Progress.[180] The text suggests that he visited Cordoba and not the Alhambra, as would tend to confirm my inability to find a trace of his passage in the visitors' book.[181] Nevertheless, if I do include him in this study, it is because he shows that Tunalı Hilmi's somewhat radical and extreme example should not be unduly generalised from. Very far from the latter's cynicism and much

---

the period is a Gendarmerie officer, who was exiled to Yemen in 1911 and reappeared – if that was still him – in 1919 in Izmir as the author of a memorandum on the atrocities committed by the Greek army during the occupation of the city, and ended up a general and chief commander of the Gendarmerie in Istanbul in 1920 (Ch. Herzog, *Osmanische Herrschaft und Modernisierung im Irak*, p. 186; BOA, HR SYS 2383/1, 4 June 1335/1919; K. Gurulkan et al. (eds), *Osmanlı Belgelerinde Millî Mücadele ve Mustafa Kemal Atatürk*, pp. 254–8). While it seems rather unlikely that a Gendarmerie officer would travel to Spain less than a month after the Young Turk Revolution, one cannot exclude this possibility.

179 The son of the palace first secretary, Ahmed Süreyya Bey, Münir Süreyya had studied at the Imperial Lycée, where he also taught French before starting a lively diplomatic career. He was appointed consul general to Barcelona (1899–1904), Syros (1904–5), rejected Niš for health reasons, and was appointed first secretary at the Legation in Bern (1905). He filled in the same position in Vienna (1906–10) and Brussels (1910), before being appointed consul general in São Paulo (1910–12), Tbilisi (1914) and Geneva (1920), and chargé d'affaires in Bern (1920–3). In 1923, he was appointed second secretary to Caliph Abdülmecid, and when the latter was exiled in 1924, he was sent as chargé d'affaires to Madrid (1925–7) and consul general in New York (1927–9) and in Piraeus (1929–31). It appears that Münir Süreyya Bey was married to a foreign subject – a Frenchwoman? – by the name of Andrée, who died in 1919 (BOA, HR UHM 205/56, 19 December 1919).

180 Münir Süreyya, 'İspanya Hatıratı'.

181 Knowing that he arrived in Cordoba on 'a glorious sunny morning of the spring of 1902' (Münir Süreyya, 'İspanya Hatıratı', p. 1,421), I have looked in vain for his signature – in any possible script –through the pages of the visitors' book of the Alhambra corresponding to that season.

closer to the mysterious Ali Kemal Sırrı mentioned above, Münir Süreyya was highly impressed by his discovery of Andalusia and filled with admiration, but also sadness, for the civilisation that was behind it. The fall of Granada was a dramatic event, embodied in a painting representing the Catholic sovereigns facing a defeated Boabdil, who presented them with the keys to his city.[182]

However, it was Cordoba that mostly drew his attention. Comparing the glory of this past metropolis of science and knowledge to the state of disrepair of what had now become a miserable provincial town, he sang the praise of those who had created this miracle: ʿAbdelraḥman I (r. 756–88), his son Hāshim [*sic*, for Hishām] (r. 788–96), ʿAbdelraḥman II (r. 822–52), ʿAbdallah bin Muḥammad (r. 888–912), ʿAbdelraḥman III (r. 912–61) and al-Ḥakam II al-Mustanṣir Billah (r. 961–76). Among all these rulers his preference was for ʿAbdelraḥman III, whose reign as an emir and then as a caliph represented the peak of the power, wealth, and cultural and intellectual influence of Cordoba.[183]

How would he not lament the fate of this civilisation? 'What is there that remains today in Cordoba of all this prosperity, a source of pride for the Arabs for all eternity?' Nothing, except that magnificent mosque, a visit to which is 'the first duty of any Muslim going to Cordoba'. That was exactly what he did, 'with tearful eyes', sighing and lamenting at the idea of the thousands of believers who used to crowd this holy site. Giving in to emotion, he could not help but pray in secret in front of a perfectly preserved *mihrab*. Once outside, he started looking for the tombs of the great and illustrious inhabitants of the city; finding none, he resigned himself to recite a *fātiḥa*, the first surah of the Koran, on the square facing the mosque 'from the bottom of my heart, for all Muslim men and women'.[184]

182 'This painting, which I had seen in a "museum" when I was in Spain, represents a cheerful location outside the gates of Granada. One can see on one side King Ferdinand and his wife Queen Isabella, both on horseback. Facing them, one recognises the vanquished King of Granada, ʿAbdallah al-Ṣaghīr, also on horseback. Their retinue stands at attention behind each sovereign: one can read [the joy of] the Spaniards on their face. Amid this impressive crowd, al-Ṣaghīr, his hand extended, takes a sorrowful look at his capital he has had to leave and surrenders the keys of Granada to Ferdinand' (Münir Süreyya, 'İspanya Hatıratı', p. 1, 420). One can easily identify this painting as the famous work by Francisco Pradilla y Ortiz (1848–1921), realised in 1882 and known as *La Rendición de Granada*.

183 Münir Süreyya, 'İspanya Hatıratı', p. 1,421.

184 Münir Süreyya, 'İspanya Hatıratı', p. 1,421.

These actions and impressions suffice to show the ideological abyss that separated Münir Süreyya, a pious visitor to Andalusia, from Tunalı Hilmi, whose comments flirted dangerously with blasphemy. And yet, by looking somewhat closer and by scratching away the rhetorical veneer of these texts, one may discover surprising and very interesting commonalities between them. Indeed, during his description of the mosque of Cordoba, Münir Süreyya insisted that 'the modifications brought by the Spaniards to this holy mosque to convert it into a church have partly destroyed the beauty of the edifice'. However, he adds, Charles V himself, when he discovered the work that had been done, 'lashed out at the priests who had deceived the government and partly destroyed this architectural wonder'.[185] We are now quite familiar with that story, as we have read it from Tunalı Hilmi's pen, who himself had borrowed it from his Baedeker guidebook. True, Münir Süreyya told it differently, but knowing that he was perfectly fluent in French and realising that his list of the greatest rulers of Cordoba followed exactly the same sequence that Baedeker gave when describing the mosque,[186] it becomes rather obvious that he had used the same travel aid as Tunalı Hilmi before him. These convergences clearly show that, despite his pious and nostalgic attitude towards the heritage of al-Andalus, Münir Süreyya remained very 'Turkish' in his approach, in the sense that he observed the remains of this past through Western sources. While he certainly attached to it a historic and highly religious value, this remained essentially abstract and ecumenical in nature, with no linkage to a contemporary political discourse, be it along the lines of Arabism or of Ottomanism. Interestingly, but perhaps not surprisingly, the only exception had to do with the painting he had admired in a museum, depicting the surrender of Granada. He wished to see an Ottoman artist paint a similar canvas, but representing the conquest of Andalusia by Ṭāriq ibn Ziyād, 'as it sprang from the ardent genius of our great poet, Abdülhak Hâmid Bey'.[187]

[185] Münir Süreyya, 'İspanya Hatıratı', p. 1,422.

[186] Baedeker, *Spain and Portugal*, pp. 310–11.

[187] As noted earlier, Abdülhak Hâmid was the author of several 'Andalusian' plays, including one on the adventures of Ṭāriq ibn Ziyād. Münir Süreyya Bey's dream was to see that this painting, once completed, would be placed in the Military Museum, in the section devoted to the glories of Islam, facing canvases depicting the bravery of the Ottomans (Münir Süreyya, 'İspanya Hatıratı', p. 1,420).

The list of Ottoman 'Turkish' visitors ends with Samipaşazade Sezai Bey (1859–1936), minister in Madrid from 1909 to 1914. His signature is strikingly revealing of the context of his visit: he simply signed 'S. Sezaï, 3 March 1914', entirely in French. Nothing else; not a single word in Turkish, no titles or functions, no comment. So much so that I had a very hard time finding it in the pages of the visitors' book. Just below, a second signature, dated 4 March clearly reads 'Mahmoud', again in French. It could very well be his brother, Mahmud Hüdayi Bey, although it seems difficult to understand why the two siblings might have visited the site separately on two consecutive days.[188] Should we deduce from the fact that Sezai Bey visited the Alhambra in the fifth year of his residence in Madrid and that he barely left a signature, that he attached little importance to the monument? Fortunately, additional sources allow for a better contextualisation of this visit. First, we have a photograph of him – a 'real' one, this time – showing him in the Court of the Lions (Figure 4.15). The diplomat is standing up very straight, next to one of the small double columns of the gallery, in a costume as Western as his signature: a tie and a starched collar, his hands deep in the pockets of a dark coat and, most strikingly, wearing a fedora. In all evidence, Sezai Bey was even more Westernised than Tunalı Hilmi, who had taken off his fez only to dress up as a Roma. He also originated from a very different social milieu. As the son of the statesman Abdurrahman Sami Pasha, he had grown up in a very grand environment. In 1880, he was appointed second secretary at the London embassy, but was dismissed in 1885 – for having worn a hat. That is when he discovered his talent as a novelist, but he ended up exiling himself to Paris in 1901 to escape from Hamidian censorship and pressure. There, he formed friendships with exiled Young Turks and eventually returned to Istanbul after the Revolution of 1908. Two men of very different ages and social milieux were thus joined by common political and cultural causes.

There was one more point of convergence between the two men. Sezai Bey, too, published an account of his travels. However, he did it with an inexplicable delay: it was only in 1927, thirteen years after his journey, that his six-page text was published in a monthly periodical under the title of 'The Great Mosque – The Alhambra'.[189] As suggested by the title, this

[188] AA, *libros de firmas*, 49, fol. 153, 3 and 4 March 1914.

[189] S. Samipaşazade, 'El-mescidi'l-Camia: Elhamra'.

Figure 4.15 Photograph of the Ottoman minister Samipaşazade Sezai Bey in the Court of the Lions, 3 March 1914. Sinan Kuneralp collection, Istanbul. The minister's relaxed pose and his fedora match his profile of a 'super-Westernised' Ottoman gentleman and intellectual of the last decade of the empire.

account covered only the mosque of Cordoba and the Alhambra, precisely the two sites that Tunalı Hilmi had omitted in his travelogue. Nevertheless, Sezai Bey's approach to the matter was somewhat reminiscent of Hilmi's style. Contemporary Spain was very present, most notably through the description of the express train to Cordoba and a comparison of the city with European cities: 'After the broad and harmonious avenues one sees everywhere in Europe, [the streets of Cordoba] seem at the same time strange and charming'.[190] The Orient lurked at the corner of each street:

> God only knows to what mysterious palace of a king or queen of al-Andalus these narrow and hidden streets will take me. I was overwhelmed by the feeling that these streets were going to make me jump over centuries and reveal the Middle Ages, Arab Spain, the secret love and passions provoked by the warm quivers of Africa.[191]

[190] Samipaşazade, 'El-mescidi'l-Camia: Elhamra', p. 12.

[191] Samipaşazade, 'El-mescidi'l-Camia: Elhamra', p. 12.

Instead of a palace, Sezai Bey came across the great mosque. A detailed description followed, with its impressive dimensions: 175 × 130 m, 'almost as large as the famous church of Saint Peter in Rome'. He counted twenty-two gates and 860 columns, forming a 'white forest'. He brought up the conversion of the mosque into a church and lamented that they should have demolished one of the *mihrab*s, 'in order to replace it, as commented Charles V, by a church altar identical to those in every church'.[192] Despite the paraphrase, there is no difficulty in identifying the source for this latter information, but also for the dimensions of the mosque and the comparison with St Peter's. Of course, Sezai Bey, too, was travelling with the Baedeker in his hands.[193]

The following day, in Granada, Sezai Bey was enthralled by the beauty of springtime, so different from Paris, Vienna, Istanbul and Madrid. He settled at the Alhambra Palace, a luxury hotel built by the very same Count of Benalúa who had hosted İzzet Fuad Pasha at his hunting parties. Sezai Bey found the hotel 'modern' (*asri*) but did not mention its neo-Nasrid style. The following day, he climbed the incline leading to the Alhambra, which, 'viewed from the exterior looks more like a fortress than a palace'. He even engaged in a digression on this characteristic of the Arab house, closed to the exterior and whose charms are turned toward the interior.[194] He described Charles V's palace, 'sturdy but coarse', the Court of the Myrtles and the beauty of the decoration of the palace halls.

> I believe one has to be an Oriental to understand and feel the Alhambra. Westerners are disappointed by this palace. They find it strange that there should be no statues and paintings on the wall, a flaw according to them. However, while Orientals may be saddened by this state, they do not find it surprising. The Europeans accuse the architects of the Alhambra of not knowing the rules of their art, or of sacrificing them to fantasy.[195]

The Nasrid motto inspired him a commentary that was, to say the least, fanciful:

192 Samipaşazade, 'El-mescidi'l-Camia: Elhamra', p. 12.
193 Baedeker, *Spain and Portugal*, pp. 312–16.
194 Samipaşazade, 'El-mescidi'l-Camia: Elhamra', p. 13.
195 Samipaşazade, 'El-mescidi'l-Camia: Elhamra', p. 16.

> However, as they kept being defeated, I believe that the rulers of al-Andalus who were trying to cling to Granada finally lost all hope of victory, [which is why] all one can see instead of statues and paintings is '*la ghāliba illā Allah*' written in the ancient Kufic calligraphy all over the walls, in every hall, in every room of the palace. And yet the Lord has never said 'I am the only victor, you are all vanquished; I am the only one to exist, you are all non-existent.' No prophet has ever transmitted such words. One should say instead: 'You should follow the behaviour of the Creator.' How can they claim that their enemies did not vanquish them? It is truly because of this great plague of the Orient, namely this pitiful and despicable resignation, that the Andalusians have been completely defeated and that the remains of their civilisation have been reduced to dust.[196]

Once again, Sezai Bay was getting most of these comments from his little red-covered guidebook. This was particularly true of the remarks on Arab homes on the place of architecture and decoration in Arab culture, and on the absence of sculpture and painting.[197] However, Baedeker was not responsible for the digression on the deeper meaning of the Nasrid motto.[198] Confident in his knowledge – apparently rather limited – of the Arabic language and Islam, Sezai Bey had built a completely fanciful theory which turned the famous motto into proof of Arab fatalism and the cause of their ineluctable defeat. And yet we know that this motto could already be seen in the Almohad Caliph

[196] Samipaşazade, 'El-mescidi'l-Camia: Elhamra', pp. 16–17.

[197] 'The Arab house, like the house of classical antiquity, is simple and reserved on the outside; its rooms all open on an internal court' (Baedeker, *Spain and Portugal*, p. 356). 'Their constructive value is small; the material, chiefly wood and plaster, is by no means solid and is frequently employed with illusive intent; the laws of architectonics seem often to exist for the architect only that he may evade or deride them' (p. 356). 'The plastic reproduction of living creatures is not only forbidden by the Koran but is foreign to the Arab nature. This is the explanation of the lack of sculpture and the absence of any intellectual stimulus connected with the plastic art. An indifferent substitute for sculpture is afforded by the use of inscriptions, mainly in the venerable Cufic character, as borders for enclosed wall-spaces' (p. 357).

[198] The only comment on this matter is: 'He [Mohammed I] was the originator of the motto "*Wala ghaliba ill Allah*" ("there is no conqueror but God"), which is so conspicuous, along with the "*plus ultra*" of Charles V, among the inscriptions of the Alhambra' (Baedeker, *Spain and Portugal*, p. 350).

Ya'qūb al-Manṣūr's (r. 754–75) banner, that it was taken up by Muḥammad I (r. 1232–73), the founder of the Nasrid dynasty, and that its meaning perfectly suited the Islamic tradition of attributing the destiny of men and nations to the divine will. After all, Muḥammad I himself had claimed the name of *Ghālib bi'llah*, or 'victor by the grace of God'.

It is clear that in Sezai Bey's eyes, the defeat of the Arabs of Spain and the collapse of their civilisation was the consequence of a form of decadence, whose principal causes he saw in the adulteration of Islam and in the character of a kingdom that had lost its martial spirit. The conclusion of this short travel account perfectly illustrates the ambiguous mix of fascination and scorn he felt before the faded splendour of the palace:

> The Alhambra gave me the impression of a tent pitched in the desert, inside of which the noblest ideas and the most delicate arts have flourished. A tent, the blue satin door of which would reveal, like a spectre, a mirage wrapped in a distant mist, the armoured and helmeted soldiers of al-Andalus, of ancient Damascus, of Baghdad and of all Arabia, the poets calling for heroism at the battlefield, feverish preachers, the scholars on whom rest civilisation and then, a people who has fallen into captivity because of its corrupt character.
>
> The Alhambra shows us that by distancing itself from reality, lost in a dream of paradise, the Arab state of Granada will have to leave forever al-Andalus, its homeland, and surrender its place, its civilisation and its lands to their former masters, the fierce and fanatical Spaniards.[199]

Clearly, Sezai Bey was combining borrowed Orientalism – his Baedeker provided him with much of it[200] – with acquired Orientalism, that famous Ottoman Orientalism that enabled 'white' Ottomans to cleanse themselves of Oriental stigmata by projecting all these clichés and stereotypes onto those they considered to be 'darker' than themselves, in this particular case, the

199 Samipaşazade, 'El-mescidi'l-Camia: Elhamra', p. 17.

200 'This Moorish palace comes to us like the resuscitation and artistic glorification of a far-distant past; the tent of the nomad Arab celebrates a late resurrection in its halls. The thin and fragile marble columns, on which rest large and apparently heavy masses of masonry, are an imitation of the tent-poles; the brilliant colours of the "arabesque" ornamentation is an echo of the gay patterns of the Oriental carpets with which the tent-interiors were draped' (Baedeker, *Spain and Portugal*, pp. 356–7).

Arabs.[201] Of course, one important question needs to be addressed. Was Sezai Bey writing this in 1927, or was he publishing what he had already written during, or just after, his journey in 1914? While it is impossible to know for sure, it seems reasonable that it was a mix of the two. The details of the journey, as well as the 'basic' Orientalism, borrowed from Baedeker, were probably contemporary of his visit, and had probably been drawn from notes taken in the moment. On the other hand, the comments on the decline and fall of al-Andalus were strongly tainted with notions that one cannot help but associate with the Turkish political agenda of the 1920s: the abolition of the sultanate (1922) and of the caliphate (1924), the first steps towards secularism (1924–6), and the rapid growth in power of Kemalism. Beyond an Ottoman form of criticism directed at the Arabs and their civilisation, Sezai Bey's text seems to include elements of republican secularism with a strong Kemalist undertone. Viewed from this perspective, the decadence observed in Spain seems to hold true for the Ottoman Empire, whose disintegration was now celebrated as a legitimate and much expected return to a Turkish revival. Together with the empire, it was also Islam that was to blame, as a cause for backwardness and weakness against the power of the West. The context was extremely different from that of the 1880s, when Ottoman intellectuals and statesmen were timidly attempting to take advantage from the Andalusian heritage to polish the image of Islam and of the Orient in order to face Europe's political and intellectual offensive. Like Tunalı Hilmi before him, Sezai Bey saw in the Alhambra splendid and charming ruins, but most of

[201] I am appropriating and adapting to the Ottoman context the expression 'white Turks' (*beyaz Türkler*), which was coined in 1992 by the journalist Ufuk Güldemir (1956–2007) in his *Teksas Malatya*. The expression was taken over by many scholars and researchers in the social sciences, who saw it as an expression of one of the major fault lines of Turkish society and politics, especially in the form of the contempt expressed by Kemalist bourgeois elites towards their 'darker' fellow citizens, from Kurds to pious Muslims, from villagers in remote Anatolian areas to headscarf-wearing women. See, T. Bora, 'Notes on the White Turks Debate'. I believe that this concept, fits perfectly in the continuum between Ottoman and Turkish Orientalism, as illustrated by many Ottoman Muslims, who, due to their allegiance to, and integration with, Western modernity, considered themselves as distinct from the masses on whom they could project Orientalist stereotypes borrowed from the West.

all he felt that these were the traces of a bygone era and of a failure from which one needed to draw a lesson.

Shortly after Sezai Bey's visit, another Young Turk, Celal Nuri [İleri] (1882–1938)[202] addressed the question of Andalusian history through a series of articles he published in his own literary magazine, *Edebiyat-ı Umumiye Mecmuası* (*Journal of General Literature*).[203] This was not a travel account, given that the author had never been to Spain. His goal was rather to provide his readers with a synthesis on the history of Muslim Spain and to connect it to that of the Ottoman Empire, which is why I have decided to include it in this study. Despite its brevity – about fifteen pages in three issues – this is the only true study on the topic published in Turkish since Ziya Pasha's translation of Viardot. Interestingly, Celal Nuri's approach to the history of al-Andalus overlaps to a great degree with the dominant trends I have already noted among the last 'Turkish' visitors of the Alhambra.

While the author expressed great admiration for the civilisation the Arabs had established in Spain and for their ability to 'constitute a Muslim nation in Europe', he insisted from the very start on the fact that 'the destiny of al-Andalus had no connection to Ottoman history', which had been his initial objective.[204] Nevertheless, using Sédillot and Ziya Pasha, he drew a very positive assessment of the military, literary, artistic and scientific achievements of Arab civilisation in Spain, continuously contrasting the prosperity and sophistication of this land to the state of barbary that characterised the rest of Europe.

[202] After graduating from the Imperial Lycée and Law School, Celal Nuri started his career as a journalist in 1909. Navigating between nationalism and pan-Islamism, he found his cause in the defence of the empire against Western imperialism. As a true globetrotter, he travelled to Russia and Scandinavia (1912), to the North Pole (1913) and to the United States (1914). He established the *Journal of General Literature* (*Edebiyat-ı Umumiye Mecmuası*) in 1916, followed by the daily *Âti* (*The Future*) in January 1918. A few months later, the defeat having brought down the Unionists, Celal Nuri fell from grace and his newspaper was suspended in February 1919. He immediately started a new one, called *İleri* (*Forward!*), from which he would get his surname in 1934. He was elected to parliament in 1919 and exiled to Malta by the Entente Powers. Upon his return in 1921, he joined the Ankara government as a deputy and contributed to the drafting of the 1924 constitution.

[203] Celal Nuri, 'Endülüs'e Dair'.

[204] Celal Nuri, 'Endülüs'e Dair', p. 337.

A passage from the text, where he listed the major scientific contributions of the Arabs is particularly interesting:

> The Arabs wearing the burnous and the keffiyeh, those Arabs we are accustomed to see in the desert in a state of sluggishness close to carelessness, would measure the meridians with compasses, correct Ptolemy's astronomical errors, produce alcohol in alembics, conduct calculations on spheres. They saved Aristotle's works from the depths of oblivion; by a constant recourse to experimentation, they discovered algebra; they were able to solve problems of geometry and trigonometry. The Arabs were the ones who spread arithmetic. Physics, mechanics, chemistry had the privilege of drawing their attention. In an era when time had no value whatsoever, the Andalusians were building the most beautiful clocks. Their travellers had discovered the four corners of the globe. Like the British and the Americans of our time, the Muslims of Spain gave much importance to *tourisme* [in French].[205]

The list was not extraordinary in itself, given that it was a rehash of most of the achievements attributed to the Arabs during the Middle Ages. However, the way these achievements were presented is truly surprising, as it rests on the contrast between the 'sluggish Arab of the desert' and his noble forbears.[206] Once again, Orientalism was at work, to describe the decline and degeneration of a civilisation, whose direct heirs were no longer worthy of it. It was therefore elsewhere that one would have to look for the Andalusian heritage, namely, in Europe, where the scientific advances borrowed from the Arabs had flourished, and in Spain, as the natural result of the human residual of a presence of almost eight centuries:

> It should be known that Islam in Spain has not been entirely destroyed like, for example, the people and structures of the Vandals. No! The Muslim civilisation of al-Andalus continues to live today in the form of Western civilisation.

[205] Celal Nuri, 'Endülüs'e Dair', 24 March 1917, p. 359.

[206] One cannot help but remember the inscription left in 1847 by a French colonist from Algiers who regretted 'not having brought a few Bedouins with him to show them what they had been capable of some centuries ago and to teach them what they should become' (see p. 87).

> The Muslims of Spain are not heirless. Those who have not migrated to Africa have changed their shape to form the new Spanish race. If we set aside their Inquisition, their auto-da-fés, their Jesuits and their violence, Spain and the Spaniards are somewhat Maghrebi: there is in the Spanish race a considerable part – which I cannot determine precisely – of blood from the Maghreb; in their way of thinking, their feelings, their ideas, their character, their customs, Spaniards – and even the three Americas [*sic*], from Mexico to Cape Horn – are a continuation of al-Andalus. The ways of life and even the faces and physiognomy of Spain remind the inhabitants of Najd, of Yemen, of Syria, of Mecca. There is, in its villages, its towns, its houses, an Arab taste. Setting aside religious fanaticism and the atrocities of the Inquisition, Spaniards today still use two thousand words in Arabic – just like Turkish and Persian![207]

Celal Nuri went on to discuss the causes of the decline and collapse of this brilliant civilisation. According to him, there were five. First, at the peak of their conquests, the Arabs had neglected homogeneity and assimilation (*tecnis ve temsil*), favouring on the contrary 'tolerance and a destructive freedom'.[208] They were also victims of a 'violent dissension' (*şiddetli tefrika*), which had always constituted an obstacle to the establishment of political unity and centralisation, a situation aggravated by the extremely fragmented geography of the Iberian Peninsula. The third cause was the rapidity with which the Arabs advanced in their conquests, which worked against a proper 'appropriation' (*istimlak*) of the territories under their rule. A fourth argument, which, he emphasised, was especially brought forward by Westerners, was that polygamy constituted a factor of corruption that weakened their notions of family and nation. Finally, the last, and in Celal Nuri's view, the most important, of all causes behind Arab decline was the geographic and military superiority of the Christians: 'Much more than their internal corruption, it is the sword of the Christians, the zeal of the Crusaders that defeated the Muslims of Spain.'[209]

Celal Nuri concluded his study with an analysis of the relations between Ottomans and Arabs at the time of the fall of Granada. He insisted that despite repeated calls for help he received from Andalusia, the Ottoman

[207] Celal Nuri, 'Endülüs'e Dair', 24 March 1917, pp. 359–60.

[208] Celal Nuri, 'Endülüs'e Dair', p. 360.

[209] Celal Nuri, 'Endülüs'e Dair', p. 360.

Sultan Bayezid II (r. 1481–1512) turned a deaf ear and did little more than a few gestures that provided no solace to his co-religionists in Spain. Had he been able to show the moral fibre of his son and successor, Selim I (r. 1512–20), 'it is quite possible that the Ottomans would have then embraced an ambitious policy of Islamic unity'.[210]

Celal Nuri's approach could hardly have been more Ottoman in almost every way. It rested strongly on sources and arguments borrowed from Europe, thus inevitably leading to a form of Orientalism, which granted the Arabs a past glory, but not its heritage. His admiration for the West caused him to attach more importance to the numerical, strategic and moral superiority of the Christians in explaining Arab defeat, than to the argument of dissension and internal strife, which he believed was too facile an explanation. His Ottoman bias also encouraged him to revisit the history of the fall of the Arab kingdoms by imagining the impact that a stronger and more determined intervention by the Ottomans might have had.

However, it was in a much less direct way that Celal Nuri's Ottoman, or rather Turkish, identity crept into his historical synthesis on the rise and fall of Muslim power in Spain. To understand this much subtler dimension of his text, one needs to know that his main objective was to explore and expose the ills that undermined the dying empire and threatened to bring it to its end. He had already published in 1914 a work, whose title was as heavy as it was dark: *A History of Ottoman Decadence and Historical Fate*.[211] In 1917, just a few months before the publication of his analysis of Andalusian history, he had published a pamphlet of more modest size, but whose long and cumbersome title was even more telling: *The Movements We Did Not Participate In: Ottoman History and the Discoveries, the Renaissance and the Reform*.[212] This comes to show how much importance Celal Nuri attached to Ottoman failure in the face of European success; but beyond this very Manichaean – and very Western – vision, it is striking to see to what extent the causes of Ottoman

[210] Celal Nuri, 'Endülüs'e Dair', pp. 372–3.

[211] Celal Nuri, *Tarih-i Tedenniyat-ı Osmaniye ve Mukadderat-ı Tarihiye*.

[212] Celal Nuri, *İştirak Etmediğimiz Harekât: Tarih-i Osmani ve Keşfiyat, Rönesans ve Reform Harekâtı*. The title page notes that this seventy-six-page booklet was published on 12 August 1917.

decline – he had a list of eight – overlapped with those he had put forward to explain the doom of Arab presence in Spain, The Ottomans, or rather the Turks, had also formed an empire at a speed that made it impossible for them to establish the solid financial and administrative bases that would have ensured the longevity of their state, for their character as warriors made them more inclined towards conquest and plunder than towards state-building; rather than assimilating and integrating the different ethnic and religious groups among their subjects, they had given preference to granting them much autonomy; the oppression of women was cause for the degeneration, or even the absence, of family life.[213]

Once again, it is striking to see to what extent this discourse differed from that of the Arabists mentioned earlier. The latter, even if they often involved some sorrow at the sight of the ruins and of the past splendours of al-Andalus, were always strongly attached to feelings of admiration and pride, which were perceived as an inspiration for Arab nationalism and the hope for an Islamic revival. After a short period characterised by a common enthusiasm and mutual interaction, Arab and Turkish intellectuals had ended up drifting apart, sometimes reaching opposite positions with respect to their vision of the political and cultural future of the region. Growing awareness of the power embedded in their linguistic and cultural identity, generally associated with a strong allegiance to Islamic values, the Arabs managed to put together a dream of grandeur and freedom, which found much of its inspiration in Arabo-Islamic medieval heritage. The Alhambra and Andalusia stood at the centre of this construct and thus became an essential reference to a golden age, which legitimised their commitment to a struggle for the emancipation of the self-proclaimed heirs of this civilisation. While the participation of several non-Muslim Arab intellectuals to this project managed to give it a cultural, rather than religious, outlook, this distinction rapidly faded away and was replaced by a vision in which Arab and Islamic identities ended up merging into a single mould.

The Turks' infatuation with the same theme was short-lived and much more superficial. This narrative never managed to take root in a culture that lacked familiarity with the linguistic, literary and historical references needed

[213] Celal Nuri, *Tarih-i Tedenniyat-ı Osmaniye ve Mukadderat-ı Tarihiye*, pp. 64–7.

to appreciate and internalise it fully. As a result, the few authors and intellectuals who dabbled with it had to draw their knowledge and information from Western sources, on which they remained dependent practically till the end. However, it is particularly in the field of ideology and politics that the Andalusian dream lost most of its power and influence on the Turkish public. While Abdülhamid's policy did lead to an Islamisation of the 'hard core' of Anatolia, with tragic consequences for the region's non-Muslim populations, it nevertheless failed to create a true unity with the populations of the Arab provinces, whose elites had already started to wander off down a very different path. For the Turks, especially after the Young Turk Revolution, if Islam remained an essential component of their identity, it was on the new Turkist ideology that the nation that was gradually invented would be built, would appropriate the empire and would eventually monopolise its heritage. Within this perspective, the Alhambra or Andalusia no longer meant much, other than the usual over-rated clichés of Western exoticism; as a result, they would soon become synonymous with the notions of decline and decadence.

If Aḥmad Zakī, Shakīb Arslān and Aḥmad Shawqī constituted a sort of crescendo in the Arabist perception and imagination of al-Andalus, Turhan Bey, Tunalı Hilmi, Celal Nuri and Sezai Bey represented the milestones of a gradual disenchantment of their Turkish contemporaries. To crown this series, I will propose the famous poem – 'A dance in Andalusia' (*Endülüs'te Raks*) – which Yahya Kemal [Beyatlı] (1884–1958),[214] the representative of the Turkish Republic in Madrid from 1929 to 1932,[215] wrote in 1933. Although we know that he visited both Granada and Cordoba and despite the fact that I have combed through the pages of the visitors' book between those dates, I have not been able to retrieve his signature. We do know, however, that in Cordoba he found nothing worth seeing, except the mosque, and that he

[214] Like many of his peers, Yahya Kemal was strongly influenced by French literature – especially the Parnassians – which he discovered in Paris where he exiled himself in 1903 to flee, like so many others, Abdülhamid's oppression and censorship. He is mostly known for his efforts to maintain, while modernising them, the forms and traditions of Ottoman poetry and for his passion for Ottoman and Turkish history, which often serves as a backdrop to his poetry.

[215] He left his post in 1931 for Paris and was considered to have resigned the following year (N. Özcan, 'Yahya Kemal Beyatlı'nın Elçilik Yılları ve Diğer Resmi Vazifeleri', p. 34).

thought the town was very 'Oriental'.[216] On the contrary, he found Granada to be 'unforgettable' and 'impossible to describe in a single letter'.[217] Nevertheless, the most memorable moment of his Andalusian journey seems to have been the flamenco show he attended in Jerez, which inspired his celebrated 'Dance in Andalusia'.[218]

> Castanets, a mantilla, and a rose. A frenzied dance in this garden . . .
> In this evening of desire, Andalusia is three times red.
>
> The magic song of love lingers on hundreds of lips.
> Spain, in its cheerfulness, resounds tonight in these castanets.
>
> With her sudden spins, like a fan one would turn,
> Full of frivolity, she arches back, pushes forward, then covers herself . . .

[216] Y. K. Beyatlı, *Mektuplar ve Makaleler*, pp. 5–6; R. Carpintero Ortega, 'Visión de España de Yahya Kemal', pp. 186–7.

[217] Beyatlı, *Mektuplar ve Makaleler*, pp. 7–8; R. Carpintero Ortega, 'Visión de España de Yahya Kemal', p. 187. It is worth noting that Yahya Kemal is one of the rare authors, who, when he speaks of 'Andalusian civilisation', insists that it is a mix of 'Arab and Berber' culture (Beyatlı, *Mektuplar ve Makaleler*, p. 11).

[218] Sermet Sami Uysal conveys Yahya Kemal's following words concerning the circumstances surrounding the poem: 'Yes, I had written that poem after seeing a show of Spanish dance, he said, and then he gave me these very interesting explanations. While I was ambassador in Spain, despite the years that had passed, I had not yet managed to attend a Spanish dance. One day I said to a marquess I knew: It has been quite some time I have been here. I still have not seen a proper Spanish dance. If I was asked about this back at home, what could I say? These words offended the marquess. The Spaniards call a marquess a wealthy individual who is fond of luxury and pleasure. [Probably a reference to "*vivir como un marqués*", to live like a marquess] The marquess asked me: Could you go all the way to Andalusia to watch a Spanish dance? I said I would. At the set date, I went to Jerez in Andalusia. In that place which some call Cerez, others Querez and others yet Djerez, there was no major town. There were only great farms. They produce a lot of wine there. The marquess had invited beautiful girls and women from the vicinity and even from Madrid. After a while, three girls started dancing. One of them danced extraordinarily well. The moonlight, too, was magnificent. However, that charming night cost me two thousand pounds with the tips. It was that night that the words "castanets, mantilla, and rose" came to my mind. I loved these words so much that first I was afraid of writing a poem about them. Then, gradually, the verses came into being. I left my post in 1932 and the poem was completed in 1933' (S. S. Uysal, *Yahya Kemal'le Sohbetler*, pp. 41–2).

Our eyes do not covet any colour, they seek red;
Tonight, Spain, continuously undulating, is all in that mantilla.

Loving kiss curls line up on her forehead,
The most beautiful rose of sweet Granada on her breast . . .

A golden cup in each hand, the sun in all the hearts;
Tonight, the existence of Spain is in this rose.

She stops halfway through the dance, starts again, as if walking;
With one move of the head, she fires a look that kills . . .

Her skin a rose, her lips embers, her charcoal eyes lined with kohl . . .
The devil tempts you; one has to embrace her and kiss her a hundred times.

The dazzling mantilla, the bewitching rose,
The sound of the castanets fills the heart, and all let out the same cry: 'Olé!'[219]

[219] The poem was first published in 1948 (Y. K. Beyatlı, 'Endülüs'te Raks'; *Kendi Gök Kubbemiz*, pp. 157–8). Translating poetry is not a skill I claim to possess. Nevertheless, I have done my best to translate this poem by keeping as close to the original as possible. Nevertheless, I have taken the liberty of translating '*zil*' (cymbals) as castanets and '*şal*' (shawl) as mantilla, as these two words seem to be more relevant in the context of a Spanish dance. For an earlier draft version of the poem, see Carpintero Ortega, 'Visión de España de Yahya Kemal', pp. 189–90.

CONCLUSION
CONNECTIONS, ENTANGLEMENTS AND INFLUENCES

'Olé!' I could not have found a better spin to conclude this long series of 'Turkish' observers and travellers with a text that went exactly in the direction of what I wanted to prove. Starting from almost total ignorance of what Andalusia represented from a historical and cultural point of view, they had gradually discovered – mostly through Western sources – a narrative and references that promised to bring a new dimension not only to their perception of the past, but also to their relations with an increasingly invasive Europe. Then, a third and final period of disenchantment, or even disappointment, was characterised by a notable decline in their initial enthusiasm, soon to be replaced by a more aesthetic, almost touristic, perception of the charm and exoticism of Andalusia. Yahya Kemal and his 'dance' represented a sort of peak in this turnaround, as embodied in the castanets and the flamenco dancers spinning on a stage in Jerez.

Of course, I can always be accused of having made an easy choice and consciously left aside the highly traditional side of Yahya Kemal's oeuvre, filled with frequent poetic references to the past glory of the Ottoman Empire, with a strong Islamic undertone. After all, if flamenco dancers triggered his senses in Jerez, in Istanbul, it was the call to prayer of the muezzin that echoed in his ears.[1]

[1] One would need only to list the titles of some of his poems: 'A *Bayram* Morning at the Süleymaniye', 'Song of Mohàcs', 'The Conquerors', 'Üsküdar, who witnessed the conquest of Istanbul [*sic*]' (Y. K. Beyatlı, *Kendi Gök Kubbemiz*).

That being said, I believe that it is precisely on this point that Turkish intellectuals stood apart from their Arab peers, given that even when they embraced a more conservative – and sometimes Islamic – ideology and political stand, their vision of the past still remained deeply anchored in an essentially Turkish geography and culture. One will always find cases of Turkish authors whose perceptions of Andalusia go against the examples I have listed earlier. While this is always a possibility, I firmly believe that even the most laudatory texts one might find in some obscure periodical or publication would still be heavily tainted with a national(ist) bias that would set them apart from not only those of Arab authors and thinkers, but even from the popular culture of Arab countries up to the present.[2] I must admit, however, that such an analysis would by far exceed my competences, my ambition, but also my concerns. I had from the very start chosen to focus on the 'long' nineteenth century, which I believe offers a form of homogeneity that earlier or later periods would have spoiled. I may have breached this rule by mentioning Moroccan travelogues of the eighteenth century and, most of all, by spilling over into the 1920s, well after the First World War. I should probably justify my decision regarding this last point. Indeed, why would I include Shakīb Arslān, whose journey took place in 1930 and was published even later, when I have excluded so many earlier travellers, such as Muḥammad Kurd 'Alī (1922), Muḥammad Labīb al-Batānūnī (1924) or Muṣṭafà Farrukh (1930)?

I could argue that the latter authors have already been studied extensively by others.[3] I could also invoke the fact that Shakīb Arslān translated Chateaubriand's *Last Abencerrage* in 1897 and that his cousin Amīn Arslān had signed the visitors' book of the Alhambra in 1910. In all honesty, it is rather obvious that the main appeal of this author has to do with the photograph he had sent in 1930 to the historian Mohammed Daoud in Tétouan, whose relevance to my study was simply too important to be discarded. I believe I can justify

[2] Many authors have focused on the repercussions and legacy of the image of al-Andalus in the Arab world throughout the twentieth century. See, among others, J. H. Shannon, *Performing al-Andalus*; Martínez Montávez, *Al-Andalus, España, en la literatura árabe contemporánea*; Granara, 'Nostalgia, Arab Nationalism, and the Andalusian Chronotope in the Evolution of the Modern Arabic Novel'; Cortés García, 'Andalucía: realidad y mito en la perspectiva intelectual árabe'; Civantos, *The Afterlife of Al-Andalus*.

[3] See, particularly, Paradela, *El otro laberinto español*, pp. 163–200.

with similar 'utilitarian' arguments my inclusion of Yahya Kemal, whose stay in Spain was even later. His poem was just too perfect a fit for a clear trend I had observed among the Young Turk generation regarding the perception of al-Andalus.

This brings me to the task of discussing the main objective of this work and to attempt an overall assessment of my findings. It is generally easier to define what one has tried to avoid. In my case, it is evident that I did not want to repeat what others had done before me. This is particularly true of the two main approaches I have observed to this day, namely, on the one hand, inventories, anthologies and other systematic studies on the Arab visitors and observers of al-Andalus,[4] and, on the other hand, a discussion of the formation, nature and meanings of the Andalusian mythos, be it in its perception throughout the Arab world,[5] or in the West and more particularly in Spain.[6] Of course, it was impossible to avoid some overlaps, even repetitions, due to the quality and scope of previous works.

However, I do believe that I can make a claim as to the difference and, I would hope, the originality of my approach and its results. First, I would have to mention its 'micro-historical' ambition, characterised by a double focus on a particular monument – the Alhambra – and a well-defined group of individuals – visitors signing this monument's visitors' book. This methodological and documentary 'squeeze' has a double, and somewhat paradoxical,

[4] Pérès, *L'Espagne vue par les voyageurs musulmans*; Martínez Montávez, *Al-Andalus, España, en la literatura árabe contemporánea*; Paradela, *El otro laberinto español*.

[5] Stearns, 'Representing and Remembering Al-Andalus'; Granara, 'Nostalgia, Arab Nationalism, and the Andalusian Chronotope in the Evolution of the Modern Arabic Novel'; Civantos, *The Afterlife of Al-Andalus*; Cortés García, 'Andalucía: realidad y mito en la perspectiva intelectual árabe'; Paradela, 'El viaje y la historia: el mito de al-Ándalus en los modernos viajeros árabes a España'.

[6] I wish to emphasise the depth of José Antonio González Alcantud's contribution to the study and critical analysis of the Spanish dimension of this myth: González Alcantud, 'Andalousie: le double regard'; González Alcantud, *Lo moro: Las lógicas de la derrota y la formación del estereotipo islámico*; González Alcantud, 'Lo moro revisitado: Dimensión estética, diversidad cultural, función crítica, fantasma social'; González Alcantud, 'La survivance du mythe de Al-Andalus dans une ville du Maghreb: Fès'; González Alcantud, *El Mito de al-Ándalus: Orígenes y actualidad de un ideal cultural*.

advantage, since, on the one hand, it narrows down the scope of analysis by focusing on one particular site, instead of the vaguer notion of Andalusia, while, on the other hand, it widens it by including a great number of individuals, who, under different circumstances, would not have attained visibility. Of course, let us not be naive: my focus on the Alhambra stems from the fact that it possesses a visitors' book dating from 1829. I would certainly not have refused to include the mosque of Cordoba had it benefited from similar documentary resources. On the other hand, it is also true that, whenever I felt it was necessary, I did resort to authors who had not signed the book, nor even visited Granada and that I have used comments concerning other sites, Andalusia or even Spain in general.

Nevertheless, it is true that the conjunction of the visitors and the site remains at the centre of this study, and that punctual digressions or diversions can only enrich it, as long as one does not lose sight of its this central focus. Several factors justify this approach. To start with, I would bring forth the simple observation that the relation between the site and its visitors creates a fertile, and generally more direct and more 'candid', context than comments and accounts of a constructed and self-conscious nature, written ex post, or even without any connection to an actual visit. Most of all, the great number of individual records that can be accessed through the visitors' book constitutes a powerful antidote against the syndrome of the 'usual suspects', whereby unavoidable but highly predictable figures end up weighing down research in history. If Pérès, Paradela, Martínez Montávez and others end up listing the same names, it is of course because their analyses are almost exclusively based on a limited number of published sources. My point is not to question the value of these texts or of the works that study them; I simply think that it would have been difficult, even impossible, to add anything new to the debate by using the same sources.

I have thus been able to work on a much wider corpus. If I am not mistaken, I have identified a total of eighty-one visits concerning a total of 199 individuals corresponding to the profile I defined at the start. It seems clear, therefore, that my sample goes far beyond the dozen or so texts that have been studied to date. I can therefore claim that I have combed a much wider area and that I have come up with more ordinary, 'real' individuals. And yet, from my point of view, it was not so much the quantity but the variety that counted.

The individuals studied to this day were almost all Arabs, almost exclusively from the Mashreq, which gave them a degree of homogeneity that was reflected in the coherence of their thoughts and discourse. They seemed to share a longing for a lost paradise and a sense of pride in their civilisation's achievements, which they deemed more advanced than that of their contemporaries. It is this image that they propped up in the face of a now powerful Europe, with dreams of a revival based on the recreation of an Arab and/or Islamic unity. Admittedly, my first 'case', Khalīl Jawād al-Khālidī, was also from the Mashreq, but my search for his inscription and signature in the visitors' book led me to the discovery of many other identities and origins, from Morocco to Istanbul.

From that point on, it was clear that this work would form around the five major categories that I could see developing along the pages of the visitors' book: the Maghreb, the Mashreq, 'Turkey', Spain and, of course, the West. The objective was no longer to understand what the Arabs and/or the Muslims thought of Andalusia, but to rummage through the records of individuals, who, faced with one of the most inspiring monuments of Muslim Spain, would become the virtual respondents of a detailed survey concerning the context and the circumstances in which their visit had taken place and, of course, the nature of the reactions it had provoked. The data thus collected would form a base on which I could graft all additional and connected information I could gather on each occurrence. Inevitably, many turned out to be extremely dry and sterile, allowing for little more than the simple recording of an anonymous presence. However, apart from the fact that even 'silent' presences are meaningful, I believe I have been able to collect enough data to free myself, at least at the beginning, from the texts of well-known or predictable authors and to manage to start to build a narrative that covered all the geographic areas and categories I have taken into consideration.

Thus was born the sequence of the book's four chapters. It seemed logical to start with the North – a better term than West, when viewed from Andalusia – since that was where the modern and romanticised version of the Alhambra was born in the first half of the nineteenth century. Combing through the visitors' book was not possible, nor really necessary, for this section, which was obviously the best documented of all. It was sufficient to remind the reader of the major sources on the Alhambra and to put them in context, but also in communication, considering that they clearly fed on each other in such a way as to end up conquering the entire Western imagination through a great variety of textual, visual and architectural reconstitutions. However, even though I did not – and could not – use it in systematic fashion, the visitors' book proved very useful in linking this grand narrative to some of its ramifications, which, although perhaps of lesser importance, helped me greatly in fulfilling some of my goals. Indeed, it is thanks to comments they left in the visitors' book that I was able to give concrete examples of quarrels pitting Frenchmen against Spaniards or conservatives against liberals, or of Maurophile or Maurophobe feelings expressed by foreign, but especially local, visitors. This is what has allowed me to address the Spanish dimension of the question, regarding the perception of Andalusia and Spain by foreign – Northern – observers, but also the emergence of a local version of Orientalism targeting the Islamic past and, at the same time, Morocco, the objective of Spain's newly discovered colonial ambitions.

This provided me with a perfect transition to the second chapter, which addressed the Maghrebi dimension of the study. Given that we already knew of documents concerning several Moroccan visitors in previous centuries and of two in the nineteenth century, a thorough search was needed to check whether the cultural and geographical proximity of this region was not at the origin of a far greater interaction than suggested by this handful of texts. The visitors' book proved me right, if one considers that the Maghrebi, most of them Moroccans, constitute by far the largest Muslim sample having visited the Alhambra during this period. Granted, their large number is offset by their discretion and silence, as they were generally content with inscribing their name without any comment. Counting heads does not allow for a discussion of an emotional or intellectual context, but the simple evidence of numbers cannot be dismissed either. Given that Granada had no other appeal to travelling foreigners than its sights and heritage, such frequent visits were bound to represent a real interest. Nevertheless, the silence of these visitors was thick enough to prevent me from filling it with assumptions, which, while probably justified, would have remained rather sterile. It was this challenge that made me sense the wealth and potential of yet another source of documentation, which I had not exploited systematically until then: the Spanish press, at national level, of course, but most of all local, from Granada itself. This turned out to be material of extraordinary wealth, which allowed me to flesh out these simple presences by adding descriptions that occasionally provided details down to the feelings and reactions of my otherwise silent visitors. Of course, there were serious risks involved, considering that Spanish observers were more than ready to take their place and ascribe them thoughts and emotions that were merely a projection of their own imagination and expectations. Yet this was a risk that a critical and careful reading could help control or minimise, with the additional advantage of delving into the issue raised in the preceding chapter of Spanish imagination in the face of Moorish and Andalusian heritage. The first two chapters have thus enabled me to engage with three very different, but complementary, types of sources: a predominantly Western general literature focusing on the Alhambra and constructing its image; a local press strongly aware of the interest in the region's historical legacy; and, finally, the Alhambra's visitors' book, the raw material forming the common thread running throughout the study. With this base set, I could move on in the direction of the two geographical areas with which I would be able to complete my 'Oriental' panorama: the Mashreq and 'Turkey'. Yet I soon realised that this distinction, while justifiable from a purely comparatist perspective, could usefully be replaced by a more dynamic sectioning, which, rather than simply cultural differences, would consider chronological discrepancies. I had already noticed that apart from a few Maronites in the 1880s, visitors from the Mashreq did not really begin to appear before the 1890s. As a result, it seemed reasonable and useful to take into account this chronological turning point in trying to establish the book's structure.

That is why the third chapter refers to the 'East'; and while it is still strongly focused on a majority of cases linked to the imperial capital and consequently rather 'Turkish', it also addresses the issue of the binary structure that stems from the European vision of a de facto division of the world into East and West. It should not be forgotten that it is in the nineteenth century that Orientalism – in the Saidian meaning of the word – reached its peak before it plunged into its own paroxysm: imperialism. It is during this century that the 'Eastern Question', centred on the Ottoman Empire and its impending doom, started monopolising the strategic, political and economic agenda of the Great Powers. Finally, it is also during this period that the Orient itself, and more particularly the Ottoman Empire, conscious of the gravity of the situation, tried to respond to this threat by adopting measures that varied from an almost servile submission to an effort to resist, if not politically, at least intellectually. This is the reason why Istanbul would have a muddled, not to say incoherent, perception of the Alhambra and, more generally, of Andalusia. This vision remained extremely vague, superficial and marginal for a long time; most importantly, it depended almost exclusively on half-digested Western sources and narratives. Even the frenzy with which the imperial architectural programme appropriated the Moresque style under Abdülaziz really boils down to little more than a 'copy–paste' transfer of European fantasies, chosen for their Oriental-cum-modern look, without the slightest reflection on their historic and cultural context.

Nevertheless, and despite all this superficiality, a handful of authors did eventually discover and begin to explore Andalusian history, albeit through the mediation of Western works and sources. It should not come as a surprise that this new phase coincided with the protracted crisis during which the empire felt cornered, nearly bankrupt and its very existence threatened; nor that most of these works adopted a clearly tragic tone. This phase lasted for about fifteen years, a little bit more than its earlier architectural equivalent. Nevertheless, it left a much deeper mark, due to a more modern awareness, and to the power of the images it brought up. That is why the last chapter is called 'Modernity', given that it analyses a decisive and somewhat final moment in the narrative, centred on the use and mobilisation of the image of al-Andalus for political and ideological purposes, as a lost paradise, but also as a symbol of an Arab and Islamic Renaissance against the colonial might of Europe.

While this modernity shared by Arabs and 'Turks' justified the inclusion of these two dimensions of the phenomenon under the same title, it was also necessary to underline a growing divergence between the intellectual currents represented by Cairo and Istanbul at the turn of the twentieth century. Although they started with a common discovery of the evocative power of Andalusian history and heritage, these two currents had ended up espousing very different, sometimes even opposite, paths. While the Arab *Nahḍa* enthusiastically embraced this rich historical, cultural and political vein, Sultan Abdülhamid's timid attempts at appropriating this heritage to feed his (pan-)Islamist policy and his claims to an ecumenical caliphate were rapidly overshadowed by the rise of Turkish proto-nationalism, soon to be relayed and amplified by the increasingly active Young Turk opposition, which would eventually seize power with the 1908 Revolution. The already significant cultural differences that set Arabs and Turks apart were now embedded in a much more tangible political divergence. While the excitement of al-Andalus seized prominent actors and activists of the Levantine and Egyptian *Nahḍa*, the Young Turk generation would roam Andalusia with the Baedeker guidebook in hand, discovering a land embodying exoticism and decay. With the establishment of the Republic, this vision had come full circle. Now officially Turks, the Ottomans had returned to the Western perception of a civilisation they had never fully understood. Is it not meaningful that when he was asking for a chance to watch a flamenco show in 1930, Yahya Kemal was pretty much repeating his illustrious predecessor Fuad Efendi's request, almost a century earlier, of attending a 'dance with castanets'?[7]

I should now conclude by attempting to assess the overall strengths and weaknesses, and the contributions and shortcomings of this study. Generally speaking, I believe that I have innovated by widening the scope of my analysis to include a vast spectrum of individuals belonging to a relatively homogeneous category defined in terms of its cultural, intellectual and emotional ties to the Alhambra and, by extension, to Andalusia. This approach has enabled me to include in a discourse generally restricted to Arab intellectuals, many visitors of very diverse origins, whose perception of this heritage varied significantly. I also hope that I have succeeded in integrating into this complex panorama a Western and Spanish presence, which, rather than standing apart, showed many overlaps and interconnections with my sample, both in terms of influences and of interactions rarely taken into a consideration to this day. Of course, I can hardly claim to have reached an exhaustive and firmly balanced vision of such diverse phenomena. The general framework of my study has remained essentially Mediterranean, and I have chosen to leave aside a few Oriental and/or Islamic figures who were too distant to be included in the sample without disrupting its relative homogeneity. This is the case of the governor (*wālī*) of Dar-es-Salaam (1900),[8] of Prince Arfa'

[7] See p. 152 above.

[8] Soliman bin Nasser bin Soliman visited the Alhambra on 25 April 1900, leaving as the only trace of his passage his name and functions in Arabic and in French: 'Soliman ben Nassar Ouali from Dar-es-Slem Deutsch Ost-Afrika near Zanzibar' [*sic*] (AA, *libros de firmas*, 46, fol. 152 v).

ud-Dowla Mīrzā Reẓā Khān (1846–1939), Iranian ambassador in Istanbul (1902),[9] or of the poet Muhammad Iqbal (1877–1938), whose famous poem on the mosque of Cordoba went down in history.[10] Even worse, for fear of dissipation and incompetence, I have had to leave aside everything that concerned a number of Jewish communities – European, American, Oriental, Levantine, Ottoman, Maghrebi – despite the frequency and visibility of their members as well as the obvious interest of the question given the importance attached to the Andalusian past among a significant number of members of these communities.

Moreover, how can I ignore the fact that the limits of my competences have unavoidably prevented me from making a full use of the wealth of documentation that was available to me. I have often repeated throughout the pages of this work to what extent I believed that the lack of familiarity of Turkish-speaking Ottomans with Arab culture, language and history constituted an obstacle to the formation of a clear and well-informed perception of Andalusian heritage. I must admit that, rather ironically, I was not very different from them in my incapacity to go beyond the surface of that documentation, in my reliance on the help of specialists to decipher some of the inscriptions in Arabic, and my often pathetic efforts at trying to guess the general meaning of the more consequential traces left by some of these visitors in the form of travel accounts, works of history or novels. With yet another touch of irony, it is precisely the works of those I wanted to avoid imitating and repeating that provided me with the means of circumventing my ignorance of the Arabic language either by reading Zakī, Farīd, Rīḥānī, Shawqī or Arslān in French, English or Spanish,

[9] This diplomat had left his post in Istanbul to represent his sovereign at Alfonso XIII's coronation on 17 May 1902. He signed the visitors' book and left a short distich in Persian: 'From the image and view of the gates and walls in ruins / Appear the traces of Arab rulers' (*Az naqsh o negār-e dar o dīvār-e shekaste / Āthār padīd ast az salāṭīn-e 'Arab-rā*). What makes this inscription particularly interesting is that the prince-ambassador had borrowed – in a completely decontextualised way – two verses from a *qaṣīda* by the poet 'Orfī Shīrāzī (1555–91) dedicated to the Prophet (*Dar setāyesh-e ḥaẓret-e Rasūl*), in which he had replaced the expression 'Persian heroes' (*ṣanādīd-e 'Ajam*) with 'Arab rulers' (*ṣalāṭīn-e 'Arab*) (AA, *libros de firmas*, 46, fol. 234 v, 28 May 1902; see also at: http://www.nosokhan.com/Library/Topic/1F23).

[10] Noorani, 'The Lost Garden of Al-Andalus', pp. 237–8, 247–51.

or by putting to profit the analyses made by my predecessors. Thanks to them, I may have managed to avoid major errors; at any rate, I am convinced that my true contribution has to do with 'Turkish' visitors, unknown or ignored to this day, and that it consists in my ability to have built a narrative that covers, for almost a century, the vicissitudes of the image and idea of Andalusia among the Ottoman intellectual and political elite.

Yet what can I say about the Maghreb? I may be credited with having demonstrated to what extent and with what frequency travellers and envoys from that area – most particularly from Morocco – had visited Granada and climbed up the incline leading to its former citadel. I have done my best with the sources I have been able to access, to give meaning to these visits, using for that purpose all the information I could gather from the contemporary local press and taking all the precautions that such an exercise required. Nevertheless, it is also true that I have not been able to go further in my quest and to look, for example, for traces these visits might have left in Moroccan sources. Are there really any? The silence of secondary and online sources suggests that there may indeed be none, or at least that they may be very rare and may have remained unexploited. We will not have an answer to this question before researchers – probably Moroccan – have started working on the topic. In similar fashion, I can only regret that I have not been able to go further than just point at the silence, on both sides of the divide, about the Amazigh/Berber dimension of Andalusian history. That, too, constitutes a limit I have not been able to cross and of which I do not even know whether it might ever be crossed by researchers having access to sources I have not been able to find or identify.

It would be an exaggeration to claim that I have developed a particular methodology to deal with such diverse and detailed sources. I believe I have navigated the waters of micro-history,[11] of connected histories,[12] of entangled history or *histoire croisée*,[13] more out of necessity and expediency than conviction and methodological rigour. Indeed, the material I have used reveals

[11] G. Levi, 'On Microhistory'.

[12] S. Subrahmanyam, 'Connected Histories: Notes towards a Reconfiguration of Early Modern Eurasia'.

[13] M. Werner and B. Zimmermann, 'Penser l'histoire croisée: entre empirie et réflexivité'; M. Werner and B. Zimmermann, 'Beyond Comparison: *Histoire Croisée* and the Challenge of Reflexivity'.

links and relations that can only be described as connections, crossings or entanglements. This is evident with respect to some of the actors, when one discovers – or assumes – that they were linked by sometimes unpredictable threads and interactions. I think I have proved beyond reasonable doubt that Khālidī visited Spain with Zakī's travel account to hand. Yet I still do not know by what mechanism he felt the urge to write down a quatrain that a Moroccan embassy secretary had scribbled in the same book ten years earlier, and which I have been able to trace back to Ṭahṭāwī seventy years earlier, to Maqrīzī in the fifteenth century or to the *Thousand and One Nights*. Some of these connections are unexpected and would probably warrant a more systematic investigation to be properly used and contextualised. It was only after having read a first draft of the present work that I realised that the recipient of Shakīb Arslān's portrait taken in a Cordoba studio, Mohammed Daoud, was one and the same as the historian from Tétouan, whose letter 'to the Spanish nation' I had discovered in a Granadan newspaper.

Of course, as much as the individuals concerned, these connections and crossings are also linked to places, texts, images or even the notions attached to them. The Alhambra itself is the most blatant example of this, if one considers that its visitors' book, as I have tried to show in several instances, becomes the catalyst of conversations or discussions between visitors with converging or conflicting views. The studios of Granadan and Andalusian photographers constitute another example of such a medium, which brought together tourists of very diverse profiles and offered them the possibility of revealing their fantasies or simply their desire to mark a significant moment in their discovery of Andalusia. I find it extraordinary, but also meaningful, that I should have been able to identify three 'Orientals' having used – two of them more than once – the services of Rafael Garzón, the dean of 'Moorish' portraits, whose legacy lives on today as part of the rituals proposed to tourists visiting the Alhambra (Figure C.1). Finally, how can one not note the influence and impact of certain texts and images, whose circulation, by means of translation, adaptation or simply reading or gazing, is greatly responsible for the creation and diffusion of a narrative of Andalusia throughout and across the cultural and religious borders of a growingly interconnected world? This is true of Viardot's and Sédillot's histories, of Chateaubriand's works, of Goury and Jones's plates and of a quantity of secondary sources that would end up

Figure C.1 Contemporary photograph of a tourist posing before the Alhambresque setting of Galería fotográfica Ruiz Linares, Granada. See at: https://alhambrafoto.com/fotografias-moderna, with kind permission of Galería fotográfica Alhambra. A closer look at the image reveals that this is actually the central section of the side gallery of Garzón's original *patio árabe*, as suggested by the juxtaposition of older and more recent tiles on both sides of the arch.

finding their way into the intellectual and sentimental world of so many scholars of the Arab and Islamic world, from Istanbul to Cairo and, who knows, from Beirut to Fez. However, among all these 'go-betweens', I would give a very special mention to Baedeker, or rather to *the* Baedeker, that little red guidebook, which I have been able to spot in the hands and minds of three of my 'Turkish' travellers, and which has ended up acquiring much greater fame and visibility than most of the more scholarly or literary publications that come to mind. Of course, Washington Irving may well be an exception, at least in the West, for it is rather striking that the *Tales of the Alhambra* should have received very little, if any, attention in the Arab and Islamic worlds.[14]

The observation of the power and influence of Western texts and authors on Oriental perceptions of the Alhambra and of Andalusia inevitably brings up the issue of a central notion in this work, which, much like the works just mentioned, runs across the entire spatial and mental environment under study. Indeed, Orientalism, that powerful ideology of the nineteenth century, can be traced back to practically every instant in the creation of a Europocentric image of the Alhambra and in the amazing semantic fluidity one can observe in the use by contemporary authors of the 'ethnic' terminology that accompanied it: Arab, Moorish, Oriental, Spanish, Andalusian, African, Turkish. However, this phenomenon is all the more complicated by the existence of local appropriations of Orientalism, not just in Spain, where it was fed by the country's colonial ambitions of the second half of the nineteenth century, but also in the Ottoman Empire, where a sort of 'Stockholm syndrome' incited a sizeable part of the elite to embrace some of the fundamental values and visions of European Orientalism.

This phenomenon is extremely interesting, because it reveals yet another level of interconnectedness and of cross-fertilisation between various participants in this intercultural dialogue. Nevertheless, it remains extremely problematic, due to its tendency to confirm and reproduce unequal and

[14] To my knowledge, the only works by Washington Irving translated into Turkish are his *Legend of Sleepy Hollow* (*Uykulu Kuytu Menkıbesi*, 1939, 2003; *Başsız Süvari*, 2007; *Hayalet Süvari*, 2015; *Uykulu Kuytu Söylencesi*, 2016), *Rip Van Winkle* (2015), and *Mahomet and His Successors* (*Hz. Muhammed*, 2012). It seems that the situation is rather comparable in the Arab world, where I have been able to identify only translations of *Mahomet and His Successors*.

hierarchical relations based on categories practically devoid of any analytical value. The consequences are often serious and can lead to the proliferation of old stereotypes updated to meet the tastes and requirements of the day, thus feeding into neo- or crypto-Orientalist currents strongly tainted with Islamophobia, against which José Antonio González Alcantud often warns us.[15] One of the major goals of the new trends in history – connected, *croisée*, entangled – is precisely to correct such inequalities by abandoning the notion of a one-way flow of transfers, from centre to periphery, from top to bottom, from West to East, and to seek, on the contrary, connections and entanglements of a much more complex and reflexive nature.[16]

While one should certainly wish for such a reversal, and while breaking down these barriers is proving to be relatively easier for the Early Modern period,[17] it seems difficult to imagine that Orientalism can be liberated from the strong hierarchisation, which, apart from being intrinsic to it, is practically its reason to exist. Crossings and transversal inter-crossings are frequent and understandably fascinating. This is true of the Spaniard who Orientalises the Moors, of the Turkish poet who finds Cordoba 'too Oriental', of the Arab intellectual who blames the Turkish hordes for having corrupted Egyptian culture, of the Ottoman diplomat who uses the exact same term, applied to Africans, to speak of the plundering of a convent in Spain, of a Young Turk who finds exoticism in a Roma costume, or of an ideologue of the same vein who wallows in the comparison between the past splendour of Andalusian civilisation and the present state of the 'sluggish Arab of the desert'. There is little doubt that the 'periphery' had perfectly internalised the principles and mechanisms of Orientalism and knew how to use them for political and ideological purposes by directing them at easier targets, already 'tested' by European Orientalism. However, whatever evidently worked 'transversally', from South to South and Orient to Orient, can hardly be applied to exchanges and relations between Europe and the areas under study, where unilateralism seems to have been the unbreakable rule. Be it in the case of the architectural

[15] J. A. González Alcantud, *Lo moro: Las lógicas de la derrota y la formación del estereotipo islámico; et El Mito de al-Ándalus: orígenes y actualidad de un ideal cultural.*

[16] See particularly, Werner and Zimmermann, 'Penser l'histoire croisée', pp. 13–17, 27–8.

[17] Subrahmanyam, 'Connected Histories'.

follies of Abdülaziz's reign, or of the stereotypes that clung to Islamic civilisation in Spain, the information flowed essentially in one direction, before being disseminated and redistributed through transversal channels. While Chateaubriand, Sédillot or Baedeker had no difficulty in finding their way across cultural borders between Europe and the Orient, Maqqarī or Zakī did not have the means to travel in the other direction.

Disappointing as this thought may be, it cannot and should not be forgotten that despite its rich historical heritage, Andalusia, as it emerged in the nineteenth century, was first and foremost a Western creation and invention, which the Orient rediscovered through European mediation before they could draw from it the material they needed for the construction of their vision and interpretation of this heritage. Some succeeded in this endeavour and carried it to its completion; others soon abandoned it to move on in the direction of other sources of inspiration; some remained much more oblivious to its appeal. That is the story I have tried to tell, by staging the most celebrated monument of this civilisation, with thousands of individuals who visited it, admired it, and perceived it as the embodiment of their dreams, their fantasies and for some, of their future.

BIBLIOGRAPHY

Primary Sources

Archival Sources

Archives of the Alhambra, Granada (Patronato de la Alhambra y el Generalife, Archivo de la Alhambra) (AA)
Libros de firmas: 42–51
Ottoman State Archives (Devlet Arşivleri Başkanlığı Osmanlı Arşivi) (BOA)
A. DVN. 9/49
BEO 999/74870; 1456/109190; 1470/110198; 1585/118804; 1591/119314; 1626/121896; 1639/122885
DH SAİDd 1/133; 2/996; 47/84; 75/80
HR İM 17/39; 105/60; 133/89
HR MKT 340/53
HR MTV 36/54; 687/1; 710/59
HR SYS 15/52; 1790/8; 1795/8; 1811/8; 2383/1; 2116/3; 2886/33
HR UHM 205/56
İ AZN 107/1330
İ DH 451/29844
İ DUİT 50/1
İ HR 27/1254; 314/20061; 316/20304; 423/23; 429/35; 433/30
İ HUS 87/84
İ MTZ (01) 3/64

İ MVL 482/21842
İ TAL 61/89; 464/18
MF MKT 394/8
MVL 534/30
Y A HUS 393/73
Y EE 31/31
Y PRK BŞK 15/60
Y PRK EŞA 7/13; 31/62; 36/44; 37/50
Y PRK HR 20/71; 29/58
Y PRK TKM 7/84

Newspapers and Periodicals

Ayine-i Vatan
Ceride-i Havadis
Chicago Tribune
Diario constitucional de Palma
Diario de Córdoba
Diario de Pernambuco
Diario oficial de avisos de Madrid
Eco del comercio
El Áncora
El Castellano
El Católico
El Clamor público
El Correo militar
El Defensor de Granada
El Día
El Espectador
El Globo
El Graduador
El Guadalete
El Heraldo
El Heraldo de Madrid
El Imparcial
El Lábaro
El Liberal
El Noticiero granadino

El Pabellón nacional
El País
El Pensamiento de la nación
El Popular
El Pueblo español
El Siglo futuro
El Triunfo
Frank Leslie's Chimney Corner
Freeman's Journal and Daily Commercial Advertiser
John Bull
Journal de Constantinople
Juvenile Companion and Sunday School Hive
L'Illustration
L'Univers illustré
La Acción
La Alhambra. Revista quincenal de artes y letras
La Campana de la vela
La Correspondencia de España
La Crónica meridional
La Discusión
La Época
La Estrella de Occidente
La Gaceta del sur
La Iberia
La Idea. Diario defensor de los derechos del pueblo
La Ilustración española y americana
La Justicia
La Mañana
La Monarquía
La Paz
La Paz de Murcia
La Política
La Presse
La Publicidad. Diario de avisos, noticias y telegramas
La Turquie
La Unión católica
Las Dominicales del libre pensamiento
Le Diable boiteux

Le Figaro
Le Miroir des spectacles, des lettres, des mœurs et des arts
Le Monde illustré
Los Debates
Maarif
Manchester Courier and Lancashire General Advertiser
Mir'at
Morning Post
New York Tribune
Night and Day. A Monthly Record of Christian Missions and Practical Philanthropy
Nottinghamshire Guardian
Official Gazette of the Government of Palestine
Porter's Spirit of the Times
Resimli Kitab
Revista de España
Revista de geografía comercial
Revue des deux mondes
Ruzname-i Ceride-i Havadis
Servet-i Fünun
Sırat-ı Müstakim
Sunday Times
Takvim-i Vekayi
The Era
The Illustrated London News
The Knickerbocker, or New York Monthly Magazine
The Ladies' Treasury
The Lady's Newspaper and Pictorial Times
The Levant Herald
The Spectator
The Times
The Town and Country Magazine, or, Universal Repository of Knowledge, Instruction, and Entertainment
The Westmorland Gazette

Newspaper Articles

'Xe congrès international des orientalistes', *T'oung Pao*, III (1892), p. 488.
'A Description of the *Alhambra*, or Palace of the *Moorish* Kings of Granada', *The Town and Country Magazine, or, Universal Repository of Knowledge,*

Instruction, and Entertainment XIII (1 February 1781), pp. 79–82; (1 March 1781), pp. 138–40.
'Acercamiento hispano-musulmán: Granada y el mundo islámico', *El Defensor de Granada* 28,933 (21 October 1933), p. 1.
'Alhambra Stove: By Stuart & Smith, Sheffield', *The Illustrated London News* 527 (1 November 1851), p. 560.
'Antonio Almagro Cárdenas', *El Defensor de Granada* (15 November 1881), pp. 1–2.
'Archaeology in Turkey', *The Times* 24,945 (8 August 1864), p. 9.
'Bal de M. d'Ofalia', *Le Figaro* 5(173) (22 June 1830), p. 2.
'Bir Medeniyet-i Münkarizenin Enkazından: Les débris d'une civilisation disparue', *Şehbal* I(11) (1/14 September 1325/1909), pp. 214–15.
'Cacería en Láchar', *El Defensor de Granada* 12,349 (26 January 1902), p. 2.
'Cacería en Láchar', *El Defensor de Granada* 12,671 (1 February 1903), p. 1.
'Congresso orientalista', *Diario de noticias* (17 June 1892), p. 1.
'Congresso dos orientalistas', *Diario illustrado* XXI(6,988) (9 September 1892), p. 1.
'Congresso em Lisboa', *Diario de noticias* (5 October 1892), p. 1.
'Coronación de Zorrilla', *El Liberal* (4 May 1883), p. 1.
'Daire-i Umur-ı Askeriye', *Âyine-i Vatan* I(2) (24 January 1867), p. 6.
'De potencia a potencia', *El Defensor de Granada* 1,158 (13 December 1883), p. 2.
'Death of Fuad Pasha', *Freeman's Journal and Daily Commercial Advertiser* (16 February 1869).
'Description of the Great Bath of the Alhambra', *The New Lady's Magazine* 8 (August 1794), pp. 314–16.
'Desde Granada', *El Liberal* (29 December 1885).
'Discours prononcé par Jean Aristoclès, membre du Grand Conseil de l'Instruction Publique à l'occasion de l'ouverture de l'Université Impériale, célébrée le 8/20 février 1870', *La Turquie* (26 February 1870), p. 2.
'Dos joyas', *El Globo* (26 June 1878), p. 1.
'Échos', *Le Rappel* 10,989 (12 April 1900), p. 2.
'El embajador marroquí visitando la Alhambra', *La Ilustración española y americana* XXI/XLVIII (30 December 1877), p. 403.
'El Mokri', *Gaceta del sur* 3,991 (2 October 1916), p. 2.
'El Mokri, en Madrid', *La Acción* I(28) (2 October 1916), p. 5.
'El viaje de los moros', *El Heraldo de Madrid* (5 March 1895).
'Elhamra Sarayında İki Hemşire Divanhanesi', *Maarif* 1(20) (7 Kânun–ı Evvel 1308/1 January 1892), p. 315.
'Embajador', *El Defensor de Granada* IV(877) (3 March 1883), p. 1.

'Esbab-ı Servet', *Mir'at* I(1) (Ramazan 1279/February–March 1863), pp. 5–11.

'Espectáculos', *La Idea: Diario defensor de los derechos del pueblo* 424 (30 November 1871), p. 3.

'Espectáculos', *La Idea: Diario defensor de los derechos del pueblo* 425 (1 December 1871), p. 3.

'Establecimiento de un museo de antigüedades en la Alhambra', *La Época* 6,890 (28 March 1870), p. 1.

'Exposition à Constantinople' *L'Illustration* 1,050 (11 April 1863), p. 230.

'Fiesta de moros', *El Defensor de Granada* 2,628 (25 September 1887), p. 2.

'Fuad-Efendi, enviado estraordinario de la Sublime Puerta', *El Pensamiento de la nación* 22 (3 July 1844), p. 351.

'Fuad-Pacha', *La Presse* (15 February 1869), p. 1.

'Fuad Pasha', *The Levant Herald* (2 March 1869), p. 2.

'Funérailles de Fuad Pacha', *The Levant Herald* (1 March 1869), p. 3.

'Funérailles de Fuad Pacha', *La Turquie* (5 March 1869), p. 2.

'Gırnata'da Elhamra Kasrı', *Servet-i Fünun* 803 (31 August 1322/13 September 1906), p. 803.

'Gran centro de fotografías', *Los Debates* 108 (28 June 1892), p. 4.

'Granada en fiestas: Correr la pólvora', *La Publicidad: Diario de avisos, noticias y telegramas* 5,039 (16 June 1900), p. 2.

'Grupo fotográfico', *La Publicidad: Diario de avisos, noticias y telegramas* 6,232 (1 May 1904), p. 2.

'Había motivo', *El Graduador* (13 December 1877).

'Kurtuba Camii', *Maarif* 1(21) (14 Kânun-ı Evvel 1308/5 January 1892), pp. 336–7.

'Kurtuba Camii ve Kilisesi', *Servet-i Fünun* 64(1680) (25 October 1928), p. 388.

'L'Andalousie au temps des Maures', *Guide Chaix: Les plaisirs et les curiosités de l'Exposition avec 20 plans et des illustrations* (Paris: Chaix, 1900), p. 260.

'L'Andalousie au temps des Maures', *L'Exposition en famille : Revue illustrée de l'Exposition universelle de 1900* I(4) (5 June 1900), pp. 142–3.

'L'islam devant le siècle', *La Turquie* (30 July 1870), pp. 1–2.

'"La Alhambra" en el Mogreb', *La Alhambra* I(3) (30 January 1884), pp. 1–2.

'La cruz en las ruinas', *El Siglo futuro* (16 October 1889), p. 2.

'La embajada', *El Defensor de Granada* (5 March 1895).

'La embajada', *El Defensor de Granada* (6 March 1895).

'La embajada marroquí', *El Defensor de Granada* (16 December 1885).

'La embajada marroquí', *El Correo militar* (12 October 1889).

'La embajada marroquí', *El Correo militar* (14 October 1889).

'La embajada marroquí', *La Correspondencia de España* (14 October 1889).
'La embajada marroquí', *El Defensor de Granada* (23 October 1889).
'La embajada marroquí', *La Iberia* (25 October 1889).
'La embajada marroquí', *La Monarquía* (25 October 1889).
'La embajada marroquí', *La Unión católica* (6 March 1895).
'La embajada marroquí', *Las Baleares* (1 February 1895).
'La embajada marroquí', *El Defensor de Granada* (28 and 29 May 1902).
'La embajada marroquí', *El Triunfo* (28 May 1902).
'La embajada marroquí', *La Publicidad* (28 May 1902).
'La embajada marroquí', *El Noticiero granadino* (12 June 1906).
'La embajada marroquí', *El Noticiero granadino* (13 June 1906).
'La embajada marroquí', *El Defensor de Granada* (13 June 1906).
'La embajada marroquí en Granada', *El Popular* (23 October 1889).
'La invención de la Santa Cruz', *El Lábaro* II(75) (3 May 1891), p. 1.
'Léon Roches', *La Dépêche tunisienne* 3,653 (11 July 1900), pp. 2–3.
'Leopoldo Cano en Granada', *El Liberal* (9 October 1889), p. 3.
'Les funérailles de Fuad Pacha', *La Turquie* (1 March 1869), p. 2.
'Lettres sur les hommes d'État de la France', *Revue des deux mondes*, 2nd series 4(6) (15 December 1833), pp. 686–725.
'Llegada del embajador estraordinario de la Sublime Porta', *La Campana de la vela* 46 (19 July 1844), p. 2.
'Los marroquíes', *El País* (25 October 1889).
'Los marroquíes en Granada', *El Isleño* (31 October 1889).
'Los moritos', *Crónica meridional* (13 December 1877).
'Los turbantes', *El Correo militar* (24 October 1889).
'Maarif-i Umumiye Nazırı devletlü paşa hazretleri tarafından irad buyurulan nutuk', *Takvim-i Vekayi* 1,192 (20 Zilkade 1286/21 February 1870), p. 1.
'Malogrado congresso orientalista em Lisboa', *Diario de noticias* (29 October 1892), p. 1.
'Mr. Burford's Panorama of Granada and the Alhambra', *The Illustrated London News* 615 (2 April 1853), p. 253.
'Nouvelles d'Orient. Mont Liban : Une courageuse entreprise', *La Terre sainte : Journal des Lieux-Saints* I(1) (15 July 1875), pp. 130–1.
'Obituary. Fuad Pasha', *New York Tribune* (15 February 1869), p. 4.
'Obituary. Mehmed Fuad Pasha', *Chicago Tribune* (15 February 1869), p. 2.
'Obra de arte', *La Publicidad: Diario de avisos, noticias y telegramas* 4,988 (12 April 1900), p. 2.

'Obra de arte', *El Defensor de Granada* 11,962 (18 October 1900), p. 2.
'Obra notable', *El Heraldo granadino* 335 (30 May 1900), p. 2.
'Opening of the Royal Panopticon', *John Bull* 1736 (18 March 1854), pp. 169–70.
'Our Spanish Correspondence: "H. P. L." in the Alhambra', *Porter's Spirit of the Times* 6(17) (25 June 1859), p. 258.
'Panorama of the "Alhambra", Leicester Square', *The Lady's Newspaper and Pictorial Times* 326 (26 March 1853), p. 193.
'Partida de caza', *El Defensor de Granada* 12,656 (17 January 1903), p. 2.
'Patio árabe', *El Heraldo granadino* 454 (20 October 1900), p. 2.
'Re-Opening of the Colosseum, Regent's Park', *The Illustrated London News* 157 (3 May 1845), p. 276.
'Recepción de la embajada marroquí', *La Época* (13 December 1885).
'Réminiscences de Fuad Pacha', *The Levant Herald* (9 March 1869), p. 3.
'Sanskritica', *Diario illustrado* XXI(6,993) (15 September 1892), p. 1.
'Sid Abdesslam Esuisi visitando el palacio de la Alhambra, el 4 del actual', *La Ilustración española y americana* XXI/XLVIII (30 December 1877), pp. 403, 413.
'Souvenirs de l'Italie', *Revue britannique* XXII (Paris: Revue britannique, 1829), pp. 308–28.
'Spain and the Moors', *The Lady's Newspaper and Pictorial Times* 688 (3 March 1860), p. 172.
'The Alhambra', *Frank Leslie's Chimney Corner* V(119) (7 September 1867), p. 233.
'The Alhambra', *The Ladies' Treasury* (1 December 1857), p. 290.
'The Alhambra Court in the Crystal Palace', *The Illustrated London News* 1,038 (30 June 1860), pp. 633–4.
'The Beautiful Alhambra Vase', *The Major & Knapp Illustrated Monthly* I(10) (1 October 1870), pp. 111–13.
'The "Beni-Zoug-Zoug-Arabs"', *The Era* (2 March 1889), p. 17.
'The Burial of Fuad Pasha', *The Levant Herald* (1 March 1869), p. 2.
'The Death of Fuad Pasha', *Nottinghamshire Guardian* 1,200 (19 February 1869).
'The Late Fuad Pasha', *Manchester Courier and Lancashire General Advertiser* 3,828 (18 February 1869), p. 6.
'The Moorish Palace of Alhambra', *Juvenile Companion and Sunday School Hive* (1 January 1864), pp. 1–4.
'The Ottoman Exhibition, Constantinople', *The Illustrated London News* 1,198 (11 April 1863), p. 416.
'The Red House of the Moorish Kings of Granada: The Finest Example of Moorish Art', *The Illustrated London News* 3,650 (3 April 1909), pp. 488–9.

'The Royal Panopticon of Science and Art, Leicester Square', *The Illustrated London News* 543 (31 January 1852), p. 96.

'Théâtres de Londres', *Le Diable boiteux* 5 (21 April 1816), p. 119.

'Variétés. Bibliographie: L'Architecture ottomane', *La Turquie*, VI(223) (30 September 1872), p. 3.

'Viaje de regreso del embajador marroquí Sidi el Arby Brischa', *La Estrella de Occidente* II(15) (1 July 1880), pp. 1–2.

'Viaje del Mokri', *El Guadalete* 20,329 (17 August 1916), p. 3.

'Visita a la Alhambra', *Las Dominicales del libre pensamiento* (5 October 1889).

'Visita del Rey á Granada', *El Defensor de Granada* 13,212 (1 May 1904), p. 1.

'Visitando la Alhambra', *La Justicia* (2 October 1889).

'Voyage pittoresque en Espagne', *Le Miroir des spectacles, des lettres, des mœurs et des arts* 855 (30 May 1823), p. 3.

Reference Material

Almanach de Gotha : Annuaire diplomatique et statistique (Gotha: Justus Perthes, 1859).

American Annual Cyclopædia and Register of Important Events, The (New York: D. Appleton, 1873).

Annuaire encyclopédique, 1869–1871 (Paris: Encyclopédie du XIXe siècle, 1872).

Annuaire oriental du commerce, de l'industrie, de l'administration et de la magistrature (Constantinople: Cervati, 1891).

Beeton's Modern European Celebrities: A Biography of Continental Men and Women of Note (London: Ward, Lock & Tyler, 1874).

Calendario manual y guía de forasteros en Madrid (Madrid: Imprenta real, 1831–41).

Catalogue de la bibliothèque de feu Ahmed Véfyk Pacha (Constantinople: Typographie et lithographie K. Bagdadlian, 1893).

Congrès internacional (sic) des orientalistes. 10ème session, circulaire du 28 April 1892.

Conseil municipal de Paris: Rapport présenté par M. Thuillier, au nom de la 3e Commission, tendant à donner l'autorisation d'occuper une partie de la rue Le Nôtre et une bande du sol du quai Debilly pour la 'Reconstitution de l'Andalousie au temps des Maures' *pendant la durée de l'Exposition de 1900* (Paris: Imprimerie municipale, 1897).

Encyclopædia Britannica, The: A Dictionary of Arts, Sciences, and General Literature (Philadelphia, PA: Maxwell Sommerville, 1891).

Explication des ouvrages de peinture et dessins, sculpture, architecture et gravure, des artistes vivans (Paris: Imprimerie des sciences et des arts, an X, 1802).

Explication des ouvrages de peinture et dessins, sculpture, architecture et gravure, des artistes vivans (Paris: Dubray, 1808).

Explication des ouvrages de peinture et dessins, sculpture, architecture et gravure, des artistes vivans (Paris: Dubray, 1812).

Explication des ouvrages de peinture et dessins, sculpture, architecture et gravure, des artistes vivans (Paris: Dubray, 1814).

Explication des ouvrages de peinture et dessins, sculpture, architecture et gravure, des artistes vivans (Paris: Imprimerie de Madame Hérissant le Doux, 1817).

Explication des ouvrages de peinture et dessins, sculpture, architecture et gravure, des artistes vivans (Paris: C. Ballard, 1822).

Guía oficial de España 1887 (Madrid: Manuel Minuesa de los Ríos, 1887).

Guía oficial de España 1888 (Madrid: Sucesores de Rivadeneyra, 1888).

Guía oficial de España 1889 (Madrid: Manuel Minuesa de los Ríos, 1890).

Guía oficial de España 1890 (Madrid: Manuel Minuesa de los Ríos, 1890).

Guía oficial de España 1901 (Madrid: Sucesora de M. Minuesa de los Ríos, 1901).

Guía oficial de España 1916 (Madrid: Sucesores de Rivadeneyra, 1916).

Guide Lemercier, publié par les concessionnaires du Catalogue officiel de l'Exposition universelle de 1900 (Paris: Ludovic Baschet, 1900).

Historia de los subterráneos de la Alhambra, o los amores de Aben-Amed, descendiente de los reyes moros de Granada (Madrid: José M. Marés, 1862).

Horrible Atrocities of Spaniards in Cuba: An Historical and True Account of the Cruel Massacre and Slaughter of 20,000,000 of People in the West Indies by the Spaniards. Written by Bishop Las Casas, an Eye-witness, translated from the French edition, printed in 1620 (New York: J. Boller, 1898).

L'Architecture ottomane: Ouvrage autorisé par irade impérial et publié sous le patronage de Son Excellence Edhem Pacha, ministre des Travaux publics, président de la Commission impériale ottomane pour l'Exposition universelle de 1873, à Vienne. Texte français par Marie de Launay. Dessins par Montani Effendi, Boghoz Effendi Chachian et Maillard. Documents techniques par Montani Effendi. Exécution matérielle par Sébah (Constantinople: Pascal Sébah, 1873).

L'Indicateur ottoman. Annuaire-almanach du commerce, de l'industrie, de l'administration et de la magistrature (Constantinople: Cervati frères et D. Fatzea, 1881).

La Constitution ottomane du 7 Zilhidjé 1293 (23 décembre 1876) expliquée et annotée par A. Ubicini (Paris: A. Cotillon, 1877).

La Vérité sur la question des lieux-saints par quelqu'un qui la sait (Malta, 1853).

Le Miroir de la cruelle, & horrible tyrannie espagnole perpetree au Pays Bas, par le tyran duc de Albe, & aultres cõmandeurs de par le Roy Philippe le deuxieme: On a adjoinct la deuxieme partie de les tyrannies commises aux Indes occidentales par les Espagnols (Amsterdam: Ian Evertszoon Cloppenburch, 1620).

Le Panorama: Exposition universelle (Paris: Ludovic Baschet, 1900).

*Lettres champenoises ou correspondance morale et littéraire rédigée par plusieurs hommes de lettres; adressée à Madame de ***, à Arcis-sur-Aube* (Paris: Pillet aîné, 1824).

Men of the Time: A Biographical Dictionary of Eminent Living Characters of Both Sexes (London: George Routledge, 1865).

Narratio Regionum Indicarum per Hispanos quosdam Deuastatum Verissima (Frankfurt: Ioannis Saurri typis, 1598).

Nouveau voyage pittoresque de la France (Paris: Ostervald l'aîné, 1817).

Relación Nueva en la que se describe el arribo y desembarco, que ha hecho en la ciudad de Barcelona el día 28. de julio de este año de 1787. exc.mo señor enviado de la Sublime Puerta Otomana. Cerca de S. M. Católica. Con la lucida comitiva que trae: osequios que se le han hecho, y otras curiosidades que se verán en este nuevo romance (Valencia: Francisco Burguete, 1787).

Views of the Crystal Palace and Park, Sydenham: From Drawings by Eminent Artists, and Photographs by P. H. Delamotte (London: Day & Son, 1854).

Publications

Ahmed Lutfi, *Vak'anüvîs Ahmed Lûtfî Efendi Tarihi*, trans. Yücel Demirel (Istanbul: Tarih Vakfı-Yapı Kredi Yayınları, 1999).

Ahmed Midhat, *Tarih-i Umumi, vol. II: Ezmine-i MutavassıtaTarihi* (Istanbul: Kırk Anbar, 1296/1879).

Ahmed Midhat, *Letaif-i Rivayat: On Birinci Cüz. (Bahtiyarlık) İsmiyle Bir Hikâyeyi Havidir* (Istanbul: Kırk Anbar, 1302/1885).

Alarcón, Pedro Antonio de, *Diario de un testigo de la Guerra de África* (Madrid: Gaspar y Roig, 1859).

Ali Tevfik, *Fezleke-i Tarih-i Umumi, vol. II: Tarih-i Kurun-ı Vusta* (Istanbul: Karabet, 1311/1893–4).

Almagro y Cárdenas, Antonio, 'El 2 de enero de 1880', *La Estrella de Occidente* II(3) (2 January 1880), p. 1.

Almagro y Cárdenas, Antonio, *Biografía del doctor D. Francisco Javier Simonet, catedrático que fué de lengua árabe en la Universidad de Granada y vicepresidente de la Comisión de monumentos históricos y artísticos de la provincia* (Granada: Paulino Ventura Traveset, 1904).

Alpinus, *Quelques pages sur Léon Roches* (Grenoble: Allier frères, 1898).

Amador de los Ríos, Rodrigo, *Inscripciones árabes de Sevilla* (Madrid: T. Fortanet, 1875).

Amicis, Edmondo de, *Constantinopoli* (Milan: Fratelli Treves, 1877).

Argote, Simón de, *Nuevos paseos históricos, artísticos, económico-políticos por Granada y sus contornos*, 3 vols (Granada: Francisco Gómez Espinosa de los Monteros, 1807[?]).

Arslān, Chakīb, *Riwāyat Ākhir Benī Sarrāj* (Alexandria: Al-Ahram, 1897).

Arslān, Chakīb, *Al-Hulal al-sundusiyya fī al-akhbār wa-l-āthār al-Andalusiyya* (Cairo: al-Maṭba'a al-Raḥmāniyya, 1936–9).

Arslan, Emir Emin, *La verdad sobre el harem* (Buenos Aires: Otero, 1916).

Aubry, *Description du château d'eau situé sur l'esplanade du boulevard de Bondi* (Paris: Aubry, 1811).

Azcárate, Gumersindo de, 'Pensamiento de un Muslim', *El Telegrama del Rif* (11 February 1906), p. 1.

Azcárate, Gumersindo de, 'Intereses político-económicos de España en Marruecos', *La Tarde* (15 February 1911), p. 1.

Baedeker, Karl, *Spain and Portugal: Handbook for Travellers* (Leipzig: Karl Baedeker, 1898).

Baedeker, Karl, *Espagne et Portugal: Manuel du voyageur* (Leipzig: Karl Baedeker-Paul Ollendorff, 1900).

Baragnon, Pierre, *Coup d'œil général sur l'Exposition nationale à Constantinople* (Constantinople: Journal de Constantinople, 1863).

Barnardo, T. J., 'The Beni-zou-zougs!', *Night and Day: A Monthly Record of Christian Missions and Practical Philanthropy* V(56) (1 December 1881), pp. 215–21.

Berger, Abel, 'Notice biographique de M. le comte Charles de Vendegies', *Mémoires de la Société d'émulation de Cambrai*, vol. LII (Cambrai: Régnier frères, 1898), pp. 359–77.

Bertrand, Louis, *Le Mirage oriental* (Paris: Perrin, 1910).

Beyatlı, Yahya Kemal, 'Endülüs'te Raks', *Aile* II(5) (1948): 2–3.

Beyatlı, Yahya Kemal, *Kendi Gök Kubbemiz* (Istanbul: Yahya Kemal Enstitüsü, 1974).

Beyatlı, Yahya Kemal, *Mektuplar ve Makaleler* (Istanbul: İstanbul Fetih Cemiyeti, 1977).

Bezirdjian, Sopon, *Albert. Fine Art Album – L'Albert: Album des Beaux-Arts* (London: John Heywood, 1889).

Bineteau, P., *Exposition universelle de 1900: Plan général* (Paris: A. Taride, 1900).

Binḥāddah, 'Abd al-Raḥīm (ed.), *Riḥlat al-Wazīr fī iftikāk al-asīr* (Tokyo: Tokyo University of Foreign Studies, 2005).

Burford, Robert, *Description of a View of the City of Granada; with the Celebrated Fortress and Palace of the Alhambra, and the Surrounding Beautiful Vega, or Plain* (London: W. J. Golbourn, 1853).

Burton, Richard F., *The Book of a Thousand Nights and a Night* (New York: Heritage Press, 1962).

Calvert, Albert F., *Granada and the Alhambra: A Brief Description of the City of Granada with a Particular Account of the Moorish Palace* (London: John Lane, 1907).

Casas, Bartolomé de las, *Brevísima relación de la destruyción de las Indias* (Seville: Sebastián Trugillo, 1552).

Castillo Tejada, Cayetano del, *Poesías, pensamientos y firmas que se encuentran en los cuatro albums de la Alhambra y los Dos genios* (Granada: José López Guevara, 1890).

Caston, Alfred de, 'Le grand mouvement architectural dans l'Empire ottoman: Règne de S.M.I. le sultan Abd-ul-Aziz-Khan. L'Arsenal de Matchka. La mosquée Azizié. S. Exc. Serkis Bey Ballian, l'ingénieur-architecte des palais et des monuments impériaux', *Revue de Constantinople* (7 March 1875), pp. 395–421.

Charmes, Gabriel, 'Un essai de gouvernement européen en Égypte: I. La formation d'un ministère anglo-français', *Revue des deux mondes* 34 (15 August 1879), pp. 776–812.

Chateaubriand, François-René de, *Itinéraire de Paris à Jérusalem et de Jérusalem à Paris, en allant par la Grèce, et revenant par l'Égypte, la Barbarie et l'Espagne* (Paris: Le Normant, 1811).

Chateaubriand, François-René de, *Aventures du dernier Abencerage* (London: Treuttel & Würtz, Treuttel fils, 1826).

Chateaubriand, François-René de, *İbni Serrac Âhir: Endülüs'e Dairdir*, trans. A. Tahir (Istanbul: Mihran, 1298/1882).

Claris de Florian, Jean-Pierre, *Gonzalve de Cordoue ou Grenade reconquise* (Paris: Antoine Auguste Renouard, 1820).

Conte, Augusto, 'Recuerdos de un diplomático', *La Época* 18,623 (18 April 1902), p. 4; 19,565 (18 November 1904), p. 4.

Contreras, Rafael, 'La Alhambra y el museo oriental', *El liceo de Granada* II(10) (15 June 1870), pp. 145–52.

Crayon, Geoffrey [alias Washington Irving], *The Alhambra*, 2 vols (London: Henry Colburn & Richard Bentley, 1832).

Crayon, Geoffrey [alias Washington Irving], 'Recollections of the Alhambra', *The Knickerbocker, or New York Monthly Magazine*, XIII(6) (June 1839), pp. 485–7.

Cunningham, Peter, *London in 1853* (London: John Murray, 1853).

Dancourt, Joseph, 'L'Andalousie au temps des Maures', *Le Livre d'or de l'Exposition de 1900* (Paris: Édouard Cornély, 1900), pp. 239–40.

Daoud, Mohamad A., 'Acercamiento andaluz: Cordial saludo de un moro de paz', *El Defensor de Granada* 27,569 (29 June 1931), p. 3.

Davillier, Charles, *L'Espagne* (Paris: Hachette, 1874).

Dethier, Philip Anton, 'Le Monument de Théodose II', *Journal de Constantinople* 4, 894 (24 January 1866), p. 1.

Dethier, Philip Anton, *Le Bosphore et Constantinople: Description topographique et historique* (Vienna: Alfred Hölder, 1873).

Disraeli, Benjamin, *Contarini Fleming: A Psychological Auto-Biography* (London: John Murray, 1832).

Dusé Mohamed, *In the Land of the Pharaohs: A Short of History of Egypt from the Fall of Ismail to the Assassination of Boutros Pasha* (London: Stanley Paul, 1911).

Echeverría, Juan de, *Paseos por Granada, y sus contornos que en forma de diálogo traslada al papel Don Joseph Romero Yranzo, Colegial del Insigne de San Fulgencio de Murcia* (Granada: Nicolás Moreno, 1764).

Echeverría, Juan de, *Paseos por Granada y sus contornos, o descripción de sus antigüedades y monumentos dados a luz por el célebre Padre Juan de Echeverría, por los años de 1764 y ahora nuevamente reimpresos e ilustrados con algunas pequeñas notas*, 2 vols (Granada: Imprenta nueva de Valenzuela, 1814).

Embasevi, Seyyid Ali ibn, 'İslam Kütüphaneleri', *Mecmua-i Fünun* V(44) (Muharrem 1284/May 1867), pp. 25–9.

Farīd, Muḥammad, *Min Miṣr ilá Miṣr: Riḥlah sanat 1901* (Cairo: Maṭba'at al-Mawsū'āt, 1901).

Fernández y González, Manuel, *Los alcázares de España: La Alhambra, leyendas árabes* (Madrid: J. J. Martínez, 1856).

Flaubert, Gustave, *Œuvres complètes de Gustave Flaubert, Notes de voyages, vol. II: Asie-Mineure–Constantinople–Grèce–Italie–Carthage* (Paris: Louis Conard, 1910).

Flaubert, Gustave, *Œuvres complètes illustrées de Gustave Flaubert: Voyage en Orient (1849–1851)* (Paris: Librairie de France, 1925).

Ford, Richard, *A Hand-Book for Travellers in Spain and Readers at Home* (London: John Murray, 1845).

Ford, Richard, *A Hand-Book for Travellers in Spain*, 5th edn (London: John Murray, 1878).

[Frashëri], Şemseddin Sami, *Seydi Yahya: Beş Fasıldan İbaret Facia* (Istanbul: Tasvir-i Efkâr Matbaası, 1292/1875).

[Frashëri], Şemseddin Sami, *Kamusü'l-A'lam* (Istanbul: Mihran 1314/1899).

Gago y Palomo, Rafael, 'El tiempo de los moros', *La Alhambra* I(21) (30 July 1884), pp. 1–2.

García, J., 'Estudios históricos: Los cristianos del Líbano. Los maronitas', *La Alhambra* 235 (3 February 1858), p. 1; 236 (4 February 1858), p. 1; 238 (6 February 1858), pp. 1–2.

Gautier, Théophile, *Voyage en Espagne* (Paris: Charpentier, 1845).

Gautier, Théophile, *Constantinople* (Paris: Michel Lévy Frères, 1853).

Gautier, Théophile, *Wanderings in Spain* (London: Ingram, Cooke, 1853).

Gautier, Théophile, 'Henri Regnault', *Œuvres de Henri Regnault exposées à l'École des beaux-arts* (Paris: École des beaux-arts, 1872).

Girard, Pierre-Simon, *État des services de M. P. S. Girard* (Paris: Renouard, 1832).

Girault de Prangey, Joseph-Philibert, *Monuments arabes et moresques de Cordoue, Séville et Grenade, dessinés et mesurés en 1832 et 1834* (Paris: Veith & Hauser, 1837).

Girault de Prangey, Joseph-Philibert, *Essai sur l'architecture des Arabes et des Mores, en Espagne, en Sicile, et en Barbarie* (Paris: A. Hauser; Brockhaus & Avenarius, 1841).

Gladstone, William Ewart, *Bulgarian Horrors and the Question of the East* (London: John Murray, 1876).

Goury, Jules and Owen Jones, *Plans, Elevations, Sections, and Details of the Alhambra: From Drawings Taken on the Spot in 1834, by Jules Goury, and in 1834 and 1837 by Owen Jones. With a Complete Translation of the Arabic Inscriptions, and an Historical Notice of the Kings of Granada, from the Conquest of that city by the Arabs to the Expulsion of the Moors, by Mr. Pasqual de Gayangos* (London: Owen Jones, 1842–5).

Hermosilla, José de (ed.), *Antigüedades árabes de España* (Madrid: Imprenta Real, 1787).

Heuser, Robert F., 'Von der Alhambra', *Das Atelier des Photographen* 7 (1898), pp. 117–19.

Hugo, Abel, *France pittoresque, ou Description pittoresque, topographique et statistique des départements et colonies de la France* (Paris: Delloye, 1835).

Hugo, Victor, *Odes et ballades*, 4th edn (Paris: Hector Bossange, 1828).

Hugo, Victor, *Les Orientales*, 5th edn (Paris: Charles Gosselin, Hector Bossange, 1829).

[İleri], Celal Nuri, *Tarih-i Tedenniyat-ı Osmaniye ve Mukadderat-ı Tarihiye* (Istanbul: 1331/1915).

[İleri], Celal Nuri, 'Endülüs'e Dair', *Edebiyat-ı Umumiye Mecmuası* 1(20) (17 March 1917), pp. 337–42; 1(21) (24 March 1917), pp. 357–60; 1(22) (31 March 1917), pp. 369–73.

[İleri], Celal Nuri, *İştirak Etmediğimiz Harekât: Tarih-i Osmani ve Keşfiyat, Rönesans ve Reform Harekâtı* (Istanbul: Cemiyet Kütübhanesi, 1917).

Irving, Washington, *Histoire de la conquête de Grenade, tirée de la chronique manuscrite de Fray Antonio Agapida*, trans. J. Cohen (Paris: Timothée Dehay, 1829).

Irving, Washington, *Tales of the Alhambra* (Madrid: Miguel Sanchez, 1832).

Irving, Washington, *The Alhambra: A Series of Sketches and Tales of the Moors and Spaniards*, 2 vols (Philadelphia: Carey & Lea, 1832).

Irving, Washington, *The Alhambra; or the New Sketch Book* (Paris: A. & W. Galignani, 1832).

Irving, Washington, *Cuentos de la Alhambra* (Valencia: Mallén y Berard, 1833).

Irving, Washington, *L'Alhambra. Chroniques du pays de Grenade*, trans. P. Christian (Paris: Lavigne, 1843).

Jones, Owen, *The Alhambra Court in the Crystal Palace* (London: Crystal Palace Library, 1854).

Jones, Owen, *The Grammar of Ornament* (London: Day & Son, 1856).

Juderías, Julián, 'La leyenda negra y la verdad histórica, España ante Europa', *La Ilustración española y americana* LVIII(VI) (15 February 1914), pp. 94–9.

Juderías, Julián, *La leyenda negra y la verdad histórica: Contribución al estudio del concepto de España en Europa, de las causas de este concepto y de la tolerancia religiosa y política en los países civilizados* (Madrid: Tipografía de la Revista de archivos, bibliotecas y museos, 1914).

[Kuntay], Midhat Cemal, 'Elhamra', *Resimli Kitab* 2(7) (15 April 1325/28 April 1909), pp. 688–9.

[Kuntay], Midhat Cemal, 'Elhamra', *Sırat-ı Müstakim*, 1/8 (19 February 1325/4 March 1910), p. 118.

Laborde, Alexandre, comte de, *Voyage pittoresque et historique de l'Espagne* (Paris: Pierre Didot l'aîné, 1812).

Laborde, Alexandre, comte de, *Projets d'embellissement de Paris et de travaux d'utilité publique concernant les ponts et chaussées* (Paris: A. Belin, 1816).

Lafuente Alcántara, Miguel, *El libro del viajero en Granada* (Granada: Sanz, 1843).

Lafuente Alcántara, Miguel, *Historia de Granada, comprendiendo la de sus cuatro provincias, Almería, Jaen (sic), Granada y Málaga desde remotos tiempos hasta nuestros días*, 4 vols (Granada: Imprenta y librería de Sanz, 1845).

Lavallée, Joseph, *Histoire des inquisitions religieuses d'Italie, d'Espagne et de Portugal* (Paris: Capelle et Renand, 1809).

Lavallée, Joseph and Adolphe Guéroult, *Espagne* (Paris: Firmin Didot frères, 1844).

Lavigne, Alfred Germond de, *Itinéraire descriptif, historique et artistique de l'Espagne et du Portugal* (Paris: L. Hachette, 1866).

Leitner, Gottlieb W., *Xme Congrès international des orientalistes*, March 1890.

León, Rogelia, *Auras de la Alhambra* (Granada: José María Zamora, 1857).

Lévy, Arthur, *Napoléon intime* (Paris: E. Plon, Nourrit, 1893).

Lewis, John Frederick, *Lewis's Sketches and Drawings of the Alhambra, made during a Residence in Granada in the Years 1833–4* (London: Hodgson Boys & Graves, 1835).

Macnaghten, William Hay (ed.), *The Alif Laila or Book of the Thousand Nights and One Night* (Calcutta and London: W. Thacker and W. H. Allen, 1839).

Maʻlūf, Yūsuf Nuʻmān, *Khizānat al-Ayyām fī Tarājim al-ʻIẓām* (New York: Maṭbaʻat Jarīdat al-Ayyām, 1899).

Marin, Scipion, *Histoire de la vie et des ouvrages de M. Chateaubriand, considéré comme poète, voyageur et homme d'État, avec l'analyse de ses ouvrages* (Paris: Vimont, 1832).

Maqqarī al-Maghribī al-Mālikī, Aḥmad, *Kitāb nafḥ al-tīb min ghuṣn al-Andalus al-raṭīb, wa-dhikr wazīrihā lisān al-dīn al-khaṭīb* (Cairo: Maṭbaʻah al-Azharīyah al-Miṣrīyah, 1302/1885).

Maqrīzī, Naqiyyuddīn Aḥmad bin ʻAlī, *Kitāb al-mawāʻiż wa al-iʻtibār bi-dhikr al-khiṭaṭ wa al-āthār* (Cairo: Matbaat al-Nil, 1324/1906).

Mehmed Kâmil, *Arusetü'd-Dünya: Coğrafya-yı Umumi-i Devlet-i Aliyye ma Hıdiviyet-i Celile-i Mısriyye* (Istanbul: chez l'auteur, 1290/1873).

Mehmed Murad, [Mizancı], *Muhtasar Tarih-i Umumi* (Istanbul: Civelekyan, 1302/1885).

Mercinier, Edgar, 'L'Égypte actuelle: aperçus de géographie sociale et économique, nationalisme et internationalisme', *Le Globe: Revue genevoise de géographie* 50 (1911): 1–31.

Miknāsī, Muḥammad ibn ʻUthmān, *Al-Iksīr fī fikāk al-'asīr* (Rabat: al Markaz al-Jāmiʻī li-l-Baḥth al-ʻIlmī, 1964).

Milá y Fontanals, Manuel, *Noticia de la vida y escritos de Don Próspero de Bofarull y Mascaró, archivero y cronista de la corona de Aragón* (Barcelona: Juan Oliveres y Monmany, 1860.

Montani, Pietro, 'La nouvelle mosquée de la Sultane Validé', *La Turquie* (31 March 1870), pp. 2–3.

Morgan, Edward Delmar (ed.), *Transactions of the Ninth International Congress of Orientalists (Held in London, 5th to 12th September 1892)* (London: Committee of the Congress, 1893).

Muallim Naci, *Musa bin Eba'l-Gazan yahud Hamiyyet* (Istanbul: Matbaa-i Ebüzziya, 1299/1882).

Murphy, James Cavanah, *The Arabian Antiquities of Spain* (London: Cadell & Davies, 1815).

Münir Süreyya, 'İspanya Hatıratı – ve – Kurtuba Cami-i Şerifi', *Beyanü'l-Hak* 2(73) (2 August 1326/15 August 1910), pp. 1,419–22.

Namık Kemal, *Külliyat-i Kemal: Birinci Tertib, 1, Rönan Müdafaanamesi* (Istanbul: Mahmud Bey Matbaası, 1326/1910).

Numan Kâmil, *İslamiyet ve Devlet-i Aliyye-i Osmaniye Hakkında Doğru Bir Söz* (Istanbul: Malumat, 1316/1898).

Oliver Hurtado, José and Manuel Oliver Hurtado, *Granada y sus monumentos árabes* (Malaga: Oliver Navarro, 1875).

Ortega-Munilla, J., 'Madrid', *El Imparcial* (21 December 1885).

Ovilo y Otero, Manuel (ed.), *Historia de las cortes, de las armas, letras y artes españolas, ó sea biografías de los senadores, diputados, militares, literatos y artistas contemporáneos* (Madrid: Francisco R. del Castillo, 1852).

Pascual, Don, 'Los moros argelinos', *El Defensor de Granada* 11,857 (16 June 1900), p. 1.

Paula Valladar, Francisco de, 'Un embajador de Marruecos en Granada en el año de 1766', *La Estrella de Occidente: Revista quincenal, órgano de la Unión hispano-mauritánica* III(46) (10 May 1891), p. 4; III(47)(31 May 1891), pp. 3–4; III(48) (15 June 1891), pp. 3–4).

Paula Valladar, Francisco de, 'El álbum de Generalife', *La Alhambra: Revista quincenal de artes y letras* V(102) (31 March 1902), pp. 707–10.

Paula Valladar, Francisco de, 'El álbum de Generalife', *La Alhambra: Revista quincenal de artes y letras* XXIV(545) (30 November 1921), pp. 325–9.

Pérez de Hita, Ginés, *Historia de los bandos de Zegríes y Abencerrajes: primera parte de las Guerras civiles de Granada* (Saragossa: Miguel Ximeno Sánchez, 1595).

Pérez de Hita, Ginés, *Histoire chevaleresque des Maures d'Espagne, traduite de l'espagnol, précédée de quelques réflexions sur les musulmans d'Espagne* (Paris: Cérioux et H. Nicolle, 1809).

Planat, Paul-Amédée (ed.), *Encyclopédie de l'architecture et de la construction* (Paris: Aulanier, 1892).

Ponz, Antonio, *Viage de España* (Madrid: Joachin Ibarra, 1780).

Poujoulat, Baptistin, *La Vérité sur la Syrie et l'expédition française* (Paris: Gaume frères & J. Duprey, 1861).

Reichard, Heinrich August Ottokar, *Guide des voyageurs en Europe* (Weimar: Bureau de l'industrie, 1805).

Renan, Ernest, *L'islamisme et la science: Conférence faite à la Sorbonne le 29 mars 1883* (Paris: Calmann Lévy, 1883).

Roberts, Davis, *Picturesque Views of Spain and Morocco: Comprising Granada, with the Palace of the Alhambra, Andalusia, Castile, Biscay, Seville, Valencia, Gibraltar,*

Tangiers, Tetuan, Morocco, the Town of Constantina, etc. (London: Robert Jennings, 1838).

Roches, Léon, *Trente-deux ans à travers l'islam (1832–1864)*, 2 vols (Paris: Firmin Didot, 1884).

Roches, Léon, *Dix ans à travers l'islam (1834–1844)* (Paris: Perrin, 1904).

Ruiz, Aureliano, 'Un poema árabe', *Revista de Andalucía* V(12) (10 May 1878), pp. 118–20.

Ṣafadī, Ṣalāḥ al-Dīn Khālīl bin Aybak, *Kitāb al-Wāfā bil-Wafiyāt* (Beirut: Dar Ihya al-Turath al-Arabi, 1420/2000).

Saint-Priest, Alexis de, *Monumens, souvenirs, mœurs de l'Espagne* (Paris: Imprimerie de H. Fournier, 1829).

Saint-Priest, Alexis de, *L'Espagne: Fragment d'un voyage* (Paris: A. Firmin Didot, 1830).

Saint-Victor, Jean-Baptiste de, *Tableau historique et pittoresque de Paris* (Paris: Librairie classique élémentaire, 1822).

Saint-Victor, Jean-Baptiste de, *Kamusü'l-A'lâm* (Istanbul: Mihran, 1314/1899).

Samipaşazade, Sezai, 'El-mescidi'l-Camia: Elhamra', *Yeni Kitab* 1(7) (31 October 1927), pp. 12–17.

Sánchez Valdivia, Rafael, *Brevísimo guía del palacio árabe y demás alcázares que deben visitarse con un estudio del álbum de la Alhambra* (Granada: José López Guevara, 1900).

Sancho y Rodríguez, Manuel, *Crónica de la coronación de Zorrilla* (Granada: J. G. Garrido, 1889).

Sanders, Lloyd C. (ed.), *Celebrities of the Century: Being a Dictionary of Men and Women of the Nineteenth Century* (London: Cassell, 1887).

Sauvaire, Henri (ed.), *Voyage en Espagne d'un ambassadeur marocain (1690–1691), traduit de l'arabe par H. Sauvaire, consul de France en retraite* (Paris: Ernest Leroux, 1884).

Scudamore, Frank Ives, *France in the East; a Contribution towards the Consideration of the Eastern Question* (London: William H. Allen, 1882).

Seco de Lucena, Luis, *Poesías y pensamientos del álbum de la Alhambra* (Granada: Francisco Reyes, 1878, 1883, 1889).

Seco de Lucena, Luis, *Practical and Art Guide of Granada* (Granada: Defensor de Granada, 1912?).

Seco de Lucena, Luis, *Idearium de la Alhambra* (Granada: Artes gráficas granadinas, 1921).

Sédillot, Louis Pierre Eugène Amélie, *Histoire des Arabes* (Paris: Hachette, 1854).

Sédillot, Louis Pierre Eugène Amélie, *Histoire des Arabes* (Paris: Maisonneuve, 1877).

Sédillot, Louis Pierre Eugène Amélie, *Khulāṣat Tārīkh al-'Arab* (Cairo: Maṭba'at Muḥammad Afandī Muṣṭafa, 1309/1892).

Silió Cortés, César, *Otro desastre más (España en París)* (Valladolid: Castellana, 1900).

Simonet, Francisco Javier, 'Francia en Siria y España en Marruecos', *La Estrella de Occidente* III(35) (15 November 1890), pp. 1–2; III(36) (30 November 1890), pp. 1–2; III(37) (15 December 1890), pp. 1–2; III(40) (31 January 1891), pp. 1–2; III(41) (15 February 1891), pp. 1–2; III(42) (28 February 1891), pp. 1–2; III(43) (15 March 1891), pp. 1–2.

Stoddard, Lothrop, *The New World of Islam* (London: Chapman & Hall, 1922).

Swinburne, Henry, *Travels through Spain in the Years 1775 and 1776 in which Several Monuments of Roman and Moorish Architecture are Illustrated by Accurate Drawings Taken on the Spot* (London: P. Elmsly, 1779).

Swinburne, Henry, *Travels through Spain, in the Years 1775 and 1776: In which Several Monuments of Roman and Moorish Architecture are Illustrated by Accurate Drawings Taken on the Spot* (London: P. Elmsly, 1787).

Swinburne, Henry, *Voyage de Henri Swinburne en Espagne en 1775 et 1776, traduit de l'anglois* (Paris: Didot l'aîné, 1787).

Ṭahṭāwī, Rifā'a Rāfi', *Takhlīṣ al-ibrīz fī talkhīṣ Bārīz* (Cairo: Dār al-Ṭibā'ah al-'Āmirah, 1250/1834).

Ṭahṭāwī, Rifā'a Rāfi', *Tahlisü'l-ibriz ila telhis-i Paris*, transl. Rüstem Besim (Cairo: Bulaq, 1255/1839).

Ṭahṭāwī, Rifā'a Rāfi', *Takhlīṣ al-ibrīz ila talkhīṣ Bārīz* (Cairo: Dār al-Ṭibā'ah al-'Āmirah, 1265/1849).

Ṭahṭāwī, Rifā'a Rāfi', *An Imam in Paris: Account of a Stay in France by an Egyptian Cleric (1826–1831)*, trans. D. L. Newman (London: Saqi, 2004).

Ṭahṭāwī, Rifā'a Rāfi', *L'or de Paris*, trans. A. Louca (Arles: Actes Sud, 2012).

[Tarhan], Abdülhak Hamid, *Nazife yahud Feda-yı Hamiyyet* (Istanbul: Tasvir-i Efkâr Matbaası, 1293/1876).

[Tarhan], Abdülhak Hamid, *Tarık yahud Endülüs'ün Fethi* (Istanbul: Mahmud Bey Matbaası, 1296/1879).

[Tarhan], Abdülhak Hamid, *Tezer yahud Melik Abdurrahman e's-Salis* (Istanbul: Mihran, 1297/1880).

[Tarhan], Abdülhak Hamid, *Riwāyat Fatḥ al-Andalus: Riwāyatun Ta'rīkhiyyatun Gharāmiyatun Tamthiliyatun* (Istanbul[?], 1323/1905).

[Tarhan], Abdülhak Hamid, *Abdullah e's-Sagir: Nazife* (Istanbul: Matbaa-i Amire, 1335/1917).

[Tarhan], Abdülhak Hamid, *İbni Musa yahud Zatü'l-Cemal* (Istanbul: Matbaa-i Âmire, 1917).

Taylor, Isidore Justin Séverin, baron, *Voyage pittoresque en Espagne, en Portugal et sur la côte d'Afrique, de Tanger à Tétouan* (Paris: Librairie de Gide fils, 1832).

[Tunalı], Ahmed Hilmi (*alias* Bu da ben), *Rezalet, Dördüncü Fasıl: Portekiz* (İhsanbol [Geneva]: n.p., 1318/1900).

[Tunalı], Ahmed Hilmi, *Rezalet, Beşinci Fasıl: Yine İspanya'da* (n.p., 1318/1900).

[Tunalı], Ahmed Hilmi, *On Birinci Hutbe* (n.p., 1318/1900).

Vahid, 'Elhamra', *Hayat* 2(46) (13 October 1927), pp. 9–14.

Vapereau, Gustave, *Dictionnaire universel des contemporains, contenant toutes les personnes notables de la France et des pays étrangers* (Paris: Hachette, 1858).

Vermont, Jean, 'La Retraite aux flambeaux du mercredi', *Le Livre d'or de l'Exposition de 1900* (Paris: Édouard Cornély, 1900), p. 239.

Viardot, Louis, *Essai sur l'histoire des Arabes et des Mores d'Espagne*, 2 vols (Paris: Paulin, 1833).

Viardot, Louis, *Les Musées d'Espagne, d'Angleterre et de Belgique, guide et mémento de l'artiste et du voyageur* (Paris: Paulin, 1843).

Viardot, Louis, *Histoire des Arabes et des Mores d'Espagne, traitant de la constitution du peuple arabe-espagnol, de sa civilisation, de ses mœurs et de son influence sur la civilisation moderne*, 2 vols (Paris: Pagnerre, 1851).

Vigny, Alfred de, *Cinq-Mars, ou Une conjuration sous Louis XIII* (Paris: Le Normant père, 1826).

Vollers, Karl (ed.), *Le neuvième congrès international des orientalistes tenu à Londres du 5 au 12 septembre 1892* (Cairo: Imprimerie nationale, 1892).

White, William, *The Illustrated Hand Book of the Royal Alhambra Palace, Leicester Square* (London: Nicholls Brothers, 1869).

Wien, Peter, *Arab Nationalism: The Politics of History and Culture and Culture in the Modern Middle East* (London: Routledge, 2017).

Willkomm, Moritz, *Zwei Jahre in Spanien und Portugal: Reiseerinnerungen* (Dresden: Arnoldische Buchhandlung, 1847).

Wood, Ruth Kedzie, *The Tourist's Spain and Portugal* (New York: Dodd, Mead, 1913).

Zakī, Aḥmad, *Al-Safar ila al-Mu'tamar* (Cairo: Bulaq, 1311/1893).

Zakī, Aḥmad, *Al-Safar ila al-Mu'tamar*, 2nd edn (Cairo: Bulaq, 1311/1894).

Zanth, Ludwig von, *Die Wilhelma: Maurische Villa Seiner Majestät des Königes Wilhelm von Württemberg* (Stuttgart: chez l'auteur, 1855[–6]).

Zavattaro, Mario, 'Caricaturas contemporáneas: Príncipe Amin Arslau (*sic*)', *Caras y caretas* XXII(632) (12 November 1910), n.p.

Zaydān, Jurji, *Fatḥ al-Andalus: Riwāyah ta'rīkhiya ghurāmiya* (Cairo: al-Hilal, 1909).

Zaydān, Jurji, *The Conquest of Andalusia*, trans. Roger Allen (Bethesda, MD: Zaidan Foundation, 2010).

Ziya Pasha, *Endülüs Tarihi*, vol. I (Istanbul: Takvimhane-i Âmire, 1276/1860); vol. II (Istanbul: Tercüman-i Ahval, 1280/1864).

Ziya Pasha, *Endülüs Tarihi*, vols I–III (Istanbul: Asır Kütübhanesi, 1304/1888); vol. IV (Istanbul: Karabet ve Kasbar Matbaası, 1305/1889).

Ziya Pasha, *Terci'-i Bend: Terkib-i Bend* (Istanbul: Mühendisyan Ohanes Matbaası, 1872).

Ziya Pasha, *Harabat* (Istanbul: Matbaa-i Amire, 1291/1874).

Ziya Pasha, *Enkizisyon Tarihi* (Istanbul: Matbaa-i Ebüzziya, 1299/1882).

Ziya Pasha, *Külliyat-ı Ziya Paşa* (Istanbul: Kanaat Kütüphanesi, 1343/1925).

Zorrilla y Moral, José, *Granada: Poema oriental, precedido de la leyenda de Al-Hamar* (Paris: Pillet fils aîné, 1852).

Secondary Sources

'El retrato morisco, un suvenir andaluz', *Museos de Terque: Apología radical de las cosas viejas* XV(171) (2020); 1–2.

'Ṭarā'if nādirat 'an: al-Cheikh Muḥammad 'Abduh', *Al-Athnayn wa al-Dunya* (June 1945).

'Abd al-Wahhāb, Ḥasan Ḥusnī, *Waraqāt 'an al-Ḥaḍārat al-'Arabiyya bi-Ifrīqiyat al-Tūnisiyya* (Tunis: Maktabat al-Manār, 1966).

Abdel Nasser, Tahia, 'Shawqi, Ahmed', in E. K. Akyeampong and H. L. Gates, Jr (eds), *Dictionary of African Biography* (Oxford: Oxford University Press, 2012), vol. 5, pp. 359–61.

Abdullah, Fevziye, 'Namık Kemal'in Midilli'de Yazdığı Manzum ve Mensur Eserler', *Türkiyat Mecmuası* 12 (1955): 57–90.

Almagro Gorbea, Antonio (ed.), *El legado de al-Ándalus: Las antigüedades árabes en los dibujos de la Academia* (Madrid: Real Academia de Bellas Artes de San Fernando-Fundación MAPFRE, 2015).

Almagro Gorbea, Antonio, 'Las antigüedades árabes en la Real Academia de San Fernando', in A. Almagro Gorbea (ed.), *El legado de al-Ándalus: Las antigüedades árabes en los dibujos de la Academia* (Madrid: Real Academia de Bellas Artes de San Fernando-Fundación MAPFRE, 2015), pp. 12–29.

Aoki Girardelli, Miyuki, 'Léon Parvillée and the Discourse on "Turkish" Architecture', *Round, 1, Jewels: Selected Writings on Modern Architecture from Asia* (2006), pp. 164–8.

Aral, Hâmid (ed.), *Dışişleri Bakanlığı 1967 Yıllığı* (Ankara: Ankara Basım ve Ciltevi, 1968).

Archilés Cardona, Ferran, '¿Una cultura imperial? Africanismo e identidad nacional española en el final del siglo XIX', *Storicamente* 12(5) (2016): DOI: 10.12977/stor621.

Arlı, Hakan, 'Âli Paşa Camii ve Sebili', *Dünden Bugüne İstanbul Ansiklopedisi* (Istanbul: Kültür Bakanlığı-Tarih Vakfı, 1994) vol. I, p. 195.

Arslan, Ceyhun C., 'Translating Ottoman into Classical Arabic: *Nahḍa* and the Balkan Wars in Aḥmad Shawqī's "The New al-Andalus"', *Middle Eastern Literatures* 19(3) (2016): 278–97.

Ateş, Sabri, *Tunalı Hilmi Bey: Osmanlı'dan Cumhuriyet'e bir Aydın* (Istanbul: Tarih Vakfı Yurt Yayınları, 2009).

'Awdāt, Ya 'qūb (ed.), *Min a'lām al-fikr wa al-adab fi Filastīn* (Amman: Wakālat al-Tawzī' al-Urduniyah, [1987]).

Ayvazoğlu, Beşir, 'Edebiyatımızda Endülüs', *Endülüs'ten İspanya'ya* (Ankara: Türkiye Diyanet Vakfı, 1996).

Aydın, Cemil, *The Idea of the Muslim World: A Global Intellectual HIstory* (Cambridge, MA: Harvard University Press, 2017).

Barrios Rozúa, Juan Manuel, *Reforma urbana y destrucción del patrimonio histórico en Granada* (Granada: Universidad de Granada-Junta de Andalucía, 1998).

Barrios Rozúa, Juan Manuel, 'El Generalife y las ruinas árabes de su contorno: Un capítulo inédito de los *Nuevos Paseos* de Simón de Argote', *Al-Qantara* XXV(1) (2014): 29–59.

Barrios Rozúa, Juan Manuel, *Granada napoleónica: Ciudad, arquitectura y patrimonio* (Granada: Editorial Universidad de Granada, 2016).

Barrios Rozúa, Juan Manuel, 'La recreación orientalista del Patio de los Leones', in J. A. González Alcantud (ed.), *Leones y doncellas: Dos patios palaciegos andaluces en diálogo cultural (siglos XIV al XXI)* (Granada: Universidad de Granada, 2018), pp. 229–45.

Batur, Afife, 'Abdülmecid Efendi Köşkü', *Dünden Bugüne İstanbul Ansiklopedisi* (Istanbul: Kültür Bakanlığı-Tarih Vakfı, 1994), vol. I, pp. 51–2.

Birinci, Ali, 'Osmanlı Devletinde Matbuat ve Neşriyat Yasakları Tarihine Medhal', *Türkiye Araştırmaları Literatür Dergisi* IV(7) (2006), *Yeni Türk Edebiyatı Tarihi I*, pp. 291–349.

Bora, Tanıl, 'Notes on the White Turks Debate', in R. Kastoryano (ed.), *Turkey between Nationalism and Globalization* (Abingdon: Routledge, 2013), pp. 87–104.

Calatrava Escobar, Juan, 'Un retrato de Granada a principios del siglo XIX: Los "Nuevos Paseos" de Simón de Argote', *Demófilo: Revista de cultura tradicional de Andalucía*, 35 (2000): 95–110.

Calatrava Escobar, Juan, 'La Alhambra, entre las luces y el romantismo', in J. A. González Alcantud and A. Malpica Cuello (eds), *Pensar la Alhambra* (Barcelona: Anthropos Editorial, 2001), pp. 182–200.

Calderwood, Eric, *Colonial al-Andalus: Spain and the Making of Moroccan Culture* (Cambridge, MA: Harvard University Press, 2018).

Cantor, Paul A., 'Tales of the Alhambra: Rushdie's Use of Spanish History in *The Moor's Last Sigh*', *Studies in the Novel* 29(3) (1997): 232–341.

Caro Baroja, Julio, *Los Judíos en la España Moderna y Contemporánea* (Madrid: Ediciones ISTMO, 1986).

Carpintero Ortega, Rafael, 'Visión de España de Yahya Kemal', *Boletín de la Asociación española de orientalistas* XXVIII (1992): 181–93.

Çelik, Zeynep, *Displaying the Orient: Architecture of Islam at Nineteenth Century World's Fairs* (Berkeley: University of California Press, 1992).

Çelik, Zeynep, 'Speaking Back to Orientalist Discourse', in J. Beaulieu and M. Roberts (eds), *Orientalism's Interlocutors: Painting, Architecture, Photography* (Durham, NC: Duke University Press, 2002), pp. 19–41.

Chejne, Anwar G., 'Travel Books in Modern Arabic Literature', *Muslim World* LII(3) (1962): 207–15.

Chejne, Anwar G., 'Amīn al-Rīḥānī and al-Andalus: A Journey into History', *Al-'Arabiyya* 9 (1976): 9–18.

Chraïbi, Driss, *Naissance à l'aube* (Paris: Éditions du Seuil, 1986).

Cirot, Georges, 'La maurophilie littéraire en Espagne au XVIe siècle', *Bulletin hispanique* 40(2) (1938): 150–7.

Civantos, Christina, *The Afterlife of Al-Andalus: Muslim Iberia in Contemporary Arab and Hispanic Narratives* (Albany, NY: SUNY Press, 2017).

Cortés García, Manuela, 'Andalucía: realidad y mito en la perspectiva intelectual árabe', in M. Á. Brelanga Fernández (ed.), *Lo Andaluz Popular, Símbolo de lo Nacional* (Granada: Universidad/Centro de Documentación Musical de Andalucía, 2009), pp. 265–308.

Crosnier Leconte, Marie-Laure, 'Oriental ou colonial? Questions de styles dans le concours de l'École des beaux-arts au XIXe siècle', in N. Oulebsir and M. Volait (eds),

L'orientalisme architectural entre imaginaires et savoirs (Paris: CNRS-Picard, 2009), pp. 43–67.

Daufresne, Jean-Claude, *Louvre & Tuileries: Architectures de Papier* (Brussels: Pierre Mardaga, 1987).

DeGuzmán, María, *Spain's Long Shadow: The Black Legend, Off-Whiteness, and Anglo-American Empire* (Minneapolis: University of Minnesota Press, 2005).

Delpechin, Davy, 'Orientalism Challenged: The Spanish Pavilion at the 1910 Brussels International Exhibition', in F. Giese and A. Varela Braga (eds), *The Power of Symbols: The Alhambra in a Global Perspective* (Bern: Peter Lang, 2018), pp. 371–84.

Deringil, Selim, *The Well-Protected Domains: Ideology and the Legitimation of Power in the Ottoman Empire, 1876–1909* (London: I. B. Tauris, 1998).

Deringil, Selim, '"They Live in a State of Nomadism and Savagery": The Late Ottoman Empire and the Post-Colonial Debate', *Comparative Studies in Society and History* 45(3) (2003): 311–42.

Dodds, Jerrilynn D. (ed.), *Al-Andalus: The Art of Islamic Spain* (New York: Metropolitan Museum of Art, 1992).

Doğru, İhsan, 'Elegy to the Balkans in Arab Poetry: Fall of Edirne, Sister of Andalucia', *Journal of Academic Social Science Studies* 54 (2017): 497–504.

Dold-Ghadar, Gabriele, *Pers-Andalus: Iranische Kulturdenkmäler in, al-Andalus al-aqṣā'. Bewertung der Forschungsergebnisse für das 8.–12. Jahrhundert* (Berlin: Klaus Schwarz Verlag, 2016).

Duffield, Ian, 'Duse Mohamed Ali and the Development of pan-Africanism, 1866–1945', PhD dissertation, University of Edinburgh, 1971, 2 vols.

Dupont, Anne-Laure, *Ǧurǧī Zaydān (1861–1914) écrivain réformiste et témoin de la Renaissance arabe* (Damascus: Institut français du Proche-Orient, 2006).

Dupont, Anne-Laure, 'How Should the History of the Arabs be Written? The Impact of European Orientalism on Jurji Zaidan's Work', in G. C. Zaidan and Th. Philipp (eds), *Jurji Zaidan: Contributions to Modern Arab Thought and Literature, Proceedings of a Symposium at the Library of Congress* (Bethesda, MD: Zaidan Foundation, 2013), pp. 85–121.

Eldem, Edhem, *Pride and Privilege: A History of Ottoman Orders, Medals and Decorations* (Istanbul: Ottoman Bank Archive and Research Centre, 2004).

Eldem, Edhem, *Consuming the Orient* (Istanbul: Ottoman Bank Archive and Research Centre, 2007).

Eldem, Edhem, 'Les Ottomans, un empire en porte-à-faux', in F. Pouillon and J-C. Vatin (eds), *Après l'orientalisme: L'Orient créé par l'Orient* (Paris: IISMM-Karthala, 2011), pp. 285–302.

Eldem, Edhem, 'Making Sense of Osman Hamdi Bey and His Paintings', *Muqarnas: An Annual on the Visual Culture of the Islamic World* 29 (2012): 339–83.

Eldem, Edhem, 'Powerful Images: The Dissemination and Impact of Photography in the Ottoman Empire, 1870–1914', in Z. Çelik and E. Eldem (eds), *Camera Ottomana: Photography and Modernity in the Ottoman Empire, 1840–1914* (Istanbul: Koç University Press, 2015), pp. 106–53.

Eldem, Edhem, 'The Changing Design and Rhetoric of Ottoman Decorations' *Journal of Decorative and Propaganda Arts* 28 (2016): 24–43.

Eldem, Edhem, 'Ottomans at the Alhambra, 1844–1914: An Investigation into the Perception of Al-Andalus by Ottoman Subjects in Times of Modernity', *Turcica* 49 (2018): 239–359.

Eldem, Edhem, 'The Ottomans and the Alhambra: Inspiration or Ignorance?', in F. Giese and A. Varela Braga (eds), *The Power of Symbols: The Alhambra in a Global Perspective* (Bern: Peter Lang, 2018), pp. 97–110.

Eldem, Edhem, 'The Search for an Ottoman Vernacular Photography', in M. Ritter and S. G. Scheiwiller (eds), *The Indigenous Lens? Early Photography in the Near and Middle East* (Berlin: De Gruyter, 2018) (*Studies in Theory and History of Photography: Schriften der Lehr- und Forschungsstelle für Theorie und Geschichte der Fotografie am Kunsthistorischen Institut der Universität Zürich*, vol. 8), pp. 29–56.

Eldem, Edhem, 'The (Still)Birth of the Ottoman "Museum": A Critical Reassessment', in M. Wellington Gahtan and E-M. Troelenberg (eds), *Collecting and Empires: An Historical and Global Perspective* (Turnhout: Brepols, 2018), pp. 258–85.

Eldem, Edhem, 'Turcos y árabes en la Alhambra: el descubrimiento otomano de al-Ándalus', in J. A. González Alcantud (ed.), *Leones y doncellas: Dos patios palaciegos andaluces en diálogo cultural (siglos XIV al XXI)* (Granada: Universidad de Granada, 2018), pp. 317–38.

Eldem, Edhem, *L'Alhambra: À la croisée des histoires* (Paris: Les Belles Lettres, 2021).

Elinson, Alexander E., *Looking Back at Al-Andalus: The Poetics of Loss and Nostalgia in Medieval Arabic and Hebrew Literature* (Leiden: Brill, 2009).

Emparán Fernández, Maria Antonieta, 'Palacio de la Alhambra: Un orientalismo chileno del siglo XIX', in F. Giese and A. Varela Braga (eds), *The Power of Symbols: The Alhambra in a Global Perspective* (Bern: Peter Lang, 2018), pp. 355–70.

Enginün, İnci, 'Edebiyatımızda Endülüs', *Araştırmalar ve Belgeler* (Istanbul: Dergâh Yayınları, 2000).

Eraktan, Halid, 'Fuad Paşa Camii ve Türbesi', in R. E. Koçu (ed.), *İstanbul Ansiklopedisi* (Istanbul: İstanbul Ansiklopedisi, 1971), vol. XI, p. 5852.

Ergüven, Rebia Akil, 'La danseuse espagnole', *Journal d'Orient* (31 December 1963), p. 3.

Ersoy, Ahmet, 'Ottoman Gothic: Evocations of the Medieval Past in Late Ottoman Architecture', in P. J. Geary and G. Klaniczay (eds), *Manufacturing Middle Ages: Entangled History of Medievalism in Nineteenth-Century Europe* (Leiden: Brill, 2013), pp. 217–38.

Ersoy, Ahmet, *Architecture and the Late Ottoman Historical Imaginary: Reconfiguring the Architectural Past in a Modernizing Empire* (Farnham: Ashgate, 2015).

Ersoy, Ahmet, 'The Sultan and his Tribe: Documenting Ottoman Roots in the Abdülhamid II Photographic Albums', in B. Öztuncay and Ö. Ertem (eds), *Ottoman Arcadia: The Hamidian Expedition to the Land of Tribal Roots (1886)* (Istanbul: Koç University Center for Anatolian Civilizations, 2018), pp. 31–64.

Espinosa Ramírez, Antonio B., 'Los judíos marroquíes vistos a través del periódico africanista *La Estrella de Occidente*', *Miscelánea de Estudios Árabes y Hebráicos* 62 (2013): see at: http://www.meahhebreo.com/index.php/meahhebreo/article/view/198/295.

Ferry, Kathryn, 'Owen Jones and the Alhambra Court at the Crystal Palace', in Glaire D. Anderson and Mariam Rosser-Owen (eds), *Revisiting Al-Andalus: Perspectives on the Material Culture of Islamic Iberia and Beyond* (Leiden: Brill, 2007), pp. 227–45.

Fontanella, Lee, *La historia de la fotografía en España desde sus orígenes hasta 1900* (Madrid: El Viso, 1981).

Frübis, Hildegard, 'Die Neue Synagoge in Berlin (1866) und die Alhambra: Die Adaption maurischer Stilelemente und die Re-Orientalisierung des europäischen Judentums', in F. Giese and A. Varela Braga (eds), *The Power of Symbols: The Alhambra in a Global Perspective* (Bern: Peter Lang, 2018), pp. 153–62.

Gallego Morell, Antonio, '"The Alhambra" de Washington Irving y sus traducciones españolas', *Revista hispánica moderna* 26(3/4) (1960): 136–42.

Gámir Sandoval, Alfonso, 'En el siglo XVIII, moros en la Alhambra', *Miscelánea de estudios árabes y hebraicos: Sección árabe-islam* 10 (1952): 51–65.

Gámiz Gordo, Antonio, 'Los dibujos originales de los palacios de la Alhambra de J. F. Lewis (h. 1832–33): J. F. Lewis's Original Drawings of the Alhambra Palaces', *Expresión gráfica arquitectónica* 20 (2012): 76–87.

García Arenal, Mercedes and Rodríguez Mediano, Fernando (eds), *The Orient in Spain: Converted Muslims, the Forged Lead Books of Granada and the Rise of Orientalism* (Leiden: Brill, 2013).

Gibson, Shimon, Yoni Shapira and Rupert L. Chapman III, *Tourists, Travellers and Hotels in Nineteenth-Century Jerusalem* (Abingdon: Routledge, 2017).

Giese, Francine, 'An Inclination for the Moorish Style: Architects and Networks in 19th-Century Germany', in F. Giese and A. Varela Braga (eds), *The Power of Symbols: The Alhambra in a Global Perspective* (Bern: Peter Lang. 2018), pp. 257–80.

Giese, Francine and Ariane Varela Braga (eds), *The Power of Symbols: The Alhambra in a Global Perspective* (Bern: Peter Lang, 2018).

Goldschmidt, Arthur Jr (ed.), *Biographical Dictionary of Modern Egypt* (Boulder, CO: Lynne Rienner, 2000).

Gómez Moreno, Manuel, 'Unas cartas de El Solitario', *Boletín de la Real Academia Española* XXXIII (1953): 214.

González, Antonio Jesús (ed.), *Los Garzón: Kalifas de la fotografía cordobesa* (Cordoba: Ayuntamiento de Córdoba, 2017).

González Alcantud, José Antonio, 'Andalousie: Le double regard', *Ethnologie française* XXX(2) (2000): 271–81.

González Alcantud, José Antonio, *Lo moro: Las lógicas de la derrota y la formación del estereotipo islámico* (Barcelona: Anthropos Editorial, 2002).

González Alcantud, José Antonio, 'El mito fallido sacromontano y su perdurabilidad local a la luz del mozarabismo de F. J. Simonet', *Al-Qantara* XXIV(2) (2003): 547–73.

González Alcantud, José Antonio, 'La maurophobie dans les cercles intellectuels andalous aux XIXe et XXe siècles', in J. A. Alcantud and F. Zabbal (eds), *Histoire de l'Andalousie: Mémoire et enjeux* (Montpellier: L'Archange Minotaure, 2003), pp. 239–63.

González Alcantud, José Antonio, 'Pasión fría y objeto fóbico: El círculo orientalista Estebánez, Cánovas, Simonet', in C. Lisón Tolosana (ed.), *Antropología: Horizontes emotivos* (Granada: Universidad de Granada, 2003), pp. 169–87.

González Alcantud, José Antonio, *La ciudad vórtice: Lo local, lugar fuerte de la memoria en tiempos de errancia* (Barcelona: Anthropos Editorial, 2005).

González Alcantud, José Antonio, 'Reflejos de la Conferencia de Algeciras en la ciudad vórtice: Granada', in J. A. González Alcantud and E. Martín Corrales (eds), *La Conferencia de Algeciras en 1906: Un banquete colonial* (Barcelona: Bellaterra, 2007), pp. 253–70.

González Alcantud, José Antonio, 'Lo moro revisitado: Dimensión estética, diversidad cultural, función crítica, fantasma social', *Revista internacional de filosofía política* 31 (2008): 29–48.

González Alcantud, José Antonio, 'La survivance du mythe de Al-Andalus dans une ville du Maghreb: Fès', in M-Th. Garcia, O. Lasserre Dempure and A. Vatrican (eds), *La Ville méditerranéenne: Entre imaginaire et réalité* (Paris: Honoré Champion, 2009).

González Alcantud, José Antonio, 'The Dream of Washington Irving in the Alhambra or the Endurance of the Myth', *Washington Irving and the Alhambra, 1859–2009* (Granada: Patronato de la Alhambra y el Generalife, 2009), pp. 31–43.

González Alcantud, José Antonio, *Social History of a World Heritage Site: The Alhambra of Granada* (Oxford: Blackwell-UNESCO, 2012).

González Alcantud, José Antonio, *El Mito de al-Ándalus: Orígenes y actualidad de un ideal cultural* (Cordoba: Almuzara, 2014).

González Alcantud, José Antonio, 'Al Ándalus y el tiempo mítico de los "Andalusíes"', in I. E. Buttitta and T. India (eds), *La definizione culturale del tempo: Atti del convegno internazionale: Palermo, 26–27 novembre 2015* (Palermo: Fondazione Ignazio Buttitta, 2016), pp. 147–69.

González Alcantud, José Antonio, 'Andalucía "en el tiempo de los moros": Flamencos en la Exposición Universal de París de 1900', *Andalucía en la historia* XIV(52) (2016): 50–5.

González Alcantud, José Antonio, 'El orientalismo de los viajeros españoles por el Marruecos decimonónico: L'orientalisme des voyageurs espagnols à travers le Maroc du XIXe siècle', in J. À, Carbonell (ed.), *Caminos del sur: Marruecos y el orientalismo peninsular. Chemins du sud. La Maroc et l'orientalisme ibérique* (Barcelona: Instituto europeo del Mediterráneo – Museu nacional d'art de catalunya – Instituto municipal de museus Reus, 2016), pp. 132–65.

González Alcantud, José Antonio, 'La reinvención "persa" del Patio de los Leones: Los laberintos antropo-imaginarios del restauracionismo', in J. A. González Alcantud (ed.), *Leones y doncellas: Dos patios palaciegos andaluces en diálogo cultural (siglos XIV al XXI)* (Granada: Universidad de Granada, 2018), pp. 247–76.

González Alcantud, José Antonio (ed.), *Leones y doncellas: Dos patios palaciegos andaluces en diálogo cultural (siglos XIV al XXI)* (Granada: Universidad de Granada, 2018).

González Alcantud, José Antonio, *Qué es el orientalilsmo: El orientalismo imaginado en la cultura global* (Cordoba: Almuzara, 2021).

González Alcantud, José Antonio and Sandra Rojo Flores, 'La Alhambra de Granada: Un fractal orientalista en clave poscolonial. Los puntos de vista local y árabe', *Estudios de Asia y África* XLIX/155(3) (2014): 693–721.

Gözütok, Zehra, 'Ziya Paşa'nın Endülüs Tarihi', Masters' thesis, University of Marmara, School of Theology, Istanbul, 2008.

Granara, William, 'Nostalgia, Arab Nationalism, and the Andalusian Chronotope in the Evolution of the Modern Arabic Novel', *Journal of Arabic Literature* XXXVI(1) (2005): 57–73.

Guerrero Moreno, Montserrat, 'Entre maurofobia y maurofilia: formación e impacto del pensamiento historiográfico de Francisco Javier Simonet', *Revista de Estudios Internacionales Mediterráneos* 27 (2019): 204–23.

Gurulkan, Kemal et al. (eds), *Osmanlı Belgelerinde Millî Mücadele ve Mustafa Kemal Atatürk* (Ankara: Başbakanlık Devlet Arşivleri Genel Müdürlüğü, 2007).

Gutiérrez Viñuales, Rodrigo, 'Alhambras americanas: Memoria de una fascinación', *Artes de México* 54 (2001): 60–7.

Güldemir, Ufuk, *Teksas Malatya* (Istanbul: Tekin Yayınevi, 1992).

Hajjar, Nijmeh, *The Politics and Poetics of Ameen Rihani: The Humanist Ideology of an Arab-American Intellectual and Activist* (London: Tauris Academic Studies, 2010).

Hamilton, James, *A Strange Business: Making Art and Money in Nineteenth-Century Britain* (London: Atlantic Books, 2014).

Hanssen, Jens, '"Malhamé–Malfamé": Levantine Elites and Transimperial Networks on the Eve of the Young Turk Revolution', *International Journal of Middle East Studies* 43 (2011): 25–48.

Herlihy-Mera, Jeffrey, 'Islamic Spain in American Travel Writing', *Revista de fililogía* 38 (2019): 125–39.

Hermes, Nizar F., 'Nostalgia for al-Andalus in Early Modern Moroccan *Voyages en Espagne*: Al-Ghassānī's *Riḥlat al-Wazīr fī Iftikāk al-Asīr* (1690–91) as a Case Study', *Journal of North African Studies* (2015): 1–20.

Herzog, Christoph, *Osmanische Herrschaft und Modernisierung im Irak: Die Provinz Bagdad, 1817–1917* (Bamberg: University of Bamberg Press, 2012).

Hirschkind, Charles, 'Granadan Reflections', *Material Religion* XII(2) (2016): 209–32.

İnal, İbnülemin Mahmud Kemal, *Osmanlı Devrinde Son Sadrâzamlar* (Istanbul: Maarif Matbaası, 1940).

Irwin, Dana, 'Sheikhs and Samurai: Léon Roches and the French Imperial Project', *Southeast Review of Asian Studies* 30 (2008): 23–40.

Irwin, Robert, *The Alhambra* (Cambridge, MA: Harvard University Press, 2004).

Jiménez Martín, Alfonso, 'Notas sobre los dibujos de las *Antigüedades Árabes* y los *Monumentos Arquitectónicos*', in A. Almagro Gorbea (ed.), *El legado de al-Ándalus: Las antigüedades árabes en los dibujos de la Academia* (Madrid: Real Academia de Bellas Artes de San Fernando-Fundación MAPFRE, 2015), pp. 30–43.

Ju'beh, Naẓmī, Al-Khālidī, Walīd and Khaḍir Ibrāhīm Salāmah (eds), *Fihris makhṭūṭāt al-Maktabah al-Khālidīyah, al-Quds: Catalogue of Manuscripts in al-Khalidiyya Library, Jerusalem* (London: Mu'assasat al-Furqān lil-Turāth al-Islāmī, 1427/2006).

Kaddouri, Abdelmajid, 'Images de l'Europe dans un genre d'écriture marocaine: la *Rihla*', *Cahiers de Tunisie* XLIV(157–8) (1989): 123–34.

Kadhim, Hussein N., *The Poetics of Anti-colonialism in the Arabic Qaṣīdah* (Leiden: Brill, 2004).

Kagan, Richard L., *The Spanish Craze: America's Fascination with the Hispanic World, 1779–1939* (Lincoln: University of Nebraska Press, 2019).

Kalmar, Ivan Davidson, 'Moorish Style: Orientalism, the Jews, and Synagogue Architecture', *Jewish Social Studies*, NS 7(3) (2001): 68–100.

Karal, Enver Ziya, *Osmanlı Tarihi, vol. VII: Islahat Fermanı Devri 1861–1876* (Ankara: Türk Tarih Kurumu, 1983).

Kayalı, Hasan, *Arabs and Young Turks: Ottomanism, Arabism, and Islamism in the Ottoman Empire, 1908–1918* (Berkeley: University of California Press, 1997).

Khalidi, Rashid, *Palestinian Identity: The Construction of Modern National Consciousness* (New York: Columbia University Press, 2010).

Khalidi, Rashid, *The Hundred Years' War on Palestine: A History of Settler Colonialism and Resistance, 1917–2017* (New York: Picador, 2021).

Koppelkamm, Stefan, *The Imaginary Orient: Exotic Buildings of the 18th and 19th Centuries in Europe* (Stuttgart: Edition Axel Menges, 2015).

Kuneralp, Sinan (ed.), *From an Ottoman Gentleman to his English Friend: The Letters of Ahmed Vefik Pasha to Sir Austen Layard (1846–1890)* (Istanbul: Isis, forthcoming).

Kuneralp, Sinan, 'El primer representante permanente otomano en Madrid', *Las relaciones turco-españolas a lo largo de la historia* (Madrid: Tam, 2008), pp. 66–71.

Kuneralp, Sinan, 'L'émigration syro-libanaise en Amérique latine et la diplomatie ottomane', *Syrian Studies Association Newsletter* 15(1) (Winter 2009–10), see at: https://ojcs.siue.edu/ojs/index.php/ssa/article/view/868/381.

Kuneralp, Sinan, *Son Dönem Osmanlı Erkân ve Ricali, 1839–1922): Prosopografik Rehber* (Istanbul: Isis Press, 2003).

Lakhdar, M., 'al-Kardūdī', in P. Bearman, Th. Bianquis, C. E. Bosworth, E. van Donzel and W. P. Heinrichs (eds), *Encyclopaedia of Islam*, 2nd edn, available at: http://dx.doi.org/10.1163/1573-3912_islam_SIM_3930, last accessed 5 April 2019.

Levi, Giovanni, 'On Microhistory', in Peter Burke (ed.), *New Perspectives on Historical Writing* (Cambridge: Polity Press, 1991), pp. 93–113.

Lewis, Bernard, 'Quelques thèmes andalous de la littérature turque au XIXe siècle', *Études d'orientalisme dédiées à la mémoire de Lévi-Provençal*, vol. I (Paris: Maisonneuve et Larose, 1962).

Lirola Delgado, Pilar, 'Al-Sumaysir, poeta satírico testigo de las taifas', *Miscelánea de Estudios Árabes y Hebraicos: Sección Árabe-Islam* 68 (2019): 197–229.

López García, Bernabé, 'Arabismo y orientalismo en España: Radiografía y diagnóstico de un gremio escaso y apartadizo', *Awraq*, annexe XI (1990): 35–69.

Losensky, Paul, ''Orfi Širazi', *Encyclopædia Iranica*, online edition, 2012, available at: http://www.iranicaonline.org/articles/orfi-of-shiraz

Makdisi, Ussama, 'Ottoman Orientalism', *American Historical Review* 107(3) (2002): 768–96.

Mardin, Şerif, 'Super Westernization in Urban Life in the Ottoman Empire in the Last Quarter of the Nineteenth Century', in P. Benedict, E. Tümertekin and F. Mansur (eds), *Turkey: Geographic and Social Perspectives* (Leiden: Brill, 1974), pp. 404–46.

Mardin, Şerif, *The Genesis of Young Ottoman Thought: A Study in the Modernization of Turkish Political Ideas* (Syracuse, NY: Syracuse University Press, 2000).

Martín Corrales, Eloy, 'Relaciones de España con el Imperio Otomano en los siglos XVIII y XIX', in P. Martín Asuero (ed.), *España-Turquía: Del enfrentamiento al análisis mutuo* (Istanbul: Isis, 2003), pp. 253–70.

Martín Corrales, Eloy, 'Maurophobie/islamophobie et maurophilie/islamophilie dans l'Espagne du XXIe siècle', *Revista CIDOB d'Afers Internacionals* 66(7) (2004): 241–54.

Martínez Bande, José Manuel, *Los años críticos: República, conspiración, revolución y alzamiento* (Madrid: Encuentro, 2007).

Martínez Montávez, Pedro, *Al-Andalus, España, en la literatura árabe contemporánea* (Madrid: MAPFRE, 1992).

Matar, Nabil, *In the Lands of the Christians: Arabic Travel Writing in the Seventeenth Century* (London: Routledge, 2003).

Matar, Nabil, *An Arab Ambassador in the Mediterranean World: The Travels of Muḥammad ibn 'Uthmān al-Miknāsī* (London: Routledge, 2015).

Matulka, Barbara, 'On the European Diffusion of the "Last of the Abencerrajes" Story in the Sixteenth Century', *Hispania* 16(4) (1933): 369–88.

McSweeney, Anna, 'Versions and Visions of the Alhambra in the Nineteenth-Century Ottoman World', *West 86th* 22(1) (2015): 44–69.

McSweeney, Anna, 'El mudéjar y el alhambresco: Pabellones españoles en las exposiciones universales y la invención de un estilo nacional', in J. A. González Alcantud (ed.), *Leones y doncellas: Dos patios palaciegos andaluces en diálogo cultural (siglos XIV al XXI)* (Granada: Universidad de Granada, 2018), pp. 203–28.

Menchinger, Ethan I., 'The Sefaretname of Ahmed Vasıf Efendi to Spain', *History Studies* 2(3) (2010): 351–67.

Méndez Rodríguez, Luís, Rocío Plaza Orellana and Antonio Zoido Naranjo (eds), *Viaje a un oriente europeo: Patrimonio y turismo en Andalucía (1800–1929)* (Seville: Centro de estudios andaluces, 2010).

Mestyan, Adam, *Arab Patriotism: The Ideology and Culture of Power in Late Ottoman Egypt* (Princeton, NJ: Princeton University Press, 2017).

Miller, Susan Gilson (ed.), *Disorienting Encounters: Travels of a Moroccan Scholar in France in 1845–1846. The Voyage of Muḥammad aṣ-Ṣaffār* (Berkeley: University of California Press, 1992).

Morales Lezcano, Víctor, 'La percepción de al-Ándalus en libros de viajes de autores árabes', in J. A. González Alcantud and A. Malpica Cuello (eds), *Pensar la Alhambra* (Barcelona: Anthropos Editorial, 2001).

Morales Oliver, Luis, *La novela morisca de tema granadino* (Madrid: Universidad Complutense, Fundación Valdecilla, 1972).

Navascués Palacio, Pedro, 'Los autores: arquitectos, pintores y dibujantes', in A. Almagro Gorbea (ed.), *El legado de al-Ándalus: Las antigüedades árabes en los dibujos de la Academia* (Madrid: Real Academia de Bellas Artes de San Fernando-Fundación MAPFRE, 2015), pp. 62–79.

Nepomuceno, Alexandra, 'Les brumes de l'orientalisme: brève histoire d'une rencontre fantomatique', *Bérose: Encyclopédie internationale des histoires de l'anthropologie* (Paris: Bérose, 2017), art. 1120.

Newman, Daniel, 'Myths and Realities in Muslim Alterist Discourse: Arab Travellers in Europe in the Age of the *Nahda* (19th C.)', *Chronos* 6 (2002): 7–76.

Noorani, Yaseen, 'The Lost Garden of Al-Andalus: Islamic Spain and the Poetic Inversion of Colonialism', *International Journal of Middle East Studies* 31(2) (1999): 237–54.

Nunley, Gayle R., *Scripted Geographies: Travel Writings by Nineteenth-Century Spanish Authors* (Lewisburg, PA: Bucknell University Press, 2007).

Orelli-Messerli, Barbara von, 'Gottfried Semper's Dresden Synagogue Revised: An Echo of the Alhambra?', in F. Giese and A. Varela Braga (eds), *The Power of Symbols: The Alhambra in a Global Perspective* (Bern: Peter Lang, 2018), pp. 139–52.

Özcan, Nezahat, 'Yahya Kemal Beyatlı'nın Elçilik Yılları ve Diğer Resmi Vazifeleri', *Bilig* I (1996): 31–8.

Öztuncay, Bahattin, *Vasilaki Kargopulo: Hazret-i Pâdişâhî'nin Serfotoğrafı* (Istanbul: BOS, 2000).

Öztuncay, Bahattin, *The Photographers of Constantinople: Pioneers, Studios and Artists from Nineteenth-Century Istanbul*, 2 vols (Istanbul: Aygaz, 2003).

Öztuncay, Bahattin, *Hâtıra-i Uhuvvet: Portre Fotoğraflarının Cazibesi, 1846–1950* (Istanbul: Aygaz, 2005).

Palazzo, Benedetto and A. Raineri, *La chiesa di S. Pietro in Galata: note storiche illustrative in occasione del 1. centenario delle consecrazione* (Istanbul: Harti, 1943).

Paradela, Nieves, *El otro laberinto español: Viajeros árabes a España entre el siglo XVII y 1936* (Madrid: Ediciones de la Universidad Autónoma, 1993; reprinted Madrid: Siglo XXI de España, 2005).

Paradela, Nieves, 'El viaje y la historia: el mito de al-Ándalus en los modernos viajeros árabes a España', *Revista de Filología Románica* IV (2006): 245–65.

Pascual del Coso, Carlos, 'El retrato a la morisca', *Alhóndiga* 4 (2017): 4–9.

Pérès, Henri, *L'Espagne vue par les voyageurs musulmans de 1610 à 1930* (Paris: Librairie d'Amérique et d'Orient Adrien-Maisonneuve, 1937).

Pérez, Joseph, *La Légende noire de l'Espagne* (Paris: Fayard, 2009).

Pérez Berenguel, José Francisco, 'Las fuentes principales de los *Viajes por España* (1779) de Henry Swinburne', *Hispania: Revista española de historia* LXIX (2009): 67–86.

Philipp, Thomas, *Ǧurǧī Zaidān his Life and Thought* (Beirut: Orient Institut der deutschen morgenländischen Gesellschaft, 1979).

Philipp, Thomas, *Jurji Zaidan and the Foundations of Arab Nationalism* (Syracuse, NY: Syracuse University Press, 2014).

Piñar Samos, Javier (ed.), *Imágenes en el tiempo: un siglo de fotografía en la Alhambra, 1840–1940* (Granada: Patronato de la Alhambra, Tf Editores, 2003).

Piñar Samos, Javier, 'Turismo emergente y mercado fotográfico en torno a la Alhambra (1842–1915)', *En la Alhambra: Turismo y fotografía en torno a un monumento* (Granada: Caja Granada; Junta de Andalucía, Consejería cultural, 2006), pp. 41–9.

Piñar Samos, Javier, *Fotografía y fotógrafos en la Granada del siglo XIX* (Granada: Caja General de Ahorros de Granada/Ayuntamiento de Granada, 1997).

Pouillon, François, *Les deux vies d'Étienne Dinet, peintre en Islam: L'Algérie et l'héritage colonial* (Paris: Balland, 1997).

Prieto Sánchez, Emilio, 'Citas y pensamientos del álbum la Alhambra', *Proa* 27, 28, 29, 30 (2, 3, 6 November and 9 December 1952).

Redondo, Augustín, 'Moros y moriscos en la literatura española de los años 1550–1580', in I. Andres-Suárez (ed.), *Las dos grandes minorías étnico-religiosas en la literatura española del Siglo de Oro: Los judeoconversos y los moriscos* (Paris: Les Belles lettres, 1995), pp. 51–84.

Rifai, Nada Yousuf al-, 'The Influence of Greco-Roman Literature on Ahmad Shawqi', *Advances in Social Sciences Research Journal* V(6) (2018): 358–78.

Roberts, Mary, *Istanbul Exchanges: Ottomans, Orientalists, and Nineteenth-Century Visual Culture* (Berkeley: University of California Press, 2015).

Roca Barea, María Elvira, *Imperiofobia y leyenda negra: Roma, Rusia, Estados Unidos y el Imperio español* (Madrid: Ediciones Siruela, 2016).

Rodríguez Casado, Vicente, 'La embajada del talbe Sidi Mohamed ben Otman en 1780', *Hispania* III (1943): 598–611.

Rogers, Benjamin, '*Andalusia in the Time of the Moors*: Regret and Colonial Presence in Paris, 1900', in J. Hackforth-Jones and M. Roberts (eds), *Edges of Empire: Orientalism and Visual Culture* (Oxford: Blackwell, 2005), pp. 181–205.

Roldán Romero, Juan Luis, '*Al-Riḥla al-Andalusiyya* de 'Alī Sālim al-Wardānī al-Tūnisī (1861–1905): Estudio preliminar', *ehumanista/IVITRA* 9 (2016): 290–9.

Romero, Emilio, 'Desde los Pirineos hasta el Atlas: nuestros apellidos', *Nueva Alcarria* (29 December 1951), p. 2.

Rubin-Dorsky, Jeffrey, '*The Alhambra*: Washington Irving's House of Fiction', *Studies in American Fiction* 11(2) (1983): 171–88.

Rushdie, Salman, *The Moor's Last Sigh* (London: Random House, 1995).

Rüstem, Ünver, *Ottoman Baroque: The Architectural Refashioning of Eighteenth-Century Istanbul* (Princeton, NJ: Princeton University Press, 2019).

Ryad, Umar, '"An Oriental Orientalist": Aḥmad Zakī Pasha (1868–1934), Egyptian Statesman and Philologist in the Colonial Age', *Philological Encounters* 3 (2018): 129–66.

Saglia, Diego, 'The Exotic Politics of the Domestic: The Alhambra as Symbolic Place in British Romantic Poetry', *Comparative Literature Studies* 34(3) (1997): 197–225.

Said, Edward, *Orientalism* (New York: Vintage, 1979).

Salameh, Khader, 'Al-Shaykh Khalīl al-Khālidī: Qāḍī Mamlakat al-Filastīn', in S. Tamari (ed.), *Madīnat al-Ḥujjāj wa-al-A'yān wa-al-Maḥāshī: Dirāsāt fī Tārīkh al-Quds al-Ijtimā'ī wa-al-Thaqāfī* (Jerusalem: Mu'assasat al-Dirāsāt al-Maqdisīyah: Markaz Dirāsāt al-Quds, 2005), pp. 40–62.

Samsakçı, Mehmet, 'Bir Savunma Psikolojisi Aracı Olarak Türk Edebiyatında Endülüs İmajı', *Sabah Ülkesi* 42 (2015): 58–62.

Sánchez Cano, David, 'Allende el Estrecho (Beyond the Straits): The Photographic Gaze on the Orient in Andalusia and Morocco', *Art in Translation* 9(1) (2017): 92–113.

Sánchez, Joseph P., *The Spanish Black Legend/La Leyende Negra Española: Origin of Anti-Hispanic Stereotypes/Orígenes de los estereotipos antihispánicos* (Albuquerque, NM: Spanish Colonial Research Center, 1990).

Saner, Turgut, '19. Yüzyıl Osmanlı Eklektisizminde "Elhamra'nın Payı"', in Z. Rona (ed.), *Osman Hamdi Bey ve Dönemi* (Istanbul: Tarih Vakfı Yurt Yayınları, 1993), pp. 134–45.

Saner, Turgut, 'Fuad Paşa Camii', *Dünden Bugüne İstanbul Ansiklopedisi* (Istanbul: Kültür Bakanlığı-Tarih Vakfı, 1994), vol. III, p. 341.

Saner, Turgut, 'Fuad Paşa Türbesi', *Dünden Bugüne İstanbul Ansiklopedisi* (Istanbul: Kültür Bakanlığı-Tarih Vakfı, 1994), vol. III, pp. 341–2.

Saner, Turgut, 'Orientalism in Architecture', *1001 Faces of Orientalism* (Istanbul: Sakıp Sabancı Museum, 2013), pp. 52–61.

Sazatornil Ruiz, Luis and Ana Belén Lasheras Peña, 'París y la *españolada:* Casticismo y estereotipos nacionales en las exposiciones universales (1855–1900)', *Mélanges de la Casa de Velázquez* 35(2) (2005): 265–90.

Schulz, Andrew, '"The Porcelain of the Moors": The Alhambra Vases in Enlightenment Spain', *Hispanic Research Journal* 9(5) (2008): 389–415.

Selçuk, Hüseyin, 'Benderli Mehmed Selim (Sırrı) Paşa'nın Hayatı, İdari ve Siyasi Faaliyetleri (1771–1831)', Masters' thesis, University of Istanbul, 2019.

Shalem, Avinoam, 'The "Golden Age" in Al-Andalus as Remembered, or How Nostalgia Forged History', in J. Anderson (ed.), *Crossing Cultures: Conflict, Migration and Convergence* (Carlton, Melbourne: Miegunyah Press, 2009).

Shamsie, Muneeza, 'Introduction: The Enduring Legacy of al-Andalus', *Journal of Postcolonial Writing* 52(2) (2016): 127–35.

Shannon, Jonathan Holt, *Performing al-Andalus: Music and Nostalgia across the Mediterranean* (Bloomington: University of Indiana Press, 2015).

Shaw, Wendy K., 'The Paintings of Osman Hamdi and the Subversion of Orientalist Vision', in Ç. Kafescioğlu and L. Thys-Şenocak (eds), *Aptullah Kuran İçin Yazılar: Essays in Honor of Aptullah Kuran* (Istanbul: Yapı Kredi Yayınları, 1999), pp. 423–34.

Simour, Lhoussain, *Recollecting History beyond Borders: Captives, Acrobats, Dancers and the Moroccan–American Narrative of Encounters* (Newcastle upon Tyne: Cambridge Scholars, 2014).

Stearns, Justin, 'Representing and Remembering Al-Andalus: Some Historical Considerations Regarding the End of Time and the Making of Nostalgia', *Medieval Encounters* 15 (2009): 355–74.

Stinglhamber, Louis, 'Chateaubriand à Grenade?' *Bulletin de l'Association Guillaume Budé: Lettres d'humanité* 11 (1952): 93–114.

Strauss, Johann, '*Kurûn-ı Vustâ*: la découverte du Moyen-Âge par les Ottomans', in F. Georgeon and F. Hitzel (eds), *Les Ottomans et le temps* (Leiden: Brill, 2012), pp. 205–40.

Strauss, Johann, 'What was (Really) Translated in the Ottoman Empire? Sleuthing Nineteenth-century Ottoman Translated Literature', in M. Booth (ed.), *Migrating Texts, Circulating Translations around the Ottoman Mediterranean* (Edinburgh: Edinburgh University Press, 2019), pp. 57–94.

Subrahmanyam, Sanjay, 'Connected Histories: Notes towards a Reconfiguration of Early Modern Eurasia', *Modern Asian Studies* XXXI(3) (1997): 735–62.

Tabbal, Sarah, 'Marià Fortunys *Die Ermorderung der Abencerragen*: Zur Alhambra als Projektionsfläche und Symbolträgerin imaginierter Vergangenheit in der Malerei des 19. Jahrhunderts', in F. Giese and A. Varela Braga (eds), *The Power of Symbols: The Alhambra in a Global Perspective* (Bern: Peter Lang, 2018), pp. 279–91.

Tanpınar, Ahmet Hamdi, *19uncu Asır Türk Edebiyatı Tarihi* (Istanbul. Çağlayan Kitabevi, 1988).

Thornton, Lynne, *The Orientalists: Painters-Travellers* (Paris: ACR, 1994).

Tofiño-Quesada, Ignacio, 'Spanish Orientalism: Uses of the Past in Spain's Colonization in Africa', *Comparative Studies of South Asia, Africa and the Middle East* 23(1/2) (2003): 141–8.

Tornielli, Pablo, 'Hombre de tres mundos: Para una biografía política e intelectual del emir Emín Arslán', *Dirāsāt Hispānicas. Revista Tunecina de Estudios Hispánicos* 2 (2015): 157–81.

Toros, Taha, 'Yapı Kredi Bankası'nın Bağlarbaşı'ndaki Mecid Efendi Köşkü', *Sanat Dünyamız* 31 (1984): 2–9.

Tuğlacı, Pars, *The Role of the Balian Family in Ottoman Architecture* (Istanbul: Yeni Çığır, 1990).

Uğurcan, Sema, 'Türk Edebiyatında Endülüs İmajı', *İslâmiyât* 7(3) (2004): 89–104.

Urquízar-Herrera, Antonio, *Admiration and Awe: Morisco Buildings and Identity Negotiations in Early Modern Spanish Historiography* (Oxford, Oxford University Press, 2017).

Uysal, Sermet Sami, *Yahya Kemal'le Sohbetler* (Istanbul: Kitap Yayınları, 1959).

Varela Braga, Ariane, 'Building a Dream: The Alhambra in the Villa of Sammezzano', in F. Giese and A. Varela Braga (eds), *The Power of Symbols: The Alhambra in a Global Perspective* (Bern: Peter Lang, 2018), pp. 293–308.

Viñes Millet, Cristina, *Granada y Marruecos: Arabismo y africanismo en la cultura granadina* (Granada: Sierra Nevada 95, 1995).

Viñes Millet, Cristina, *La Alhambra que fascinó a los románticos* (Granada: Patronato de la Alhambra, 2007).

Vives, Jaime Vicens, *An Economic History of Spain* (Princeton, NJ: Princeton University Press, 1969).

Volait, Mercedes, 'Appropriating Orientalism? Saber Sabri's Mamluk Revivals in late-19th century Cairo', in D. Behrens-Abouseif and S, Vernoit (eds), *Islamic Art in the 19th Century: Tradition, Innovation and Eclecticism* (Leiden: Brill, 2005) pp. 131–55.

Volait, Mercedes, 'Dans l'intimité des objets et des monuments: l'orientalisme architectural vu d'Égypte (1870–1910)', in N. Oulebsir and M. Volait (eds), *L'orientalisme architectural entre imaginaires et savoirs* (Paris: CNRS-Picard, 2009), pp. 233–51.

Volait, Mercedes, 'L'ingénieur, le réformateur et le collectionneur: trois figures égyptiennes de l'orientalisme architectural au Caire au tournant du XXe siècle', in S. Basch, P. Chuvin, M. Espagne, N. Seni and J. Leclant (eds), *L'orientalisme, les orientalistes et l'Empire ottoman de la fin du XVIIIe siècle à la fin du XXe siècle: Actes du colloque international réuni à Paris, les 12 et 13 février 2010, au palais de l'Institut de France* (Paris: Académie des Inscriptions et Belles-Lettres, 2011), pp. 275–91.

Walker, Dennis, 'Egypt's Arabism: Mustafa Kamil's 1893 Play (*Fatḥ al-Andalus*) on the Muslim Conquest of Spain', *Islamic Studies* 33(1) (1994): 49–76.

Werner, Michael and Bénédicte Zimmermann, 'Penser l'histoire croisée: entre empirie et réflexivité', *Annales: Histoire, sciences sociales* 58 (2003/1): 7–36.

Werner, Michael and Bénédicte Zimmermann, 'Beyond Comparison: *Histoire Croisée* and the Challenge of Reflexivity', *History and Theory* 45 (2006): 30–50.

Wharton, Alyson, 'The Balyan Family and the Linguistic Culture of a Parisian Education', *International Journal of Islamic Architecture* 5(1) (2016): 39–71.

Wharton, Alyson, 'The Unknown Craftsman Made Real: Sopon Bezirdjian, Armenian-ness and Crafting the Late Ottoman Palaces', *Études arméniennes contemporaines* 6 (2015): 71–109.

Wharton, Alyson, *The Architects of Ottoman Constantinople: The Balyan Family and the History of Ottoman Architecture* (London: I. B. Tauris, 2015).

Wien, Peter, *Arab Nationalism: The Politics of History and Culture and Culture in the Modern Middle East* (London: Routledge, 2017).

Yalçınkaya, Alper, *Learned Patriots: Debating Science, State, and Society in the Nineteenth-Century Ottoman Empire* (Chicago: University of Chicago Press, 2015).

Yenişehirlioğlu, Filiz, 'Continuity and Change in Nineteenth Century Istanbul: Sultan Abdülaziz and the Beylerbeyi Palace', in D. Behrens-Abouseif and S. Vernoit (eds), *Islamic Art in the 19th Century Tradition, Innovation and Eclecticism* (Leiden: Brill, 2006), pp. 57–89.

Yetiş, Kâzım (ed.), *Yahya Kemal İçin Yazılanlar*, vol. I (Istanbul: İstanbul Fetih Cemiyeti, 1998).

Ziriklī, Khayr al-Dīn (ed.), *Al-A'lām: Qāmūs Tarājim li-Ashhar al-Rijāl wa-al-Nisā' min al-'Arab wa-al-Mustaghribīn wa-al-Mustashriqīn* (Beirut: Dār al-'Ilm lil-Malāyīn, [1969], 2002).

Ziter, Edward, *The Orient on the Victorian Stage* (Cambridge: Cambridge University Press, 2003).

Websites

Alhambra Foto, Galería fotográfica Ruiz Linares, desde 1886: https://alhambrafoto.com.

All dialects: The weather is hot: https://forum.wordreference.com/threads/all-dialects-the-weather-is-hot.3573430.

Carmen de los Mártires: https://es.wikipedia.org/wiki/Carmen_de_los_Mártires.

Casa de los Tiros: https://es.wikipedia.org/wiki/Casa_de_los_Tiros.

Chorrojumo: https://es.wikipedia.org/wiki/Chorrojumo.

Cid Hiaya: https://es.wikipedia.org/wiki/Cid_Hiaya.

Colorized photograph of Ahmad Zaki Pasha (1867–1934), also known as the Dean of Arabism: https://commons.wikimedia.org/wiki/File:Ahmad_Zaki_Pasha.jpg.

Contract signed by Jean-Antoine Melhamé in 1925: http://earsiv.sehir.edu.tr:8080/xmlui/bitstream/handle/11498/16293/001635770019.pdf?sequence=1&isAllowed=y.

Dar setāyesh-e hazrat-e Rasul: http://www.nosokhan.com/Library/Topic/1F23.

Espada de Boabdil: https://es.wikipedia.org/wiki/Espada_de_Boabdil.

Estudio fotográfico Garzón y Señán: https://rinconesdegranada.com/estudio-fotografico-garzon-senan.

Famille Poupart de Neuflize: https://fr.wikipedia.org/wiki/Famille_Poupart_de_Neuflize.

Galería fotográfica Abelardo Linares: https://rinconesdegranada.com/galeria-fotografica-abelardo-linares.

Jarrones de la Alhambra: https://es.wikipedia.org/wiki/Jarrones_de_la_Alhambra.

Khalidiyya Foundation: http://khalidi.org.

La Estrella de Occidente: https://es.wikipedia.org/wiki/La_Estrella_de_Occidente.

Libros de firmas de la Alhambra: https://www.alhambra-patronato.es/ria/handle/10514/813; https://www.alhambra-patronato.es/ria/handle/10514/822.

Liste des préfets de Vaucluse: https://fr.wikipedia.org/wiki/Liste_des_préfets_de_Vaucluse.

Louis Bertrand (écrivain): https://fr.wikipedia.org/wiki/Louis_Bertrand_(écrivain).

Los jarrones tipo Alhambra: historia y vicisitudes: https://www.alhambra-patronato.es/jarrones-tipo-alhambra.

Marwat ʿAlī Ḥusayn, نساء الأسرة العلوية ودورهن في المجتمع المصري: https://books.google.com.tr/books?id=je48DwAAQBAJ&pg=PT66&lpg=PT66&dq=» توحيد + السلحدار »&source=bl&ots=DPNkOYif5b&sig=ACfU3U0la8vqNlNktNqhUBwfc3j_PcePTQ&hl=en&sa=X&ved=2ahUKEwjV0-33ktTrAhUCXRUIHcy6DPg4ChDoATADegQICBAB#v=onepage&q=» توحيد السلحدار »&f=false.

Mohamed Tawfik Naseem Pasha: https://en.wikipedia.org/wiki/Mohamed_Tawfik_Naseem_Pasha.

Nagdat Fatḥī Ṣafwat, حكايات دبلوماسيّة: https://books.google.com.tr/books?id=JVndDwAAQBAJ&pg=PT22&lpg=PT22&dq="توحيد + السلحدار"&source=bl&ots=SRyg-RFGGU&sig=ACfU3U0RaPeZBGCTSWdwflpq1kVz4tpiug&hl=en&sa=X&ved=2ahUKEwjV0-33ktTrAhUCXRUIHcy6DPg4ChDoATAAegQICRAB#v=onepage&q="3%" توحيد السلحد Dfalse&f=false.

Obispos y arzobispos de Granada: https://es.wikipedia.org/wiki/Anexo:Obispos_y_arzobispos_de_Granada.

Puerto del suspiro del moro: https://es.wikipedia.org/wiki/Puerto_del_Suspiro_del_Moro.

Rifʿat al-Saʿīd, فرح أنطون يعلمنا كيف يكون الثوري رومانسيًا, https://www.albawabhnews.com/2232430.

Ryad, Umar, Sophie Spaan, Andrei Tirtan and Mehdi Sajid, 'Muslims in Interwar Europe': https://muslims-in-interwar-europe.com/Gallery3.html.

Tadros, Fanny Emma, Zionsfriedhof Jerusalem: https://commons.wikimedia.org/wiki/File:Tadros,_Fanny_Emma_Zionsfriedhof_Jerusalem.jpg.

TECOP, Textos e contextos do orientalismo português, X Congresso de Lisboa: http://tecop.letras.ulisboa.pt/np4/congLisboa.html.

Tomb of Fuad Pasha: http://community.fansshare.com/pic103/w/pasha--hinduism-/369/23969_tomb_of_fuad_pasha_istanbul_turkey.jpg.

Un bulo para poder lucirse: https://www.ideal.es/granada/prensa/20070302/provincia/bulo-para-poder-lucirse_20070302.html.

INDEX

Note: The names of individuals found in the visitors' book of the Alhambra are in **bold**, followed by the date of their visit

Abbas Hilmi II, Khedive of Egypt, 248n57, 250n67, 269
Abbasid, 48, 281
ʿAbd al-Wahhāb, Ḥasan Ḥusnī, Tunisian historian, 231
ʿAbdallah al-Saghīr, 298n182; *see also* Boabdil el Chico
ʿAbdelkerīm bin Slīmān, secretary of a Moroccan legation (1895), 113–14, 120, 130–2, 258, 260
ʿAbdelraḥman III, Caliph of Cordoba, 131, 190, 257–8, 260, 298
ʿAbduh, Muḥammad, Egyptian reformist sheikh, 276–7
Abdülaziz, Ottoman sultan, 167, 174–5, 177, 189, 193n144, 194n146, 197–202, 210, 213, 216, 218–19, 221–2, 321, 329
Abdülhak Hâmid [Tarhan], Ottoman poet and playwright, 189–92, 224, 250, 299
Abdülhamid II, Ottoman sultan, 79, 117–18, 175, 177, 183, 193n144, 231–2, 234, 236, 243–4, 262–3, 271, 275, 278–83, 285n141, 289, 293n170, 295n173, 311, 321
Abdülmecid, Ottoman sultan, 145, 199–200
Abencerrage, 25n11, 26, 32n39, 33, 35, 55–6, 58, 78, 154n27, 162
  Adventures of the Last Abencerrage (*Aventures du dernier Abencerage*), novel by Chateaubriand (1826), 26–7, 29, 50, 88, 191, 263, 315
  Massacre of the Abencerrages (*La matança dels Abenserraigs*), painting by Fortuny (ca 1870), 57n120, 58
  see also Chateaubriand; *Summary Execution*; Fortuny; Pérez de Hita; Regnault
ʿAbīd, Ibrāhīm Ṣāleḥ, Maronite visitor (1879), 169
Abu Yuhanna bin Suf, Maronite priest, 170
Admiralty, Kasımpaşa, Istanbul, 209
Adrianople *see* Edirne
Africa, African, 15, 17, 38n58, 51–2, 57, 59–62, 64–5, 70–2, 77, 87, 94, 102n91, 121–2, 124, 130, 133, 135, 137, 139–42, 144, 153, 157, 166, 168, 219n208, 228–9, 301, 308, 327–8
  Berlin Conference for the partition of Africa, 71, 139
  see also Pan-Africanism
africanismo, 71, 94, 135, 140–2, 253; *see also* colonialism

Aguirre, Joaquín de, Spanish *arbitrista*, 46
Aḥmad bin Shuqrūn, military attaché of a Moroccan legation (1885), 99–100, 104
Aḥmad bin Aṣaf ʿAbdallah, Arab visitor (1919), 120
Ahmed Midhat Efendi, Ottoman author, 223–4, 261n93
Ahmed Vasıf Efendi, Ottoman envoy to Spain, 145, 167, 284
Ahmed Vefik Efendi, Ottoman statesman, 215–16
Alarcón, Pedro Antonio de, Spanish author, 139–40
Albaicín, district of Granada, 107–8, 128
álbumes de la Alhambra see visitors' book of the Alhambra
Alcázar of Seville, 60, 65, 75, 116, 219, 223, 253, 266–7
Alfonso VI, King of Leon, Galicia and Castile, 287
Alfonso XII, King of Spain, 81
Alfonso XIII, King of Spain, 92, 139, 323 n9
Algeciras Conference, 141–2
Algeria, Algerian, Algiers, 59, 63–4, 87, 93–6, 250, 255; *see also* Maghreb
Alhambresque, 16, 39–41, 53, 55n119, 66, 68, 193–4, 216n203, 217, 222, 326; *see also* Moresque, Mudejar
ʿAlī ben Muḥammad, manager of the Beni Zoug-Zoug company of acrobats (1871), 94–5
Ali Kemal Bey, Ottoman journalist and author (1899), 274–6
Ali Kemal Sırrı, Ottoman visitor (1908), 296, 298
Âli Pasha, Ottoman statesman, 146, 148, 209
Aliaga Romarosa, Pedro, Spanish visitor (1879), 90
Almagro y Cárdenas, Antonio, Arabist from Granada (1885, 1889), 102, 106, 110, 112, 134n184, 135–6, 138, 140–1, 170–1
Almaric, Adrien-Augustin, comte de Mailly, marquis d'Haucourt et de Nesle, prince d'Orange, former French governor of the Alhambra (1833), 84–5
Almohad,154, 303 ; *see also* Yaʿqūb al-Manṣūr
Amazigh, 254, 324; *see also* Berber; Chraïbi; Ṭāriq ibn Ziyād
America, American, 13, 44–5, 47, 80, 85n33, 183, 266, 307–8, 323; *see also* Indies; United States
anarchism, 291
Anatolia, 189, 193, 199, 217, 221, 273n124, 278, 305n201, 311; *see also* Turkey
al-Andalus, 1, 19, 42, 48, 71, 77, 118, 159, 161, 167, 173, 177, 179 182–3, 185–6, 188–91, 202, 204, 224, 226, 228, 230, 233, 239, 242–3, 246, 250–2, 255, 262–3, 267–70, 280, 282–3, 286, 299, 301, 303–8, 310, 311, 315n2, 316, 321–2; see also *History of al-Andalus*
Andalusia, Andalusian, 7–8, 11n14, 14, 16, 19, 24, 28, 33, 42–3, 46, 48–51, 54, 57, 59–66, 68, 75, 77, 80–1, 88, 98, 115, 117, 119–20, 123–4, 127, 132, 135, 142, 150, 157–60, 166–8, 170–1, 175–6, 178–9, 183–9, 192–3, 196, 199, 202, 207, 214, 217, 224–6, 228–33, 240, 242, 245, 250, 252–5, 257, 259–60, 263, 265–72, 279–81, 284–6, 297–9, 303, 305–12, 314–18, 320–5, 327–9
Andalusia under the Moors (L'Andalousie au temps des Maures), section of the 1900 Paris exhibition, 60–6
Anichar, Moses, member of a Moroccan delegation (1885), 100, 104
Antoni, Gustav, German visitor (1897, 1899), 92
apostasy, 293
Arab and Moorish Monuments of Cordoba, Seville and Granada (*Monuments arabes et moresques de Cordoba, Séville et Grenade*) by Girault de Prangey (1837), 33–4
Arab Antiquities of Spain (*Antigüedades árabes de España*), by Hermosilla (1787), 23–4

Arabian Antiquities of Spain, by Murphy (1815), 24–5, 74–5, 110n 115
Arabism
ideology, 244, 249–50, 252, 254, 263, 268, 276, 278, 299, 310–11
philology, 92, 101–2, 106, 112, 140n208, 169, 237, 238n32
Aramoun, village of Mount Lebanon, 170–1
archaeology, 153, 155, 166, 215
archbishop's palace, Granada, 150–1
architecture, 13, 16, 19, 23–7, 29, 31–41, 54, 58–61, 68, 70, 72–4, 77, 82, 84, 86, 100, 119-20, 140, 151–2, 167, 193–224, 253, 287, 299, 302–3, 319, 321, 328–9
Arfaʿ ud-Dowla Mīrzā Reẓā Khān, Iranian ambassador in Istanbul (1902), 322–3
Argote, Simón de, Granadan author, 28
Armenians, Armenian, 172–3, 199, 212, 275n128; *see also* Balian
Arslān, Amīn, Ottoman Druze diplomat (1910), 263, 315
Arslān, Shakīb, Druze intellectual, Arabist, 142n215, 263–5, 311, 315, 325
Asia, Asian, Asiatic, 51–2, 206
autocracy, 231, 244, 262n95, 281; *see also* Abdülhamid II
Azancot, Carmen (1885), 101–2; *see also* **Bula y Azancot**

Baedeker guidebooks, 108n111, 178n98, 277, 283, 287–9, 291, 295n172, 299, 302–5, 322, 327, 329
Baghdad, 48, 95n69, 174n89, 185–6, 210, 304
Balian, Agop and Sarkis, Ottoman Armenian architects, 197–8, 201, 209–11, 213, 218
Balkans, 178, 188–9, 251, 268–70
Baragnon, Pierre, French journalist in Istanbul, 205–6
barbarian(s), barbaric, barbarism, barbary, 25, 42, 45, 47, 60, 86, 90, 118–19, 124, 165, 185–6, 188, 250, 306
Barcelona, 148–9, 151, 159, 175–6, 269, 272, 286, 290–1, 297
Bayezid II, Ottoman sultan, 309
Bedouin(s), 55, 87, 307n206
Beirut, 1, 170–1, 251, 259, 327
Belgium, Belgian, 173, 221
Benalúa, Count of, 272, 302
Benderli Mehmed Selim Sırrı Pasha, Ottoman grand vizier, 247
Beni Zoug-Zoug, company of acrobats (1871), 94–5
Benton, Charles William, American academic (1894), 92
Berber, 63, 94, 139, 254, 312n217, 324; *see also* Amazigh
Bertrand, Louis, French author and traveller, 252–3
Beyatlı, Yahya Kemal *see* Yahya Kemal [Beyatlı]
Beylerbeyi Palace, Istanbul, 209, 215n198
Bezirdjian, Sopon, Ottoman Armenian artist and craftsman, 197–9
Billecocq, de, secretary of the French embassy in Madrid (1829), 82–3
Black Legend (*leyenda negra*), 41–50
Boabdil (Moḥammed XI), Nasrid Emir of Granada, 27, 154
Boabdil el Chico (Moḥammed XII), last Nasrid Emir of Granada, 30n30, 33, 84, 123, 125, 192n143, 235, 298
sword, 106, 111, 128–9
Bonforti, C., French colonist and visitor from Algiers (1847), 87
Bourgeois, Marie Auguste Antoine, French architect, 204–8, 213
Brīsha, ʿAbdelkerīm, Moroccan ambassador (1895), 112, 130
Brīsha, Lʿarbi, Moroccan ambassador (1880), 99, 120, 123–5
British *see* Great Britain
Browne, Edward Granville, Persian instructor at Cambridge (1900), 92
Buḥturī, Walīd ibn ʿUbayd Allāh, Syrian poet, 269
Bula y Azancot, Isabel (1885), 101–2
bullfighting, 113, 120, 285n141
Burford, Robert, British artist and entrepreneur, 37
Burton, Decimus, British architect, 36–37

Cairo, 38–9, 63, 132, 185, 217–19, 242, 244, 246, 249, 251–2, 255, 259–60, 274–5, 321, 327
caliphate, 228, 232, 234–6, 243, 245, 252, 278, 305, 321
Camino, José, Granadan photographer, 103, 109
Campana de la vela, Granadan newspaper, 150–1, 153, 158
Cano y Masas, Leopoldo, Spanish poet (1889), 89–90, 124, 296
Cano, Alonso, Spanish artist, 151, 155
Cárdenas *see* Almagro Cárdenas
Carlism, Carlist, 89, 102, 157
Carlos III, King of Spain, 23, 75
Cartali, Themistocles, Greek philanthropist (1900), 172
Cartuja (Charterhouse) of Granada, 153, 157
Casado, José, Chief of the section for the development of Granada (1885), 100–1
Casas, Bartolomé de las, Dominican priest and critic of Spanish colonisation in America, 45
Casiri de Gartia, Miguel, Spanish Arabist of Maronite origin, 24, 70, 169–70
Castillanos, Manuel Pablo, Spanish visitor (1876), 90
Castrillo, Alonso, Governor of Granada (1885), 100–1
cathedral, 49, 221, 250, 287
  Granada, 23, 42, 113, 150–1, 155
  Lisbon, 289
Celal Nuri [İleri], Young Turk intellectual, 306–11
Cemile Hanım, Ottoman visitor (1907), 274n127, 296–7
chapel of Santo Cristo de la Luz, Toledo, 287
Charles V, Habsburg emperor, King of Spain, 85, 89–90, 125n165–6, 284, 287–8, 299, 302
  Charles V's Palace at the Alhambra, 67, 89, 98n77, 109, 128, 136, 246
Chateaubriand, François-René de, French author, 26–7, 29, 33, 50, 53, 68, 88, 162, 191, 263, 315, 325, 329
Chorrojumo, (Mariano Fernández Santiago), 'Prince of the Gypsies', 107, 293–5
Chraïbi, Driss, Moroccan author, 254
Christian, Christianity, 29, 37, 48–9, 62, 68, 76, 78, 88, 102n92, 116–18, 124, 133–4, 138, 143, 169, 171–2, 180, 185, 189, 222, 231, 233, 246–7, 250–2, 254, 270, 281, 288, 308–9
  Catholicism, Catholic, 39, 45, 47n86, 50, 68, 70, 90n46, 92, 109n114, 124–5, 140–1, 152, 155, 162, 169–70, 172, 176, 185, 212, 253n78, 298
  Christian Arabs, 168–72, 233, 246, 251
  see also Maronites
Çinili Köşk (Tiled Pavilion), Istanbul, 206, 208
Cinq-Mars, novel by Alfred de Vigny (1826), 50
Çırağan Palace, Istanbul, 200, 209, 222
civilisation, 35, 47–8, 50–2, 54–5, 60, 66–7, 71–2, 77, 88, 117–19, 123–4, 128, 143–4, 154–6, 168, 175–6, 185–6, 188, 191–3, 201, 224, 227–9, 235–6, 239, 251–5, 296, 298, 303–8, 310, 318, 322, 328–9
Claris de Florian, Jean-Pierre, French author, 22
Clarke, Edward Marmaduke, British entrepreneur, 38
colonialism, colonies, 14, 59, 62–3, 66, 157, 216, 219, 244, 251, 255, 263, 269–70, 277, 321
  French, 62–3, 87, 253, 255
  Spanish, 41, 44, 66, 70–1, 134, 139–41, 255, 319, 327
  see also africanismo; imperialism
Committee of Union and Progress, 249–50, 297; *see also* Young Turks
connected histories, 324, 328; *see also* entangled history; *histoire croisée*
Constantinople *see* Istanbul
Contreras Granja, Mariano, architect of the Alhambra (1885), 100
Contreras y Muñoz, Rafael, caretaker of the Alhambra, 54
Cordoba, 23–4, 26, 40, 60, 75–6, 79, 81, 90, 105–6, 114n133, 116, 118–19, 126,

131, 176, 185–6, 190, 221, 230–2, 250, 257–8, 264–6, 270, 283, 286–7, 297–9, 301, 311, 317, 323, 325, 328
costume, 1, 5–11, 49, 52, 57, 62–3, 72, 100, 104, 107, 109n114, 149–50, 264–6, 276, 291, 293–5, 300; *see also* fez; hat; turban
Court of the Lions (*patio de los Leones*), Alhambra, 22–3, 25, 27, 32, 35–6, 38n58, 41, 54, 59, 60–2, 72–4, 98, 102–3, 121, 130, 258, 300–1
  fountain, 31–2, 70, 106, 109, 154, 168
  pavilions (*templetes*), 54, 74, 103
Court of the Maidens (*patio de las Doncellas*), Alcázar of Seville, 65, 267
Court of the Myrtles (*patio de los Arrayanes*), Alhambra, 51, 59, 81, 108, 122, 302
Crusades, Crusaders, 87, 156, 189, 221, 244, 308
Crystal Palace, London, 35–8
Ctesiphon *see* Khosrow's Palace

Dampierre, Salvador Amadeo, representative of the government of Granada (1844), 148
dance, 25, 29, 47, 49–50, 61–3, 152, 322
  Dance in Andalusia (*Endülüs'te Raks*), poem by Yahya Kemal Beyatlı (1933), 311–4
  see also flamenco; *jaleo*
Daoud, Mohammed, Moroccan historian from Tétouan, 142–3, 263–5, 315, 325
Dāvud, ʿAbdallah Khalīl, Christian Arab visitor (1849), 168–9
decline, decadence, degeneration, 191–2, 222, 243, 281, 296, 304–5, 307–11
Defensor de Granada, Granadan newspaper, 94, 100, 102, 104–6, 110–14, 126, 129–31, 135–6, 142, 258, 264
Delaunay, French visitor (1879), 85
Dethier, Philipp Anton, director of the Ottoman Imperial Museum, 207
Diebitsch, Carl von, German architect, 40, 217–18
Dimitriadis, Mikhail, ambassador Fuad Efendi's servant (1844), 145–7
Dinet, Étienne, French artist, 63–4
Disraeli, Benjamin, British statesman (1830), 49, 53
Dolgorukov, Dimitri Ivanovich, Russian prince (1829), 82–4
Dolmabahçe Palace, Istanbul, 200, 216
Doré, Gustave, French artist, 59, 66
Druze, 262–3, 270; *see also* Arslān
Dusé Mohamed, Egyptian intellectual of Nubian origin, 253–4
Duval, Albert, French visitor (1878), 86

East, Eastern *see* Orient
Echeverría, Juan Velázquez de, Granadan author, 28, 170
eclecticism, 37–9, 200, 204–5, 217, 223, 264
economy, 76, 183, 228, 320
Edhem Pasha, Ottoman statesman, 179, 196, 221
Edirne (Adrianople), 268–9
Egypt, Egyptian, 31, 33, 35, 59, 79, 132, 148, 211, 217–19, 237–8, 244–55, 262, 268–71, 273–6, 322, 328; *see also* Cairo; nationalism
Elias, Edward, Egyptian visitor (1895), 246
England, English *see* Great Britain
entangled history, 324, 328; *see also* connected histories; ***histoire croisée***
Ersoy, Ahmet, art historian, 179n101, 196, 197n153, 220
Essay on the Architecture of the Arabs and Moors (*Essai sur l'architecture des Arabes et des Mores*) by Girault de Prangey (1841), 34
Estébanez Calderón, Serafín, Spanish Arabist, 102
Estrella de Occidente, Granadan periodical, 141, 170–1
ethnography, 61, 77
Eugénie de Montijo, Empress of France, 209–11, 217
Europe, European, 25, 27–8, 38, 41–2, 44–7, 49–2, 65, 69–70, 94, 106, 117, 120, 127, 149–50, 156, 163, 165, 168, 171, 174–5, 182, 185–9, 191–4,

198, 200–2, 204–6, 209, 211–19, 222–3, 231, 241, 244–5, 250–1, 254, 277, 281, 289, 291, 301–2, 305–7, 309, 314, 318, 320–1, 323, 327–9; *see also* West
exile, 32, 125, 175, 177, 187, 189, 235, 247, 251, 269, 289, 300
exoticism, 16, 29, 34, 46, 59, 62, 70, 72, 88, 94, 115, 129, 135, 149, 216, 223, 236, 239, 293–4, 311, 314, 322, 328

fanaticism, 50, 89, 176, 296, 304, 308
fantasia, 62, 93–4
Farīd, Muḥammad, Egyptian author and politician (1901), 249–50, 255, 323
Fāssī, Muḥammad bin Aḥmad, member of a Moroccan delegation (1889), 105
fatalism, resignation, 49, 57, 121, 303
Favart, Antoine-Pierre-Charles, French artist and author (1829), 82
Ferdinand II of Aragon and V of Castile, 29, 42, 87, 129, 152, 156, 189, 298n182
Feridun Bey, Ottoman minister in Madrid (1896), 271–2
Fernández de Córdoba y Aguilar, Gonzalo, general serving the Catholic rulers in 1492, 22, 29–30, 85
Fernández Santiago, Mariano *see* Chorrojumo
Fernández y González, Francisco, professor of literature in Granada (1857), 90
Fernández y González, Manuel, Spanish author, 67
Ferrero, J. Emilio, Spanish visitor (1899), 88–9
fez, 149–50, 154, 175, 291, 300; *see also* costume, hat, turban
flamenco, 66, 312, 314, 322; *see also* dance; *jaleo*
flamenquismo, 66; *see also* Orientalism
Forbin, Auguste, comte de, French artist and author, 29–30
Ford, Richard, British author of guidebooks, 49–51, 54–5
Fortuny, Marià, Catalan artist, 57–8, 107n108
France, French, 22–3, 26, 29–30, 43–4, 50, 54, 57, 62–3, 67, 82, 84–8, 93–4, 96, 108, 115, 117–18, 138–9, 143–5, 147, 149, 151, 153–4, 156–8, 161–3, 175, 177, 179, 186, 203–4, 207, 209–11, 214, 221, 228, 233–4, 237, 241–2, 245–6, 252–5, 266, 272–6, 278, 284, 287, 299–300, 307, 319, 323
Francoism, 143
Franks *see* Christian
Frashëri, *see* Şemseddin Sami [Frashëri]
Frémond, Georges, abbot, canon of Alger (1893), 87
Friller, Ramón, Spanish visitor (1879), 90
Fuad Efendi/Pasha, Ottoman envoy and statesman (1844), 144–68, 172–8, 199, 202–4, 271–2, 322
mausoleum, 166–7, 199, 202–4

García, José, brigadier in the Spanish regiment of invalids, 31
Garzón Rodríguez, Rafael, photographer in Granada, 7–12, 1, 208–9, 257, 264–6, 291–5, 325–6
Gautier, Théophile, French author, 51, 53, 57–8
Gavilanes, Joaquín, substitute mayor of Granada (1885), 100
Generalife, 10, 25, 59, 81, 91, 97, 99, 110–12, 116, 221, 295
Georgia, Georgian, 87–8
Germany, German, 22, 38–9, 60, 153, 207, 221, 268
Gérôme, Jean-Léon, French artist, 5, 52–3
Gezirah Palace, Cairo, 217–18
Ghassānī, al-Wazīr, Moroccan envoy, 77
Ghāzī, Qaddūr, Moroccan ambassador (1906), 114, 129n175
Ghazīrī, Mikhail *see* Casiri de Gartia
Ghazzāl, ʿAbu'l-ʿAbbas Aḥmed ibn al-Mahdī al-Fāsī al-Andalusī al-Ḥimyarī, Moroccan envoy, 75–8
Ghrīssī, ʿAlī bin al-Bachīr al-Charīf al-Husnī, Maghrebi visitor (1863), 95–6, 121n156

Giralda, Seville, 60, 65, 219
Girault de Prangey, Joseph-Philibert, French artist and photographer, 33–4
Gladstone, William, British statesman, 189
Gómez Carrión, Fulgencio, officer in the Guardia Civil (1916), 90–2
González Alcantud, José Antonio, anthropologist and historian, 54, 328
Gonzalo of Cordoba *see* Fernández de Córdoba y Aguilar
Gothic, Neogothic, 37, 39, 47–8, 86, 106, 182, 196, 217, 219, 221–2
Goury, Jules, French architect (1834), 33–4, 84, 325
Grammar of Ornament by Jones (1856), 35, 198
Granada, 22–3, 25–8, 30–3, 37, 41–2, 47, 50, 54, 57, 59, 61, 67–9, 73, 75–8, 81–2, 84–5, 88–91, 93, 95–9, 102–3, 105–7, 111–13, 115–16, 119, 123–6, 128, 133, 135–6, 141–2, 144–5, 147–8, 150–8, 167, 170, 173–4, 176–7, 180, 189, 219, 221, 225–6, 228–9, 236, 239, 242, 246, 253, 263, 271–2, 282, 285-6, 292, 294, 302–4, 311–13, 317, 319, 324–5
  fall of, 29, 85, 125, 141, 189, 250, 268, 282, 298–9, 308
Great Britain, British, England, English, 22–3, 37–9, 59, 67, 70, 92, 95, 108, 119, 139, 144, 163, 174, 197, 203, 207, 214–15, 221, 245, 250, 253–4, 266, 269, 278, 307, 323
Greece, Greek, 26, 35, 52, 60, 145–6, 150, 169, 172, 174, 228
Griffin, Henry, British visitor (1900), 92
Gypsy, 34, 47, 57–9, 61–2, 81, 107, 293–5, 300, 328; *see also* Chorrojumo

Hagia Eirene, Istanbul, 156
Hagia Sophia, Istanbul, 156, 289
Hall of the Ambassadors (*sala de los Embajadores*), Alhambra, 31n34, 98, 109, 121–2
Hall of the Boat (*sala de la Barca*), Alhambra, Alhambra, 108
Hall of the Kings (*sala de los Reyes*), Alhambra, 154
Hall of the Two Sisters (*sala de las dos Hermanas*), Alhambra, 108–9
Hamelberg, Gustav von, German visitor (1829), 84
Hand-Book for Travellers in Spain by Ford (1845), 49
Ḥarīshī, L'arbī bin Aḥmad, Moroccan ambassador (1908), 114
hat, 73–4, 175, 276, 293, 300; *see also* fez, turban
Heffernet, Henry, American academic (1901), 92
Hilmi *see* Tunalı Hilmi Efendi
Hispano-Mauritanian Union, 102, 141
histoire croisée, 324, 328
History of al-Andalus (*Tarih-i Endülüs*) by Ziya Pasha (1859), 167, 179–83, 186–7
History of the Arabs and Moors of Spain (*Histoire des Arabes et des Mores d'Espagne*) by Viardot (1833), 179–81
History of the Factions of the Zegri and the Abencerrages (*Historia de los bandos de Zegríes y Abencerrajes*) by Pérez de Hita (1595), 27
Hugo, Joseph Sigisbert Léopold, French officer, father of Victor Hugo, 30
Hugo, Victor, French author and poet, 51–3
Hünkâr İskelesi, Istanbul, 209–10
Hüseyin Hüsnü Sermed, *see* Sermed Efendi

ideology, 70–1, 137, 140–1, 172, 192, 194, 214, 220, 243, 245–6, 249, 252–3, 276–7, 284, 299, 311, 315, 321, 327–8
Ilbīrī , Abū al-Qāsim Khalaf bin Faraj *see* al-Sumaysir, 242
İleri *see* Celal Nuri [İleri]
Ilustración española y americana, 81, 121–2
Immaculate Conception by Cano, 155
Imperial Café, Toledo, 286–7
Imperial Museum, Istanbul, 156, 207
imperialism, 251, 263, 270, 320
India, Indian, 59, 253
Indies, 45–6
Inquisition, 45, 89, 184–5, 308
Iran *see* Persia

Irving, Washington, American author (1829), 32–4, 37, 41, 46–51, 53, 67–8, 82, 113, 266–7, 327
Irwin, Robert, historian, 55–7
Isabella I, Queen of Castile, 78, 85, 87, 129, 152
Isabella II, Queen of Spain, 145, 148, 160, 162
Islam, Islamic, Muslim, 28–9, 42, 48–9, 60, 67–8, 70–2, 74–9, 85–6, 91, 93, 107, 116–20, 124, 127, 133, 139, 143–5, 150, 152–5, 167–9, 172, 174–6, 179, 183–9, 191–2, 194, 199–201, 219, 222, 224, 225–31, 233–6, 239, 241–4, 246–7, 250–3, 255, 263, 269–71, 277–8, 280-1, 283, 286, 288, 293, 296–8, 303–11, 314–15, 318–19, 321–2, 327–9; *see also* pan-Islamism
Ismail Pasha, governor and khedive of Egypt, 217–18, 222, 275
Istanbul, 30, 41, 54, 60, 156, 160, 162–3, 166, 172–3, 193, 195–8, 202, 204–7, 209–12, 214, 216–17, 219, 223, 229, 232, 243–4, 259, 271, 274–5, 278–9, 281, 283, 289, 300, 302, 314, 318, 320–1, 323, 327
Italy, Italian, 32, 41, 47, 149, 228
İzzet Fuad Pasha, Ottoman officer, minister in Madrid (1903), 272–3, 279, 302

jaleo (chorus of Flamenco musicians and dancers), 152
Jerez, 171, 230, 312, 314
Jerusalem, 1, 163, 246, 259, 262
Jews, Jewish, 41, 61, 100, 102, 158, 185, 323, 213, 216–18, 325
Jones, Owen, British architect (1834), 33–5, 37, 84, 197–9, 201
Journey to al-Andalus (*Riḥla ila'l-Andalus*) by Aḥmad Shawqī (1919), 270
Juderías, Julián, Spanish author, 43–5, 66

Kaddouri, Abdelmajid, historian, 117
Kagan, Richard, historian, 47
Kâmil Bey, Fuad Efendi's secretary and brother-in-law (1844), 145, 147, 158, 271
Kāmil, Muṣṭafa, Egyptian nationalist, 249, 252
Karatheodori, Stephanos/Étienne, Ottoman Greek diplomat (1882), 173–4
Kardūdī, Abu al-ʿAbbās Aḥmad, secretary of a Moroccan legation (1885), 100, 104
Kardūdī, Aḥmad bin Muḥammad bin ʿAbdelqāder Kardūdī, secretary of a Moroccan delegation (1885, 1889), 79, 93, 99–100, 103–6, 108–9, 112, 114, 116–17, 120, 126–7
Kardūdī, Muḥammad bin Aḥmad, member of a Moroccan delegation (1910), 114
Keçecizade *see* Fuad Efendi/Pasha
Kemalism, 277, 305
Kerckhove, Eugène de, Ottoman diplomat of Belgian origin, minister in Madrid (1859), 173–4
Khālidī, Khalīl Djawād, Ottoman Palestinian judge and scholar (1904), 1–5, 7–15, 255–61, 266–7, 291–2, 318, 325
Khālidī, Rāgheb, Palestinian scholar, 12
Khālidī, Rūḥī, Ottoman Palestinian scholar and diplomat (1907), 261–2
Khedive Ismail's palace, Altunizade, Istanbul, 222–3
Khosrow's Palace at Ctesiphon, 180, 269
Khūrī Ilyās, Nicolas, Greek Orthodox from Bethlehem (1881), 169
Khūrī Ilyās, Panayot, Greek Orthodox from Bethlehem (1881), 169
Kitrānī, ʿAbdallah, Moroccan notable, 78
Koran, 73–4, 106, 121, 145, 154–5, 226, 232, 234–5, 280, 298, 303n197
Kufic script, 153, 155, 168, 182, 232, 303

Lā ghāliba illā Allah (There is no victor but God), Nasrid motto, 87, 91, 155, 222, 303n198, 304
Laborde, Alexandre, count of, French archaeologist and scholar, 23–7, 32, 39, 72–5
Láchar, Granada, 272

Lafuente Alcántara, Miguel, historian of Granada, 152–5
laments, 26, 28, 42, 75–8, 84, 89, 109, 120, 128, 156, 184, 188, 235, 236, 241–2, 247, 250, 255, 258–9, 266, 268, 288, 296, 298, 302; *see also* Moor's sigh; sighs; tears
L'arbī bin Ḥussain, Moroccan qaid (1885), 100
lead books of Sacromonte, 69, 170
Lebanon, Lebanese, 61, 169–70, 266–7, 270, 276
León, Rogelia, Granadan poet, 67
Les Orientales, collection of poems by Victor Hugo (1829), 30, 51–2
Levant, Levantine 26, 169, 171, 255, 262, 271, 322–3; *see also* Lebanon; Mashreq; Palestine; Syria
Lévy, Arthur, French historian, 43–4
Lewis, Bernard, British historian, 183
Lewis, John Frederick, British artist, 33–4
Lewis, Thomas Hayter, British architect, 38
leyenda negra see Black Legend
Leyla Şerife Hanım, daughter of Halil Şerif Pasha and Marie-Anne Detourbay (1899), 274–7
libros de firmas see visitors' book of the Alhambra
Lisbon, 82, 236–7, 286, 288–9
London, 29, 35–9, 148, 197, 237, 245, 300
Lussy, Édouard de, French architect (1829), 82

Ma'lūf, Yūsuf Na'mān, Christian Arab from New York, 164–5
Madrid, 23, 82, 84, 90, 99, 104, 113, 116, 135, 139, 145, 150, 159, 162, 173, 225–6, 227, 230, 232, 271, 273, 279, 285, 300, 302, 311
Maghreb, Maghrebi; see also Algeria, Morocco, Tunisia, 26, 72–144, 159, 198, 229, 231, 233, 243, 254–5, 271, 284, 308, 318–19, 323–4
Malek Salem, poet from Tétouan (1876), 133–43, 227, 239
manuscripts, 79, 106, 116–18, 130, 164, 184, 230
Maqqarī, Aḥmad Moḥammad, Algerian historian, 131–2, 242, 260, 261n91, 269, 277, 329
Maria II, Queen of Portugal, 148, 162–3
Marin, Scipion, French author, 27
Maronites, 24, 70, 169–72, 233, 262n95, 266, 320
Mashreq, 138, 144, 233–41, 246, 249, 254, 270, 281, 318, 320; *see also* Lebanon; Levant; Palestine; Syria
Matar, Nabil, historian, 78, 255
Mauritania, Mauritanian, 79, 102, 117–18
Maurophilia, Maurophobia, 70, 85–92, 124, 127, 319
Mecidi order, 200
medievalism, 29, 46, 159, 201
Medina Azahara (Madīnat al-Zahrā), 132, 242
Mediterranean, 60, 169, 233, 322
Mehmed II, Ottoman sultan, 156
Mehmed Kâmil Bey bin Numan, fifth secretary at the Imperial Palace (1892), 233–7, 239, 244, 246, 271
Melhamé, Jean-Antoine, solicitor in Beirut (1910), 262
Mema'a, Ḍoumit, Maronite visitor (1883), 169
Mérali, doctor, Georgian physician of the Negus of Ethiopia (1919), 87
al-Mo'aṭī bin 'Abdelkebīr Mezāmsī, Moroccan ambassador (1889), 104–12
micro-history, 316, 324
Middle Ages, 54, 185, 199, 290, 301, 307
Midhat Pasha, Ottoman statesman and grand vizier (1877), 174–8, 189, 210, 227
Mīkhā'il, Yūhanā, Maronite visitor (1881), 169
Miknāsī, Muḥammad ibn 'Uthmān, Moroccan envoy, 77–9, 93
Misfīqī, 'Abdelqāder bin Houari, member of a company of Algerian horsemen (1900), 93
modernity, modern, 38, 42–3, 47, 65–6, 68–9, 99, 109, 112, 118, 148, 154, 156, 168, 176, 178, 188, 194, 202, 219–20, 223–4, 225–313, 318, 321

Mokrī, Muḥammad, Moroccan grand vizier (1916), 114
Monasa, Elias, language teacher at the School of Fraternal Charity in Aramoun (1880), 170–1
Monastery of San Jerónimo, Granada, 151
Montani, Pietro, Italian architect serving the Ottoman government, 207n181, 213, 220–2
Moor's sigh (*suspiro del moro*), 125, 129; *see also* laments; sighs; tears
Moors, Moorish, 22–3, 25, 28, 34, 37–8, 42, 47–9, 54–6, 60, 62–3, 65–9, 72, 74–5, 86–7, 89, 94–7, 108, 113, 115, 123–6, 128–9, 135, 142, 153–4, 176, 229, 253, 264, 291, 293, 320, 325, 327–8; *see also* Arabs; Moresque; Moriscos; Saracens
Moresque, 9, 11, 13–14, 19, 27, 29, 32, 34–5, 37–42, 47, 51–2, 60, 61, 68, 73, 166, 193–202, 204–22, 321; *see also* Alhambresque, Mudejar
Moriscos, 42, 62, 68–9, 77, 109n114, 250
Morocco, Moroccan, 62–3, 70–1, 73–4, 76–9, 93–145, 148, 153, 155–6, 159, 168, 176, 199, 229, 232, 237, 243, 250, 255, 258, 260, 315, 318–19, 324–5; *see also* Maghreb
mosque(s), 38, 99, 160, 184, 195, 203–4, 209, 246, 287–9
  Aissaoua, Tétouan, 60
  Alhambra, 67, 126
  Cordoba, 23, 76, 79, 81, 105, 116, 118, 126, 231, 250, 264–6, 270, 283–4, 287, 298–302, 311, 317, 323
  Pertevniyal Valide Sultan, Aksaray, Istanbul, 220–2
  Rüstem Pasha, Istanbul, 5–6
  Tangier, 60
Mowāz, Aḥmed, Moroccan ambassador (1910), 114
Muallim Naci, Ottoman author, 191–2, 251
Mudejar, 40, 75; *see also* Alhambresque, Moresque
Muḥammad bin Jalūl, member of a company of Algerian horsemen (1900), 93
Muḥammad bin Madanī bin Nīs, secretary of a Moroccan legation (1889), 104–5
Muḥammad I, founder of the Nasrid dynasty, 304
Muḥammad III, Sultan of Morocco, 75, 77–8
Muḥammad IV, Sultan of Morocco, 139
Muḥammad XI *see* Boabdil
Muḥammad XII *see* Boabdil el Chico
Mulāy Ḥasan, Nasrid Emir of Granada, 154
Münir Süreyya Bey, Ottoman consul in Barcelona, 297–8
Murphy, James Cavanah, Irish architect, 24–5, 42, 74–5
Mūsà ibn Nuṣayr, commander of the Muslim conquest of Spain, 190
museum, 287, 299
  Alhambra, 98n77, 110, 128
  Istanbul, 156, 207
Muslim *see* Islam

Nafiz Bey, notable from Chios, 232–3
Nahḍa (Arab awakening), 243–4, 251, 253–5, 262–3, 270–1, 276–7, 321–2
Na'īm, Ibrāhīm, Maronite visitor (1879, 1883), 169–70
Namık Kemal, Ottoman author, 186–7
Napoleon I, French emperor, 30, 43–4
nationalism, nationalist, 44, 124, 185, 189, 254
  Arab, 167, 172, 193, 249, 252–3, 263, 276, 310
  Egyptian, 249, 250–3, 268–9
  Turkish, 167, 193, 321
  see also Arabism; pan-Arabism; pan-Islamism
Nazlı/Nazli, Egyptian princess (1899), 274–7
Necib Pasha, Ottoman minister in Madrid, 271
Newman, Daniel, historian, 117
Noailles, Nathalie, Countess of, Count of Laborde's sister, 26–7
nostalgia, 46, 77, 88, 90, 94, 130, 134–5, 138, 145, 202, 204, 233, 239, 242–3, 252, 255, 269, 270, 278, 283, 289, 299
Nubia, Nubian, 52, 100, 253

O'Donnel, Leopoldo, Spanish officer and statesman, 70, 139
Orient, Oriental, East, Eastern, 30, 37–8, 41, 48–54, 57–8, 60, 62, 66–7, 72, 124, 136–7, 144, 148–50, 158, 162, 164, 167, 170–1, 173, 176, 178, 192, 194, 198–203, 207, 209, 211, 214, 217, 219, 221–3, 226, 231, 243, 253–5, 264, 266, 276, 279, 281, 286, 295, 301–5, 312, 320–3 325, 327–9
Orientalism, Orientalist, 4–5, 7–8, 11, 13–14, 16, 30, 33, 38, 41, 49–71, 87–8, 92, 129–30, 140, 157, 162, 167, 193–4, 200, 214, 216, 236–7, 245, 257, 265–6, 272–3, 278–9, 293, 304–5, 307, 309, 319–20, 327–8
  Congress of Lisbon, 236–7
  Congress of London, 237–8, 240, 245
  Ottoman/Turkish, 4–5, 66–7, 69–70, 157, 272–3, 278–9, 304, 305n201, 307, 309, 327–8
  Spanish, 16, 66–7, 70, 94, 129–30, 140, 319, 327–8
  see also *flamenquismo*
Osman Hamdi Bey, Ottoman artist and director of the Imperial Museum, 4–7
Osmani order, 200–1, 233
Ottoman Architecture (*L'Architecture ottomane*) (1873), 196–7, 220–1
Ottoman Empire, Ottoman, Ottomans, 144–228, 231–4, 243–5, 247–9, 251, 261, 263, 267–78, 284–6, 289–90, 299–301, 304, 305–6, 308–10, 314, 320, 322–4, 327–8
Ottoman Exhibition of 1863 in Istanbul, 204–7
Ouled Naïl, Algeria, 63–4

Palestine, Palestinian, 1, 33, 255, 257, 260, 266
pan-Africanism, 253
pan-Islamism, 243, 263, 271, 278
Paradela, Nieves, historian, 239, 317
Paris, 31–2, 40, 57, 60–6, 104, 112, 114, 132, 146, 158, 221, 240, 260, 263, 274–7, 290, 300, 302
Parvillée, Léon, French artist serving the Ottoman government, 206, 213
patio árabe (Arab courtyard), 2, 7–10, 266, 291–4, 326; *see also* Garzón Rodríguez
patriotism, 70, 186, 192, 252, 267
Paula Valladar, Francisco de, Granadan author, 96–7
Pera, district of Istanbul, 209, 212, 223
Pérès, Henri, French Arabist, 75, 77–9, 99, 116–17, 239, 255, 317
Pérez de Hita, Ginés, Spanish author, 27, 68
Persia, Persian, 38-9, 52, 54, 92, 156, 171, 180, 198, 221, 228, 308; *see also* Arfa' ud-Dowla Mīrzā Reẓā Khān
photography, photographs 1–5, 7–12, 102–3, 107–9, 130, 220, 256–9, 263–7, 276–7, 291–5, 300–1, 315, 325–6; *see also* Garzón Rodríguez; Girault de Prangey
Picturesque and Historical Travels to Spain (*Voyage pittoresque et historique de l'Espagne*) by Laborde (1812), 23, 25–7, 32, 72–3
Picturesque Travels in Spain (*Voyage pittoresque en Espagne*) by Baron Taylor (1832), 32
Plateresque, neo-Plateresque, 39–40, 66
poetry, 2-4, 52-3, 55, 59, 67, 78, 79, 84, 88-90, 117–18, 128, 130–2, 134–43, 148, 161–5, 180, 183, 186–7, 226–7, 239, 241–43, 257–60, 268–70, 293, 295, 299, 304, 311–14, 316, 323, 328
polygamy, 308
Portugal, Portuguese, 148, 162–3, 236, 284–7
Poupart, Auguste, French visitor (1841), 87
prayer, 75, 78, 87, 95, 99, 105, 111, 227, 234, 284, 298, 314
press, 32, 37, 38n58, 44, 63, 89, 93, 97–100, 102–5, 111–15, 121, 123–8, 135-6, 140, 147–8, 150–3, 156–9, 161–3, 167–8, 170–1, 175–6, 197, 203–4, 206–7, 211, 214–15, 219–20, 225, 231, 239, 255, 319–20, 324; see also *Defensor de Granada, Estrella de Occidente*
Prim, Juan, Spanish officer and statesman, 57–8

Protestantism, Protestant, 45
Protestant College of Beirut, 251

qaid, 100, 103–5, 112

racism, 140, 253
railroad, 106, 112–13
Ramón Benítez, Salvador, Spanish visitor (1913), 90
Rauda (garden), Alhambra, 110
Reconquista, 29, 67–8, 94, 117, 129, 141, 143, 189
Regnault, Henri, French artist, 55–9
Renan, Ernest, French historian and philologist, 187–8
Rīfī, ʿAbdelṣādeq bin Aḥmad, governor of Tangier, Moroccan ambassador (1885), 100, 229
Rīḥānī, Amīn, American author of Lebanese Maronite origin, 266–8, 323
riḥla, 75, 77, 79–80, 239, 250, 255, 261, 270; *see also* travel accounts
Roberts, David, British artist, 33–4
Roches, Léon, French orientalist and Arabist, 96–7
Rojo Flores, Sandra, historian, 54
romanticism, romantic, 22, 26, 29, 32–4, 37, 46–7, 51, 55, 127, 137, 144, 156, 159, 318
Rome, 32, 35, 37, 302; *see also* Saint Peter
Roseyro, Jean-Samuel, French entrepreneur and impresario, 63–5
Ross, Edward Denison, Persian instructor at London University (1900), 92
Royal Alhambra Palace/Theatre of Varieties, London, 37–8
Royal Panopticon of Science and Art, London, 38–9
Russia, Russian, 82, 163, 189

Safadī, Khalīl bin Aybak, Mamluk historian, 131
Safvet Pasha, Ottoman statesman, 186
Saïd, Edward, scholar and intellectual, 52, 55, 69, 320
Saint Peter, Rome, 302
Saint-Priest, Alexis, Count of, French ambassador in Lisbon (1829), 82
Saints Peter and Paul, church in Galata, Istanbul, 184
Salomé, painting by Regnault (1870), 57–8
Samipaşazade Mahmud Hüdayi Bey, brother of Samipaşazade Sezai Bey (1914), 300
Samipaşazade Sezai Bey, Ottoman author, minister in Madrid (1914), 300–6, 311
San Fernando Royal Academy of Fine Arts, Madrid, 23–4, 41
San Marzano, Ermolao Asinari di, secretary of the Sardinian legation in Madrid (1829), 82
Sánchez Sarabia, Diego, Spanish artist, 23
Sánchez Ximénez, Manuel, Spanish artist, 23
Saracen(ic) style *see* Moresque
Sarasate, Pablo de, Spanish composer and violinist (1881), 169
Sazkâr, slave/companion of Princess Nazlı (1899), 274–5
School of Fraternal Charity, Aramoun, Lebanon, 170–1
Sébastiani, Horace, French officer and diplomat, 28n25, 30, 54, 157
secularism, 289, 296, 305
Sédillot, Louis-Pierre-Eugène, French historian, 250, 306, 325, 329
Selim I, Ottoman sultan, 309
Şemseddin Sami [Frashëri], Ottoman Albanian author and lexicographer, 164, 189, 224
Seraskerat (War Ministry), Istanbul, 207–9
Sermed Efendi, Ottoman minister in Madrid (1883), 225–6, 273
Seville, 41, 47–9, 54, 60, 65, 75, 82, 116, 119, 158, 219, 221, 230, 242, 253, 266–7; *see also* Alcázar of Seville
Seydi Yahya by Şemseddin Sami [Frashëri] (1875), 189
Shawqī, Aḥmad, Egyptian nationalist poet (1919), 79, 268–70, 311, 323
Shinqīṭī, Moḥammed Maḥmūd ibn al-Talāmīd al-Turkuzī, Mauritanian scholar (1887), 79, 117–18, 230, 243, 271
Shorby, poet from Tétouan, 139–40

sighs, 124–5, 128–9, 176, 236, 298; *see also* laments; Moor's sigh; tears
Silaḥdār, Muḥammad Tawḥīd, Egyptian author, journalist and diplomat (1897), 246–9
Silió, César, Spanish politician, 65-6
Siloé, Diego de, Spanish architect and sculptor, 151
Simonet, Francisco Javier, Granadan Arabist (1885), 102, 106, 119, 140, 170n77, 171n78
slavery, 100, 133, 135, 239, 274–6
Souza, Gerardo de, Spanish diplomat (1844), 147–8
Spain, Spanish, Spaniard, 22–5, 26–7, 30–3, 37, 39–55, 57–63, 65–73, 75–9, 81–2, 85–94, 97, 99–100, 102, 104–5, 107, 113, 115, 117–21, 123–4, 127–30, 132–6, 138–42, 145, 147–9, 151, 153–5, 159–65, 168–71, 175–7, 180, 183–7, 189–90, 192–3, 198, 199, 207, 215, 224–8, 230, 232, 235–6, 239, 242–3, 245, 247, 250–1, 253–5, 263–4, 268–71, 283–7, 289–91, 294–6, 299, 301, 304–10, 312–13, 316–20, 322–3, 325, 327–9
Spain (*L'Espagne*) by Davillier (1874), 59
Spath/Chbat, Gabriel, founder of the School of Fraternal Charity in Aramoun (1880), 170–1
Strolls in Granada and its Surroundings (*Paseos por Granada y sus contornos*) by Echeverría (1764), 28, 70
Sumaysir, Granadan poet, 242
Summary Execution, painting by Regnault (1870), 55–7
Sūsī, ʿAbdesselām, Moroccan ambassador (1877), 98, 121–3, 176
Swinburne, Henry, British author and traveller, 24, 41–3, 46
Sylvester II, Pope, 185
synagogue, 41, 202–3, 216
Syria, Syrian, 169, 171, 233, 236–7, 247, 270, 280–1, 308

Tadros, Dimitri Nicolas, travel agent in Jerusalem (1897), 246
Ṭahar ben ʿAbdelqāder, member of a company of Algerian horsemen (1900), 93
Ṭahṭāwī, Rifāʿa, Egyptian author and scholar, 132, 240–1, 260, 325
Talavera, Felipe de, Spanish visitor (1849), 90
Tales of the Alhambra, collection of stories by Washington Irving (1832), 32–4, 46–8, 67, 266, 327
Tamṭamun, Muḥammad, member of a Moroccan delegation (1895), 113
Tangier, 60–1, 94, 100, 102
Ṭanjawī, Aḥmad ben Muḥammad, member of the Beni Zoug-Zoug company of acrobats (1871), 94
Tarhan, Abdülhak Hâmid, *see* Abdülhak Hâmid [Tarhan]
Ṭāriq ibn Ziyād, Berber conqueror of Spain, 77, 119, 189–90, 254, 299
Taylor, Isidore, baron, French intellectual and philanthropist, 32
tears, 73–5, 98, 121, 123, 125, 128, 133, 156, 176, 227, 231, 235, 241–2, 258, 279, 284, 293, 298; *see also* laments; Moor's sigh; sighs
Tétouan, 60, 70, 100, 124, 134, 136, 139, 142–3, 239, 263–4, 315, 325; *see also* Shorby; Daoud; Malek Salem; mosque
The Black Legend and Historical Truth (*La leyenda negra y la verdad histórica*) essay by Julián Juderías (1914), 43–5
The Grief of the Pasha (*La Douleur du pacha*), painting by Jean-Léon Gérôme (1885), 52–3
The New Andalus (*Andalus al-Jadīda*), poem by Aḥmad Shawqī (1912), 268
The Tunnels of the Alhambra (*Historia de los subterráneos de la Alhambra, o los amores de Aben-Amed*), anonymous Spanish chapbook, 68–9
Thousand and One Nights, 132, 325
tiles, 23–4, 109–10, 157, 206, 208, 326
Tiṭwānī, Muḥammad, member of the Spanish legation in Morocco (1885), 100

Toledo, 40, 47, 60, 119, 176, 230, 286–88; *see also* Chapel of Santo Cristo de la Luz, Imperial Café
Toledo, Eduardo de, Granadan journalist (1885), 102
tourism, tourists, 33, 80, 86, 93, 107, 119, 173, 181, 246, 253, 264, 272, 276, 288, 290–1, 293, 295, 307, 314, 325–6
Tower of the Candle/Watch Tower (*torre de la Vela*), Alhambra, 81, 107–8, 113, 126
Trad, Benjamin, Lebanese priest and trader (1884), 169, 171
translation, 24, 28, 45, 67, 70, 92, 106, 135–8, 148, 153, 160, 171, 179–80, 184, 190–2, 196–7, 208, 245, 250–1, 263, 271, 306, 315, 325
Trapani, Captain L. (1907), 296
travel accounts, travelogues, 24–6, 32–3, 41, 75–80, 132, 239–42, 245, 250, 257, 259–62, 269, 284–6, 288, 301, 306, 315, 323, 325; see also *riḥla*
Travels in Spain (*Voyage en Espagne*) travel account by Théophile Gautier (1845), 51
Tuğlacı, Pars, historian, 198
Tunalı Hilmi Efendi, Young Turk author and activist (1900), 272–3, 279–97, 299–301, 305, 311
Tunisia, Tunisian, 59, 62–3, 79, 93, 117–18, 120, 231; *see also* Maghreb
turban, 63, 72–3, 150, 154, 264; see also fez, hat
Turhan Hüsnü Bey/Pasha, Ottoman minister in Madrid (1889), 226–33, 235, 239, 241, 245, 271, 311
Turkey, Turkish, Turks, 50, 52, 88, 145, 147, 149–50, 154, 160, 162–3, 165, 167–8, 171, 174. 176–7, 179, 189, 191–3, 198, 200, 206–8, 211, 214–15, 221, 224–6, 228, 231, 233–4, 243–4, 248–50, 252, 263, 270–316, 318, 320–4, 327–8; *see also* Anatolia

United States, 41, 66, 202, 266, 268; *see also* America
universal exhibitions, 39, 54, 66, 204, 214
- London 1851, 35
- Paris 1867, 40
- Vienna 1873, 40, 196, 220–1
- Paris 1878, 40
- Paris 1889, 63, 104, 112
- Paris 1900, 40, 60–3, 65–6
- *see also* Crystal Palace; Ottoman Exhibition of 1863

Valencia, 150, 176
Vapereau, Gustave, French biographer, 162–5
vases of the Alhambra, 110n115
Vendegies, Charles de, French orientalist and dilettante (1846), 88
Viardot, Louis, French historian, 179–81, 186, 196, 306, 325
Vigny, Alfred de, French poet and author, 50, 53
visitors' book of the Alhambra, 3, 11–12, 14–15, 80–5, 89, 91, 93–5, 97, 99–101, 103, 105, 110–18, 127, 129, 131, 133–4, 136–7, 141, 144, 147–8, 155, 167–73, 176–7, 199, 225–7, 229, 233–4, 237–8, 241–5, 255, 257–60, 262, 268, 271–2, 279–80, 284, 297, 300, 311, 315–20, 325
visitors' book of the Generalife, 97, 111–12
Vivanco, Emilio, secretary of the government of Granada (1885), 100

Wardānī, Alī ibn Sālim, Tunisian scholar (1887), 79, 117–20, 230–2, 243, 271, 284
Wāṣif Mawlānā, Moroccan qaid (1885), 100
Watch Tower, see Tower of the Candle
West, Western, 22, 28, 48–9, 52, 66, 70, 72–3, 85–6, 118–19, 127, 138, 145, 148, 156–60, 164–5, 167, 171–2, 178, 184, 185, 188, 192–4, 200–2, 213–14, 216, 219, 221–3, 228, 231, 233, 240–1, 244, 252–4, 263, 266, 268, 277, 279, 299–300, 302, 305, 307–9, 311, 314, 316, 318–22, 327–9
- Westernisation, 67, 148, 158–9, 187–8, 194, 200, 213, 273–4, 276, 300–1
- *see also* America; Europe; France; Germany; Great Britain; United States

Wetzstein, Johann Gottfried, German Arabist (1870), 92
Whiff of Perfume of the Flowery Branch of al-Andalus (*Kitāb Nafḥ al-Ṭīb min Ghuṣn al-Andalus al-Raṭīb*) historical work by Maqqarī, 242, 131n179
Wien, Peter, historian, 117, 264–6
Wilhelma Palace, Stuttgart, 213
Wilkie, David, British artist, 47–8
Wilkomm, Heinrich Moritz, German botanist, 153–4, 157
wine, 107, 111, 158
World War I, 268, 278, 296, 315

Yaʿqūb al-Manṣūr, Almohad caliph, 303–4
Yahya Kemal [Beyatlı], Ottoman/Turkish poet and diplomat, 311–14, 316, 322
Yazīd, sultan of Morocco, 78
Yıldız Palace, Istanbul, 236, 280–2, 285, 295
Young Turks, Young Turk Revolution, 249, 263, 274–5, 278–9, 281, 300, 306, 311, 316, 321–2, 328; *see also* Committee of Union and Progress

Zakī, Aḥmad, Egyptian scholar and bureaucrat (1893), 79, 237–46, 250, 257–60, 269–70, 277, 285, 311, 323, 325, 329
Zanth, Ludwig von, German architect, 38–9, 201
Zaragoza, 40, 286, 289–90
Zaydān, Jurji, Lebanese novelist, 251, 254
Zendreras, Antonio, lieutenant colonel of the Cuban infantry in Granada (1885), 100–1, 103–4
Ziya Pasha, Ottoman poet, author and bureaucrat, 167, 179–88, 193, 196, 208, 215, 224, 306
Zorrilla, José, Spanish poet, 67, 136, 239
Zōzō, ʿAbdesselām, member of a Moroccan delegation (1885), 105
Zugasti Dickson, Juan Vicente, Spanish consul in Larache (1885), 100–1

EU representative:
Easy Access System Europe
Mustamäe tee 50, 10621 Tallinn, Estonia
Gpsr.requests@easproject.com

www.ingramcontent.com/pod-product-compliance
Lightning Source LLC
Chambersburg PA
CBHW050158240426
43671CB00013B/2175
* 9 7 8 1 3 9 9 5 2 4 8 8 9 *